READINGS IN
ARKANSAS POLITICS AND GOVERNMENT

Readings in Arkansas Politics and Government

EDITED BY
JANINE A. PARRY AND RICHARD P. WANG

The University of Arkansas Press
Fayetteville
2009

ISBN-10 (cloth): 1-55728-902-6
ISBN-13 (cloth): 978-1-55728-902-5

ISBN-10 (paper): 1-55728-903-4
ISBN-13 (paper): 978-1-55728-903-2

13   12   11   10   09   1   2   3   4   5

Designed by Liz Lester

⊗ The paper used in this publication meets the minimum requirements of the American National Standard for Permanence of Paper for Printed Library Materials Z39.48-1984.

LIBRARY OF CONGRESS CATALOGING-IN-PUBLICATION DATA

Readings in Arkansas politics and government / edited by Janine A. Parry and
    Richard P. Wang.
        p.   cm.
        Includes bibliographical references and index.
        ISBN 978-1-55728-902-5 (cloth : alk. paper)—ISBN 978-1-55728-903-2
    (pbk. : alk. paper)
        1. Arkansas—Politics and government—1951–   I. Parry, Janine A., 1971–
    II. Wang, Richard P., 1946–
        JK5116.R43   2009
        320.9767—dc22
                                            2008053227

For Diane Blair, *with great admiration;*
for our colleagues, *with gratitude;*
and for our families, *with love.*

CONTENTS

PART I:
Foundations and Context in
Arkansas Politics and Government

PART II:
Policymaking Institutions in Arkansas Politics and Government

PART III:
Practicing Politics in Arkansas Politics and Government

PART IV:

Policy Issues and Political Patterns for the Twenty-first Century in Arkansas Politics and Government

ACKNOWLEDGMENTS

Every book is the product of the work of many more people than those whose names appear on the cover. In the case of this edited volume, the number of people deserving of thanks is likely in the hundreds. In the interest of space, we first extend our gratitude to the writers and scholars who, together with their heirs and publishers, have made such a fine collection of work available to us. Their contributions (as well as the dozens more we could have included) have proven invaluable to our own understanding of, and appreciation for, Arkansas politics and government. We suspect that our students and the many political hobbyists populating the state will be equally grateful to have this collection for their backpacks and bookshelves.

We also wish to thank David Pryor, one of Arkansas's most distinguished public servants, for supplying such a gracious introduction to the volume. We owe a debt of gratitude as well to our colleague, historian Michael Dougan, at Arkansas State University, for his role in setting the stage for this collection. Equally deserving of our thanks are students Victoria Adams, Anne Diallo, Timothy Evans, and Jeffery Kearney at the University of Arkansas, as well as Larry Malley and Julie Watkins at the University of Arkansas Press for their patient, capable assistance.

Finally, we thank our families for their patience, as well as their encouragement and understanding.

JANINE A. PARRY AND RICHARD P. WANG

FOREWORD

It has been more than ten years since students—and practitioners—of Arkansas politics were treated to a compilation of the most current historical, legal, and social science research. Now, with the publication of *Readings in Arkansas Politics and Government,* Janine Parry and Richard Wang make a major contribution to the study and practice of Arkansas government by retaining key readings from past collections while exposing us to just how many changes the state's politics have undergone in just a decade's time. What we see is that though many of Arkansas's unique political intricacies remain intact, the advent of term limits, a wholly revised judicial branch, increased party competition, and new scholarship on the political activities of historically disadvantaged groups have reformed much of the governmental landscape.

That said, this volume is much more than an updated reference source. It is a compilation of the writings and research of many astute observers of Arkansas and its treasured political lore. The book not only treats in some depth all branches of our state's government with vivid illumination, but its policymakers as well. Authors specializing in public policy, legal history, election analysis, social movements, and more shed light on changing demographics and voting patterns and altered public institutions that affect every Arkansan. Even more, *Readings in Arkansas Politics and Government* addresses several long-lived issues, recounting their ultimate outcomes together with the subtle individualized acts of political courage and vision, the latter of which might well fade from memory were it not for the reprinting of scholarly accounts in collected works such as this.

This volume should be mandatory reading for scholars, students and practitioners alike. It provides a timely, critical look at our state's history and its decision-making process as influenced by our 1874 Constitution and long-standing custom of retail politics—and does so early in a new century, when this audience of scholars, students, and practitioners is perhaps most open to studying change and the evolution of power in the state. *Readings in Arkansas Politics and Government* is destined to become one of the major cornerstones of study and practical application within the sphere of the Arkansas political system.

DAVID PRYOR

INTRODUCTION

Devotees of Arkansas politics and government are as passionate as they are numerous. The editors of this collection have long felt a strong kinship with the hundreds—even thousands—of reporters, editors, academics, jurists, pollsters, teachers, lawmakers, bureaucrats, and others scattered across the state, now and in decades past, who share our insatiable appetite for all things Arkansas. *Readings in Arkansas Politics and Government* is, in this sense, offered as a bit of indulgence in a shared obsession.

This new collection would not be possible were it not for the efforts of others, both past and present, to author scholarly accounts of Arkansas politics and government. These individuals include David Yancey Thomas, who headed up the Department of History and Political Science at the University of Arkansas in Fayetteville for the first half of the twentieth century and founded the *Arkansas Historical Quarterly,* from which so many of our selections are drawn. Professor Thomas was instrumental in establishing the significance of the rigorous—and necessarily critical—study of the state's political traditions and practices. The work of Henry M. Alexander, a professor of government for more than 30 years, also supplied many important treatments of the subject in both article and book form, including various editions of *Government in Arkansas: Organization and Function at State, County, and Municipal Levels,* setting the stage for the systematic investigation of politics and policy in this state.

Also of extraordinary value over the decades have been the *Historical Report of the Secretary of State* publications, painstakingly produced by the executive branch for much of the twentieth century; Walter Nunn's *Readings in Arkansas Government* from 1973 together with the 1997 collection by Michael Dougan and Richard Wang, *Arkansas Politics: A Reader;* the launch of the *Arkansas Political Science Journal* in 1980 and its several incarnations since; the various editions of *Governors of Arkansas* compiled by historians Timothy Donovan, Willard Gatewood, and Jeannie Whayne; and, of course, the many biographies and autobiographies of the state's rich harvest of fascinating political figures including Bill Fulbright, Fulbright's mother and long-time newspaperwoman Roberta Fulbright, Sid McMath, Orval Faubus, Winthrop Rockefeller, Dale Bumpers, and David Pryor, among others. Finally, we must direct readers to the remarkable contribution of Diane Blair in producing *Arkansas Politics and*

Government: Do the People Rule? in 1988, a volume that quite possibly stands alone among textbooks nationwide in its perfect pairing of substance and form. We are profoundly grateful to Jay Barth of Hendrix College for completing the second edition when Diane became ill; we hope this collection is a worthy complement to their incomparable book.

We divide the selections included in this volume into four sections. The first examines the state's historical foundations and political context, with a particular focus on regional culture, constitutional history, and several conflicts long central to the state's development: racial tension, rigid social values, and political corruption. The second section investigates the structure and operations of Arkansas's policymaking institutions, devoting much attention to both change and stability in the legislative, executive, and judicial branches. The third section aims to shed light on the practice of politics in Arkansas. We include fascinating accounts of five of the most influential political figures of the twentieth century (governors Faubus, Rockefeller, Bumpers, Pryor, and Clinton) as well as detailed treatments of several particularly illuminating elections and policy debates. The final section reflects our projections for the political patterns and issues sure to play a central role in the state's future: partisan and regional voting patterns and education policy in the post-*Lake View* era.

Considered independently, each of these twenty-one works contributes much to our knowledge of contemporary Arkansas politics and governance. Taken together, we believe the collection lays a firm foundation for real understanding of the subject. By drawing upon the efforts of historians, lawyers, pollsters, journalists, practicing public servants, and political scientists, we have tried to paint a richer picture than otherwise would be possible. We hope readers come away with a deeper appreciation for what has changed in Arkansas politics since the mid–twentieth century, and what has not; for the things we assumed everyone knew, and yet perhaps all did not; and for what is predictable about Arkansas politics, and what—deliciously—is not. We especially hope that students from across the state emerge from their classroom experiences with a heightened awareness of the tremendous possibilities for this state's political future, and for their own remarkable potential for shaping that future.

I

Foundations and Context in Arkansas Politics and Government

Political Culture, Political Attitudes, and Aggregated Demographic Effects

Regionalism and Political Ideology in Arkansas

Janine A. Parry and William D. Schreckhise

Regionalism—specifically, the distinct social, political, and economic patterns that distinguish the Arkansas Ozarks from the Arkansas Delta—has long been an important factor in Arkansas politics. What are these differences and why do they exist? This selection reviews past empirical work on Arkansas regionalism and further investigates the notion of political culture among distinct geographic regions in the state. In addition to identifying attitudinal differences among regions, the authors test competing explanations of the source of such variations. Is it the influence of long-standing regional-level effects (that is, "political culture") or are the political differences among Arkansas's regions instead a product of the individual characteristics of people who share the same space? Both contextual data and the results of a statewide poll are used to address these questions. Though the statistical relationships found are modest, the findings recommend the individual-level model of explanation rather than the regional, or cultural, one. Parry and Schreckhise conclude that political culture is best understood as the aggregation of shared demographic characteristics of a region's residents, which are, in turn, shaped by past social, economic, and political forces.

Janine A. Parry and William D. Schreckhise, "Political Culture, Political Attitudes, and Aggregated Demographic Effects: Regionalism and Political Ideology in Arkansas," *Midsouth Political Science Review* 5 (2001): 61–75. Reprinted with permission.

The notion of politically and culturally distinct intrastate regions has long been a subject of interest in subnational political science research. The state of Arkansas has been the target of several such investigations, and the concept yet plays a very integral role in its politics.[1] Specifically, a sense that there are certain characteristics that differentiate west from east, north from south, and—most particularly—Ozark from Delta is pervasive in the state's academic and popular rhetoric. It is interesting that much of the conversation about the state's regional variations centers upon explanation as much as characterization. The small-town charms and the concentrated poverty said to distinguish Southeast Arkansas, for example, are widely explained as remnants of its cotton plantation legacy and thus its connection to the "Old South" both economically and culturally. Popular characterizations of Northwest Arkansas paint a contrasting picture of a frontier land that long bordered "Indian Territory" and is distinguished by its individualistic mentality and raw, rugged flavor. The latter area's booming industry and haughty isolation from its sister regions are likewise attributed to those much-chronicled early roots.

More interesting still, from a political science perspective, is the tendency of Arkansans to explain the political differences that yet remain between Delta and Ozark by relying upon these distinctive historical legacies. There is perhaps no better illustration of this phenomenon than the widely reported divergent party preferences of the two regions. Since the New Deal, conventional wisdom waxes, Democrats have held the day in the counties bordering the Mississippi River and its westward stretching plains out of grateful loyalty for poverty-quelling government programs. For their support, Republicans—who planted their roots in the state's antislavery forested uplands during the Civil War—have been able to court only the northern and western mountainous regions. Contemporary voter turnout rates are likewise said to be reflective of the state's two distinctive cultural traditions. Participation rates in eastern and southern Arkansas remain precipitously low (relative even to other southern states), partly in deference to a still resonant plantation, *noblesse oblige* mentality. Voting rates in the west and northwest corner, in contrast, are often competitive with national averages reflecting, perhaps, the rugged individualism of bygone days.[2]

The scholarship that addresses these matters has indeed generated a good deal of evidence that describes and delineates the state's political divides, especially between the Northwest and the Southeast.[3] The causes of the phenomenon, however, remain something of a puzzle. Are contemporary differences in political preferences between "Ozark" and "Delta" chiefly a product of their distinctive historical legacies? Or, does the real answer lie in factors much less sublime, such as the differences in the demographic composition of two areas?

These are questions, of course, with which political science has grappled for some time, most expressly by scholars working with the concept of "political culture." Defined by Daniel J. Elazar in 1966 as "the particular pattern of orientation to political action in which each political system is imbedded,"[4] the notion traditionally has been more heavily tied to historical research than most social scientists would prefer. Measured and tested in various ways since Elazar's entrepreneurial work, the concept has been demonstrated to have some utility in predicting the policy choices, institutional character, and other politically relevant phenomena among the American states.[5] What scholars have not figured out, however, is the degree to which such differences genuinely are the product of distinctive collective cultural legacies and not simply a matter of the preferences and actions of the individuals who happen to live in a common space.

Although resolving this conflict is far beyond the reach of this paper, we do aim to shed a little more light on the characteristics and causes of political regionalism within Arkansas. We proceed in this way: First, by using county-level social and economic data, we attempt to characterize distinct regions within the state. Second, we test the significance of these regions for individual political preferences in the form of a "conservatism index" crafted from recent survey data.[6] Third, we attempt to determine whether it is the distinctiveness of these regions that affects the political attitudes of their residents, or whether it is instead the case that such attitudes are more properly linked to the demographic characteristics of the individuals who live there.

Regionalism in Arkansas Politics: The Literature

As noted above, there have been a number of studies in the Arkansas politics literature that have confirmed the presence of a political divide between Northwest and Southeast Arkansas. Robert L. Savage and Richard J. Gallagher for example, revealed three regions: one on either side of an imaginary diagonal line running from Texarkana to Jonesboro, as well as a central urban region (confirming much of the prevailing wisdom in the state)[7]. The counties of Northwestern Arkansas generally demonstrated higher citizen participation rates in elections, and populations that were older and more highly educated than found in other parts of the state. Citizens of this "Ozark" region also were more likely than those in other regions to support Republicans in state and national elections. The counties to the east and south, in contrast, contained younger and less-educated residents who, as might be expected, were less likely to register and to vote, though when they did vote it was for Democratic candidates. Residents of these "Delta" counties also were more impoverished than their northwestern neighbors. According to Savage and Gallagher, the final, "Urban," region revealed by their analysis was more difficult to characterize. Much smaller in number (only five of the state's seventy-five counties fell into this category), Arkansas's urban counties showed some propensity toward lower birth rates, higher levels of educational attainment, a greater proportion of people engaged in managerial-professional occupations, and the like.

Building from the preliminary descriptive findings of Savage and Diane D. Blair, Blair, William D. Mangold, and Savage also found considerable evidence for regionalism in Arkansas politics.[8] Broadly speaking, the primary observation they provide is that while there are great similarities within the Arkansas electorate, attitudinal variations among the geographic regions of the state are indeed detectable and, in some cases, are of considerable magnitude. The residents of the state's eastern and southern counties were discovered to be socially conservative on questions of criminal punishment, gender equity, school integration, and abortion; they also were markedly pessimistic about their economic futures. Arkansans of the western and northern counties, in contrast, were—for the most part—more cheerful about economic conditions and also were more inclined, relative to their Delta counterparts, to take a liberal position on social issues such as racial and sexual equality.

The work of Blair, Mangold, and Savage is particularly important to this study, not only because of the additional evidence they discovered for intrastate variations in public opinion, but because they reached beyond the bounds of the past literature and sought to *explain* the differences they observed. Specifically, after acknowledging the tremendous difficulty of sorting through the respective roles of historical legacy, contemporary contextual conditions, and individual-level demographic differences (especially given their access to aggregate-level data only), they managed to hold two theoretically interesting demographic variables constant in their analysis. These were: (1) each region's level of educational attainment, and (2) its proportion of "native" (as opposed to transplanted) Arkansas residents. From these efforts, Blair and her colleagues arrived at the tentative conclusion that regional opinion differences in Arkansas are, at least in part, a product of what they call "compositional effects." Their research suggests that to the degree the political attitudes collectively expressed by one section of a state are distinct from those expressed by another, it is quite likely that in addition to being an outcome of distinctive cultural legacies, such results reflect the individual-level characteristics of people who happen to live in the same space.

Explaining Regionalism in Arkansas Politics

Again, the goals of this article are threefold: first, to discern the presence of distinctive regions within the state of Arkansas; second, to test the significance of these regions on individual political preferences; and third, to sort through the causes of those variations. To determine first whether distinctive intrastate regions would emerge from data collected in the 1990s as they did in the 1970s and 1980s, county-level social and economic variables were collected on each of the state's seventy-five counties. When a principal components analysis was employed on these data (see table 1), three factors emerged, factors strikingly similar to those seen in Savage and Gallagher's study. The first component, featured in the first column of table 1, clearly reflects an Ozark-Delta division. Counties receiving a higher score on this component demonstrated slower economic growth than the rest of the state, more pronounced economic impoverishment, a sizable number of African American residents, and steady population decline. Nearly all of the counties that received a score above the median on this component, were adjacent to the Mississippi River, shared a border with a county adjacent to the Mississippi River, or were located in the extreme southern part of the state[9] (see table 2). A "Delta" region, then, remains clearly identifiable in contemporary Arkansas.

TABLE I

Principal Components Analysis of Arkansas's Region

| | COMPONENT | | |
	DELTA	URBAN	RURAL
% Below poverty 1996	**0.902**	-0.120	0.308
Per capita income support 1990	**0.826**	-0.138	0.366
% Black 1990	**0.833**	0.265	-0.009
% Unemployed 1994	**0.779**	-0.156	-0.070
% Change in population 1997–98	**-0.759**	-0.017	-0.026
Median income 1996	**-0.700**	0.498	-0.288
% Workforce in skilled trade occupation 1990	**-0.536**	**-0.536**	-0.202
Total county population 1990	-0.173	**0.813**	-0.152
% Workforce in management occupation 1990	0.043	**0.756**	-0.342
% Own homes 1990	-0.462	**-0.729**	-0.272
Per capita income 1993	-0.388	**0.716**	-0.221
Per capita earnings from agriculture 1990	-0.070	-0.200	**0.867**
% Workforce agriculture 1990	0.250	-0.268	**0.859**
% Workforce in farm occupations 1990	0.174	-0.333	**0.795**
% Farmland 1992	0.180	0.258	**0.688**

The next component revealed by our analysis reflects the "urbanness" of the county. As featured in the second column of table 1, urban counties possess larger populations, their residents earn higher-than-average incomes, and are more often employed in managerial or professional occupations. At the same time, urban county residents are less likely to own their own homes. The third component suggests the level of a county's dependence upon agriculture in its economy. As featured in table 1's third column, the residents of these "rural" counties receive more of their per capita income from agricultural production, are more likely to labor in the agricultural industry, and engage in farm-related occupations with great frequency. Likewise, a larger portion of the land in these counties is used for farming.

TABLE 2

Component Score by County

	DELTA	URBAN	RURAL
Arkansas	-0.445	1.086	1.974
Ashley	0.131	0.010	-0.735
Baxter	-0.637	0.046	-0.958
Benton	-2.047	1.552	0.282
Boone	-0.473	0.531	-0.014
Bradley	0.883	-0.280	-1.421
Calhoun	0.667	-1.081	-1.831
Carroll	-0.960	0.015	0.618
Chicot	2.272	0.219	1.212
Clark	0.499	1.079	-0.793
Cleburne	-0.743	-0.941	-0.548
Cleveland	-0.629	-1.262	-0.676
Columbia	0.960	0.005	-1.309
Conway	-0.205	-0.151	0.276
Craighead	-0.783	1.667	0.489
Crawford	-0.737	-0.463	-0.736
Crittenden	0.899	1.204	0.236
Cross	0.120	0.272	1.468
Dallas	1.121	-0.689	-1.855
Desha	1.372	0.354	1.406
Drew	0.605	0.250	-0.688
Faulkner	-1.119	1.421	-0.654
Franklin	-1.448	-0.777	0.819
Fulton	0.138	-1.218	0.258
Garland	-0.236	1.109	-1.053
Grant	-1.173	-0.655	-1.448
Greene	-0.889	-0.102	0.000
Hempstead	0.349	-0.493	-0.274
Hot Spring	-0.301	-0.565	-1.165
Howard	-0.767	-0.202	0.830
Independence	-0.637	0.045	-0.288
Izard	-0.058	-0.955	-0.214
Jackson	0.891	0.357	0.660
Jefferson	1.207	1.232	-0.975
Johnson	-0.526	-0.456	-0.433
Lafayette	1.554	-0.958	-0.625

Lawrence	0.191	-0.496	0.613
Lee	2.503	0.128	1.678
Lincoln	0.757	-0.366	0.806
Little River	0.253	0.299	-1.481
Logan	-0.571	-0.716	-0.301
Lonoke	-1.524	0.776	0.774
Madison	-1.446	-0.690	2.358
Marion	-0.914	-0.584	0.009
Miller	0.289	0.156	-0.893
Mississippi	1.027	1.073	0.407
Monroe	1.718	0.454	1.453
Montgomery	-0.763	-1.373	0.952
Nevada	0.403	-0.675	-0.356
Newton	0.426	-1.458	-0.339
Ouachita	1.344	-0.117	-1.995
Perry	-0.860	-1.725	0.364
Phillips	2.797	0.814	0.386
Pike	-0.698	-0.672	0.179
Poinsett	0.054	-0.108	1.543
Polk	-0.603	-0.556	0.060
Pope	-0.916	0.647	-0.529
Prairie	-0.412	-0.321	2.530
Pulaski	-0.344	4.753	-0.693
Randolph	-0.148	-0.784	-0.349
Saline	-1.532	0.592	-0.865
Scott	-0.151	-0.542	-0.061
Searcy	0.524	-1.242	0.760
Sebastian	-0.869	1.081	-0.266
Sevier	-0.398	0.126	-0.526
Sharp	-0.383	-1.308	-0.014
St. Francis	2.064	0.359	0.126
Stone	0.128	-0.536	0.507
Union	0.266	0.639	-1.543
Van Buren	0.448	-0.900	-0.821
Washington	-1.190	2.471	0.395
White	-0.666	0.230	-0.301
Woodruff	1.307	0.361	1.512
Yell	-0.683	-0.534	0.533

Having established that there are still identifiable regions into which Arkansas counties may be rather easily sorted (and that they are very similar to those uncovered in past research), we can now turn our attention to our second task: identifying a relationship between the aggregate character of each region and the political attitudes of the individual respondents residing within them. To do so, we created an index—a new variable —that reflects the relative "conservativeness" of each respondent in our survey sample. The index itself is a simple additive scale of seven dichotomous variables. The dichotomous variables were generated from the responses to ideological-type poll questions on matters such as taxes, abortion, flag burning, and gun control (see figure 1). Conservative responses on each question were coded "1," liberal or moderate responses were coded "0," and the values were then summed. Respondents with a conservative index score of "7" thus were clearly identifiable as very conservative, whereas those who received a "0" for their index score were not at all conservative.[10] Table 3 displays a frequency distribution for the conservatism index.

FIGURE 1: Conservatism Index

1. Property taxes in Arkansas are too high. (Agree=1; Disagree=0)

2. Property taxes in Arkansas should be: increased (0), kept the same (0), reduced (1), or abolished (1).

3. Would you say you favor stricter gun control (0), or less strict gun control (1)? (No change=0)

4. Do you favor laws that would make it more difficult for a woman to get an abortion (1), favor laws that would make it easier to get an abortion (0) or should no change be made to existing abortion laws (0)?

5. And, do you favor or oppose passing a Constitutional amendment that makes it illegal to burn the American flag? (Favor=1; Oppose=0)

6. Do you approve (1) or disapprove (0) of taking the state sales tax off of food purchased at a grocery store?

7. And, how do you feel about legalizing casino gambling here in Arkansas? That is, do you favor (0) or oppose (1) legalizing casino gambling in our state? Or haven't you thought much about this matter?

To determine whether an individual's political attitudes (that is, degree of conservatism) were related to the characteristics of his or her region of

TABLE 3

Conservatism Index Frequency Distributions

		FREQUENCY	PERCENT	CUMULATIVE PERCENT
Least Conservative	0	7	0.9	0.9
	1	29	3.5	4.4
	2	78	9.5	14.0
	3	120	14.7	28.6
	4	226	27.7	56.3
	5	187	22.9	79.2
	6	138	16.9	96.1
Most Conservative	7	32	3.9	100.0
TOTALS:		817	100.0	

residence, the conservatism variable was correlated with the county component scores, now transformed into three separate variables: the Delta component score, the Urban component score, and the Rural component score. As table 4 suggests, there appears to be little relationship between the individual-level conservatism scores and the county-level characteristics. Specifically, although the correlation coefficient is statistically significant for the "urban" scores and individual conservatism index scores, the relationship is very weak, accounting for less than one percent of the variance. This suggests that a respondent's region has little to do with his or her political ideology. If a person is from a Delta county, he or she may indeed hold different political views than someone from the Ozarks; these differences, however, cannot be attributed to their respective geographic locales. Another look at the remaining relationships tested in table 4 indicates that the same conclusion holds true for urban and rural counties.

It would appear that our findings so far contradict a good deal of prevailing wisdom, a collective "sense" among Arkansas citizens and among most of the community of scholars studying political culture in the state that cultural differences contribute much toward explaining the divergent political perspectives of east and west. Even more, the finding is counterintuitive in that it defies what we know (and can point to empirically) about vote choice in Arkansas over the past fifty years. Residents of the Delta always have voted more fervently Democratic than the rest of the state, and residents of the Ozarks have long been a Republican candidate's best hope of support.[11] How can it be that our data reveal little difference between the ideological preferences of the two regions' residents? That is our most puzzling question still.

TABLE 4

Pearson's Correlation Coefficients, Regional Components Scores and Conservatism Index

	DELTA FACTOR	URBAN FACTOR	RURAL FACTOR
Conservatism Index			
Pearson Correlation	-0.042	-0.094	-0.01
Sig. (2-tailed)	0.228	0.007	0.769
N	817	817	817

It seems there are two possible explanations. First, what if the relationship does not materialize because Arkansans are ideologically uniform? It was V. O. Key who proposed, "Arkansas exhibits a case of political consensus in exaggerated form."[12] We have not, after all, tested respondents' party identification against the regionalism concept; Democrat or Republican, perhaps all Arkansans are conservative? We are confident this is not the case. Though they are not illustrated here, there were wide differences on many of the policy questions included in our survey. Gun control and abortion were particularly divisive within the sample. A quick return to the results of table 3, in fact, illustrates this point. Though the distribution of the conservatism index leans a little to the right, it is a respectable curve with substantial variance. In other words, Arkansans varied significantly in their responses to the ideological indicators we asked them.

That said, we hypothesized that the answer could very well lie in the demographic characteristics of the individuals who reside in the distinctive regions of the state. To test this idea, we regressed (using an ordinary least squares model) regional component scores for each county, along with individual level demographic data, onto respondents' scores on the conservatism index variable. The results for the first regional factor, the Delta factor, are displayed in table 5. Although the model itself holds no great predictive power and the relationships revealed are weak, if we look at the specific variables within the equation, some insight into the dynamics of regional political culture is revealed. Specifically, the race and education variables were significant, while the Delta factor's score was not. This means that respondents' race and education are better predictors of their political attitudes than is region. Stated more broadly, people who share similar racial characteristics and attain like levels of education will have similar political attitudes, a fact that obscures any potential regional

TABLE 5

Delta Component (OLS) Regression Analysis of Political, Socioeconomic, and Demographic Variables

	UNSTANDARDIZED COEFFICIENTS		STANDARDIZED COEFFICIENTS	t	SIG.
	B	STD. ERROR	BETA		
(Constant)	4.507	0.302		14.935	0.000
Age	0.000	0.003	0.003	0.080	0.937
Sex	-0.034	0.112	-0.011	-0.302	0.763
Income	-0.001	0.033	-0.001	-0.019	0.985
Race	0.422	0.151	0.109	2.794	0.005
Education	-0.151	0.044	-0.143	-3.442	0.001
Delta Factor	-0.011	0.061	-0.007	-0.175	0.861

R=.175

R Square=.031

Adj. R Square=.022

influence. African Americans and the better educated, for example, tend to hold more liberal ideological orientations, while less-educated whites tend to be more conservative. The results for the equations in which the "urban" and "rural" regions were tested were likewise disappointing for proponents of culture as an independent variable in political science research (see tables 6 and 7). At least within Arkansas, then, knowing the region from which a respondent hails is of very little predictive utility for political attitudes when individual-level demographic information is included in the analysis.

Discussion and Conclusions

The investigation of regionalism within Arkansas is a line of research with a rich history. It has firmly established that the long-perceived intrastate regions—particularly the Ozark-Delta split—are very real, in that they connote not only different historical legacies, but also divergent contemporary realities. Despite increasing in- and out-migration in the state in the 1980s and 1990s, our findings support this distinctive regional identities thesis. Past research also has confirmed that these

TABLE 6

Urban Component (OLS) Regression Analysis of Political, Socioeconomic, and Demographic Variables

	UNSTANDARDIZED COEFFICIENTS		STANDARDIZED COEFFICIENTS	t	SIG.
	B	STD. ERROR	BETA		
(Constant)	4.570	0.303		15.068	0.000
Age	0.000	0.003	-0.001	-0.035	0.972
Sex	-0.044	0.111	-0.015	-0.393	0.694
Income	0.002	0.033	0.002	0.049	0.961
Race	0.392	0.149	0.102	2.633	0.009
Education	-0.141	0.044	-0.133	-3.177	0.002
Urban Factor	-0.054	0.034	-0.062	-1.613	0.107

R=.185

R Square=.031

Adj. R Square=.026

TABLE 7

Rural Component (OLS) Regression Analysis of Political, Socioeconomic, and Demographic Variables

	UNSTANDARDIZED COEFFICIENTS		STANDARDIZED COEFFICIENTS	t	SIG.
	B	STD. ERROR	BETA		
(Constant)	4.482	0.303		14.808	0.000
Age	0.000	0.003	0.003	0.066	0.947
Sex	-0.032	0.111	-0.011	-0.286	0.775
Income	0.000	0.033	-0.001	-0.014	0.989
Race	0.444	0.149	0.115	2.986	0.003
Education.	-0.152	0.044	-0.143	-3.454	0.001
Rural Factor	-0.065	0.069	-0.035	-0.948	0.344

R=.178

R Square=.032

Adj. R Square=.024

regions demonstrate some degree of meaningful political differences. But are such differences a product of regional culture?

Our polling data, at least as compressed into the single "conservatism index" featured here and tested as a simple correlate with the Delta, urban, and rural regions, suggest that regional political differences in Arkansas may be a product of the ecological fallacy when inferred onto individual residents. That is, using county-level election outcomes as the dependent variable in regional explorations obscures the individual-level preferences that can be revealed by survey data. To this end, one more step in the investigation proved revealing. Switching to regression analysis and using the individual conservatism index as our dependent variable, we were able to probe not just the presence, but also the cause of the geographically based distinctiveness in our sample. Although further analysis will be required to better support the findings presented here, it appears that the source of the of ideological distinctiveness of Arkansas's regions is not so much a matter of regional circumstance as it is an issue of each region's ethnic and educational composition.

This raises an interesting question, one that has both a "temporal" and a "level of analysis" quality, and which has long been troublesome to scholars working with the political culture concept. If culture is measured in a traditional, Elazarian fashion, much of it is historical in nature: which people settled where and when; what were the expectations—especially of the elite[13]—of economic, social, and political institutions; and in what ways were leaders and citizens constrained in their preferences and choices? These historical developments, some from decades and some from centuries ago, manifest themselves today largely as demographic facts. The Delta region of Arkansas, for example, is poor, under-educated, and black as a direct consequence of the plantation economy that operated there from the 1800s until (including the sharecropping system) the 1940s. Regional culture, then, manifests itself in demographics, and demographics—as we have demonstrated here—help explain the attitudes and behaviors that most interest political science. We are compelled to conclude, then, that for social scientists who seek to study contemporary attitudes and behaviors, regional culture is somewhat suspect as an autonomous concept, an independent variable with predictive powers in its own right. Instead culture tempers and shapes the contemporary characteristics of the individual people who happen to share the same space.

The Proposed Arkansas Constitution of 1970

ROBERT W. MERIWETHER

Arkansas's current constitution is its fifth. Adopted in 1874 on the heels of "Radical Reconstruction," the antiquated document long has been an object of derision for civic groups, journalists, and scholars. Yet each attempt to replace it with a new charter has been rejected by the voting public. Here, Prof. Robert Meriwether— who served on the constitutional study commission of 1967, was elected as a delegate to the constitutional convention of 1969, and volunteered to direct the group formed to secure ratification in 1970—chronicles the origins, features, and rejection of one attempt to replace Arkansas's governing charter. Interestingly, just as Meriwether notes that many of the changes proposed in the failed charter revision of 1917–18 were adopted gradually over the next decade, many—though hardly all—of the changes described here have been adopted by constitutional initiative or referred amendment since 1970.

At the November 1970 general election, the voters of Arkansas decisively rejected a revised state constitution. The proposed Arkansas Constitution of 1970 had been drafted by the Seventh Arkansas Constitutional Convention and had been endorsed by ninety-eight of its one hundred delegates. Both major political parties, both major party candidates for governor, the two leading state newspapers, and such influential groups as the Arkansas Bar Association, the Arkansas Chamber of Commerce,

Robert W. Meriwether. "The Proposed Arkansas Constitution of 1970," *Nebraska Law Review* 50 (1971): 600–621. Reprinted with permission.

the Arkansas Farm Bureau Federation, the League of Women Voters, the Arkansas Jaycees, the National Association for the Advancement of Colored People, and some thirty other statewide organizations had all endorsed the proposed charter. The group formed to campaign for the proposed constitution was headed by a former Democratic governor and the incumbent Republican lieutenant governor. "Arkansans FOR the Constitution of 1970" spent one hundred and thirty thousand dollars in cash on the campaign and received "in kind" contributions of at least twenty thousand dollars more; local committees and supporting organizations spent hundreds more and contributed many hours of labor.

In contrast, the opponents of the proposed charter seemed disorganized and few in number. The American Independent Party spent some of its time denouncing the revised constitution, but its gubernatorial candidate polled less than 7 percent of the votes in the general election. A statewide organization consisting of a few lawyers and judges, supported by some Little Rock real estate interests, spent only a fraction of the sum expended by the proponents: less than twenty thousand dollars. And yet the proposed constitution was approved by the voters in only eleven of the state's seventy-five counties, and by a respectable margin in only three of these. What went wrong? This article will attempt to answer that question.

I.

The Constitution of 1874 is Arkansas's fifth constitution. The first charter was drafted in 1835 and went into effect the following year when the state was admitted into the Union. Subsequent constitutions were adopted when the state joined the Confederacy, under "Presidential Reconstruction," and under "Radical Reconstruction."

The Constitution of 1874 was written in reaction to real and imagined corruptions in state and local government during Reconstruction. As such, it is rather typical of state constitutions adopted during this period, especially in the South.[1] Highly restrictive and detailed, it was perhaps very well suited to the needs and expectations of Arkansans in the 1870s; however, many of these restrictions seem unnecessary and even detrimental to those who wanted vital and responsive state and local government in the 1970s.

The original 1874 Constitution has some 21,500 words; its fifty-three amendments have more than doubled its length to some 46,000 words. It is easy to amend, especially since the adoption of the constitutional initiative in 1910. Most amendments, however, have perpetuated its restrictive details: raising a property tax limit a few mills, increasing a salary a few hundred dollars, creating a new constitutional agency, altering slightly a feature of the state's electoral laws, or changing the duties of a county official. At some periods in the state's history amendments have been frequent (six were adopted in 1938), while at other times amendments have fared poorly. Since 1958, only one of the fifteen amendments proposed by the Arkansas General Assembly has been approved by the voters; three other successful amendments were proposed through the initiative. These last four amendments were necessary to (1) permit the use of voting machines, (2) establish a voter registration system, (3) permit the establishment of community colleges supported in part by local property taxes, and (4) permit the establishment of kindergartens and adult education programs in the public schools.

Several abortive efforts have been made to revise the 1874 Constitution. Prior to 1969, the greatest effort was made in 1917–18 when the Sixth Arkansas Constitutional Convention drafted a document that was rejected overwhelmingly by the voters in a special election. It is of some interest to note that of the twenty-four major changes proposed by this convention, twenty were instituted by statute or constitutional amendment within the following decade.[2]

II.

As in many other states, interest in constitutional revision was reactivated in Arkansas in the early 1960s. In the general assembly a small group of advocates was led by Rep. Virgil Butler and included the present congressman from the Fourth District, David Pryor. Interest was spurred by the dean of the School of Law at the University of Arkansas,[3] and by the foremost academic authority on Arkansas government, Henry M. Alexander,[4] a professor of government at the university.

Efforts toward constitutional revision were stifled by the generally negative attitude of Gov. Orval Faubus, but in 1966 the people of Arkansas elected their first Republican governor since Reconstruction, Winthrop Rockefeller. Rockefeller had called for constitutional reform during his election campaign. Among the measures he presented in 1967 to the overwhelmingly Democratic legislature was a bill to create a study commission. With the support of Butler and other Democratic legislators, a statute was passed creating the Arkansas Constitutional Revision Study Commission.[5]

The thirty-member study commission was given a little less than ten months to make its report. Ten members were appointed by the governor, and five each by the speaker of the house, the president pro tem of the senate, the chief justice of the Arkansas Supreme Court, and the president of the Arkansas Bar Association. There was mild surprise when Rockefeller appointed only two Republicans to the commission; as a result, the commission had twenty-seven Democrats and one "independent." Among the more prominent members were Robert A. Leflar, dean emeritus and distinguished professor at the University of Arkansas School of Law, Edward F. McFaddin, a recently retired associate justice of the supreme court, and Representative Butler.

The commission elected Leflar as its chairman and, with a one hundred thousand dollar appropriation, went at its work with dispatch and diligence.[6] A Little Rock attorney, George Campbell, was hired as executive secretary and headed a staff of three researchers and one secretary. Meeting frequently in the state Senate chamber during the summer and fall, the commission reached its January 1 deadline with a thorough one hundred and fifty page report, which not only contained detailed recommendations for the calling of a constitutional convention, but also a complete revised constitution for the consideration of a convention.[7]

Governor Rockefeller called a special session of the General Assembly in February 1968. Among the measures submitted by the governor were two prepared by the study commission: a bill submitting to the voters at the 1968 general election the question of whether to call a constitutional convention,[8] and another bill providing for the holding of such a convention if approved by the people.[9] The General Assembly passed both bills with relatively few alterations, but one change had considerable significance: any proposals submitted by the convention to the people would be voted upon at the general election of 1970 rather than a special election in 1969.

A small organization, "Arkansans for a Revised Constitution," was formed to secure a favorable vote on the call for a constitutional convention at the November 1968 general election. Rockefeller, running for reelection, supported the call and helped finance the campaign from his personal resources. By adroit maneuvering, the convention supporters induced the Democratic gubernatorial nominee, Marion Crank, to make a last-minute endorsement. The convention call passed by the narrow margin of 227,429 to 214,432. Nearly 240,000 Arkansans who voted in the presidential and gubernatorial contests failed to mark their ballots for or against the convention.

At the same general election the voters elected one hundred delegates to the convention from the same districts as were elected members of the Arkansas House of Representatives. Since few people really thought the convention call would pass, and because of the great interest in the presidential and gubernatorial contests, many delegate races were either uncontested or of low voter interest.

The Seventh Arkansas Constitutional Convention held a two-day organizational meeting in the house of representatives on January 6 and 7, 1969. Eleven members of the old study commission had been elected as delegates, including chairman Leflar, vice-chairman C. Randolph Warner, and executive secretary Campbell. These men had also been the three members of the Constitutional Convention Advisory Commission, which had been crated by the legislature to prepare for a convention. It was a foregone conclusion that Leflar would be elected president of the convention. These circumstances, plus the presence of the study commission's recommended revised constitution, gave rise to fears that the members of the study commission would dominate the convention. To forestall this possibility, a group of noncommission delegates formed a coalition.

Leflar was elected president, as expected, but then the coalition pushed through changes in the proposed rules that limited the authority of the president by transferring some power to an Administrative Committee. Election contests for the convention's four vice presidencies and membership on the Administrative Committee developed between study commission members and nonmembers. Warner was elected one of the vice-presidents and Campbell was elected to the Administrative Committee, but the coalition was successful in gaining control of the important posts. Leflar showed his administrative and political skill by cooperating with the collation so that, after a short time, the distinctions and suspicions between study commission members and nonmembers largely ceased to exist.

The convention created eleven substantive committees to study various parts of the 1874 Constitution and make recommendations. All delegates were polled as to their choice of substantive committee assignments and, after the appointments were made by the Administrative Committee, each delegate was given the opportunity to request a change. Only one did so, and the convention approved the change before adopting the Administrative Committee's appointments. The committee chairmen and vice-chairmen were also designated by the Administrative Committee, and the convention gave unanimous approval. Four former study commission members were made substantive committee chairmen, but only one (Butler on the Legislative Branch Committee) was thought to chair a really significant committee.

The procedural committees, and their duties, were as follows:

Administrative. Chaired by the president and consisting of the four vice presidents (one from each congressional district) and seven members elected by congressional districts, this was the most influential committee. The committee chose Little Rock attorney Philip E. Dixon as secretary-director (this appointment was confirmed by the convention) and supervised the selection of the staff, supervised the budget, served as the committee on committees, supervised the general day-to-day operation of the convention, and made the long-range plans. It was particularly proud of the fact that more than $120,000 of the $605,200 appropriated for the convention was returned to the state treasury.[10] All of its decisions were subject to the review of the convention, but the delegates never overturned an Administrative Committee decision. Its major difficulty concerned the work of the convention reporter and the preparation of the transcript.

Rules and Resolutions. The rules, originally proposed by the Constitutional Convention Advisory Commission, were revised by this committee and approved by the convention.[11] Further minor revisions occurred from time to time. On several occasions the presiding officer called on the Rules Committee chairman to help straighten out procedural snarls, but there were few, if any, parliamentary "tricks" or delaying tactics. Individuals and minorities were heard; majorities worked their will. On only one occasion was debate terminated abruptly; the issue was the abolition of capital punishment and the question was never raised again.

Public Information. This committee never really "got off the ground," to a large extent because so many delegates, including the president, felt that no public funds should be expended for publicity purposes. The rules provided that all convention sessions, committee hearings, and meetings be open to the public. Press coverage by the state's two major newspapers, the *Arkansas Gazette* and the *Arkansas Democrat,* was thorough, accurate, and favorable. Radio and television coverage was as superficial as such local news coverage usually is; the few "in depth" shows were aired either late at night or on Sunday morning. Local newspaper coverage, generally supplied by the wire services, varied considerably according to the inclination of local editors. The Arkansas general public was not well informed about the activities of the convention, but this was primarily because the public was not interested and little, if anything, was done to make them interested.

In an effort to stir up public interest and participation, the convention held a number of regional hearings throughout the state. These were usually sparsely attended and resulted in little local news coverage.

Agenda. This committee, with the president as chairman, was created when it appeared that the placement of measures on the calendar would be difficult. In actual practice this did not develop and the Agenda Committee really did not function frequently as a committee.

Style and Drafting. This was a very important, hard-working committee. Before measures were brought up on second or third reading they were subjected to thorough study by this committee. Revisions made by the committee were reported to the convention, and occasional votes were taken when it was alleged that substantive changes had been made. Fortunately, the convention learned it could trust this committee, which is almost a must.

Committee to Prepare the Report to the People (also called the "Comments" Committee). The last committee appointed, this committee did much of its work after the convention adjourned. It prepared the report that contained the text of the proposed constitution and an explanation, supposedly without bias, of each provision.[12] The explanation generally consisted of comparisons with the 1874 Constitution. Four hundred thousand tabloid and one hundred and fifty thousand booklet copies of the report were printed for distribution (there were around eight hundred thousand registered voters). Despite efforts by the delegates,[13] the convention staff, and the supporters of the proposed charter, over half of the reports still sit in a storeroom in the basement of the state capitol. Most of the bulk disposition went to schools and was distributed through the Farm Bureau. Generally speaking, the people of Arkansas showed little interest.

In addition to the two-day organizational meeting in January 1969, the convention met in regular session for three months during the summer and for thirty days in January and February of 1970. During the four-month break in the autumn the convention, with the cooperation of the *Arkansas Democrat,* distributed thousands of tabloid editions of the proposed constitution as it appeared after the second reading. Hopes of the delegates that the people would respond to the proposals and offer criticism were soon dashed; the voters of Arkansas were just not interested. Generally, the changes made on third reading were few in number and were destined to meet the more vehement objections of certain pressure groups.

With only one black and seven (later eight) women delegates, the convention could not be characterized as a cross section of Arkansas voters. Although elected on a nonpartisan basis, the membership was overwhelmingly Democratic, with five or six Republicans, a scattering of independents, and one member of the American Independent Party. In political philosophy, however, the group did range from conservative to liberal; it might best be characterized as a "moderate-to-conservative" assembly, which was representative of the political philosophies of at least the Arkansas white middle-class voters. Nearly half the delegates were licensed attorneys.

The two organizations that worked the hardest, and were the most successful, in getting their members elected as delegates were the Arkansas Chamber of Commerce and the Arkansas Farm Bureau Federation. Only one delegate was a member of a labor union; he was appointed during the convention as the state labor commissioner. Business and banking interests were well represented, and the convention proved particularly responsive to pressure from professional groups such as the medical doctors. There were also a handful of professional educators on the panel, including the president and two committee chairmen.

The convention was markedly free from personal invective. Groups that formed on one issue would divide on the next, though, naturally, delegates found themselves frequently allied with the same fellow delegates. Despite the presence of a former governor (Ben T. Laney, 1945–49), a future federal district judge (G. Thomas Eisele), the next attorney general (Ray Thornton), and a few experienced politicians, the convention was not strong in practical grassroots politics. This was amply demonstrated during the ratification campaign, when most of the delegates were unable to reach the "average" Arkansas voter.

III.

The proposed Arkansas Constitution of 1970 was composed of twelve articles and a three-part schedule, with 13,573 words in the main body and 3,190 words in the schedule. Following is a résumé of the major points and changes in the document, with special emphasis on those that figured prominently in the ratification campaign.

Preamble. There was no change from the 1874 Constitution preamble, which includes the statement that the people of Arkansas are "grateful to Almighty God." Later, when the foes of the proposed document were complaining of the omission of "Almighty God" from the freedom of religion provision, the supporters ran television and radio spots that began with a quotation from the preamble with emphasis on the reference to the deity.

Principles of Government. A minor innovation of the proposed charter was the inclusion of a separate article containing the usual state constitutional provisions about the source of political power, inherent and inalienable rights, the separation of powers, and so on. These were thus distinguished from the individual rights contained in the Declaration for Rights.

One addition, which proved unfortunate, was the "powers of the state" provision recommended in the Model State Constitution.[14] Opponents of the proposed constitution seized upon this and claimed it gave unprecedented and dangerous power to the state. Supporters of the document were never able to explain this provision satisfactorily to the voters.

Declaration of Rights. Among the relatively few substantive changes made from the 1874 Constitution were a protection against unreasonable invasions of privacy, the guarantee of preliminary hearings in felony cases, a clearer expression of protections of the accused in the areas of right to counsel and double jeopardy, and a broader ability for individuals to file taxpayers' suits.

In an effort to broaden the protections of the freedom of religion section, the convention dropped the reference to the deity from the phrase "All men have a natural right to worship *Almighty God* according to the dictates of their own consciences." The proposed constitution also omitted the provision in the 1874 Constitution that prohibited atheists from holding public office or witnessing in court, which, insofar as is known, has never been enforced. Opponents of the proposed document made much of these omissions. In a state like Arkansas, where people are quite conscious of the symbols of piety if not the practice, there is no doubt that this hurt on election day.

Legislative Branch. This article made several significant changes.

1. It permitted, but did not require, annual sessions of the General Assembly.

2. It required single member districts and provided for a three-to-one ratio between House and Senate seats (102–34) in order to facilitate apportionment.

3. It allowed the General Assembly to call itself into special session.

4. It required a three-fifths vote, rather than a simple majority, to override the governor's veto.

5. It allowed the General Assembly to set its own salaries.[15]

6. It required a three-fifths vote to levy or raise taxes. Under an amendment adopted in 1934, the General Assembly could raise some taxes, for example, the income tax, only by a three-fourths vote, while it takes only a simple majority to raise others, such as a sales tax.

7. It required open meetings of the General Assembly and its committees.

With the exception of the salary provision, this article did not cause much opposition. The present General Assembly has included an amendment very similar to this article as one of the three it will submit to the people at the 1972 general election.

Executive Branch. Among other things, this article combined the elective offices of lieutenant governor and secretary of state (the new officer would not preside over the state Senate) and those of auditor and treasurer; the state land commissioner would no longer be elected. The two officers, along with the governor and attorney general, would be elected for four- (instead of two-) year terms and their salaries would be set by the General Assembly rather than the constitution.[16] The governor would be limited to two consecutive terms.

A highly controversial provision in this article mandated the reorganization of the executive branch[17] into no more than twenty principal departments, with the educational, quasi-judicial, and professional licensing and disciplining boards exempted unless required by the General Assembly. Several professional groups objected to this section, which was also opposed by leaders of the educational establishment. It is interesting to note that, at the strong insistence of newly elected Gov. Dale Bumpers, the General Assembly, in February 1971, reorganized the executive branch into thirteen principal departments, although excluding the professional licensing and disciplining boards.

Against its better judgment, the convention continued the provisions of two constitutional amendments from 1944 and 1952, which give a high degree of independence to the state game and fish commission and the state highway commission. To have tampered with these two "sacred cows" would, no doubt, have ensured the defeat of the proposed constitution.[18] Despite these concessions, many of the most sincere opponents of the revised charter felt it gave the governor too much power and encouraged the building of a powerful state political machine.

Judicial Branch. A good case could be made that the provisions of this article were the most damaging to the fate of the proposed constitution. Briefly, the changes were as follows.

1. The Arkansas Supreme Court was given increased supervisory control over the lower courts, including some powers that now are exercised by the General Assembly.

2. Circuit, chancery, probate, and county courts were combined into district courts.[19] The boundaries and subject matter jurisdiction of these courts were to be determined by the Supreme Court. The present circuit judges and chancellors would become district judges.

3. County trial courts were created in each county to have the functions of municipal, juvenile, mayor's, police, and justice of the peace courts. Arkansas juvenile courts are presently presided over by the county judge, an official who need not be a lawyer and who is usually elected on his ability to build and maintain county roads and bridges. The present municipal judges would all have become county trial court judges.

4. A Judicial Ethics Commission was created with the power to investigate charges against judges and to recommend their removal by the Supreme Court.

5. Payment to all court officials from fees and fines was prohibited.

6. A court of appeals (an intermediate appellate court) could be

created by the joint action of the Supreme Court and the
General Assembly.

7. District attorneys (now styled "prosecuting attorneys") would
be prohibited from the private practice of law.[20] The Supreme
Court, by classification, could prohibit the private practice of
law by county trial court judges.

8. Magistrates, limited to preliminary criminal processes and
proceedings, could be appointed by the district judges.
Commissioners could be appointed by the district judges in
those counties that did not have a county trial court judge.

The most spirited and learned debate in the convention took place
on whether some variation of the Missouri Plan should be adopted in
place of the popular election of judges. In large part because it knew such
a change would be almost impossible to sell to the voters, the convention retained the elective system, although on a nonpartisan basis and
with some increase in the length of terms.

Many of the changes in the judicial article had been proposed by an
Arkansas Judiciary Commission study in 1965,[21] and the Constitution of
1970 was approved without a dissenting vote at the annual convention of
the Arkansas Bar Association in June 1970. But the lawyer opponents of
the proposed charter were simply biding their time and, when the autumn
campaign began, many attorneys worked effectively on the local level to
defeat the document. The most open opposition came from some of the
chancery judges. Significantly, no judicial officeholder at any level came
out publicly in support of the revised constitution. Even the endorsement
of the incumbent president of the American Bar Association, Edward L.
Wright of Little Rock, failed to rally significant support for the proposed
document from the Arkansas legal fraternity.

Local Government. This article contained provisions concerning both
counties and municipalities, which will be treated separately.

1. County government. It would take a lengthy dissertation to
discuss the many provisions of the 1874 Constitution and its
amendments that pertain to the operation of Arkansas counties and to indicate how these were altered by the proposed
constitution. Although the revised charter increased the terms
of elective county officials from two to four years, eliminated
the five thousand dollar annual salary limitation, crated a true
county legislature with real authority,[22] increased the taxing

powers of counties, and included just about all of the recommendations of a publication of the National Association of
Counties,[23] it was effectively opposed by the great majority of
county officials in Arkansas. Many objected to the provision
that county officials would no longer be paid on the basis of
fees, a practice that is almost universally used to get around
the salary limitations. The county judges were reluctant to
lose the judicial immunity they enjoy by issuing warrants
against the county treasury as an order of the county court.
Most county officials viewed the proposed county legislative
body with suspicion. And county officers simply feared any
changes that might upset their way of doing business. As was
the case in Maryland in 1967–69,[24] first the convention and
then the supporters of the revised constitution failed miser-
ably in communicating and working with the Arkansas
county officials.

2. Municipal government. The convention and its product were
definitely oriented toward the needs and the future of Arkansas
municipalities. "Dillon's rule" was specifically reversed, municipal tax limitations were removed, and other sources of taxation
were opened. Some municipal powers could be withheld by the
General Assembly only by a three-fifths vote.

The removal of the municipal property tax limitation[25] was one of
the major issues that helped defeat the proposed charter. Prominent Little
Rock real estate interests led and helped finance the opposition. The
Arkansas Municipal League was rather ineffective in rallying the mayors
and city councils in support of the proposed constitution.

Again it is interesting to note that, again with the support of Governor
Bumpers, the 1971 General Assembly has passed statutes repealing "Dillon's
rule" and granting municipalities the authority to levy income and payroll taxes.

The possibility that cities might levy sales tax was one factor in the
lack of enthusiasm of the state AFL-CIO for the proposed charter.
Ironically, organized labor had actively supported the calling of the convention and had long advocated constitutional reform. The possibility
of a municipal sales tax, plus inclusion of the "right to work" provision
(to be discussed later), kept the AFL-CIO officially neutral during the
ratification campaign, though there is some evidence that the leadership
and rank and file were opposed.[26]

The possibility that cities might levy a sales tax and that both municipalities and counties might raise their property taxes also bothered top
officials in the state Department of Education and the Arkansas Education
Association. They reasoned that any increased tax income for other local
governmental units would lessen that which would be available for the
public schools. Although the AEA Board of Directors, in response to the
opinions of many "civic minded" teachers, eventually endorsed the proposed constitution, support for the document was noticeably lacking
among educational leaders on both the state and local levels.

Finance and Taxation. Several of the provisions concerning finance and
taxation have been discussed, above, under "Legislative Branch" and "Local
Government." The convention attempted to bring together and clarify,
with slight modifications and "reforms," the many detailed provisions of
the 1874 Constitution and its amendments concerning property assessment, bonds, bond and tax elections, industrial development bonds, and
so on. Even the delegates were perplexed by many of the provisions, and
scarcely 1 percent of the voters would reasonably be expected to compre-
hend all of the technical language and its practical implications.

However, the opponents of the proposed constitution were successful in attaching a "high tax" label to the document during the ratification
campaign. Detailed, often strained, and sometimes not altogether truth-
ful explanations by the supporters fell on confused or deaf ears. The average voter had to take the claims of proponents and opponents on faith,
not reason. The general attitude might be summed up: "We don't want
higher taxes; the Constitution of 1970 permits higher taxes." The result:
"Against."

Education. This article of the proposed charter contained little of substance which differed from the 1874 Constitution. However, two "minor"
alternations—one that lessened the independence of state institutions of
higher learning, and the other which altered a provision in the recently
adopted "kindergarten" amendment—served to increase the distrust of
some educational leaders for the entire document.

Suffrage and Elections. The convention witnessed a colorful fight to
lower the voting age and ended up with a compromise: keeping the voting age at twenty-one but allowing the General Assembly to lower it to
eighteen. Surprisingly, and in contrast with the experience of other states,
the question was not an issue in the ratification campaign.

One interesting change was to require that, in order to be elected in a general election, a candidate must receive a majority of all votes cast for that office. This provision reflected the entry of the American Independent Party into Arkansas politics and was considered by some delegates insurance that the AIP would not elect a "minority" candidate. Although the AIP fought the proposed constitution, this provision was not mentioned.

The 1874 Constitution requires the numbering of paper ballots, and there have been many alleged abuses of the system.[27] The convention adopted a "secret ballot" provision that many delegates hoped would attract wide support. Its main effect seemed to be to give some county politicians another reason to fight the entire charter.

Initiative and Referendum. This article contained no substantial changes from the amendment adopted in 1920.

General Provisions. This important "catchall" article contained several provisions that figured prominently in convention debates and/or the ratification campaign.

A rather innocuous provision making the General Assembly "the guardian and conservator of the water resources of the state" was attacked during the campaign by a state senator who said that "by the time a farmer gets a permit to dig a well from the legislature, all his cows will be dead." The entire natural resources section aroused opposition which was quite surprising to the delegates.

The usury provision, which effectively limits the interest on all contracts to no more than 10 percent, stayed in the revised document. Portions of the Arkansas business and banking community made strong efforts to get the convention to soften this section, and would have succeeded if an offer by the Arkansas Bankers Association to finance the campaign for ratification had not backfired.

The so-called "right to work" amendment adopted in 1944 stayed in the proposed constitution despite efforts by organized labor to at least get the provision out for a separate vote. The main reason labor had worked for the calling of a convention was to remove this provision, and their failure to influence the convention went a long way toward labor's disenchantment with the final product.

An amendment to the 1874 Constitution in 1956 makes lawful parimutuel wagering on horse racing at Hot Springs. Rather than court massive opposition from Garland County voters, the convention decided to leave the provision in the revised constitution. Mindful of the public's dislike for legal casino gambling, the past inclination of the General Assembly to be influenced by professional gamblers, and the exhortations of a group of Methodist ministers who wanted the delegates to take a stand on this "moral" issue, the convention voted to outlaw all forms of gambling except that presently authorized. Then, as a result of adroit vote swapping and ardent lobbying, the Crittenden County delegates got the convention to give constitutional sanction to the currently authorized pari-mutuel wagering on dog races at West Memphis. Surprisingly, the gambling issues never became important in the campaign, but the forces for the proposed constitution allegedly received a substantial contribution from Crittenden County.

Constitutional Amendment and Revision. The 1874 Constitution contains no article on amendment and revision and is one of the few in the nation that does not authorize the calling of a constitutional convention. This article in the proposed constitution contained no novel or controversial provisions.

Schedule. A Committee on Schedule and Transitional Provisions, which was composed of members from each of the ten other substantive committees, had general jurisdiction over the schedule; however, in practice, the convention and its committees worked directly on this part of the document.

Ray Thornton, who was later to be the successful Democratic candidate for attorney general, was the delegate largely responsible for the idea of a "three part" schedule: (I) provisions that could be changed by a majority vote of each house of the general assembly; (II) provisions that could be changed by a two-thirds vote of each house; and (III) temporary provisions that provided for the transition from the 1874 to the 1970 Constitution.

Little would be gained here by a detailed description of the many different items in the schedule, but its perusal is recommended to drafters of revised state constitutions. Not only is the three-part schedule the one major innovation of the proposed Arkansas charter, but the convention used the schedule to do a little "legislating"—most of which created more enemies than friends.

Four items in the schedule allegedly figured in the financing of the pro- and anti-constitution organizations, but were not campaign issues as far as the general public was concerned:

> 1. A Schedule I item gave some relief to Arkansas fish farmers from the supposedly authoritarian decrees of the state Game

and Fish Commission.

2. Another Schedule I section voided all laws fixing prices of consumer goods, thus incurring the wrath of the wholesale and retail liquor dealers who have for years enjoyed the protection of the state's so-called "fair trade" liquor law.[28] Later it was discovered that the section also struck down fair trade laws on milk and cigarettes, to the discomfiture of some wholesale grocers.

3. A Schedule II provision eliminated the practice of "bond conversions," which is practiced only in Arkansas. This provision was opposed by the state's large bond brokers.

4. Another Schedule II section provided for the "nondiversion" of revenue collected from highway users to any other use except for highways, and so on. Major highway users, contractors, and others were ardent advocates of this provision.

The provisions of the schedule designed to provide for a smooth transition from one constitution to another seemed to be adequate, but, since the proposed charter failed, we will never know for sure. The committee also did some work on legislation that would have been necessary if the proposed constitution had been adopted.

IV.

The Seventh Arkansas Constitutional Convention adjourned *sine die* on February 10, 1970, nearly eight months before the November general election. During the convention, few delegates had given much thought to an organization in support of ratification. During the next several weeks there were phone calls and informal meetings to see if some sort of an organization could be started. Finally, Governor Rockefeller called a meeting of several civic and political leaders from both major parties. Eventually an organization known as "Arkansans FOR the Constitution of 1970" was formed to promote the document. Former Democratic governor Sid McMath and Republican lieutenant governor Maurice "Footsie" Britt agreed to serve as co-chairmen. The author, a college professor with no previous campaign experience who had served on the study commission and as a delegate to the convention, was the unpaid director. Shirley McFarlin, a former president of the state League of Women Voters, a study commission member and a convention delegate, and an active worker in the campaign to call the convention, volunteered to work part-time and organize a speakers' bureau. The chief full-time employee was Walter H. Nunn, who had been on the staff of the study commission, the Constitutional Convention Advisory Commission, and the convention.[29]

"FOR" hired one of the state's leading public relations firms to handle its campaign and used the services of the state's most well-known pollster to advise it on campaign techniques and issues. Two Little Rock business and civic leaders headed the finance committee. Although he was in a tough, eventually unsuccessful, campaign for a third term, Governor Rockefeller made substantial cash and "in kind" contributions. FOR was assisted materially by the state Farm Bureau organization[30] and, to a lesser extent, the state Chamber of Commerce. Outside the League of Women Voters, none of the other thirty-odd supporting groups contributed much toward the campaign in money or manpower —the lack of enthusiasm of the Arkansas Jaycees was particularly disappointing.

The campaign for adoption of the proposed constitution never really got off the ground. The director later characterized the effort as "amateurish, uninspiring, and ineffective." Although following the advice of the pollster and advertising firm, the campaign caught no one's attention or imagination. The speakers' bureau helped provide scores of speeches, all to civic groups who were generally disposed in favor of the constitution anyway. Indications were that the proposed charter had the support of about 40 percent of the voters in February, May, and November.

The FOR organization relied mainly on "endorsement" advertisements that went into little detail about the constitution itself. The supposition was that the "average voter" would not read a detailed explanation of so complicated a document, and would not understand it if he did. Therefore, he would depend on the endorsement of political and civic leaders and organizations. There is little evidence that this sort of campaign picked up any support. Local groups were organized in about fifteen counties, usually on the initiative of convention delegates. Some worked diligently, but the proposed constitution seemed to fare no better in most of these counties than it did where there was little visible local activity.

Governor Rockefeller and the state Republican Party actively supported the ratification campaign, but with the Democrats it was a different story. Democratic gubernatorial candidate Dale Bumpers sincerely wanted the constitution to be ratified, and, after his expected primary victory over former governor Orval Faubus, hopes ran high. However, the opposition of local Democratic officeholders at the Democratic State Convention in September forced a watered-down endorsement of the charter in the party platform. The Democrats did not make the constitution an "article of faith" on either the state or local level, and the FOR organization received no cooperation or support from the Democratic leadership during the last two months of the campaign. One result was that the constitution suffered two of its worst defeats in the home counties of Bumpers and Thornton, the party nominee for attorney general, while the candidates were racking up impressive majorities over the Republicans and the AIP.

The question "For" or "Against" the proposed Constitution of 1970 was on the ballot between two other issues. One was an initiated act to repeal the state's 1907 railroad "full crew" law. The campaign for "Act 1" was heavily financed and easily tripled in volume the advertisements for the proposed constitution. Toward the close of the campaign the railway brotherhoods and other labor groups launched a massive attack against Act 1. There is some indication that union men, conducting an active door-to-door campaign against Act 1, also used the opportunity to oppose the constitution.

The other issue concerned the issuance of bonds for the construction of a state library building and a trifling corporation tax to pay for the bonds. No one came out in opposition to the two measures, both of which had to pass before the project could be undertaken.

Act 1 and the two library propositions went down to defeat with the revised constitution as thousands of voters marked "Against" right down the ballot.

The campaign against the proposed constitution seemed splintered. An eastern Arkansas lawyer announced the reactivation of a committee to oppose the document, but the "committee" seemed to limit its work to one county. A municipal judge and a state senator in central Arkansas also formed a "committee." Outside a few appearances on television panel shows, this committee's work seemed confined to personal contacts.

Former Supreme Court associate justice Edward F. McFaddin, who had been a member of the study commission, headed the main group in opposition to the proposed charter. McFaddin, who said the document was the "first step toward a Fascist state" and that it would "destroy the finest state court system in the country," was assisted by a few Little Rock lawyers and real estate brokers. Other identified members of "Save Present Constitution" included two chancery judges and the one convention delegate who had voted against adoption of the constitution, Patsy Robinson, a south Arkansas attorney. The group taped two television shows and ran a number of radio spots and newspaper advertisements, as well as distributing some hand literature. These stressed primarily the "high tax" issue. Several of their charges were characterized by the advocates of the constitution as half-truths and outright lies.

The other major group openly opposing the proposed constitution was, as previously mentioned, the American Independent Party. The AIP stressed taxes, "Almighty God," and a few other relatively minor points. Col. John Norman Warnock, the only delegate who was a member of the AIP, had abstained on the final vote when the convention approved the proposed constitution 98–1, but he later came out in opposition. Warnock was the AIP candidate for attorney general, but he spent most of his time and effort fighting the revised charter. Warnock considered the omission of the delineation of the state's boundaries a serious defect and a blow at "states' rights." Although the convention had also omitted the so-called "interposition" amendment adopted in 1956 (but never implemented), this was not an open issue in the campaign.

A few small county newspapers were in opposition to the document. The large Palmer chain in southwest Arkansas stayed neutral, but was generally considered to be opposed. At the last minute, the influential Don-Rey chain in Northwest Arkansas came out in opposition, primarily over the tax issue. With these exceptions, practically all of the so-called "leading" local newspapers supported the constitution.

As mentioned earlier, the most effective opposition to the constitution came from county and judicial office holders who felt their positions threatened. Few came out in open opposition, but they worked quietly and effectively behind the scenes, primarily with voters who never heard the civic club speeches made by the proponents.

On November 3, 1970, the voters of Arkansas defeated the proposed Arkansas Constitution of 1970 by a vote of 223,334 to 301,195 (42.6 percent for). Approximately 85,000 people who voted in the governor's race did not go down to the middle of the ballot to vote on the constitution. If they had, the great majority would probably have voted against. Thus the proposed charter was saved from a worse defeat by being "buried" on the ballot.

V.

Why was the constitution, which had so much going for it, defeated? Some critics believe that a separate vote on some controversial issues might have defused opposition to the main document. The convention considered three separate issues: the voting age, the usury provision, and "right to work." The first was not a damaging issue and the separation of the second and/or third would probably have brought more opposition than support. One observer said that the constitution was defeated by "God and taxes." Should these have been the separate issues?

Some observers believe that the voters of Arkansas were unable to give sufficient attention to the constitution in a general election that saw well over one million dollars spent on the governor's race and an additional half a million dollars on the "full crew" repeal. Press, radio, and television coverage of the gubernatorial race dwarfed the relatively few references to the constitutional question. Explanations and advertisements on the proposed constitution were lost in the tremendous outpouring of political propaganda on other races, state and local. And, what people do not understand, they vote against.

To this author, there is one obvious conclusion: the voters of Arkansas were not convinced that they suffered appreciably under the 1874 Constitution or that they would be benefited by the proposed 1970 Constitution. Another thing seems obvious: state constitutional revision—from the inception of the idea, through study commissions, legislative enactments, constitutional conventions, educational programs, ratification campaigns, or what have you—require more political sophistication and maturity than any other type of state political endeavor. Arkansas, in 1967–70, just didn't have it.

Intelligible, Honest, and Impartial Democracy

Making Laws at the Arkansas Ballot Box; or, Why Jim Hannah and Ray Thornton Were Right about May v. Daniels

STEVE SHEPPARD

In the 2004 election, state voters were asked not only to support an incumbent president's bid for a second term but, also to give their approval to a proposal amending the Arkansas Constitution to define marriage as consisting "only of the union of one man and one woman" and establishing that relationships not consistent with this definition would not enjoy legal standing in Arkansas. The state's voters, to almost no one's surprise, consented heartily to both propositions.

In this research note, Steve Sheppard, a member of the University of Arkansas Law School faculty, argues that the initiated proposal ("An Amendment Concerning Marriage") at least was misleading in both its popular name and ballot title and should have been recognized as such by the Arkansas Supreme Court in its response to a challenge to the proposal by a taxpayer group (May v. Daniels). *Finding plenty of support for his position in the opinions of the two dissenting justices in the case, the author offers his views on the essential elements of "intelligibility, honesty, and impartiality," and argues that these elements were not inherent in either the ballot proposal or the majority decision in* May v. Daniels. *As such, he concludes, "the ballot amounts to a fraud, or a trick, and there can be no basis for believing that the law really represents the will of the people."*

Previously unpublished. Used by permission.

There is a long-standing tension in America between the ideals of direct democracy and the rule of law. In its simplest form, rule by democracy requires that the majority gets what it wants, but the rule of law requires not only respect for certain procedures but also, as we know it today, respect for those who would oppose the majority.[1]

Nowhere in Arkansas law does one see this tension as clearly as in our perennial disputes over ballots for initiatives proposing new statutes or constitutional amendments.[2] Initiatives have been used to enact statewide and municipal laws since 1925.[3] As the basis for constitutional amendment[4] and even for statutes, laws passed by ballot have a particular political allure because they are immune from veto.[5] Initiatives, in particular, were and remain heralded for their peculiar legitimacy as representing the direct voice of the people,[6] but they spark a continuing concern for their potential to enact laws that impose the will of the majority, which may be prone to sway by populists and demagogues.[7] Nonetheless, both initiatives and constitutional referenda have grown more popular as a means of enacting laws in the state, and initiatives on the ballot as a result of petition have fared about as well as those proposed by the legislators.[8] Over forty statutes and amendments have been enacted by vote since the 1938 election.[9]

The powers and procedures for initiatives are governed by Amendment Seven of the Arkansas Constitution:

> The legislative power of the people of this State shall be vested in a General Assembly, which shall consist of the Senate and House of Representatives, but the people reserve to themselves the power to propose legislative measures, laws and amendments to the Constitution, and to enact or reject the same at the polls independent of the General Assembly; and also reserve the power, at their own option, to approve or reject at the polls any entire act or any item of an appropriation bill.[10]

The exercise of this power of initiative and of the related power of referendum differ somewhat. Initiative, or the popular creation of a new law or amendment, requires a petition to be signed by sufficient voters in sufficient counties to be placed on the ballot.[11] Referendum, in itself, is a ballot either to repeal an established statute or appropriation brought by petition or a legislative referral of a constitutional amendment to a popular vote.[12]

The lion's share of disputes before the courts over such measures arises in challenges to two aspects of the procedures in Amendment Seven that apply to initiated acts and amendments. The sponsoring individual or group must write or attach the ballot title and the text of the proposed law to each petition presented for signature.[13] The popular name, ballot title, and text must be presented to the state attorney general, who must either authorize the use of the title on the petition and ballot, draft a substitute, or require redrafting.[14] The attorney general also prepares an abstract of the proposed law to appear on the ballot, as well as altering or assigning its popular name; the secretary of state assigns its number.[15] The state Supreme Court is required to hear appropriate appeals of the certification of the ballot title and the ballot, which may come before it in mandamus as well.[16]

Actions challenging the popular name and ballot title have become a matter of near routine for initiated acts and amendments. Commencing in the election to pass what would become Amendment Seven itself, the sufficiency of the petition, the fitness of the name, and the fairness of the ballot language have routinely been challenged, for statewide as well as for local elections.[17]

Indeed, only months after Amendment Seven was initially adopted, the supreme court vacated a trial court's mandamus ordering the secretary of state to allow an initiative on the relocation of the county seat of Dallas County.[18] Chief Justice McCulloch considered both the amendment and its enabling act and found the proposed act was outside the scope of the amendment as it was then written. He concluded: "The act clearly makes it the duty of the court, on an application for mandamus, to inquire whether the proposed measure falls within the terms of the Constitution as amended, and, if it does, to compel submission to the people; otherwise to restrain the submission of it to the people."[19]

In the first of many such cases to challenge a ballot title, the court in 1931 relied on the law of Oregon and Massachusetts to determine that a ballot was misleading, and so in violation of the amendment.[20] The way in which that ballot was misleading is instructive. The ballot read as if it allowed divorce for people who had been in the state "for ninety days only," rather than to anyone who had been in the state at least ninety days. The court noted that anyone who even casually read the statute would understand the limit of the law, but that such a cure was insufficient. The "great body of the electors, when called upon to vote for or against an act at the general election, will derive their information about it from the ballot title. This is the purpose of the title."[21]

Misleading information was not the only problem to vex early ballot titles. Information that might have been the basis for a voter's decision but that was missing from the ballot killed an initiative to establish a tax to assist the blind.[22] The bill would have enacted a sales tax, but its title described these only as "an act to provide for the assistance of aged and/or blind persons and funds therefore, the administration and distribution of same." The court found this insufficient to explain the act's general purposes. Again, that a citizen might otherwise have familiarity with the act could not save it from this constitutional defect.[23]

Similar problems arose over the popular name. In one of the most interesting name or title cases, the court held that in the popular name of "Modern Consumer Credit Amendment," which was to repeal Arkansas's famous limit on usury, the term "modern" was pure salesmanship. As Justice George Smith wrote for the court,

> It is certainly not descriptive of the amendment, unless we are to say that every amendment is modern merely because it is new. Rather, the word is used as a form of salesmanship, carrying the connotation that the original constitution is old-fogeyish and outmoded, while the proposed amendment is modern and therefore desirable. Even though the popular name need not be as explicit as the ballot title . . . it should not be used as a vehicle for unnecessary praise of the measure. In studying his ballot the voter is not bound by the rule of caveat emptor. He is entitled to form his own conclusions, not to have them presented to him ready-made.[24]

Despite such clear language, the court has sometimes applied its principles in confusing manners. Indeed, there are several hairs split so finely among the cases that one is tempted to see in the precedents that there are forces at work more dependent on the issue than the process. In the early decades attacks on revenues were looked on favorably, though in recent years, bills that would abrogate taxes appear to have a higher threshold to cross. Bills favoring social causes once had to cross a similarly high barrier, unless the bill favored banks or railroads.

Yet the Arkansas Supreme Court has never acknowledged such ends-oriented thinking in its opinions. There are several cases in which one can easily see the courage of judges voting to strike from the ballot bills they liked or to leave on bills they despised. The principles of a ballot that is intelligible, honest, and impartial have never gone completely away. Rather, these principles have evolved from the earliest cases with slight expansion and general acceptance.

These principles differ for the review of the popular name and the ballot title. For the popular name, the standard is fairly relaxed:

1. The popular name fails if it communicates a meaning contrary to the burdens actually created by the act.

2. The popular name cannot contain catch phrases or slogans that tend to mislead or give partisan coloring to a proposal. A single word that sells the measure through distraction from its core purpose is misleading.

3. Deference, though far from absolute deference, is given to the approval of a popular name by the Attorney General.

The standards for a ballot title are stricter than those for the popular name. The bulk of the cases that have overturned a ballot have turned on an insufficient or misleading ballot title:

1. The ballot title must contain every essential idea needed to be sufficient to explain the effects of the law to anyone of ordinary intelligence. The ultimate issue is whether the voter, while inside the voting booth, is able to reach an intelligent and informed decision for or against the proposal and understands the consequences of his or her vote based on the ballot title.

2. The ballot title must be free from any misleading tendency, whether of amplification, of omission, or of fallacy, and it must contain no partisan coloring.

3. Ballot titles that depend on information outside the ballot to make sense are insufficient.

4. Ballot titles that use salesmanship, language that leads the voter toward one outcome or another, are misleading.

5. Ballot titles containing a word or phrase, particularly when seen in the light of the word or phrase in the popular name, that acts as a lure or obscures a single important effect of the law, are misleading.

6. Ballot titles that omit information regarding the effect of the law on a burdened group, particularly costs that the group will bear or liabilities the group will face, are misleading.

7. Ballot titles that omit information regarding the effect of the law on taxes, or on other rights, powers, or duties under the law, are misleading.

8. Ballot titles that omit information regarding the effect of the proposed law on other rights, powers, or duties under other provisions of the law, are misleading.

9. Ballot titles that omit information regarding the effect of the law on government services provided to citizens are misleading.

10. Ballot titles that omit information regarding the effect of the law, that change the authority or responsibility of government officers or agencies, are misleading.

11. Ballot titles that are so long and complex as to not be understandable in the brief time available to the voter for reading them are misleading. While length alone will not render the ballot insufficient, length coupled with omission or complexity does.

12. Some acts are just too long and complex to be fairly presented in any valid ballot title.

Applying all of these principles, we may consider the decision by the Arkansas Supreme Court in a recent ballot matter, *May v. Daniels.*[25]

In *May,* the attorney general accepted the popular name and ballot title of "An Amendment Concerning Marriage."[26] The stated purpose of the law was to create a constitutional amendment limiting marriages to a male and a female. The underlying purpose of at least some of its sponsors was to increase partisan turnout for the general election, as part of a nationwide attempt to inflame conservative voters who were angered by a recent decision of the Massachusetts Supreme Judicial Court that led to the recognition of marriages between two people of the same gender.[27]

The wider political role of the placement of the issue on the ballot is not material to the court's evaluation of the ballot title or its popular name. Even so, that political context ensured that the fundamental purpose of the measure was to forbid gay marriage in Arkansas, although the law went farther, regulating or potentially regulating all of the rights related to marriage.

The ballot title was:

A PROPOSED AMENDMENT TO THE ARKANSAS CONSTI-
TUTION PROVIDING THAT MARRIAGE CONSISTS ONLY
OF THE UNION OF ONE MAN AND ONE WOMAN; THAT

LEGAL STATUS FOR UNMARRIED PERSONS WHICH IS IDENTICAL OR SUBSTANTIALLY SIMILAR TO MARITAL STATUS SHALL NOT BE VALID OR RECOGNIZED IN ARKANSAS, EXCEPT THAT THE LEGISLATURE MAY REC-OGNIZE A COMMON LAW MARRIAGE FROM ANOTHER STATE BETWEEN A MAN AND A WOMAN; AND THAT THE LEGISLATURE HAS THE POWER TO DETERMINE THE CAPACITY OF PERSONS TO MARRY, SUBJECT TO THIS AMENDMENT, AND THE LEGAL RIGHTS, OBLIGATIONS, PRIVILEGES, AND IMMUNITIES OF MARRIAGE.[28]

A group of citizen taxpayers sought a declaration that both the popular name and the ballot title were insufficient and misleading under Amendment Seven.

The majority of the court did not agree and refused to bar the amendment from the ballot.[29] The popular name was compared to the standards applied to strike down a proposed abortion law in 1984, which had "unborn child" in its popular name.[30] The court held that

> The popular name of Proposed Amendment 3, "An Amendment Concerning Marriage," clearly and concisely identifies the measure to the voters. It is intelligible, honest, and impartial and does not contain inflammatory language, political catchwords, or partisan coloring. It merely alerts the voters to the subject on which they will be voting, without attempting to influence them one way or the other. Contrary to Petitioners' urging, we do not believe that the term "marriage" evokes the same type of emotional reaction as the phrase "unborn child."[31]

It similarly rejected complaints that the popular name was incomplete, as the name made no mention of the rights beyond the act of marriage itself that would be altered by the new law. According to the court, the relationship of section two, which altered other rights that arise as a result of marriage, was sufficient for the popular name.[32]

The ballot title was upheld in light of the higher scrutiny demanded by precedent. After reciting the various standards, the court held that the ballot title was neither vague or misleading nor omitting of essential effects of the law. Although the court agreed the ballot could have been written more clearly, it found none of the terms complained of, especially "marital status" or "rights," were vague or misleading in context.[33]

More interestingly, the court also rejected the argument that the ballot failed to describe its effect on unmarried and some married people and to describe its effective repeal of the guarantee of equal protection as it applies to many persons. The court held that the petitioner's arguments amounted to speculation concerning how the law may be interpreted to bar gay couples from the homestead exemption for heads of families. This argument, the court held,

> amounts to nothing more than an assertion that some current laws may be affected or even impliedly repealed with the passage of Proposed Amendment 3 . . . the laws allegedly implicated in this case are by no means certainly implicated, such that the ballot title must inform the voters of this. Accordingly, the ballot title does not fail in this respect.[34]

The court also rejected a complaint that the ballot failed to disclose that the amendment would preclude the legislature from future recognition of gay marriages.[35]

Then-associate justice, now chief justice, Jim Hannah, and Associate Justice Ray Thornton dissented. Justice Thornton's first concern was that the popular name really did nothing at all to signal the right in issue for those who would be barred from marriage, which he found to be insufficient and misleading. The effect of section two made the amendment more than an attack on gay marriage alone, which is what the voter would probably have thought the vote to amount to. A more complete popular name, he argued, "would have informed voters that the amendment was broader than a prohibition of same-sex marriages and that it would also have an effect on unmarried persons, without regard to their gender or sexual orientation."[36] Further, he saw the ballot title as insufficient because it was so likely that the amendment "could repeal or modify a number of Arkansas statutes that affect the rights of unmarried persons and I believe that the voters have a right to some warning that this proposal could limit the rights of single persons under Arkansas law."[37]

Justice Hannah separately dissented, facing squarely the real issue of the amendment. "[I]t is apparent that the goal of the proponents of Amendment 3 is to preclude statutory adoption of any state-recognized and state-protected union of persons such as domestic partners and civil unions."[38] That goal, he noted, was nowhere stated in the popular name or the ballot title. "The issue before this court is simply a lack of candor in the popular name and ballot title, and I believe that this court should compel drafters of popular names and ballot titles to be forthright and clear."[39]

Noting that marriage is more than the estate of matrimony, and that the law has long recognized its contractual aspects, Justice Hannah was specific in analyzing the effects of the amendment that could not be known by reading it alone, but which required a knowledge of the wider Arkansas law to determine its effects. After reviewing a variety of recent cases of ballot titles that were more candid than Amendment 3 but which the court had rejected, he concluded, "Neither the popular name nor the ballot title meet the statutory requirements. They are one-sided, and only present a partial description of the proposed change to the Constitution."[40]

The dissenters were right. The ballot title and the popular name in *May* were patently inadequate. The mere fact that they did not mention the people on whom the burden of the law would fall is a hint.

The reasons offered in the dissents are quite clear and compelling, but even these arguments are not, I think, as strongly put as the law demands.[41] When a ballot title does not make clear the burdens of the law to be passed, it is insufficient.[42] The simplest point of comparison is to the court's refusal to allow the ballot title in 1958 for a bill that would require railroads to install lights and gates at crossings.

In *Johnson v. Hall*[43] the court considered a constitutional amendment called "The Safety Crossing Amendment—An amendment to require adequate safety devices at all public railroad crossings." The ballot title was found defective for two reasons: because it conveyed to the voter that the current protections and laws requiring them were insufficient and because it did not make clear that the law would require expensive installations at all 3,600 roadways that cross railroads in the state, and that this expense would fall on the railroads. There is no way to reconcile that precedent with *May.* If the burden to a railroad of a law on railroads is not disclosed in the ballot title, which is quite lengthy in what it required of railroads,[44] how could the burden to singles and gays in this title be disclosed when they are never mentioned at all?

The dissent was correct that the popular name was defective as well. The word that distracts the voter need not be obvious; it needs only to mislead. A word that directs the attention to a positive outcome of the law to the neglect of the burdens it creates is misleading. For this reason, the court rightly struck the popular name in an attempt to raise the usury limits entitled "The Modern Consumer Credit Act."[45] That title was as related to its purpose as "An Amendment Concerning Marriage." But the court realized that "modern" had a pleasing connotation that belied the changes to the law that were not described within the name or title. Here, "marriage" is clearly a good thing, and merely saying it makes people likely to vote for it. Anyone is more likely to vote for "Concerning Marriage," but many such voters would not have voted for "An Amendment to Bar Committed Couples from Marriage on the Basis of Gender."[46]

The court has often and rightly said that there is no perfect formula for a ballot title or popular name. That is true. On the other hand, it has given lip service to standards of intelligibility, honesty, and impartiality that have real meaning. Here are some essentials of that meaning:

1. If a voter is asked to do something the voter might regret with further information, the voter did not have enough information.

2. If the proposed amendment or law creates a likely burden or harm on a person or group, that person or group must be identified.

3. If the proposed amendment or law creates a likely burden or harm on a person or group, the harm must be identified.

4. If a person trained in law would know about likely effects of the proposal that are not clear to a nonlawyer, these effects must be clearly identified.

If these meanings are not inherent in the ballot by which a voter creates a law, the principles of law cannot be maintained. The ballot amounts to a fraud, or a trick, and there can be no basis for believing that the law really represents the will of the people.

It might be easy for observers to claim, perhaps even easy for lawyers or judges to believe, that the proper role for the courts when confronted by a ballot dispute is to bow out, to leave the matter somehow to the will of the people. This is a dreadful conclusion.

The will of the people must be a fundamental basis for the legitimate exercise of law in the American legal system. Yet, for this exercise to be legitimate, the people must be asked fair and reasonable questions, from which their answers can have clear meanings. It is an abuse of the will of the people to submit to them a ballot that risks deceit, confusion, or bias to any voter, much less a large number of them. Just as it is an abuse of the will of the people to send them a ballot that would encourage them to vote for an act or amendment that would be unconstitutional in the federal system (an abuse beyond the focus of this note), the officials of the state abuse

TABLE I

Laws Brought to the Ballot Box: Arkansas
Legislative Referenda and Initiated Referenda, 1938–2004
with Decennial Averages of Passage

YEAR	LP	LF	RATIO	IP	IF	RATIO	TOTAL PASS	TOTAL FAIL	AVE-RAGE	DECEN-NIAL AVERAGE
1938	2	2	0.50	4	3	0.57	6	5	0.55	0.53
1940	2	4	0.33	2	3	0.40	4	7	0.36	
1942	1	2	0.33	2	1	0.67	3	3	0.50	
1944	0	0	0.00	4	3	0.57	4	3	0.57	
1946	1	1	0.50	1	1	0.50	2	2	0.50	
1948	2	0	2.00	3	2	0.60	5	2	0.71	
1950	0	0	0.00	1	3	0.25	1	3	0.25	0.41
1952	2	1	0.67	0	2	0.00	2	3	0.40	
1954	0	3	0.00	0	1	0.00	0	4	0.00	
1956	0	2	0.00	7	3	0.70	7	5	0.58	
1958	3	0	1.00	1	1	0.50	4	1	0.80	
1960	0	3	0.00	0	1	0.00	0	4	0.00	0.14
1962	1	3	0.25	0	3	0.00	1	6	0.14	
1964	0	3	0.00	2	2	0.50	2	5	0.29	
1966	0	0	0.00	0	1	0.00	0	1	0.00	
1968	1	2	0.33	2	2	0.50	3	4	0.43	
1970*	0	1	0.00	0	1	0.00	0	2	0.00	0.60
1972	0	0	0.00	1	0	1.00	1	0	1.00	
1974	2	1	0.67	0	1	0.00	2	2	0.50	
1976	3	0	1.00	1	0	1.00	4	0	1.00	
1978	1	0	1.00	0	1	0.00	1	1	0.50	
1980*	1	0	1.00	0	2	0.00	1	2	0.33	0.55
1982	3	1	0.75	0	0	0.00	3	1	0.75	
1984	1	2	0.33	1	2	0.33	2	4	0.33	
1986	1	0	1.00	1	2	0.33	2	2	0.50	
1988	3	0	1.00	2	1	0.67	5	1	0.83	
1990	1	3	0.25	1	0	1.00	2	3	0.40	0.71

YEAR	LP	LF	RATIO	IP	IF	RATIO	TOTAL PASS	TOTAL FAIL	AVE- RAGE	DECEN- NIAL AVERAGE
1992	3	0	1.00	1	0	1.00	4	0	1.00	
1994	0	0	0.00	1	0	1.00	1	0	1.00	
1996	2	1	0.67	2	1	0.67	4	2	0.67	
1998	1	2	0.33	1	0	1.00	2	2	0.50	
2000	3	0	1.00	1	1	0.50	4	1	0.80	0.52
2002	1	1	0.50	0	2	0.00	1	3	0.25	
2004	1	1	0.50	1	1	0.50	2	2	0.50	
TOTAL	42	39	0.52	43	47	0.48				

Key: LP=Legislative Passed. LF=Legislative Failed. IP=Initiative Passed. IF=Initiative Failed

*Years of constitutional conventions, both of which failed by popular ballot.

the will of the people by allowing it to be hijacked by the clever lawyers who write unconstitutional ballots.

The people are to judge the issue on the ballot. They should not have to assess the fairness of the ballot. Indeed they cannot, for all they can do is cast a vote that seems to be about the issue itself. It is the proper role of the law and of the courts to ensure that the ballot is fair, clear, and honest. If it is not, then regardless of the allure or danger of the issue the ballot presents, it is the responsibility of the courts to send the ballot back for revision.

It would be wrong to prevent a fair ballot lawfully initiated on a constitutionally acceptable question to go to the people. It would be as wrong to send a ballot that will be misunderstood, or that cannot be fully appraised, or that contains propaganda, no matter how artfully cast in innocuous words or casual omissions. In either case, the state would be interfering in the democratic process. In either case, the officials of the state would violate its constitution.

In 2004, the majority of the court was somehow distracted from these basic truths. We must hope that they will not be distracted for long.

TABLE 2

Selected Actions Challenging State-wide and Local Ballots in Arkansas in the Supreme Court of Arkansas, 1912–2004

CASE	BALLOT LANGUAGE	CLAIMS AGAINST THE POPULAR NAME, BALLOT TITLE, OR TEXT	COURT'S RULING
Hodges v. Dawdy 149 S.W. 656 (Ark. 1912)	See Appendix, note 1	Whether "each municipality" and "each county" in then Amendment 7 allowed local municipalities to enact local legislation, thus allowing an initiative to move the county seat.	No. The amendment was a reservation of power and not a delegation of power. "The people of each municipality and county, never having possessed the sovereign legislative power, apart from the other people of the state, could not reserve such power." *Hodges*, 149 S.W. at 660.
Westbrook v. McDonald. 43 S.W.2d 356	See Appendix, note 2	Whether the ballot title was barred because it "appears to describe the act as one permitting that granting of decrees of divorce to applicants who have resided in the state for ninety days *only*," when the true purpose was to permit divorce by persons who have resided in the state for at least ninety days.	Yes. "The ballot title . . . ought to be free from any misleading tendency, whether of amplification, of omission, or of fallacy, and that it must contain no partisan coloring. . . . As the ballot title here submitted might mislead, we have concluded that it was defective and insufficient, and that the amendment was not sufficiently complied with in this respect." *Westbrook*, 43 S.W.2d at 360, citing *In Re Opinions of the Justices*, 171 N.E. 294.
Walton v. McDonald 97 S.W.2d 81 (Ark. 1936)	See Appendix, note 3	Whether a ballot title fails that did not explain that it would require the levy of a tax in order to assist the blind.	Yes. "While the ballot title need not be so elaborate as to set forth the details of the act, it must identify the proposed act and recite its general purposes." The title does not explain how a provision is to be made or where the money will come from. *Walton*, 97 S.W.2d at 82.

CASE	BALLOT LANGUAGE	CLAIMS AGAINST THE POPULAR NAME, BALLOT TITLE, OR TEXT	COURT'S RULING
Bradley v. Hall 251 S.W.2d 470 (Ark. 1952)	See Appendix, note 4	Whether the Modern Consumer Credit Act's popular name was defective, incomplete, and misleading, that it conveys a false idea of the proposed law, and that it contains half truths and partisan coloring.	Yes. The act to allow credit that was barred by usury law was not sufficiently described. Both the ballot title and the popular name were insufficient. The popular name, "Modern Consumer Credit Amendment," was misleading because no one provided a justification for the use of the word "modern." *Bradley,* 251 S.W.2d at 472. "Modern" implied better, and that the rule in place was outdated, which is a form of salesmanship in the title. The language "authorize, define, and limit charges," tended to lead the voter to believe that the amendment would give the legislature powers to curb charges in addition to interest, which was not true.
Moore v. Hall 316 S.W.2d 207 (Ark. 1958)	See Appendix, note 5	Whether the popular name of an antiunion act called the "Freedom to Hire Amendment" was misleading, as the actual effect of the amendment would be to curb the number of employees and the number of new hires.	Yes. "The sufficiency of the title is directly related to the degree to which it enlightens the voter with reference to the changes that he is given the opportunity of approving. . . . Where the popular name conveys a meaning that is in direct conflict with the proposed amendment which would actually restrict and curtail the number and hiring of employees, it has a tendency to mislead voters and contains partisan coloring. . . . Freedom is an enchanting and bewitching word to every citizen of a democracy." *Moore,* 316 S.W.2d 208–09

CASE	BALLOT LANGUAGE	CLAIMS AGAINST THE POPULAR NAME, BALLOT TITLE, OR TEXT	COURT'S RULING
Johnson v. Hall 316 S.W.2d 197 (Ark. 1958)	See Appendix, note 6	Whether "An Amendment to Require Adequate Safety Devices at All Public Railroad Crossings" is misleading because it implies that existing protections at crossings and laws requiring them are inadequate.	Yes. The ballot title suggests to the voter "that present railroads were not using adequate safety devices at all public crossings and that our present statutes do not provide adequate protection for the highway traveler." The title also did not state that all Arkansas railroads would have lights and gates at crossings or the "heavy expense on the railroads" required by the law. *Johnson*, 316 S.W.2d at 198.
Arkansas Women's Political Caucus v. Riviere 677 S.W.2d 846 (Ark. 1984)	See Appendix, note 7	Whether the popular ballot name, "The Unborn Child Amendment" is partial and misleading to the extent that the electorate will be deceived.	Yes. "The requirements for the popular name are not as stringent as those for the ballot title." But catch-phrases would confuse voters, such as "unborn child" in the ballot name, which would mislead voters who follow different schools of thought for what that means. And, the ballot name did not mention the amendment's bar of public funds for abortions. *Arkansas Women's Political Caucus*, 677 S.W.2d 848-4.
Christian Civic Action v. McCuen 884 S.W.2d 605 (Ark. 1994)	See Appendix, note 8	Bill title to establish a state lottery challenged as too long and too abstract.	The deliberate avoidance of common terms for "racetrack," "bingo," and "casinos" was misleading and colored the ballot. "A ballot title must, as we have stated, convey an intelligible idea of the scope and significance of a proposed change in the law. . . . Viewing in the context of the ballot title's considerable length the specialized terminology, which obscures meaning, and the artful amplifications and omissions, which conceal the proposed amendment's potential effect, we must hold that the ballot title manifests a fatal misleading tendency." *Christian Civic Action*, 884 S.W. 2d at 610.

CASE	BALLOT LANGUAGE	CLAIMS AGAINST THE POPULAR NAME, BALLOT TITLE, OR TEXT	COURT'S RULING
Kurrus v. Priest 29 S.W.3d 669 (Ark. 2000)	See Appendix, note 9	Whether the ballot for an amendment to abolish sales and use taxes without voter consent is too long and complex or misleading to voters, or tinged with partisan coloring.	Yes. "The ballot title does not inform the voter of the far-reaching consequences of voting for this measure." For example the definition of "tax increase" in both the ballot title and the text of the amendment does not convey the legal difference between the terms "tax" and "fee." It is thus not clear that the amendment's prohibitions would extend, for example, to taxes imposed by school districts, whereas the ballot title would cover those taxing entities." The ballot title, considered along with its popular name, was misleading, "both by its amplification and omission." *Kurrus*, 29 S.W.3d at 673–675.
Ward v. Priest 86 S.W.3d 884 (Ark. 2002)	See Appendix, note 10	Whether an amendment to abolish taxes on food and medicine refers to matters outside the ballot title that are insufficient to inform the voters concerning the choice they are called upon to make, fails to inform the voters about the fiscal consequences of the proposed amendment, and has definitions of the terms "food" and "medicine" that are inaccurate and misleading.	No. The ballot title clearly informs the voters "that a loss of services or an increase in taxes or both may occur with passage of the amendment." The definitions of "food" and "medicine" are based on long-existing government programs. The language in the ballot title follows the same course as that in the amendment itself, and "the most accurate way to reflect what is contained in the proposed amendment is to nearly repeat the proposed amendment word for word" in the ballot title. The clear language of the proposed amendment would abolish taxes on food and medicine, and it even specifically tells the voter that the proposed amendment "will result in a loss of revenue for state, county, and city governments, as well as school districts." *Ward*, 86 S.W.3d 884 at 891–96.

CASE	BALLOT LANGUAGE	CLAIMS AGAINST THE POPULAR NAME, BALLOT TITLE, OR TEXT	COURT'S RULING
May v. Daniels 2004 Ark. LEXIS 554 (Ark. . 2004)	*See* Appendix, note 11	Whether in "An Amendment Concerning Marriage" the popular name is insufficient because it contains partisan language and misleads the voter into believing that the proposed amendment deals exclusively with marriage, omitting the limitations that the amendment will impose on the rights of unmarried couples or single persons or of the impact the amendment will have on the legal recognition of any future union or partnership.	No. "The term 'marital status' is not vague because it can be understood by the voters within the context of the ballot title." "The voters are sufficiently informed that the legislature will further interpret the amendment in the future. "In sum, our job is not to review the relative merit or fault of the proposed initiative, nor is it to fashion a perfect or even a better ballot title. Rather, we are to review the ballot title liberally, using common sense, with an eye toward the purpose of Amendment 7, which is to reserve to the people the right to adopt or reject constitutional amendments or legislation." *May,* Ark. LEXIS 554, at 13, 15.

Notes Related to Ballot Cases*

1. That section one, article five, of the Constitution of the state of Arkansas be amended so as to read as follows:

"Section 1. The legislative powers of this state shall be vested in a General Assembly, which shall consist of the Senate and House of Representatives, but the people of each municipality, each county and of the state, reserve to themselves power to propose laws and amendments to the Constitution and to enact or reject the same at the polls as independent of the Legislative Assembly, and also reserve power at their own option to approve or reject at the polls any act of the Legislative Assembly. The first power reserved by the people is the initiative, and not more than 8 percent. of the legal voters shall be required to propose any measure by such petition, and every such petition shall include the full text of the measure so proposed. Initiative petitions shall be filed with the Secretary of State not less than four months before the election at which they are to be voted upon.

"The second power is a referendum, and it may be ordered (except as to laws necessary for the immediate preservation of the public peace, health or safety) either by the petition signed by 6 percent. of the legal voters or by the Legislative Assembly as other bills are enacted. Referendum petitions shall be filed with the Secretary of State not more than ninety days after the final adjournment of the session of the Legislative Assembly which passed the bill on which the referendum is demanded. The veto power of the Governor shall not extend to measures referred to the people. All elections on measures referred to the people of the state shall be had at the biennial regular general elections, except when the Legislative Assembly shall order a special election. Any measure referred to the people shall take effect and become a law when it is approved by a majority of the votes cast thereon and not otherwise. The style of all bills shall be, 'Be it enacted by the people of the state of Arkansas.' This section shall not be construed to deprive any member of the Legislative Assembly of the right to introduce any measure. The whole number of votes cast for the office of Governor at the regular election last preceding the filing of any petition for the initiative or for the referendum shall be the basis on which the number of legal votes necessary

---

*A fuller table of ballot cases is in *2005 Arkansas Law Notes.*

to sign such petition shall be counted. Petitions and orders for the initiative and for the referendum shall be filed with the Secretary of State, and in submitting the same to the people he and all other officers shall be guided by the general laws and the acts submitting this amendment until legislation shall be specially provided therefor[e]." *Hodges* 149 S.W. 656 at 657 (Ark. 1912).

2. Ballot title: "To permit the granting of decrees of divorce to applicants who have resided in the State for a period of only three months."

3. "An Act to provide for the assistance of aged and/or blind persons and funds therefore, the administration and distribution of same, penalties for the violation of Act, and for other purposes." *Walton,* 97 S.W.2d 81 (Ark. 1936).

4. "A proposed constitutional amendment to amend Article XIX, Section 13 of the Arkansas Constitution of 1874 by empowering the General Assembly to enact laws to authorize, define, and limit charges, in addition to interest, in connection with the lending of money and commercial transactions." *Bradley,* 251 S.W.2d 470, 471 (Ark. 1952).

5. Popular name: "Freedom to Hire Amendment." Ballot title: "An amendment prohibiting practices that require or induce an employer to employ a greater number of persons than the employer deems necessary to carry on his business." *Moore,* 316 S.W.2d 207 (Ark. 1958).

6. "Proposed Constitutional Amendment No. 52 (By Petition) Safety Crossing Amendment—An amendment to require adequate safety devices at all public railroad crossings. Section 1. The practice of operating trains and locomotives over railroads in this state across highways, public roads, crossings and city streets at high rates of speed without adequate protection to the vehicular and pedestrian traffic at such crossings is detrimental to the safety and welfare of the people and contrary to the public policy of this state. Section 2. Every railroad company in this state whose line or lines are more than one hundred miles in length who operate trains in excess of twenty-five miles per hour over said lines shall install and maintain at each public road crossing or street electrically controlled warning signals which flash red for an approaching train and shall provide and maintain electrically controlled boards or gates on each side of such roads, crossings or streets as a further protection. Section 3. Failure to provide or maintain such warning signals or electrically controlled boards or gates shall create an inference and presumption of civil negligence to any such

railroad company in any civil action for damages to persons or property against such company arising out of accidents at such public roads, crossings or streets. Filed: July 3, 1958 C. G. 'Crip' Hall Secretary of State." *Johnson,* 316 S.W.2d 197 (Ark. 1958).

7. "The Unborn Child Amendment." *Arkansas Women's Political Caucus,* 677 S.W.2d 846 (Ark. 1983).

8. "AN AMENDMENT TO AUTHORIZE A STATE LOTTERY, NONPROFIT BINGO, PARI-MUTUEL WAGERING, AND ADDITIONAL GAMES OF CHANCE AT RACETRACK SITES." *Christian Civic Action Committee,* 884 S.W.2d 605 (Ark. 1994).

9. Popular name: "An Amendment to Abolish the State and Local Sales and Use Tax on Used Goods, to prohibit the increase of taxes without voter approval at a general election, to provide for a three year statute of limitations for actions to recover taxes, by the taxing authority or by an aggrieved taxpayer, to provide procedural safeguards for taxpayers, and for other purposes." Ballot title: "AN AMENDMENT TO THE ARKANSAS CONSTITUTION ABOLISHING THE STATE AND LOCAL SALES AND USE TAX ON USED GOODS; AUTHORIZING THE COLLECTION OF SALES AND USE TAX ON GOODS USED TO MAKE REMANUFACTURED GOODS, BUT NOT ON THE SALE PRICE OR MARKET VALUE OF THE REMANUFACTURED GOODS; PROVIDING THAT THIS AMENDMENT SHALL NOT BE CONSTRUED TO PREVENT THE IMPOSITION OF SALES AND USE TAX UPON OTHERWISE TAXABLE GOODS, OR THE SALE OR USE OF SAME, WHICH HAVE NOT BEEN PREVIOUSLY SUBJECT TO ANY SALES OR USE TAX BY ANY GOVERNMENT ENTITY; PROVIDING THAT THIS AMENDMENT SHALL NOT BE CONSTRUED TO PROHIBIT THE COLLECTION OF TAXES FOR WHICH LIABILITY ACCRUED PRIOR TO THE EFFECTIVE DATE OF THIS AMENDMENT; PROHIBITING THE IMPOSITION OR INCREASE OF ANY TAX, OR THE DIVERSION OF ANY FUEL TAXES OR OTHER REVENUE SOURCES PRESENTLY USED FOR ROAD OR BRIDGE CONSTRUCTION OR MAINTENANCE TO OTHER PURPOSES, WITHOUT THE APPROVAL OF A MAJORITY OF THE QUALIFIED ELECTORS, OF THE STATE OR THE AFFECTED LOCAL GOVERNMENTAL ENTITY, FREELY VOTING AT THEIR ABSOLUTE UNFETTERED DISCRETION UPON THE ISSUE AT A REGULARLY SCHEDULED STATEWIDE ELECTION;

PROVIDING THAT THE REDUCTION OR ELIMINATION OF
EXEMPTIONS OR CREDITS, OR THE CHANGING OF ANY LAW
OR RULE WHICH RESULTS IN THE COLLECTION OF ADDI-
TIONAL REVENUE FROM SOME OR ALL TAXPAYERS, SHALL BE
DEEMED A TAX INCREASE TO THE EXTENT THAT SAID LAW
RESULTS IN INCREASED TAX OR EXACTION; PROVIDING THAT
THE TERM "MAJORITY OF THE QUALIFIED ELECTORS," AS
USED IN THIS AMENDMENT, MEANS A MAJORITY OF THE
QUALIFIED ELECTORS WHO ACTUALLY APPEAR AND VOTE
UPON THE PERTINENT QUESTION; ABOLISHING THE RULE
AGAINST RECOVERY BACK OF VOLUNTARY PAYMENTS, AS
APPLIED TO ILLEGAL EXACTIONS; PROVIDING FOR A THREE (3)
YEAR STATUTE OF LIMITATIONS FOR THE CITIZENS' RECOV-
ERY BACK OF ILLEGAL EXACTIONS, AND FOR A THREE (3) YEAR
STATUTE OF LIMITATIONS ON ALL CIVIL, CRIMINAL, OR
OTHER ACTIONS BY ANY STATE OR LOCAL GOVERNMENT TO
COLLECT DELINQUENT TAXES; PROVIDING THAT IN ANY ILLE-
GAL EXACTION LAWSUIT, ALL PERSONS SIMILARLY SITUATED
TO THE NAMED PLAINTIFF SHALL BE ENTITLED TO RECOVER
BACK ANY SUMS FOUND TO HAVE BEEN ILLEGALLY EXACTED,
LESS COSTS AND REASONABLE ATTORNEY'S FEES, UPON SUCH
CONDITIONS AS THE COURT MAY FIND JUST; EXPANDING THE
DEFINITION OF ILLEGAL EXACTION TO INCLUDE NOT ONLY
ILLEGAL IMPOSITION, LEVYING, ASSESSMENT, OR COLLEC-
TION OF TAX OR ENFORCED GOVERNMENTAL OR QUASI GOV-
ERNMENTAL EXACTIONS, BUT ALSO ERRONEOUS OR
EXCESSIVE IMPOSITION, LEVYING, ASSESSMENT, OR COLLEC-
TION OF TAX OR ENFORCED GOVERNMENTAL OR QUASI GOV-
ERNMENTAL EXACTIONS OF ANY KIND WHATSOEVER,
PROVIDED, HOWEVER, THAT SUCH SHALL NOT INCLUDE ANY
LEGAL TAX IF THE TAXING AUTHORITY REASONABLY
ATTEMPTED TO COMPLY WITH ALL LAWS, REGULATIONS, AND
REQUIREMENTS FOR THE ASSESSMENT OR COLLECTION OF
TAX, AND THE CIRCUMSTANCES ARE SUCH THAT THE TAXPAY-
ERS IN FAIRNESS AND EQUITY OUGHT NOT TO ESCAPE LIABIL-
ITY FOR THE TAX; PROVIDING THAT SOVEREIGN IMMUNITY,
FAILURE TO EXHAUST ADMINISTRATIVE REMEDIES, FAILURE
TO APPROPRIATE MONEY FOR REPAYMENT, OR PAYMENT

OVER TO ANOTHER ENTITY, CONSTITUTE NO DEFENSES TO
AN ACTION FOR ILLEGAL EXACTION; PROVIDING FOR LIB-
ERAL CONSTRUCTION IN FAVOR OF THE TAXPAYER, SEVER-
ABILITY, AND GENERAL REPEALER OF CONFLICTING
PROVISIONS; PROVIDING THAT THE AMENDMENT IS SELF-
EXECUTING AND SHALL TAKE EFFECT IMMEDIATELY, EXCEPT
AS OTHERWISE PROVIDED; PROVIDING THAT ALL PROTEC-
TIONS FOR THE TAXPAYER, RELATED TO LITIGATION, SHALL
APPLY TO ALL ACTIONS BROUGHT TO JUDGMENT AFTER THE
DATE OF PASSAGE OF THIS AMENDMENT, EXCEPT AS TO
ACTIONS IN WHICH A NEW TRIAL WOULD BE REQUIRED IN
ORDER TO DETERMINE FACTS ESSENTIAL TO THE JUDGMENT,
OR ACTIONS IN WHICH THE JUDGMENT WAS ALREADY FINAL
ON THE DATE OF THE PASSAGE OF THIS AMENDMENT; AND
FOR OTHER PURPOSES." *Kurrus,* 29 S.W.3d 669, 678–79 (Ark. 2000).
10. The initiative's popular name is "Amendment Eliminating Taxes on
Food and Medicine." Its ballot title is "AN AMENDMENT TO THE
ARKANSAS CONSTITUTION, ABOLISHING AND PROHIBITING
TAXATION ON FOOD AND MEDICINE; DEFINING 'FOOD' TO
MEAN 'ANY ITEM THAT WAS ELIGIBLE FOR PURCHASE WITH
FEDERAL FOOD STAMPS ON APRIL 1, 2001 OR IS OTHERWISE
AVAILABLE UNDER ANY STATE OR FEDERAL NUTRITION
ASSISTANCE PROGRAM AS EXISTING ON APRIL 1, 2001;' DEFIN-
ING 'MEDICINE' TO MEAN 'ANY ITEM BEING FURNISHED OR
AVAILABLE AT A REDUCED COST UNDER ANY STATE OR FED-
ERAL HEALTH CARE ASSISTANCE PROGRAM ON APRIL 1, 2001;'
PROVIDING THAT ALL NEW, ADDITIONAL, OR INCREASED
TAXES NOT EXEMPTING FOOD AND MEDICINE SHALL BE
VOID; PROVIDING THAT TAXES ON FOOD AND MEDICINE
ESTABLISHED BEFORE THE EFFECTIVE DATE OF THIS AMEND-
MENT SHALL EXPIRE ON JULY 4TH 2003, EXCEPT THAT THOSE
REQUIRED TO SECURE BONDS OR OTHER CONTRACTUAL
OBLIGATIONS MAY BE EXTENDED TO SATISFY THOSE OBLIG-
ATIONS; AND REQUIRING THAT ALL REVENUE FROM SUCH
TAXES REGARDLESS OF SOURCE SHALL BE USED EXCLUSIVELY
TO FULFILL AND TERMINATE SUCH CONTRACTS AT THE EAR-
LIEST POSSIBLE DATE. THIS AMENDMENT ABOLISHES ALL
FORMS AND TYPES OF TAXES ON FOOD AND MEDICINE (AS

THOSE TERMS ARE DEFINED HEREIN) AND WILL RESULT IN A LOSS OF REVENUE FOR STATE, COUNTY, AND CITY GOVERN-MENTS, AS WELL AS SCHOOL DISTRICTS, WITH THE RESULT THAT A REDUCTION IN THE SERVICES PROVIDED BY THOSE ENTITIES AND/OR AN INCREASE IN OTHER TAXES MAY BE REQUIRED." *Priest v. Kimball.* 86 S.W.3d 884 at 890 (Ark. 2002).

11. The initiative's popular name is "An Amendment Concerning Marriage." Its ballot title is "A PROPOSED AMENDMENT TO THE ARKANSAS CONSTITUTION PROVIDING THAT MARRIAGE CONSISTS ONLY OF THE UNION OF ONE MAN AND ONE WOMAN; THAT LEGAL STATUS FOR UNMARRIED PERSONS WHICH IS IDENTICAL OR SUBSTANTIALLY SIMILAR TO MARI-TAL STATUS SHALL NOT BE VALID OR RECOGNIZED IN ARKANSAS, EXCEPT THAT THE LEGISLATURE MAY RECOG-NIZE A COMMON LAW MARRIAGE FROM ANOTHER STATE BETWEEN A MAN AND A WOMAN; AND THAT THE LEGISLA-TURE HAS THE POWER TO DETERMINE THE CAPACITY OF PERSONS TO MARRY, SUBJECT TO THIS AMENDMENT, AND THE LEGAL RIGHTS, OBLIGATIONS, PRIVILEGES, AND IMMU-NITIES OF MARRIAGE."

I am grateful for the help of Blake Rutherford in his third year, and of Dan Oberste and Timothy Evans in theirs, for their research assistance. During the writing of this note, the law school lost a leader, the bar lost a mentor, and my family and I lost a dear friend in the death of Richard Atkinson. This note is a small token toward the memory of a great man.

The Antievolution Law

Church and State in Arkansas

CAL LEDBETTER JR.

*This case study was written a quarter of a century ago by one of the state's most respected intellectuals and political activists. Though the study itself is dated, the issues it raises are as salient today as they ever were. The proximate issue enjoined in this study is the constitutionality of Arkansas's antievolution law, approved by the voters as Initiated Act No. 1 in 1928. This act outlawed the teaching in any Arkansas public school or public institution of higher learning the theory that "mankind ascended or descended from a lower order of animal." The issue became a much celebrated controversy when the law was successfully challenged in the courts almost forty years after its enactment on the grounds that it violated the Establishment Clause of the First Amendment to the U.S. Constitution [*Epperson v. Arkansas (1968)].*

*Interestingly, Epperson did not settle the conflict in Arkansas over the teaching of Darwin's theory, as the legislature passed, and Gov. Frank White signed into law, another "monkey law" only months after Professor Ledbetter's study, reproduced here, was first published. This law was also struck down by the federal courts [*McLean v. Arkansas (1982)].*

Some three years before the United States Supreme Court struck down the Arkansas antievolution law as unconstitutional,[1] Harry Pearson, a reporter for the Pine Bluff *Commercial,* had this to say about that particular law:

Cal Ledbetter Jr., "The Antievolution Law: Church and State in Arkansas," *Arkansas Historical Quarterly* 38 (Winter 1979): 299–327. Reprinted with permission.

> There is a law in Arkansas that forbids the teaching of the theory of
> evolution in the public schools. It is an unenforceable law; it is a dis-
> regarded law, but its very existence in the Arkansas statute books is
> a symbol. To the fundamentalist it is a symbol that the state tacitly
> endorses his concept of religion. To the liberal it is a symbol of dark-
> ness and witches and monkey trials. To the professional educator.
> . . . it is an affront to the principle of academic freedom.[2]

The antievolution law in Arkansas has managed to generate intense emotions long after the passing of the historical period that prompted its
adoption. In 1959, a state representative from Pulaski County, at the
request of a young high school student, introduced a bill to repeal the
antievolution law.[3] The bill was withdrawn three days later [4] after unexpected opposition developed, and the sponsor of the repealing legislation stated that "It now appears to me that the majority of the people of
my county do not wish to grant the academic freedom these young
people requested."[5] On June 28, 1966, sixteen hundred people attended
a meeting in Little Rock that lasted three and a half hours and featured
a general debate on the subject of evolution.[6] One reason for this article
is to explore the causes and consequences of these still strong feelings
produced by a law passed a half century ago.

It is also interesting to look at Arkansas as a case study of the only
state to pass an antievolution law by popular vote. This action came at
a time when the national movement to embody antievolution sentiment
in law had probably peaked. Nevertheless, when an initiated act is passed
that can only be changed by a two-thirds vote of the legislature,[7] it poses
serious problems in strategy for those who may wish to challenge the
protection that a popularly passed law can give to theological position.
Commenting on this problem, John T. Scopes, an expert in these matters, said that once such a law gets on the books it is next to impossible
to change because "no politician is going to go out on a limb and try to
repeal it."[8] The question of what strategy was pursued to get the law
removed from the books, and why, will be another focus of the article.

Although the United States Supreme Court decision striking down
the Arkansas antievolution law was unanimous, there were three concurring opinions. Some members of the United States Supreme Court
also seemed quite critical of the Arkansas Supreme Court for not dispos-
ing of the case adequately, and, consequently, forcing the nation's highest court to choose between the conflicting legal values of a state's power

over curriculum and an individual's right to freedom of speech and ideas and the guarantee that church and state be kept separate. The legal questions raised by this case will be also explored.

It is hoped, too, that a study of the Arkansas antievolution law can produce insights into the strongly held values that led to its passage, the problems faced in the implementation and repeal of such a law, and the legal consequences that arise when church and state are mixed.

Background

By the beginning of the twentieth century, urbanism, industrialization, and expanding education had begun to threaten the traditional values of rural and small-town America. Many thought that traditional religious values were especially jeopardized by social gospelism, scholarly Biblical criticism, and the spread of the teaching of evolution through the nation's colleges. To counter these new trends, supporters of social and religious orthodoxy presented their views in a set of twelve pamphlets published from 1909 to 1912 and titled *The Fundamentals: A Testimony to Truth,* and hence the name "fundamentalists."[9]

To compensate for the ground lost in the colleges and to prevent the spread of the teaching of evolution to the more numerous students in high schools, state legislatures were approached by fundamentalists in the south and middle west to outlaw the teaching of evolution in state-supported schools. A contributing factor to the urgency of this move was the realization that the number of high schools in the country had doubled between 1897 and 1912 and that a high school diploma was now becoming a prerequisite for success in life.[10]

Evolution seemed to incorporate all the evils, real or imaginary, against which the defenders of the social and religious status quo were battling. It threatened their religious viewpoint because one tenet of fundamentalism was an infallible Bible, literally interpreted,[11] and the logical corollary of that belief is that if any portion of the Bible is not literally true, none of it may be true. The teaching of evolution in the public schools undermined the values of their children, and hence, put the family as an institution in danger. Evolution was identified with science, science was identified with materialism, and materialism was seen as eating away the moral fabric of society, particularly in the 1920s.[12] To the fundamentalists, evolution became the hated symbol of all that was threatening in a modern and increasingly urban society, and their efforts to turn back the tide in the 1920s were focused on such projects as banning the teaching of evolution in public schools, preserving prohibition, defeating Al Smith in 1928, and supporting William Jennings Bryan in his struggle to preserve traditional values in the Scopes trial and elsewhere. Perhaps the menace of evolution to the fundamentalists is best described by Bryan, who said in 1924 that "All the ills from which America suffers can be traced back to the teaching of evolution. It would be better to destroy every other book ever written, and just save the first three verses of Genesis."[13]

William Jennings Bryan was the charismatic leader around whom the antievolution movement coalesced and it was not until he "entered the conflict in 1920 that the movement became one of national importance."[14] Support for the movement was strong in the middle west, and, at least for a time, it probably also had "the active support and sympathy of the overwhelming majority of the Southern people."[15] One goal of the movement was to use this popular support to pressure state legislatures into passing antievolution laws and into becoming major instruments in the revolt against modernity.

Many different techniques were used to ban the teaching of evolution in the public schools from 1920 to about 1926. Three states (Arkansas, Mississippi, and Tennessee) passed specific statutes to accomplish this, either by action of the legislature or vote of the people.[16] The Florida legislature, by joint resolution, condemned the teaching of evolution in the public schools and, in Oklahoma, the textbook law was amended to outlaw the teaching of evolution.[17] In North Carolina and Texas, state boards with educational responsibilities banned textbooks that made reference to evolution.[18] The same result was accomplished by Louisiana by order of the state superintendent of education.[19] Nationwide, in the eight-year period from 1921 to 1929, thirty-seven antievolution bills, resolutions, and riders were introduced in twenty state legislatures.[20] In addition, "Informal restrictions through the censorship of textbooks by superintendents of education, local school boards, etc., were widely applied."[21]

The antievolution movement, despite its initial successes in the south from 1920 to 1925, experienced near disaster in July 1925. The unfavorable publicity that came from the Scopes trial that began July 13, 1925, and the death of William Jennings Bryan two weeks later were two events that had a crippling effect on fundamentalism and the antievolution movement. The loss of Bryan was especially devastating, not only because of his eloquence and charisma, but also because he was the most important national figure associated with the antievolution cause. The necessity of defeating Al Smith in 1928 also diverted time and effort from the antievolution cause. By 1930, even though religious orthodoxy remained, the kind of fundamentalism that held antievolution as its central component had collapsed as an organized movement.[22] This made the Arkansas experience even more interesting since it came at a time when the antievolution movement was in decline.

The 1927 Legislative Attempt

As early as 1924 the Arkansas State Baptist Convention had officially gone on record as totally rejecting the theory of evolution.[23] By spring 1926, petitions began to circulate in several communities requesting that legislators enact a bill similar to the Tennessee Antievolution Law,[24] and by summer 1926 it was fairly clear that a bill would be introduced in the 1927 session.[25] The two individuals most identified with the bill to be proposed were State Rep. Astor L. Rotenberry of Pulaski County and the Rev. Ben M. Bogard, pastor of the Antioch Missionary Baptist Church in Little Rock and chairman of the Antievolution Committee of the Arkansas Association of Missionary Baptist Churches, a group that had officially separated from the Arkansas State Baptist Convention in 1902 but still shared with the convention a common opposition to evolution.[26] Another strong supporter of an antievolution bill was the Rev. James Seth Compere, editor of the *Baptist Advance,* the official publication of the Arkansas Baptist State Convention. Compere not only contributed editorials to the cause but was instrumental in drafting and passing resolutions against evolution at Baptist state conventions from 1924 to 1927.

On December 19, 1926, Representative Rotenberry released his bill to the newspapers and asked for public comment on its provisions. The proposed bill did not contain references to the Biblical story in Genesis, but it did make it unlawful for the theory of evolution to be taught in the public schools or for a teacher or textbook commissioner to use or adopt any textbook that teaches that mankind descended from a lower species of animal. Penalty provisions included a fine not to exceed one thousand dollars and revocation of the license to teach.[27]

Before the legislative session began, letters to the editor in the

Arkansas Gazette dealing with the proposed new law developed both sides of the issue. Those favoring the proposed bill advanced the arguments that people who pay taxes to the public schools need to have a voice in what is taught there and that evolutionists may teach their doctrine, but not in the public schools. Opponents stressed the difficulty of legislating against theories or doctrines, and one letter writer who opposed the Rotenberry bill hoped that Arkansas would not become "the laughing stock of the educated world by passing such a law."[28] Ministers were also divided in their comments. Dr. Hay Watson Smith, minister of the Second Presbyterian Church in Little Rock, quoted the scientist Luther Burbank to the effect that "Those who would legislate against the teaching of evolution should also legislate against gravity, electricity, and the unreasonable velocity of light,"[29] while Calvin B. Waller, pastor of Little Rock's Second Baptist Church, said "There is no common ground of compromise between evolution and the Bible."[30]

On January 12, 1927, Rep. Thomas P. Atkins of Prairie County introduced an antievolution bill (House Bill No. 4) on the first day of the 1927 session of the Arkansas legislature.[31] The Rotenberry bill was introduced the very next day, January 13, and became House Bill No. 34.[32] The major difference between the two bills was that the Atkins bill prohibited the teaching of any theory that conflicted with the biblical story of creation[33] while the Rotenberry bill prohibited only the teaching that men descended from a lower order of animals.[34] At any rate, Atkins became a cosponsor, along with four others, of the Rotenberry bill and apparently decided not to actively push his bill. The Rotenberry measure was referred to the House Education Committee on January 13, 1927.[35]

A hearing on the bill was set for the night of January 28, 1927, to begin at seven thirty. The *Arkansas Democrat* was not pleased with what was about to take place and reported:

> Arkansas will take the stage in the "monkey business" entertainment that has been going the rounds in various states, Friday night when the house committee on education will hold a public hearing on Representative Rotenberry's antievolution measure. The meeting will be held in the house chamber at the state capitol, and the curtain will be raised promptly at 7:30 o'clock. There will be no preliminaries or orchestral numbers, the whole program being devoted to the drama itself.[36]

On the night of the hearing, the house galleries were packed and the meeting continued until eleven. Eleven people testified for and against, with the proponents being led by the Rev. Ben M. Bogard and the major opponent being Hay Watson Smith, the Presbyterian minister. The committee adjourned without taking any action, but the chairman announced that it would meet again.[37] Another public meeting was scheduled for February 2, 1927, but interest was apparently waning. The crowd was not nearly as big, and only four of the thirteen committee members were present when the hearing opened, and one of these left before the hearing was finished.[38] Fourteen people testified, equally split between those for and against, and at the conclusion of the meeting, the chairman announced that no more open hearings would be held but that the committee would meet at a later date and prepare its report.[39]

Perhaps anticipating that the committee vote would be negative, Bogard had a circular placed on every legislator's desk on February 2, 1927. It began with the phrase "Fair Warning" and ended with the admonition that if the Rotenberry bill did not become law "the war has just started. We shall appeal to the people to make it an issue in every county for the next two years."[40] The circular was signed by Bogard as chairman of the Antievolution Committee of the Arkansas Association of Missionary Baptist Churches. The House responded by passing a resolution by a vote of forty-three to thirty-four stating that "We do condemn such methods endeavoring to coerce the passage of any bill whether we are for or against the proposed measure."[41] Bogard's reaction to the resolution was to thank the House members for the free publicity given to the antievolution law and to repeat his warning.[42]

The House Education Committee gave a "do not pass" recommendation to the Rotenberry bill on February 3, 1927.[43] Only seven of the thirteen members of the committee attended the meeting at which the vote was taken, and six of the seven who attended voted "no" and one voted "yes." The lone dissenter at the committee meeting was later joined by a second member who was not at the meeting in a minority report recommending that HB No. 34 "do pass."[44] After an unsuccessful attempt by opponents to amend the bill to prohibit any library supported with tax funds to have on its shelves any books "relating to biology, anthropology or genetics, or any other phase of evolution,"[45] the measure was first made a special order of business on Monday, February 7,

1927.[46] A motion to table was defeated by a vote of thirty-eight in favor and fifty-three against, and the bill was then made a special order of business on Wednesday, February 9, 1927, at two in the afternoon.[47]

Some confusion still lingers as to the outcome of the vote on that Wednesday afternoon. Debate lasted about three hours, with Rep. Harney M. McGehee from Crawford County arguing for the bill because "the legislature is the guardian of the state's children and has a right to say what shall be taught in the public schools"[48] and Rep. H. Jordan Monk of Jefferson County arguing against the measure because "the bill strikes at the heart of freedom of thought and speech."[49] Although the first roll call seemed to indicate that the bill had been defeated by one vote, some quick maneuvering switched two no votes, those of Arthur J. Jones of Pulaski County and W. E. Spencer of Drew County, to the affirmative column so that the final official total showed that the bill passed by a vote of fifty-one to forty-six with three absent and not voting.[50]

The bill went to the Senate in the late afternoon of February 9, 1927, and as soon as the bill was read a second time there on February 10, it was tabled by an overwhelming voice vote.[51] The entire process took less than fifteen minutes.[52] On February 15, 1927, an attempt was made in the Senate to take the measure from the table, but after it was discovered that the bill had been returned to the House, another motion was made to return the bill so that the Senate could still take some action on it. This attempt was probably an effort to put senators on record one way or another, and the final test came on a motion to table the motion to return the bill from the House. The motion to table carried by a vote of seventeen for, fourteen against, and four absent and not voting.[53] Opponents of the bill voted to table, while proponents voted not to table, and the result was the final defeat of the Rotenberry bill.

The *Arkansas Democrat* was pleased with the outcome and declared that the Senators who had voted against the antievolution bill deserved to be placed on an honor roll for political courage and commended the senate itself for deciding that "the province of the legislature is not to settle debates over theology."[54] Representative Rotenberry was not so pleased with the performance of the Senate and recommended that the initiative now be used so that the issue could be settled by popular vote. He felt the Senate had not responded to the popular will and that the use of the initiative would give the people an "opportunity of bringing into being an antievolution law with teeth in it."[55] Ben Bogard was equally unhappy with the results and he quickly incorporated an organization called the American Antievolution Association, with himself as president. One purpose of the organization was to get enough signatures so that an initiated antievolution measure could be put on the ballot in November 1928.[56]

The 1928 Campaign

Securing the number of names to place an initiated act on the ballot in November 1928 was not really a difficult problem, given the high emotional content of such an issue and the low number of names required. An initiated act required signatures equaling only 8 percent of the votes cast for governor in the last preceding general election.[57] Since general elections in Arkansas in the 1920s for the office of governor seldom involved any real Republican challenge to the Democratic nominee, the turnout was minimal, and in the general election of 1926, only 111,656 people voted for the office of governor.[58] This meant that fewer than nine thousand legal voters could place an initiated act on the ballot. Representative Rotenberry, Bogard, and Dr. John F. Hammett, president of the Arkansas Antievolution League, were the chief sponsors of the initiated act. The provisions were almost identical to the Rotenberry bill.[59] The proposed initiated act outlawed in any college or public school financed in whole or in part with state or local taxes, the teaching of "the theory or doctrine that mankind ascended or descended from a lower order of animal."[60] It was also made illegal for teachers or textbook commissioners to select textbooks that taught the prohibited theory to be used in any state institution. Teachers or textbook commissioners violating the law were guilty of misdemeanors and, upon conviction, had to vacate their positions and were subject to fines not to exceed five hundred dollars.

In May 1927, Rev. Ben Bogard began sending out letters with petitions enclosed[61] and by November 1927, he announced that petitions were being circulated over the state and that the required percentage nearly had been achieved.[62] Bogard and Rotenberry stumped the state to secure petitions and support for the proposed initiated act. The Rev. James Seth Compere, editor of the *Baptist Advance,* gave both his editorial endorsement and his personal support to the movement. Compere, at the time, was a powerful figure at Baptist state conventions, and his stand with Bogard and Rotenberry gave significant assistance to the campaign for an initiated act. In May 1928, the *New York Times* reported that the Arkansas Antievolution League claimed to have four thousand more names than required.[63] On June 6, 1928, petitions with more than 19,000 names were filed in the secretary of state's office.[64] This was more than sufficient and the antievolution measure appeared on the November 1928 general election ballot as Initiated Act No. 1.

The opponents of Initiated Act No. 1 formed a statewide Committee Against Act No. 1 with Charles T. Coleman, a Little Rock attorney and judge, as chairman. The college establishment of the day was well represented on the committee, and its membership included many prominent academic figures such as Charles H. Brough, former governor and president of Central Baptist College at Conway; John C. Futrall, president of the University of Arkansas; John Hugh Reynolds, president of Hendrix College at Conway; Virgil Jones, dean of the College of Arts and Sciences at the University of Arkansas; and Dr. Frank Vinsonhaler, dean of the Arkansas Medical School at Little Rock. Other members included John Netherland Heiskell, editor of the *Arkansas Gazette,* and the Rev. Hay Watson Smith, minister of the Second Presbyterian Church in Little Rock. The Committee Against Act No. 1 took out a series of newspaper advertisements beginning on October 7, 1928, and ending on November 6, 1928. The advertisements stressed the general acceptance of evolution in the scientific and intellectual communities, and the idea that evolution and religious faith were not incompatible. Above all, they pleaded with the voters to avoid making Arkansas look ridiculous and to protect "our schools from foolish and futile legislation and the good name of our state from ridicule."[65]

The idea that evolution was atheistic was a theme stressed by the supporters of Initiated Act No. 1 and was an argument that the opponents of Initiated Act. No. 1 sought to counter in their advertisements. The opponents were sorely distressed by the arrival in the state of Charles Smith of New York, who was president of the American Association for the Advancement of Atheism. Smith, a native of Sebastian County, had returned to Arkansas during the first week of October 1928 to campaign against the initiated act.[66] A flamboyant individual who did identify evolution with atheism, Smith set up an atheist headquarters in Little Rock as part of his campaign. He was arrested and fined for breach of the peace, then went to jail rather than pay the fine, and while in jail went on a hunger strike to protest his own arrest and the proposed antievolution act. He was finally released from jail, but opponents of the initiated act devoted much of the space in their advertisements attempting to avoid any identification with the out-of-state atheist and his campaign.

Other support for the opponents of the antievolution act came from both Little Rock newspapers. The *Arkansas Democrat* editorialized on October 28, 1928, about the unfairness of applying the proposed law only to state-supported institutions, pointing out that it would have no effect on private schools. The *Arkansas Gazette* deplored the tendency to equate evolution with atheism and urged its readers not to "make Arkansas the Monkey State."[67] The University of Arkansas, which would be directly affected by the law, probably took the leading role in the fight against it with President Futrall, Dean Jones, and Dean Vinsonhaler all actively involved. The faculty members at Fayetteville also participated individually through the American Association of University Professors.[68] Ironically enough, the University of Arkansas was attempting to secure a chapter of Phi Beta Kappa at this time.[69]

The supporters of the antievolution act had overwhelming support both from official Baptist groups and undoubtedly from rank-and-file Baptists in the state. In fact, popular support was so strong that occasional tirades by Bogard to the effect that the move to teach evolution had been brought about by the John D. Rockefeller Foundation, "which has been controlled by skeptics and infidels and atheists"[70] didn't seem to matter. The proponents of Initiated Act No. 1 spent very little money on newspaper advertising and had only one advertisement in the *Arkansas Gazette,* headed simply "The Bible or Atheism, which?" The advertisement stressed the theme that atheism equals evolution and stated that "All atheists favor evolution. If you agree with atheism, vote against Act No. 1. If you agree with the Bible, vote for Act No. 1."[71] The piece concluded: "The *Gazette* said Russian Bolshevists laughed at Tennessee. True, and that sort will laugh at Arkansas. Who cares? Vote FOR ACT NO.1."[72]

In the 1928 November general election, Initiated Act No. 1 carried by a vote of 108,991 to 63,406.[73] The margin of approval was 63 percent, and the antievolution act lost in only five counties. Although the measure lost in Pulaski County by a vote of 5,374 in favor and 7,662 against, it carried four other urban counties (Jefferson, Garland, Sebastian, and Washington) by a substantial margin. The vote in those counties was 11,324 to 7,025.[74] Even though opposition to the act was led by the

University of Arkansas, the *Arkansas Gazette* reported that the act "obtained a majority in the ward where the university is located."[75] For the rest of the nation, reactions to the victory of the antievolution act ranged from outrage to acceptance. "For the first time in the history of the world the teaching of a scientific theory has been made a statutory offense by a vote of the people," declared Maynard Shipley in *Current History*.[76] But the *New York World* voiced approval: "Foolish as a referendum on such a subject may appear, the ultimate right of the taxpayers to say what shall be taught in their schools cannot be denied unless we are able to repudiate Democracy."[77]

Shortly after the victory of the antievolution act, J. P. Womack, state superintendent of public instruction, said that he thought the law would have no effect on the public schools since no state-approved textbooks in the public schools contained any reference to Darwin's theory.[78] Later, however, Womack wrote a letter to county and city school superintendents notifying them that the state Department of Education approval had been withdrawn from *World Book Encyclopedia,* pending a court decision, because it contained statements that might be in violation of the new law. He also said that the act raised questions concerning dictionaries, encyclopedias, and other reference works and that the word "teach" in the law needed to be clarified, as well as the word "textbook."[79]

The issue raised by Womack had bothered others also, and there was speculation in the *Arkansas Gazette*[80] that a group of lawyers, businessmen, and physicians might bring suit to determine not only the constitutionality of Initiated Act No. 1 but whether it prohibited mentioning and explaining the theory of evolution so long as it was not taught as fact or truth. Just at this point, Ben Bogard, in his capacity as president of the American Antievolution Association, wrote a letter to the *Arkansas Gazette* stating that "the law does not prohibit teaching what evolution is, so that students may know what it is. . . . To tell a student what a theory is vastly different from telling him that the theory is true."[81] Although this obviously was not the final legal judgment in the matter, this opinion from Bogard that evolution can be mentioned or explained so long as it is not taught as fact seemed to dampen the enthusiasm for a lawsuit. This interpretation that the law did not prohibit mentioning or explaining the theory of evolution came to be accepted by those who had to enforce the law, and was one of the important factors that blunted intellectual anger and allowed the antievolution act to stay in place for forty years.

1928–1968

There were other historical factors that helped to leave the antievolution law untouched for forty years. Major historical events during this period, such as the Depression, World War II, and the changing international situation after World War II diverted energy and attention elsewhere. The unofficial policy that no one would be bothered so long as he or she did not teach evolution as truth amounted almost to a "no enforcement" policy. As a columnist for the *Arkansas Democrat* noted in 1966: "The law had been dormant and all but forgotten for years, literally repealed from neglect,"[82] particularly since there had never been any prosecutions under the act. This failure to enforce kept dissatisfaction at tolerable levels. There was also the difficulty of finding a teacher plaintiff for a lawsuit since a teacher's time, money, and even job could all be involved. The requirement that an initiated act can be changed only by a two-thirds vote of the legislature gave strong protection to the antievolution act, and two legislative attempts, one in 1937[83] and one in 1959,[84] failed before even coming to a vote. All these factors assisted in keeping the antievolution act on the statute books.

A more serious legislative attempt was made in 1965. Even though the outcome was the same as previous attempts, this effort in 1965 seemed to act as a catalyst. Rep. Nathan Schoenfeld of Garland County introduced House Bill No. 275,[85] which would have repealed Initiated Act No. 1 of 1928. Schoenfeld said the 1928 act was "blatantly wrong"[86] and the *Arkansas Gazette* editorialized that Schoenfeld's bill was a means of "rectifying the ancient error."[87] Although Schoenfeld had not contacted any of the education groups that might have been interested in repeal before introducing his bill,[88] the Arkansas Education Association (AEA), the Arkansas School Boards Association, and the Arkansas Congress of Parents and Teachers decided to support his bill.[89] Forrest Rozzell, executive secretary of the AEA, drafted a statement on behalf of these three groups for Schoenfeld's use in case his bill came to a vote. The bill was never voted on, but it apparently stimulated the thinking of those most interested in repealing the antievolution law.

According to Forrest Rozzell,[90] the unsuccessful 1965 attempt convinced him that any legislative approach to repeal could not succeed and that the judicial route must be pursued. Newspaper discussion of the Schoenfeld bill and its lack of success had aroused many to write and say that the antievolution act should be enforced, and had also left some doubt in the minds of teachers as to whether the law was still a dead letter. The public debate aroused by the Schoenfeld bill convinced Rozzell that the issue of the antievolution act had to be resolved finally, and strengthened his resolve to go to court. He consulted Eugene R. Warren, attorney for the AEA, and they made plans to bring a suit.[91]

The first move in the new campaign to repeal the 1928 law was a "personal position" statement issued by Rozzell at a news conference on September 14, 1965. His statement was very similar to the one that had been made available to Representative Schoenfeld, stressing that religious beliefs should not be coerced by the state and that an understanding of the environment in which people live is necessary for survival.[92] It recommended, of course, that the law be repealed. Reaction was favorable from state Commissioner of Education Arch Ford, who said that "the law was a dead issue and there was no reason for keeping it on the statute books."[93]

The *Arkansas Gazette* commended Rozzell for tackling the 1928 law and commented further that "The reason that Mr. Rozzell is a state resource of first importance is that once he has set his mind on this kind of problem, he is likely to peel it like an onion."[94] Gov. Orval Faubus was less complimentary, feeling that the law should not be repealed but should be kept "as a safeguard to keep way out teachers in line."[95] Public debate on the issue had begun, and the foundation was being laid for a lawsuit.

The strategy pursued by Rozzell and Warren was to keep the legal case as local as possible. This meant finding a plaintiff who had roots in Arkansas, finding an Arkansas group and an Arkansas attorney to undertake the financing and trial of the case, and keeping national groups that might be interested in the case for reasons of ideology or political belief out of the case as sponsors. The AEA agreed to sponsor the case,[96] and its attorney, Warren, agreed to try the case charging only for his expenses.[97] National groups such as the National Education Association and the American Civil Liberties Union were not allowed to join the suit as sponsors because of the emphasis on local origination. Costs of the suit paid by the AEA amounted to only $2,500.[98]

The most crucial matter, however, was a plaintiff who had an impeccable Arkansas background. The person finally chosen met that requirement and also had many other attributes that helped the case greatly.

Susan Epperson was in her second year of teaching biology at Central High School in Little Rock when she was approached about being the plaintiff in the case. She was contacted first by Virginia Minor, a fellow teacher at Central High School, who was also president of the Little Rock chapter of the American Association of University Women, a group that had supported the Schoenfeld bill in 1965.[99] Epperson was then interviewed by Rozzell and Warren[100] and agreed to become the plaintiff. She was a native of Clarksville, Arkansas, who had graduated from the College of the Ozarks, a Presbyterian school in Clarksville, where her father was a professor of biology. She was married to an Air Force officer who was stationed at the Little Rock Air Base. She was also a religious person who saw no conflict between her religious beliefs and evolution; although in the classroom she taught evolution only as theory and not as fact.[101] For those interested in overturning the antievolution act, Epperson was a dream come true.

In November 1965, a "John Doe" complaint was sent by Eugene Warren to Floyd Parsons, superintendent of the Little Rock Public Schools, indicating generally what kind of legal issues would be raised in the forthcoming lawsuit. This was designed to alert the Little Rock school system since the members of the Little Rock School Board and Superintendent Parsons would technically be defendants in the case. On December 6, 1965, a suit was filed in Pulaski County Chancery Court by Susan Epperson seeking a declaratory judgment that the Arkansas Antievolution Law (Initiated Act No. 1 of 1928) was unconstitutional. It was a civil suit, to be heard in chancery court without a jury. Epperson said at the time the suit was filed that if she obeyed the law she would neglect "the obligations of a responsible teacher of biology. This is the sure path to the perpetration of ignorance, prejudice, and bigotry."[102] In March 1966, Hubert H. Blanchard, associate executive secretary of the AEA, entered the case on behalf of his two sons, who were both attending the North Little Rock Public Schools at the time.[103] This was done to show that damage was occurring to students as well as teachers because of the Arkansas act.

Under Arkansas law, the attorney general of the state is involved whenever the validity of Arkansas law is challenged. The attorney general at that time, Bruce Bennett, was eager to get involved and showed signs initially of wanting to turn the case into a second Scopes trial. Bennett quickly began lining up witnesses to attack the validity of the evolution theory and wrote Judge Murray O. Reed, the chancellor in the *Epperson* case, that "Mrs. Epperson was the only person since the law was approved to 'clamor' in favor of teaching that man evolved from monkeys, apes, sharks, porpoises, seaweed, or any other form of animal or vegetable."[104] In a pretrial hearing before Judge Reed, Warren accused Bennett of trying to make a joke of the case and encouraging the "carnival atmosphere or the buffoonery that went on in Tennessee to go on in Arkansas."[105] Judge Reed, at this time, saw the case as primarily a question of law in which private beliefs about evolution were not relevant. Bennett argued that Epperson wanted to "advance an atheistic doctrine."[106]

As time went on and the date of the trial approached, Bennett seemed to alternate between saying that the main issue in the case was simply the legal question of whether Epperson's freedom of speech outweighs the people's right to prescribe the subjects to be taught in school,[107] and, on the other hand, attacking the theory of evolution as an atheistic doctrine whose validity had great bearing on the case. Apparently irritated by a letter sent to him by the Executive Committee on Christian Education of the Arkansas Presbyterian Church that commended Epperson for bringing the suit and expressed deep concern about Bennett using the case for political propaganda and "giving Arkansas an undeserved reputation for backwardness,"[108] he said that he planned to offer in evidence the views of fourteen scholars on the validity of Darwin's theory. He also warned that if the antievolution act was ruled unconstitutional, the public schools would be thrown open to the "haranguing [sic] of every soap box orator with a crackpot theory of evolution" even extending to the "'God is dead' theory, or the theory that man came from a gorilla."[109]

The trial of the case before Judge Reed was scheduled for April 1, 1966. On the day before the trial, Karr Shannon, a columnist for the *Arkansas Democrat*, was not encouraged about the prospects, writing that: "The monkey trial to open in Judge Murray O. Reed's court tomorrow will not only be a waste of the taxpayer's money but will net Arkansas a slush of adverse publicity that may require decades for recovery."[110] The results were otherwise, as Judge Reed ruled that the question of whether evolution is true or false was not before the court and sustained more than fifty objections by Warren that blocked Bennett's efforts to question the validity of the evolution theory.[111] The trial took only two hours and twenty minutes, and the only witnesses to appear were Epperson and Blanchard for the plaintiff and four school superintendents for the defendants, who testified that the 1928 law did not have any adverse effect on their schools.[112] Warren argued for the plaintiff that the law infringed freedom of speech, violated the separation of church and state, and was vague and indefinite. Bennett argued for the defendants (the Little Rock School Board members and the superintendent) that the state, as Epperson's employer, was entitled to tell her what she could teach while on duty in the public schools.

At the conclusion of the trial, Judge Reed announced that he would render no decision for at least a month and gave the attorneys thirty days to file briefs. Although the courtroom was packed during the trial, with about one hundred people crowded into a room that seated fifty comfortably,[113] the consensus seemed to be that the trial was dignified, decorum was maintained, and the carnival atmosphere of the Scopes trial never materialized.[114]

On May 27, 1966, Judge Reed issued a nine-page memorandum opinion holding that Initiated Act No. 1 of 1928 was unconstitutional because it violated the constitutionally protected right of free speech and tended to "hinder the quest for knowledge, restrict the freedom to learn, and restrain the freedom to teach."[115] He further stated that the issue presented was whether Initiated Act No. 1 of 1928 conflicted with freedom of speech and expression and not whether the theory of evolution was true or false.[116] Judge Reed also distinguished the Scopes case[117] saying that later decisions of the United States Supreme Court had made the ruling in that case obsolete.[118] Notice of appeal by the state was given on June 21, 1966.

Briefs in the case were filed before the Arkansas Supreme Court on October 7 and October 21, 1966. Warren's brief on behalf of Susan Epperson concentrated on five major points. The first point argued was that school teachers are entitled to all the guarantees of both the state and federal constitutions. At the time the Scopes case was decided, the Tennessee court had held that the state, when dealing with its own employees and their conditions of employment, is not hampered by the "due process" constitutional guarantees of either the state or federal constitutions.[119] The argument of the brief for the appellee (Epperson) was that United States Supreme Court decisions since the Scopes case had greatly modified the decision of the Tennessee Supreme Court in 1927. A second argument was that the antievolution law violated the free speech guarantees of both the federal and Arkansas constitutions. The third point raised was that the law violated the equal protection clause of the Fourteenth Amendment to the United States Constitution, since it only applied to public schools and did not include private schools. The fourth point related to the third and raised the question of violation of the due process clause of the Fourteenth Amendment to the United States Constitution. This argument was that since Initiated Act No. 1 of 1928 imposed criminal penalties, its language had to be definite, certain, and clearly understood, but such was not the case because of ambiguity surrounding such words in the antievolution act as "to teach" and "textbooks." The fifth argument was that the law violated the religious freedom guarantees of both the Arkansas and United States constitutions, in that the state cannot prohibit the teaching of a theory in order to assist religion.

The brief for the state of Arkansas, the appellant in the case, was filed by Attorney General Bennett and Fletcher Jackson, an assistant attorney general. The argument for the state was briefly that the act in question was constitutional because it was "a reasonable regulation of the conduct of a public employee, a school teacher, and a reasonable regulation of the curriculum in the public schools.[120] Since the state provided part of the money for local school districts, it had some authority to control curriculum and to determine what subjects should be taught. Initiated Act No. 1 of 1928 became part of the contract that Epperson signed and under which she worked, since one provision in her contract was that "Both parties hereto agree that this contract shall be construed in accordance with all applicable laws and regulations governing the employment, compensation, and conduct of teachers."[121] The concluding argument for the state pointed out that freedom of speech is not absolute, particularly when it is curtailed on the basis of the employer-employee relationship. Examples were given of the Hatch Act and certain state laws prohibiting state employees, including college staff and faculty, from running for political office. The argument was that laws like the Hatch Act and the antievolution act were valid even though they interfere to some extent with freedom of speech.

On June 5, 1967, the Arkansas Supreme Court upheld the constitutionality of Initiated Act No. 1 of 1928 with one judge (Lyle Brown) dissenting and one judge (Paul Ward) concurring.[122] In a one paragraph decision, the court said:

> Upon the principal issue, that of constitutionality, the court holds
> that Initiated Measure No. 1 of 1928 is a valid exercise of the state's

power to specify the curriculum in its public schools. The court
expresses no opinion on the question whether the Act prohibits any
explanation of the theory of evolution or merely prohibits teaching that the theory is true; the answer not being necessary to a decision in the case, and the issue not having been raised.[123]

Judge Ward concurred in the decision because he agreed with the first
sentence in the opinion but thought that the second sentence cast some
doubt on the clear meaning of the first sentence. A petition for rehear-
ing was denied by the Arkansas Supreme Court on July 26, 1967.

Epperson v. Arkansas

Once the decision of the Arkansas Supreme Court was made, there was
no doubt that the case would be appealed to the United States Supreme
Court.[124] The Supreme Court agreed to hear the case March 4, 1968,[125]
and oral arguments were held on October 16, 1968. By the time for oral
arguments, friend-of-the-court briefs had been filed on behalf of Susan
Epperson, now the appellant in the case, by the National Education
Association, the National Science Teachers Association, the American
Civil Liberties Union, and American Jewish Congress.[126] According to
Eugene Warren, still attorney for Epperson, the written briefs he and the
attorney for the state of Arkansas submitted to the United States Supreme
Court were very similar to the ones submitted to the Arkansas Supreme
Court earlier.

In the time between the decision of the Arkansas Supreme Court and
oral arguments before the United States Supreme Court, a new attorney
general, Joe Purcell, had been elected in Arkansas, and he did not seem to
have the same degree of enthusiasm for this case as his predecessor. Oral
arguments in the case and the brief for the appellee, now the state of
Arkansas, were handled by Don Langston of the attorney general's office.
Langston stressed that the case had gone to trial under a previous administration, and, according to a *New York Times* report, he also made it clear
that he was defending the case for the state of Arkansas only because state
law required it.[127] Langston did concede during the questioning before the
court that in his opinion, Initiated Act No. 1 made it a crime not only to
teach that the theory of evolution is valid but even to inform students that
such a theory existed, saying that "if Mrs. Epperson were to tell her students that there is a Darwin's theory of evolution, then I think she would

be liable for prosecution."[128] This turned out to be a very damaging admission for the state's case.

The oral arguments took only thirty-five minutes, mainly because Langston did not use all the time allotted to him.[129] Warren and Langston were the only two attorneys involved in the oral arguments, and at the conclusion of the arguments, Warren felt that the judges were favorably inclined, with the exception of Justice Hugo Black who had been the most critical.[130] Justice Thurgood Marshall seemed amazed by the brief decision by the Arkansas Supreme Court and suggested facetiously that the United States Supreme Court should write a one sentence opinion and upstage the Arkansas Supreme Court.[131] A reporter concluded that the judges by their questioning were trying to find as narrow a ground as possible for their decision.[132]

On November 12, 1968, the United States Supreme Court struck down Initiated Act No. 1 as unconstitutional because it violated the separation of church and state provision of the First Amendment.[133] Justice Abe Fortas wrote the majority opinion, and there were three concurring opinions written by justices Hugo Black, John M. Harlan, and Potter Stewart.

Although Justice Fortas sounded a note of restraint at the beginning of his opinion by cautioning that "Judicial interposition in the operation of the public school system of the Nation raises problems requiring care and restraint,"[134] nevertheless, he said that when basic constitutional values are involved, there can be court intervention. In the present case, the opinion concurred, there is a narrower issue of violation of the establishment clause of the First Amendment on which the decision can be based. The antievolution act unconstitutionally aided religion because it prevented teachers "from discussing the theory of evolution because it is contrary to the belief of some that the Book of Genesis must be the exclusive source of doctrine as to the origin of man."[135] The state's right to determine curriculum for the public schools does not include the power to prohibit "the teaching of a scientific theory or doctrine where that prohibition is based upon reasons that violate the First Amendment."[136] Justice Fortas concluded the opinion of the court by stating that the Arkansas law attempted "to blot out a particular theory because of its supposed conflict with the Biblical account, literally read. Plainly, the law is contrary to the mandate of the First, and in violation of the Fourteenth, Amendment to the Constitution."[137]

Justice Black concurred in the decision reached but had grave reservations about the whole matter. He questioned whether an actual "case or controversy" was involved since no attempt to prosecute under the antievolution act had ever been attempted and the theory of evolution was presumably taught openly without punishment in the public schools. He was upset by the "pallid, unenthusiastic, even apologetic defense of the Act"[138] presented by the state of Arkansas. He was worried about federal intrusion into state power to determine curriculum and had grave doubts that "'academic freedom' permits a teacher to breach his contractual agreement to teach only the subjects designated by the school authorities who hired him."[139]

He preferred to rest his own concurrence on the vagueness of the Arkansas statute since it was unclear whether the statute allowed discussion so long as it was not contended that the theory was true, or whether it precluded even a mention of Darwin's theory. Black felt that "the statute is too vague for us to strike it down on any grounds but that: vagueness."[140]

Justice Harlan concurred with the majority on the ground that the establishment clause had been violated. However, he wished to disassociate himself from the language of the majority opinion discussing the extent to which freedom of speech guarantees apply to school teachers, since it was not necessary to the decision in the case. He also was very critical of the Arkansas Supreme Court, saying that he found it "deplorable that this case should have come to us with such an opaque opinion by the State's highest court"[141] and that the Arkansas Supreme Court's handling of the case "savors of a studied effort to avoid coming to grips with this anachronistic statute and to 'pass the buck' to this Court."[142] Justice Stewart's concurrence followed Justice Black's line of reasoning that the Arkansas law was so vague as to be unconstitutional.[143]

There were several themes that seemed to recur throughout the *Epperson* decision in both the majority and the concurring opinions. One theme was that of restraint, a reluctance to get involved in the sensitive area of the power of a state over curriculum and the related area of the extent of a teacher's free speech guarantees when they clash with the state's power over curriculum. The result was that these areas were touched on only so far as was absolutely necessary to decide the *Epperson* case. In fact, the decision was narrowed to a separation of church and state question, which is much easier to decide and which sets a precedent fairly narrow in scope.

Another theme found in both the majority and concurring opinions about which the court was not so reluctant was its general dissatisfaction with the Arkansas Supreme Court and the way it had decided the *Epperson* case. These criticisms ranged from subtleness in the case of Fortas to bluntness in the cases of Harlan and Black, where such language as a "studied effort to pass the buck" is used. This also probably reflected the court's reluctance to intrude into the area of curriculum and their resentment at being compelled to decide a case that forced them into this area. The justices undoubtedly felt the case should have been decided in a more thorough and complete manner by the Arkansas Supreme Court in the first place.

Reaction to the decision of the Supreme Court ranged from favorable on the part of Epperson, who said that Arkansas schoolteachers could now "teach the full subject of biology with an open and clear conscience"[144] to unfavorable from the Rev. M. L. Moser Jr., pastor of the Central Baptist Church in Little Rock, who said that now "someone who believes in the creation should also be present when evolution is taught."[145] Forrest Rozzell was pleased because the decision had been based on the establishment clause, which killed the issue once and for all, rather than the "vagueness" objection favored by Black and Stewart, which might have left the issue still dangling.[146] The *Arkansas Gazette* commended Epperson again for her efforts "to remove from the books an obstacle to quality education that was rooted in ignorance and perpetrated through 40 years of legislative indifference."[147] Perhaps the most memorable quotation of all came from John T. Scopes, the defendant in that famous trial in Tennessee in 1925, who was now sixty-eight years old and living in retirement in Shreveport, Louisiana. Scopes said that he was pleased with the decision in the Epperson case but that "The fight will still go on with other actors and other plays. You don't protect any of your individual liberties by lying down and going to sleep."[148]

Low Villains and Wickedness in High Places

Race and Class in the Elaine Riots

JEANNIE M. WHAYNE

In the fall of 1919, the small Phillips County town of Elaine, Arkansas, became the scene of one of the most violent racial conflicts the country had ever to that time experienced. Not surprisingly, the Elaine Race Riot has generated numerous scholarly efforts over the years and continues to fascinate researchers, and trouble citizens, to this day. Noting that the written descriptions of the event have produced wildly contradictory accounts of the underlying causes of the riot, failing to generate even a "common narrative" of events surrounding the affair, historian Jeannie Whayne does not offer here her own account of the riot. Rather, she critiques several of the most high-profile accounts, finds some of them inadequate and others downright misleading, and argues that each of these flawed narratives is a product of the historical context within which it was written.

Whayne argues that the key to understanding the Elaine riot is to place the event in proper historical context. For her, this context must include, for example: the pressures generated by the expanding plantation system in Phillips County and other Delta counties during the years leading up to the riot; the changed attitudes and aspirations of returning black and white World War I veterans; and class conflict within the white community, especially, the planters versus landless whites.

Jeannie M. Whayne, "Low Villains and Wickedness in High Places: Race and Class in the Elaine Race Riots," *Arkansas Historical Quarterly* 58 (Autumn 1999): 285–313. Reprinted with permission.

Perhaps no event in the history of the Arkansas Delta has received as much attention and been the subject of more speculation than the Elaine Race Riot of 1919. Historians, struggling with a mass of rich but contradictory and even tainted evidence, have failed to arrive at a common narrative of events. One noted account amounts to little more than propaganda for the planter elite of Phillips County, while another, a contemporary essay written by a future black leader, focused on exposing the evils of the plantation system.[1] As varied as their interpretations have been, however, virtually all share a common shortcoming. The only exception is to be found in a novel based on the Elaine riot by an Arkansas protégé of Norman Mailer—and that book failed to find an American publisher.[2]

Competing interpretations of the riot emerged almost as soon as it had ended. Walter White, assistant secretary—and, later, executive secretary—of the National Association for the Advancement of Colored People, visited Phillips County incognito in mid October 1919 in order to secure material for an article he later published in the *Nation*. White's interest in the riot almost cost him his life. An African American who, with his blue eyes and blond hair, passed for white, he barely escaped a lynch mob that had discovered his true identity.[3] White took exception to the official version of the riot embraced by white officials and published in Arkansas newspapers. This version insisted blacks intended to murder certain white planters and take their land. Whites, it was said, had discovered the plot accidentally after two deputies whose car had broken down were fired upon by blacks attending a meeting of a sharecroppers' union at Hoop Spur church outside Elaine. Walter White countered that African Americans had organized the Progressive Farmers and Household Union of America to sue planters for a fair settlement of their crops, that whites had fired into the church at Hoop Spur in order to disrupt a meeting of the union, and that blacks had returned fire only in self defense.[4]

However the incident really began, one deputized white official, W. A. Adkins, lay dead, and another, Charles Pratt, was seriously wounded. Several days of brutal violence ensued. A posse was quickly raised and rushed to the scene. White men from other parts of Arkansas, as well as from Mississippi and Tennessee, joined in the hunt for the alleged "insurrectionists," some of whom fought back. Local white leaders wired Gov. Charles Brough asking for federal troops from Camp Pike to restore law and order. Col. Isaac C. Jenks commanded the 583 soldiers who were dispatched early in the morning of October 2 and were accompanied by Brough. Immediately upon his arrival, Jenks disarmed all blacks as well as white civilians and set about quelling the violence. Martial law was declared, and federal troops patrolled the streets of Elaine and Helena and scoured the countryside. By the time order was restored two days later, five whites and at least twenty-five blacks lay dead. Several hundred blacks were incarcerated in Elaine and Helena. When the Phillips County grand jury convened on October 27, 1919, over one hundred were still being held. In subsequent trials twelve were sentenced to death for first-degree murder and another sixty-seven to prison terms. The white community celebrated the trials and convictions as evidence of the rule of law over mob violence.[5]

Most of the facts in the official version of the riot were disputed not only by Walter White but by lawyers who appealed the convictions of the twelve black men sentenced to death. Yet the official version showed some staying power. One account written forty years after the riot essentially reiterated it. In 1961 J. W. Butts and Dorothy James published "The Underlying Causes of the Elaine Riot of 1919," in the *Arkansas Historical Quarterly*, arguing that a few disgruntled and misled African Americans hatched a plot to murder white planters and take their land, that this "insurrection" was discovered before the conspirators could bring their plans to fruition, and that the white community responded reasonably given the situation. Butts and James, who relied largely on interviews with white Phillips County residents and references to reports of unidentified "negro detectives" from Chicago, took pains to establish that the black sharecroppers of Phillips County, rather than being exploited, were actually "rather prosperous" and contented with their situation. The trouble was caused by an outside agitator and confidence man, Robert L. Hill of Winchester, Arkansas, who founded the Progressive Farmers and Household Union of America strictly for the purpose of "making easy money" from the members through an assortment of "schemes." Although Hill escaped prosecution, the other guilty parties, a few disgruntled and misguided souls, according to Butts and James, secured fair trials and were subsequently convicted.[6]

Butts and James were writing specifically to counter an article, "The Elaine Race Riots of 1919," by O. A. Rogers Jr., which had appeared in the *Arkansas Historical Quarterly* less than a year earlier. The first of the modern accounts to appear in print, Rogers's introduction promised to place the Elaine Race Riot within the context of the 1919 "Red Summer" of racial and union violence. He failed, however, to develop that theme. Instead, in addition to a brief overview of the riot, his article focused attention on the exploitation of African Americans on Phillips County plantations as the basic reason for the creation of the Progressive Farmers and Household Union of America.[7] As such, it was a credible extension of Walter White's argument, and it stood in direct contrast to the planter perspective supported by Butts and James.

These two schools of thought, the planter versus the black perspective, were elaborated upon in two books published in 1970 and 1988, respectively. The first, *Union, Reaction, and Riot: A Biography of a Rural Race Riot,* by B. Boren McCool, referred to both the essays written in 1960 as "propaganda," and began with a lengthy discussion of social and economic conditions in Phillips County. While he took issue with Butts and James in the matter of whether blacks were being economically exploited in the sharecropping system and dismissed the notion of an insurrectionary plot, he largely accepted their general narrative of events as they developed after the incident at Hoop Spur Church. In doing so, McCool failed to consider crucial evidence undermining that narrative. Perhaps because he drew heavily upon a collection of documents held by J. W. Butts, his rendering of the violence tended to affirm the planter perspective.[8] The other full-length study of the riot, Richard C. Cortner's *A Mob Intent on Death,* returned to the themes pursued by White and Rogers, but had as its ultimate goal an explication of the appeals arising out of the convictions. A scholar interested in the legal significance of one of the cases, Cortner drew heavily upon Arthur I. Waskow's account in *From Race Riot to Sit-In,* published in 1966. Though Waskow devoted only fifty-three pages to the Elaine Race Riot, his deeply researched and cogently argued account stands as the best counter to the planter perspective and is a useful vehicle for addressing the main issues raised by Butts and James.

Was the Progressive Farmers and Household Union of America intent upon murdering unsuspecting planters, or did it merely intend to file lawsuits against planters believed guilty of cheating the union's black members—as Waskow, following White, believed? Most of the Phillips County white population certainly believed that a black insurrection was at hand, and the *Helena World* employed language that echoed the hysteria that surrounded rumors of imminent slave rebellions in the antebellum South. White women and children were dispatched in a special train to the safety of Helena; others were gathered in buildings heavily guarded by white men. Even some local whites sympathetic to blacks were scared. The family of musician Levon Helm believed the "rumor that all the white farmers and their families were going to be murdered by the rioters." Helm's father and grandfather armed themselves and prepared to defend their homes, but "the riot never did come down the road."[9]

As all the facts came to light in the months and years following the riot, the existence of an insurrection plot grew less plausible. While some blacks had clearly fought back, there was little evidence of African Americans hunting down white targets or assaulting white institutions— as insurrectionists would presumably do. Even John E. Miller, the attorney who led the successful prosecution of the Elaine blacks, indicated in an interview in 1976 that events in Phillips County "had every appearance of [a black insurrection] until you got in and went to the bottom of it." He believed that the planters were determined to crush the union, and that the death of W. A. Adkins outside the church gave them the excuse to do so. "When that boy was killed they decided to crush it." Although Miller continued to believe that the convicted blacks had committed murder, he said "I'm awful glad the court reversed" the convictions. "While they were guilty all right, technically, but hell if there was a provocation, they had a provocation."[10]

Other prominent white Arkansans, certainly not beholden to the NAACP perspective, also came to repudiate the insurrection theory. David Yancey Thomas, a professor of history and political science at the University of Arkansas and the first editor of the *Arkansas Historical Quarterly* after a lengthy correspondence with a variety of individuals connected to both sides, eventually rejected the story that the events in Elaine were an insurrection. At first, Thomas had stopped short of rendering such an opinion. Immediately following the riot, he corresponded with several individuals in an effort to discover the facts behind the alleged insurrection. At the time of one of these queries Thomas was representing the University of Arkansas at a meeting of the University Race Commission in Tuskegee, Alabama. Although, as Arthur Waskow suggests in his book, Thomas may have had doubts about the official version as early as February 1920, he only repudiated it publicly some ten years later with the publication of his *Arkansas and Its People.* In that book he remarked that the insurrection plot idea "was later shown to be incorrect" and that the report that it was an insurrection "only aggravated the situation."[11]

This judgment—rendered in a well-known history text—makes the Butts and James article all the more curious. In spite of the doubt cast on the insurrection theory by a prominent Arkansas historian, they relied on suspect contemporary newspaper accounts, confessions of blacks and the testimony of witnesses that had been shown—decades before Butts and James wrote—to have been coerced or falsified, and the unsubstantiated testimony of individuals interviewed forty years after the events.[12]

Waskow, on the other hand, judiciously dismissed the newspaper accounts as hysterical, repudiated the coerced confessions, and relied heavily on the affidavits of two white witnesses who had recanted the testimony they had given at the time of the trial and told a version of events that supported the black perspective. The testimony of both T. K. Jones and H. F. Smiddy was offered in support of the appeals of six of the black men convicted and sentenced to death. Jones and Smiddy lived in Helena at the time of the riot and were "co-workers of the first man killed at Hoop Spur," W. A. Adkins.[13] According to Jones, a party of white men fired upon the church with the express purpose of breaking up the union meeting, and, according to Smiddy, the black trustee accompanying Adkins and Charles Pratt told him the next day that the white men had fired first.[14] In direct contradiction to the story broadcast by the newspapers and authorities at the time and later repeated by Butts and James, Smiddy further testified that the literature found in the church contained "nothing to indicate a criminal or unlawful purpose on the part of the organization."[15] Both men witnessed and participated in the torture applied to secure damning testimony from blacks taken into custody, and both men described whites systematically hunting down and shooting blacks, armed or unarmed. So "out of control" was one group that Smiddy suggested at least one of the white casualties was at the hands of "a member of our own posse."[16]

John E. Miller, the prosecuting attorney in Helena, later supported this view of the source of the bloodshed. The Mississippians who joined the posse, he said, "came over with blood in their eye."[17] Certainly a letter in the Brough Papers (cited but misread by McCool) suggests that whites were the ones on the rampage and that some local authorities likely did little to restrain them. Harry Anderson of Bon Air Coal & Iron Corporation in Nashville, Tennessee, wrote Governor Brough that he had lived in Phillips County twenty years earlier, described himself as a "rough rider" there, and indicated that "knowing Frank Kitchens

[Phillips County sheriff] and his crowd as well as I do, I am quite sure your action was the direct cause of saving a great number of lives—both white and black down there. Nothing would have suited Frank better than to have been given free hand to hunt 'Mr. nigger' in his lair and in-as-much as the negroes seem to have been well prepared, I am of a firm belief that your action nipped a small war in its bud."[18]

Given the apparent murderous intent of the white posse, it is little wonder that some blacks resisted. That they were armed at all was not evidence of the existence of an insurrectionary plot, but rather emblematic of a rural culture dependent in part on hunting for subsistence. For Waskow—as for other partisans of the "black" perspective—their resistance suggests not rebellion but a determination to defend themselves in the face of a hostile force of whites.[19]

This hostile white mob, though, warrants closer scrutiny than it has received. As varied as they are, all historical accounts take for granted something that very much needs to be explained. Few have noted that the white assault represented a phenomenon rare in the Delta outside periodic lynchings: an alliance of white planters and working-class whites against black sharecroppers. Even prosecutor Miller believed that planters played a role in the violence—at the very least by using the shoot-out at Hoop Spur as an excuse to destroy a union that had been worrying them for some time.[20] But the posses clearly included more humble whites—clerks, veterans, tenant farmers, lumbermen, railroad workers—with few ties to the planter class. With the exception of the Arkansas novelist Francis Irby Gwaltney, though, those who have written about the events at Elaine have tended to view the white community within Phillips County as one monolithic whole.[21] Some have recognized divisions within the black community, divisions briefly overcome in the aftermath of the riot, but no one has grasped the class conflict within the white community, a conflict only temporarily surmounted in the brutal suppression of the Progressive Farmers and Household Union of America.[22]

Behind this conflict was an expansion of the plantation system in Phillips County between 1880 and 1920, an expansion challenged by a violent campaign on the part of landless whites. Phillips County had long been dominated by the plantation, but as the lumber industry boomed in the last decades of the nineteenth century, land was being reclaimed, and many new immigrants to the Arkansas Delta, both black and white, looked for opportunity there. While the number of acres in

cotton increased from 42,654 in 1880 to 92,944 in 1920, the percentage
of farm owners decreased from 70.3 percent in 1880 to 18.8 percent in
1920.[23] Lumbering operations were bringing new land into production
in the southern portion of the county—that area rocked by violence during the riot—but draining and developing cleared land was expensive,
and even those who could afford to engage in such an enterprise usually
did so through borrowing large sums of money.[24] Expense doubtlessly
undermined many whites' efforts to secure land—as did the decline after
1910 in the amount of land coming into cultivation. Frustrated in their
ambitions to own land, many whites found that neither could they rent
it. Black sharecroppers rather than white owners or tenants cultivated
the vast majority of acres in Phillips County because planters preferred
black to white labor; the former was cheaper and, given legalized dis-
franchisement and segregation, blacks were regarded as more tractable.
The result was growing animosity on the part of landless whites toward
those who controlled most of the land, the planters. In the mid-1890s,
landless whites who had pinned their hopes on the "agricultural ladder"
—by which they could work their way up from the ranks of tenancy to
proprietorship—struck at the planter class by terrorizing sharecroppers
who had secured places on Phillips County plantations. Just as planters
viewed blacks as more tractable, working class whites recognized blacks
were an easier, intermediary target through which they could more safely
strike at planters.

In February 1898 at Connell's Point, less than ten miles north of
Elaine, "a gang of irresponsible [white] men" began to terrorize "the
defenseless negroes of that vicinity until they have actually succeeded in
driving the majority of them out of the neighborhood. They [the whites]
profess to be actuated by a desire to rent land at reasonable prices, and
say they cannot do so because the negroes will take it at the prevailing
prices." Planters were eager to protect their cheap labor supply, but,
according to the *Helena World*, "when a gang of hoodlums circle around
the back end of large plantations at the hour of midnight and fire into
negro cabins and then disappear, it is difficult to swear who did the nefar-
ious work." Four men arrested in early February had been "discharged for
lack of sufficient evidence to hold them." The alleged whitecappers were
accused not only of terrorizing black sharecroppers, but also of destroy-
ing the property of plantation owners. One of the discharged men, Jones
Strawn, had lost his tenancy on a plantation that subsequently witnessed

depredations against its black sharecroppers and suffered the burning of five thousand pounds of seed cotton. The *Helena World* declared itself "morally sure" that Strawn, along with the other arrested whites, were guilty. In another incident a year earlier, the barn of another planter "was burned, resulting in the loss of two fine mules, wagons, tools, feed, a new buggy, etc." By February 1898 the situation had become so unstable that the *World* editor, a reliable spokesman for the planter perspective, was moved to suggest that "if a few of [the white nightriders] were shot to death when they are out marauding, it would have a wholesome effect," and that "if they are caught while at their unlawful work, they should be shot down like dogs, for the man who would burn his neighbor's barn and substance is worse than an assassin."[25]

Such violence was not confined to Phillips County, rather, it accompanied the expansion of the plantation in all parts of the Arkansas Delta. Whitecappers struck in Cross and Poinsett counties in 1902, in Crittenden County in 1904, and periodically plagued Mississippi County from 1908 to 1921. Two cases involving nightriders in Cross and Poinsett counties were well publicized in Phillips County in 1903 and 1904 because they were tried in federal court in Helena. In the Cross County case, planters hired white detectives to track down nightriders who were attempting to drive blacks from plantations. The fifteen men arrested in Poinsett County were charged with attempting to drive African American workers away from a sawmill. Although no convictions were secured in the first case, three men were convicted in the Poinsett County case. When the Supreme Court overturned the convictions in 1905, planters were again left without adequate protection against such white marauders and successfully pressed the state to pass a nightriding law in 1909. Although the law provided local authorities with a new weapon, it by no means ended nightriding activities, and planters continued to complain about such depredations.[26]

Nightriding persisted because white men looking for the main chance in the Arkansas Delta continued to be doomed to disappointment. An examination of the manuscript census of population for the three Phillips County townships (Tappan, Mooney, and Searcy) where most of the fighting occurred in 1919 is quite revealing.[27] Although the number of white farmers in these townships increased from 36 in 1900 to 155 in 1920, those owning farms dropped from 60 percent to 19.1 percent. The number of black farmers, meanwhile, increased from 289 in

1900 to 1,132, with only 92 (8.4 percent) owning farms. White farmers were greatly outnumbered by African Americans, and they were less likely than ever to own the farms they operated. The ground was shifting beneath them, and the plantation was advancing on all fronts. The majority of these farmers, both white and black, were not native to Arkansas, had lived only a few years in these townships, and likely knew very little about one another. Only 23.9 percent of the white farmers had been born in Arkansas. Most of the rest hailed from Mississippi (32.3 percent) and Tennessee (11 percent). Only 7.1 percent came from outside the south. As for black farmers, 25.2 percent were native to Arkansas, with 39.9 percent from Mississippi and 14.8 percent from Louisiana. Only 0.7 percent were non-southern. These statistics had changed very little from 1900, but, interestingly enough, less than 10 percent of the whites or blacks listed in these townships in 1900 remained in 1920. This was a community in turmoil.[28]

This turmoil and the diminishing opportunities available to many whites may have intensified that community's hostility, not only toward black croppers and tenants, but also toward African Americans in general—such that by 1919 accomplished blacks of the professional classes could likewise be targets of an enraged white mob. One of the most controversial aspects of the Elaine riot involved the deaths of Dr. D. A. E. Johnston, a wealthy black dentist and druggist from Helena, and his three brothers. Two of his brothers lived with him and ran an automobile business, a third, Dr. L. H. Johnston, was a physician from Oklahoma who had the misfortune to be visiting at the time of the riot. According to the official version, the heavily armed Johnston brothers were "driving in a car south of Elaine" on October 2 when warned of the trouble there. They boarded a train for Helena, but when that train stopped at Elaine, the four Johnstons were arrested. They were placed in a car with Orley R. Lilly, who intended to take them to Helena, with several deputies following in a separate car. On the way to Helena, Dr. D. A. E. Johnston was alleged to have grabbed Lilly's gun from his holster and shot and killed him. The whites in the other car then opened fire and killed all four Johnstons.[29]

But even Bessie Ferguson, who wrote a thesis on the riot generally sympathetic to the planter perspective, rejected that version of the Johnstons' deaths.[30] Her rendering more nearly resembles that of Ida B. Wells-Barnett, the black crusader against lynching who investigated the Elaine riot in 1920 and offered a more chilling account of the incident.

According to Wells-Barnett, the four Johnstons were returning from a successful hunt for game—which explains the guns—when they were warned of the trouble in Elaine, turned back, and boarded a train at Ratio. Taken off the train at Elaine, the Johnstons were bound with ropes and placed in the car with Lilly. As the car pulled away, the white mob opened fire, killing everyone in the car, including Lilly.[31] The newspapers reported the official version, however, and even implicated Dr. D. A. E. Johnston in the insurrection plot. According to the *Arkansas Gazette*, "a dozen high-powered rifles and hundreds of rounds of ammunition were confiscated" from his dental office after the incident.[32] This report both supported the contention that there had been insurrection plans and further legitimized the killing of the Johnstons. Because there was no coroner's inquest, neither the high-powered rifles nor any other evidence of the Johnstons' purported involvement in the plot was ever produced, however.[33]

The attempt to justify the deaths of the Johnstons by implicating them in an insurrection plot is simply ludicrous. The social distance between wealthy blacks and poor sharecroppers was just too great.[34] Elite black men like the Johnstons were more likely to found benevolent organizations and engage in charitable activities than to lead a rebellion of black sharecroppers. Though the Johnstons' deaths must have stunned the rest of Helena's black upper class—which included one of the most prominent black Baptists in the country, Dr. E. C. Morris—elite blacks seem not to have been cowed by those deaths. Morris, who was pastor of the Centennial Baptist Church in Helena and the founder of both Arkansas Baptist College and the National Baptist Convention, apparently "lost the confidence" of the local white community when he refused to participate in the interrogation of the black defendants. The Committee of Seven, made up of prominent Phillips County white citizens, including Sheriff Kitchens, "tried to prevail upon various of the negro leaders to question the prisoners here, to read over the written evidence, and to verify the data collected by our committee, but in no single instance were we successful."[35] Dr. Morris probably understood that he would be party to a whitewash or risk retaliation if he differed with the white investigators. Other black leaders in Helena also refused to participate in what they likely regarded as a kangaroo court and likewise suffered the "loss of confidence" of the white community.[36] In correspondence with the NAACP, Morris went so far as to straightforwardly repudiate the white version of events. Although black leaders throughout the Arkansas delta denounced violence and reassured

whites that they did not support union activities, Helena's black elite subsequently contributed to the defense fund established by the NAACP
through Scipio Jones, a black attorney in Little Rock who helped represent the black defendants in their appeals.[37]

A rare instance of whites transcending class differences in order to
crush a black union had, it seems, led to an instance of blacks transcending their own class differences. When called upon to aid the white community in railroading black sharecroppers, local black leaders indulged
in an uncommon display of race consciousness trumping class consciousness. The potential for this may well have made the continuing violence
increasingly worrisome to the white elite. The greater solidarity among
different classes in the African American community that the killing of
black professionals might forge could not have been understood as serving the interests of white planters.[38]

That the circle of violence had widened to include not only the black
union members who clearly threatened planter interests but also some
of the most accomplished blacks in Helena puts the telegraph to
Governor Brough requesting aid in a different light.[39] Although the
Johnstons were not to die until October 2, the situation in Phillips
County was already deteriorating rapidly when the first telegraph was
dispatched to Brough the day before. Officials in Elaine wired the governor at noon on October 1 that they were "having race riots here in
Elaine and need some soldiers at once. Several white men and Negroes
killed last night and this morning."[40] Subsequent urgent messages from
Helena followed up on that initial request for troops with one indicating
"one hundred and seventy-five negro prisoners are expected to arrive at
any moment among white men." As Arthur Waskow suggests, "it is not
clear . . . whether the local authorities hoped that the troops would help
in tracking down Negro 'insurgents,' or would protect the prisoners from
white lynch mobs, or both."[41] The fact that Colonel Jenks ordered that
white civilians as well as all blacks be disarmed is suggestive. Waskow indicates that Jenks was too easily convinced by local authorities that a black
insurrection was taking place, but the colonel did establish as one objective "preventing lynchings of Negro prisoners" and of O. S. Bratton, the
only white man held in jail in connection with the riot.[42]

With the possible exception of Waskow, historians have assumed that
white leaders in Phillips County required federal troops to subdue the black
population, either because they were engaging in an insurrection or at least

fighting back against whites. Harry Anderson's letter to Governor Brough suggests another possibility. In congratulating Brough for taking "prompt measures," Anderson expressed his conviction that the governor's actions had prevented the loss of black as well as white lives.[43] Furthermore, the messages to Brough implying a fear that the jailed African Americans might be lynched suggest that some planters may well have been as concerned with protecting their labor force from whites run amuck as with protecting themselves from blacks run amuck. Planters had been very much interested in the suppression of the union, and that interest could for a time make common cause with the grudges and fears that working class whites harbored toward African Americans. But planters may have become alarmed as the violence escalated. Certainly in the weeks after peace was restored it became clear that the mob had done its work too thoroughly, at least as far as planter interests were concerned. An unknown number of blacks had fled the area, and planters in Phillips County complained about the cotton going unpicked in the fields. They had been so successful in supplanting white with black labor that they had few options open once their black labor force was dispersed. In the townships where most of the violence occurred, black sharecroppers outnumbered white plantation laborers 1,003 to 123, and the whites who had swarmed into Arkansas to put down the so-called insurrection apparently had no interest in remaining behind to labor on plantations.[44] Accordingly, some planters felt compelled to post bond for blacks jailed in the aftermath of the riot.[45] What common purpose whites found in the initial suppression of the black union apparently faded quickly.

The defection of Smiddy and Jones serves as another example of the fragility of the alliance that planters and working-class whites had forged in the interest of suppressing the union. Both men were employed as special agents for the Missouri-Pacific Railroad at the time of the incident and Jones supervised Smiddy and Adkins, the white man killed at the Hoop Spur church.[46] By their own admission they were very much involved in the events that transpired during the riot, but they later gave affidavits that discredited the "official" narrative of events. Afterward they received threats from Phillips County whites and were branded as "low villains" by Justice James McReynolds, a Tennessean on the U.S. Supreme Court.[47] The alliance between planters and men such as Smiddy and Jones was tenuous at best and did not survive those few horrifying days in early October 1919, largely because it was at odds with more than two decades of tension existing between planters and working-class whites.

In addition to recognizing how divisions within the white community complicated events, understanding what happened at Elaine very much depends on a closer examination of the relationship between planters and their sharecroppers than is to be found in much of the existing literature. Butts and James portray that relationship as nonexploitative. Virtually every other historian suggests otherwise, yet neither side examines that relationship as it existed in the Arkansas Delta in detail. McCool relies on data largely drawn from the printed census, while Rogers, Waskow, and Cortner merely assume exploitation within Phillips County. The fact is that planters sometimes acted as the protectors of African Americans against whitecappers, but their actions in suppressing the union in 1919 were not out of character. Their prime concern had always been to maintain a reliable supply of labor, and some of them had used every means at their disposal to hold black workers in place. At the same time that federal judge Jacob Trieber was convicting whitecappers in 1904 in Helena, a federal investigation of peonage resulted in several arrests and some convictions of planters in nearby Ashley County. U. S. Bratton, the attorney who was later engaged by the Progressive Farmers and Household Union of America to file suits for fair settlement, was an assistant U.S. attorney investigating peonage in Arkansas in 1905. In July of that year, writing to the U.S. attorney in Texas concerning a case that crossed state lines, he declared, "We have had a number of peonage cases in this State recently."[48]

Many years later, Bratton would have cause to recall this investigation into peonage. In answer to a letter from David Y. Thomas, who in 1921 was still attempting to uncover the facts behind the Elaine riot, Bratton indicated that he had learned when he was an assistant U.S. attorney that "large plantation owners were practicing what is known as 'peonage,' and which is nothing more than slavery."[49] Bratton claimed to have secured "convictions or had pleas of guilty entered," on peonage charges, but, peonage was difficult to prove, and Arkansas law, similar to laws in other southern states, armed planters with potent weapons. Vagrancy laws provided for the arrest of apparently unemployed blacks who could be put to work on plantations in the locale where they were apprehended. Other laws established the planter's lien as superior to that of any other creditor and prohibited a sharecropper owing a debt from leaving the employ of a planter. John Miller, the man who prosecuted the Elaine cases, conceded that conditions in Phillips County "came as near a feudal state as ever existed."[50]

Clearly, Butts and James's apparent endorsement of the notion that sharecroppers' circumstances were satisfactory cannot be sustained. Debt was an endemic problem. The authors of one study of Arkansas plantations reported that "those workers who approach full share cropper status have little capital of their own upon which to draw for living expenses from the time the crop is started until the cotton is sold in the fall. As a matter of necessity, therefore, the plantation operators must furnish either money or supplies while they are engaged in making the crop."[51] John Miller indicated "never was a bigger fraud on any set of people then was perpetrated on those sharecroppers [in Phillips County]. The deducts, as they call it . . . they [the planters] got all the money and everything else, they sold the crop." According to Miller, "there isn't any question but the sharecroppers were being defrauded."[52]

It was at crop settlement time that problems sometimes surfaced. Many planters did not furnish a written accounting to sharecroppers even though far many more could read by the turn of the century than was true at the time of emancipation. There was plenty of room for misunderstanding and for outright fraud on the part of planters. Southern planters did not extend credit interest free, and some historians have concluded that the interest charged sometimes amounted to over 40 percent.[53] Bessie Ferguson showed that interest rates were that high in Phillips County, listing figures from the firm of Dowdy and Longnecker of Elaine. Like many merchants, Dowdy and Longnecker had one price for cash and another for credit, and their interest rates hovered around 50 percent. For example, a cash customer paid $1.00 for twenty-four pounds of low-grade flour. A credit customer paid $1.50. Some items carried even higher interest. A pair of work shoes cost $2.50 if a customer paid cash and $4.00 if the transaction involved credit.[54] A planter having an arrangement with such a merchant would pass the cost of the credit along to his sharecroppers and sometimes add a carrying charge. As Henry Lee, an African American immigrant to the Arkansas Delta put it, sharecroppers traditionally "got figured clean out" by planters at settlement time.[55] The Department of Agriculture reported in a 1901 study that those sharecroppers who succeeded in "getting out of debt at the end of the crop year" became indebted "again almost immediately" because they would have to pay for the coming year's "meat, meal, tobacco, molasses and other things necessary."[56]

U. S. Bratton described how black sharecroppers, aware that he was prosecuting peonage cases, "came by the droves to my office telling their stories as to how they were being robbed by the landlords, who took their crops at their own prices, charged whatever they saw fit for the supplies furnished, and as a final consummation of the whole thing, refused to make any kind of settlement with them whatever, the end being that they received a statement, written upon blank tablet paper as a rule, showing 'balance due' in a lump sum."[57] Bratton also illustrated how a sharecropper's obligations could travel from one plantation to another, thus perpetuating the vicious cycle of debt. He said "that the planters refused to consider making any arrangements with one of these people who happen to live upon an adjoining farm, without first ascertaining how much the balance due is claimed to be. If the planter is willing to pay the balance due, or in other words buy him at that price, then he is at liberty to take him; but the custom is so well established that it is not proper to take one with a balance due unpaid, that this is rarely done."[58]

Whatever Butts and James's sources may have told them, other Phillips County whites were not necessarily under any illusions about the circumstances of local sharecroppers in the years immediately preceding the Elaine riot. Charges of mistreatment of black sharecroppers in Phillips County surfaced in 1916 in an unlikely place. According to the *Helena World*, the Rev. Burke Culpepper, a white preacher holding a revival over several days in Helena, at one point "took up another line of spiritual wickedness in high places in this community, in the unfair treatment of labor, especially colored farm labor, on the part of those whose positions as financial and social leaders should make them above such practices." In a rare admission for the generally proplanter *Helena World*, the editor remarked that "the evangelist evidently knows that some large fortunes in Helena have been founded on unfair and unrighteous treatment of negro farmers."[59]

Regardless of whether union organizers were engaged in a money-making scheme, they had clear grievances to build on. The organization of the sharecroppers' union in Phillips County did not, furthermore, represent the first instance of black resistance to this state of affairs, yet few who have written on the Elaine Race Riot have grasped that fact. Waskow came closest to appreciating that long-standing tensions existed between planters and their black sharecroppers and that the Elaine Race Riot was one manifestation of a long struggle over settlement of the crop. His evidence, however, does not include specific examples of earlier resistance in Phillips County. O. A. Rogers went so far as to suggest that until the formation of the Progressive Farmers and Household Union, the blacks of Phillips County were simply "illiterate and docile tenant farmers and laborers."[60] In fact, 73.3 percent of the adult black men in the townships where most of the violence occurred in 1919 reported in the 1920 census that they could read.[61] If not necessarily illiterate, neither were these men always docile.

Long before the Elaine Race Riot, some Phillips County African American sharecroppers became frustrated enough to confront planters at settlement time. The results were usually disastrous. For example, in October 1898, Charles Munn, an African American tenant in Phillips County, confronted the planter he sharecropped for, Frank DuBarry. He "went over to Mr. Frank's house and axed him ef he had looked at his book to see how much he owed me. He said no and took and lit it and cussed me and told me to get outer his house unless I wanted him to kill me. Then I hit him." Munn confessed to burning DuBarry's house to the ground while DuBarry lay unconscious within it. Munn was arrested, convicted, and executed.[62] Another conflict involving a planter and black sharecropper was reported in the *Helena World* the same day as the Munn/DuBarry affair, but according to the planter it involved a quarrel brought on when the planter demanded that his sharecropper haul his cotton to the gin before an expected rain began. "The negro demurred, and finally told Mr. Ferrell he would haul the cotton when he d— pleased to do so. This brought on a quarrel and the negro finally became so infuriated at what he considered an invasion of his personal rights that he ran to one of his cotton baskets and got out a butcher knife and made for Ferrell. The latter ran back a few steps until he could get his pistol from his pocket when he fired, the ball entering the left side just below the heart." There were no witnesses to the incident, and Ferrell was not charged with any crime in the "unfortunate affair."[63]

Tensions persisted throughout the Arkansas Delta well into the twentieth century. By 1916 a federal study of plantation conditions in Arkansas was warning that "as a result both of the evils inherent in the tenant system and of the occasional oppression by landlords, a state of acute unrest is developing among the tenants and there are clear indications of the beginning of organized resistance which may result in civil disturbances of a serious character."[64]

The existence of tensions severe enough to warrant fears of serious civil disturbances prior to World War I suggests that some historians may be attributing too much to the experience of that war and the postwar "Red Summer" in attempting to explain the emergence of the Progressive Farmers and Household Union of America and the Elaine Race Riot. To be sure, the form that longstanding discontent took was influenced by the war and its aftermath. Black veterans and civilians were conditioned by black participation in World War I, and their horizons had been expanded. Participation in the war also influenced the white response. The American Legion, an organization founded by returning veterans, played an instrumental role in fashioning that response, issuing a call to arms and generally massing white veterans in the offensive against black sharecroppers. But the legion could no more control the wild and undisciplined white mob that descended upon Phillips County than could the planters who must have been, once the initial scare was past, aghast at their behavior. Nevertheless, planters publicly closed ranks, asking for troops—troops who disarmed white civilians as well as blacks—and then touted an official version of the riot that concealed what really transpired. Such a version served to obscure the abuses of the sharecropping system and to restore the delicately balanced white class structure, dominated at the top by planters.

Just as the official version of events was concocted within a certain historical context, its adoption by Butts and James forty years later cannot be divorced from events taking place in the late 1950s and early 1960s. Butts and James were writing just three years after the Central High crisis and in the midst of a swelling civil rights movement. The Arkansas Delta soon became the center of a voting rights campaign by the Student Nonviolent Coordinating Committee, and, again, the white community there felt besieged. It is only within this context that Butts and James's wildly contradictory portrait of Robert Hill, the union organizer described as a con man and troublemaker, can be understood. He is seemingly presented as a forerunner of the civil rights era's "outside agitators," come—in the minds of many white southerners—to muddy the "peaceful relations between the races."[65] Hill was an ambiguous figure whose motivations troubled even sympathetic historians and whose demeanor, behavior, and origins disquieted class-sensitive NAACP officials. Yet the convoluted scenario created by Butts and James is implausible at best. They would have it that Hill created the union simply as a money-making scheme. Yet at the same time, they argue he forged an insurrectionary force and hatched a plot to murder planters. Complicating these two obviously contradictory lines of thinking, Butts and James insisted that Phillips County sharecroppers were neither exploited nor unhappy. Their explanation of why Phillips County blacks joined the union rests on the condescending assumption that they were ignorant and easily duped by a smooth-talking black con man. Butts and James, furthermore, failed to note that, on the morning of the Hoop Spur incident, Robert Hill, unaware of the violent turn of events at the church, was meeting O. S. Bratton, son of attorney U. S. Bratton, at the railroad station in McGehee, Arkansas. Hill had earlier approached the senior Bratton to represent union members in the suits they planned to file, and the younger Bratton was on his way to Phillips County to secure information. Butts and James never explained why a con man would hire an attorney, especially one with U. S. Bratton's credentials, to represent the individuals the alleged con man was swindling.[66]

In portraying black southerners bestirring themselves at long last to resist their oppression, O. A. Rogers Jr., president of Arkansas Baptist College, a black institution in Little Rock, was likely influenced in his own way by the momentous events swirling around him. He discovered all too quickly that there were some in the Phillips County white community who still held to the traditional narrative of events. Rogers was acquainted with novelist Francis Irby Gwaltney, who claimed in a letter to his literary agent to have helped him research his essay, and Gwaltney was to discover that even a fictionalized account of the riot would receive a cool reception in certain quarters.[67] The reaction of American publishers to Gwaltney's novel about Elaine, *The Quicksand Years,* suggests that they too found the topic problematic for reasons other than the book's literary quality. If Butts and James refused to acknowledge that the planters had brought events upon themselves, those more sympathetic to civil rights had little reason at this point to dwell on the legitimacy of black armed response. One publisher thought the premise was too farfetched, and another described the story as "too unreal."[68] Gwaltney was forced to go to a London publisher, and the book came out to some very good reviews in the summer of 1965.[69] By that time, the events it described may have seemed not "unreal" but all too real. In October 1965, just two months after the Watts riot rocked Los Angeles, Gwaltney's Hollywood agent reported on his failed efforts to sell producers on the idea of a movie based on the Elaine Race Riot. "I realize you really did not expect any other reaction," the agent wrote, but "without exception" the response from producers was "that the material is beautifully written, but quite impossible to do as a motion picture in this town at this time."[70]

Arthur Waskow, publishing a year after Gwaltney's Hollywood rejection, was seeking to understand governmental attempts to control individual and group violence, and thus was more consciously viewing the Elaine Race Riot from the perspective of the 1960s. B. Boren McCool, writing four years later, had witnessed more urban rioting and the assassination of Martin Luther King Jr. These developments perhaps led McCool to recognize a greater degree of militancy on the part of Phillips County African Americans in 1919, which stands in contrast to Rogers, who saw them as simply defending themselves from white attacks.

What this suggests, in fact, is that history is constantly being rewritten and reinterpreted, and that no historian, including the one writing this essay, can escape the influence of the environment in which he or she lives and writes, no matter how much one strives for objectivity. The Elaine Race Riot reminds us that violence has been a part of almost every age, including our own. This violence can be triggered by a complex of social, economic, ethnic, racial, psychological, and other factors. Behind the events in Elaine is a "white" story as well as a "black" story, and understanding what motivated groups of landless whites to rampage against blacks at the beginning of the twentieth century may be crucial to understanding why minorities continue to be the targets of racial violence at the end of the twentieth century—and not simply in Arkansas or Jasper, Texas, but in Howard Beach, New York, and Chicago, Illinois.

A Place at the Table

Hot Springs and the GI Revolt

PATSY HAWTHORN RAMSEY

Most readers will be at least broadly familiar with Arkansas's long history of political corruption. Garland County—Hot Springs, in particular—was the home of an especially blatant example of crooked politics well into the twentieth century. Relying largely upon the manipulation of poll tax receipts as a way of engineering election outcomes and protecting the lucrative gambling industry, the political machine of Hot Springs led by mayor Leo P. McLaughlin finally was defeated in 1946 by a group of returning World War II veterans and their allies. In this selection, the author details the backgrounds, motivations, and career paths of Sid McMath, Q. Byrum Hurst, I. G. Brown, and other members of the "GI Revolt." While Ramsey paints a more complicated picture of the men and the movement than past accounts, she concludes that their legacy was indeed one of cleaner elections, though not a Hot Springs free of gaming interests.

On June 14, 1946, the *Arkansas Gazette* reported that a retired marine, Lt. Col. Sid McMath, and a group of his fellow World War II veterans, were staging a "GI Revolt" in Garland County. They intended to oust the entrenched political machine of Hot Springs mayor Leo P. McLaughlin, who was identified as the kingpin of a corrupt and illegal gambling industry in the spa city.[1] Subsequent newspaper articles and historical narratives continued to use the term "revolt" to describe the entrance of World War II veterans into Arkansas politics, citing McMath and the Garland County

Patsy Hawthorn Ramsey, "A Place at the Table: Hot Springs and the GI Revolt," *Arkansas Historical Quarterly* 59 (Winter 2000): 407–28. Reprinted with permission.

GIs as the pioneers and the most conspicuous examples of this phenomenon. Encouraged by the rhetoric of the GIs themselves, writers have
repeated the story that the GIs, having so recently fought totalitarianism
abroad, were eager to make Arkansas safe for democracy by bringing fair
and honest government to their own communities.[2] A number of accounts
do acknowledge that a more complex mixture of idealism and ambition
went into the revolt, but few have taken a very close look at the personalities and backgrounds of the men involved.[3]

The war-hero imagery that the veterans themselves indulged obscures
what appears to have been profound differences within the Garland
County group that fought the McLaughlin machine. Although some of
them were war heroes, others were not even veterans. Some among the
GIs wanted to rid Hot Springs of illegal gambling while others supported
it. Some of the candidates may have decided to seek office because of their
war experiences, but at least two of them were pursuing longstanding
dreams of holding public office. And while some invited themselves to the
table, others took a place already set for them. Still, whatever their motives
or background may have been, the GIs possessed a common interest in
securing honest elections in Garland County in 1946. Accomplishing that
would earn them a place in Arkansas history.

Garland County was certainly a community in need of political
change. For as long as most citizens could remember, political and economic power had been concentrated in the hands of Hot Springs mayor
Leo P. McLaughlin's political machine, which protected and was supported by an illegal but open casino gambling industry.[4] While many
local citizens did not necessarily object to gambling, which provided jobs
in a rather underdeveloped area, they were dissatisfied with the attendant corruption in their local government and their limited access to the
political process.

The little resort's gambling history reached as far back as the late
1800s. After several interruptions, legal pari-mutuel betting on horse races
became a permanent fixture in 1934. Fashionable casinos and back street
dives openly offered illegal gambling both to high rollers and penny-ante
players.[5] Places such as the Belvedere Club and the Tower Club on the
edge of the city and the chic Southern Club on Central Avenue catered
to casino gambling as well as bookmaking. Slot machines were stuck in
back rooms of small cafes and taverns, out of the way, but certainly not
hidden. There was no need to hide the gambling devices because local

officials, including those in law enforcement, accepted illegal gaming as part of the heritage of Hot Springs, and state officials often pretended to be completely unaware of it. Occasionally, in response to social reformers or political pressure, the gambling halls were raided and closed briefly. They never remained so for long.[6]

Since his election as mayor in 1927, McLaughlin and cohorts such as circuit judge Earl Witt and municipal judge Vernal Ledgerwood had operated a tightly controlled political machine that directed city and county politics and regulated the illegal gambling industry.[7] Many people thought Ledgerwood actually ran the machine while McLaughlin was merely its figurehead. Street talk sometimes credited unknown gangsters or underworld gambling figures with calling the shots for the whole operation. Yet, despite the presence of such figures as Owney Madden in Hot Springs, no one has offered proof of such control.[8] Regardless of who the real decision maker was in the political machine, Leo Patrick McLaughlin enjoyed being its titular head. Flamboyant in dress and personality, the mayor, wearing a signature red carnation on his lapel, often drove down Central Avenue in his viceroy showbuggy drawn by matching horses named Scotch and Soda.[9]

The machine more than merely tolerated illegal gambling. By what Jim Lester terms a "gentlemen's agreement," entertainment businesses that wished to avoid problems with local law enforcement paid regular "fines," essentially semimonthly fees, with a portion going to the city and part going to McLaughlin's group. Former bookmakers testified in the 1947 bribery trial of Hot Springs city attorney Jay Rowland that they had paid regular "fees" to Rowland or to the secretary of former mayor McLaughlin.[10] In return for the fees, McLaughlin allowed these establishments to operate without fear of police raids or other legal interference. McLaughlin openly promoted Hot Springs as a vacation spot for people interested in gambling.

Of course, McLaughlin could not provide such protection to the gambling industry without completely controlling local government. The machine hand-picked candidates for political offices. Persons seeking office knew they had little chance of winning without the blessing of "the Administration," as the machine was often called."[11] In turn, the machine made sure its candidates were elected. Its means of control was fraudulent manipulation of the poll tax, Arkansas's unofficial means of voter registration. Everyone desiring to vote, except citizens in military service, had to pay the tax. By Arkansas law, a person could pay any eligible voter's tax by proxy. Law required that the tax receipts be turned over to the prospective voters within five days of purchase.[12] Liquor stores and other small businesses sometimes bought blocks of receipts, handing them over to customers as they came in to shop. In a small city where not everyone had regular transportation to the courthouse such a practice was a convenience, a kind deed, and a means of garnering business and political loyalty. But with no voter registration or identity verification system in place, abuse of the system was inevitable. The Hot Springs machine routinely purchased large blocks of poll tax receipts and found voters to redeem them for ballots on election day. For the unscrupulous politician, it was not a large step from having poll tax receipts on hand for potential voters to signing up people who should be voting but were not. Apparently for many politicians, moving on to signing authorizations for deceased or absent voters was not so large a step either. To carry out the scheme, the county clerk, collector, and election officials had to be involved in the plan, choosing not to check the legitimacy of poll tax receipts in the hands of their political friends. Clearly, many local citizens also knew the truth but chose either to ignore it or to participate in its effacement.[13]

The McLaughlin regime met its first real political challenge with McMath's decision to run for prosecuting attorney in 1946. McMath later said that he had two motives in seeking office that year. His ambition since youth had been to hold public office, possibly that of governor, and he was ready to pursue that goal at this point in his life. But he also wanted to rid Hot Springs of the corrosive gambling industry. As a young man, McMath had spent many hours listening to former circuit judge C. T. Cotham talk about his own frustration at being unable to stem the corruption that accompanied open gaming in the city. McMath vowed to himself that one day he would do what Judge Cotham had been unable to do.[14] To carry out that goal, McMath called upon his fellow veterans and former classmates to join him on his self-appointed mission. Some of those who joined him shared his disgust with gambling. Others simply shared McMath's ambition for office. Either way, accomplishing their purposes necessitated the toppling of the McLaughlin machine.

In the winter of 1945, McMath met with a group of veteran friends at the Elks Lodge in Hot Springs to discuss his hopes of winning office and reforming local politics. His goal, he told them, was to establish honest government in their city and county. McMath convinced the men that together they could secure county and city offices and eliminate the McLaughlin machine.[15] Adopting the name "Government Improvement League," which was aptly, and perhaps opportunistically, shortened to GI League, the men began working toward their goal of winning the Democratic preferential primaries to be held that July. By the end of April, they had chosen their slots and announced their candidacies.

The GI League consisted of approximately twenty to thirty men. Most of them were, indeed, returned veterans. Of those who filed for county positions in the Democratic preferential primary, only Leonard Ellis, a longtime friend of McMath and candidate for circuit and chancery clerk, was not a veteran. Two other notable nonveterans in the group, Scott Wood and William Bouic, both local attorneys, worked on the campaigns but were not candidates.[16] Those in the group who had served in the war were not necessarily typical of the state's veteran population, however. Four of the veteran candidates were practicing attorneys: McMath, Clyde Brown, David Whittington, and Q. Byrum Hurst. A number of prominent members of the group who were not candidates were likewise attorneys, including Julian Glover and Richard Hobbs, who helped with legal work for the group.[17]

McMath filed to run for prosecuting attorney for the eighteenth judicial circuit, composed of Garland and Montgomery counties. His opponent was incumbent Curtis Ridgeway, a McLaughlin insider. Because of its power to bring criminal cases to court, control of the prosecutor's office was essential to political reform. McMath's law partner, Clyde H. Brown, ran for the other key county position, circuit judge of the eighteenth circuit, against incumbent Earl Witt, an integral part of the McLaughlin machine.[18] I. G. Brown (no relation to Clyde) opposed incumbent sheriff Marion Anderson. J. O. Campbell drew no opposition for tax collector in the primary but expected an independent opponent in the general election, Filmore Bledsoe, a McLaughlin supporter.[19] GI attorney Q. Byrum Hurst ran for county judge against long-time incumbent Elza Housley. W. J. Wilkins opposed the machine's county treasurer, Henry Murphy. Veteran Ray Owen, owner of the Hot Springs Credit Bureau, ran for tax collector against Mack Wilson. In the state senate race, local attorney and veteran David B. Whittington challenged Ernest Maner, who had served six terms in the state legislature. Nonveteran Ellis challenged John Jones for the position of circuit and chancery clerk that Jones had held since 1912, and E. M. Houpt (Hurst's uncle) ran for county clerk against fifteen-year incumbent Roy Raef.[20] The smallest race on the ticket was for the position of constable within the city of Hot Springs. Veteran Tommy Freeman, an ex-navy petty officer and former welterweight boxing champion of the world, ran for that position.[21]

Not all politically active veterans enlisted in the GI League. The Garland County sheriff's race drew another war veteran candidate, Charles "Stuffy" Dugan, who campaigned in decided opposition to the GI group. Dugan, twenty-five and a highly decorated flyer, was a student at Henderson State College during the campaign season.[22] His rather limited campaigning appeared to center around accusations that Hurst and GI attorney Scott Wood had engineered the GI effort in order to continue their own control of the gambling industry.[23] That belief was apparently not shared by a large number of other people. No other person knowledgeable about the era has suggested that Hurst was anything more than one of the followers of the group.

In spite of considerable talk about McLaughlin not being the real head of the machine and the fact that the mayor's office was not on the July ballot, he was the main target of the GI campaign. According to McMath, the GIs felt that if they could expose McLaughlin, the rest of the machine would fall with him. Other than eliminating that machine, these ambitious young men, ranging in age from mid-twenties to mid-thirties, had no real political agenda or cohesive political philosophy.[24] Some of the men opposed illegal gambling, but some of them, notably Hurst and I. G. Brown, openly supported gambling because of its strong positive impact on Hot Springs's economy.[25] Accordingly, the GI campaign focused on political corruption and said next to nothing about gambling—as inextricably linked as the two phenomena were.

As real as the problem of corruption was, some GIs seem to have been driven chiefly by a sense that it was time to resume career trajectories that prior political interest, family connections, and professional background had charted but the war had delayed. Hurst, for example, had dreamed of holding public office since his youth. The son of a well-known Church of God minister who was active in local politics and the real estate market, Hurst spent many evenings at county Democratic party meetings listening to men talk politics. Hurst entered the army in 1943, serving as a counselor to men preparing for discharge but not participating in any overseas military action.[26] The GI movement presented a golden opportunity for Hurst to enter the political fray with group support and the prestige of wartime military service on his résumé.

By Hurst's own account, some of the incumbents were "good men" who were challenged chiefly because he and other veterans wanted their positions. He remembered Curtis Ridgeway, the circuit judge who used his court to protect machine members, as a "dear man," and not part of the McLaughlin machine (McMath disagreed, insisting that Ridgeway was definitely a McLaughlin man who assisted in the maintenance of corrupt government). Former sheriff Mack Wilson and former county judge Elza T. Housley, whom Hurst put out of office, were likewise not corrupt, he said, but instead were honorable men who tried to steer clear of the taint of McLaughlin. When asked why he worked so hard to win the office from Housley, Hurst laughed and replied, "I wanted his job."[28] Some of the support the GIs received also apparently partook of this "outs vs. ins" spirit. Without naming names, McMath recalled in a 1996 interview that he had received contributions in 1946 from "people who were mad at the Administration because they were not part of it."[29]

Furthermore, the distinct battle lines drawn between the GIs and the McLaughlin group obscured the personal and family connections that existed between the veterans and the old regime. Most of the veterans had grown up in Garland County and had family on both sides of the gambling issue. Some had family members who worked in some aspect of the gaining industry or for the local government. Circuit judge candidate Clyde Brown was married to the daughter of Sam Watt, former owner of the Belvedere Club, the most elegant of the gambling establishments.[30] Brown's father was Hot Springs assistant fire chief, Cap. Riley Brown, a McLaughlin appointee. Captain Brown expected to lose his job after the election and had considered retiring before the election, but McLaughlin chose to be magnanimous, letting him know that he would not be fired because he was a good man and could not help what his son was doing.[31]

Whatever their backgrounds or reasons for participating in the revolt, the GIs needed to prove to voters that the McLaughlin regime was indeed corrupt. They knew they could not possibly win if machine candidates continued the unscrupulous practice of ballot box stuffing by means of illegal poll tax receipts. They set about looking for evidence of poll tax fraud. Knowing that a challenge under state election laws would be heard in Circuit Judge Earl Witt's court, a court under the control of the McLaughlin machine, they found a candidate for the local congressional seat so that they could mount a challenge under federal election laws. Patrick Mullins of Dumas agreed to be a write-in candidate against unopposed incumbent W. R. Norrell in the August preferential primary. They began preparations to challenge the validity of one-third of Garland County's poll tax receipts in federal court.[32]

Meanwhile, the official campaign opened on July 4, 1946, with the equivalent of a twenty-one gun salute. Using a World War II propaganda technique, I. G. Brown flew over the small community of Lonsdale, a few miles east of Hot Springs, dropping campaign leaflets inviting people to attend the GIs' first rally, to be held that night at the Colony House in Lonsdale. Presumably, they bypassed Hot Springs for their opening night in order to avoid problems with McLaughlin. Before an audience of the loyal and the curious, the handsome and eloquent McMath promised voters that his group would clean up the corruption that kept good citizens from enjoying democracy as it should be. To the more than eight hundred persons there, he vowed to "protect you against the violation of your civil rights; I will champion the rights of the people against all opponents—yes, against his majesty Der Fuehrer of Hot Springs."[33] On stage with him, the lineup of exuberant and sincere young candidates in their military uniforms seemed to present a picture of America at its best.

As members of the audience left the rally to drive away in their automobiles and pickup trucks, they were reminded of the sinister forces the GIs were fighting. While people were inside listening to speeches, someone had sneaked into the parking lot and salted it with roofing tacks.[34] In her memoir of growing up in Hot Springs, author Shirley Abbott related her father's assertion that "Leo's boys"—in plainclothes rather than policemen's uniforms—had scattered the tacks.[35] People certainly assumed McLaughlin was responsible. The young veterans who had so enthusiastically promised to respond to the needs of their community had their first opportunity to do so right then. They ended their evening changing flat tires for their audience.

While the candidates were busy pursuing votes, other GI League members worked to gather evidence of fraudulent use of poll tax receipts. Five candidates for office (Leonard Ellis, Tommy Freeman, I. G. Brown, Egbert M. Houpt, and Patrick Mullins) and three taxpayers (Brad O. Smith, Jr., John T. Kilgore, and Oliver Livingston) filed suit in U.S. District Court complaining that nineteen individuals had made block purchases of poll tax receipts, then forged ineligible or fictitious names on them for the purpose of "stuffing" the ballot boxes of Garland County. Tax Collector Mack Wilson and County Clerk Roy C. Raef were also named in the suit because of their roles in poll tax sales. So were three Garland County election commissioners accused of knowingly certifying the illegal poll tax receipts. Defendants alleged to have purchased blocks of receipts included black ward boss Will Page, casino operator Jack McJunkin, Walter Weldon, Mrs. Fannie McLaughlin, A. J. Karston, Erb Wheatley, Elmer Walters, George Young, Arthur Young, Ben Rogers, George Pakis, R. Manning, Charles Dieckriede, Mike Baucher, H. A. Bledsoe, Charles Appleton, Ross B. Adams, Bill Abbott, and Frank Grant.[36]

Three days before the trial began, a man robbed GI campaign workers Oliver Livingston and Earl Fulton of a briefcase containing depositions of persons who said their names had been used on receipts without their permission. The pair identified McLaughlin's special deputy assessor Ed Spears as the person who held them at gunpoint and took the briefcase.[37] GI leaders promptly paid a visit to the mayor's office, demanding the return of their briefcase. Two hours later, the case was returned, contents intact. McLaughlin knew that keeping the case would not stop the GIs but apparently wished to use their information against them. Several individuals whose depositions were in the case would appear in court three days later as witnesses for the defense. Ed Spears later admitted to, and was convicted of, stealing the briefcase.[38]

The poll tax fraud trial opened July 8 in Judge John E. Miller's federal court. Presenting the contents of the rescued briefcase as evidence, the plaintiffs charged that 3,825 poll tax receipts issued to the defendants were illegitimate. Some of the signatures were of persons who were deceased or had moved from Garland County years before, others belonged to persons who swore that their names had been forged.[39]

Even after getting the briefcase evidence to court, the GI attorneys had to fight to prove it credible. The defense produced several witnesses whose signed affidavits were in the case but who suddenly "remembered" on the witness stand that they had authorized purchase of their poll taxes. Club operator and defendant Jack McJunkin admitted, however, that he had personally signed more than two hundred authorizations, which had been purchased in a block. Other defendants admitted making similar purchases and signing them, using ineligible and unauthorized names. Garland County Collector Mack Wilson testified during the trial that he had issued many illegal poll tax receipts in his years in office but defended himself by insisting that such practices were common all over the state.[40]

The largest block of poll tax receipts in contention was held by Will Page, a black ward boss and gambling house operator who had 1,483 receipts issued over a period from May 29 to August 24, 1945. They were numbered in a way designed to impede detection. Anne McMath and J. O. Campbell discovered a pattern of skips while working through the night to decipher the code of receipt entries. When Campbell testified in court, the defense attorneys did not even cross-examine him; they knew they had lost.[41] Handwriting expert W. H. Quakenbush of the Kansas Bureau of Investigation had already testified that "an overwhelming majority of the signatures of authorizations held by Will Page were signed in the same writing." He gave the same testimony about names on the McJunkin list, a fact to which McJunkin readily admitted. The evidence against Page turned the case in the GIs' favor. On July 11, Judge Miller canceled 1,607 Garland County poll tax receipts, 776 of those held by Will Page and 831 of those obtained by other followers of McLaughlin.[42] The first battle had been won. The veterans were closer to an honest election.

In an attempt to further curb the power of McLaughlin, GIs immediately filed another suit, this time in circuit court, to remove Mayor McLaughlin as chairman of the Garland County Democratic Central Committee. With McMath and Clyde Brown acting as their attorneys, the GI plaintiffs contended that officeholders or candidates could not be members of the central committee. Citing section nineteen of the Arkansas Democratic Party rules, McLaughlin responded that he was not an elected member of the committee. Instead, he had been appointed and, though chairman, did not have voting privileges.[43] In a rather heated exchange with GI attorney David Whittington, the mayor drew a laugh from the audience when he told Whittington, "If you're questioning our legal methods I'll remind you that for years one of our best legal advisors was your daddy."[44] The late George Whittington had indeed been an attorney for and supporter of Leo McLaughlin. Not surprisingly, the GIs' claim was denied by Circuit Judge Earl Witt, a principal in the machine, and the mayor continued as chairman of the Garland County Democratic Central Committee.[45]

The three weeks between the poll tax trial and the Democratic primary saw local opinion sharply divided and tensions reaching the boiling point. Supporters of both sides were reported to be carrying weapons. Members of labor unions and the "entertainment industry" supported McLaughlin, but the GIs appeared to have captured the popular imagination. At a final rally the night before the election, a crowd of nearly six thousand listened to the veterans promise clean government. At a rally for the incumbents held at the city auditorium, only a few hundred people showed up to hear members of the old regime plead to be returned to office. Neither side knew for sure what to expect the next day.[46]

Voters going to the polls on July 30 for the Democratic preferential primary saw a sight they had not seen in a long time, if ever, in Garland County. Poll watchers for both sets of candidates were carefully monitoring the proceedings. Supporters of the veterans used home-movie cameras to record citizens going into the voting stations. When Mayor McLaughlin tried to enter the sixth ward polling station (not his voting place) a poll watcher stopped him and informed him that he could not proceed. When the mayor protested that as chairman of the Democratic Central Committee he had a right to enter the polling place, the poll watcher still refused. McLaughlin was so "flabbergasted" that he shook the man's hand twice before he hurriedly left the room.[47] Hot Springs native James Holt remembers that his father and other GI workers stationed themselves in buildings adjacent to the polling places, armed with shotguns to make sure no one tampered with the ballot boxes. McLaughlin forces took the same precaution.[48]

Yet, in spite of the GIs' vigilance, what had probably been the most honest election in Garland County in years did not overturn the McLaughlin regime. Only the charismatic McMath defeated an "Administration" incumbent, unseating Curtis Ridgeway with a vote of 3,900 to 3,375. Veteran J. O. Campbell was unopposed in his bid for tax assessor after incumbent Roy Gillenwater resigned from office and left town. Votes from Montgomery County, the other part of the local judicial district, probably secured McMath's victory.[49] Clyde Brown came within three hundred votes of upsetting incumbent circuit judge Earl Witt, mostly through the support of Montgomery County voters. Brown's loss probably reflected the fact that Witt was viewed by the public as a much more honorable man than McLaughlin or Ridgeway. The candidates who depended upon votes exclusively from Garland County lost by larger margins.[50]

Charges of election fraud emerged immediately. Poll tax receipts that had been canceled by Judge Miller in the July federal court decision were used for voting in two black wards that went heavily for the incumbents. The margins in these two wards brought the defeat of circuit judge candidate Clyde Brown and I. G. Brown, candidate for sheriff. GIs claimed that they had film of black voters going into the polls with receipts to which pink slips had been attached instructing them how to mark their ballots. The veterans announced plans to contest the election in court. In turn, "Administration" candidates accused the GI camp of intimidating legitimate voters, keeping some from the polls.[51] Their threats to have ballot boxes impounded amounted to little, however, since they had won most of the elections.

Following the primary, McMath declared in a public statement that he would continue the fight to clean up Garland County and Hot Springs government. "The war for free government has just begun," he said.[52] The GIs' plan now called for the defeated veterans to enter the general election race as independent candidates. The move would allow opponents in later campaigns to question these men's loyalty to the Democratic Party, but running as independent candidates seemed a more fruitful option than filing a lawsuit contesting the vote. Judge Miller's federal court would not have jurisdiction over an election that did not involve any federal offices, so this time the case would have to be heard in circuit court. The veterans, however, did announce plans to ask the Arkansas Supreme Court to remove McLaughlin as chairman of the county Democratic committee. For its part, the McLaughlin camp threatened to enter an independent candidate against McMath, but he ended up being unopposed in the November general election, except for the token write-in candidacy of Jay Rowland, the "Administration's" city attorney.

The general election of November 5, 1946, put Garland County GI candidates in all county offices and in the circuit judge and prosecuting attorney positions. In a solidly Democratic state and county, all county and circuit judicial officers were elected as independents. Voters apparently saw the single win in the primary election as a signal that new leadership was possible in their counties. A record sixteen thousand voters cast ballots that day. Clyde Brown's loss changed to victory by a 2,008 vote margin in the circuit judge's race. I. G. Brown won the sheriff's position from incumbent Marion Anderson. Q. Byrum Hurst beat Elza T. Housley to become county judge. Ray Owen won as tax collector, and E. M. Houpt secured the county clerk position. Leonard Ellis beat John E. Jones for circuit clerk. Only two veterans failed in their races. Attorney David

Whittington lost his bid for state senator to the twelve-year incumbent, Ernest Maner, and Tommy Freeman lost his race for constable, presumably because his contest was restricted to city voters, among whom McLaughlin was stronger.[54]

In a radio address following the election, Municipal Judge Vern Ledgerwood admitted that the McLaughlin regime had come to an end.[55] The implicit message was that without the support of the circuit judge and prosecuting attorney the machine would be unable to manipulate the court system. Without the cooperation of the county tax assessor, clerk, and collector they would have no control over the electoral process. For his part, McMath proclaimed that the era of machine politics was over in Garland County and Hot Springs. Responding to speculation that the young veterans might become the next machine, McMath stated, "There's a difference between an organization and a machine. Yesterday's election was proof that the residents of this county will not bow to another machine in the next 20 years."[56]

On November 7, the *Arkansas Gazette* reported the GIs' "course for the future." It included defeat of Mayor McLaughlin in the 1947 municipal elections, grand jury investigation of multiple unspecified charges against McLaughlin, and a straw vote after the city election to ascertain citizen support of open gambling.[57] Such a vote would have no legal standing because all gambling except restricted pari-mutuel betting at Oaklawn Park was illegal by state law. But the GI campaign had been quite cautious with respect to the gambling issue, and some of the veterans seem to have been eager at this point to assure their constituents that they were not opposed to it.

It turned out that the transfer of power from the McLaughlin machine to the GI forces would be completed even before the municipal elections of 1947. Knowing their regime had ended, Vern Ledgerwood announced he would not seek reelection.[58] McLaughlin attempted another campaign for mayor but saw his political support shrivel up along with the gambling industry. GI Earl Ricks, part owner of Ricks-Clinton Buick dealership, quickly announced his candidacy for the mayoralty. Following the seating of a special grand jury to investigate his administration, McLaughlin publicly admitted that he had allowed illegal gambling and withdrew from the race. Voters elected Ricks that spring in a landslide vote, along with a new slate of aldermen.[59]

In March the grand jury returned thirty-two indictments against

McLaughlin. It also indicted his secretary, Hazel Marsh, for perjury and his brother, George McLaughlin, for wrongfully receiving public funds.[60] McLaughlin's city attorney, Jay Rowland, was charged with bribery in multiple gambling cases. Former circuit judge Earl Witt and former municipal judge Vern Ledgerwood, rumored "brain" of the old machine, escaped any indictments and retired to their respective private law practices. Witt died of throat cancer a short time later.[61]

In Rowland's bribery trial, which took place on October 10, 1947, Prosecuting Attorney McMath focused on the corruption associated with gambling. He called six former operators of gambling establishments to the stand to give testimony about their payments to the city for operating privileges. Otis McGraw, former operator of the Southern Book Club and the Ohio Club, admitted that he paid Rowland a retainer of fifty dollars each month for very little legal work. A. J. Karsten, of the White Front Club, testified that he also paid fifty dollars per month to the city attorney during 1946. He delivered the payments to McLaughlin's secretary, in the mayor's office. Karsten and McGraw stated that when their businesses were raided by state police in previous years Rowland represented them in circuit court and arranged for the return to them of 50 percent of the cash seized in the raids. Rowland retained the other half for the "Administration." City Clerk Emmett Jackson stated from the witness stand that local gamblers contributed $60,757.25 in monthly fees during 1945 and 1946 for licenses to operate. Each gaming establishment paid $131.30 a month, with $100 going to the city and $25 going to the city attorney. Jackson had no explanation for where the remainder went.[62] The fifty dollar retainer to Rowland paid by some gamblers was apparently a separate payment from the "licensing fee" paid to the city.

Rowland's first trial ended in deadlock, but Judge Maupin Cummings granted McMath's immediate request for a new trial, which brought a conviction. The attorney was sentenced to a year in state prison and a fine of $750.[63] Ultimately, Rowland would be the only "Administration" defendant to receive jail time.

McLaughlin's attorneys requested and were granted a change of venue for his trial on charges of malfeasance of office and bribery. The trial was moved to Mount Ida, the seat of Montgomery County, which had furnished majorities to McMath and Circuit Judge Brown. Yet, on November 19, 1947, McLaughlin was acquitted of the malfeasance charges, which centered around his brother George being on the city payroll without actually engaging in any work. One year later, Circuit Judge Cummings declared a mistrial when a second jury deadlocked in its deliberations on the bribery charges. Prosecutor McMath immediately dropped all charges against the former mayor.[64]

In *The Bookmaker's Daughter,* Shirley Abbott recalled a conversation with Earl Witt in which he claimed to have engineered McLaughlin's acquittal. After the jury was chosen, Witt said, he sent some cattle buyers to visit each juror's farm, with offers to buy cattle at more than twice the market price, in cash. The trial was not mentioned, and no promises were asked for or offered. "You'd be surprised at what a little money can do," Abbott remembered Witt saying.[65]

In the jury's defense, however, it might be noted that the evidence to convict on the malfeasance charge was scanty. George McLaughlin's own trial had ended in a hung jury. Witnesses had testified that George McLaughlin showed up in municipal court every day, although he engaged in no courtroom activities other than "standing there." Mayor McLaughlin stated that his brother had been hired as an "undercover" agent to keep track of gamblers and gangsters visiting the city. When giving instructions to the jury, the judge admonished members that they could not convict a man for not earning his paycheck but only for getting a fraudulent salary.[66]

Despite losing his battle to convict McLaughlin, Sid McMath was able to use the trials as a stage for his next political venture. He appointed Julian Glover and Richard Hobbs as deputy prosecuting attorneys to handle the eighteenth circuit's caseload and hit the road making public appearances in as many Arkansas towns as he could. Leaning upon his name recognition and prestige among veterans, McMath invited GI political organizations that had sprung up in other counties—including Yell, Crittenden, Jefferson, Cleveland, and Montgomery—to join the Young Democrats of Arkansas, of which he was president, in taking their revolt to the state level. He had not announced for governor, but that was not far away.

Even with only one local political campaign in his portfolio, McMath had enough political savvy to know that he needed more than just GI identification and support to get elected. Campaigning on promises of better roads and education, McMath courted traditional Democrats with a tone of moderate conservatism and built support by welding together coalitions of regionally powerful political leaders.[67] His strategies were effective, and, after a tough gubernatorial race, McMath went to the governor's office, where he served two terms (1949–53). Leaving hometown ties behind, the new governor distanced himself from his former political allies and avoided entanglement in the controversies over gambling and corruption that still swirled around Garland County politics. The state police under McMath staged a few raids on Hot Springs gambling establishments, but those raids made little difference in the amount or types of gambling taking place.

Of the other original GI candidates, Leonard Ellis, Ray Owen, and Q. Byrum Hurst enjoyed lengthy careers in politics. J. O. Campbell served three terms as tax assessor and I. G. Brown two terms as sheriff before they each moved on to other interests. W. J. Wilkins left the treasurer's office after two terms.[68] Clyde Brown spent one lackluster year as circuit judge, then returned to private law practice. He had a reputation as a heavy drinker who "lived off his wife's money." His wife had received a substantial inheritance from her father, gambling club owner Sam Watt.[69]

The GIs of Garland County achieved their primary goal—securing honest elections that displaced the McLaughlin machine. Balloting on November 2, 1946, was probably the cleanest in many years—and the most honest for some years to come, if some poll watchers are to be believed. After the GI victory, the machine quickly withered. For some among the GI group, that was enough. But those among them interested in more enduring political reform and, especially, those interested in doing away with illegal gambling, would find their ambitions frustrated.

The men who had campaigned against the corruption of the McLaughlin machine would have some problems keeping their own political organization clean. Honest elections did not guarantee honest or good government. Some of the GIs tried to perform the jobs to which they were elected honorably and efficiently. Others took the opportunity to build political power and reap economic rewards through public office. After serving at least six terms as tax collector, Ray Owen was convicted of poll tax fraud and sentenced to prison.[70] Leonard Ellis, a supporter of open gambling from the start, moved in 1955 from the circuit clerk's office to that of sheriff, where he stayed for many years. By reputation, Ellis was "Dane's man," meaning he received election support from Dane Harris, a prominent gambler and casino owner in Hot Springs, in return for political favors.[71] In 1959, Harris and Owney Madden opened the Vapors, a sophisticated supper club and casino that presented Las Vegas quality entertainment and casino gambling without interference from law enforcement. The club operated openly as a premier illegal gambling spot until 1967, when newly elected Republican governor Winthrop Rockefeller carried through with a promise to shut down illegal gambling in Hot Springs.

Near the end of his single term as county judge, Q. Byrum Hurst, elected as a GI in 1946, sold the county road equipment and pocketed the proceeds. A grand jury indicted him on a charge of malfeasance of office, and several taxpayers filed suits against him in an effort to recover the $7,950 that he received and some of the equipment. He returned at least part of the money and avoided a jail term. Hurst then ran for prosecuting attorney the following spring and narrowly lost the Democratic nomination in a run-off with his GI colleague Julian Glover. Interestingly, Hurst's strongest show of support came from Hot Springs's second ward, where more than a thousand illegal poll tax receipts had been disqualified in 1946, thanks to the GI effort. In the that ward, Hurst received 1,103 votes, Glover 214 votes, and a third candidate 127 votes.[73] The voters, or at least the ballot boxes, of Garland and Montgomery counties did not hold Hurst's transgressions against him for long. A short time later he ran for state senator of that district, won, and served in that position for many years. While he was senator, he faced more criminal charges, this time for federal income tax evasion. Hurst won acquittal on those charges when several Hot Springs businessmen, including gambler-gangster Owney Madden, testified that the income in question came from substantial loans they had made to Hurst over a period of years, rather than from payment for professional services. In his last trip to federal court, Hurst was not so fortunate. After he retired from the state senate in the late 1970s he was convicted of misuse of bank funds in a savings and loan scandal and was sentenced to time in a federal penitentiary.

Though some among the GI group, such as McMath, seemed genuinely to oppose illegal gambling, the impact of their clean sweep of county government on gaming seems to have been only temporary. Shortly after the 1946 election the gambling houses quietly closed their doors and ceased operation. The GIs did not ask them to leave or threaten them, but, stripped of the friendly protection of Earl Witt and Vern Ledgerwood, casino operators must have been unsure of their future in Hot Springs. Not knowing who controlled the police, or if anyone did, gamblers kept under cover. Some of the gambling houses would open again in the spring, but only secretively and irregularly. In separate interviews, people who were involved in Hot Springs public life assert that the only gambling in town in the late 1940s was hidden. One of the most prominent casino operators of the 1950s referred to the gambling of 1947 to 1950 as "sneak gambling," in which people surreptitiously placed bets and played the horses in garages and back rooms. The casinos had closed, though "people knew where to find [gambling] if they wanted it."[75]

In early 1948, the Garland County grand jury issued a statement insisting that laws prohibiting illegal gambling be enforced and praising the men who assumed office after January 1, 1947, for "the courageous, efficient, and honest efforts they have made and are making to enforce the ordinances of Hot Springs."[76] The city jail docket for 1946–47 suggests that arrests for gambling decreased in 1947. In November 1946, twenty men were arrested for gambling, with fines of fifty dollars noted by the names of twelve of them. Only the first six of those men, arrested November 2, paid their fines. In December, thirteen people were arrested for gambling, with fines of fifty dollars or one hundred dollars each, though none of these fines were paid. On February 3, 1947, thirteen men (no repeats from those of the previous year) were arrested, with fine of ten dollars, not paid. No other gambling arrests were recorded until June, with one, and July, with four arrests. These June and July arrests also ended in fines of ten dollars, none paid, and the cases were dismissed. City policeman Captain Young signed the book in 1946 as the arresting officer in all the arrests for that year. "Sheriff's office" was the entry for arresting officer in all of the 1947 cases.[77]

It might be that, rather than illegal gaming being in decline, law enforcement personnel were just not pursuing gamblers. But it appears that by the beginning of 1948 the future of gaming was sufficiently uncertain that the divisions over gambling that had always existed within the GI group became public. On January 16, 1948, the *Arkansas Gazette* reported that a new political party, the Business Man's Party, had formed in Hot Springs to work for election of "candidates who will serve Hot Springs rather than themselves." Referring to the new party as "Another chapter . . . in the bitter fight that has been going on for more than a year to restore commercial gambling to Hot Springs," the article detailed the growing conflict between Prosecutor McMath and Business Man's Party leaders, including County Judge Hurst and Tax Collector Ray Owen, both former GI group members.[78]

Whatever decline had occurred in the immediate aftermath of the GI Revolt, open commercial gambling had returned to Hot Springs by 1951 with the reopening of the Southern Club casino, one of the oldest and most prominent of the McLaughlin-era establishments. Soon other gambling houses sprang up, and Hot Springs was on its way to reestablishing its reputation as an entertainment resort. The Belvedere, the Southern, the Ohio, Stute's, and other clubs opened under slightly different rules from those of McLaughlin's day. The highly structured system of "licensing" used earlier gave way to a less organized system of individualized bribery, payoffs, and officials looking the other way.[79] After his election as governor in 1956, Orval Faubus sent a message that he would not interfere with the city's local affairs. City leaders again imposed a system of fines on gambling establishments and prosperity reigned for another decade.[80] Sheriff Leonard Ellis, Tax Collector Ray Owen, and State Senator Hurst were the only GIs still holding local office by 1956. All were both supporters and beneficiaries of the gambling industry.[81]

The men of 1946 rode onto the field of Arkansas politics upon white chargers of honor and justice and free elections. But if they used their war hero images to generate political support, they were simply employing a campaign strategy that had been effective since the days of George Washington. American voters have a long tradition of expecting war heroes to be good political leaders, and World War II's victory over totalitarianism made heroes of many young men. If ambition, even opportunism, intertwined with idealism in some or most of them, they were not so very different from many politicians nor, indeed, from some of American history's greatest statesmen. And if some seem to have betrayed the group's principles, one should remember the distinctive environment in which they operated. When asked if any of the GI politicians ever compromised their integrity, Q. Byrum Hurst responded, "Yes, some of us did. The people demanded it."[82] The people of Garland County had voted to clean up local politics, but many among them supported— perhaps even depended upon—the illegal gambling industry, which could hardly exist if every politician did his duty honestly and well.

II

Policymaking Institutions in Arkansas Politics and Government

"The Great Negro State of the Country"?

Black Legislators in Arkansas, 1973–2000

JANINE A. PARRY AND WILLIAM H. MILLER

Scholars thus far have paid little attention to African American political participation at the state level. Here, Parry and Miller provide an introduction to black legislative activity in the state of Arkansas with a focus on descriptive and substantive representation issues. Specifically, the article investigates the presence and role of black Arkansans in the state's General Assembly since the 1960s, assessing their acquisition of legislative seats, their ascendancy to committee and chamber leadership positions, and —especially—their attempts to present an influential voting bloc. The authors conclude that although African American legislators in Arkansas are disadvantaged by their small numbers, there are ways for them to exercise power, including playing the "spoiler" in close votes, sensitizing the white majority to African American concerns, and crafting strategic alliances with institutional leaders and/or occupying such posts themselves.

Scholarship on African American political participation—like research on political participation generally—has focused largely on the national-level preferences of citizens and policymakers.[1] Considerably less attention has been paid to such dynamics in the American states.[2] Here we provide an introduction to black legislative activity in the state of Arkansas with an eye on descriptive and substantive representation issues. Specifically, we investigate the presence and role of black Arkansans in the state's General Assembly in the post-1960s era of civil rights reforms, assessing their

Janine A. Parry and William H. Miller, "'The Great Negro State of the Country'? Black Legislators in Arkansas: 1973–2000," *Journal of Black Studies* 36 (July 2006): 833–72. Reprinted with permission.

acquisition of legislative seats, their ascendancy to committee and chamber leadership positions, and—especially—their attempt to present an influential voting bloc.

Central to our examination is the context within which the state's black legislators operate. On one hand, scholars of Arkansas's political history have long argued that the 1957 events surrounding Little Rock's Central High School—events that came to stand for the South's stubborn insistence on the preservation of segregation—belie a history of relative racial toleration in the state. In the late 1800s, for example, a bishop in the African Methodist Episcopal Church declared that Arkansas was "destined to be the great Negro state of the Country" and that "the Colored people have a better start there than in any other state in the Union."[3] Indeed, half a century later some of the earliest and most peaceful experiments with school integration occurred in Arkansas, most just a few years before the Little Rock crisis. Key (1949) presented evidence that white Arkansans also were less stalwartly obstructionist about voting practices at mid-century than their peers in other states. Yet Arkansas is a state of the Old Confederacy. As such it "manifested all the major symbols of southern segregation and white supremacy" including Jim Crow laws, inferior public services for its black citizens, a white primary and other restrictions on political activity, and lynchings.[4] Compound these considerations with the fact that the state maintains a relatively low statewide African American population—pre–and post–Civil War—and the prospects for black legislative success become even cloudier.

Research Design

As this primarily is a descriptive project, our first step was to document every African American elected to the Arkansas state legislature after Reconstruction. Similar to other southern states, the first twentieth-century Arkansas elections that included substantial African American participation did not occur until after the civil rights movement and accompanying political reforms of the 1960s. This opened the way for greater participation in the last twenty-five years of the century. We compiled data on African American legislators for each chamber independently, taking note of the party (all were Democrats, other than the two house terms served by Christene Brownlee, a Republican), sex, committee assignments, leadership posts, and years of service of each member.

Our second step involved looking for patterns in the legislators' voting behavior. Using two chief criteria, we selected twenty-seven policy proposals of the tens of thousands considered by both chambers during the period in question. Our first criterion was that the proposal had to have been subjected to significant news coverage, a quality we determined by examining the pages of the two newspapers with statewide circulation (though the *Arkansas Gazette* was folded into the *Arkansas Democrat* in 1991). Because Arkansas remains one of only a handful of states to depend on biennial legislative meetings, we focused on articles appearing in the week before and after the official adjournment dates in each odd-numbered year.[5] The "session wrap-up" articles produced by the state's journalists with regularity were particularly helpful.[6] Our second criterion was to try to represent as many policy areas as possible, some of general interest to all policymakers, and some likely to be of greater interest to African Americans. These areas were education; crime, health, and abortion; race and/or ethnicity; economic development; and government reform.

Descriptive Representation in Arkansas

Integration of Arkansas's legislative chambers arrived with little fanfare in 1972 when a handful of the eleven African Americans who had appeared on the general election ballot were elected to office. Only the four Democrats prevailed—all against black, Republican opponents—supplying African American representation in the Arkansas General Assembly for the first time since 1893, and making Arkansas the last southern state to elect a black legislator.[7] Among the four was Dr. Jerry Jewell, a Little Rock dentist and past president of the Arkansas chapter of the National Association for the Advancement of Colored People, who was elected to serve in the state senate (and would serve as its sole African American member for more than twenty years). Jewell, who also was the first African American to serve on the Little Rock Civil Service Commission, won the post by defeating businessman Sam Sparks, who had run unsuccessfully for a Senate seat just two years earlier.[8] Entering the state house were Richard Mays, a partner in the state's first multiethnic law firm and a former prosecuting attorney; Dr. William Townsend, an optometrist and veteran civil rights activist[9]; and professor Henry Wilkins III, a political science professor at the University of Arkansas at

Pine Bluff (the state's historically black college) who had been the only African American member of the state's 1969 constitutional convention. Mays and Townsend were elected to serve the multimember and majority black Third District of eastern and central Little Rock, whereas Wilkins scraped out a narrow victory to represent the northern region of Pine Bluff, a city just southeast of the capital with a large African American population.[10] The proportion of African American members in the Arkansas General Assembly held fast at just 3 percent of each chamber (one of thirty-five in the Senate and three of one hundred in the House) through the 1970s, rendering the prospect of future diversification less than promising. One long-time political observer and pollster, Jim Ranchino, observed in 1977 that if "you want to run for office in the state and lose, then simply be a woman, a black, a Jew, or a Republican—in that order."[11] Indeed by 1989, the percentage of African American house members had inched up to just 5 percent, as Senator Jewell continued to be the only African American member of the Senate. Growth was accelerated, however, by a court ruling later the same year declaring that past legislative redistricting plans (a process completed in Arkansas by the governor, the secretary of state, and the attorney general sitting together as the Board of Apportionment) had violated the national Voting Rights Act.[12] The remedy ordered was the creation of black-majority legislative districts, a directive the board met by creating—and maintaining despite further court challenge—thirteen such House districts and three such Senate districts.[13] The action was smaller in scale than many black activists preferred but spurred a new wave of African American representation in Arkansas politics nonetheless.[14]

The resulting forward thrust of African Americans being elected to the state legislature was marked (see tables 1 and 2). Specifically, the 1990 election brought the number of black representatives to nine as two additional African American members joined Jewell in the Senate. Two years later, the House proportion grew to 10 percent, and House and Senate held steady at 10 percent and 9 percent, respectively, until the 1998 election, when the House increased by still two more African American members, though the Senate dropped back by one member. Given his extended term of service, it is worth noting that Jewell was not among the state Senators around to usher in a new century. An African American opponent (Rep. Bill Walker) defeated him in the primary election of 1994. After a bitter battle, the twenty-two-year veteran legislator confided "It was hell being here . . . alone."[15] Heading into the 2000 election cycle, then, the number of African Americans in the Arkansas General Assembly stood at two senators and twelve representatives, a grand total of fourteen—or 10.4 percent—of one hundred and thirty five state legislators. This was an improvement but still fell short of the approximately 16 percent of the state's population composed of African Americans.

The General Assembly's small number of black members did not easily acquire leadership positions once elected. Ethnicity, however, was not the major obstacle. Until the implementation of term limits in 1998, Arkansas manifested a low legislative turnover rate compared to other states. According to the National Conference of State Legislatures, for example, while the average turnover nationally among state senators between 1987 and 1997 was 72 percent, Arkansas's was just 57 percent, making it the fourth most stable in membership. As leadership opportunities for newcomers were unlikely in such a context, the early African American members of the General Assembly generally were appointed as rank-and-file members mainly of the Education, Legislative Affairs, and Judiciary committees. Yet by 1979, Representative Townsend and Senator Jewell had been elevated to committee vice chairs; and by the mid-1980s, Jewell was chairing the Senate Committee on Agriculture and Economic Development.

The 1990s found additional African Americans serving as committee vice chairs, including the elevation of Rep. Irma Hunter Brown (D-Little Rock), the first African American woman to serve in the Arkansas General Assembly, to second in command on the House Revenue and Taxation Committee.[16] Of perhaps greater significance, at least symbolically, was Senator Jewell's election as the president pro tempore of the senate in 1993, a post traditionally held by the member with the most seniority who has not previously served in the position.[17] Representative Townsend was elevated to chair of the House Aging and Legislative Affairs Committee in the same year and continued in that post through the 1995 session. In the last half of the decade, senators Jean Edwards (D-Sherrill) and Roy C. "Bill" Lewellen (D-Marianna) chaired the upper chamber's committees on city, county, and local affairs and aging and legislative affairs, respectively, and Reps. Ben McGee (D-Marion) and Joe Harris Jr. (D-Osceola), each served a term heading up the House's Public Transportation Committee. A timeline of African American committee chairs in both chambers is presented in tables 3 and 4.

TABLE 1

African American Legislators in the Arkansas House of Representatives

1981–1982	1983–1984	1985–1986	1987–1988	1989–1990	1991–1992	1993–1994	1995–1996	1997–1998	1999–2000
Brown	Brown	Brown	Brown	Brown	Brown	Bennett	Bennett	Bennett	Bennett
Richardson	Richardson	Hunter	Townsend	McGee	Brownlee	Brown	Booker	Booker	Easton
Townsend	Townsend	Townsend	Wm. Walker	Townsend	McGee	Brownlee	Brown	Brown	Harris
Wilkins, III	Wilkins, III	Wilkins, III	Wilkins, III	Wm. Walker	Roberts	McGee	Harris	Harris	Johnson
				Wilkins, III	Smith	Roberts	McGee	McGee	Jones
					Townsend	Smith	Roberts	Roberts	Lewellen
					Wm. Walker	Townsend	Smith	Smith	Steele
					Wilkins, III	Wm. Walker	Townsend	W. Walker	Thomas
					Wilson	J. Wilkins	J. Wilkins	J. Wilkins	W. Walker
						Wilson	Wilson	Wilson	White
									Wilkins, IV
									Willis
4 members	4 members	4 members	4 members	5 members	9 members	10 members	10 members	10 members	12 members
4% of House	4% of House	4% of House	4% of House	5% of House	9% of House	10% of House	10% of House	10% of House	12% of House

Note: The last two rows indicate the total number of African Americans in the state House, and their percentage of the total chamber membership of one hundred members. The complete names of African American members in the twentieth century are: M. Dee Bennett, Michael D. Booker, Irma Hunter Brown, Christene Brownlee (the sole African American Republican legislator during the period under study), John Eason, Joe Harris Jr., Clarence Hunter, Calvin Johnson, Steve Jones, John Lewellen, Ben McGee, Richard L. Mays, Grover C. Richardson, Jacqueline Roberts, Judy Seriale Smith, Tracy Steele, Lindbergh Thomas, William Townsend, William Walker, Wilma Walker, Robert White, Henry Wilkins III, Henry "Hank" Wilkins IV, Josetta E. Wilkins, Arnett Willis, and Jimmie L. Wilson. Of these twenty-six individuals, six (23 percent) are female.
Source: Various legislative guides, Arkansas History Commission; photograph collection, Arkansas Black History Advisory Committee.

TABLE 2

African American Legislators in the Arkansas Senate

1981–1982	1983–1984	1985–1986	1987–1988	1989–1990	1991–1992	1993–1994	1995–1996	1997–1998	1999–2000
Jewell	Jewell	Jewell	Jewell	Jewell	Edwards	Edwards	Edwards	Edwards	Edwards
					Jewell	Jewell	Lewellen	Lewellen	Wm. Walker
					Lewellen	Lewellen	Wm. Walker	Wm. Walker	
1 member	1 member	1 member	1 member	1 member	3 members	3 members	3 members	3 members	2 members
3% of Senate	3% of Senate	3% of Senate	3% of Senate	3% of Senate	9% of Senate	9% of Senate	9% of Senate	9% of Senate	6% of Senate

Note: The last two rows indicate the total number of African Americans in the state Senate, and their percentage of the total chamber membership of thirty-five members. The complete names of African American members in the twentieth century are: Jean C. Edwards, Jerry D. Jewell, Roy C. "Bill" Lewellen, and William L. "Bill" Walker.

Source: Various legislative guides, Arkansas History Commission; photograph collection, Arkansas Black History Advisory Committee.

TABLE 3

African American Committee Chairs in the Arkansas House of Representatives

1981–1982	1983–1984	1985–1986	1987–1988	1989–1990	1991–1992	1993–1994	1995–1996	1997–1998	1999–2000
None	None	None	None	None	None	Townsend—Aging and Legislative Affairs	Townsend—Aging and Legislative Affairs	McGee—Public Transportation	Harris—Public Transportation
0 chairs	0 chairs	0 chairs	0 chairs	0 chairs	0 chairs	1 chair	1 chair	1 chair	1 chair
of 16 total committees	of 17 total committees	of 17 total committees	of 16 total committees	of 18 total committees	of 18 total committees	of 18 total committees	of 18 total committees	of 17 total committees	of 17 total committees
0% of total	0% of total	0% of total	0% of total	0% of total	0% of total	6% of total	6% of total	6% of total	6% of total

Note: The last three rows indicate the total number of African American committee chairs, the total number of committees in the state House (including select committees), and the percentage of committees chaired by African Americans.
Source: *Arkansas Legislative Digest*, Arkansas General Assembly.

TABLE 4

African American Committee Chairs in the Arkansas Senate

1981–1982	1983–1984	1985–1986	1987–1988	1989–1990	1991–1992	1993–1994	1995–1996	1997–1998	1999–2000
None	Jewell—Agriculture & Economic Develop	Jewell—Agriculture & Economic Develop	Jewell—Agriculture & Economic Develop	Jewell—Agriculture & Economic Develop	Jewell—Joint, Retirement and Social Security	Jewell—Education	Lewellen—Aging and Legislative Affairs	Edwards—City, County, and Local Affairs	Edwards—City, County, and Local Affairs
						Jewell—also President Pro Tempore			
0 chairs	1 chair	1 chair	1 chair	1 chair	1 chair	1 chair	1 chair	1 chair	1 chair
of 18 total committees	of 17 total committees	of 17 total committees	of 17 total committees	of 18 total committees	of 19 total committees	of 19 total committees	of 19 total committees	of 18 total committees	of 17 total committees
0% of total	6% of total	6% of total	6% of total	6% of total	5% of total	5% of total	5% of total	6% of total	6% of total

Note: The last three rows indicate the total number of African American committee chairs, the total number of committees (including select committees) in the state Senate, and the percentage of committees chaired by African Americans.
Source: *Arkansas Legislative Digest*, Arkansas General Assembly.

Although it had existed as an unofficial network for many years, the Arkansas Legislative Black Caucus was officially incorporated in 1989. Instrumental to its establishment was Rep. Henry Wilkins III.[18] The Caucus's official mission

> is to provide a major forum primarily for African American state legislators interested in improving the quality of life for African American and other disadvantaged people in Arkansas; to provide an organizational framework for the passage of legislation; to oversee a more beneficial operation of state agencies; and to provide an additional channel for constituent input.[19]

In keeping with a key tenet of the organization's objectives, caucus members formulated an official list of shared legislative priorities for the 2001 legislative session. Increased teacher salaries and other investments in education topped the list.[20] Further signs of the unit's greater "institutionalization" are found in the weekly meetings held by the caucus, regular gatherings in the "off season," and sustained collaborations with an organization of significantly wider membership (that is, not simply current state legislators), the Democratic Black Caucus.[21] The latter is an official auxiliary organization of the Democratic Party of Arkansas.[22] Such developments no doubt play a role in Kerry L. Haynie's report that the Arkansas legislature has experienced a dramatic increase in the political incorporation of African Americans in recent years.[23]

Of course, the caucus has not been free of criticism. When a prominent civil rights lawyer entered the race for state senator in 2002 against caucus chair Rep. Tracy Steele, he sharply criticized the caucus for failing to "raise issues and make advocacy" on behalf of the state's African American population. Caucus members responded by pointing to recent policy successes including changes to the state's plans for a large tobacco settlement and setting aside a day to honor a prominent civil rights activist.[24] Additional evidence of the caucus's growing significance in the Arkansas political environment lies in the fact that the support of its members was actively courted by U.S. Senate candidates in a close election in 2002.[25]

Substantive Representation in Arkansas

Although widely examined to answer innumerable questions in the political science literature, roll call votes possess many obvious limitations.

The two most significant we encountered were (a) the overwhelming propensity of legislators to vote with unanimity by the time measures came to a floor vote and (b) the tendency of members to be absent or to vote "present" when a consensus emerges on a controversial issue and they find themselves on the losing side of that consensus. Future research stands to fill in the gaps left by such practices. Still, several patterns emerged and we discuss them below.

Tables 5 though 9 provide a summary of twenty-seven roll call votes on key pieces of Arkansas legislation between 1973 and 1999. The tables are divided by the issue areas noted earlier: education; crime, health, and abortion; race and/or ethnicity; economic development; and government reform. What is perhaps most striking about the data, at first glance, is the degree of relative consensus in the African American vote across time and issue area. Black delegates diverged from one another on thirteen measures (or 48 percent of the time), and five of these were inter-chamber-only disputes in which intra-chamber voting was unanimous among African Americans. Although not insubstantial, such cumulative discord is far less than the twenty-one measures (or 78 percent of the time) in which white Democrats cast ballots in opposition to other white Democrats. Also worth noting is that disagreement among African American legislators increased as their numbers increased; 62 percent of the measures in which a split is evident, for example, occurred during the last ten years of the study (1989 to 1999).

We turn now to a more in-depth look at the five issue areas in our analysis. With regard first to the seven education measures examined in table 5, the 1983 teacher testing bill represents well the intense debate surrounding the state's most significant education reform to date, as well as the multifaceted position of the state's black leadership on education matters. A special session was called in the fall of that year to address a public education system widely considered to be in crisis. A 1978 study on school finance commissioned by the legislature had concluded, for example, that "the average child in Arkansas would be much better off attending the public schools of almost any other state in the country."[26] Buoyed by this report, by an ad hoc Education Standards Committee (chaired by Hillary Clinton), and by a state Supreme Court decision declaring the state's school funding system unconstitutionally inequitable,[27] Governor Clinton pitched a wide-ranging package of reforms to the special session. These proposals included raising teacher salaries, establishing a more rigorous core curriculum, mandating smaller class sizes, implementing a longer

TABLE 5

Roll Call Votes in the Arkansas General Assembly on Education Issues

	HOUSE OF REPRESENTATIVES			SENATE		
	BLACK DEMS	WHITE DEMS	REPUB-LICANS	BLACK DEMS	WHITE DEMS	REPUB-LICANS
1973 Free kindergarten measure						
For	100%	69%	—	100%	100%	100%
Against	0	31	—	0	0	0
N= Total voting members	(3)	(89)	(0)	(1)	(25)	(1)
1977 School funding formula						
For	100%	22%	100%	100%	100%	100%
Against	0	88	0	0	0	0
N= Total voting members	(3)	(88)	(4)	(1)	(33)	(1)
1979 Aid to schools						
For	100%	78%	50%	100%	76%	—
Against	0	22	50	0	24	—
N= Total voting members	(3)	(83)	(6)	(1)	(34)	(0)
1983 Teacher testing						
For	0%	74%	67%	0%	65%	33%
Against	100	26	33	100	35	67
N= Total voting members	(4)	(76)	(6)	(1)	(31)	(3)
1985 Home schooling						
For	100%	97%	100%	0%	72%	100%
Against	0	3	0	100	28	0
N= Total voting members	(2)	(71)	(9)	(1)	(29)	(4)

	HOUSE OF REPRESENTATIVES			SENATE		
	BLACK DEMS	WHITE DEMS	REPUB-LICANS	BLACK DEMS	WHITE DEMS	REPUB-LICANS
1989 School choice						
For	50%	53%	82%	0%	52%	50%
Against	50	47	18	100	48	50
N= Total voting members	(4)	(80)	(11)	(1)	(29)	(4)
1991 School choice						
For	17%	89%	100%	0%	56%	75%
Against	83%	11	0	100%	44	25
N= Total voting members	(6)	(79)	(7)	(3)	(16)	(4)

Note: In the Senate vote on the 1989 school choice bill, the tie-breaking vote in favor of the measure's passage was cast by Lt. Gov. Winston Bryant, a white Democrat. One of the House Republicans voting on the 1991 school choice bill was an African American.
Source: House and Senate journals of the Arkansas General Assembly, 1973–91 volumes, Secretary of State's Office.

school day and a longer school year, elevating standards for high school graduation, and requiring kindergarten statewide.[28] Three major varieties of tax increases served as the companion bills to fund such reforms; only one of them—the first one-cent hike in the state sales tax in more than twenty years—eventually passed. In exchange, the governor promised, and delivered, a comprehensive battery of teacher testing.[29]

Although broadly supportive of improved public education in Arkansas, members of the Arkansas Legislative Black Caucus criticized many of the reforms, especially teacher testing. In a meeting with the caucus in early October, Clinton told the members that the onetime "inventory" of all presently certified teachers would "go a long way to restoring public confidence in what . . . is still the most important profession in our country."[30] The governor further explained to the members that although he recognized that "there are people who have been victimized by institutional racism and institutional limitations in the past," he rejected "the notion that any group of people . . . have any inherent, God-imbedded limitation."[31] He concluded that "given the proper opportunity, everybody can pass this test and can prove that our people are just as capable as any people in the country."[32] Caucus members were unpacified, however, and closed the meeting with votes to oppose the examination requirement for current teachers as well as to oppose the sales tax increase unless exemptions for food and utilities were made.[33] They later made good on these resolutions with a unanimous—if futile, in light of the white majority's support for the measure—no vote on teacher testing during the session.

Also of particular interest among the education measures examined was the 1989 school choice bill, the only education issue to evoke yes and no votes (and one nonvote) among the African Americans in the Arkansas legislature. (This division was particularly significant because the measure passed only narrowly in both chambers.) The precise cause of the divide among the black caucus on the measure remains unclear; however, an interview with former representative Ben McGee, who was in his first term that session and voted yes, revealed several related possibilities. The first was that rural legislators—black and white—were not particularly concerned with parents in their communities pulling kids out of one school to the perceived detriment of another. In most cases, McGee noted, there was not another school for many miles, so school choice "wasn't really feasible" in his district. Combine this practical reality with the fact that rural legislators often were frustrated with the cost of desegregation efforts in the central Arkansas region, and the protest of Little Rock public school advocates failed to resonate with McGee. "I was not a fan of the Little Rock district," he admitted, saying that voting for the School Choice Act and against the preferences of many of his urban, black colleagues, was not particularly troubling. Rep. Irma Hunter Brown confirmed this analysis, identifying the divide as largely "a geographic thing," a consequence of the fact that legislators—black or white—often strive to serve the interests of constituents with markedly different demographics.[34]

With regard to the no votes, a successful effort to expand the School Choice Act two years later is further revealing. An element of governor Clinton's legislative package for the 1991 session, HB 1449 promoted expansion of school choice and was raised amid concerns that it would enlarge, rather than diminish, racial and ethnic segregation in Arkansas schools.[35] Many urban, black legislators were especially vocal against its passage, citing the risk of "white flight."[36] "I am unalterably opposed to this legislation because it is not progressive" noted Senator Jewell at the time. "It provides an opportunity for discrimination against white kids and black kids."[37] McGee countered in an interview that most of the whites likely to flee from an integrated public school system "had already bought a house at Cabot," a small, homogenously white town northeast of Little Rock that experienced explosive growth in the 1980s.[38]

On crime, health, and abortion issues, the African American Senate delegation experienced one break in their ranks while members of the house were consistently unified (table 6). Of the four (of six) measures in this category on which black legislators split (either between or within chambers), a 1991 conflict over the availability of contraceptives in school-based health clinics and the adoption in 1995 of a "two strikes" criminal justice reform measure merit further investigation. Specifically, the former was a provision embedded in the state health department's budget that erupted in the final days of the 1991 session. Several House members—including Gus Wingfield (D-Delight) and John Miller (D-Melbourne), both white—supported amending the budget to prevent the purchase and/or distribution of condoms in school-based health clinics, a restriction the Senate refused to support.[39] Although a compromise eventually emerged (the language only forbade the use of state funds for condom purchase and distribution, leaving school nurses free to use federal funds for such purposes), only six Black house members (including Rep. Christene Brownlee, the sponsor of a controversial antiabortion measure in the same session) voted for it (three others abstained), and one of the three African American senators voted against it.[40]

Such division was surprising. After all, the state's black political leadership had been among the strongest supporters of sex education throughout the 1980s, and the measure's most vocal proponent was Dr. Jocelyn Elders, an African American female and director of the state Health Department.[41] Recalling the conflict in an interview, Elders explained the divide as a consequence of some members "voting their minister." African American legislators would not have wanted to vote "against her," she said; however, they did not want to vote "against the church," either. Abstention on the controversial vote was the sensible solution.[42]

Positions virtually flipped on the 1995 criminal punishment reform measure that established a minimum prison sentence of forty years for people convicted of more than one violent crime. Backed by Democratic governor Jim Guy Tucker, the measure received support from all three

TABLE 6

Roll Call Votes in the Arkansas General Assembly on Crime, Health, and Abortion Issues

	HOUSE OF REPRESENTATIVES			SENATE		
	BLACK DEMS	WHITE DEMS	REPUB- LICANS	BLACK DEMS	WHITE DEMS	REPUB- LICANS
1983 Loosened parole						
For	0%	100%	100%	100%	100%	100%
Against	100	0	0	0	0	0
N= Total voting members	(2)	(64)	(6)	(1)	(20)	(3)
1985 Restricted abortion						
For	100%	100%	100%	0%	96%	100%
Against	0	0	0	100	4	0
N= Total voting members	(3)	(81)	(8)	(1)	(28)	(4)
1985 Indigent health care						
For	100%	93%	33%	100%	100%	100%
Against	0	7	67	0	0	0
N= Total voting members	(4)	(72)	(6)	(1)	(30)	(4)
1991 Birth control clinics						
For	100%	86%	100%	67%	85%	100%
Against	0	14	0	33	15	0
N= Total voting members	(5)	(79)	(8)	(3)	(27)	(4)
1995 Two strikes						
For	0%	91%	100%	100%	100%	100%
Against	100	9	0	0	0	0
N= Total voting members	(7)	(74)	(12)	(3)	(24)	(7)

	HOUSE OF REPRESENTATIVES			SENATE		
	BLACK DEMS	WHITE DEMS	REPUB-LICANS	BLACK DEMS	WHITE DEMS	REPUB-LICANS
1995 Drive-by shooting						
For	100%	100%	100%	100%	100%	100%
Against	0	0	0	0	0	0
N= Total voting members	(6)	(75)	(10)	(3)	(24)	(7)

Note: One of the House Republicans voting on the 1991 birth control clinics bill was an African American.
Source: House and Senate journals of the Arkansas General Assembly, 1983–95 volumes, Secretary of State's Office.

African American senators; however, the seven voting House members broke with 91 percent of their white, Democratic colleagues to vote against it (three other black representatives abstained). McGee could not recall, in a 2002 interview, exactly why he was among the abstainers, but suggested his vote had been tied to some other piece of legislation. "People don't pass legislation . . . because it's good policy," he said. Often, they take a position based instead on the fact that somebody will owe them later, or as a show of support for a particular individual."[43] The measure's chief sponsor, Rep. Lisa Ferrell, a White Democrat from Little Rock, confirmed McGee's recollection. Specifically, she remembered that Sen. Bill Walker, a member of the Black Caucus in his first term in the upper chamber, had introduced another criminal justice reform measure during the same session, one that required persons convicted of serious crimes to serve at least 70% of the time sentenced. "Some of the sentiment in the Caucus," she said, was "'we've got to support Bill Walker,' so we can't support the other bill." Noting that she did not feel the bills were mutually exclusive, she also characterized the split as "not at all rancorous."[45] Ferrell added that there likely was a more substantive consideration driving the black caucus's opposition: concern about the disparate impact of a two-strikes law on African American males. Although Ferrell disputed that hers was the "harsher" measure of the two bills, she acknowledged that its effect on black men was a clear worry among many caucus members. This response is not surprising in light of a special session on Tucker's anticrime package the previous summer, a session that had produced several measures that allegedly "targeted young blacks" and had generated considerable concern among the Assembly's African American membership.[45] Representative Brown attributed her no vote to exactly this context. "No one condoned criminal activity by anyone—black or white," she said. However, many of the "tough on crime measures," often used, in her view, to justify ballooning corrections budgets, seemed to be aimed at young African Americans, particularly those who were economically disadvantaged and lacked access to good legal representation.[46]

Our efforts uncovered only three overtly race-relevant issues that made it to a vote of the full assembly and received notable publicity in the period under study (table 7). The first two measures passed with unanimous African American support. The establishment of a Human Resources (or Civil Rights) Commission had been a failed administration measure of Democratic governor David Pryor previously but was shepherded to passage by African American lawmakers in the 1977 session: Rep. Henry Wilkins and Senator Jerry Jewell. During the days just prior to adjournment, three white senators spoke in opposition to the commission's establishment, all going to some length to deny that their opposition had anything to do with race. Ultimately, it was adopted by the chamber, eighteen to five, with twelve senators not voting (May, 1977).[47]

A 1989 vote to approve a $118 million settlement over the Little Rock school desegregation conflict—a measure Representative McGee, the first Black house member from the Arkansas Delta since Reconstruction, called "an opportunity (finally) to put '57 behind us"—proved even more contentious in the chambers, though not among the African American membership.[48] The matter stemmed from a federal court order mandating that the state help finance desegregation efforts in Little Rock's three major school districts because the state had facilitated the segregation of Pulaski County schools. The state's financial portion concentrated mainly on magnet schools and remedial programs.[49] Although several white legislators balked at the steady increase of the settlement total during the session, the final vote demonstrated the eagerness of the entire Assembly to put thirty years of school-related racial strife to rest.

The third overtly race-relevant measure—the Civil Rights Act of 1993—caused considerable strife among the state's African American lawmakers. The breach centered on how much to compromise in Arkansas's struggle to leave Alabama as the only state to lack an antidiscrimination statute. Senator Bill Lewellen's bill emerged early as the most stringent of the measures introduced in the 1993 session. The two primary bills circu-

TABLE 7

**Roll Call Votes in the Arkansas General Assembly
on Race/Ethnicity Issues**

	HOUSE OF REPRESENTATIVES			SENATE		
	BLACK DEMS	WHITE DEMS	REPUB- LICANS	BLACK DEMS	WHITE DEMS	REPUB- LICANS
1977 Human resources commission						
For	100%	100%	100%	100%	76%	100%
Against	0	0	0	0	24	0
N= Total voting members	(3)	(79)	(4)	(1)	(21)	(1)
1989 Desegregation settlement						
For	100%	95%	90%	100%	97%	50%
Against	0	5	10	0	3	50
N= Total voting members	(5)	(73)	(10)	(1)	(30)	(2)
1993 Civil rights act						
For	100%	98%	100%	0%	100%	75%
Against	0	2	0	100	0	25
N= Total voting members	(7)	(66)	(8)	(3)	(27)	(4)

Note: One of the House Republicans voting on the 1993 Civil Rights Act was an African American.
Source: House and Senate journals of the Arkansas General Assembly, 1977–93 volumes, Secretary of State's Office.

lated in the House, by Rep. Bill Walker and by Rep. Bob Fairchild (a white Democrat from the northwest corner of the state), lacked the Lewellen bill's public accommodation protection for gays and lesbians and its hate crimes provision. Both House measures also mandated that only businesses of fifteen or more employees would be subject to the law, rather than Lewellen's nine employee count. With such differences still intact, all three proposals had cleared either the House or the Senate by the end of February, clearing the path for an inter-chamber battle of epic proportions.[50]

Senator Lewellen's bill received a cold reception indeed in the House. It was immediately referred, for example, to the Public Health Committee, on which Walker and Fairchild sat, rather than to the more hospitable Judiciary Committee.[51] Furthermore, though Democratic governor Jim Guy Tucker endorsed Lewellen's proposal early in the session, by late March he was actively lobbying senators to accept one of the House measures. The ensuing debate was exceptionally rancorous, with Walker and Lewellen repeatedly blocking consideration of the other's bills in their respective chambers. Members of the black caucus suggested—anonymously—that the standoff was a personal dispute between Walker and Lewellen. The charge was denied by both as Lewellen assured reporters that the "Black Caucus itself is making moves to compromise the two bills."[52] Ultimately, however, printed news accounts placed the credit—or blame—for crafting a deal with Governor Tucker. In the closing days of the session, Tucker pushed the Walker bill through the senate, leading Rep. Jimmie Wilson, a Lewellen ally, to lash out at the governor and fellow caucus members. The governor, he said,

> led Rep. Walker down the primrose path to sponsor and encourage passage (of) legislation that would be the infamy of all African Americans. . . . I would hate for any African-American across this nation to read our so-called civil rights law and think that was the best people of color in this state could propose.[53]

Despite the opposition of all three African American senators and abstentions by Representative Wilson and one other African American member, the measure was adopted by a wide margin in both chambers.[54]

Arkansas's black legislators also experienced considerable conflict on four of the six economic development measures analyzed (table 8). The 1983 adoption of Gov. Bill Clinton's enterprise zones sparked opposition from two African American house members; another abstained while Senator Jewell joined three fourths of his white colleagues in approving it. Jewell likely was persuaded, as was Benjamin Hooks, executive director of the Arkansas NAACP, by the argument that the plan's tax breaks and other incentives might address depressing employment figures among African Americans.[55] Representatives Brown and Richardson, together with *Gazette* columnist Ernie Dumas, seem to have reasoned instead that tax breaks for corporations were unlikely to improve the structural unemployment problems plaguing the state's poor. "Education and a stronger econ-

TABLE 8

Roll Call Votes in the Arkansas General Assembly
on Economic Development Issues

	HOUSE OF REPRESENTATIVES			SENATE		
	BLACK DEMS	WHITE DEMS	REPUBLICANS	BLACK DEMS	WHITE DEMS	REPUBLICANS
1973 Tax exemption for poor						
For	100%	96%	—	100%	100%	100%
Against	0	4	—	0	0	0
N= Total voting members	(3)	(81)	(0)	(1)	(31)	(1)
1977 Minimum wage increase						
For	100%	100%	100%	100%	100%	100%
Against	0	0	0	0	0	0
N= Total voting members	(2)	(82)	(3)	(1)	(28)	(1)
1983 Enterprise zones						
For	33%	65%	67%	100%	73%	50%
Against	67	35	33	0	27	50
N= Total voting members	(3)	(84)	(6)	(1)	(26)	(2)
1987 Quarter-cent sales tax increase						
For	25%	27%	11%	100%	61%	0%
Against	75	73	89	0	39	100
N= Total voting members	(4)	(85)	(9)	(1)	(28)	(4)
1995 Five-cent gas tax increase						
For	80%	79%	25%	33%	64%	100%
Against	20	21	75	67%	36	0
N= Total voting members	(10)	(76)	(12)	(3)	(25)	(7)

	HOUSE OF REPRESENTATIVES			SENATE		
	BLACK DEMS	WHITE DEMS	REPUB- LICANS	BLACK DEMS	WHITE DEMS	REPUB- LICANS
1995 Bonds for roads						
For	100%	87%	42%	33%	68%	43%
Against	0	13	58	67	32	57
N= Total voting members	(8)	(75)	(12)	(3)	(25)	(7)

Source: House and Senate journals of the Arkansas General Assembly, 1973–95 volumes, Secretary of State's Office.

omy," Dumas argued, "will put more Blacks to work than tax subsidies."[56] Irma Hunter Brown added that she was dubious about who such business incentives actually would reach. "Many of the folks that truly needed to be targeted," she said "would not have received those breaks."[57] In particular, she recalled that the definition of minority was being expanded at that time to include women. "Otherwise-majority businesses," she said, were putting women up front on their applications because they could then qualify for the enterprise zone incentives. The result, in her view, was great risk that the benefits would not go to people who were genuinely economically disadvantaged.[58]

A 1987 one-quarter-cent sales tax increase produced similar division, though in that case most black legislators joined a large majority of their white counterparts in defeating Clinton's plan for raising additional revenue for education and other social programs. News accounts of the marathon battle over the measure noted much concern with the impact of an increased sales tax on "blacks and poor whites."[59] Reacting to Governor Clinton's speech to the full legislature on the matter, however, Senator Jewell advocated the additional revenue generation as a "way to take care of our children." "Their needs are the increased funding of the schools, more efficient operation of the schools, (and) qualified teachers," he said.[60]

Similar arguments accompanied the two 1995 measures. The five-cent increase in the diesel gasoline tax and the bond package were key components of Governor Tucker's large-scale road construction plan. The governor insisted that transportation upgrades were essential to economic development. Despite general support for the improvement of Arkansas highways, some Republican and African American lawmakers were concerned about a tax increase and the state's debt load. Bill Walker, the House member who had authored the winning civil rights bill two years earlier and had defeated Jerry Jewell for a state Senate seat in 1994, was a leading opponent of the roads plan, voting against both measures.[61] Despite eventual adoption by the legislature, voters resoundingly rejected the package in a special election the following year.

Finally, just one of the five government reform measures we identified appears to have been a matter of significant dispute, among African Americans or white legislators (table 9). Similar to most such efforts in southern states, the 1991 congressional redistricting plan for Arkansas's four U.S. House seats raised questions about the historic disenfranchisement of the black population and appropriate remedies at the congressional-district level. Rep. Ben McGee (D-Marion) put forward a plan that would have put 87 percent of the state's African American residents into one district (the Fourth), resulting in a district with a 42 percent minority population. The vast majority of the black caucus supported the idea, as did the state Republican Party; however, it found little support elsewhere in the legislature.[62] Although these rather strange political bedfellows presented several versions of this "black influence district" concept during the course of the 1991 session, white Democrats preferred a plan that would bring little change to the lines drawn ten years earlier.

Racial rhetoric was central to the debate. Republicans and Black Democrats charged that the state Democratic Party historically had "fractured" the bulk of Arkansas's African American population among three different districts (the First, the Second, and the Fourth) and, thus, diluted their voting strength.[63] "They put enough Blacks in those districts . . . by running fingers of them" into the Delta and through the Black neighborhoods of Little Rock, asserted Representative McGee, "so a White male who says he's a Democrat could get elected."[64] Such Democrats, in McGee's view, then pay only "lip service" to their black, Delta constituents to avoid alienating the conservative, white voters who compose the rest of the district. White Democrats parried that consolidating the African American vote in the way McGee proposed actually would reduce overall black political influence in Arkansas's congressional delegation. They added that the black caucus–Republican alliance was disingenuous, charging that Republicans simply desired to unseat Democratic congressional incumbents "and to create an apartheid Black district under the guise of being

TABLE 9

Roll Call Votes in the Arkansas General Assembly on Government Reform Issues

	HOUSE OF REPRESENTATIVES			SENATE		
	BLACK DEMS	WHITE DEMS	REPUB- LICANS	BLACK DEMS	WHITE DEMS	REPUB- LICANS
1977 Freedom of information act expansion						
For	100%	100%	—	100%	100%	100%
Against	0	0	—	0	0	0
N= Total voting members	(1)	(71)	(0)	(1)	(28)	(1)
1987 Move primary/Super Tuesday						
For	100%	99%	100%	100%	96%	100%
Against	0	1	0	0	4	0
N= Total voting members	(4)	(79)	(7)	(1)	(26)	(4)
1991 Congressional redistricting						
For	20%	92%	71%	0%	96%	100%
Against	80	8	29	100	4	0
N= Total voting members	(5)	(72)	(7)	(2)	(27)	(4)
1995 Ethics violations fines						
For	100%	100%	100%	100%	100%	100%
Against	0	0	0	0	0	0
N= Total voting members	(10)	(76)	(12)	(3)	(25)	(7)
1995 Motor voter						
For	100%	100%	100%	100%	100%	100%
Against	0	0	0	0	0	0
N= Total voting members	(10)	(73)	(12)	(3)	(25)	(7)

great friends of blacks."[65] A conference committee in late March brought victory to the white Democrats in the form of the status quo, majority-backed bill, a plan that shuffled only six counties among the state's four congressional districts. The only no votes on the committee came from its three black members—Representative McGee and Senators Jewell and Lewellen.[66] It is important to note not only did all but one member of the black caucus later vote against the redistricting plan upon final roll call in their respective chambers (though five abstained) but also all except Representative Wilkins (who was ill with cancer and missed most of the 1991 legislative session) participated as plaintiffs or interveners in a subsequent lawsuit filed by the state Republican Party.[67] The U.S. Supreme Court, however, rejected the challenge.

It is interesting to add that a similar conflict and alliance between some black caucus members and the state Republican Party emerged with the 2001 redistricting effort at the state legislative level. Republican governor Mike Huckabee (who is white) put forward a redistricting plan that would have increased the number of majority-black districts in Arkansas to fifteen in the House and five in the Senate, figures not far off from the NAACP's goals of seventeen and six, respectively. White Democrats Sharon Priest, secretary of state, and Mark Pryor, attorney general, preferred a plan that placed the number at thirteen in the House and four (up one) in the Senate. Rep. Tracy Steele (D-North Little Rock), chair of the black caucus, supported the Democratic plan because "Huckabee wanted more black-majority districts . . . [to] dilute Democratic voting strength in other districts."[68] Dale Charles, state NAACP president, countered that Steele, director of the state's Martin Luther King Jr., Commission, was "the rabid mouth of racism for the Democratic Party."[69] The issue generated much controversy among African American political leaders and likely played a role in a three-way primary race among Steele, former representative Wilma Walker, and civil rights attorney John Walker for one of the majority-black Little Rock Senate seats in May of 2002. Steele won with 56 percent of the vote, a victory pundits attributed to his "harmony-seeking demeanor."[70]

Note to table: The one African American House Republican voting on the 1991 congressional redistricting plan joined the one white House Republican in opposing the plan, while five white House Republicans favored it.
Source: House and Senate journals of the Arkansas General Assembly, 1977–95 volumes, Secretary of State's Office.

Conclusions and Implications

This preliminary effort to catalog and analyze the presence and behavior of African American legislators in the Arkansas General Assembly produced two key findings. First, the proportion of black state legislators increased steadily following the voting rights reforms of the 1960s. This process was accelerated, significantly, by the court-ordered, race-conscious legislative redistricting of the late 1980s. Still, although a state legislative membership that is 10 percent black (12 percent of the House and 6 percent of the Senate) may be an improvement over thirty years ago, the goal of full descriptive representation for African Americans in the Arkansas legislative process has yet to be realized. Although it is true that most southern states long have had, and continue to maintain, African American populations of at least twice the size of Arkansas's, this is not ample justification for the state's still-low ratio of black legislators to black residents. If indeed Arkansas was "destined to be the great Negro state of the country" at the dawn of the past century, such promise remains unfulfilled with regard to their descriptive representation at the dawn of the next.

That promise remains unfulfilled in terms of substantive representation as well. Specifically, our second—and most important—finding is that African Americans in the Arkansas General Assembly have been unable to exercise consistent influence over policy outcomes. In part, this is because African Americans—like any demographic group—have not been wholly homogenous when it comes to policy preferences. (In fact, the greater the degree of chamberwide contention over the policy questions included in this analysis, the greater the propensity of black legislators to take opposing positions among themselves.) However, as noted earlier in the chapter, African American members have voted together more often than not and have presented a unified front far more frequently than white Democrats.

The chief obstacle to black influence in Arkansas lies primarily in the small proportion of the total state legislative membership composed of African Americans. One senior member, a white Democrat who was influential throughout the 1980s and 1990s, indicated that the Arkansas Legislative Black Caucus was simply never big enough to "really kill anything." From time to time, he intimated, they wielded enough votes that the governor or the senior member shepherding a measure through the chamber would indeed need to court them on controversial issues. They did so, however, largely on an individual basis. This was because the Arkansas legislature was not traditionally a place in which members "caucused off"; efforts to do so were, in fact, seen as a bit of an "irritant" by senior members who, until the adoption of term limits in 1992, controlled the Arkansas legislative process.[71] The only measure on which the member could recall leverage exercised by black legislators as a group was on a redistricting plan for the state Court of Appeals debated through the mid- and late-1990s. Caucus members pressed for black-majority districts and although "they didn't get their way," the majority did have to postpone its actions.[72]

Interviews with African American leaders active during the period of investigation confirmed that black legislators in Arkansas have been too few in number and have not occupied the necessary leadership positions to wield much observable influence. Former state health director (and, later, U.S. surgeon general) Dr. Joceyln Elders noted, for example, that although most of the black legislators "were very proud to be there . . . representing their constituents," few of them took positions not already congruent with the white majority's preferences. The fact that the Assembly was controlled by "four old, white leaders, [who, if they] couldn't get it done, it wasn't going to get done," contributed to an inhospitable environment for the black caucus.[73] Former state representative McGee echoed this sentiment, noting first that with just "thirteen black folks in the House and fifty-one needed for passage, getting all the black folks wasn't going to help you."[74] He also concurred that the lack of numbers was not the only—or even the most significant—part of the equation. Rather, a measure stood little chance during his term of service unless "kissed" by at least one of the senior members of the body. Among these was Lloyd George, a white Democrat from Danville, who, McGee reported, was ultimately responsible for the passage of the much-disputed 1993 Civil Rights Act. According to McGee, George agreed to cosponsor the measure by Rep. Bill Walker (after McGee delivered an unrelated favor and a promise that it would not apply to gays and lesbians). Suddenly, introduced and rejected at the committee level every session for many years, the Arkansas Civil Rights Act—with the George imprimatur—"flew through the house."[75]

Few in number and not counted among the "network of senior members," it is thus not surprising that in each of the eight times in which the majority of the black caucus split with the majority of white Democrats on the twenty-seven measures examined, they lost.[76] And, by at least one measure, the future does not look much more promising. The state's African American population is small, now less than 16 percent. Even if the proportion of Black legislators grows to match that figure, it will still play only a minor role in the vast majority of roll call votes. Under such circumstances, perhaps the caucus's best hope is to pursue a three-pronged strategy. First, their current numbers allow them to play the spoiler on closely divided votes such as the appellate court dispute noted above, and—very nearly—the 1989 school choice measure. Rep. Tracy Steele, the current chair of the black caucus (and the executive director of the Arkansas Martin Luther King Jr. Commission), offered the state's recent debate over the use of its share of the national tobacco settlement money as an additional example. "Obviously [the black membership] is not enough to pass bills, but it is [now] enough to stop them on a close vote."[77] Dissatisfied with the insufficient level of attention paid to minority needs in the major tobacco settlement plan crafted in a special legislative session, they did just that in April of 2000.[78] Playing this card too often, of course, could turn their white peers off to future cooperation; however, black caucus members will be increasingly well positioned to successfully impede distasteful measures as the Assembly's partisan balance becomes more evenly weighted between Democrats and Republicans.

African American legislators also can continue to play the "sensitizer" role identified by former representative Brown. The election and service of people who long have been political minorities sensitizes "those who had not had to think about certain things before."[79] This idea was firmly reiterated by former representative and chair of the Women's Caucus, Lisa Ferrell, a white Democrat. "It helps to have folks who bring other worlds to the table," she said. In her view, this is not to suggest that other legislators purposely ignore nonmajority groups. Instead, it is "a question of educating [the white, male majority] about the needs of various populations."[80] The success of this role rests, in part, on the black caucus's ability to "galvanize community support for the issues . . . outside the halls of the Capitol."[81] An important tactic of the current caucus, in fact, is to appeal to their white colleagues for cooperation by reminding them of the proportion of minorities in their districts.

Finally, Arkansas's black legislators can look toward crafting strategic alliances[82] with the major players in the General Assembly, a strategy made easier and more difficult by the full implementation of term limits with the 2002 election cycle. Senior members similar to Reps. Lloyd George and John Miller have disappeared from the state's political landscape. Black legislators now must negotiate—for policy victories, committee assignments, and leadership posts—with white Democrats who have no more than four (in the House) or six (in the Senate) years of experience in the respective chambers. They also must negotiate with a white, Republican governor and a much-expanded Republican legislative delegation that has benefited from term limits and a population boom in the white, conservative, business Mecca of Northwest Arkansas.

Their success in such an environment will depend heavily on the elevation of African American members to legislative leadership posts, an area in which they had some success in recent sessions. African Americans have chaired the Public Health, Welfare, and Labor committees in both chambers. Black caucus members have served as vice chairs for the house Education and Management committees as well, and Senator Bill Lewellen recently chaired the legislative caucus for the central Arkansas region.[83] If the state's African American legislators can aggressively retain and expand their influence in this manner and continue to play the spoiler and education roles, the Arkansas political landscape stands—finally—to be significantly transformed.

Term Limits in Arkansas

Opportunities and Consequences

ART ENGLISH

Ignoring warnings, some from the academic community, that establishing limits on the number of terms candidates for state offices can serve could have dire consequences for state government (for example, they could upset the balance of power between the legislative and executive branches, or could increase the influence of special interests in the state capitol), Arkansas voters went to the polls in 1992 and, by a large margin, approved what would become Amendment 73 to the Arkansas Constitution, the "Term Limits Amendment." In this brief study, veteran political scientist Art English notes the changing demographics of the General Assembly—especially the increase in seats held by women and African Americans and the growing number of Republicans serving in both chambers—in the decade following adoption of term limits and speculates as to the role of Amendment 73 in spurring these changes.

His conclusion, in short, is that term limits have resulted in increased opportunity for public service, which has, in turn, produced a more diverse legislative body. But this has come at the expense of the experienced leadership many view as essential to the efficient and effective operation of the legislative branch of government. Note: The proposed change to Amendment 73 noted here by Professor English as a pending proposal that would have retained term limits but increased the number of terms allowed Arkansas legislators, was soundly rejected by the voters in the 2004 election.

Art English, "Term Limits in Arkansas: Opportunities and Consequences," *Spectrum: The Journal of State Government* 76 (Fall 2003): 30–33. Reprinted with permission.

In April 2003, the Eighty-fourth Arkansas General Assembly, following one of its most hectic and disorderly sessions in the last twenty-five years, submitted a constitutional amendment that would extend the potential for House and Senate service from six to twelve years and from eight to twelve years respectively. While the vote on the new term limits amendment will not take place until the November 2004 general election, the Assembly's action has added more fuel to the ongoing debate over the merits of term limits in Arkansas.

It is fair to say that the Arkansas General Assembly was not a likely candidate for term limits in the first place. Arkansas has a citizens' legislature that is required to meet only sixty days every odd-numbered year. Arkansas legislators are not professional legislators. They are part-time, have other full-time vocations, and are not the beneficiaries of full-time salary or extensive staff support. However, Arkansas during the last half of the twentieth century had a very senior legislature. Compared to most state legislatures its turnover rate had been low, seldom averaging over 15 percent from session to session. Senior legislators were especially dominant in the Senate, where power coalesced around the floor leader, the pro tempore, and those senators who controlled the rules, budget and efficiency committees. In the House, power was somewhat more decentralized around the long-serving senior committee chairs and the Speaker of the House as the institutional symbol and leader of that chamber.[1]

During the 1980s power became more fractured in the Senate as a new breed of legislator challenged the old bulls for control. In part, the number of senior legislators in the Arkansas General Assembly during this period may have provided fodder for the term limits movement that was aimed at professional-congressional types of legislators who were reelected year after year. With 59.9 percent of the voters supporting a term limits amendment in 1992, which also limited constitutional executive officers to no more than eight years in office, it could hardly be doubted how the electorate felt over a decade ago. Certainly the expectation among term limit supporters was to even out the playing field for challengers, stimulate more balanced party competition, generate new blood and ideas, eliminate complacent and unresponsive legislators, and produce a more efficient and effective legislative process. Opponents of term limits responded that there would be a loss of leadership and institutional memory, members would become less rather than more responsive, and the legislative process would become more subordinate to interest groups and the executive branch. Based on twenty-three interviews with legislators, legislative leaders, and prominent staff members,[2] coupled with observations of some fundamental legislative trends over the last two decades, this analysis is aimed at assessing some of the recent effects of term limits on the Arkansas General Assembly.

Sessions

One of the apparent effects since the introduction of term limits has been longer legislative sessions. Legislative sessions in Arkansas are constitutionally mandated for sixty days but they can be extended by a two-thirds vote of the legislature. Longer sessions have occurred prior to term limits, however. In the nineteenth and early twentieth centuries, legislative sessions were commonly ninety days or more and that was certainly the case with the Eighty-fourth Arkansas General Assembly, which had to confront not only severe revenue shortfalls but also the seemingly intractable problem of school consolidation. Nonetheless, the pattern before term limits was not characterized by long sessions. From 1953 to 1991—a total of 20 legislative sessions—only one exceeded 90 days with the average length of session being 70.1 days. However, since term limits were implemented in 1992, four out of the six and three out of the last four sessions have lasted 90 days or more, with an average session length of 88.3 days, 18 legislative days longer than the average over the previous 20 sessions. One of the common themes of our interview data was that under term limits, members accelerated the introduction of legislation in the expectation that they would have less time to achieve its passage. Several of our respondents noted that you had to hit the ground running when your entire legislative life was limited to just 180 regular session days in the House and 240 in the Senate. Among the various impacts of term limits, this was one of its most unexpected consequences.

Bills

Bill and act totals reflected the more frenetic and heavier "lawmaking" pace the Arkansas General Assembly has worked under since the invocation of term limits. The first session under term limits produced an increase of more than one hundred bills from the Seventy-eighth Assembly, which suggested that perhaps some legislators were getting the

quick start message and that less powerful committee chairpersons could
not stop as many bills emerging from their committees. But it was not
until the term-limited members from 1993 began to get close to completing their terms and new members began to enter the House and
Senate in 1999 and 2001 respectively that bill introductions began to
increase at their most rapid rate. Two hundred more bills were introduced in the Senate in 1999 than the previous session and there were
steady increases of almost three hundred bills in each of the last two
House sessions from the preceding sessions.[3] The increase in bill passage
should also be noted, although the Arkansas General Assembly has long
had a high batting average when it comes to passing bills. This characteristic of the state's political culture, in combination with the more equitable distribution of power in the House because of term limits—as
several of our respondents noted—is likely responsible for the increase
in bill introductions and passage in the Arkansas General Assembly.

TABLE 1

Bills Introduced and Passed: 1981–2003

YEAR	SESSION	SENATE BILLS	HOUSE BILLS	TOTAL	ACTS
1981	73rd	629	1,018	1,647	994
1983	74th	572	1,011	1,583	937
1985	75th	705	1,069	1,774	1,097
1987	76th	681	1,079	1,760	1,072
1989	77th	618	958	1,576	995
1991	78th	743	1,125	1,868	1,246
1993	79th	837	1,144	1,981	1,319
1995	80th	855	1,168	2,023	1,358
1997	81st	756	1,285	2,041	1,362
1999	82nd	967	1,291	2,258	1,598
2001	83rd	988	1,655	2,643	1,843
2003	84th	979	1,906	2,885	1,816

Demographic and Party Change

Proponents of term limits also anticipated fundamental changes in the demographic and partisan characteristics of the Arkansas General Assembly, a legislature that for virtually all of its history was overwhelmingly white, male, and Democratic. Some of these effects have taken place, but not all of them can be attributed to term limits. The South has seen a rise of Republicans in state legislatures overall because of party realignment, although it has proceeded at a slower pace in Arkansas. And legislative reapportionment, which has resulted in the drawing of more black-majority districts, has had an effect on the larger number of minority legislators in the Arkansas General Assembly. The increased number of African Americans, women, and Republicans in the Assembly is evident nonetheless and it appears that at least some of these increases can be attributed to the effects of term limits. In analyzing table 2, the big jump in the number of females in the 135-member body actually started to take place in the early 1990s when the number more than doubled those from the 1980s sessions, culminating with the election of twenty-two women in 1997 and twenty in 1999 as term limits began to take effect for the 1993 members.

TABLE 2

**African Americans and Women in the
Arkansas General Assembly: 1981–2003**

	1981	1983	1985	1987	1989	1991	1993	1995	1997	1999	2001	2003
AFRICAN AMERICANS												
House	3	3	4	4	5	9	10	9	10	12	12	12
Senate	1	1	1	1	1	3	3	3	3	3	3	3
Total	4	4	5	5	6	12	13	12	13	15	15	15
WOMEN												
House	4	6	9	8	7	8	12	16	22	20	14	15
Senate	1	1	1	1	2	1	1	1	1	0	4	7
Total	5	7	10	9	9	9	13	17	23	20	18	22

Term limits do not seem to have had a dramatic effect on the overall number of women in the legislature since, however, as other women elected in 1995 and 1997 have been term limited and in some cases have

been replaced by male legislators. However, this analysis is a bit misleading in respect to the impact of term limits on women in the Assembly.
The number of women in the Senate has increased dramatically from
one, for most of the last twenty years, to four women in 2001 and seven
in 2003. What is interesting about the larger number of women in the
2003 Senate is that five of them have served in the House, so the effect
of term limits may be more subtle than direct. Now that there are open
seats in the Senate because of term limits, more women with House experience are running for them. The number of African Americans in the
Assembly, however, has remained flat since a doubling in their numbers
took place in 1991. Term limits do not seem to have had an appreciable
effect on the number of blacks in the Arkansas General Assembly, and
as term-limited African Americans leave the legislature, there is no guarantee black legislators will replace them.[4]

Where term limits in Arkansas have had a significant effect—indeed
the desired impact by many who supported them—is the much larger contingent of the minority party in the Arkansas legislature and the dramatic
increase of new members—turnover in other words—from previous legislative sessions. While Republicans were gaining seats in the legislature
before term limits, table 3 documents that in 1999, when term limits first
took effect, the number of Republicans increased in the Assembly by 50
percent from the previous legislature. If term limits were intended to help
balance out the partisan playing field in one-party-dominated legislatures,
then it has helped move toward that goal in Arkansas. And while new, fresh
ideas cannot be correlated with raw numbers, the increase in the number
of new legislators in the Arkansas General Assembly has been extraordinary. In 1999, sixty-one new legislators were elected, forever transforming
a senior-dominated body. Consider, for example, that as recently as 1993
(the first Assembly to live under term limits) turnover was only about 9
percent. Since 1999, however, when turnover approached a remarkable 50
percent of the membership, better than a third of the Arkansas General
Assembly has been new members.

TABLE 3

Republican and New Member Representation: 1981–2003

	1981	1983	1985	1987	1989	1991	1993	1995	1997	1999	2001	2003
REPUBLICANS												
House	5	6	7	7	11	9	10	12	13	24	21	30
Senate	1	3	4	4	5	4	5	7	7	6	8	8
Total	6	9	11	11	16	13	15	19	20	30	29	38
NEW MEMBERS												
House	17	17	16	7	10	18	18	29	20	56	32	35
Senate	5	11	5	2	2	6	4	7	5	5	16	16
Total	22	28	21	9	12	24	22	36	25	61	48	51

Leadership Changes

Since the introduction of term limits, the changes that have taken place in the Arkansas General Assembly have been stunning. Once the territory of legislators in their sixties with twenty and even forty years of service, the Arkansas General Assembly has seen an influx of young legislative leaders with few legislative sessions under their belts. Since term limits, legislators with only four years of experience have chaired standing committees in the House. The 2003 pro-tem of the Senate is only in his second term, when the usual number of years experience for assuming that office has been sixteen to twenty years. The real and symbolic effects of term limits have been even more dramatic in the House. In 2001, the Speaker of the House assumed the office with just two completed terms and at the tender age of twenty-eight years, just half the average age of speakers of the last thirty years, almost all of whom have been in their fifties or sixties when they took office. The 1999 session Speaker was only thirty-three when he was elected Speaker. Interestingly both of these youthful leaders took early steps to combat the perceived problems of term limits. They instituted training sessions for new legislators well before the session started. They met frequently with new and veteran members to smooth the socialization process, and they worked closely with legislative staff to enhance communications, technology, and procedures so that new members could adapt to legislative life as quickly as possible. The trade-off, then, in Arkansas has been experience versus new members. Term limit supporters have argued that new members translate into new ideas and a more responsive legislature. Those opposed to term limits point out that it is experience that is the stuff of effective lawmaking and representation.

Recruitment and Departure

Where have the new legislators been coming from? Where have the former legislators gone? These are important questions to ask because they help us assess whether the fundamental goals of term limits are being met. While this question cannot be fully answered because this is still an experiment in progress, the preliminary findings are nonetheless interesting and instructive.

Table 4 indicates that more new legislators seem to be coming at least with county legislative experience. County legislative districts in Arkansas are single member, and county legislators serve part-time like their state legislative counterparts. The transition, then, to the state legislature, these numbers suggest, would seem to be a relatively natural one.[5] A glance at the overall experience levels in the state legislature however, especially since term limits, would show that a large number of new legislators come with local and county government experience. They are not just county legislators but also county judges, mayors, city directors, aldermen, and school board members. What the term-limited legislatures do not lack is prior governmental experience. Indeed, one recent study found that forty legislators in the 1981 session had local government experience while sixty-six did in the 2001 session.[6] If anything, term limits have opened up the Arkansas General Assembly to a host of local government officials who want to be legislators.

TABLE 4

County Legislative Experience in the Assembly and Previous House Experience in the Senate: 1985–2003

YEAR	1985	1987	1989	1991	1993	1995	1997	1999	2001	2003
County legislative experience	8	10	11	12	15	17	17	18	21	17
Senators with House experience	9	8	8	6	7	9	8	8	21	29

And what of the legislators who leave? Where do they go? As table 4 indicates, many of them run successfully for the upper house. Twenty-nine of the 2003 members of the Senate have served in the House, including the 1999 and 2001 Speakers, while the average number of state senators with House experience from 1985 to 1997 was a mere eight.[7] Other legislators find it hard to give up public life and seek jobs in state government. Several resigned before their term was over—since they cannot come back—to take positions as lobbyists and in state government.

Others give up their House term before it ends to run for the Senate. Two long-term members of the Senate have actually come back to the House when their Senate terms ended. Three recent legislators (Tim Hutchinson, Vic Snyder, Mike Ross) ran successfully for Congress, while several others have tried the waters of federal elected service without success. Many state legislators who otherwise would have run for their legislative seats again have sought other public opportunities. Other legislators, however, without the right connections and timing, have seen their legislative and political careers end while they still believed they had much to contribute.

Discussion: Opportunities and Consequences

The Eighty-fourth (2003–4) regular legislative session was a frayed one. It was long and acrimonious for the most part. Some in and out of the legislature blamed term limits for its foibles. They argued that the new legislators did not know how to get along in the legislature and use its information sources. Some of our respondents added that the new legislators were not experienced enough to ask penetrating questions of the staff and executive agency heads. The press (while not supporting the extension of term limits) printed articles criticizing the more individualistic styles of the legislators, who they said were more interested in pork for their districts and advancing their own electoral careers than the good of the state. In truth, much of the debate over the worth of term limits was obscured by the difficult issues the assembly was facing: school consolidation, revenue shortfalls, and executive branch reorganization. Supporters of the legislature cited the large number of bills as an indication of the hard work the new legislators were doing. Interestingly, some of our respondents suggested that the legislature was a kinder and gentler one for staff, that the new legislators were more respectful and courteous than the senior legislators of the past—and more reliant on them. Other respondents pointed to the deficit of lawyers left in the Senate after term limits—the Senate having been known for its legal eagles who could rewrite or stop bad legislation before it became law. Overall more research will need to be done to assess whether term limits have produced positive benefits. More state analyses with more precise public policy linkages need to be looked at. For the present, though, it appears that the Arkansas General Assembly has accepted term limits as a part of its political system for many more years. The current constitutional amendment, if approved by the people, would not abolish term limits; it would only extend them to twelve years of possible service. In part the legislators that adopted this amendment seem to be saying that they can and will have to live with term limits. It has brought more people into legislative life that hopefully will have the energy and ideas to produce good public policy. While that important part of the term limits enigma remains to be more fully evaluated, it also seems fair to say that greater flexibility in term limits may be the best way to tandem experience and opportunity in Arkansas and the other state legislatures.

Arkansas Governors in the Twentieth Century

A Ranking and Analysis

CAL LEDBETTER JR. AND C. FRED WILLIAMS

Americans seem to like to rank-order everything—sports teams ("Top Twenty College Football Programs"), academic institutions ("Best and Worst American Universities"), cities ("One Hundred Most Livable Communities in America"), restaurants ("Ranked Number one for the Last Ten Years"), and more. There have even been serious attempts to rank America's presidents from best to worst. The authors of this work adapted the design of one such effort, based on a poll of experts, to rank Arkansas governors, up to and including the administration of the state's first post-Reconstruction Republican governor, Winthrop Rockefeller. Respondents, primarily academics (political scientists, historians), journalists, and lawyers, were asked to refer to a number of focusing questions (such as, "What kind of people did he appoint to office?", "What did he achieve as governor?", "Did he abuse the power of his office?") in evaluating each governor. Based on the responses, the author of this article ranked the governors from "great" to "poor." No governor was ranked "great" and only one was ranked "below average." The reader may be surprised by a few of the rankings, but the article as a whole provides a fascinating overview of Arkansas politics in the twentieth century.

Cal Ledbetter Jr. and C. Fred Williams, "Arkansas Governors in the Twentieth Century: A Ranking and Analysis," *The Arkansas Political Science Journal* 3 (1982): 36–58. Reprinted with permission.

Despite the fact that the office of the American presidency was modeled somewhat along the lines of the office of governor in New York, the presidency has consistently overshadowed the state office that helped give it birth. It is certainly not surprising that the president receives more attention than governors, given the power and scope of the office, its leadership role in foreign affairs, and the function of the office in symbolizing the country's history and greatness. The office of governor in most states lacks the potential for political drama found in the presidency and, in addition, is burdened with legal handicaps not experienced by the presidency, such as independently elected executives at the state level (a check and balance system within one branch of government) and state agencies with varying degrees of autonomy. In fact, the change is so complete that many reformers at the state level now attempt to remodel the office of state governor along presidential lines.

Because the presidency throughout American history has held the attention of both the public and academics, there are periodic attempts to poll experts and ask them to rank American presidents in categories ranging from "great" to "failure." Broad standards of evaluation are usually provided to help the experts measure achievement in the executive office, and the presidents are usually ranked in order from the one who is ranked as the greatest through the one who is deemed to be the worst. The most famous polls of this nature were those done by Arthur M. Schlesinger Sr., in 1948 and 1962. Although any poll of this kind is bound to be subjective and relatively unscientific, it can provide some measurement of historical judgment at a particular moment in time and can be useful for comparison purposes in the future. Nevertheless, polls that rank chief executives seem to be confined to presidents, and the purpose of this article is to use the Schlesinger approach to rank state governors.

It is hoped that a poll of this kind can be useful in a variety of ways. Even though most governors, in comparison with presidents, barely penetrate the historical consciousness, it still is helpful to find which governors in a particular state like Arkansas have captured some historical attention and why. Since professional historical research in Arkansas has not been extensive, a poll may identify areas, individuals, and historical periods where further investigation is needed. It also can provide a reference point for the future, since the consensus reached in 1980 on governors will undoubtedly be substantially revised by 2020.

The Schlesinger model does present certain problems, however, when it is applied to a state. Each one of the presidents in the "great" category seems to have interpreted the powers of his office broadly and left the office greatly strengthened after his departure.[1] This kind of achievement is difficult for a governor of a Southern state with a Reconstruction constitution even to approach, because the legal powers of the office are usually carefully circumscribed. The ambiguity of the United States Constitution that allows presidents to read their powers liberally is not present in the 1874 Arkansas Constitution. In fact, the Arkansas Constitution may so severely limit the governor that the likelihood of one of them having a significant impact on history and events is greatly reduced.[2]

All of the presidents in the "great" category in the Schlesinger polls of 1948 and 1962 were "activist" presidents. The Arkansas poll should give some interesting comparisons as to whether this same judgment is made at the state level, particularly in view of Watergate and a consequent climate of opinion more favorable toward restricting the powers of the presidency. Will a "Whig" type governor who emphasizes dignity, honor, and restraint at the expense of significant political achievements rank higher in this post-Watergate era, or will the emphasis still be placed by the panelists upon the activist who achieves concrete political results? Are attitudes any different at the state level in regard to executive power today, or is it still an unsolved dilemma "between the people's fear of executive power and their confidence in its necessity and capacity for good?"[3]

Before discussing the mechanics of this Arkansas poll, some historical background on the office of governor in the state will help put the office in perspective. Under the 1868, or Reconstruction Constitution in Arkansas, the governor was elected for a four-year term with a salary set by the legislature. The Republican Party, then new to the state, attempted during Reconstruction to establish a centralized state government because "it did not have the local organizations to carry out its functions throughout the state."[4] One method used to accomplish this centralization was to increase the appointing power of the governor, and his appointing powers under the 1868 Constitution were breathtaking.[5] The governor appointed the tax assessors, prosecuting attorneys, all judges in the state with the exception of Supreme Court judges, and all precinct and township officials. With the return of Democratic rule in 1873, the inevitable reaction occurred; under the new constitution approved in 1874, the term of office was cut from four to two years, the salary was set in the constitution itself, and the powers of appointment were cut back sharply.

The office as delineated in the 1874 Constitution is relatively unchanged today. The governor has a two-year term, the salary is still set in the constitution, and any veto can be overridden by a majority vote of the legislature. The governor shares executive power with six other elected executive officials and numerous independent boards and commissions. Two of these independent agencies, the Highway Commission and the Game and Fish Commission, not only are administratively independent by constitutional amendment[6] but are fiscally autonomous as well, since their operating revenues are generated by special taxes (gasoline and hunting and fishing licenses) earmarked for highway and wildlife purposes.

Even though constitutional and legal powers define only one dimension of a governor's office, this dimension is important because the governor's lack of strong legal and constitutional powers can inhibit great accomplishments in office and cause low historical ratings. As described by the Arkansas Constitutional Revision Study Commission in 1968:

> Presently Arkansas' governors do not have constitutional powers commonly associated with the concept of "chief executive," although many have had great influence as political leaders. . . . Short term of office, weak veto, meager salary, competing and independently elected executives at the State level, and a proliferation of agencies subject to little executive control have significant bearing on gubernatorial influence both in policy matters and in administrative management. These and other limitations hinder the ability of a governor to fulfill public expectations for responsible accomplishment of programs for which he has received a recent popular mandate.[7]

In choosing the respondents for the Arkansas Governors Poll, an attempt was made to include experts who had taught, published, or shown an unusual interest in Arkansas history and government. Although most of the individuals asked to participate were college teachers, the group included journalists, political advisors, and others with expertise in this area, even though not necessarily engaged in teaching or research.[8] Forty-one responses were received from a mailing of fifty-three—a return rate of 78 percent. The Schlesinger model was used, in that the evaluation was based on only what a governor did while in office, and evaluation standards were suggested for use by the respondents.[9] The poll included only governors since 1900 in order to limit evaluation to sixteen governors rather than to a total of forty, which would be the case if 1819 (the year Arkansas became a territory) were selected. In addition to making a respondent's task more manageable, beginning the poll in 1900 focuses attention on an historical period nationally, a time when executive leadership at the state level became increasingly active and the policymaking role of the governor became more visible. Governors who served less than a year or who had been out of office for less than ten years were not considered. At the suggestion of the respondents, Governor John S. Little, who served only several months before his health failed, was also excluded from the poll.

Respondents were asked to rank governors of Arkansas since 1900 on a five-point scale with five given for great, four for good, three for average, two for below average, and one for poor.[10] The authors established the following categories and necessary ranking:

> Great: 5.0 to 4.5
> Good: 4.4 to 3.5
> Average: 3.4 to 2.5
> Below average: 2.4 to 1.5
> Poor: 1.4 and below

A governor's rank in the poll was determined by dividing the total points he received by the number of respondents who chose to evaluate him. Written comments on the governors were encouraged.

The poll results are shown in table 1. Each governor is listed by rank and category. Table 1 shows total points obtained as well as the number of individuals who evaluated each governor.

Background and Analysis[11]

The seventy years served by the Arkansas governors in the poll roughly correspond to three periods in American history: the Progressive Era (1900–1920); the period between the wars (1920–40), and the post–World War II period (1945–70). Each period had its own distinctive characteristics nationally, and some discussion of these periods may be helpful in identifying a particular Arkansas governor with that period of American history during which he served and to see the impact of national trends on a state administration.

The Progressive Era was held together by a fairly sophisticated reform movement that showed three major tendencies. Politically, the

TABLE 1

Arkansas Governors in the Twentieth Century

	NO. OF REPLIES	RANKING	CATEGORY	TOTAL
Charles H. Brough	31	4.16	Good	129
George W. Donaghey	29	4.10	Good	119
Winthrop Rockefeller	35	3.97	Good	139
Sid McMath	35	3.86	Good	135
Carl E. Bailey	31	3.74	Good	116
Thomas C. McRae	27	3.56	Good	96
Ben T. Laney	33	3.33	Average	110
John E. Martineau	24	3.21	Average	77
Jeff Davis	27	3.15	Average	85
Orval Faubus	34	3.12	Average	106
George W. Hays	24	2.88	Average	69
Francis Cherry	35	2.83	Average	99
Homer M. Adkins	30	2.80	Average	84
J.M. Futrell	29	2.76	Average	80
Harvey Parnell	29	2.59	Average	75
Tom J. Terral	24	2.04	Below Av.	49

Fifty-three questionnaires mailed; eighty-five responses by questionnaire; six responses by letter

reformers wanted to eliminate graft, corruption, and "boss rule" while making the political process more open and responsive to the general public. Economically, progressives sought to break up corporate monopoly where necessary, regulate business activities wherever possible, and foster competition when there was an opportunity to do so. Socially, leaders of the period worked for improving conditions of the poor, including better education, health care, and housing, eliminating child labor, and securing voting rights for women. It was a time when public opinion generally supported the concept of a strong president and vigorous executive leadership. Governors Jeff Davis, George Donaghey, George Hays, and Charles Brough all served during the progressive era.

The second historical era, the period between the wars, can be almost equally divided into two sections of ten years each. The 1920s witnessed the flowering of American business and increasing world trade. An expanding domestic market and lack of governmental interference combined to produce a decade of prosperity. Gone was the progressive spirit of reform and regulation. Instead, a mood of laissez-faire prevailed, perhaps best illustrated by president Calvin Coolidge's statement that "the business of government is business."

The 1930s brought a reversal in both political and economic trends. From an economic standpoint, the decade was a time of depression characterized by high unemployment, sluggish capital expansion, and general pessimism. Politically, however it was one of the most active decades in United States history. President Franklin D. Roosevelt, with personality and programs, led the Congress in implementing a broad-based plan to ease, if not break, the economic stagnation. Thomas McRae, Tom J. Terral, John Martineau, Harvey Parnell, J. M. Futrell, Carl Bailey, and Homer Adkins held office in Arkansas during the period between the wars.

The post–World War II era has been characterized by America's growing involvement in world affairs. The Cold War caused the nation's political leaders to seek alliances around the world and stockpile nuclear weapons. Defense spending became an integral, essential part of the budget. Domestically, Americans came to be increasingly concerned with civil rights in general and minority rights in particular. The domestic economy, spurred by international trade, an expanding home market, and a rapidly increasing population, provided businessmen with a new wave of prosperity. Ben Laney, Sid McMath, Frances Cherry, Orval Faubus, and Winthrop Rockefeller were the Arkansas governors during this time.

Of the top five governors in the poll (Brough, Donaghey, Rockefeller, McMath, McRae), two served during the Progressive Era when the national mood was reformist in tone, two served in the post-World War II period when the national emphasis was on improved race relations and industrial growth, and one served during the decade of the Great Depression (the period between the wars) when concern for the problems of rural America and the poor was particularly evident. Although diverse in occupation (two businessmen, two lawyers, and one college professor), they shared several characteristics. All were strong personalities, had well-conceived programs before taking office, and worked tirelessly to gain legislative approval for their ideas. That each was also sensitive to the national mood is perhaps indicative of his place in the poll.

Charles Hillman Brough (1917–21) ranked first in the poll. Born in Mississippi, Brough came to Arkansas as a professor of economics at the University of Arkansas. His most immediate problem as governor was an acute economic crisis brought on by a severe shortage of state income. After gaining legislative approval for securing a short-term loan to meet emergency needs, he then moved on a broad front to create a budget system for state government, revise the schedule for property assessments and establish a standardized accounting system for county government. On other matters, Brough called for a convention to draft a new state constitution and took the lead in movements to improve public education, eliminate adult illiteracy, adopt Prohibition, and increase the availability of health services. Partially as a result of his actions, the legislature created the Arkansas Illiteracy Commission and the Textbook Commission, passed the "Bone Dry Law" for prohibiting the sale of alcoholic beverages, and established the State General Hospital to provide free health care for qualified patients.

Brough's term coincided with Woodrow Wilson's second term as president. Both were college professors and served during the Progressive Era, when voters supported strong and vigorous executive leadership. Wilson finished among the top five presidents in the 1962 Schlesinger poll.

George W. Donaghey (1907–11) finished second in the rankings. A building contractor from Conway, Donaghey was elected initially because of his promise to complete the new state capitol building. He once remarked that he would rather build the capitol than be governor. His first term was almost totally devoted to the construction issue. In his second term he devoted a major portion of his attention to education, particularly in rural areas. With his leadership the legislature chartered four agricultural schools, widely separated geographically, in the effort to encourage more young people to attend school. The General Assembly also created a department of public health, established a tuberculosis sanitarium, and approved a constitutional amendment authorizing initiative and referendum petitions.

Donaghey's administration ran concurrently with William Howard Taft's tenure as president. The governor's business background was apparently more in line with voter sentiment than Taft's cautious approach toward problem solving. Taft, trained as a lawyer, took a legalistic approach toward executive leadership and finished far down in the presidential poll, in the average category.

Winthrop Rockefeller (1967–71), a transplanted New York businessman, finished third. He first got into politics by serving as director of the Industrial Development Commission under Orval Faubus. After breaking with Faubus on the race issue, Rockefeller made an all-out effort to rebuild the Republican Party in the state. His activities were rewarded in 1966 when he became the first Republican governor of the state since Reconstruction. Once in office, Rockefeller focused his attention on reform. He closed casino gambling in Hot Springs, made major changes in the prison system, and sponsored a bill in the legislature providing for tighter regulation of the sale of securities in the state. He also attempted to reorganize and consolidate state agencies, but was thwarted by the General Assembly.

Rockefeller's terms as governor came during the presidential administrations of Lyndon B. Johnson and Richard M. Nixon. Neither of these presidents was included in the Schlesinger poll.

Sid McMath (1949–53), an attorney from Hot Springs, was fourth in the poll. He first claimed statewide attention while prosecuting attorney of Garland County. In that position he earned the reputation of being a reformer, opposed to machine politics and an advocate for equal protection under the law. As governor he continued his reform efforts by sponsoring antilynching legislation, repeal of the poll tax, a new system of voter registration and a new election code. He also made a major commitment to expand the highway system. Unfortunately for his program, all of McMath's proposals except the highway proposal were defeated by the legislature. McMath was defeated while seeking a third term as governor.

McMath served as governor while Harry S Truman was president. They held similar views on race relations and political reform. For a time McMath was rumored to be under consideration for a position in the Truman cabinet. Truman was ranked in the near great category by the Schlesinger poll.

Carl E. Bailey (1937–41) ranked fifth in the poll. Although born in Missouri, he lived at several locations in Arkansas before opening a law office in Little Rock. As governor he inherited the highway debt problem that had plagued Arkansans for a decade. Like his predecessors he also adopted a plan for refinancing the debt. On other matters he sought to increase state services, gain legislative support for a 2 percent sales tax, and increase support for the public schools and old age assistance, while reducing the state tax on property. The legislature also approved the first workman's compensation law during his tenure in office.

Bailey was governor during Franklin D. Roosevelt's third term as president. In the later 1930s Roosevelt's administration increasingly turned to reform in social welfare, labor, and agriculture. Roosevelt finished in the top five in the Schlesinger poll, which put him in the great category.

Thomas C. McRae (1921–25), an attorney from Prescott, placed sixth in the governor's poll. A fiscal conservative, he repeatedly advocated a philosophy of "make no appropriation until funds are in sight to meet it." During his four years in office he called the legislature into special session on three different occasions. But despite this political activity McRae succeeded in getting only two major programs adopted. One provided for increased funding for public schools through a special tax on cigars and cigarettes; the other established the basis, without funding, for a state highway system.

McRae was governor during the administrations of Warren G. Harding and Calvin Coolidge. Both presidents were also fiscal conservatives and the national mood shifted decidedly in favor of business and away from reform while they were in office. In the Schlesinger poll, Harding rated as a failure and Coolidge was listed in the below average category.

Ben T. Laney (1945–49), a businessman from Camden, was rated as the seventh best governor by the respondents. His administration was perhaps best remembered for the Revenue Stabilization Act which Laney sponsored. The effect of this proposal was to create a single fund to operate the state government and most of the state agencies. Laney also pushed for major consolidation and reorganization of the various state boards and commissions. A Public Service Commission and a Resources and Development Commission resulted from this action. Initiated Act 1, which provided for major consolidation in the public school system, also became law during his administration.

Laney served as governor during the transition between Franklin Roosevelt and Harry Truman. He strongly disagreed with Truman on the race issue and led in the formation of a third party, the Dixiecrats, to oppose Truman for the presidency in 1948.

John E. Martineau (1927–28) finished eighth in the poll. An attorney and public school teacher from Lonoke, he was elected after campaigning on a slogan of "good roads and good schools." He succeeded in at least part of his program when he persuaded the legislature to approve the "Martineau Road Law," which created a comprehensive road system with a continuous source of funding. The remainder of Martineau's program was cut short when President Coolidge appointed him federal judge for the eastern district of Arkansas.

Jeff Davis (1901–7), an attorney from Russellville, finished ninth in the poll. He was the first Arkansas governor to be elected for a third term. Although in office during the Progressive Era in American history, Davis demonstrated no consistent pattern of reform behavior. An executive with an activist philosophy, he once vetoed some three hundred bills as a direct challenge to legislative authority. On the other hand, he sponsored no major program of his own. An outspoken critic of the convict lease system, Davis pardoned numerous prisoners. But at the same time he strongly opposed efforts by the Prison Board to acquire the Cummins Plantation, a move that would provide more space and improve conditions for inmates. Although an opponent of excessive waste and expenditures in state government, he nevertheless campaigned vigorously against efforts to build a new capitol building—even when it was apparent that the original capitol had become overcrowded and inadequate for transacting the state's business.

Other progressive measures enacted by the General Assembly during Davis's administration included a reform school for youthful offenders, a child labor law and recognizing Labor Day, the first Monday in September, as a holiday. In each instance, however, Davis's role was minimal.

Theodore Roosevelt was president at the time Davis was governor. The two men were sometimes compared because of their similar, flamboyant styles in campaigning. However, their similarities ended there. Roosevelt was a much more effective administrator than Davis. In the Schlesinger poll, Roosevelt rated in the near great category and finished seventh in a field of thirty-one.

Orval E. Faubus (1955–67) finished tenth in the poll. A newspaper publisher from Madison County, he was elected six times and served more years as governor than any other chief executive in Arkansas history. His administration may well be divided into two periods: before and after the Little Rock Central High School crisis. In his early years as governor, Faubus provided major assistance to public schools, welfare assistance, and roads for rural areas. He also integrated the state Democratic Party by appointing six blacks to the central committee. He worked closely with the Industrial Development Commission in an attempt to attract industry to the state. After the Little Rock Central High School Crisis, however,

Faubus turned increasingly to racial issues and many of his earlier programs were deemphasized. He voluntarily retired from the governor's office after serving twelve years in that post.

Faubus's tenure as governor coincided with the presidential administrations of Dwight D. Eisenhower, John F. Kennedy, and Lyndon B. Johnson. Eisenhower was the only one of the three rated by the Schlesinger poll, and he finished in the average category.

George W. Hays (1913–17), a Camden attorney, placed eleventh in the poll. Initially elected to fill the unexpired term of Joe T. Robinson, Hays was then reelected for a full term in 1915. As governor he faced a growing deficit in the state treasury. In an effort to increase revenue, he tried, unsuccessfully, to get county officials to raise property assessments and thereby eliminate the need for a general tax increase. Funding for state government continued to be a problem throughout his administration. Hays was governor during Woodrow Wilson's first term as president.

Francis Cherry (1953–55) was ranked twelfth in the poll by the respondents. Born in Texas and educated in Oklahoma, he performed a variety of jobs before opening a law practice in Little Rock. As governor he sponsored legislation to create a new fiscal code for the state that required "strict accountability" for expenditures. He also supported efforts by Arkansas Power and Light Company to gain a rate increase from the Public Service Commission, and he endorsed a bill requiring that names of welfare recipients be made public. The latter two issues proved to be particularly unpopular, and Cherry was denied reelection to a second term by state voters. He was only the second governor in the twentieth century to fail in such a bid. He served as governor during the transition between Dwight Eisenhower's first and second administrations.

Homer M. Adkins (1941–45), a pharmacist from Jacksonville, served two terms as governor during World War II and placed thirteenth in the poll. Although leading the state in the war effort, he offered little by way of legislative programs, and local politics was almost totally overshadowed by world events at the time. Federal funds and employment opportunities in war industries greatly improved the state's economy. Even so, Arkansas received less federal funding (more than 25 percent less than Mississippi, the next lowest) than any other state in the South. Adkins served as governor during Franklin Roosevelt's fourth and last term as president.

J. M. Futrell (1933–37) rated fourteenth in the poll. A public school teacher and lawyer from Greene County, Futrell was governor during the depths of the Depression. He campaigned on a platform of reducing state expenditures by 50 percent. Once in office he set out to reach that objective by ordering all state agencies to "live within their income." He also sought to have the highway indebtedness refunded and insisted that the state prison become economically self-sufficient. Futrell's austerity, coupled with a massive infusion of federal money, allowed officials to get the state's economy under control. The price paid in terms of lost services, however, worked a hardship on many Arkansans—particularly small farmers.

Futrell served as governor during Franklin D. Roosevelt's first term as president. The two men could not have been more dissimilar in either personality or executive leadership.

Harvey Parnell (1928–33) finished fifteenth in the poll. A farmer from Dermott, he was the first lieutenant governor under the 1874 constitution. He assumed office during one of the most difficult periods in the state's history. The Martineau Road Law had obligated the state to an indebtedness of more than one hundred million dollars, payable in yearly installments. Unfortunately between 1927 and 1930 Arkansas suffered a cycle of devastating floods and droughts that all but destroyed the state's agriculture. That, coupled with the business depression that followed the stock market crash, severely hampered the economy. In an effort to meet these needs Parnell ordered a 20 percent reduction in state expenditures and twice called the legislature into special session to consider reduction in cotton acreage and highway refunding. The legislators were cooperative but all efforts did little to check the state's growing indebtedness. Parnell did not seek reelection for a second term.

Herbert Hoover was president during Parnell's tenure as governor. The two men showed much of the same philosophy about governmental responsibilities and programs in proposing solutions to the problems of the Depression. Hoover finished in the average category in the presidential poll.

Tom J. Terral (1925–27) finished last in the poll. Born in Louisiana, he spent most of his adult life in Little Rock, where he worked as an attorney. As governor he sponsored no programs of consequence and achieved only mild success in gaining additional funding for the public schools. He was the first governor in the twentieth century to seek reelection to a second term and be defeated. Terral was governor during the presidential administration of Calvin Coolidge.

On the basis of the number of respondents, Rockefeller, McMath, and Cherry were the best-known of the governors. Each was evaluated by thirty-five of the forty-one people who completed the survey. Terral, evaluated by twenty-four respondents, was the least known. Rockefeller received the highest number of points, 139, based on the rating scale, and Terral, with 49, received the least number of points.

Comments of Respondents

The comment section deals only with the observations by the respondents who cared to put their thoughts about various governors in writing. Since this was usually less than half of those who evaluated a particular governor, these comments should not necessarily be read as typical of the entire group who made the evaluation. An attempt has been made to briefly summarize these comments and to quote verbatim in certain situations.

According to the respondents in the Arkansas governors' poll, the two best governors in Arkansas since 1900 were Charles H. Brough, with a 4.16, and George W. Donaghey, with a 4.10. Both governors ranked well above the midpoint (4.00) in the "good" category.

Charles H. Brough, in the opinion of the respondents, was a progressive in the Woodrow Wilson tradition of the scholar-politician who worked for such causes as a new constitution, women's suffrage, penal reform, and administrative reorganization. Most respondents saw him as a highly intelligent and articulate person who possessed great speaking skills. The only blot on the record was his handling of the Elaine Race Riot. One of those offering comments about Brough seemed to catch the consensus of those who did comment when he said: "Aside from the 1919 tragedy in Elaine, Brough appears to have been a highly positive governor who was much more active than other Arkansas governors during the first half of the twentieth century."

Comments about Donaghey were not as extensive as those about Brough. Donaghey was given credit for ending the convict leasing or convict labor system and for completing construction of the state capitol and rescuing that project "from the mess in which Jeff Davis had left it." Donaghey was perceived as an able administrator and a thoroughly honest man. In fact, even though ten people made written observations about Donaghey, it is remarkable that virtually all of these were in a positive vein.

Winthrop Rockefeller got a 3.97 ranking in the poll, but this verdict was more mixed than in the cases of Brough and Donaghey. He was praised for a more positive national image, more professional appointments, better race relations, and a climate of reform that valued openness and new ideas. This was offset by what many of the respondents saw as his political ineptness and limited administrative ability. The handicap of being a Republican in Arkansas and the problem that this caused in working with the legislature was also mentioned. Nevertheless, the overall evaluation was much more positive than negative. As one of the respondents put it: "Unquestionably, Arkansas is better off today as a result of Win Rockefeller having been governor at the particular time during which he served."

Sid McMath finished fourth in the poll, with a ranking of 3.86. McMath was commended for his handling of race relations, the positive national image that he projected, and the reform legislation that he supported. The consensus of those who made comments about McMath, however, was that his promise was unfulfilled because of the highway scandal and that this episode prevented a "great" ranking.

Carl E. Bailey received a ranking of 3.74, which kept him well within the range (4.4 to 3.5) of the "good" category. The respondents who saw Bailey in a favorable light mentioned as evidence his ability as an administrator and his support for a civil service law and free textbooks through the eighth grade. He was also viewed as a governor who understood the needs of a Depression-era state and how to meet those needs. The only negative factor stressed about Bailey was the consuming ambition that led him into mistakes of judgment, such as his unsuccessful attempt to become a U.S. Senator in 1937 after Joe T. Robinson's death. Bailey had the Democratic State Committee select him as their nominee rather than calling a special primary to pick the nominee. This tactic was resented and Bailey was defeated in a special election to fill Robinson's seat by John E. Miller, who ran as an independent candidate.

Thomas C. McRae was the last governor in the "good" category, and the respondents chose to make only a few observations about him. They were mostly to the effect that McRae was mildly progressive for the twenties, that he favored more money for education, and he began a modern road-building program. He seems almost, however, to be damned with faint praise.

The next category was the one designated as "average," and, as might be expected, it contains most of the governors since 1900. Nine governors fall in the 3.4 to 2.5 range. In this "average" category and ranked right next to each other are Jeff Davis and Orval Faubus, the two most divisive and charismatic personalities in the seventy years covered by the poll. Ben T. Laney was the governor with the highest ranking (3.33) in the "average" category. The respondents took a generally favorable attitude toward Laney, pointing out that during his campaign he promised to bring a business-like administration to state government and that he did what he said he would do. He was praised for his sound fiscal management and for the passage of the revenue stabilization act (an act that guarantees the state cannot spend more money than it takes in). Most criticism of Laney focused around his attitude on race, but this seemed to be outweighed by his administrative and fiscal accomplishments. One respondent phrased it this way: "His fiscal management was superb and the revenue stabilization act was an inspired piece of legislation. This offsets his negative position on race."

John E. Martineau also ranked high (3.21) in the "average" category. Evaluation of his administration was particularly difficult since he resigned during this first term to accept a federal judgeship. Only seven respondents wrote anything about Martineau, and their comments were almost split equally between those who said that the Martineau road pro-gram was a blessing and those who said it was disaster. The road legisla-tion sponsored by Martineau unified the highway system in the state and provided that the state would assume the debts of the local highway improvement districts and would finance new construction through the sale of bonds. The program was caught by the flood of 1927 and the depression two years later, hence the split verdict. The Martineau road program was almost the only thing mentioned in the evaluations.

Jeff Davis falls in the middle range of the average category. The con-sensus of those who commented was that he was more talk than action, and though perhaps possessing progressive instincts, his measurable accom-plishments were few. His deeds failed to match his rhetoric and "like some of Arkansas' more contemporary politicians, Davis seemed to enjoy 'get-ting' elected more than experiencing the powers of office."

Ranking just below Jeff Davis was Orval Faubus at 3.12. Over half the respondents expressed their opinions about Orval Faubus, and they range over the spectrum from those who felt that he should be ranked "as a good to great governor primarily based upon his strength in admin-istrative leadership and accomplishments" to some who felt that his administration was "the low point in all American history." Most evaluations, however, clustered around a middle position that acknowledged Faubus's achievements (broadening the tax base, economic development, mental health efforts, a state building program, and expansion of state services) but felt they were overshadowed and outweighed by the 1957 Central High School crisis. This middle position is summarized in the following quote:

> [He is] the hardest governor to evaluate due to the mixed results of his tenure. The first four years would be classified as "good." The remaining eight years are mixed. The most overwhelming impact of his administration was the tremendous adverse publicity resulting from the 1957 [Central High] school crisis. During 1958–59, Arkansas experienced a crisis which adversely effected the development of the state for a decade or more. More than anyone else, Faubus bears the responsibility for the situation which developed. Despite many positive accomplishments, the overall impact of Orval Faubus' 12 years in office can only be considered negative.

George W. Hays was ranked at the midpoint (2.88) in the average category. Only five respondents chose to make remarks about Hays, so it is difficult to get any insights into the reason for his ranking. Two respondents considered him mildly progressive because of his attempts at property tax reform, while two others thought him undistinguished although very popular with the public. The fifth respondent was noncommittal about Hays.

Francis Cherry was ranked below the midpoint in the average category and there was a surprising unanimity among the respondents that Cherry was sincere and honest but also insensitive, tactless, and poorly equipped for political life. He lacked executive ability and political skills and "did such a poor job that he was defeated for a second term."

Homer Adkins, in the judgment of those who made written comments, was strictly a machine politician with little foresight and few ideals. He received a ranking of 2.80 which puts him well below average in the average category.

J. M. Futrell was praised for keeping the state from bankruptcy but criticized for his insensitivity to the needs of the people in a time of economic crisis. The consensus seemed to be that he "did good work in keeping the state from bankruptcy, but possessed the wrong economic outlook for depression times."

Harvey Parnell was the governor ranked last in the average category. Although a few of the respondents were sympathetic toward Parnell's attempts at leadership during the Depression, most felt that he was simply the wrong person to cope with the staggering problems of the Depression. The highway scandal during his administration was also mentioned.

Tom J. Terral was the only governor placed in the "below average" category. He drew little comment from the respondents except where it was emphasized that he was not elected to a second term.

Conclusion

Prior to preparing the questionnaire, the authors reviewed several potential problems. One concern was the extent to which respondents would be familiar with the governors. Unlike the Schlesinger presidential poll, which had the advantage of having well-publicized subjects and a broad national sample, Arkansas governors have not, traditionally, received a great deal of attention. Also, the governor's survey involved fewer subjects, sixteen, and there was a smaller reservoir of individuals to poll than in the Schlesinger presidential poll. As anticipated, respondents were generally less familiar with those individuals serving prior to World War II. If respondents' comments were any guide, however, governors during the Progressive Era were reasonably well known. Clearly respondents were less familiar with chief executives of the 1920s and 1930s.

Another concern was the extent to which the post-Vietnam, post-Watergate distrust of executive power would influence the ratings. Specifically, the question was raised as to whether a governor might be penalized for an activist administration. This concern proved unfounded, as reflected in the fact that the top four governors were all activists in terms of legislative programs and political action. The least active governor also received the lowest rating.

There was also a curiosity as to whether any governor would be ranked in the "great" category. In preparing the guidelines the authors determined that to be considered "great" a governor must receive a "great" ranking from at least fifty percent of the respondents. While that formula appears to be a most lenient one, in reality none of the governors achieved a ranking of great. Perhaps the primary reason behind this lack of distinction is reflected in a comment on one of the questionnaires. As the respondent noted, the "conservative nature of the legislature and the frequency of gubernatorial elections made it difficult for any Arkansas governor to be rated great." It is also possible that the office, created during Reconstruction when distrust of executive power was prevalent, simply lacks the constitutional authority and broad legal powers that can enhance the place in history of a talented governor.

Finally, as many respondents noted, there is a great need for more research on Arkansas governors—both on the office and the individual governors. The governor's role in federal-state relations, regional planning, and economic development, to name just a few areas, has been largely unexplored by the state's academic community. A systematic evaluation of individual issues such as education, the prison system, the highway program, and race relations, among others, has also been neglected by researchers in terms of executive leadership. Perhaps this poll will have the effect of focusing more attention on the governor's office in the future. At least it offers an opportunity to establish a benchmark for evaluating the state's chief executives eight decades into the twentieth century.

A Practitioner's Guide to Arkansas's New Judicial Article

Larry Brady and J. D. Gingerich

In introducing this selection in its original form, the editors of the University of Arkansas at Little Rock Law Review wrote "The passage of Amendment 80 on November 7, 2000 was a watershed event in the history of the Judicial Department of this state. Jurisdictional lines that previously forced cases to be divided artificially and litigated separately in different courts have been eliminated. This fundamental change naturally brings with it a whole host of issues, both theoretical and practical, concerning the form and structure of our court system."[1] The fusion of the state's two trial-level courts was of course only one of several changes included in the voters' overhaul of the judicial article of the Arkansas Constitution; others included removing political party labels from judicial elections, lengthening the terms of office for prosecuting attorneys, and consolidating the many layers and kinds of local level courts. In this short essay on Arkansas's early efforts to implement Amendment 80, Brady and Gingerich illuminate the challenge of carrying the state's overhauled judicial branch into operation. Given recent attention by both the state Supreme Court and the legislature to the use of magistrates and the funding of local-level "district" courts, it is likely that implementation issues will require attention for years to come.

On November 7, 2000, members of the Arkansas bench and bar[2] and other interested citizens completed an odyssey that had begun more than thirty years earlier to bring comprehensive change to the state's court

Larry Brady and J. D. Gingerich, "A Practitioner's Guide to Arkansas's New Judicial Article," *University of Arkansas at Little Rock Law Review* 24 (2002): 715–26. Reprinted with permission.

system.[3] Similar efforts had been attempted but defeated by the voters or the Arkansas General Assembly in 1970,[4] 1980,[5] 1991,[6] and 1995.[7]

While the effort to study and draft the new proposal and secure its passage was the result of substantial contributions, both personal and financial, by the Arkansas bench and bar, the ultimate passage of Amendment 80 by such a large majority of the voters came as a surprise to both the supporters and detractors of the amendment. Due to a history of so many failed attempts, the large number of other items that appeared on the election ballot,[8] and the tendency of Arkansas voters to defeat long and complicated ballot measures, most were surprised by the successful outcome.

One result of this tendency to expect that the amendment would be defeated was a failure to prepare for its success. Neither the Arkansas Bar Association and the Arkansas Judicial Council, the main supporters of the Amendment, nor the Arkansas Supreme Court, the body primarily responsible for its implementation, performed any serious work to plan for or study the actions that would be necessary in the event of the amendment's passage. In light of what was, in retrospect, a very short period between passage and implementation,[9] this failure to plan for the next steps, while understandable, made the implementation process much more difficult.

Despite this lack of preparation, a considerable amount of work has been done to implement the changes. The Arkansas Supreme Court has promulgated a number of administrative orders and rule changes, and the Arkansas General Assembly has adopted a package of legislation. This article begins by explaining the process that the Supreme Court has established for the implementation of Amendment 80. Next, it describes the new trial court structure that Amendment 80 created. The new rules regarding court administration, pleading, and practice are covered next. Finally, the article notes some of the unresolved issues that the Supreme Court and the bar will face as implementation of Amendment 80 continues.

The Process and Timing of Implementation

When the voters approved Amendment 80, the Arkansas Supreme Court recognized that it had the primary responsibility to implement it.[10] Within three weeks following passage, the Supreme Court appointed a nine-member committee to oversee the implementation process.[11] The committee immediately held a series of meetings and began to adopt both a short-term and long-term strategy for Amendment 80's implementation. The committee determined that, with Arkansas's biennial session of the General Assembly beginning in less than one month, the consideration of necessary action by the legislative branch should be the first order of business. The committee considered and ultimately endorsed a package of legislation that was proposed to the General Assembly. The proposals that were ultimately signed into law included a clarification of the qualification of justices and judges,[12] the repeal of all statutes relating to the Court of Common Pleas,[13] a designation for election purposes of each of the divisions of trial courts,[14] an amendment to various provisions of the juvenile code,[15] and a comprehensive act setting out the process for nonpartisan judicial elections.[16]

While the General Assembly was considering this legislation, the committee continued to review action to be taken by the Supreme Court. The central recommendation concerned the structure of trial court administration and the management of cases, resulting in the Supreme Court's adoption of Administrative Order No. 14, issued on April 6, 2001.[17] The court also received recommendations from its Committee on Civil Practice and Committee on Criminal Practice. As a result, the court revised each of its administrative orders that were affected by Amendment 80[18] and adopted amendments to the Rules of Civil Procedure and the Inferior Court Rules,[19] the Rules of Criminal Procedure,[20] the Rules of Appellate Procedure—Civil, and the Rules of the Supreme Court,[21] and, most recently, a new rule to allow for the certification of questions of Arkansas law to the Supreme Court by any federal court of the United States.[22]

During the process of study and review by the Amendment 80 Committee, it became clear that the full implementation of Amendment 80 by the time of its effective date, July 1, 2001, was next to impossible. The committee noted that county governments, which were responsible for funding most of the operations of Arkansas trial courts, operated on a calendar year budget. Computer software programs would need to be reprogrammed, printed docket books and other court forms would have to be revised, some modifications in physical facilities might be required, and judges, lawyers, and court personnel would have to be educated. As a result, the Supreme Court, based upon the recommendation of the committee, established the first of two transition periods.

For the period of July 1, 2001, through December 31, 2001, all judges are circuit judges and may hear any type of case, but during this period of transition, circuit judges shall continue to be assigned the types of cases each was being assigned prior to the effective date of Amendment 80 of the Arkansas Constitution.[23]

The result of the court's order was that, during the transition period from July 1, 2001, through December 31, 2001, the circuit court became the unified court of general jurisdiction. Chancery and probate courts ceased to exist.[24] As to the filing and management of cases, however, judges continued to hear the same type of cases they previously had heard.[25] The court's dockets remained in place, and the required cover sheets from pre–Amendment 80 days continued to be used. By June 1, 2001, judges in each of the judicial circuits submitted the plans for court administration for their circuits, as required by Administrative Order No. 14. On June 28, 2001, the Supreme Court adopted the plans. In its consideration and review of the plans, however, the court found that several practical issues and substantive public policy questions needed answers before a full implementation of Amendment 80 and its purpose was possible. As a result, the court established a second period of transition from January 1, 2002, until July 1, 2003, during which all of the provisions of Amendment 80 would be in force, but evaluation and refinement of the procedures could also take place.

In formulating their administrative plans, the judicial circuits have recognized that the Arkansas judiciary is in a transitional stage. We have considered this fact in passing judgment on their proposed plans. Identifying these practical problems at the front end will hopefully permit the General Assembly, as well as county quorum courts, to work with us in formulating answers to these issues, including the appropriation of necessary funding. Thus, we believe that a realistic target date for completing implementation of the new unified court system should be July 1, 2003. On that date, we expect all circuit judges to be available to try all "justiciable matters."[26]

Trial Court Structure

With the passage of Amendment 80, Arkansas voters reduced the number of states with separate law and equity jurisdiction from four to three and joined the majority of states that have each created a unified court of general jurisdiction.[27] As of July 1, 2001, all Arkansas courts became circuit courts and all chancery and circuit/chancery judges became cir-

cuit judges.[28] There is no longer a division between law and equity jurisdiction. A judge hearing a case has full authority to dispose of any and
all issues in the case.

As of January 1, 2002, the Supreme Court also mandated the establishment of five subject matter divisions in each circuit court. They are
criminal, civil, juvenile, probate, and domestic relations.[29] The court out-
lined the scope and purposes of these divisions as follows:

> A circuit judge shall at all times have the authority to hear all mat-
> ters within the jurisdiction of the circuit court and has the affirma-
> tive duty to do so regardless of the designation of divisions. . . . The
> designation of divisions is for the purpose of judicial administra-
> tion and caseload management and is not for the purpose of sub-
> ject-matter jurisdiction. The creation of divisions shall in no way
> limit the powers and duties of the judges as circuit judges. Judges
> shall not be assigned exclusively to a particular division so as to pre-
> clude them from hearing other cases which may come before
> them.[30]

Court Administration

One of the major unanswered questions raised by Amendment 80's adoption is the nature and structure of the administration of the trial court.
Arkansas has little, if any, history of trial court administration. The lack of
state and local resources for personnel and a long tradition and expectation by trial judges that they will operate their courts in an autonomous
fashion have created a wide variation in the level and nature of administration from circuit to circuit. With the removal of chancery and probate
courts and an expansion of jurisdictional authority for all judges, a new
system is required. Who or what should determine the types of cases a particular judge will hear? In multi-judge circuits, how are decisions made?
Should the system be uniform from circuit to circuit? The specific language of Amendment 80 did not answer these and many other questions.

Shortly after the approval of Amendment 80, the director of the
Administrative Office of the Courts contacted the National Center for
State Courts for an evaluation of the amendment and a recommendation
on the issues that would need to be addressed for successful implementation. This report identified the establishment of a plan for trial court
administration as the central issue for any successful implementation:

> The major issue will be creating an administrative structure. . . . The judicial article brings about organizational unification and some degree of administrative unification. The problem is that the Supreme Court cannot manage a statewide court system from Little Rock. The best the high court can do is set guidelines and policies. There has to be a local system of judicial administration or the reform will flounder. There is no unified court system in the United States without local administrative judges, and some of these judges are supported by court administrators. With two sets of elected clerks, the circuit courts will already have problems of administrative cohesion, not to mention the consolidation of various courts that were formerly separate from one another. It is hard to envision how this can be done through en banc administration.[31]

The Amendment 80 Committee faced this issue early in its deliberations and received a significant amount of input from judges, clerks, and other court officials. It became clear to the committee, as evidenced by its recommendation to the Supreme Court, that the role of the Supreme Court should not be one of becoming involved in the day-to-day affairs of the trial court administration; rather, the supreme court should establish a uniform set of overriding goals and principles that should form the basis of each circuit's administrative structure. In this way, each circuit takes into account significant local issues or customs. The procedure adopted by the Supreme Court to carry out this role was the creation of local administrative plans. Administrative Order No. 14 required each multijudge judicial circuit to submit a plan for circuit court administration to the Supreme Court by June 1, 2001.[32] In the plan, the circuit judges were required to set out the process by which they will determine case management and administrative procedures. All of the judges must unanimously agree on the manner in which decisions will be reached under the plan, but the decision-making structure agreed upon does not require unanimity for subsequent decisions. For example, the judicial circuit could hold periodic meetings among the judges with a majority, supermajority, or unanimity being required to bind the circuit. Alternatively, an administrative judge or an administrative committee could be established. In other words, the Supreme Court did not require any particular decision-making structure, but only that the structure adopted at the local level be clear and in writing.[33]

The heart of the plan is a policy on case assignment and allocation. Administrative Order No. 14 requires the following:

> The plan shall describe the process for the assignment of cases and shall control the assignment and allocation of cases in the judicial circuit. In the absence of good cause to the contrary, the plan of assignment of cases shall assume (i) random selection of unrelated cases; (ii) a substantially equal apportionment of cases among the circuit judges of a judicial circuit; and (iii) all matters connected with a pending or supplemental proceeding will be heard by the judge to whom the matter was originally assigned.[34]

Pursuant to the requirements of Administrative Order No. 14, judges in twenty-one judicial circuits submitted their proposed administrative plans to the court. Four judicial circuits were single-judge circuits and did not have to submit a plan.[35] Three judicial circuits could not agree on a plan to submit.[36] The plans submitted offered a wide range of methods of case administration and case distribution. In some cases, a new position as administrative judge was designated. In others, a system of rotation between divisions was established. These variations were, to some extent, a result of the very different circumstances that existed from circuit to circuit.

On June 28, 2001, the Supreme Court issued a per curiam order in which it announced its decision on each plan.[37] Sixteen of the twenty-one submitted plans were approved, although the court required two of these circuits to provide clarification on or before August 15, 2001.[38] Five plans were rejected, primarily for their continuation of the distinction between law and equity cases in their case assignment plan.[39] These circuits were ordered to submit amended plans to the court on or before August 15, 2001. Each of these circuits ultimately had its plans approved. In the three circuits where no agreement was reached and no plan was submitted, the Supreme Court developed a plan for each circuit and appointed an administrative judge to implement the plan.

Because the administrative plans set out the types of cases that each judge will hear and the method for case allocation and management within each circuit, these are important documents that any practicing attorney should review. The plans must be filed in the office of each circuit clerk; copies are available through the Arkansas Judiciary Web site.[40]

Pleading and Practice

Effective July 1, 2001, all pleadings filed in the circuit courts should be styled "In the Circuit Court of County." The pleading should be so styled even if it is the continuation of a matter that had previously been filed in a chancery or probate court.[41] As of January 1, 2002, when a case is filed, it will be assigned to one of the five subject matter divisions of circuit court: criminal, civil, probate, domestic relations, or juvenile. Pursuant to Administrative Order No. 8, a cover sheet must accompany all initial filings. There is a separate cover sheet for each of the divisions. Because of the expanded jurisdiction of the circuit court, it is possible that there could be issues in a pleading that would allow it to be filed in more than one division. In this case, the administrative order provides: "If a complaint asserts multiple claims which involve different subject matter divisions of the circuit court, the cover sheet for that division which is most definitive of the nature of the case should be selected and completed."[42] To commence an action, the attorney or pro se litigant filing the initial pleading is responsible for the completion of the filing information on the appropriate cover sheet. The court clerk cannot accept the pleading unless the reporting form accompanies it.[43]

Cover sheets take on a greater importance in the Amendment 80 environment. Because there are no longer separate chancery and probate courts through which to filter cases, all cases are filed in circuit court. In order for the clerk to understand the type of case and to properly assign the case to the appropriate judge, the clerk will have to rely on the information contained in the cover sheets.[44]

When a case is filed, it will be docketed pursuant to Administrative Order No. 2. Cases shall be assigned the letter prefix corresponding to that docket and a number in the order of filing. Beginning with the first case filed each year, cases shall be numbered consecutively in each docket category with the four digits of the current year followed by a hyphen and the number assigned to the case beginning with the number "1." For example: criminal CR2002–1, civil CV2002–1, probate PR2002–1, domestic relations DR2002–1, juvenile JV2002–1.[45]

Circuit clerks then assign the cases to particular circuit judges based upon the provision of the circuit's administrative plan. One complicating factor in the process of filing cases has to do with where the pleading is to be filed, that is, which clerk is responsible for receiving and filing the court record. Arkansas's circuit and county clerks are constitutional officers,[46] but Amendment 80 did not amend or repeal any of the constitutional language regarding clerks. The role of each clerk is, at best, unclear after Amendment 80's abolishment of probate court, which had been the responsibility of the county clerk.[47] The Supreme Court received a recommendation from its Committee on Civil Practice that the circuit clerk be designated as the sole clerk for all circuit court matters, eliminating any role for the probate clerk. The Supreme Court Committee on Amendment 80 also debated this issue. As this discussion took place, the Association of County Clerks pursued legislation before the 2001 General Assembly, which eventually enacted Act 997 of 2001.[48] The act provides that if the Supreme Court creates a probate division, then the county clerk will continue to serve as the clerk for the probate division. The act designates the county clerk as the ex officio clerk of the probate division of circuit court. When the Supreme Court eventually adopted the probate division as one of the five divisions of circuit court in Administrative Order No. 14, this statutory role for the county clerk became effective. However, because the five subject matter divisions did not go into effect until January 2002, a gap existed in the statutory responsibility of county clerks. A transitional provision added to Rule 3 of the Arkansas Rules of Civil Procedure remedied this gap. This provision states that for the period of July 1, 2001, through December 31, 2001, probate matters shall continue to be filed with the same clerk for such matters as were filed prior to July 1, 2001.[49] Administrative Order No. 8 now incorporates this notion:

> Court Clerk means the elected circuit clerk . . . except in the event probate matters are required by law to be filed in the office of the county clerk, then the term clerk shall also include the county clerk for this limited purpose.[50]

Unfinished Business

Much has been accomplished in the sixteen months since passage of Amendment 80, but the implementation of Amendment 80 is an evolving process. Decisions that have been made may need to be reconsidered,[51] and questions that have not yet been asked will need to be answered. Some issues can be resolved by legislation or court rule while others will be decided in the context of appellate court decisions. Issues that are currently on the table include the implementation by January 1, 2005, of the new district court system,[52] and the appointment of masters, referees, and magistrates.[53]

Some of the more vexing of the unresolved issues are those raised by the Supreme Court in its June 28, 2001, per curiam order.[54] One question that confronted the court in weighing the merits of the various plans was how a judge's experience and specialization should be balanced with the potential for burnout as a factor in the assignment and allocation of cases.[55] Another issue was the matter of juvenile proceedings and whether they should be treated differently from other cases. The court took note of the "state apparatus" related to these proceedings, "such as the prosecutors, public defenders, probation officers, DHS attorneys and caseworkers, attorneys ad litem, CASA volunteers, intake officers, and so forth."[56]

Is it necessary or desirable to keep these types of cases segregated in order for the system to operate efficiently? If so, should there be a regular rotation system whereby a circuit judge may be assigned to the juvenile or criminal division of circuit court for a specified period of time, at the end of which he or she would be assigned to other cases?[57]

The court also expressed concern over the practical issues related to facilities, staff, and education.

Even if all the theoretical questions were answered, we could not immediately implement the necessary changes because of time and financial constraints. We must allow time for incumbent and newly elected circuit judges to participate in judicial education programs to train them in areas of the law with which they are not as familiar since all such judges must become available to try any type of case.[58]

These issues remain unresolved, but will have to be addressed very soon to allow the 2003 General Assembly to enact necessary legislation and to meet the court's directive for full implementation of Amendment 80 by 2003.

Conclusion

With the adoption of Amendment 80, the Arkansas judicial system has experienced comprehensive and fundamental change. While many of the basic structural issues were made clear by the language of the amendment, numerous other important issues were not. The Supreme Court and its committees and the members of the circuit court bench have accomplished an extraordinary amount during a short period of time. It is incumbent upon the bench and bar, however, to become familiar with both the changes that have been wrought and the issues that have yet to be addressed in order to successfully implement Arkansas's new judicial article.

History, Political Culture, and Constitutional Reform in Arkansas

GARY D. WEKKIN AND DONALD E. WHISTLER

Arkansas's 1874 Constitution, one of the oldest among the fifty states and dubbed the "Thou Shalt Not" Constitution, is woefully inadequate to the increasing demands on state government in the early twenty-first century. This, quite simply, is the judgment of most students of Arkansas government and politics, including the authors of this study. That judgment has generated, not surprisingly, serious efforts to bring about state constitutional reform—four times in the twentieth century. Each of these efforts has been rejected by the voters, who, when asked to ratify a finished product, or merely give their approval of a proposed way ahead, have said "no" to constitutional reform in Arkansas.

In an attempt to explain this pattern of resistance on the part of state voters, Wekkin and Whistler argue that previous explanations, mostly focused on resistance to change on the part of powerful interest groups or other political actors, are incomplete. Their argument, supported by data from public opinion polls, is that there is a "politocultural" explanation for the state electorate's consistent rejection of constitutional reform; reform efforts have failed, they argue, because voters do not trust the state's political elites, and this popular distrust of elites has "struck voters as a reason to retain, not replace, the limited government framework of the 1874 Constitution."

Gary D. Wekkin and Donald D. Whistler, "History, Political Culture, and Constitutional Reform in Arkansas," *Midsouth Political Science Review* 5 (2001): 21-38. Reprinted with permission.

Introduction

If democratic political institutions are to be supported over time, citizens must believe that they are organized and operated properly. David Easton refers to this as diffuse support for a political system.[1]

An important indicator of whether citizens support their political institutions is the *trust* they express in the political institutions. Yet Americans have always had a principled mistrust of government. The 1787 constitution makers constructed national government and the compound republic (federalism) on the premise that "power corrupts, and absolute power corrupts absolutely"; but at the same time, they understood that government is necessary and that it can be institutionalized by reason predicated on human experience.[2] That is, government must be given enough power to govern, but not enough to tyrannize. Properly limited by internal checks and by regular accountability to voters, government can be more beneficial than harmful to human well-being. Thus, popular trust in government is an indicator of the public's evaluation of the effectiveness and accountability of government to the governed.

Over time, general trust in government has, along with trust in the particular levels of government within the federal system, gone through several stages. The initial stage, which we could style the First Republic, was one of principled distrust of government but acquiescence in its ineluctable necessity, after the worldview modeled by the constitutional drafters and their anti-Federalist doubters. This stage would survive from the Federal period until the expansive transformations of the role of the Washington government during the New Deal.

A second stage, consisting of heightened trust in the national government and lessened trust in state governments, began in the early 1930s and culminated in the Great Society of the mid-1960s. This period of confidence in the national government, which coincides with the period that Richard E. Neustadt styles the modern presidency (for example, the introduction of Keynesian political economy, intergovernmentalist domestic policy, and internationalist foreign policy), is one of not only numerous successes for the Washington government (such as the New Deal, World War II, selective incorporation of the Bill of Rights, the Civil Rights and Voting Rights Acts) but numerous embarrassments for the state governments as well (like segregation, malapportionment, rampant organized crime, eco-pollution), all of which subsequently gravitated onto the agenda of organs of the national government. Research performed in the 1960s thus showed trust in the national government to be roughly twice as great as that in the states or their local appendages.[3] But such trust in the national government began to plummet in the 1970s, as the Vietnam War, the bureaucratic expansion fueled by Great Society programs, the taxes and inflation fueled by the effort to have both guns *and* butter, and Watergate eroded evaluations of the national government's effectiveness, cost efficiency, and accountability to voters.[4]

A third stage, rooted in the post-Watergate climate of morality of the 1970s and still prevalent at the turn of the century, finds Americans happier with their state governments—which have developed greater institutional capacity to perform expanded governing tasks since the upgrading of governors' offices in the 1950s and 1960s, legislatures in the 1960s and 1970s, and fiscal and institutional capacities—than with the national government, which has subjected the public to a seemingly never-ending cycle of partisan scandal-mongering (Watergate Abscam, Koreagate, Iran-Contra, Whitewater, Monica and Bill, and so on) and gridlock that accounts for not only declining trust but declining voter participation, as well.[5] State governments are now perceived to be capable of delivering governing services with greater cost efficiency and responsiveness to voters than would the denizens of the self-absorbed world on the Potomac: asked which level of government they trust "to do a better job running things," 61 percent of a 1995 national sample chose their own state government, while only 24 percent chose the national government.[6]

Thus, our historic principled distrust of government has returned, nested within which is the tendency to trust most the levels of government that are closer to the people.[7]

History and Political Culture in the "49th State"

In Arkansas, however, we find a history of state government performance almost calculated to cause inhabitants to look *beyond* state boundaries for trustworthy governance. Victimized since statehood by the Conway-Rector-Sevier-Johnson dynasty of slave-owning cotton-planters (also known as "the Family" or "Sevier's Hungry Kinfolk") who burdened the state with debt following the failure of an economic development scheme involving state-issued bonds, and then by still more state and local debt as a result of the taxes and land transfer schemes of Gov. Powell Clayton and his cronies under the "Carpetbag Constitution" adopted in

1868, the first thought of Arkansans when Reconstruction ended was to replace that power-centralizing document with one "specifically designed to protect citizens from possible oppression by their own state government."[8] To ensure popular control over government, many offices previously appointive were made elective, terms were reduced from four to two years, maximum salaries for officials from capitol to courthouse were set, the General Assembly was limited to one sixty-day session every other year, and "taxing and spending powers were circumscribed with every prohibitive device imaginable" in the Arkansas Constitution of 1874.[9]

After promulgation of this document a new set of elites ruled, consisting initially of exconfederates who were soon supplemented by white agrarians, small-town businessmen, lawyers, and agents of out-of-state companies or individuals who owned property in Arkansas (that is, timber and railroad interests). Their policies aimed chiefly at trying to attract some northern business capital by keeping labor costs, public services, and taxes low, but not so much outside investment that their own political preeminence would be threatened. Populist opposition to these policies of the post-Reconstruction elites became endemic among poor farmers in Arkansas as elsewhere throughout rural America in the last third of the nineteenth century. However, elites in Arkansas, as elsewhere throughout the South, were able to reduce the political potential of these poor whites as well as of poor blacks by means of economic coercion, electoral devices such as poll taxes and the white primary, and *de jure* segregation that impeded biracial coalescence of the poor. This domestic order remained in effect, except for the brief "rule of the rustics" during the administrations of Jeff Davis (1901-7), until the Great Depression visited even more pervasive hardship upon the have-nots of the state. In response to this emergency, the posture of the Delta landholders and business/financial elites who controlled state and local government was to cut services and wait on federal relief programs, disregarding or even dispersing popular protest activities to the contrary.[10]

Only when World War II carried a generation of Arkansas GIs beyond the state's boundaries and back, determined to create in their home state the quality of life they had found elsewhere, did the spirit of public service begin to burn brighter than that of self-service among Arkansas's political class. Ex-GIs such as Gov. Sid McMath, who cleaned up the organized crime haven of Hot Springs; Gov. Francis Cherry, who refused to bow to the interests of the local Democratic machines and was dumped for it; and

Gov. Orval Faubus, who for a time displayed New Deal tendencies, ran for office to make Arkansas a better place.[11] Then Faubus, in an astounding desertion of his own values in order to preserve his political career,[12] brought on the Little Rock school integration crisis of 1957–59 that would, fairly or not, define Arkansas in the American mind until the Clinton presidency.

Not surprisingly, then, the leading students of contemporary Arkansas political culture have found, based upon a 1982 Arkansas Household Research Panel sample,[13] that while Arkansans have the "least faith" in the national government (49.5 percent), followed by local government (25.8 percent) and state government (16.6 percent), they nevertheless select local government (37.7 percent), rather than state government (22 percent), as the level in which they have the "most faith."[14] Indeed, even the national government, at 31 percent, supersedes state government's share of those indicating the level of government in which they have the "most faith" (see table 1). Robert L. Savage and Diane D. Blair conclude from this anomaly that "Presumably state government is less salient" to Arkansans than either their local government or the national government.[15]

Research by Donald E. Whistler and Gary D. Wekkin based upon a more recent (1997) and larger sample (N=703) of central Arkansas youth found that these distributions of confidence in the different levels of government continued to prevail in Arkansas in the late 1990s.[16] Their sample of eighteen-year-olds found 55.9 percent identifying the national government as the level in which they had the least confidence, and only 27.4 percent identifying the national government as the level in which they had the most confidence (see table 1). Clearly, local governments, which are appendages of the states in constitutional doctrine, enjoy much more political support than does the national government among young adults, and by proportions very similar to those reported in the Arkansas Household Survey of 1982. Where Whistler and Wekkin's results differed from those reported by Savage and Blair is in the somewhat higher level of confidence in state government versus the national government, which is significantly different than the 31 to 22 percent edge that the national government enjoyed over state government in the 1982 Arkansas Household Survey sample. This turnabout is consistent with survey data throughout the nation that show a similar refocusing of Americans' emphasis upon state and local government.[17]

We contend that this ambivalence toward state government is, instead,

TABLE I

Comparative Political Trust of Arkansans, As Measured in 1982 Arkansas Household Panel and 1997 UCA Sample of Central Arkansas High School Seniors

SAMPLE YEAR	LOCAL	STATE	NATIONAL	DON'T KNOW	N
1982 (most trust)	37.7%	22.0%	31.0%	9.4%	523
1997 (most trust)	44.8%	27.7%	27.4%	n/a	674
1982 (least trust)	25.8%	16.6%	49.5%	8.0%	523
1997 (least trust)	24.9%	19.2%	55.9%	n/a	687

Source: Data from 1982 Arkansas Household Panel adapted from Savage and Blair, 1984, 82, table 18. Data from 1997 UCA Sample adapted from Whistler and Wekkin, table 5. Question wording: Which of the following levels of government do you have the most (least) faith and confidence in?

a logical consequence of being socialized within a national political culture that distrusts government in general, conjoined with a mutative state political subculture grown accustomed to the dismal legacy of state governmental performance summarized above. While most Arkansans may not be able to cite chapter and verse their state's history of class division and state governmental indifference, they nonetheless have undergone prolonged exposure to a populist atmosphere of distrust of native political elites, and therefore insist on maintaining constitutional limits upon the power of state government over their lives.

Our argument is that the continuing reluctance of Arkansans to replace the constraining constitution of 1874 reflects, in part, this history of dismal governance. Since its adoption, Arkansas voters have firmly rejected every attempt at wholesale reform of that constitution and the limited government that it allows. The fruits of state constitutional conventions in 1918, 1970, and 1978 were rejected at the polls (the latter vote actually occurred in 1980) by margins of 61 to 39 percent, 57.4 to 42.6 percent, and 62.7 to 37.3 percent, respectively; and Governor Jim Guy Tucker's 1995 call for a miniconvention of twenty-six appointed legislators who would consider "limited" constitutional reform was defeated on December 12, 1995, by a resounding 80 to 20 percent of the electorate.[18]

This string of defeats is conventionally explained in the literature of Arkansas politics as occurring because of interest groups trying to preserve their vested interests by investing in publicity campaigns aimed at exciting public fears of tax increases, bloated government bureaucracy, and so on. During the campaign to ratify the 1970 draft constitution, county judges opposed ratification out of fear of loss of administrative power to newly strengthened county legislatures, chancery judges resisted out of fear of consolidation with courts of law, and Realtors raised the specter of increases in property taxes.[19] Liquor dealers feared loss of their price monopoly on liquor, bond buyers and out-of-state land investors feared various tax increases, and pro-gambling interests in Hot Springs financed an opposition advertising campaign,[20] a principal component of which warned that the proposed new constitution "provides 22 new ways to increase your taxes."[21] In 1980, the Arkansas Education Association feared loss of independence (from the governor's office) for the Department of Education, organized labor feared that the state's 10 percent usury limit would be lifted, fundamentalists feared that revision of the constitutional equal protection clause would facilitate backdoor adoption of equal rights for women—and, of course, everyone was susceptible to the fear that higher taxes would be the inevitable result of modernizing and strengthening the state government.[22]

The recent overwhelming electoral repudiation of Governor Tucker's 1995 call for a miniconvention illustrates that popular resistance to constitutional reform continues to exist in Arkansas despite the numerous socioeconomic transformations presently underway in the state since 1980, and grows even stronger (by nearly 20 percent) at the prospect of a convention dominated by a few hand-picked legislative elites, despite the promise of a "limited" agenda of change.

Problem Statement

Based upon an objective review of the pace of socioeconomic change in Arkansas and the limited institutional capacity of Arkansas state government to match that pace, one might expect, political culture aside for a moment, that Arkansans would support constitutional reform to bring about greater state government capacity to cope with the rate of change in the twenty-first century. The population growth and development of the "collar counties" surrounding Little Rock, the even larger population and economic boom in the state's northwest corner, the state's central location within the strategic midsouth, and its position astride the major rail and highway arterials linking eastern Canada, the northeastern United States, and Mexico are bringing unprecedented economic and social diversification, along with overcrowded roads and freeways. Midwestern retirees and Hispanic jobseekers are entering the state in force. Public schools are bursting at the seams even as increasing numbers of Arkansans are choosing private schools or home schooling for their children. These are but a few of the new challenges vying for attention alongside older, familiar problems that never seem to go away, such as prison overcrowding and school funding.

The Arkansas state government, as presently organized, is overmatched by such changing needs and popular demands. Its executive branch, at 52 agencies and 388 boards and commissions,[23] is too large and unwieldy to lie within the "span of control" of its chief executive officer (governor), whose appointive, administrative, and legislative powers could use strengthening: at present, the governor has the power to appoint only twenty-one of the heads of the fifty-two agencies that listed underneath his or her office, must suffer the administration of major policy areas (highways and game and fish) by officials accountable to independent boards rather than the governor's office, and has a line-item veto that can be overridden by a mere majority in both legislative chambers.[24] Popular accountability and administrative flexibility of the executive branch is also weakened by the usual plural-executive arrangement of independently elected constitutional offices (attorney general, secretary of state, treasurer) that could as well be appointed by the governor.[25] Such problematic institutional arrangements are a standing invitation to constitutional reformers bent on rationalizing the state's institutional capacity to the modern, ever-changing socioeconomic circumstances the state finds itself in.

On the other hand, factoring Arkansas's history and political culture into the equation, it is not so surprising that constitutional reformers should see their proposals come to naught time and again at the polls, for it is not the institutions of government themselves but rather the political elites who inhabit them that are distrusted by the public. Such distrust of elites is explicit not only in the increased margin by which Tucker's plan was rejected in 1995, but also in the electorate's passage in 1992, with 60 percent of the vote, of an amendment to the state constitution establishing term limits for all state elected offices.

Distrust of the state's political class can be expected to have survived, rather than abated, since that time as prominent state government officials such as Attorney General Steve Clark (1990), Secretary of State Bill

McCuen (1994), and Governor Jim Guy Tucker (1996) have been indicted
and convicted, federal prosecutors investigated the possible involvement
of Bill and Hillary Clinton in the Whitewater real estate/savings and loan
scandal, and several powerful senior state legislators have been indicted
and convicted.[26] A sample taken in May 1996, after Tucker's conviction,
found Arkansans listing the "Governor situation" (at 13 percent) as "the
single most important issue facing Arkansas today," trailed by crime, education, unemployment, and "corruption/honesty in government" (at 6 percent). Further down the list followed the "Whitewater problem" (in
fifteenth place, at 2 percent) and "President Clinton" (twenty-first, at 1 percent) as separate, but perhaps related variants on the broader theme of trust
in government.[27] Then in August 1996, a statewide sample found 46 percent of respondents agreeing and 39 percent disagreeing with the statement that "One party rule by the Democrats in Arkansas has led to
corruption and it's time for change."[28] Evidence that this continues to be
the case is provided by 1999 "Arkansas Poll" results showing that, despite
elite commentary assuring us that term limits truncate legislators' experience and increase their dependence on interest group inputs, Arkansans
are twice as likely to feel that the "large number of new state legislators"
has improved the legislature (30 percent), rather than detracted from its
quality (16 percent). Moreover, 65 percent of them approve of continuing
to include direct democracy measures (initiatives and referenda) on the
ballot.[29]

Consequently, we argue that there is a politocultural explanation of
Arkansans' consistent pattern of rejecting large-scale constitutional
reform that has been ignored in the efforts of participants and historians to itemize every interest group that contributed to the defeat of a
particular plan. A constant variable that may have figured in each of the
four ratification failures is that popular distrust of political elites struck
voters as a reason to retain, not replace, the limited government framework of the 1874 Constitution.

Data and Methods

We cannot travel back in time to verify that Arkansans' opposition to constitutional reform in 1918, 1970, 1980, and 1995 was indeed informed by
populistic distrust of elites. We can, however, draw useful, if not definitive lessons from existing data that may serve to demonstrate whether contemporary Arkansans' resistance to greater empowerment of governing

officeholders is rooted in a condition of ignorance of, or awareness of, the state's antiquated institutional capacity (for example, executive organizational structure and operating procedures). The data consist of the results of a battery of questions about the powers of the Arkansas governor's office that were asked of respondents in a May, 1998, random telephone sample funded by a University of Central Arkansas Foundation grant for general public service research. The sample was random digit dialed and drawn from all current Arkansas telephone exchanges, with interviews recorded on CATI facilities in the Social Science Microcomputer Laboratory of the University of Central Arkansas. Interviews were conducted by salaried employees with prior telemarketing experience, under the direct supervision of one of the coauthors, who has directed more than twenty telephone surveys.[30] The sample size, at 433, is slightly larger than that of professional tracking polls, and is broadly representative of the state. Although African Americans are underrepresented at 11 percent of the sample, the distributions for gender, age groups, educational achievement, and partisan orientation of the respondents are quite accurate and well within sampling error.

Findings

The data contain some evidence of popular confusion about the nature of the organization of Arkansas's executive branch. For example, 64 percent of the respondents think that Arkansas has a cabinet-style government, which is not really the case, given the governor's limited powers of appointment to the very large number of units underneath him in the state organizational flowchart (see Appendix). Moreover, while 80 percent of the respondents correctly identified the governor as the chief executive officer of the state government, only one-third of the respondents identified the governor as "responsible for seeing to it that laws and policies are implemented" (this question was, however, asked *before* respondents were asked, "which state official is the chief executive of the state government?").

However, there also is compelling evidence of opposition to constitutional revision of the executive branch and its powers despite considerable public awareness of the various restrictions upon that branch as presently arranged. The Arkansas public is not unaware of several of the specific structural problems that prevent the governor's office from conducting cabinet-style government (even if they think that the Arkansas governor does have a cabinet). For example:

- 65 percent of the telephone sample agreed (and only 23 percent disagreed) that the state's executive branch of fifty-two agencies were too many for a governor to manage

- 62 percent agreed (and 23 percent disagreed) that "the governor's power over state agencies should be strengthened in order to keep them responsible to the public"

- 69 percent (compared with 26 percent who disagreed) felt that the state's independent highway commission "should . . . answer to the governor"

- 61 percent (as opposed to 29 percent) agreed that the state's independent game and fish commission "should . . . answer to the governor" (see Appendix for complete data and full text of questions)

However, when subsequently asked "Do you think the state constitution should be amended in order to strengthen the powers of the Governor's Office, reduce the powers, or should they be left as they are," only 23 percent of these same respondents voted for amending the constitution to strengthen the governor's powers, compared to 49 percent who voted for leaving the constitution and the governor's powers thereunder alone, and 10 percent who actually wanted to reduce the powers of the office.

More specifically, although 80 percent of the sample correctly identified the governor as the chief executive officer of the state, only 21 percent selected "the Governor" when asked "who should have the responsibility to see to it that . . . funds are spent as directed," and only 46 percent endorsed the idea that the governor *should* appoint the heads of all of the agencies beneath him in the executive branch. The latter figure is interesting because 63 percent of this same sample believed that the Governor of Arkansas at present has the power to appoint the heads of all fifty-two of the agencies that are supposed to be accountable to his office, whereas in fact the governor has the power to appoint the heads of only twelve departments without the approval of the state Senate or a state board, the heads of another nine departments with Senate approval, and the head of one department (the Arkansas Economic Development Commission) with the approval of both a board and the Senate.[31] Obviously, this datum suggests the existence of some public ignorance or confusion about the appointment powers of the governor; however, it also suggests, when compared to the 46 percent who felt that the governor *should* have the power to appoint all subordinate managers, that perhaps as many as 17 percent of the respondents might favor constitutional revision to weaken, rather than strengthen, the governor's appointive powers.

Nor was there very much sentiment for strengthening the governorship by replacing the Jacksonian concept of an elected plural executive with a gubernatorially appointed cabinet. Majorities of 79 percent, 78 percent, 74 percent, and 69 percent, respectively, favored continuing to elect the state attorney general, secretary of state, state treasurer, and state auditor,[32] rather than filling such posts by gubernatorial appointment. To be sure, such support for electing, rather than appointing, such officials is normal in the Jacksonian-influenced American states—but it should not be forgotten that not long prior to the collection of these data, an Arkansas attorney general and a secretary of state, respectively, had been convicted for defrauding the state during their terms in office. Those events do not seem to have weakened support very much, if at all, for the elected plural executive plan in the Arkansas statehouse.

Finally, the legislative powers of the governor's office did not fare much better than the aforegoing managerial powers did with the sample respondents, 52 percent of whom agreed with the 1874 Constitution's requirement that a majority vote in both houses of the legislature may override a gubernatorial veto. Only 42 percent felt that it should take more than a mere majority of both chambers to override a gubernatorial veto, and of these just 7 percent would support the U.S. Constitutional norm of two-thirds of both chambers as the minimum necessary to override a governor's veto.

Conclusion

Four times in the century just passed (1918, 1970, 1980, 1995) Arkansans have rejected wholesale changes in the state's restrictive constitution, a constitution ratified in 1874. Our polling data show continued strong sentiment against lifting the most important of the constitutional restrictions imposed on state government, namely, restrictions on the governor's legal authority. Moreover, they express this opposition in the face of rapid changes in the socioeconomic situation within the state, and despite the fact that (like Americans generally) Arkansans have recently refocused their trust from the national level of government to the state and local levels.

The governmental inefficiency in Arkansas seems to be viewed not as a reason for replacing or revising the state's archaic Constitution of 1874, but rather the reason for maintaining it. As long as state government remains disorganized, inefficient, and therefore weak, state officeholders cannot do much harm, regardless of whether their names be Rector, Sevier, and Conway, or Powell and John Clayton, or Clark, McCuen, and Tucker.

Our data strongly support (although do not conclusively prove) the interpretation that the long history of Arkansas elites governing in their own interests has given rise to a public distrust of its elites, which is probably the key to understanding why Arkansans continue to refuse to approve wholesale constitutional changes. This (along with Democratic Party domination of the General Assembly) also may explain why the very recent publicity-seeking activities of the Arkansas Citizens' Commission to Streamline State Government (aka the Murphy Commission) have come to naught. Over the two-year period of 1997 to 1999, this reform group, consisting mainly of business elites, released numerous studies critical of the growth of state government bureaucracy, state taxation and spending levels, and specific state policy outputs,[33] all in the name of promoting governmental restructuring. Pointing out what is allegedly wrong with state government, however, does not earn any points for reform with Arkansas voters, who see the government's problems not structural but rather as a problem with the elites themselves.

Of course, distrust of government is an old antifederalist theme that is a part of the generic heritage of all Americans, including Arkansans, but distrust of elites is a populist theme that is a part of the specific heritage of Arkansans.[34] Even so, when convinced that it is in the public interest, Arkansans have been willing to approve specific changes to the 1874 Constitution—they have, after all, approved seventy-five amendments to it. Before any further attempts at major constitutional reforms are undertaken in Arkansas, professional students of opinion and political culture and political activists should thoroughly understand and take steps to sufficiently counter the legacies of distrust among Arkansans.

Appendix: Wording of Questions

Items drawn from May, 1998 statewide random digit dialed sample, UCA Social Science Microcomputer Laboratory.

1. "Who do you think is responsible for seeing to it that state laws and policies are implemented?" (open-ended)

"The governor"	32%
"The legislature"	22%
"The courts"	5%
"Law enforcement officials"	9%
"The people"	9%
"Other"	8%
"Don't know"	16%

N = 430

2. "Which state official is the chief executive of the state government?" (Interviewer: If respondent cannot reply, begin to read response categories to respondent.)

"Governor"	80%
"Lieutenant governor"	3%
"Attorney general"	3%
"Secretary of state"	1%
"Other"	1%
"Don't know"	12%

N = 432

3. "Does the governor have a cabinet consisting of the heads of the major departments?"

"Yes"	64%
"No"	11%
"Don't know/not sure" (combined)	25%

N = 433

4. "Currently the governor heads an executive branch made up of fifty-two agencies. Do you think this is too many agencies to manage?"

"Yes"	65%
"No"	23%
"Don't know/not sure" (combined)	12%

N = 433

5. "Who do you think appoints the heads of all of these executive agencies?" (Interviewer: Read response categories to respondents.)

"The governor appoints all"	63%
"Independent commissions appoint . . ."	2%
"Civil service selects . . ."	2%
"The legislature names . . ."	4%
"A combination of the above picks . . ."	15%
"Don't know"	14%

N = 431

6. "Who do you think should appoint the heads of these agencies?"

"The governor"	46%
"Independent commissions"	7%
"Civil service"	2%
"The legislature"	8%
"A combination of the above"	23%
"Don't know"	15%

N = 422

7. "Once the legislature has authorized funds to be spent, who should have the responsibility to see to it that those funds are spent as directed: the governor, or the head of the agency receiving the funds, or the legislators?"

"The governor"	21%
"The head of the agency"	32%
"The legislators"	24%
"All of these should be responsible"	15%
"Don't know/not sure" (combined)	7%

N = 430

8. "Currently the state's game and fish populations are managed by an independent commission. Should this commission answer to the governor?"

"Yes"   61%
"No"   29%
"Don't know"   9%
N = 429

9. "State highways are run by an independent commission. Should this commission answer to the governor?"

"Yes"   69%
"No"   26%
"Don't know"   5%
N = 428

10. "Members of the highway commission are appointed to serve for ten years. Do you think this term in office is too long?"

"Yes"   65%
"No"   30%
"Don't know"   5%
N = 426

11. "Do you think the state constitution should be amended in order to strengthen the powers of the governor's office, reduce the powers, or should they be left as they are?"

"Strengthen"   23%
"Reduce"   10%
"Leave as they are"   49%
"Don't know/not sure" (combined)   19%
N = 424

12. "Do you think that the state commissioner of lands should be elected, or appointed by the governor, or chosen some other way, or should the position be eliminated?"

"Elected"	45%
"Appointed by governor"	14%
"Chosen another way"	9%
"Eliminate the position"	17%
"Don't know/not sure" (combined)	15%
N = 424	

13. "Do you think that the state treasurer should be elected, or appointed by the governor, or chosen some other way, or should the position be eliminated?"

"Elected"	74%
"Appointed by governor"	13%
"Chosen another way"	7%
"Eliminate the position"	3%
"Don't know/not sure" (combined)	4%
N = 424	

14. "Do you think that the state auditor should be elected, or appointed by the governor, or chosen some other way, or should the position be eliminated?"

"Elected"	69%
"Appointed by governor"	12%
"Chosen another way"	9%
"Eliminate the position"	5%
"Don't know/not sure" (combined)	5%
N = 424	

15. "Do you think that the state attorney general should be elected, or appointed by the governor, or chosen some other way, or should the position be eliminated?"

"Elected"	79%
"Appointed by governor"	12%
"Chosen another way"	4%
"Eliminate the position"	2%
"Don't know/not sure" (combined)	3%

N = 424

16. "Do you think that the secretary of state should be elected, or appointed by the governor, or chosen some other way, or should the position be eliminated?"

"Elected"	78%
"Appointed by governor"	12%
"Chosen another way"	3%
"Eliminate the position"	3%
"Don't know/not sure" (combined)	5%

N = 424

17. "Currently it takes a majority vote in both houses of the legislature to override the governor's vetoes. Do you think it should require more than a majority, such as two-thirds of both houses, or remain as is?" (Interviewer: read response categories to respondent.)

"Require a majority (remain as is)"	52%
"Require more than majority, but less than two-thirds"	35%
"Require two-thirds or more"	7%
"Don't know"	6%

N = 422

III

Practicing Politics in Arkansas Politics and Government

Orval E. Faubus

Out of Socialism into Realism

ROY REED

*Gov. Orval E. Faubus was arguably the best loved, the most hated,
and, according to Roy Reed at least, the most misunderstood public figure of twentieth-century Arkansas. Influenced by the politics
of his father, a former secretary of the Madison County Socialist
Party, Faubus developed radical politics as a young man but
evolved quickly into one of a long line of Arkansas "hill-country
populists." In this essay Reed focuses on the political beliefs of the
six-term governor who, despite his socialist roots and his instrumental role in bringing New Deal–style liberalism to Arkansas,
will be forever defined by his part in the Little Rock Crisis of 1957
and the southern resistance to attempts to force desegregation of
public schools in the South.*

Orval E. Faubus was reared a liberal. His father, Sam Faubus, was a
Socialist who detested capitalism and bigotry with equal fervor. The son's
critics, myself included, have accused him through the years of selling
out the beliefs of his father on both race and economics. The story may
be less straightforward than that.

Orval Faubus came to power in Arkansas after World War II when
two things were happening:

First, the old Populist revolt that had inflamed the hills for several generations was burning itself out.[1] The end of Faubus's own radicalism coincided almost perfectly with the decline of radicalism among his people,
not only in the Ozarks but right across the southern uplands. Prosperity,

Roy Reed, "Orval Faubus: Out of Socialism into Realism," *Arkansas
Historical Quarterly* 54 (Spring 1995): 13–29. Reprinted with permission.

meager as it was, finally intruded into the hills and nudged out not only the Socialists like his father but also the intellectually tamer populists who had used their hill-country base to shower invective on the Delta planters and their establishment cohorts in banking, business, and industry. Resentment slowly began to give way to the other side of the populist coin, hope. Hope and appetite and a belief still current, vestigially populist: that our fellow hillbilly Sam Walton made it and, with a little luck, I can make it, too.

Second, a national phenomenon with far-reaching consequences was coming to a head during the 1950s. The racial equilibrium of the South was being extraordinarily disturbed, not merely by local agitation but more importantly by external forces that eventually would sweep away the entire breastwork of white supremacist defenses. The liberal Faubus might have thrown in with the national mood, a growing impatience with southern heel-dragging. Realistically, however, how much can he be blamed for choosing to be seen as defender of the local faith, no matter how little he shared that faith? What would have been the fate of a governor who chose the other side? Some of my heroes have argued that he could have exerted leadership for the rights of blacks and survived. Or that, at the least, he could have died an honorable political death.

Maybe so. But Orval Faubus had seen quite enough of honorable struggle for lost causes in his boyhood home. And there was something else. By the time he was grown, he had seen enough fear, loss, and death to last a lifetime.

Literally from the beginning, Orval Eugene Faubus's life was threatened. He weighed two-and-one-half pounds when he was born the night of January 7, 1910, and was so frail that the midwife expected him to die before morning. One night when he was a year old, he caught the croup and stopped breathing. His father rushed him outside into the cold air and plunged a finger into his throat to save his life. The toddler was just learning to talk when he wandered from the house and fell into a deep spring of water and somehow did not drown but climbed out just as his mother got there.

Danger continued to surround him as he grew and became part of the community. The year he was seven, one playmate died of diphtheria and another was crushed to death by a falling tree. During another year flux swept the community and killed two children in a neighboring family.

Life was not only perilous at Greasy Creek; it was also hard. Southern Madison County was like most of the Ozarks at that time. The residents scraped by. The towns had a small prosperity, but the countryside provided little more than subsistence. Rural people like the Faubuses raised almost all their food. Shoes and coats were practically luxuries because they had to be bought with cash, and cash was pitiably scarce. Even kerosene for the lamps was so dear that, after John D. Rockefeller cornered the market and raised the price, young Orval had to walk behind the wagon and carry the filled can the two miles from Combs to Greasy Creek, so as not to spill any—or so he recollected in 1964 when Rockefeller's grandson Winthrop tried to wrest the governorship of Arkansas from him.

Even granted that poverty and fear may be goads to ambition, it still seems extraordinary that a youngster could rise from such circumstances in such a place to be governor of his state, to keep the job longer than any other person, and to become a public figure known around the world.

Greasy Creek was, in every sense, the end of the road. Orval had to walk twelve miles to his first job across mountain trails; no roads went there from his home. Communication was primitive. News in Greasy Creek—that is, any report that reached beyond Madison County and the community grapevine—was limited to what certain elders deemed worth passing on from the occasional mail subscription to the Kansas City *Weekly Star* or the even rarer subscription to the *Arkansas Gazette* or the *Daily Oklahoman*. Politics was conducted almost entirely face-to-face, man-to-man, in a kind of slow-motion pulsation radiating from the county seat at Huntsville. Politics was also an important diversion, and there we have a clue to his escape and survival.

From his earliest years, young Orval carried a double burden of shyness and pride. He was not strong enough to excel in physical competition. He turned to the private world of words and found that he had a talent not only for language but also for retaining information. Through reading magazines and books, he learned of a world far different from the hillside farm of his father. He dreamed of entering that world.

There were two ways out for a young man of his background and temperament: teaching and politics. His mother and father together pushed the shy son toward the first. His father pushed him, perhaps unwittingly, toward the second.

John Samuel Faubus was anything but shy. He came from a large,

loud, sometimes boisterous family of fifteen children, counting stepsib-
lings. He claimed to have a fourth-grade education, but that was a flexible interpretation of the record. He once confessed that he had attended
only three or four months of school by age eleven and that he did not learn
to write until he was twenty, about the time he married. But before the
last of his seven children was born, Sam Faubus had become known as one
of the best-informed people in his part of Arkansas. The same year Orval
was born, Sam took the lead in one of the most baffling political movements in the history of the state. He and two friends signed up most of
the voting-age population on Greasy Creek as members of the Socialist
party.

   Not that socialism itself was baffling, although many people do not
appreciate how significant a hold it had on Arkansas at that time. The
southwestern states of Oklahoma, Louisiana, Texas, and Arkansas provided
a substantial vote for the Socialist party candidate for president, Eugene
V. Debs, in the election of 1912. The mystery is how Marxian socialism
penetrated to the fastnesses of Greasy Creek, twenty-five miles from the
nearest county seat, seventy years before the first pavement would be laid
on the one dirt road to the place. The best guess is that it was imported
by a gentlemanly old bachelor from the North, probably from Illinois, one
O. T. Green. After a sojourn in a boarding house at Combs, where his
socialist views caused a few embarrassing arguments, Green settled on a
small farm near Sam Faubus's place. He raised goats and peacocks, corresponded with Socialist acquaintances in other states, and befriended the
young neighbor whose inquiring mind intrigued him.[2]

   From whatever source, Socialist publications began to appear in the
Faubus household.[3] And Sam, once convinced that the big corporations
controlled the American economy and that capitalism was his enemy,
became an outspoken advocate of the socialist system. He and his friend
Arch Cornett, a teacher, wrote eloquent letters to the editor of the
Huntsville newspaper denouncing the entrenched interests.[4] Their concern spread to political reform; Sam circulated petitions calling for women's
suffrage, old-age pensions, and abolition of the vote-restricting poll tax.

   In May 1910 Sam and his friends formally established the Mill Creek
Local of the Socialist party. The charter from the state committee was
addressed to "the comrades of Combs" and carried the names of ten men,
four of them named Faubus. Whoever copied the names apparently
inverted Sam's initials so that he is listed as S. J. Faubus. The post of sec-

retary, carrying with it the responsibility of chief organizer, went to him. Arch Cornett, O. T. Green, and Sam Faubus became the most devoted members of the south Madison County local.[5]

As many as thirty people, including some from neighboring communities, might have been members of the Mill Creek Local at one time. The party had a majority of the adult residents of the Greasy Creek community. The local was large enough to provide the swing vote in district election contests between the Democrats and Republicans.[6] Madison County had at least two other thriving Socialist locals, one at Witter and the other at Kingston. Several other locals sprang up across the Ozarks.[7]

Sam and Arch joined other Socialists in opposing World War I. They almost went to prison for their troubles. Just before the war ended, the two men were arrested for distributing literature protesting the war. The charge was serious: violating the Alien and Sedition Act. Only the timely end of the war and the help of a good lawyer kept them out of the penitentiary. Sam has been referred to in recent years as an "old-time mountain Socialist." The designation suggests that people like Sam Faubus were too innocent to fully understand the implications of socialism. The old man would be indignant at that condescension if he were alive. It is probably true that the Socialists of the Southwest were less rigorous in the faith than their comrades in the industrial East. But they were apparently earnest in their attempt to change capitalism in the United States. Their hatred of Wall Street and capitalism was as intense as that of their hero Debs and any of the eastern Marxists.

Sam's interest in public affairs rubbed off on his eldest child. Orval read the Socialist party literature that came to the house. He even joined his father on at least one occasion when the two of them debated the merits of socialism with a pair of teachers at nearby Saint Paul.

In 1935, after he was married and had been teaching for several years, Orval indulged in his most serious flirtation with the political left. He hitchhiked to Commonwealth College, a labor self-help school near Mena, with the intention of gaining there the college education that he had not been able to afford elsewhere. The college comprised Socialists, Communists, labor organizers of various persuasions, and a smattering of unaffiliated idealists. They apparently had in common a conviction that the American economic system, then in collapse, was basically flawed.

How long Faubus remained on the campus has been disputed, but he was there long enough to give a May Day speech and be elected president of the student body. He says he never formally enrolled, but simply took part in campus activities in what sounds like a walk-on role.

Whatever the case, there is little doubt that young Faubus about that time began to develop a streak of political realism that was largely missing in his father. He shook the dust of Commonwealth from his feet after a few weeks or at most a few months. Instead of turning him into a crypto-Communist, as some of his later enemies put it, the close encounter with Marxism seems to have left him eventually disenchanted. It might be argued that the Commonwealth experience, far from producing a Communist subversive, was actually the beginning of a slow swing to the right that would send him into the conservative orbit more than twenty years later.

Back at Greasy Creek, Sam continued to urge socialism on his son. But Orval understood early that if he wanted a future in politics, a minority party with a radical reputation was not the way to go. And he was definitely interested in a political career.

Luckily, he was offered an alternative by national developments. Franklin D. Roosevelt was elected president in 1932. The New Deal, with its extensive social programs, co-opted some of the Socialist party's more appealing ideas. Orval became a New Dealer. Eventually, so did Sam.

Orval remained a Democrat, at least nominally, throughout his long career. He remained a liberal of declining intensity until his second term as governor.

Faubus entered public life just as his part of America, the South, was starting to revive after three-quarters of a century of lassitude. In the language of economics, the South was entering the take-off stage in 1940—just when young Faubus was proving himself in county politics and entering his own take-off stage.[8] He had been elected circuit clerk of his county in 1938 and had hopes of moving up to county judge—or even higher, with a little luck. Along with his growing success in politics, it would be his fate to come to maturity while his region was seeing its first real love affair with capitalism. The affair would bring greater prosperity to more people than the South had ever seen. It would also bring the evils of make-it-fast go-getterism: industrial pollution, runaway greed, corruption of institutions, and what is probably misnamed as conservatism in politics. As governor during the 1950s and 1960s, Faubus would preside over his state's immersion in all this, the good and the bad.

For starters, he plunged headily into the race for industrialization. He saw that the only way backward Arkansas could ever catch up with the rest of the country was to build a base of industrial production to balance the state's traditional and always uncertain agricultural base. He induced the conscience-ridden Baptist playboy Winthrop Rockefeller, who had fled to Arkansas to escape a disastrous marriage and his family's disapproval, to head up Arkansas's program for attracting industry. They made a good team, the compassionate capitalist and the Socialist-reared hillbilly. Steadily, out-of-state industry moved into the state and enriched its payroll. Faubus later estimated that one hundred and twenty-five thousand industrial jobs had been added during his twelve-year administration. The new industry also, in many cases, exploited the state's resources and fouled its air, water, and forests. Not much thought was given to regulation of industry in those days. A people who had never had any easy factory jobs—easy compared to subsistence farming—was not concerned with unfortunate consequences. Neither was the governor, except for a few notable instances when his Ozarks upbringing asserted itself, as it did, for example, when he threw in with the environmentalists and stopped the Corps of Engineers from damming the Buffalo River.

The business establishment of Little Rock was openly contemptuous of the country boy from Madison County when he first became governor. He swallowed his pride and set out to win them over. Within a year he had made peace with many of the capital's go-getters, including some who had held him up as a figure of amusement at posh cocktail parties. Even after he had made peace with them, many of the country club set continued for years to poke fun at his country speech and country ways.

Faubus never became a country clubber. He built his own set of affluent friends and associates. At the center of his set was another self-made man, a country boy who took his own revenge against the city sophisticates by simply piling up a larger fortune than any of them had. W. R. (Witt) Stephens was already a behind-the-scenes power in Arkansas politics when Faubus became governor. He and Faubus quickly formed an alliance of mutual benefit.

For Stephens the alliance provided friendly, profitable treatment from state agencies and administration allies in every institution from banks to the state legislature to scores of courthouses and city halls across the state. Early in 1957, when the state Supreme Court struck down a lucrative pricing arrangement for Stephens's Arkansas Louisiana Gas Company—one that Faubus's complaisant Public Service Commission had approved—the legislature, equally complaisant, overruled the court and passed a law reinstalling the pricing arrangement. The entire exercise, from the court decision to the governor's signature on the new law, took only a week. Stephens got the same friendly reception when his various enterprises needed official help on other matters. For example, bonds for municipalities, school districts, and other public bodies were almost always handled through Stephens, Inc., or one of its allies.

For Faubus the alliance provided vital support during the increasingly expensive election campaigns that he was obliged to run. Stephens not only contributed heavily to Faubus's campaigns, but he also cajoled, conned, and arm-twisted his many wealthy friends around the state and persuaded them to throw their collective weight behind Faubus. With the wealth of the Stephens combine behind him, Faubus became almost unbeatable. Faubus spread the benefits to his friends. An ally who headed the state Democratic party became the lawyer for a large Stephens gas company in Fort Smith.[9] A number of Faubus administration officials, including members of the governor's staff, became owners of cheap Ark-La stock before the stock price, inspired by action of the Public Service Commission, increased substantially.[10]

Among the most reluctant power bases to come around to Faubus was the Arkansas Power and Light Company. AP and L had had its way with the state's politics for many years. Gov. Francis A. Cherry had been the latest in a long series of public figures who had been in the utility's debt. He found the association so congenial that he raised no objection when AP and L, with customary arrogance but uncharacteristic ineptness, raised its electric rates during the 1954 election campaign. Faubus leapt on the issue. He had already come to the utility's attention as a gnat-like irritant several years earlier when he had had the gall to editorialize in his *Madison County Record* against the company and in favor of publicly owned electric cooperatives. Now that he was governor, Faubus knew that he could expect no favors from the power company.

The flexible Witt Stephens had become a Faubus man in a matter of hours after the voters turned out his man Cherry in the Democratic primary. The men who ran AP and L were more stiff-necked. It took a while for them to absorb the new reality. Within one eighteen-month period during Faubus's first term, the Public Service Commission—not yet dominated by him, but certainly alert to his growing power—granted two rate increases to Stephens's gas company. One of those allowed Stephens to sharply boost his rates to AP and L for the gas used in power generation. The power company objected, to no avail. During the same eighteen months, AP and L applied to the Public Service Commission for two increases of its own. It was turned down each time. When the power company persisted and applied a third time, the commission finally allowed it a fraction of its requested increase—just enough, it turned out, to pay for the rise in its gas bill. Witt Stephens made no secret of his satisfaction at lining his pockets with money from his adversaries at AP and L.

It can be argued that Faubus, with Stephens providing the goad, broke the generations-long dominance of AP and L over the state of Arkansas. Once the men in charge there understood their new situation, they lined up behind the hillbilly governor. Years later, Faubus could speak of the men at AP and L with friendly warmth. They became good corporate citizens, he said, with no discernible trace of triumph in his face.

There were many others from the moneyed establishment whom he came to count as supporters and, in some cases, social friends. They included builders, developers, insurance and real estate executives, bond dealers, road builders, heavy machinery sellers, printing company owners, newspaper publishers, and high-powered lawyers. They also included a disproportionate share of the wealthy landowners of the plantation country. These last helped to push the socialist-reared, egalitarian man from the hills in an unexpected direction on the most explosive domestic issue of the mid-twentieth century.

Race had been the defining quality in southern politics from the beginning. A dominant consideration of the white leaders of the deep South had been to assure the subordination of the black population. The issue might lie dormant for long years, then erupt when something threatened the racial equilibrium. Much of the middle and upper South was not dominated directly by the race issue, but such was the political strength and determination of the low-country black belt—"a skeleton holding together the South," V. O. Key called it—that all of the region was in its grip.[11]

The Populist revolt divided the hills from the black belt. The latter allied itself with the conservative business forces in the cities and towns to beat down the radicals flourishing in the hills. That schism continued into the twentieth century. Rebellion simmered in the uplands, but the lowlands seldom lost control of the state governments. Alabama might throw up a Hugo Black or a Jim Folsom, but the "big mules" of the cities and the planters of the black belt finally dominated. The same was true in Arkansas. The hills produced political figures of prominence—J. W. Fulbright, Brooks Hays, J. W. Trimble, Clyde Ellis, Sid McMath—but none of them succeeded without the support of the powerful forces of the Delta and their business allies. Any who resisted those forces were punished.

Faubus was the latest in a line of hill-country progressives. The Delta landowners were suspicious of him. In the early 1950s few questioned their ability to punish their opponents at the state capital. And yet there were signs that Arkansas was beginning to turn away from the Delta domination and toward a more racially neutral politics. Key, writing in the late 1940s, thought that Arkansas, along with Texas and Florida, seemed destined to develop a non-southern sort of politics, one no longer ruled by the negative influence of race.[12] On the other hand, there was no doubt that race still had the power to inflame large numbers of white voters, and not just in the lowlands. In Arkansas, Jim Johnson demonstrated as late as the gubernatorial campaign of 1956 that white feelings were still intense, especially in the wake of the 1954 Supreme Court decision requiring school desegregation. Indeed, it was Johnson's strong showing against him in 1956 that persuaded Faubus to pay more attention to the voice from the Delta.

But if anyone had been listening for nuance and not simply volume in that voice, he might have detected a note of weakness and even desperation. From the beginning it had been the white fear of being overrun by blacks that had inspired the success of the Delta's political oppression. The term black belt referred to a swath of southern counties where African Americans had a majority of the population. Arkansas, admittedly one of the least "threatened" states, had fifteen counties with black majorities in 1900. That number declined steadily as the century wore on: eleven in 1920, then nine in 1940.[13] By 1950 the state had only six counties where blacks predominated.[14] Yet those six counties, relying on the racism of varying virulence to be found in Little Rock and elsewhere, effectively imposed their politics of race on the other sixty-nine counties. Looking back across these forty years, racial fear seems to have been given more authority than it deserved. Alongside the numerical decline in the black "threat," the state was becoming increasingly urban and presumably more politically sophisticated. It was also poised to industrialize and prosper. Altogether, Arkansas was just at the take-off stage in both politics and economics and might have been expected finally to cast off the burden of racial politics. Thanks to a convergence of currents, national and local, it did not.

What happened is well known. The Little Rock School District was ready to desegregate its first public school in the fall of 1957. A few other Arkansas districts, bowing to the Supreme Court's *Brown* decision of 1954, had already taken that step, and Faubus had accepted their decisions. He balked at Little Rock. Saying he had reason to fear violence if the plan went forward, he ordered out the National Guard to block the nine black pupils assigned to Central High. President Dwight D. Eisenhower sent army troops to suppress segregationist mobs, protect the black youngsters, and enforce the authority of the federal courts that had ordered desegregation. The event dominated headlines for months, not only in Arkansas but around the world. Faubus, by forcing the federal government to intervene first in Little Rock and then in other places around the South, probably hastened the end of the southern resistance to black civil rights. His action also ensured him six two-year terms as governor and earned him a reputation, fairly or not, as a sellout to the politics of fear that had been exploited long and effectively by the Delta planters.

It might be argued that Orval Faubus captured the Delta as certainly as the Delta captured him; that the influence of the lowlands was on the wane, and that this canny hill man stepped in at the historically propitious moment and took over the whole state, the Delta included. Not much stretch of his sympathies was required. He had always felt warmly toward the poor people of his own section. It was easy to include the poor white people of the Delta, along with their betters, in his affections. That his sympathies were not expansive enough to include a public declaration of friendship for the poor black people of the Delta might have seemed to him a small price to pay. In any event, a kind of regional harmony ensued that Arkansas had not seen since the swamps were slashed and burned and turned into plantations, to be worked and in a perverse way dominated by slaves and the fear they engendered. For the first time, lowlanders and hill people were not competing for control of the capital. They shared control of the governor's office and, through the harmony Faubus imposed, the legislature as well.

The race issue, after its last sensational eruption in 1957, finally lost its grip on the Arkansas mind. With the election of Winthrop Rockefeller, the aberrant moderate Republican who succeeded Faubus, the black population pretty well ceased to exercise the power of fear that it had had on the state's politics throughout its history. Black voters achieved this paradoxic loss of control through the happy circumstance of becoming important in the state's electoral system. They had voted in some numbers for several years, but those in the Delta had had no real choice on election day. Rockefeller brought blacks into the system in large numbers, voting more or less freely and in any case jubilantly, although there were those who claimed that the millionaire New Yorker voted his blacks as surely as any Delta planter ever had. The difference was this: Rockefeller made it worthwhile financially, in some cases, to vote right; the old planter voting his field hands had made voting right a condition of employment.

Before Rockefeller, no statewide candidate who was perceived as soft on the Negro question could attain and hold office if any creditable opponent insisted on exploiting that softness. Since Rockefeller, no candidate has achieved any lasting success without the approval of black voters. Interestingly enough, that change began during the last years of Faubus's administration. He quietly achieved a rapprochement with many black leaders, including L. C. Bates, the husband of his old nemesis, Daisy Bates, who led the Arkansas branch of the National Association for the Advancement of Colored People. L. C. Bates frequently offered advice to Faubus during the mid-1960s, and on at least one occasion, according to Faubus, urged him to run for re-election.[15] The Faubus administration also supported a reform of the voter registration laws that paved the way for relieving the Delta planters of the burden of buying thousands of poll tax receipts and trucking all those black workers to the polls every election day.

Faubus accommodated to the prevailing political realities as he saw them. He continued into old age to insist that he was a true liberal, meaning a New Dealer. But he kept up a running flirtation with Republicans and conservatives during the decades following his tenure in office. He offered advice to such Republicans as John Connally of Texas and Rep. John Paul Hammerschmidt of Arkansas.[16] He had friendly contacts with the Nixon White House and expressed his gratification that Nixon had carried Arkansas in 1972.[17] He was friendly with the conservative administration of Harding College, a Searcy, Arkansas, institution connected to the Church of Christ.[18] He was active in the presidential campaign of George C. Wallace in 1968.

Did Faubus betray his father's idealism when he abandoned the left wing and opted for the more conservative mainstream? This is a more difficult question than it appears to be at a glance. Answering it requires going beyond historical evidence and making a speculative leap of judgment. The heart of the question is this: What kind of Socialist was Sam Faubus? Was he a revolutionary Marxist who would have been at home in Eastern Europe? Or was his socialism more American, that is, more diluted? Even some of America's Socialists were fairly dedicated Marxists; was Sam one of those? If Sam Faubus wanted to overthrow the American capitalist system and install a government-controlled economy, then how could he bear to see his famous son become an established part of the system he hated? But if Sam was actually a Populist who liked to call himself a Socialist, then his son's success would have pleased him.

While the more determined Socialists worked for a fundamental change in the economic system, many Populists merely raged against its inequities. Remove whatever was causing them a momentary discontent—unfair banking practices, railroad domination, trusts—and large numbers of the populist farmers would subside and let capitalism go on its way.[19]

It is hard to know what to make of Sam's beliefs. They probably fell somewhere between populist and socialist. On the one hand, he could write with apparent earnestness, after Franklin D. Roosevelt became president, "This country is owned and controlled by a few bankers and other capitalists and the quicker Mr. Roosevelt takes over all industry the better it will be for the country."[20] During the same season, his friend and fellow Socialist Arch Cornett was denouncing private ownership by "the few" of mines, mills, shops, storehouses, transportation lines, steamship lines, and electric light and water systems.[21] Whether these Madison County Socialists seriously advocated government ownership of those enterprises is not clear, but it seems fair to infer that they did.

On the other hand, southwestern Socialists like these, while generally more emotionally volatile than their comrades in other regions, tended to be less intellectually doctrinaire.[22] At times, it appeared that they would have been satisfied with a throughgoing reform, rather than a radical rebuilding, of the economic and political system. They were a little like their hero Eugene V. Debs. He embraced socialism gradually, like a swimmer entering a spring-fed pool. Debs had begun as a Democrat and a craft unionist. Then he supported the Populist Party in 1896 before joining Victor L. Berger to organize the Social Democratic Party. That was the forerunner of the Socialist Party, on whose platform he ran four times for

president. The Socialists of Arkansas, Texas, Oklahoma, and Missouri idol-
ized the fiery but undoctrinaire Debs.[23]

The platform of Arkansas's own Socialist Party contained the usual
railings against an unjust economic system, but it also carried a number
of reform ideas that in time would be considered middle of the road.
Socialists here opposed the death penalty and corruption in elections. They
favored the initiative and referendum, women's suffrage, and the graduated income tax.[24] Sam Faubus worked hard for those reforms. How hard
he would have fought in an armed revolution to overthrow the government is anybody's guess. I think he would stopped far short of that. He
was willing to go to prison for his beliefs when he agitated against World
War I—and almost did—but I have trouble seeing him at the barricades
trying to bring down the government of Calvin Coolidge. Once Roosevelt
launched the New Deal, which ameliorated some of the discontents that
Sam had suffered, he became a New Dealer. By the time of John F.
Kennedy's presidency, he was an enthusiastic Democrat.

Orval became as devoted a New Dealer as his father. The New Deal
may seem quaint to today's young liberals, but in its time it stirred fierce
emotions. Those emotions had not subsided entirely by the time Orval
Faubus became governor. He spent substantially of his political capital to
move Arkansas along in its own version of the New Deal, a movement
that had been pursued fitfully in the state during the previous twenty
years. Faubus most notably stood up to powerful forces—including those
of the Delta—and pushed through the legislature a 50 percent increase
in the sales tax to finance improved education and other state services.
He brought more compassion to the state welfare system. He was generally friendly to labor. He spent state funds generously to improve the lot
of the mentally ill and retarded. These and other accomplishments are
what he had in mind when he described himself as a true liberal as
opposed to the present-day liberal who is concerned—unduly, Faubus
believed—with the rights of various cultural, racial, ethnic, and sexual
minorities.

One final question remains: If Orval Faubus did not betray his father
and the father's idealism, did he then betray his own class? Probably not.
The populist, hill-country class that he came from is always ready to for-
give the person who escapes it. Far from seeing escape as betrayal of one's
fellows, as it was and to some extent remains in the more class-encrusted
nations of Europe, rising from one's class is seen with approval in

America. David A. Shannon put it this way: "Americans have generally believed it easier and more desirable to rise *from* their class rather than *with* their class."[25] Orval Faubus escaped into the world he had dreamed of as a boy, a world of fame, power, and material comfort. He never came close to entering the traditional establishment, but there is no doubt that he learned to traffic with the capitalists and power brokers that his father had hated. It could be argued that far from betraying his class, he fulfilled its secret yearnings.

Noblesse Oblige and Practical Politics

Winthrop Rockefeller and the Civil Rights Movement

CATHY KUNZINGER URWIN

As the first Republican to serve as governor of Arkansas (1967–71) since Reconstruction, a transplant from New York, and a member of one of the most prominent families in America, Winthrop Rockefeller has generated more than his share of attention from the scholarly community. In this essay, Urwin focuses on Rockefeller's attitudes toward race and his actions during two terms as Arkansas's governor during the early years of the civil rights movement. Her assertion that Rockefeller's personal commitment to civil rights was long-standing and genuine is hardly controversial. She attributes this commitment to both his family's established support for racial tolerance and to his membership in the liberal wing of the GOP, long committed to equal opportunity and racial justice.

The author then turns to Rockefeller's actions as governor, focusing on the goal of desegregating the state's public schools and "busing" as a public policy tool to aid in achieving that goal. With reference to these issues, she considers Rockefeller's civil rights record "erratic." But she also argues that, in the Arkansas of the 1960s, his overall position on race relations was liberal, and that, in the words of a contemporary, Rockefeller made racial toleration "acceptable and respectable in Arkansas."

On Sunday, April 7, 1968, Arkansas Gov. Winthrop Rockefeller stood hand-in-hand with black leaders on the steps of the state capitol and sang

Cathy Kunzinger Urwin, "*Noblesse Oblige* and Practical Politics: Winthrop Rockefeller and the Civil Rights Movement," *Arkansas Historical Quarterly* 54 (Spring 1995): 30–52. Reprinted with permission.

"We Shall Overcome." Approximately three thousand people, two-thirds of whom were black, had gathered at this prayer service to remember Dr. Martin Luther King Jr., slain three days earlier in Memphis. In his eulogy the governor asked the assembled crowd to "not forget that we are all creatures of God." Rockefeller was the only southern governor to publicly eulogize King in the days following the assassination.[1]

Winthrop Rockefeller was unique in Arkansas history. Elected in 1966 and reelected in 1968, he was the state's first Republican governor since Reconstruction. But it was in the field of civil rights that Rockefeller made one of his greatest contributions to the state's history. It was not political expediency that moved Rockefeller to adopt the cause of civil rights. In fact, he repeatedly downplayed his association with civil rights during his political career in Arkansas in order to avoid alienating the segregationist vote. Winthrop Rockefeller championed the cause of civil rights because he was raised to do so. Helping to advance African American rights, particularly in education, was a family tradition. John D. Rockefeller, Winthrop's grandfather, made his first gift to African-American education in June 1882, when he gave two hundred and fifty dollars to the Atlanta Female Baptist Seminary, a school for black women. On Winthrop's paternal grandmother's side, the fight to uplift African Americans predated the Civil War. As a girl, Laura Spelman Rockefeller, with her family, helped runaway slaves as part of the Underground Railroad. Atlanta Female Baptist Seminary was renamed Spelman College in 1884 in honor of Laura's parents. John D. Rockefeller continued to give money and land to both Spelman College and its counterpart for men, Morehouse College.[2]

This family commitment to African American causes intensified in succeeding generations. Winthrop's father, John D. Rockefeller Jr., was one of the founders of the United Negro College Fund. The Rockefeller family became involved with the National Urban League in 1921. Winthrop joined the executive board in 1940 and in 1947 became chairman of the Urban League Service Fund's corporate division.[3] In 1952 he donated Standard Oil of California stock worth approximately one hundred thousand dollars for the purpose of purchasing a league headquarters building. Rockefeller's connection to the National Urban League, actively and financially, continued until his death.[4]

Rockefeller involved himself in other civil rights issues and organizations long before he ever thought of moving to Arkansas. In 1936, while learning the oil business in Texas, he tried unsuccessfully to establish a local community health organization that would be run by blacks for blacks. His interest had been aroused when his black maid suffered an appendicitis attack. Through a letter to his father, Rockefeller enlisted the aid of both the Rockefeller Foundation and the Rosenwald Foundation, but ultimately failed because of disinterest on the part of the white trustees of the local black hospital.[5]

Rockefeller toured the United States for the secretary of war in 1946, surveying veterans' readjustment problems. James "Jimmy" Hudson, a black private detective from Harlem who had been working for Winthrop since 1937, accompanied him. At each stop on the tour, Hudson collected data on the problems faced by black veterans, and this information was incorporated into the final report. In the report Rockefeller stated that the black veteran faced great difficulty reverting to civilian life because "his color nullifies the fact that he is a veteran." The report asked the armed forces to help combat racial prejudice at home.[6]

Throughout the late 1940s and early 1950s, Rockefeller promoted the cause of fair employment practice legislation both in federal employment and in American industry. In a 1952 speech to the National Urban League Conference, he called fair employment practice legislation a "very useful tool" against discrimination. He called for an educational campaign to awaken people to the immorality and economic waste of racial discrimination.[7]

In 1953 Winthrop Rockefeller moved to Arkansas, and while he may have changed his state of residence, the causes and values he championed did not change. His move south was closely followed by the events that have been heralded as the start of the modern civil rights movement: the Supreme Court decision *Brown v. Board of Education* and the Montgomery, Alabama, bus boycott. Gov. Orval Faubus appointed Rockefeller the first chairman of the Arkansas Industrial Development Commission (AIDC) in 1955, and the following year Rockefeller warned publicly that southern opposition to integration would have a negative effect on industrialization.[8] Those words would prove prophetic in 1957 when Little Rock became the site of one of the most significant desegregation cases of the modern era—the Central High Crisis. When Governor Faubus used the Arkansas National Guard to prevent the integration of Central High by nine African American students, he forced a very reluctant President Eisenhower to send the 101st Airborne Division to the school to protect the nine students. A month after the crisis began, Rockefeller issued a statement that the crisis was damaging industry. In fact, not one major firm moved to Little Rock in the three years following the crisis.[9]

The Central High Crisis gives a clear indication of how important segregation was to white voters in Arkansas. Orval Faubus got what he wanted out of the crisis—a third term as governor—making him the first to win a third term in fifty years. The voters of Little Rock closed the city's high schools for the entire 1958–59 school year rather than continue integration. And seven-term congressman Brooks Hays, who had tried unsuccessfully to reach a compromise between Eisenhower and Faubus, was defeated in his bid for reelection in 1958 by a segregationist write-in candidate who announced his campaign just one week before the election.[10] These lessons would not be lost on Rockefeller when he decided not long afterward to become actively involved in his adopted state's politics.

Nineteen sixty-four was an important year in the history of American race relations. The Twenty-fourth Amendment to the United States Constitution was ratified, abolishing the poll tax. Three civil rights workers were murdered in Mississippi, and President Lyndon Johnson pressed the Civil Rights Act through Congress. In Arkansas Winthrop Rockefeller ran for the first time as a Republican candidate for governor.

Rockefeller did not win the 1964 election, but garnered 43 percent of the vote against incumbent Orval Faubus. Race was an issue that Faubus used successfully against Rockefeller. Rockefeller's involvement with the National Urban League and his family's history of interracial philanthropy were well known. A preelection poll showed that compared with the 49 percent of the voters statewide who felt that Faubus could do the best job of keeping racial peace in Arkansas, only 28 percent thought Rockefeller most likely to do so.[11] Rockefeller was very careful not to come out in favor of integration. The 1964 Arkansas Republican party platform mentioned the illegality of separate schools, but called for correcting the inequality in funding for these separate schools, which, "it is realistic to assume" would "exist for years to come." The only mention in the platform of civil rights was a statement that "human relations problems can best be solved on the local level and, in this area, the greatest permanent progress can be made through patient, good-faith, voluntary action rather than through violence, coercive legislation or court order."[12]

In part, the carefully worded appeal for voluntary gradualism in the 1964 Republican party platform was political, but it must be noted that it also reflected Winthrop Rockefeller's own philosophy. Rockefeller opposed the 1964 Civil Rights Act on the grounds that it granted extraordinary powers to the executive branch of government.[13] He believed that in the long run, moral persuasion would be much more effective in bringing about racial equality. Rockefeller learned racial justice from his parents at least thirty years before the modern civil rights movement began. In the context of the 1960s, therefore, he was not a liberal. He did not believe in giving blacks any special favors to correct existing injustices but rather providing them the opportunity and education to compete on an equal footing with whites.

Rockefeller ran for governor again in 1966, this time against "Justice Jim" Johnson, a hard-core segregationist and one of the founders of Arkansas's White Citizens Council. Johnson did not back away from his segregationist views, but by 1966 most white Arkansans had accepted the existence of the civil rights movement and the futility of trying to stop it. Johnson's extremism was certainly a major factor in Rockefeller's victory. This was the first gubernatorial election under the new voter registration system, which eliminated block purchases of poll tax receipts, and approximately 90 percent of Arkansas's black voters cast their ballots for Rockefeller. But Rockefeller also defeated Johnson in about half of the state's rural counties, where segregationist support had traditionally been greatest.[14]

Rockefeller's years as governor, 1967–71, coincided with vast changes in the direction, tone, and goals of the civil rights movement. Largely because of those changes, Rockefeller found greater success in working for and with the black community in Arkansas during his first term in office than he would find during his second. As governor, Rockefeller's main emphasis was on creating an equal playing field, to create an atmosphere in the state where blacks and whites would be considered solely on merit rather than race. This meant giving black Arkansans a voice in government by appointing them to state boards and commissions and hiring blacks for positions of power, not just the traditional custodial jobs.

High on the list of the new governor's priorities was the creation of a Human Resources Commission, the purpose of which would be to determine if the state was discriminating on the basis of race. Rockefeller attempted to have this commission created as an agency of the executive branch by the Sixty-sixth General Assembly in its regular 1967 session. The bill creating the commission passed the House, but was tabled by a voice vote in the Senate. When it was brought up in the Senate, one member inquired: "Isn't that that civil rights bill?"[15] Undeterred, Rockefeller created the Governor's Council on Human Resources by executive order in June 1967. The council first met that September; its goal was to upgrade "the employment opportunities available to our people, and make the best possible use of the state's human resources."[16] But, as John Ward, Rockefeller's public relations director and biographer noted, "the organization, for all its high purposes, never did much."[17] The council, created by executive order and not legislation, had no enforcement power; its purpose was to advise and recommend. By publicizing its goals, it could provide moral support and encouragement to those who already believed in its goals and advice to those with the power to change the status quo, but it could do little more.[18] In June 1968 Rockefeller appointed an African American, Ozell Sutton, as executive director of the Governor's Council on Human Resources. Sutton, a native Arkansan, took a one-year leave of absence from his job with the United States Justice Department to work for Rockefeller. Sutton tried unsuccessfully to obtain legislative authorization for the council. He also focused on improving relations between the police and the minority community through a suggested "Code of Conduct" sent to Arkansas chiefs of police, and worked hard within the executive branch to increase minority appointments and state jobs.[19]

Rockefeller dramatically improved the number of blacks appointed to state boards and commissions. Prior to his election the only boards or commissions with any minority representation were those dealing with black institutions or those with federal financing where pressure from Washington made minority representation necessary.[20]

By far the most dramatic change came in Arkansas's draft boards. Rockefeller nominated Col. Willard A. Hawkins as state director of the Selective Service of Arkansas in January 1967. One of Colonel Hawkins's primary goals was to put minority representation on Arkansas's draft boards, which to that point had had none. Although the selective service was a federal agency, it was up to the governor and Hawkins to nominate members of the local draft boards and the two state appeals boards. Like the Hawkins appointment, those nominations would then be approved by the president. By October 1969, forty-eight African Americans and one Asian American were on local boards, and one African American sat on each of the two appeals boards. More than 85 percent of Arkansas's minority population was under the jurisdiction of local draft boards.[21] Integrating draft boards was relatively easy, since no one in Arkansas (that is, the State Senate) had to approve the appointments aside from Hawkins and Rockefeller. However, there was opposition, much of which came from members of Arkansas's Republican Party. Their objections rested on their view of selective service board appointments as political patronage plums awarded at the discretion of the Republican Party county chairmen. In a long December 1968 letter to the executive director of the Arkansas Republican Party, Hawkins explained that while he was "most happy to receive any recommendations for appointments at any time from county chairmen or others in the county," he had other considerations and responsibilities. These included not only his and Rockefeller's commitment to integrating the draft boards, but also the reality of seeing that "the coming legislature work[s] in harmony with the administration." In other words, the predominantly Democratic legislators needed to be consulted regarding appointments in their counties in exchange for their support for the governor's legislative program.[22] In spite of the political realities, the integration of Arkansas's draft boards was the most successful of Rockefeller's attempts to bring blacks into state government.

In November 1969 Rockefeller named William "Sonny" Walker head of the state Office of Economic Opportunity, making Walker the first black department head in Arkansas and the first black state OEO director in the South. Walker publicly admitted that it was "lonely" being the first and resigned after one year in office, citing other job offers as well as the refusal of the Legislative Council to increase his salary—a salary that was paid in federal funds and was the lowest in the region for a state OEO director. The council authorized a salary, also federally funded, $1,680 higher than Walker's for his assistant. Walker told the press that one legislator had remarked that "$15,000 was too much to pay a nigger."[23]

In terms of hiring blacks to fill white collar jobs in state government, Rockefeller was often criticized for not doing more. More than one year after assuming the governorship, Rockefeller publicly admitted that discrimination against blacks in state offices did exist. Although in 1968 blacks represented 21.9 percent of the population, they held less than 3 percent of the seventeen thousand available state jobs.[24] Rockefeller refused to order department heads to hire more blacks, relying instead on "persuasion and leadership."[25] Even Colonel Hawkins, with his impressive record of integrating draft boards, had no black employees in his office until January 1968.[26]

Rockefeller's refusal to impose hiring quotas on state department heads created a situation in which long-standing prejudices would often win out. Rockefeller's first director of the Office of Economic Opportunity, appointed in January 1967, was Glen Jermstad, an influential member of the state Republican Party. In August 1967 Jermstad fired a black employee of the agency whose employment had preceded Rockefeller's election. An investigation by the regional Office of Economic Opportunity followed, revealing that the fired employee had a valid case in claiming discrimination. Though the black man was told there was no place for him in the proposed reorganization of the office, as he lacked the "background or the qualifications," the white employee who was retained and given the job in the OEO's department of education had far fewer qualifications. The fired black employee had a college degree and twenty-five years teaching experience, while the white man had no degree and had been a grocer. In spite of attempts to involve Rockefeller, the case still had not been resolved in May 1968.[27]

The lack of blacks in state jobs was a major topic of a meeting between the governor and approximately thirty leaders of the African American community held on April 9, 1968, in the wake of Dr. Martin Luther King Jr.'s death, as an attempt to prevent violent reaction to the assassination. At the meeting Rockefeller acknowledged that more needed to be done to improve the number of blacks hired by state agencies and promised to look into charges of discrimination by local State Employment Security Division offices but once again backed off from any promises to force state agencies to hire blacks.[28] During the 1968 campaign Rockefeller was criticized by Dr. Jerry Jewell, head of the Arkansas NAACP. Jewell told the *New York Times* that the black vote would not be a sure thing for Rockefeller, stating "He hasn't come out for the Negro. He could have done so much." Regarding the governor's black appointments, Jewell said "Sure it's a 'new thing,' but they're nothing but pets. We have more than our share of Toms."[29]

By 1969 the frequent pressures of black leadership had begun to pay off. The state revenue commissioner promised to fire any employee who discriminated in hiring practices and to adopt a system whereby all people would be notified of revenue office job openings rather than continuing the practice of making appointments to these jobs based on political patronage.[30]

The middle to late 1960s saw an eruption of urban riots and violent protests across the nation as the civil rights movement turned its attention from legal segregation to economic discrimination, hopelessness, and despair. Though protests in Arkansas did not compare to the death and destruction of Watts or Detroit, the state saw its share of protests. As governor, Rockefeller usually found himself involved in these disturbances. Following the death of Martin Luther King Jr., on April 4, 1968, riots flared up in 110 cities across the United States. Aside from a minor disturbance in Pine Bluff, Arkansas avoided the violence at that time, largely because of Rockefeller's own involvement in the memorial service at the state capitol. The service had been held at the suggestion of Rockefeller's wife, Jeannette Edris Rockefeller, following a request by black leaders for a marching permit. It is also important to note that while the service may have prevented violence, Rockefeller's presence created problems for him among some white Republicans.[31]

Little Rock did experience several days of violence in August 1968 after an eighteen-year-old black youth was killed by a white trusty at the Pulaski County Penal Farm. The trusty was charged with manslaughter. Rockefeller called out the National Guard and imposed a curfew on the county. The disturbances ended after a few days.[32]

The largest and most significant racial disturbances to take place during Rockefeller's governorship occurred not in Little Rock, but in Forrest City, a town approximately forty miles west of Memphis. Forrest City in 1969 had a population of fourteen thousand, 50 percent of whom were black. White intransigence to racial equality was especially strong in eastern Arkansas, a legacy of the plantation system. The black population of Forrest City itself had increased in recent years as mechanization forced tenant farmers into town in search of industrial jobs. In 1968 members of the John Birch Society gained control of the Forrest City school board, and in March the district fired, with no explanation, Rev. J. F. Cooley, a black, who had taught for eleven years at the city's all-black Lincoln Junior–Senior High. Cooley's problems seem to have stemmed from his activities in the civil rights movement. In December 1968 Cooley, along with Rev. Cato Brooks Jr., formed the Committee for Peaceful Coexistence with the purpose of better expressing black grievances to the white community. Cooley had also helped organize peaceful demonstrations and worked with young black males to prevent juvenile delinquency. In January the school board dismissed Cooley as black juvenile probation officer, a position he had held for eight years. After Cooley's March dismissal from his teaching position, junior high students vandalized Lincoln, breaking every window in the building, tearing down lockers and vending machines, and scattering debris in the halls. Cooley publicly condemned the riot, and Rockefeller called in the state police. Four youths were sentenced to juvenile training schools.[33]

The March incident was the beginning of a long year in Forrest City. In April the Committee for Peaceful Coexistence issued a list of ten grievances against the "community power structure," and asked for assistance from federal and state civil rights groups. The Forrest City mayor's reaction was that "They're just like all these groups. They can't come up with anything."[34] The mayor's response helps illustrate why change was so slow in coming to Forrest City; the white community refused to see that any inequities existed. A grand jury empanelled to investigate the Lincoln school riot failed "to conceive any justification for either the riot in March or a student walkout in April."[35]

Racial tension continued unabated throughout the summer, fed by the threat of a "poor people's march" from Forrest City to Little Rock. The march, scheduled for August 20 to 24, was meant to "dramatize outdated conditions black people are forced to live in throughout the state of Arkansas," according to its organizer, Brooks.[36] Rockefeller became directly involved, holding a meeting on August 6 with leaders from both sides of Forrest City's community. Rockefeller hoped to prevent the march by offering to travel to Forrest City with state department heads in an attempt to "find some solutions to problems that have been aggravating."[37] The governor went to Forrest City as promised and also met twice with Brooks before the minister agreed on August 19, to postpone the march because the governor needed time to make good on his promises of change and because the level of racial tension and fear of the marchers on the part of whites "makes it dangerous at this time."[38] Rockefeller, prior to his August 19 meeting with Brooks, consulted with department heads as promised and issued a lengthy response to Brooks's complaints and requests. These complaints centered around the absence of equal opportunity and racial parity in both state services and jobs.[39]

Rockefeller had been under enormous pressure from various groups to see to it that the "poor people's march" did not take place—especially the State Police, who feared outbreaks of violence along the marchers' route, and prominent Republicans, who had objected to Rockefeller's meeting with Brooks, preferring that the governor meet with Forrest City's "good Negroes," blacks the white community was willing to accept.[40]

Despite the pressure and Rockefeller's apparent success on August 19, the march did take place as scheduled, but with different leadership. Renamed a "walk against fear," and beginning in West Memphis, it was led by Lance "Sweet Willie Wine" Watson, the leader of a militant Memphis group called the Invaders. Watson had been in Forrest City at the invitation of Brooks, helping to organize a summer boycott of white businesses by the town's black population. While Brooks had promised to arm his marchers only with prayer books, Watson told the press that he and his group would "survive and defend ourselves if necessary."[41] Rockefeller urged all Arkansans, black and white, to "completely ignore the marchers," and declared a state of emergency in Prairie County, where violent white reaction seemed most likely. The marchers were escorted by plainclothes state policemen, and although Watson had promised a marching force two hundred strong, only five people accompanied him. The march ended without incident in Little Rock on August 24.[42]

The march aggravated the racial climate in Forrest City, and several incidents in the week that followed made it much worse. After two white women were raped, allegedly by black youths, and several members of Watson's Invaders were arrested for beating, stabbing, and robbing a white grocery store clerk, a white protest erupted in violence. Between five hundred and one thousand whites gathered in front of City Hall, beating at least seven people, including Watson. Rockefeller declared a state of emergency and sent in the National Guard to prevent further violence. One white businessman told the *New York Times* that what the crowd wanted was "for the police to shoot some Negroes. And while they know that can't be, they do demand some show of force, and it's all very frustrating."[43] Not a single white was arrested as a result of the incident, but Watson was charged with and convicted of disorderly conduct. In September, following protests and boycotts by white students at the junior and senior high schools, the school board closed Forrest City's schools "indefinitely," but reopened them after four days.[44] Racial unrest and fear continued in Forrest City, Rockefeller having been unable to find a middle ground that would appease the many factions within the community. But a study of the unrest in Forrest City by a non-profit group called the Race Relations Information Center praised Rockefeller for "repeatedly putting himself on record in favor of equal opportunity and justice."[45]

Many of Forrest City's problems revolved around the schools. The 1954 *Brown v. Board of Education* decision declaring "separate but equal" schools unconstitutional had not ended segregation. Southern schools frequently adopted one of two methods to meet the letter of the law, while ignoring the spirit of it. One was gradualism, desegregating a few children at a time, as in the Little Rock Central High case of 1957. The other, and most common, was "freedom of choice" integration, as at Forrest City. Students, both white and black, were free to attend whatever school they wanted to. But few whites were likely to choose to attend an academically and physically inferior black school, while few blacks were willing to accept the social isolation and harassment that went with being one of the few to attend the white schools. In Forrest City the black schools were still all black in 1969, while the white schools were approximately 83 percent white.[46]

Rockefeller did not publicly condemn freedom of choice integration, in spite of the fact that it was an obvious attempt at avoidance. The governor was under tremendous pressure, even before his election, to allow school districts to maintain local control over desegregation. And Rockefeller himself had disagreed with the 1964 Civil Rights Act, considering it too vague, with too much power concentrated in the executive branch of the federal government.[47] During the 1966 gubernatorial election, Rockefeller's advisors urged him to support legal assistance for school districts fighting the federal government's guidelines for integration, either personally or as governor. Considering the nature of the statements being suggested, Rockefeller's public statement of August 30 was relatively mild. He expressed disapproval for the "Federal Guidelines as they exist today" but suggested that the remedy lay in electing to Congress "those candidates who will reflect the attitude of the people."[48]

In the May 1968 special session of the Arkansas General Assembly, Rockefeller supported a bill that would permit the state to help pay the legal costs of school districts fighting integration in the courts. The legal fund had first been established in 1959, but required reappropriation each legislative session. The regular session of the General Assembly in 1967 had passed Act 655, reimbursing up to 50 percent of the expenses incurred in 1965 and 1966. Almost all of the money went to the Little Rock law firm of Smith, Williams, Friday, and Bowen, which handled most of the desegregation lawsuits and drew up the new bill. This bill would extend payment through 1969. Two circumstances created a firestorm around the new bill: Rockefeller's sponsorship of the bill and the changes in many people's attitudes by 1968. The bill was defeated in the House. One state representative who spoke against the bill opposed it on the grounds that it financed resistance "to what now seems to be the law of the land."[49] Black leaders criticized Rockefeller for supporting the bill, and the *Arkansas Gazette* noted that support for the governor had weakened in the black community.[50]

Rockefeller regained some of that support the following year. Under the terms of the 1964 Civil Rights Act, dual school systems had to be merged or desegregated by September 1969 or lose federal funds. When it became apparent that President Nixon planned to relax the guidelines, Rockefeller sent him a telegram asking him to reconsider "because it breaks faith with the black community and compromises to a disturbing degree the position of those who have courageously gone ahead with objectivity and a sense of justice—if not always with enthusiasm—in the implementation of federal desegregation guidelines."[51]

The Nixon administration relaxed the guidelines by extending the deadline for those districts with "bona fide educational and administrative problems."[52] In April 1970 Rockefeller was notified that forty-nine Arkansas districts operated dual school systems and were not in compliance with the Civil Rights Act of 1964. As part of his continuing attempt to appease both sides of this passionate debate, Rockefeller asked the Justice Department to delay formal action in order to give the districts time to comply with the order voluntarily. The Justice Department's reply gave the Arkansas districts until September 1970 to achieve "full desegregation." The Justice Department also wrote to the Arkansas Board of Education as "the appropriate agency to be called upon to adjust the conditions of unlawful segregation and racial discrimination existing in the public school systems of Arkansas."[53] This was significant, because the state Board of Education had thus far adamantly refused to take an active role in achieving integrated schools. The board believed that "the right to require the interpretation of the court decision as applied to individual school districts cannot be questioned," and had consistently refused to advise school districts on matters of desegregation except upon request, claiming that "it is not our function or legal right to question the wisdom of legal decisions by local boards."[54] By the time school began in September 1970, all forty-nine districts were at least minimally desegregated, only three of them by court order.[55]

The most controversial aspect of desegregation was busing. The United States Supreme Court ruled in October 1969 in *Beatrice Alexander* et al., *petrs. v. Holmes County (Mississippi) Board of Education et al.*, that school districts must end segregation "at once." In December the court used this ruling to order six school districts in four states to desegregate by February 1, 1970.[56] These decisions increased pressure on politicians to take a stand on busing. In September 1969 the Southern Governors' Conference had passed a resolution calling for "restraint and good judgement" in the use of busing to desegregate. Rockefeller voted for the resolution after being the only abstention on a failed resolution that would have condemned busing.[57] But the October and December court rulings revived public fear of and opposition to busing. In January Rockefeller issued a statement regarding busing: "It should be used and used with discretion, but neither do I think we should blatantly disregard the usefulness of the bus in implementing the court orders and the law working toward sound integration." The *Arkansas Gazette* praised Rockefeller for not "joining in the hypocritical cry suddenly heard throughout the South after whole generations of whites and blacks alike were bused all over kingdom come to keep schools totally segregated."[58]

Rockefeller's courage and moderation regarding busing did not last long. Opposition to his statement was immediate and strong. State politicians, both Democrat and Republican, publicly disagreed with the governor. Rockefeller received petitions with the signatures of 4,495 people from one county disagreeing with his stand on busing and assuring him "that your statements will be publicized should you consider reelection."[59] A member of the governor's staff noted: "Politically, this misunderstanding seems to be costing a lot of votes."[60] Consequently, Rockefeller issued a new statement February 21 to clarify what he called the "distortion" of his position:

> I endorse the position wholeheartedly which the Southern governors have taken on the resolution [of September 1969], and I want to make it perfectly clear that I have *not* recommended busing—and am *not* recommending it now. . . .
>
> The decisions will be made in the local school districts, and the responsibility for carrying out those decisions also rests with each individual school board, working within the limitations of the law and the various court orders.[61]

Rockefeller had obviously backed down on the busing issue in an effort to avoid alienating conservative white voters. This was a deliberate political decision, as later recalled by Robert Faulkner, who was Rockefeller's executive secretary in 1970: "I was one of them that suggested, and it was strictly a political [move], that he modify, or 'fuzzy' if you will, his support of busing." In retrospect, Faulkner reflected "that may have been a mistake."[62] Rockefeller received criticism for his about-face, both from the press and civil rights groups. Even though Rockefeller's announcement that he would seek a third term as governor was still six weeks away, discussion of another campaign had been going on for months. If Rockefeller's Democratic opponent had been Orval Faubus as expected, the governor's backpedaling on busing might not have done as much damage. But when the Democratic candidate turned out to be a young liberal Democrat named Dale Bumpers, Rockefeller was in trouble. Faubus had accused Bumpers in the primary runoff of being probusing; nonetheless, Bumpers won an easy victory over Arkansas's symbol of white opposition to integration.[63]

Rockefeller lost decisively to Bumpers in the 1970 general election. The primary reason for Rockefeller's defeat was the return of white moderates to the Democratic fold.[64] But there was almost certainly a loss of support for Rockefeller among black voters. One survey showed that in Little Rock, Rockefeller received only 49 percent of the black vote in 1970, as compared with 81 percent in the 1966 election.[65]

Winthrop Rockefeller died February 22, 1973. At his memorial service on March 4 one of the eulogies was delivered by William "Sonny" Walker. Walker credited Rockefeller with treating black Arkansans as "full and equal partners to progress. . . . While Win Rockefeller helped free the black man from the oppression of Jim Crow, he helped free the white man from the prison of prejudice."[66]

Governor Rockefeller's record regarding civil rights was erratic. He promoted color blindness in state appointments and jobs but refused to require state agency heads to do the same. He applauded the spirit of the Civil Rights Act of 1964 but criticized its reliance on the executive branch of the federal government for implementation. He reversed his public support of busing in an obvious attempt to gain votes.

Rockefeller was not a liberal, but in Arkansas in the 1960s his actions in race relations were liberal. As a former Democratic legislator put it: "Probably his greatest accomplishment was to make racial toleration acceptable and respectable in Arkansas."[67] Considering the racial climate in the state during his term in office, Rockefeller showed great moral and political courage in his almost continual support of racial equality by example. When he stood on the steps of the State Capitol and eulogized Martin Luther King Jr., he did so at tremendous political risk. The same can be said of his handling of the disturbances at Forrest City. In September 1969 Rockefeller met with Arkansas's congressional delegation and briefed them on his efforts to ease racial tension in the state. Afterward, Rockefeller told the press that the delegation had "pledged to support his efforts."[68] Three days later, the governor was forced to tell the press that his earlier statement was a "misunderstanding," that he had not asked for, nor had he received any support, "either direct or implied."[69] The retraction should not come as a surprise considering that Congress passed four major civil rights bills between 1957 and 1968, and all passed without a single vote from an Arkansas congressman or senator.[70] In the field of civil rights, Arkansas politicians, Democrat and Republican, liberal and conservative, were afraid of the political repercussions of endorsing civil rights actions or legislation. Rockefeller stands as a marked exception to that generalization.

There were concrete advances made as a result of Rockefeller's actions. In 1968 the United States Department of Health, Education, and Welfare conducted a review of Arkansas's compliance with the 1964 Civil Rights Act in the area of state health and welfare services. Their report to the governor stated: "The review team was pleased with the evident progress in Arkansas in matters affecting compliance with Title VI of the Civil Rights Act. Overt, obvious forms of discrimination have almost disappeared. The attitude and desire of State people generally to achieve a nondiscriminatory treatment of people were gratifying."[71] Much of the progress made by Rockefeller was done despite attempts by other politicians, particularly state legislators, to stop it. Even before Rockefeller became governor, Arkansas and Mississippi were the only states in their region without state human relations commissions.[72] But the legislature refused to create one, so Rockefeller formed his own. In 1967 the legislature refused to consolidate the segregated state juvenile training schools despite the threatened loss of federal funds. So in 1968 the Juvenile Training School Board integrated the girls' schools without legislative authorization. The legislature protested, with one state senator remarking, "They're not going this fast in the public schools." But the schools remained integrated, without incident.[73]

Certainly Rockefeller could have done more to improve race relations in Arkansas. But considering the political climate in Arkansas and Rockefeller's own aversion to both big government and affirmative action, he accomplished a great deal. And most importantly, he did make racial toleration "acceptable and respectable" in Arkansas. This was a tremendous legacy in and of itself. In 1987 Robert McCord wrote that Arkansans have "made much of the fact that Arkansas never experienced the violence that occurred in so many other American cities during the civil rights struggle. . . . The credit for this goes to Winthrop Rockefeller, who brought blacks into the mainstream of our society for the first time."[74] The credit rightly belongs primarily to those people who fought year in and year out to improve race relations and civil rights. What makes Winthrop Rockefeller so unique and so important is that he was the first major political figure in Arkansas to listen and try to help.

The Arkansas Electorate

JIM RANCHINO

In 1968 Arkansas voters simultaneously returned an anti-Vietnam Democrat to the U.S. Senate, retained their first post-Reconstruction Republican in the governor's mansion, and cast their electoral college votes for the segregationist nominee of the American Independent Party. It was this "schizophrenic" election that led Jim Ranchino to write Faubus to Bumpers: Arkansas Votes, 1960–1970, the larger work of which this selection is a part. Arkansas's unpredictable political preferences are a subject about which many have speculated but few have studied. Here, Ranchino makes two important contributions to the study of Arkansas politics. First, he offers some of the earliest survey-based research on the Arkansas electorate, concluding that "Mr. Average Voter" is—above all things—a moderate, and a Democrat. Second, he uses county-level election registration and turnout data to highlight the importance of regional influences in the state's politics. Savvy students of recent elections will note, however, that many of the political heavy-hitters of the 1960s have played a lesser role of late.

The elections of 1968 focused national attention on voting habits in Arkansas. Added to Winthrop Rockefeller's victory in the race for governor was the state's plurality for presidential candidate George Wallace and a resounding majority for Senator J. William Fulbright. This combination of a Republican with massive black support, an American Independent with an antiblack following, and a dovish Democrat made for a strange victory party in the New South.

Jim Ranchino, "The Arkansas Electorate," in *Faubus to Bumpers: Arkansas Votes, 1960–1970* (Arkadelphia, Ark.: Action Research, Inc., 1972). Reprinted with permission.

Some accused Arkansans of going to the polls blindfolded; others were less kind and described the response as political schizophrenia. At least three scholars of national reputation took one look at the precinct returns in the official records of the Secretary of State's office in Little Rock and walked away with a dull headache and an unbelieving shake of the head. The results simply made no sense.

Whatever triggered such a curious set of voting results may never by fully known (I am not at all convinced that we will ever completely know why people vote for certain candidates and reject others). However, there are some known factors about the Arkansas electorate in the 1960s that are worth discussing, and when combined with a detailed breakdown of major state elections, some distinctive clues as to what happened do appear.

Who is the Arkansas Voter?[1]

If you had to describe the "average" Arkansas voter in detail, the voter who actually participates regularly in the democratic process (which is only about 32 percent of those of voting age), it would go something like this.

That voter is a white, male, Baptist, about forty-nine years of age, who stopped his formal education after graduation from high school, holds down a white collar job in an office, or a blue collar job at a minor supervisory position, has an income of $6,500 a year, and lives in either the northwestern part of Camden, or in eastern Jacksonville.

He considers himself a Democrat, and usually votes for the party's nominees, although his party loyalties are less then deep, especially at the national level. He has, on occasion, voted for a Republican in state races, especially when he examines the qualities of the candidates, and prides himself in knowing that the party doesn't control his vote. After all, he does appreciate that "different" kind of candidate who is an individual, not a fanatical party man.

He is not extremely concerned with who wins an election, but says he does have an average to strong concern. His participation in politics is primarily that of a spectator. Every two years, he simply watches a little closer. If he has bought tickets to a banquet or breakfast to help finance a campaign's efforts, he doesn't attend the meeting. He has never written a letter to a public official and doesn't actually believe it would have much effect anyway.

On the race issue, he considers himself a mild integrationist, although he isn't quite sure of the exact implications of that stand. It does mean that he's moved into a little better white neighborhood in the last ten years and doesn't care for blacks to move into that area.

Most of his information about a candidate comes from what he sees on the television screen, although a bit here and a bit there are picked up by headline browsing the newspapers. He does little or no research into the candidate and the issues, and frankly admits that television images influence his final decision on how to vote. Besides, daily living, the family, sports, the church, the job, and the needed money are all a great deal more important than politics and much easier to understand. So goes Mr. Average Voter in Arkansas.

This brief picture of an average voter has its flaws, as all average descriptions do. It doesn't allow for the individual nuances, the personal prejudices, and the many motives that make all voters separate and definable entities. Nor does it give much credit to the impact of issues on the voting public. But it does present some revealing faces of the Arkansas electorate that deserve discussion.

There has been much talk in the last four or five years about the "independence" of Arkansas voters. Some estimates have been published that as high as sixty percent of the voters are independent. The term "independent" is somewhat misleading, for while it may imply that the individual will make up his own mind about candidates, it does not mean a sharp divorce from party identification or preference.

When asked, "Generally speaking, what do you usually think of yourself politically regardless of how you vote?," those surveyed responded in the following way:

8 percent strong Republican
9 percent not very strong Republican
24 percent Independent
31 percent Not very strong Democrat
28 percent Strong Democrat

The Democratic Party of Arkansas still maintains a majority identification in the state. Almost 60 percent consider themselves Democrats, regardless of that meaning or the way they vote. Identifiable Republicans number less than two out of ten, and those willing to admit no party label were slightly less than one out of four. In everyday terms these percentages proclaim clearly that if a Republican wins a statewide race, Democrats elect him by providing the essential majority.

It is also worth considering the response to this question: "Have you always voted for the same party, mostly for the same party, or equally divided your vote?"

21 percent Always the same party
57 percent Mostly for the same party
22 percent Equally for each party

A revealing 86 percent of those who admitted some party identification in the prior question answered this question "mostly for the same party." Arkansas is still influenced, but not dominated, by party loyalties, and the discerning politician or politician-to-be should underscore that point.

The lack of active, concerned participation in the political arena by "average voters" is reflected in a series of responses: "Did you give any money, or buy any tickets to help a party or candidate pay campaign expenses in the past year?"

9 percent Yes
91 percent No

"How many letters have you written to public officials this year?"

78 percent None
15 percent One or two
4 percent Three or four
3 percent Five or more

"Did you go to any political meetings, rallies, or dinners, etc., this year?"

70 percent None
16 percent One
11 percent Two to four
3 percent Five or more

Apathy and lack of involvement in the political process is present in Arkansas as in the remainder of the nation. Overall, relatively few voters get involved in the action in a meaningful way; it's just not that important.

Television has replaced the political machine, the radio, and the newspapers in providing information and guidance to Arkansas voters. The influence of this electronic media is so overwhelming in a statewide race that the wise politician of the future would do well to measure carefully his own expertise and talent in this element of the campaign. Too, it is the most expensive area of campaigning. The poll asked: "Of all the ways to gain information about a candidate or a campaign, which one would you say you got most information from?"

30 percent Newspapers
6 percent Radio
59 percent Television
5 percent Other

"Which of the following influences you most in your decision to vote?"

25 percent Newspapers
5 percent Radio
62 percent Television
8 percent Other

The racial issue, a crucial one for years in southern politics, and perhaps the real decisive force in defining a liberal, a moderate, and a conservative in Arkansas, seems to have been muffled across much of the state, at least in most areas. When asked to rate themselves on the issue of integration, the following breakdown resulted:

19 percent Strong segregationist
30 percent Mild segregationist
40 percent Mild integrationist
11 percent Strong integrationist

No majority for segregation was recorded, and a very slight majority gave integration the nod. Statistically there is no difference; politically, the moderate on the race issue is the man of the future in Arkansas. The extremists, on either side, are the losers. The blatant segregationist may still have his way in his own backyard, but the statewide candidate who builds his campaign with racial overtones is now appealing to a distinct minority. Arkansas simply will not give a majority to an extremist on the issues of race. And that goes for all candidates on all issues, says Mr. Average Voter.

Arkansas politicians, with as much expertise as is found in any part of this country, have practiced for years the art of clouding and confusing the voter on issues (it has always been much safer to give voters what they desire—no controversies). They have seldom taken a strong stand on a particular issue, and when they did, defeat was usually around the corner. It can be safely argued that most voters simply do not care about

issues, or at least don't understand them enough to make crucial electoral decisions based on them. When asked, "When you cast your vote,
what primarily determines your choice of the candidates?" the replies
were revealing:

> 57 percent The candidate
> 14 percent The party of the candidate
> 26 percent The issues involved
> 3 percent Not sure

Most voters discover that issues are often too difficult to define; at
that point the voter's psyche responds to the one clear object he perceives
—how a candidate looks, how he speaks, and how he relates to the per-
ceiver's experiences. Issues play a role in the final decision, but seldom
dominate that decision. The Rockefeller/Fulbright/Wallace victory has
to be understood, partly, in the candidate's image, rather than bed-rock
issues.

On the basis of this assertion, some critics of the Arkansas electorate
have argued for a cardinal principal: "Never underestimate the ignorance
of the voter." What is defined as ignorance, however, is most always lack
of discernment and comprehension of the issues. Arkansas voters are not
ignorant of the differences in the images they receive from the candidates. It takes a good deal of sophistication to vote for candidates of different parties—split-ticket voting—and that's exactly what the state
electorate has been consistently doing in the last decade. The candidates,
furthermore, have had sharp differences in their political philosophies.
"Ignorant" voters would have great difficulty establishing such a voting
pattern.

Finally, even if the issues are confusing, they are important to
Arkansas voters when they directly involve the voter. Economic and racial
problems dominate for Mr. Average Voter; education and crime rank
just behind as important issues in the survey. Prison concerns, ranking
very low on the scale, reflect the assumption that the less personal and
less related the issue is, the lower the concern. But even at that, Mr.
Average Voter of Arkansas, with moderate concern, and moderate understanding, would prefer a moderate candidate with a moderate stance on
the issues. No extremists, please!

Where the Votes Are

As in all parts of the United Sates, the majority of Arkansas voters live in a small area. The widely dispersed rural vote, which at one time dominated the selection of state officeholders, as well as the state legislature, is no more. The 1970 registration figures illustrate the growing concentration of potential voters. Only sixteen counties contain more than 50 percent of the registered voters, and thirty counties have almost 70 percent of the vote (table 1).

TABLE 1

Arkansas Counties by Number of
Registered Voters, June 1, 1971

COUNTIES	REGISTERED VOTERS	PERCENT OF STATE TOTAL	CUMULATIVE PERCENT
Pulaski	108,895	13.0	13.0
Jefferson	36,775	4.4	17.4
Sebastian	34,222	4.1	21.5
Washington	28,526	3.4	24.9
Garland	25,376	3.0	27.9
Craighead	21,344	2.5	30.4
Union	21,251	2.5	32.9
Mississippi	21,166	2.5	35.4
Benton	21,033	2.5	37.9
White	16,712	2.0	39.9
Crittenden	15,969	1.9	41.8
Ouachita	15,563	1.9	43.7
Saline	14,615	1.7	45.4
Faulkner	14,550	1.7	47.1
Phillips	14,456	1.7	48.8
St. Francis	13,591	1.6	50.4
Miller	13,563	1.6	52.0
Greene	12,507	1.5	53.5
Pope	12,169	1.4	54.9
Crawford	11,280	1.3	56.2
Lonoke	11,181	1.3	57.5
Independence	11,135	1.3	58.8
Hot Spring	10,771	1.3	60.1
Poinsett	10,758	1.3	61.4

COUNTIES	REGISTERED VOTERS	PERCENT OF STATE TOTAL	CUMULATIVE PERCENT
Ashley	10,505	1.3	62.7
Columbia	10,215	1.2	63.9
Clay	9,948	1.2	65.1
Clark	9,938	1.2	66.3
Arkansas	9,592	1.1	67.4
Baxter	9,406	1.1	68.5
Hempstead	9,360	1.1	69.6
Boone	9,320	1.1	70.7
Conway	9,050	1.1	71.8
Jackson	8,975	1.1	72.9
Lawrence	8,648	1.0	73.9
Logan	8,159	1.0	74.9
Chicot	7,661	.9	75.8
Desha	7,590	.9	76.7
Johnson	7,498	.9	77.6
Cross	7,431	.9	78.5
Lee	7,332	.9	79.4
Polk	7,077	.8	80.2
Monroe	7,045	.8	81.0
Drew	6,798	.8	81.8
Yell	6,792	.8	82.6
Franklin	6,434	.8	83.4
Carroll	6,355	.8	84.2
Madison	6,062	.7	84.9
Bradley	6,057	.7	85.6
Cleburne	5,871	.7	86.3
Randolph	5,800	.7	87.0
Howard	5,537	.7	87.7
Lincoln	5,355	.6	88.3
Van Buren	5,204	.6	88.9
Nevada	5,127	.6	89.5
Woodruff	5,066	.6	90.1
Grant	5,040	.6	90.7
Lafayette	5,022	.6	91.3
Dallas	4,840	.6	91.9
Prairie	4,836	.6	92.5

COUNTIES	REGISTERED VOTERS	PERCENT OF STATE TOTAL	CUMULATIVE PERCENT
Searcy	4,791	.6	93.1
Sevier	4,761	.6	93.7
Sharp	4,558	.5	94.2
Scott	4,563	.5	94.7
Izard	4,497	.5	95.2
Little River	4,376	.5	95.7
Pike	4,320	.5	96.2
Fulton	4,298	.5	96.7
Marion	4,262	.5	97.2
Stone	4,069	.5	97.7
Newton	3,927	.5	98.2
Montgomery	3,660	.4	98.6
Cleveland	3,340	.4	99.0
Perry	3,174	.4	99.4
Calhoun	3,026	.4	99.8
TOTAL	839,976		

Some differences appear when ranking actual voter turnout, but the concentrated strength still exists (table 2). In the 1968 gubernatorial contest, the largest vote to ever be cast in Arkansas, 615,595 voted[2] and sixteen counties represented over half the vote. The wise politician who desires a statewide office will spend his budget and time accordingly—where the votes are.

TABLE 2

Arkansas Counties by Size of Votes Cast

COUNTIES	VOTES CAST	PERCENT OF STATE TOTAL	CUMULATIVE PERCENT
Pulaski	78,192	12.7	12.7
Sebastian	26,930	4.4	17.1
Jefferson	23,785	3.9	21.0
Washington	21,824	3.5	24.5
Garland	20,167	3.3	27.8
Union	16,904	2.7	30.5
Benton	15,945	2.6	33.1
Craighead	15,556	2.5	35.6

COUNTIES	VOTES CAST	PERCENT OF STATE TOTAL	CUMULATIVE PERCENT
Mississippi	15,245	2.5	38.1
White	12,187	2.0	40.1
Ouachita	11,860	1.9	42.0
Phillips	11,371	1.8	43.8
Saline	11,215	1.8	45.6
Faulkner	10,922	1.8	47.4
Crittenden	10,430	1.7	49.1
Miller	10,427	1.7	50.8
St. Francis	8,792	1.4	52.2
Pope	8,621	1.4	53.6
Columbia	8,126	1.3	54.9
Hot Spring	8,027	1.3	56.2
Poinsett	8,003	1.3	57.5
Ashley	7,993	1.3	58.8
Greene	7,977	1.3	60.1
Independence	7,851	1.3	61.4
Lonoke	7,692	1.2	62.6
Arkansas	7,611	1.2	63.8
Boone	7,378	1.2	65.0
Hempstead	7,301	1.2	66.2
Clark	7,150	1.2	67.4
Crawford	7,110	1.2	68.6
Jackson	6,945	1.1	69.7
Baxter	6,895	1.1	70.8
Conway	6,534	1.1	71.9
Logan	6,496	1.1	73.0
Lawrence	6,208	1.0	74.0
Clay	6,201	1.0	75.0
Desha	5,757	.9	75.9
Cross	5,700	.9	76.8
Chicot	5,644	.9	77.7
Yell	5,214	.8	78.5
Johnson	5,174	.8	79.3
Polk	5,154	.8	80.1
Carroll	5,073	.8	80.9
Madison	4,991	.8	81.7

COUNTIES	VOTES CAST	PERCENT OF STATE TOTAL	CUMULATIVE PERCENT
Monroe	4,818	.8	82.5
Lee	4,799	.8	83.3
Bradley	4,792	.8	84.1
Drew	4,769	.8	84.9
Franklin	4,602	.7	85.6
Randolph	4,214	.7	86.3
Cleburne	4,131	.7	87.0
Howard	4,016	.7	87.7
Nevada	3,898	.6	88.3
Lincoln	3,834	.6	88.9
Sevier	3,752	.6	89.5
Grant	3,681	.6	90.1
Van Buren	3,674	.6	90.7
Lafayette	3,622	.6	91.3
Woodruff	3,621	.6	91.9
Dallas	3,568	.6	92.5
Prairie	3,553	.6	93.1
Sharp	3,476	.6	93.7
Searcy	3,407	.6	94.3
Scott	3,385	.6	94.9
Little River	3,324	.5	95.4
Pike	3,308	.5	95.9
Marion	3,281	.5	96.4
Fulton	3,227	.5	96.9
Izard	2,983	.5	97.4
Newton	2,945	.5	97.9
Stone	2,751	.4	98.3
Cleveland	2,694	.4	98.7
Montgomery	2,515	.4	99.1
Perry	2,288	.4	99.5
Calhoun	2,189	.4	99.9
TOTAL	615,595		

The figures are for the largest vote cast in the past ten years, the election for Governor, 1968. The presidential figure would have been larger, except for the error in Jefferson County's reported results.

TABLE 3

Voter Registration and Participation: Arkansas and the Nation, 1960–1970

ARKANSAS 1960	1962	1964	1966	1968	1970
Voting-age population					
1,041,000	1,073,000	1,109,000	1,126,000	1,142,000	1,168,000
Registered voters[a]					
603,795	601,991	715,528	687,631	769,704	821,122
Votes cast					
428,509	308,092	592,050	563,527	615,595	609,198
Percent voting of voting age					
41.2	28.7	53.4	50.0	53.9	52.2
Percent of registered voters voting					
71.0	51.2	82.7	82.0	80.0	74.2

UNITED STATES	1960	1964	1968
Voting-age population			
	107,597,000	112,184,000	116,535,000
Registered voters[b]			
	79,000,000	82,000,000	90,000,000
Votes cast			
	68,838,219	70,644,510	73,211,562
Percent voting of voting age			
	64.0	63.0	62.8
Percent of registered voters voting[c]			
	87.1	86.2	81.3

[a] Arkansas had no permanent voter registration law until after 1964. Figures for the preceding years represent poll taxes paid.

[b] Some states require no registration at all, and these figures are estimates.

[c] The advance statistics, available from the U.S. Census Bureau, state that approximately 55 percent of the voting-age population participated in the 1970 elections. The figures indicate the usual massive drop of interest in voting in non-presidential years. Arkansas proved somewhat of an exception to this rule in 1970.

The Non-voter in Arkansas

Arkansas, like so many of her southern sisters, has been plagued in the past by low voter participation in the electoral process. Disenfranchisement of blacks, lack of serious party competition, the dominance of the Democratic primary, and the poll tax were some of the guarantees that only a small part of the voting-age population would go to the polls.

In the 1920s, only a fraction over 20 percent participated in state and national elections. In school board contests, the figure remains under 20 percent even today (in one year, only 174 ballots were cast in a North Little Rock city election, and 59 in Fayetteville).

With increased party competition at the end of the Faubus era, voter participation increased. Blacks registered in a massive Republican drive in the mid-1960s that added to the turnout. The overall results indicated some increase at the polls from 1960 through 1970, although national levels of participation remained higher (table 3).

Some Arkansas counties voted over eight out of ten of those registered in 1970, a figure that parallels national efforts (table 4). Other counties, including Pulaski, Garland, Ouachita, Miller, Mississippi, Union, Craighead, St. Francis, Phillips, and Crittenden, some of the larger counties in the state, had very poor participation. This raises a question whether urbanization, education, and a higher income are exclusive incentives for voting more. Good habits of regular voting are still a goal for most Arkansans, and future politicians could reap a bonanza by spending more money and time on turning out the voting potential than competing for those who turn out regularly.

TABLE 4
Voter Participation of Registered Voters by County, 1970

RANK	COUNTY	PERCENTAGE	RANK	COUNTY	PERCENTAGE
1	Baxter	89.4	39	Crawford	74.5
2	Lee	86.5	40	Woodruff	74.2
3	Johnson	85.7	41	Pulaski	74.0
4	Saline	82.0	42	Sevier	73.4
5	Searcy	81.6	43	Prairie	72.9
6	Van Buren	81.3	44	Yell	72.9
7	Newton	80.2	45	Garland	72.7
8	Washington	80.1	46	Little River	72.7
9	Logan	79.8	47	Ouachita	72.7
10	Pope	79.1	48	Sharp	72.7
11	Arkansas	78.9	49	Nevada	72.6
12	Faulkner	78.3	50	Mississippi	72.4
13	Scott	78.3	51	Union	72.4
14	Sebastian	78.2	52	Hempstead	72.2
15	Dallas	77.5	53	Ashley	72.1
16	Bradley	77.4	54	Cleburne	72.1
17	Cleveland	77.4	55	Randolph	71.5
18	White	77.4	56	Madison	70.8
19	Lonoke	77.2	57	Craighead	70.1
20	Boone	77.2	58	Lawrence	69.9
21	Jefferson	77.1	59	Pike	69.9
22	Benton	77.0	60	St. Francis	69.5
23	Conway	76.7	61	Montgomery	69.2
24	Independence	76.6	62	Phillips	69.0
25	Hot Spring	76.3	63	Cross	68.8
26	Howard	76.2	64	Miller	68.8
27	Franklin	76.0	65	Izard	68.7
28	Grant	76.0	66	Lafayette	68.4
29	Carroll	75.7	67	Drew	67.8
30	Lincoln	75.7	68	Crittenden	67.1
31	Marion	75.5	69	Jackson	67.0
32	Stone	75.2	70	Greene	65.8
33	Calhoun	75.1	71	Chicot	65.4
34	Desha	75.1	72	Poinsett	64.6
35	Columbia	75.0	73	Polk	64.3
36	Monroe	74.8	74	Clay	64.2
37	Perry	74.7	75	Fulton	61.2
38	Clark	74.5			

"What Women Wanted"

Arkansas Women's Commissions
and the ERA

Janine A. Parry

Women's commissions, government-authorized task forces charged with studying and advancing the status of women, have a long history within the United States and abroad. Here, the author examines Arkansas's experience with these public agencies, focusing on their participation in the vigorous 1970s debate over ratification of the national Equal Rights Amendment. Relying on a decade's worth of newspaper accounts and government reports as well as interviews with both pro- and anti-ERA activists, Parry concludes that although the activities of women's commission members, including their advocacy for ERA ratification, were attacked by antifeminist women, the conflict was hardly a "ladies'" war. But casting it as such offered long-serving, conservative male legislators a way to avoid taking a position on the expansion of women's rights, a cause—as revealed here—they did not support. The death of the ERA eventually led feminists to abandon women's commissions as a tool for change in Arkansas.

An important but often overlooked element of the women's movements of the late twentieth century is the women's commission. Broadly defined as a government-appointed task force charged with studying and improving the status of women, the first such unit established in the United States was a Kennedy administration initiative: the President's Commission on the Status of Women (PCSW).[1] Chaired by former first lady Eleanor

Janine A. Parry, "'What Women Wanted:' Arkansas Women's Commissions and the ERA," *Arkansas Historical Quarterly* 59 (Autumn 2000): 265–98. Reprinted with permission.

Roosevelt, the PCSW was officially in operation from 1961 to 1963, and in 1965 produced a much-publicized report of findings and policy recommendations titled *American Women*.[2] The more lasting legacy of the PSCW, however, was the role it played in stimulating the wave of state and local women's agencies that sprouted throughout the United States in the 1960s and 1970s. Together with the National Federation of Business and Professional Women's Clubs and the U.S. Women's Bureau, the PCSW pursued a vigorous, and fruitful, campaign to persuade states to establish their own advisory commissions.[3] Michigan was the first state to establish its own women's commission, in 1962. Washington, Indiana, and Illinois quickly followed suit, and the movement burgeoned. By the end of the life of the Kennedy commission in 1963, ten state counterparts had been established. By 1967, all fifty states, the District of Columbia, the Virgin Islands, and Puerto Rico had created women's agencies.[4]

Arkansas established its first women's commission in January of 1964 under Gov. Orval Faubus. Its task, like the President's Commission on the Status of Women that spawned it, was to "explore the social, political, economic and legal problems of women," but on the state level.[5] Issuing its first report in mid-November of 1965, the commission focused on women's economic and educational needs. The report expressed concern, for example, about "the low wages earned by women, the limited jobs available to them, and the pay discrimination in some fields between men and women wage earners." Greater encouragement for women to attend college and vocational schools, more generous tax breaks for widows (and widowers) left with children to tend to, an increased minimum wage, and more stringent laws regulating employers of domestic help were among the commission's recommended remedies.[6] Though Faubus retained the commission through the end of his administration, the unit received little attention and was not credited with any discernible change in the status of Arkansas women. The title of an *Arkansas Gazette* article about a November 15, 1966, commission meeting attended by the governor is illuminating: "Faubus Lavishes Praise on Women, Statistics Don't."[7]

Another women's commission was established under the administration of Gov. Winthrop Rockefeller, the state's first post-Reconstruction Republican chief executive. Again charged with studying "state labor laws on the employment and wages of women, differences in the legal treatment of men and women with regard to political, civil and property rights and practices in education, government employment and family relations," the unit was chaired by the immediate past president of the Arkansas Federation of Republican Women, Leona Troxell.[8] In February of 1968, forty-two women and men, including the four female members of the state legislature (Senator Dorathy Allen and Representatives Vada Sheid, Bernice Kizer, and Gladys Martin Oglesby), were appointed to serve on the commission.[9] Jeane Lambie, who was not a member of the Rockefeller commission but was asked by its members to chair a committee on employment issues, recalled that the unit's main project was a report on women in state government, the conclusions of which were disheartening. "Single mothers were living together," she said, "and pooling all their resources to live." Rockefeller became very interested in the study, and it was, in Lambie's view, a central reason the governor pushed for increased state employees' salaries during his administration.[10] Dorothy Stuck, a "Rockefeller Democrat" and member of the commission for its first eighteen months, later noted only that the group gave "women's issues a little visibility." She added "I don't remember feeling that we were a very powerful or successful group. But, then, things were just beginning to open up."[11]

The commission did not survive the end of Rockefeller's governorship. As the American women's movement picked up momentum in the early 1970s, however, another Arkansas Governor's Commission on the Status of Women was established. It was revived and guided for nearly a decade by a small but growing cadre of professional and feminist women, and achieved a notable degree of success in bringing publicity to, and sometimes meeting, its objectives. Resistance follows results, however, and by the late 1970s a band of resolute antifeminists was actively sparring with the "women's libbers" for the ear—and the votes—of the state's mostly male political elite. The exchange became particularly heated over the ratification of the proposed Equal Rights Amendment (ERA) to the U.S. Constitution. As in other states across the country, proponents and opponents of change battled to define "what women wanted." Tax-supported women's commissions often got caught—or stood—in the crossfire. The Arkansas women's unit was one of these and consequently was abandoned by decade's close.[12]

Diane D. Blair, previously Diane Kincaid, Democratic party activist and professor of political science at the University of Arkansas, recalled in a May 1998 interview that the idea of a women's commission was introduced to her at a conference on women and politics she attended in Dallas in 1971. A component of the program, she recounted, was discussion of the commissions on the status of women that had been active in most states since the mid-1960s. Reports of their impact on policy change and the facilitation of women's participation in public life were mostly positive.[13] Upon her return, Blair telephoned a contact who was the head of the state's Department of Finance and Administration—the most important appointment in Arkansas government—to ask if the state currently had a women's commission. The answer was "no."

Blair's contact was Max Milam, a former chairman of the political science department at the University of Arkansas. Milam requested that she write a memorandum on the need for a women's unit in Arkansas. He agreed with the arguments she presented and encouraged her to contact Gov. Dale Bumpers, another acquaintance, whose administration was just a few months old at the time of her request. Blair had been "an early Dale Bumpers supporter," and the man to whom she was then married, Hugh Kincaid, had recently been elected to the Arkansas legislature. Relying upon these connections (a situation that would later be a source of criticism from women's movement opponents), Blair proposed a women's commission to the governor. He was supportive of the idea.[14]

According to Blair, events surrounding the actual establishment of the commission evolved quickly. Bumpers and his influential appointments advisor, Irene Samuels, decided that the governor should create the commission by executive order rather than risk confrontation with the legislature. The latter body, observed Blair, "was pretty Neanderthal at the time." The new commission was granted a budget of five thousand dollars from the Governor's Emergency Fund, though no travel expenses were to be paid for the volunteer commissioners. Samuels arranged working space in the Capitol, and the employment of an executive secretary to the commission, Harryette Dorchester.[15] Blair was named chairwoman and civil rights activist and writer Sara Murphy became vice chair. With these particulars completed, the Governor's Commission on the Status of Women (GCSW) officially was (re)instituted on May 12, 1971. It was charged with "examining the role of women in Arkansas and finding ways by which women might become fuller participants in our State's economic, political and social institutions."[16]

Two conflicts emerged within a few weeks, one of minor import and the other a harbinger of larger troubles to come. In the first instance, as Blair laughingly recalled it, the newspapers picked up on a criticism she had levied at the Bumpers administration for not naming enough women to departments within the executive branch. Her remarks had come just weeks after "this big, splashy announcement" about the establishment of the commission and her appointment as its chair, a rich twist of timing that prompted the *Democrat's* Jon Kennedy to craft a political cartoon suggesting a dampening of relations between the governor and his new appointee. Though Blair apologized to Bumpers at a September meeting of the commission for her "rather churlish remarks," the commission still issued a report in December noting that the number of women employed in the executive branch of state government had declined slightly since Bumpers took office.[17] The relationship proved buoyant, however, and Bumpers remained a supporter of the work of the commission throughout his two terms of office.

The second conflict to make waves early in the life of the reactivated commission came cloaked in a relatively benign package. Pulaski County Clerk Jerome Climer charged that the governor was "keeping women out of politics."[18] Specifically, Climer—a Republican—accused Bumpers of "removing" Republican members of the Governor's Commission on the Status of Women, presumably by not reappointing those who had served under the Rockefeller administration. Though the partisan affiliations of commission members were not identified in news accounts or official documents, the Bumpers commission did return only four of his predecessor's appointees. Blair dismissed the concern, calling it "almost amusing" and insisting that commission appointments had been made exclusively on the basis of demonstrated competence and/or interest in an area covered by the unit's mission. The political affiliations of the appointees, she insisted, had been "virtually" ignored.[19] In a later interview, Lambie, who served as an appointee to both commissions, did not recall the disbanding of the Rockefeller-appointed unit as having been politically motivated. "I don't remember it," she said. "And I would have recalled that sort of thing. I think it just kind of petered out."[20] Climer was later invited by Blair to come to the commission's September meeting. He and Democrat Ted Boswell did attend and together were introduced by Blair as "prominent politicians from opposite sides of the fence."[21]

The controversy did not end there, however. A few months later, just after the release of the December report regarding the status of women in the Bumpers administration, Jerri Pruden, president of the Arkansas Federation of Republican Women, issued a news release warning the governor that he had better improve his record of employing women in state government or he would be committing "political suicide."[22] "It's high time for Governor Bumpers to de-politicize the Status of Women Commission and to give women a fair chance at state jobs," the release said. The report indeed showed a decline in the number of women working for the state, from 5,716 in January of 1971 to 5,657 later in the year, a drop of about 1 percent. But such a small decrease, together with the reference to the women's commission (which had produced the report Pruden cited), suggests that Bumpers's critics were aggravated at least as much by the "who" of his official commission as by the "what" of its findings with regard to the situation of women. The news release explicitly charged that Bumpers had "reorganized" the Governor's Commission on the Status of Women to install only loyal Democrats as its officers. Often cited as evidence of the partisan nature of the commission was chairwoman Diane Blair (then Kincaid) herself, the wife of one of Bumper's strongest campaign supporters.[23] This theme of unfair influence, together with the argument that the commission offered a distorted representation of women's wants and needs, would reappear on a grand scale a few years later.

Nevertheless, said Blair, "we just went to work."[24] Among the early activities commissioners embarked upon was a research project on the legal status of Arkansas women, a subject of little study prior to their efforts.[25] Women in Arkansas had been partly enfranchised shortly before the passage of the national women's suffrage amendment in 1917.[26] In the decade immediately following, Arkansas joined the national government and other states across the nation in enacting—often at the behest of women's civic and service groups—various forms of "protective" legislation, especially on labor issues, that affected only females.[27] Among these were laws providing for the imprisonment of female, but not male, alcoholics; a female-specific minimum wage law (set at $1.25 per day in 1917); restricted nightclub admittance for unchaperoned girls under eighteen; protection for women from prosecution for crimes committed under coercion by their husbands; and stricter regulation of overtime, maximum hours, and continuous labor.[28] The flip side of "protection," however, was overt discrimination. Arkansas statute and convention, for example, long prevented women from practicing law in the state, even after the first female law student graduated from the University of Arkansas Law School in 1912.[29] The GCSW's Legal Task Force, chaired by Little Rock lawyer Virginia Tackett, also pointed to inequitable laws relating to rape and prostitution penalties, and a stringent abortion law.[30]

Another central goal of the commissioners was to secure federal monies under Title I of the Higher Education Act Amendments of 1965 to facilitate a statewide dialogue among its female citizens about women's status.[31] They were successful. With more than ten thousand dollars in federal and matching money, the GCSW proceeded to organize a series of five regional workshops at Southern State College in Magnolia, Hendrix College in Conway, Arkansas State University in Jonesboro, Agricultural, Mining, and Nursing College in Pine Bluff, and the University of Arkansas in Fayetteville. Blair's subsequent statement of the goals of the meetings cautioned: "The purpose of this project was not to bring Arkansas women to the boiling point but rather, by a series of statewide conferences featuring some of America's most prominent women, to stimulate awareness of and interest in the tremendous transformations taking place in woman's world, so that more people could be intelligently planning for the many implications of these changes."[32]

The Higher Education Act funds were used to bring in nationally known female speakers to each of the workshop locations. One of these was Dr. Cathryn Clarenbach, the past chairwoman of both the Wisconsin Governor's Commission on the Status of Women and the National Organization for Women. At the time of her speech in Fayetteville, Clarenbach was the president of the Inter-Association of Commissions on the Status of Women, the forerunner of the National Association of Commissions for Women, a membership organization of state, county, and city-level women's commissions. Other conference speakers included Virginia Allen, chairwoman of President Nixon's Task Force on Women's Rights and Responsibilities (a descendant of the Kennedy PCSW); Osta Underwood, president of the National Federation of Business and Professional Women's Clubs; U.S. Rep. Martha Griffiths (D-Michigan); and LaDonna Harris, cofounder of the Women's Political Caucus and a Comanche Indian activist. Packets of materials provided to conference registrants included fact sheets from the United States Women's Bureau on major legislation and executive orders related to sex discrimination, a bibliography of sex- and gender-related reading materials, and a GCSW-produced pamphlet on women and the law in Arkansas, the product of the group's earlier legal research.[33]

In arranging these regional meetings, commissioners had sought not only to arouse interest in such issues as equal pay, widow's benefits, access to credit, and improved educational and occupational opportunities but "to arouse interest in women likely to interest and inform others."[34] The gatherings promised to have that effect. Many attendants, in their written evaluations, noted their intentions to share the information they had obtained. Indeed, the workshops seem to have stimulated a minor industry in studying women's status and linking people who wanted to see it improved. After the meetings concluded, correspondence and inquiries about such subjects to both the GCSW and the office of Governor Bumpers reportedly increased. The contacts included letters of thanks, requests for more information, encouragement for more female appointments in other departments of government, boards, and commissions, questions about establishing local commissions on the status of women, and invitations to speaking engagements.[35] Conference sponsors were convinced that the response was so positive because women's opportunities to share their experiences prior to the GCSW initiative (and other nationwide efforts burgeoning at the time) had been so limited. "Golly, we'd go to these meetings and those women would preach heresy," Nan Snow, a meeting participant and an appointee to the GCSW, noted in a 1998 interview. "We were up and cheering. It was an exciting time for women. All of us approached it with an evangelical fervor."[36]

Between 1972 and 1975, the Arkansas GCSW—taking a lot of cues and receiving substantial assistance from the U.S. Women's Bureau—gathered up the observations it had collected from women all over the state and embarked upon an impressive number and variety of tasks. With the assistance of Snow, the state's federal women's program coordinator of the U.S. Civil Service Commission, who was "on loan" to the GCSW, the commission completed a comprehensive study of the status of women in state government employment. Commission members also produced a number of informational publications. These included "Possibilities for Action," a list of recommendations for local groups interested in improving women's status in their communities; "The Status of Women in Arkansas," an address made to the League of Women Voters based upon the commission's research; and a report on the "perceptions, expectations, and aspirations" of school-age girls in the state.

In all, the GCSW's research projects led to policy recommendations in the areas of employment, education, government, politics, legal rights, health, and family and child care.[37] The commission's suggestions, as detailed in the two-year summary report delivered to Governor Bumpers in July 1973, included greater publicity about complaint procedures in cases of employment discrimination; an increased federal minimum wage; an expansion of the national Fair Labor Standards Act to cover domestics, childcare workers, and people employed in similar occupations; the elevation of more women to policy positions in the state's educational system; an executive order issued to schools to eliminate discriminatory practices and stereotyped textbooks; greater action by both major political parties toward the inclusion of women in their activities; congressional action to eliminate sex-based discrimination in Social Security benefits and the availability of credit, loans, mortgages, and insurance; a state-funded study of child care in Arkansas; a review of school policies restricting the attendance and working privileges of pregnant students and teachers (an issue on which much action already had been taken by 1973); and ratification of the Equal Rights Amendment. The last of these recommendations would be the most controversial. Commission members had become prominently identified with the ERA, a move that ultimately contributed to the commission's unraveling.[38]

It is important to note that, other than support for the ERA, Blair's approach to leading the GCSW was a consciously conservative one throughout her tenure. The commission membership itself—nearly fifty Arkansas women from a broad range of professional, economic, regional, and racial backgrounds—signaled an effort to make the unit representative of women's experiences in Arkansas. Represented among the membership were twenty Arkansas communities, labor force members and stay-at-home women, professionals, students, and retirees, politicians and activists. Eight of the appointees were black.[39] The overall disposition of the women gathered also was strikingly non-radical. As Blair observed, the women involved in the commission's activities were not "bra-burners." They were married (most with children), active in their churches, and members of reputable civic organizations. The GCSW was "an acceptable, useful place to put their energies."[40] News accounts of the workshops held around the state support this description. Commissioners, invited speakers, and participants alike, for example, were often quoted as emphasizing that the "woman's role as wife, mother and homemaker should still have top priority," a sentiment—both praised and criticized—that had been pervasive in the concluding report of the first national women's commission ten years earlier.[41]

In the commission's articulation of its objectives and projects, too, a calculated effort was made to project a moderate image. Announcing the commission's goals upon her appointment as its chair, for example, Blair identified its central one as "public education" about the opportunities that existed for women. She added in the same newspaper interview that she did not agree with the feeling among some members of the women's movement that the status of women was due to an "organized conspiracy on the part of men."[42] The GCSW's mission, she concluded, was not to drive "anyone out of their home," because women were needed to care for husbands and children. In keeping with these traditional themes, Blair also was careful to invite professional and civically active speakers with relatively noncontroversial backgrounds and agendas to the 1972 workshops.[43] Speaking of her disappointment over the cancellation of a scheduled talk by Liz Carpenter, who had been the personal secretary to Lady Bird Johnson, for example, Blair noted "Liz would [have known] how to 'do southern.'"[44] Carpenter had been invited on the knowledge that she would be a tactful and gracious ambassador for the social change that necessarily would accompany the elevation of women's status in Arkansas. The decision to include her and women like her in GCSW events was a deliberate effort to bolster the commission's legitimacy.

Blair herself proved to be an accomplished study of how to "do southern," when she stepped down as chair of the commission in 1975, with the pending failure of her marriage to attorney and former state legislator Hugh Kincaid, though she remained an important member.[45] She had children to care for and pressing job-related decisions to make, but she also was acutely aware that a divorced woman should not head the Arkansas Governor's Commission on the Status of Women. It could only hurt her cause to continue to fill the post she had created. In short order, however, Blair's role as the immediate past chairwoman of the GCSW and a respected university instructor would place her in the position to debate the nationally prominent antifeminist, Phyllis Schlafly, on the floor of the Arkansas state legislature.[46] The topic was the state's ratification of the national Equal Rights Amendment.

Congressional passage of the ERA had been secured in 1972, almost fifty years after it was drafted by suffragist Alice Paul and introduced as a constitutional amendment in the U.S. House. Though nearly half of the states, and almost two-thirds the number needed for ratification, had voted to accept the proposed amendment in that same year, its progress had substantially slowed by the mid-1970s.[47] Arkansas's deliberation over the amendment demonstrated a similar pattern. With ratification by the General Assembly considered to be "virtually assured" in mid-January of

1973, approximately thirty El Dorado women, who had just returned from a Daughters of the American Revolution meeting at which Schlafly had spoken, arrived by bus at the state capitol building on January 15. Calling themselves the Committee for the Protection of Women, they expressed profound objections to the radical social changes they claimed the ERA would invoke. The group's concerns were becoming familiar in the American political scene. They included the drafting of women (specifically, "mothers" and "daughters") into military service, the institution of same-sex public bathrooms, undue interference in state-level affairs by the national government, the destruction of the nuclear family, the repeal of rape laws, and an end to homemakers' rights and protective labor legislation for women. The group claimed to speak for "98 percent" of Arkansas women, but asserted that they were "just not as organized as the other side."[48]

News accounts reported that the El Dorado group was joined by smaller contingents of opponents from around the state and that their presence came as a surprise to many legislators who, up to that point, had heard almost exclusively from pro-ERA forces, including the Federation of Business and Professional Women, the League of Women Voters, the Arkansas Women's Caucus, and the Governor's Commission on the Status of Women.[49] For some legislators, the change of heart the opposing group evoked was swift and personal. One member, Rep. Jack W. Phillips of Ozark, was reported on the day of the El Dorado group's arrival to be "frantically searching" for the bill's primary sponsor, Paul Van Dalsem of Perryville, so he could have his name removed from the list of co-sponsors.[50] Asked by a reporter about his rush, Phillips attributed the change of heart to his wife: "She said if I vote for that bill not to bother to come home."[51] Amid this commotion, the resolution's sponsors and supporters learned that Senator Guy "Mutt" Jones of Conway was attempting a surprise maneuver to block it from further consideration. His plan was to remove the resolution from the Senate Committee on State Agencies and Governmental Affairs and amend it to read "of employment" after the declaration of "equality of rights."[52] Any change to the proposed amendment's wording, of course, stood to nullify an affirmative ratification vote by the state.

A measure that previously had caused little dissension among the members of the Assembly thus was quickly transformed into a contentious "hot potato." As additional groups mobilized against an affirmative vote for ratification—including Women Who Want to be Women, the American Party, and the Arkansas Citizens' Council—a few groups mobilized in favor of the amendment. Significantly for many Arkansans, this latter collection included the *Arkansas Gazette* (with some reservation) and several local newspapers, and a number of the mainstream southern churches: Baptist, Methodist, Presbyterian, Catholic, AME, AME Zion, Episcopal, Lutheran, Jewish, and Unitarian.[53] Within a matter of days, pro- and anti-ERA forces were locked in a steady sequence of lobbying individual legislators, testifying before committees, and writing letters to the editors of the state's newspapers.

Central among the themes raised in the ensuing debate was whether the Equal Rights Amendment was necessary to protect the situations and rights of women. Opponents of the measure insisted that women already had gained all of the legal rights they needed with the passage of the Equal Pay Act in 1963, Title VII of the 1964 Civil Rights Act, and the Equal Employment Opportunity Act of 1972.[54] The Fourteenth Amendment to the U.S. Constitution also was mentioned as providing that "no state shall abridge the privileges or immunities of citizens of the United States." Congress, it was argued, thus already had the power to ameliorate any remaining inequities between men and women. What was really needed, argued the *Gazette* in an important qualification of its arguably affirmative position, was a responsible Congress and a diligent Supreme Court.[55] Anti-ERA champion Phyllis Schlafly often articulated a similar position in her remarks, cautioning that the measure only stood to deny women the "extra" rights and privileges they had been granted, particularly in matters related to the workplace and military service.[56]

Advocates of ratification acknowledged the text of the Fourteenth Amendment but pointed to the Supreme Court's failure to interpret its provisions as strictly in sex discrimination cases as it had in cases related to race or ethnicity. University of Arkansas professor of law William Lancaster wrote an elaborate letter to this effect to the editor of the *Gazette* in February of 1975. The letter was important to this component of the debate and was cited, by both proponents and opponents, in later skirmishes over the amendment. The author explained that the Fourteenth Amendment had been interpreted by the Supreme Court such that it applied its highest level of scrutiny to race. The court had for a century dealt far more gingerly with allegations of discrimination on the basis of sex. Professor Lancaster concluded that advocates of women's rights were advancing the ERA "to achieve by Constitutional amendment what the courts had thus far avoided deciding."[57]

Another critical issue of some dispute was whether adoption of the ERA would reduce the rights and privileges of women or, instead, expand those rights and privileges granted to men. Before a hearing held by the Senate's State Agencies and Governmental Affairs Committee on January 23, Schlafly and other opponents argued the former position, charging that the amendment threatened to nullify existing laws that afforded "special protection" to women. Among these, according to their analysis, were the rights of women to be supported by husbands and women's dower rights to their husbands' property.[58] Another oft mentioned charge was that the amendment would, presumably automatically, subject women to the draft. Senator Jones captured the latter fear by warning his fellow legislators in a blustery burst of chamber oratory that they would not "want to see these sweet, tender little bodies with their heads torn off by shrapnel."[59] Senator Virgil Fletcher of Benton summed up the position by declaring that governments throughout history had adopted laws "to protect the lady, [or] to make a lady out of 'em . . . but [the ERA] wipes 'em all out."[60]

Proponents of ratification countered that the vast majority of legal changes required by the amendment's passage were likely to take the form of female-specific laws being extended to males. John Lavey, a lawyer for the state Department of Labor, spoke specifically to the protective labor laws that had applied only to women employees since the early 1900s. As long as protections such as mandatory rest periods, maximum working hours, and more closely regulated overtime could be extended to men, he testified, the laws would not be rendered unconstitutional by the ERA. Proponents added that only laws that prohibited workers from higher paying jobs or certain kinds of promotions on the basis of sex without evidence that sex characteristics were a "bona fide occupational qualification" (such as a dressing room attendant at a clothing store) would be struck, and most of them already had been rendered unlawful by Title VII of the 1964 Civil Rights Act.[61] In the case of military service, expert testimony seemed to agree on the fact that because the U.S. Selective Service Act of 1967 required only males to register, in the event of any subsequent changes or extensions to the law, it would indeed have to be equally extended to females under the ERA. A U.S. Senate Judiciary Committee report was careful to note the following, however: "Of course, the ERA will not require that all women serve in the military any more than all men are now required to serve." Women who were physically unable or unqualified, who were conscientious objectors, or who were exempt due to particular responsibilities (for example, certain public officials or those with dependents) would not have to serve. "Thus," the report concluded, "the fear that mothers will be (drafted) into military services if the Equal Rights Amendment is ratified is totally and completely unfounded. Congress will retain ample power to create legitimate sex-neutral exemptions from compulsory service."[62] Parenthood, the committee suggested, might be among these.

A third critical issue in the debate was the degree to which the ERA's passage would alter traditional relations between women and men. Opponents suggested that the assigning of surnames to children—a matter of social convention, not law—would become muddled, placing nearly insurmountable obstacles in the way of tracing their lineage later in life. Men might even feel forced, it was alleged at one state Senate hearing, to take their wives' last names upon marriage.[63] Proponents countered that the amendment required equality in legal matters only, not in cultural customs. The latter would be negotiated, as historically had been the case, between the individuals involved. "It is important to note that the only kind of sex discrimination which the Equal Rights Amendment would forbid is that which exists in law," reassured U.S. Senator Marlow Cook (R-Kentucky). "Interpersonal relationships and customs of chivalry will, of course, remain as they have always been, a matter of individual choice. The passage of this amendment will neither make a man a gentleman nor will it require him to stop being one."[64] In her brief testimony early in the 1973 session, activist Shirley McFarlin, who was joined by GCSW member Ann Henry, agreed, assuring the House Committee on State Agencies and Governmental Affairs that the amendment pertained to "legal rights only, not social customs."[65] Charlene Tipton, Arkansas state president of the Business and Professional Women's Clubs, added that "Men are still going to open doors for women, and women are still going to open doors for elderly men."[66]

Such disputes over the meaning and implications of the ERA signaled the two camps' radically different notions of what women wanted. Proponents of ratification, including members of the GCSW, had approached Arkansas's members of Congress early on and convinced them that a blanket statement of equal rights under the law for women and men was long overdue. Despite their concerns about the potential threat to the protective labor provisions women themselves had rallied for earlier in the century, powerful men like U.S. Senator John McClellan conceded that the women who approached him to gain his pledge of support for the measure's congressional passage were "aware of the possible loss of certain legal advantages they now enjoy, but feel that the gains to be realized from this amendment far exceed its potential drawbacks. Women today are seeking more independence and apparently want to assume the rights and responsibilities exercised by men."[67] Opponents clearly disagreed with this conclusion and felt betrayed by the assumption that the views of the pro-ERA women's groups who had mobilized right away in the conflict were representative of all, or even most, Arkansas women. Carrying placards reading "From the breadmakers to the breadwinners" during later lobbying efforts, the anti-ERA contingent focused its message on the traditional, and reputedly Bible-based, vision of femininity. An unidentified opponent delivering a speech in the state capitol in 1975 declared it was "very ungodly that anyone could even come up with anything so ridiculous" as the ERA.[68]

The situation was widely perceived to be, to quote a passage from observer and editorialist Bob Lancaster, "a war between women and women." The active membership of both the pro and anti forces was indeed mostly female. And the mostly male legislators who found themselves in the middle were made very uncomfortable indeed. Most of them, according to Lancaster's analysis, "had prematurely signed up in support of the amendment . . . because it appeared a happy, non-controversial way to make a little political capital. They had supposed it would be a popular thing among women voters to declare them full legal equals with their men." An advocate of the amendment, Lancaster continued, "legislators might have anticipated token opposition from admirers of Ernest Hemingway and from the few remaining Spanish-American war vets who remember the halcyon days when Teddy Roosevelt was president and all virtues were considered masculine virtues and women were regarded as something of a necessary evil, useful mainly as a diversion and as floor-moppers."[69]

The members of the Arkansas General Assembly, in short, did not anticipate that opposition would come from other female members of their constituencies. Later interviews offered some support for this conclusion. "I think they were very surprised," confirmed Rachael McKinney in an interview conducted in 2000. A member of the Committee for the

Protection of Women, McKinney noted that legislators initially "didn't think women were really fighting it."[70] However, Nan Snow, ERA advocate and GCSW member under Bumpers, provided a slightly different line of analysis. "They were glad," she said, referring to the male legislators. In her view, the arrival of a few dozen vocally anti-ERA women gave them the "out" they needed.[71] Either way, the anti-ERA forces, wrote Lancaster, "declared that they spoke for 98 percent of the women in Arkansas, an undocumented statistic no doubt, but one of sufficient magnitude to cause the typical legislator to swallow his cigar."[72]

Lancaster's analysis was glib but astute. Due partly to the dynamics he described, the Equal Rights Amendment in Arkansas had swiftly moved from being perceived by many observers as "virtually assured" of ratification in January of 1973 to being openly reviled at the next legislative session. A news account of debate over a civil rights commission proposed to "trouble-shoot racial problems" in March of 1975, for example, ended by noting that Governor David Pryor's administration had amended the relevant bill to relabel the agency the "Human Affairs Commission," rather than the "Equal Rights Commission," because "it would avoid confusion with the Equal Rights Amendment, which is unpopular in the legislature."[73]

Accordingly, after a flurry of legal maneuvering in the state Senate in the 1973 session that led to the ratification measure's death (a majority of senators eventually approved a hostile amendment that protected women from the draft, a change that made the ratification issue moot) and a failure to put the matter to a vote in the House, coverage of the ERA in Arkansas dwindled for a time.[74] But, in November of 1973, the state chapter of the League of Women Voters announced the launch of a unified campaign of more than two dozen organizations that would prepare the way for the amendment's ratification in the 1975 legislative session. The league had decided, declared the group's spokeswoman, "very affirmatively that we shall not be caught shorthanded again." More specifically, the group contended, "We were taken by surprise by the anti-ERA forces, and were not geared to adequately counter the barrage of half truths and emotional argument raised by the opponents."[75]

Opponents countered the announcement with an attack the next month on the most visible member of the pro-ERA coalition, the publicly funded Governor's Commission on the Status of Women. A pair of spokeswomen for the El Dorado group that had arrived unexpectedly at the state capitol earlier in the year called the commission a "waste of taxpayers' money." They also directly criticized a former ally of one of the commission task forces, Patricia Cromwell of Little Rock, who according to a newspaper account had written a report for the commission asserting that the biggest problem facing women in the paid labor force was "lack of high standard, affordable day care facilities for their children."[76] The El Dorado group alleged that Cromwell was a member of the left-leaning Progressive Labor Party, and was affiliated with a professor at the University of Arkansas at Little Rock who had announced earlier that he taught his history courses from a communist point of view.

The overarching charge levied at the GCSW was that, as a "tax-supported" institution, it was too liberal and therefore unrepresentative. ERA activist and commission ally Shirley McFarlin later disputed the significance of the commission's receipt of public funds, however. "I don't think we worried about that. There was very little money involved." The five thousand dollars from the Governor's Emergency Fund mainly paid the salary of the part-time executive secretary to the commission, she recollected. Any other activities the GCSW or its commissioners engaged in—pro-ERA or otherwise—were paid for by private contributions. "We put out a newsletter when we had received enough individual donations to do so." [77] Nevertheless, commission opponents continued to suggest that GCSW members lobbying for the ERA amounted to political advocacy at the taxpayers' expense.

Only a smattering of news articles about either the GCSW or the Equal Rights Amendment appeared during 1974. In August, a report of the Legislative Council staff delineating which state laws would be affected by passage of the ERA garnered some attention from both sides of the debate. Nearly fifty laws were identified, almost all of them state constitutional provisions or statutes that afforded more protection for women than for men, in divorce, property and inheritance, working conditions, and criminal laws. The report did not take a position on the ERA itself but instead tracked the changes to state law that its ratification likely would require. Changes to many, such as an obscure voting rights provision that required women be designated as "Mrs." or "Miss" upon registration and an out-of-date measure providing fifty dollars per month in pension benefits to Confederate widows, were acknowledged to be unlikely to make many waves. Other issues, such as the legal presumption that mothers should receive custody after divorce proceedings,

the constitutional provision that women could not be compelled to perform jury duty, the fact that widows, but not widowers, automatically
had rights to their deceased spouses' property, and the many existing
female-only work protections such as comfortable seats, two ten-minute
break periods, handrails on stairs, a minimum of forty-five minutes for
lunch, and mandatory overtime pay for a workday longer than eight
hours were likely, according to *Arkansas Gazette* news accounts, to provide fodder for the anti-ERA position.[78] The prediction proved to be off
the mark, however, when Shirley McFarlin of the Equal Rights
Amendment Coalition praised the report as "honest and objective," and
opponent Charlene Felt called it biased and incomplete.[79] The latter
noted that the Arkansas employment laws reviewed by the Legislative
Council staffers had been interpreted according to standards established
by the U.S. Department of Labor's Citizen's Commission on the Status
of Women, which, she said, was pro-ERA. "So what you have," she proposed, "is the Council using the yardstick of the ERA promoters to determine what laws would be affected by the passage for the ERA."[80]

Wary that such resentment was still running high in the state, pro-
ERA forces, including the GCSW, garnered a few more allies as they pre-
pared for the 1975 legislative session. In December of 1974, the United
Methodist Women announced publicly that they would be supporting
ERA ratification through telephoning and writing letters to legislators
and attendance at capitol committee meetings.[81] Also of interest was the
formation of a new group calling themselves "Men for ERA" in early
January of the next year. Dr. M. Francis Christie, academic dean of
Hendrix College, spoke for the group of about twenty at a January 11
press event. He emphasized that the ERA was "not just an issue for
women" but rather "an issue for people." He indicated that the group
had been formed out of frustration with the rather superficial nature of
the conflict thus far which, he said, had "fed on personality clashes and
disputes which are irrelevant to the basic issue—equality for men and
women before the law." He added, "we're quite serious about this and
also are serious about overcoming some of the flippant way in which
some of this was handled in the previous session."[82]

It was in this context that the 1975 session of the Arkansas legislature was called to order. The first move made on the ERA issue took
many observers by surprise. Representative John Hoffman of Royal, considered one of the most conservative members of the Assembly, intro-

duced a resolution for ERA ratification on January 15. Proponents were surprised by the action and were suspicious that Hoffman was maneuvering to prevent, rather than promote, serious consideration of the measure. Their concern arose from a standing practice of the legislature that only the sponsor of a measure could bring it up for a vote, and that identical resolutions could not be introduced.[83] Democrat David Pryor, who had ascended to the governor's office in January and had made a "clear ERA vote" a priority of his administration, in fact would not accept Hoffman's resolution as his candidate for an "administration bill."[84] Two weeks later, after House Speaker Cecil Alexander of Heber Springs ruled that there was not a written prohibition on identical resolutions, Representative Robert Johnston of Little Rock stepped forward with another ratification resolution. Pryor asked that Johnston's measure be designated as the administration's bill.[85]

Despite a February 11 poll conducted by Representative Cliff Hoofman of North Little Rock indicating that sixty-one members of the House had decided against ERA ratification, a previously scheduled joint session of the Arkansas General Assembly gathered on February 14 to observe a debate on the matter. National antifeminist activist Phyllis Schlafly would speak in opposition and the GCSW's former chairwoman Diane (Kincaid) Blair would support the ERA. In front of a packed floor and gallery, the two women repeated the central issues long discussed in the deliberation: the ERA's necessity, women in combat, and the fate of the various protective labor provisions under the measure. News coverage noted that the issue probably was moot, however, given the results of Hoofman's poll. So printed accounts focused upon legislators' appreciation of the quality of the presentations ("They couldn't get two smarter ladies," one member was quoted as saying), the speakers' attire (Schlafly wore a "rose knit dress"), and the seating of the "pro" (west gallery) and the "anti" (east gallery) women. Much ado also was made about the "appropriateness" of the date for the "ladies'" debate, Valentine's Day.[86] Not long after the performance, Representative Johnston's ratification resolution was reported to be languishing in committee, while Representative Hoffman withdrew his bill.[87]

Blair later called the failure of the 1975 Arkansas legislature to ratify, or even seriously to consider, the ERA "almost like a rejection of me personally."[88] It is more likely that the outcome was both a product of the legislature's negligible commitment to equal rights and a symptom of the broader changes in the state and national political environment. In

the first case, the fact that Paul Van Dalsem had been the early champion of the amendment in the House was telling. Van Dalsem was widely
perceived, and himself admitted, to be pushing ratification only as a
means of atonement among women voters for an infamous 1963 declaration to the Little Rock Optimist Club that women who interfered in
politics should be kept "barefoot and pregnant."[89] Van Dalsem's 1973
efforts to advance the measure apparently broke down, however, when
he angered several legislators by persuading the Education Committee
to delay a vote on providing free textbooks to the upper four grades of
the public schools. A *Democrat* account noted that "It was reported [by
legislative sources] that the angry representatives planned to attempt to
sidetrack the women's rights amendment into the Judiciary Committee
if Van Dalsem brought it up."[90] The latter learned of this and opted not
to raise the ERA issue in the House, at the very moment at which it had
the best chance of passing.

In terms of the broader environment, the changing political atmosphere that undermined the ERA also began to undermine commission
leaders' own confidence in the efficacy of bodies like the GCSW. It seems
that the great majority of the work of the commission under Blair's leadership had been either perceived favorably or was hardly noticed. After all,
only the commission's regional "consciousness raising" conferences (covered in a handful of articles), its study of women's legal status (one article),
and its work on changing discriminatory policies against pregnant school
girls and teachers (a half dozen articles) had garnered any media attention.[91] Instead, it was commissioner activism in support of state ratification of the Equal Rights Amendment that made headlines, fostering a
growing perception that the Governor's Commission on the Status of
Women was a radical organization. Thus, what had seemed to commissioners to be a simple endorsement of equal rights for women and a natural extension of their efforts in the areas of education and employment
had been transformed into a plebiscite on changing social conditions, particularly women's greater participation in the paid labor force, the attendant changes in their family role, and potential contributions to the
military. This shift spelled the beginning of the end for the GCSW.

Though another Governor's Commission on the Status of Women
was instituted in mid-December of 1975 under the administration of
Democrat David Pryor (1975–79), interest in such units as an effective
means for facilitating changes in women's status waned in the late 1970s,

in Arkansas and elsewhere. In fact, few of the women's commissions and councils established in the United States in the 1960s were in continuous operation through the 1970s.[92] Many expired with the term of office of the appointing governor. Others were repealed by hostile or disinterested legislators, or simply experienced a gradual waning in their activity levels.[93] By the start of 1972, for example, seven states or territories (Connecticut, Indiana, Montana, New Mexico, North Dakota, Tennessee, and Puerto Rico) were without active commissions.[94] By 1976, Alaska, Arizona, Texas, and the Virgin Islands, were added to the list.[95] Still, members of the Arkansas GCSW continued to be fairly active throughout the mid- and late-1970s. Under the leadership of the commission's former part-time executive secretary, Harryette Dorchester, the group gathered for its first meeting in January of 1976. Composed of thirty-two members, the commission again was touted by the Pryor administration and by Dorchester as having been consciously designed to represent a cross section of Arkansas women. In announcing the appointees, age and regional diversity were emphasized, as was economic status. "The Commission has had trouble involving low income women in its activities in the past. I hope we can correct this," Dorchester said in a *Gazette* interview.[96] The inclusion of more conservative women, however, was not mentioned.

At the Pryor GCSW's first meeting, the group agreed that among their goals would be the timely implementation of Title IX of the 1972 higher education amendments to the 1964 Civil Rights Act, which provided for sex equity in educational institutions, and the establishment of a speakers' bureau to educate the public about the commission's activities. The group also reentered the ERA debate, voting unanimously to "endorse and work for ratification of the proposed Equal Rights Amendment" at the next legislative session.[97] Likewise, the twenty-eight commissioners present voted to cooperate with the state Coalition for the Ratification of the ERA formed two years before. As chair, Dorchester stressed that public funds would not be used to pursue this component of the commission's goals, noting that "any lobbying [will be] done on an individual basis."[98] Still, a December 1976 announcement of "ERArkansas" as the new organization leading the proratification campaign noted that Alice Glover, a retired teacher, and Margie Ann Chapman, an attorney, would cochair the group. Both women were identified in news accounts as being affiliated with the GCSW, Glover under the Bumpers administration and Chapman at the time of the announcement.[99]

With just four more states needed in the ratification push by ERA proponents nationally, the Arkansas General Assembly again took up the issue early in its 1977 regular session. Though the body's more optimistic pro-ERA members (who were dwindling in number) insisted the measure still had a "50–50 chance," most observers agreed that it lacked support. Media attention thus came to focus upon whether the resolution introduced in the House would come to a vote, or instead would be left to languish in the State Agencies and Governmental Affairs Committee as it had in 1975.[100] Governor Pryor continued to insist that the issue should be brought to a vote of the floor, again making it an "administration bill."[101] Even a vote of the committee was delayed repeatedly, however, often due to the existence of a related resolution offered by Representative Boyce Alford of Pine Bluff. An unabashed delaying tactic, Alford's measure called upon the committee to recommend a statewide referendum on ERA ratification.[102]

It was during this period that ratification advocates gained an unexpected ally. Representative Carolyn Pollan of Fort Smith, according to a February 1977 *Gazette* interview, became a member of yet a third "minority" group in the state legislature when she cosponsored and actively lobbied her peers on behalf of the ERA. Already one of only five Republicans and just three women in the Assembly, Pollan was credited with making one of the most effective pro-ERA speeches of the prolonged debate. At a four-hour hearing of the House State Agencies and Governmental Affairs Committee in mid-January, she based her support of the amendment on religious grounds. Angered at a letter she had received that declared "A Christian cannot support the ERA," Pollan told the committee that "In God's sight" she was "the same as any man. Christ did not say," she continued, "'Carolyn, if you want to come into the Kingdom of Heaven, you will need to have your husband or father or brother or sons at the door with you to ask for admittance.'" God gave her "equal rights for salvation" and she insisted that the Arkansas legislature grant her that same measure of equality."[103]

Though the committee eventually did pass the resolution on for consideration by the full membership of the House, it did so only by voice vote, making the identification of advocates and opponents nearly impossible.[104] This remained the case two weeks later as opponents of ratification proposed that the resolution, with its "do pass" recommendation from the State Agencies Committee, be referred to the House Rules

Committee, an unfriendly venue sure to spell its defeat. After a voice vote of the full membership seemed to indicate that a majority favored the hostile referral, ERA supporters insisted on a call of the roll so the positions of all members would be on record. House Speaker James Shaver recognized Representative Ernest Cunningham of Helena instead, however, and Cunningham proposed an alternative counting maneuver called a "division of the House." Members favoring the referral then quickly stood to be counted, followed by members opposing it. Via this technique, the House was recorded as voting forty-four to twenty-eight in favor of sending the ERA resolution to the Rules Committee. A journalist present at the melee noted that at least two members stood up twice during the count.[105]

In the face of members' apparent eagerness to kill the ERA without actually voting against it, Representative Thomas Sparks of Fordyce insisted that the House vote on the ratification resolution and not delay the matter further with a referendum. Speaking about the Alford proposal, Sparks said "This dad-blasted bill is the worst piece of trash I have ever seen in my life" and challenged "the guts" of legislators trying to skirt the issue by considering a referendum. In the end, the issue was moot as Alford's resolution to call for a public referendum in November 1978 was also exiled to the Rules Committee.[106]

Though ERA proponents tried a few days later to pry the resolution out of the committee, they again failed on a series of procedural points.[107] The *Gazette* scolded the House, as did Bob Lancaster's column in the *Democrat,* both suggesting it had fled "pell-mell from its obligation."[108] And women's groups supporting ratification—still led by past GCSW member Alice Glover—angrily vowed to make lack of consideration of the ERA a central political issue for each House member in the next election.[109] But, after a searing floor speech by Representative Pollan—met with polite applause—about politicians "abdicating responsibilities," the resolution finally succumbed for the year.[110]

As the ERA faded, so, too, did the women's commission. Tellingly, the last reference to the Arkansas Governor's Commission on the Status of Women to appear in the *Gazette* was in the form of a full-page advertisement for the Equal Rights Amendment. Printed on April 10, 1977, the ad was paid for by ERArkansas. It featured the text of the amendment, a statement of the organization's objectives and beliefs, and an extensive list of supporting organizations and individuals. The GCSW was listed among the three dozen or so organizations that endorsed the ERA.[111] Interviews and official documents suggest that subsequent to the ad, the commission's activities began to dwindle to two tasks after the spring of 1977. First, the unit had applied for and received in December 1976 a fifty thousand dollar, eleven-month federal grant to study employment issues in Arkansas. The GCSW convened a meeting for that purpose in Hot Springs on June 25.[112] Second, and more significantly, members of the GCSW, together with other women's groups and activists, helped organize a federally funded state convention commemorating International Women's Year. At the convention, delegates were to be selected to attend the National Women's Conference to be held in November of 1977.[113]

The conference, dubbed "AWARE" (Arkansas Women: Accomplishments, Realities, Expectations) by organizers, opened on June 10 amid allegations that it was misusing "taxpayers' money to promote women's lib."[114] Specifically, a group calling itself the Arkansas International Women's Year Citizens Review Committee claimed that only feminist groups had been invited to attend the meeting. The group's spokeswoman, Judy Freeman, and two dozen supporters were present at the sessions as "monitors" of the tone and message of the event. Though by Freeman's own admission most of the charges were not borne out, and despite complaints by others that the more "radical wing" of the women's movement had been excluded, the resentment felt by many antifeminist groups about the IWY gathering did not subside.[115] The situation culminated in a seven-hour closing session of the conference at which resolutions supporting the Equal Rights Amendment and legal abortion, and condemning discrimination against gays and lesbians, were resoundingly adopted.[116] The conference also voted to send eighteen delegates to the national IWY Houston conference, all seemingly feminist and five with ties to recent Governor's Commissions on the Status of Women (Jeane Lambie, Sara Murphy, Diane [Kincaid] Blair, Leona Troxell, and Margie Chapman). The anti-ERA group failed to have anyone from its slate of delegates selected.[117]

Though dozens of organizations remained active in Arkansas's ultimately unsuccessful ERA ratification push as the amendment moved closer to the original March 1979 deadline, received a controversial three-year extension, and finally fell short of ratification by just a handful of states in June 1982, the Governor's Commission on the Status of Women was not

among them.[118] The network of actors associated with the GCSW grasped
that the environment that had nurtured—or at least tolerated—public
sponsorship of their goals had changed, and together with other participants in the women's movement in Arkansas, they subsequently adopted
new strategies. By 1978, as antifeminist women found their political voice
and as the conservative tide rose nationally, the efforts of Arkansas feminists had consciously come to center upon private associations, less conspicuous commissions and study groups, and organizations geared toward
electing women to public office. Chief among these was the Arkansas
Women's Political Caucus, which rallied feminists and groomed women
for public office.[119] Also launched was the Arkansas Press Women's Club,
which flourished in the 1970s and served to promote network-building
among female journalists, editors, and publishers (who were prohibited
from membership in the mainstream professional association until
1970).[120] A Council of Women in Higher Education, commissions on the
status of women on at least two university campuses (the University of
Arkansas and the University of Arkansas at Little Rock), and the Arkansas
Association of Business and Professional Women also had been established,
or had grown substantially, in the same decade. Additionally, the GCSW
under Pryor, and later the state Department of Labor, continued to pub-
lish a legal handbook on women's rights.[121]

Further, even as feminists turned to private associations, increasing
numbers of women were to be found in public positions (other than
appointments to the women's commission). At the local level, 4 percent
of school board members were female by 1977 (up from just 0.5 percent
two years earlier), and twelve women had become school board presidents. Women also made up 5 percent of all justices of the peace and
were found to be making gains as elected city executives. Moreover,
approximately 140 women were serving as alderwomen or members of
city boards of directors throughout the state.[122] On a statewide level,
Arkansas was served in 1977 by a female state treasurer and three women
members in the General Assembly. Though they lost, two other women
had made bids in 1974 for the office of lieutenant governor and for the
congressional seat of Wilbur Mills. Governors Bumpers and Pryor also
had appointed women to a couple of key administrative posts. Of special note was Governor Pryor's selection of a female appointments aide,
ERA activist and GCSW ally Shirley McFarlin, who substantially facilitated the effort to place women onto the state's many other boards and

commissions. Blair quipped that this choice was a coup d'etat for women, concluding: "I mean that was putting the fox in the henhouse."[123]

Such changes did not immediately shift the cumulative male/female balance of power in the state, but momentum was building by the close of the 1970s. This altered atmosphere, together with the continued countermobilization of conservative organizations in the state, finally led Blair, Snow, Lambie, and other GCSW allies to abandon commissions as mechanisms for the advancement of women altogether. One reason for this change was that conservatives had begun to demand equal representation on the commission and commission supporters believed "this was a recipe for disaster."[124] Another was the feeling among some that an official commission charged with studying the status of women was an easy alternative to substantive action.[125] It is difficult to determine which of these concerns may have prevailed among the most prominent members of the women's movement in Arkansas; Lambie later suggested, simply, that "both were very important," and others echoed her conclusion.[126] What is clear is that rather than allow the commission to become a forum for feminism's opponents, or allow its existence to distract elected leaders from concrete policy change, a conscious decision was made to let it die.

In fact, Blair, Snow, and Betsey Wright, a Clinton campaign strategist and trusted advisor to the governor during the 1980s, later recalled that newly elected governor Bill Clinton and his staff offered in early 1979 and again during subsequent terms to authorize another commission if the women were interested in its continuation. They declined.[127] The controversy that had arisen over the ERA struggle and the combative atmosphere that occurred during the International Women's Year events had proved to be too much.[128] Additionally, the commission had enjoyed substantial success, and in many ways there no longer was a need for "the constant nagging" commissioners were providing. "It became easier," Blair concluded, "to let things dissolve and to go ahead . . . and continue the work we were doing through different means."[129] Former commissioner Snow echoed this perspective. "Governor's commissions were increasingly becoming targets" of conservative groups; they were "lightning rods" in a stormy social and political environment. "We weren't dampened in enthusiasm . . . we just did our thing in other ways."[130]

Arkansas's war over what its women citizens wanted thus continued into the 1980s, but without a Governor's Commission on the Status of

Women as a player. Though McFarlin volunteered in an interview that she was "not sure at all that endorsing the ERA had anything to do" with the unit's disappearance, a review of the decade's events suggests otherwise.[131] McFarlin's assessment that the commission received "tacit" but not "aggressive" support from the governor's office over the years was probably accurate. Yet, several of the quotes from members of the antifeminist, anti-ERA contingent were revealing as to the impact upon the GCSW that the ERA-countermobilization had. One of the El Dorado spokeswomen who convened the December 1973 news conference demanding that the Bumpers GCSW be made more "representative," for example, took pains to point out that the commission "was supported by the National Organization for Women," an organization that had expressed strong support for the Equal Rights Amendment. "I'm against the ERA very definitely," she was quoted as saying.[132]

In fact, a common theme among anti-ERA forces until the measure's 1982 death was that by means of entities such as the GCSW public resources had been, in their view, hijacked to provide platforms for the feminist ideology. Members of an Arkansas chapter of FLAG (Family, Life, America, and God) traveled to Washington, D.C., in 1978, for instance, to find out how much money the U.S. State Department had spent on materials for the International Women's Year conference and to ask the state's congressional delegation not to approve any more federal funds for women's meetings.[133] Likewise, in the midst of the battle over an extension of the ERA ratification deadline in the summer of 1978, Schlafly asserted that "The ERA would be dead after repeated rejections by fifteen state legislatures and rescissions by four other state legislatures if it were not for the artificial respiration breathed into it by federal employees using taxpayers' money."[134] Both federal and state expenditures were a concern of Schlafly and her peers, as evidenced by the innumerable state actions and nine federal lawsuits eventually filed against the IWY state conferences and the Houston event.[135] The suits originated in a conviction encapsulated by FLAG organizer Marilyn Simmons in a later telephone interview: "That whole time it was like the deck was stacked. Everybody high up was pushing it."[136]

In many ways, this was true. It was indeed members of the publicly sponsored GCSW, especially Margaret Kolb, who had led representatives of nearly two dozen other state organizations to lobby U.S. Senator John L. McClellan in February of 1972 (the Senator was a member of the Senate Judiciary Committee considering the ERA after its passage in the House of Representatives in October of 1971).[137] McClellan and the rest of the Arkansas congressional delegation later voted to send the amendment to the states, and governors Bumpers, Pryor, and Clinton included the amendment's ratification in their legislative packages for several consecutive sessions.[138] To the antifeminists, the game looked fixed. To members and allies of the GCSW, their successful campaign in getting some of the "high ups" to support the amendment was a natural extension of their other activities: research, consciousness-raising, and public education on economic and educational opportunity, all aimed at elevating women's status. Which group was right?

In the end, it did not matter. The decision—through a series of non-decisions—not to ratify the amendment was made by a mostly male body of legislators, most of whom were hardly emphatic supporters of "women's liberation." Lawmakers who allowed themselves to be swayed early on by the perception that supporting ERA would bring political rewards quickly moved in the other direction when antifeminist opposition emerged. Projecting the image that they were mere arbiters of a "women's war" became a powerful tool in achieving the result that many members had perhaps desired from the start. As former GCSW commissioner Snow recalled, "I never got the sense . . . that there would be passage. Oh, it depended on the individual. Some were absolutely hostile to it and some were solicitous, but none I talked to ever said they'd vote for it."[139] Several accounts printed in both the *Democrat* and the *Gazette* support Snow's assessment, likewise emphasizing legislators' lack of interest in, or hostility to, the issue.[140] Among the more telling instances were the treatment of one-time House sponsor Paul Van Dalsem's efforts at redemption and subsequent punishment over an unrelated bill and Senator Mutt Jones's anti-ERA declaration that the United States already had demonstrated its high esteem for womanhood by setting aside a "special day . . . to do honor to the mothers of our children."[141] It was this combination of attitudes that graciously invited "the ladies" into government in the form of the Governor's Commission on the Status of Women but then ensured that they would show themselves out.

A Crime Unfit to Be Named

Arkansas and Sodomy

W. BROCK THOMPSON

This essay is about sodomy in Arkansas—or, more accurately, it is the story of three decades of cultural and legal change in the state (and nation) with respect to gays and lesbians and sexual privacy. As presented by the author, the events that most directly define this changing environment include: (1) The adoption of a new Arkansas Criminal Code by the state legislature in 1975 that decriminalized sodomy, a practice which had been outlawed in Arkansas since statehood (1836); (2) an act of fellatio on February 12, 1976, committed by two men being held in a Pulaski County "drunk tank"; (3) the signing of a bill by Governor David Pryor on March 28, 1977, recriminalizing sodomy in Arkansas; (4) the U.S. Supreme Court decision in Bowers v. Hardwick *(1986) upholding a Georgia law banning homosexual sodomy (and containing Chief Justice Burger's characterization of homosexual sodomy as "a crime not fit to be named"); (5) the Arkansas Supreme Court decision in Jegley v.* Picado et. al. *(2002), which declared the state's law against sodomy unconstitutional; and (6) the announcement by Attorney General Mark Pryor, son of the governor who had signed the antisodomy bill into law, that the state would not seek a review of the case by the U.S. Supreme Court.*

The author weaves these events together and, in the process, tells a fascinating story. The reader should take particular note of the author's argument that changing national attitudes toward sexual freedoms (from the Sexual Revolution of the 1960s to the

W. Brock Thompson, "A Crime Unfit to be Named: Arkansas and Sodomy," *Arkansas Historical Quarterly* 61 (Autumn 2002): 255–71. Reprinted with permission.

*"backlash" of the 1980s) had an impact on the events that make
up this story—and, thus, on the policymaking process in Arkansas.*

The turbulent decade of the 1970s witnessed extraordinary and hotly
contested transformations in American attitudes toward sex and sexuality. The values of "free love" and tolerance that had sprouted during the
1960s began to take root in everyday life in the 1970s. The gay and lesbian movement, prospering from the successes of earlier protest movements, gained many legal victories across the nation. Queer visibility was
on the rise.[1] In 1972, for instance, moviegoers were charmed by director
Bob Fosse's *Cabaret,* one of the first American films that openly dealt
with the homosexuality of its characters.[2] On December 15, 1973, the
American Psychiatric Association unanimously approved a referendum
removing homosexuality from its list of mental illnesses.[3] This development had a tremendous impact on the public perception of homosexuality, not to mention the self-esteem of gays and lesbians living in the
United States. Yet a conservative element, personified by orange juice
huckster Anita Bryant, soon unleashed a backlash that would wash over
the state of Arkansas.

Early in 1977, the *Arkansas Gazette* reported that the Arkansas House
of Representatives had "discovered sex" and "intends to do something
about it."[4] During the first seven days of the session, legislators introduced
four bills dealing with sexual conduct. Rep. Arlo Tyer of Pocahontas took
credit for the first two bills: House Bill 237 sought to prohibit "R" and "X"
rated movies within the state, and House Bill 238 would levy a tax of $1,500
on men and women who lived together without having married. This latter bill sought, according to the *Gazette,* to make the point that while "such
cohabitation is now common in many communities," it was not to be condoned by the state. Besides paying the tax, the couple would also be
required to undergo blood tests and obtain a permit from a chancery judge
to continue cohabiting. The judge would only issue the "living together
permit" if the couple were able to show "good cause."[5] The third bill,
House Bill 191, introduced by Rep. Earl Jones of Texarkana, sought to cen-
sor sexually explicit material in the state. The "comprehensive obscenity
bill" would outlaw books and magazines that had no redeeming social or
artistic value. The fourth bill was written hastily in reaction to a development that disturbed Rep. Bill Stancil, a high school football coach from

Fort Smith. Two men had been caught in a sexual act by a police officer but apparently had broken no law.[6]

On February 12, 1976, James Black (Sammy to his friends) began drinking early. After several complaints from neighbors, Little Rock police took him into custody for public drunkenness. They put Black in the "drunk tank" at three thirty in the afternoon. An hour later, Willie Henderson, who had been arrested for driving under the influence of alcohol, joined him. The two men were not alone. Besides the jailers who periodically patrolled the drunk tank and its surrounding cells, about fifteen other detainees waited to sober up. But these circumstances did not diminish Black and Henderson's attraction to one another. An hour after Willie Henderson arrived in the drunk tank, patrolman Hugh Gentry noticed the two men engaged in an act of fellatio.

As it turned out, the behavior of the two men was perfectly legal, or at least no longer illegal. At midnight on January 1, 1976, the Arkansas Criminal Code had changed. The new code held no statute making sodomy a crime. The two men could not be charged with sodomy, as they could have been before January 1. Nor could the men be prosecuted for indecency, which was defined under the new code as follows: "a person commits public sexual indecency if he engages in any of the following acts in a public place or public view: (a) an act of sexual intercourse; (b) an act of deviate sexual activity; or (c) an act of sexual contact."[7] On February 13, 1976, Municipal Judge Jack Holt Sr., long known for his liberal views, ruled that the Little Rock city jail was not a public place. In an interview with *Arkansas Gazette* reporter George Bentley, Judge Holt remarked that "a public place is a place that the public has access to at any time, no matter who they are."[8] The judge continued, "in any criminal offense, if the statute says the person so charged must commit it in a public place, that will be my ruling, if the crime is sexual deviation or drunkenness, or no matter what it is." Judge Holt remarked that "if someone slipped a bottle of liquor to a prisoner and he got drunk, you couldn't charge him with public drunkenness."[9] Thus the two men could not be charged with any sex crime.

At the time, no one publicly took issue with this. However, many police officers privately expressed dissatisfaction with the judge's ruling, and Chief Deputy Prosecuting Attorney Wilbur C. "Dub" Bentley worried that the city jail would soon turn "into a gay bar."[10] The case went otherwise unnoticed for several weeks. Deputy Prosecuting Attorney Jack

Magruder, who at the time handled the state of Arkansas's cases in municipal court, declined to report the ruling to his supervisors in the prosecutor's office. He said he tended "to agree with the decision."[11] Judge
Holt had given Magruder the option of declining to prosecute the
charges against the two men or having the judge dismiss the charges himself. Magruder opted not to prosecute.

Under the law, however, the state had one year to file charges against
the two men. After a *Gazette* reporter brought the case to the public's
attention, the state did refile—but with the same result. Circuit Judge
William J. Kirby ruled that the city jail's drunk tank was indeed not a
public place and dismissed the charges of "public sexual indecency"
against Sammy Black and Willie Henderson. Arkansas's new criminal
code defined "public place" as "a public or privately owned place to which
the public or substantial numbers of the public have access." The new
criminal code also defined "public view" as "observable or likely to be
observed by a person in a public place."[12] Under the new criminal code,
Kirby ruled, the two men committed no real crime.

Under the old criminal code, the two men could have been charged
with sodomy, whether the act had been committed in a private or public space. The Arkansas sodomy statute that was repealed in 1976 had
been on the books since Arkansas achieved statehood in 1836 and had
been upheld by the Arkansas Supreme Court as recently as 1973.[13] The
statute read: "*Sodomy* or *Buggery*. Every person convicted of sodomy, or
buggery, shall be imprisoned in the penitentiary for a period not less than
five years nor more than twenty-one years."[14] The statute was ambiguous in three respects. First, it did not define what exactly constituted
"sodomy or buggery." It was unclear if the statute outlawed anal penetration, oral penetration, or both. Second, the statute made no distinction between public or private space. Third, the sodomy statute was not
same-sex specific. Indeed, given the language of the statute, it was not
sexually specific at all. It did not pertain specifically to either homosexual or heterosexual acts. Under the older statute, sodomy was a crime
and sodomites were criminals, whatever their sexual orientation.

When the state's new criminal code was enacted, the sodomy law
was not the only statute that was removed. Across the country, debates
over state criminal code reformation had been going on for several years.
It was clear to many that the American criminal justice system was dan-
gerously haphazard. Many states' legal codes included antiquated laws

written in the colonial period, they themselves vestiges of English common law. In response to this crisis, the American Law Institute completed the Model Penal Code, a guide to help states modernize their existing penal codes by removing old and unnecessary laws from the books. This independent group of judges, lawyers, and law professors sought to "modernize American law in almost all aspects."[15] Though the institute did not have any formal control over legislative decisions, its recommendations carried a great deal of weight. While only one state, Illinois, adopted the code as written, many states, including Arkansas, used it as a guide in reforming their criminal statutes.[16]

The state of Arkansas formed the Arkansas Criminal Code Revision Commission, consisting of lawyers, law professors, and law enforcers, as well as ministers and Catholic priests. The commission drafted the 1976 Arkansas Criminal Code for consideration by the state legislature. Practically every major offense underwent at least minor definitional revision. With respect to sex offenses, the Revision Commission decided that any sexual activity committed by consenting adults in private would not be illegal. The code it drafted borrowed directly from the Model Penal Code in forbidding sexual activities with minors, in public spaces or in public view, or with non-consenting parties. The new criminal code prompted little scrutiny. It easily passed both houses of the Arkansas legislature and was signed by Gov. David Pryor to go into effect January 1, 1976.[17]

A year later, Representative Stancil claimed he had been hoodwinked. After learning that Sammy Black and Willie Henderson had technically committed no crime, he had discovered to his amazement that he had voted for this new criminal code that essentially legalized sodomy. He soon took action to rectify the situation. In haste, he drafted House Bill 117, which would define sodomy as any deviate sexual behavior and make it a class C felony punishable by as many as ten years in prison.[18] The bill and its author soon drew criticism from legislative colleagues. Rep. Art Givens of Sherwood noted that the new criminal code had decriminalized sodomy because it was a "victimless" crime. He argued before the House Judiciary Committee that Stancil's bill would potentially make criminals out of many husbands and wives in the state and warned that "everything except what is done strictly for reproduction may be criminal in nature."[19] Givens suggested that Stancil consult the Arkansas attorney general's office for its opinion, but Stancil responded that he was not particularly interested in the attorney general's opinion. Nevertheless, Stancil agreed to amend the bill to define sodomy more precisely and to reduce the penalties with which it could be punished. As amended, House Bill 117 made bestiality and sodomy class D felonies, carrying prison terms of as long as five years, and defined sodomy as an act between two members of the same sex.[20]

Deputy Prosecuting Attorney John W. Hall of Little Rock spoke against the measure, saying that the state had no compelling interest in prosecuting sex acts between consenting adults. Hall argued that any such law would surely be struck down by the courts for violating the Arkansas constitution's guarantees of equal protection and the individual's right to privacy. He noted that under the amended bill, a homosexual couple committing a sexual act in the privacy of their own home could be found guilty of a felony, while a heterosexual couple committing a sexual act in public would only be guilty of public indecency, a misdemeanor.[21] Despite this plea, the Judiciary Committee adopted the amended bill and sent it to the floor with a "do pass" recommendation.[22]

Despite the debate over the bill in committee, it seemed that few legislators took it seriously. During the committee's proceedings, the room often exploded with laughter. Committee vice chairman N. B. "Nap" Murphy of Hamburg, who was presiding, continually pleaded for dignity. The giggles continued and, at one point, the hilarity was so intense that the course of business became difficult to follow. Murphy, repeatedly striking his gavel, pleaded: "Gentlemen, I do not know what is going on at this time."[23]

Though the bill passed the House Judiciary Committee, it was clear that once it arrived on the House floor it would have to be amended even further. Hall's argument with respect to the disproportionate penalties applied to sodomy convinced many House members, despite their reckless discourse while the bill remained in committee. Stancil agreed to change the proposed statute to define sodomy as a misdemeanor rather than a felony. This would carry a maximum penalty of up to a year in prison and a one thousand dollar fine.[24]

When the bill came up for a vote on the floor of the Arkansas House of Representatives, Stancil feared there still was a possibility of it being defeated. To convince his fellow lawmakers, he took to the floor and produced from his briefcase copies of both the King James Bible and the Arkansas Constitution. Stancil paced the floor of the House waving the two works and shouting: "One of these can be amended, but the other can't." The bill passed the Arkansas House of Representatives on a vote of sixty-six to two.[25]

When the bill arrived on the floor of the Arkansas Senate, it was treated in the same manner as it had been in the House Judiciary Committee. The bill's sponsor, Senator Milt Earnhart of Fort Smith, remarked apologetically that he did not "have any live demonstrations" to accompany his explanation of the bill.[26] The Senate chamber erupted with laughter and applause. Earnhart added that the bill was "aimed at weirdos and queers who live in a fairyland world and are trying to wreck traditional family life."[27] The Senate, on a vote of twenty-five to zero, passed the bill.

Eleven days later, on March 28, 1977, representatives of the American Civil Liberties Union and the Quakers met with Gov. David Pryor's legal advisor, Larry Yancey, and urged the governor's office to reject the bill. Several gay and lesbian organizations, as well as the governor of California, Edmund G. Brown Jr., telephoned Pryor's office to inquire after the bill.[28] Their efforts were unsuccessful. Pryor signed House Bill 117 into law that very afternoon. As enacted, the law declared that "A person commits sodomy if such performs an act of sexual gratification involving: (1) The penetration, however slight, of the anus or the mouth of an animal or a person by the penis of a person of the same sex or an animal; or (2) The penetration, however slight, of the vagina or anus of an animal or person by any body member of a person of the same sex or an animal." Sodomy was defined as a Class A misdemeanor, punishable by a jail term of up to one year and a fine of up to one thousand dollars.[29]

"Every governor bows to political pressure," Yancey later explained, "and no one, including the governor, wanted a 'nay' vote on their record, especially when it came to sodomy."[30] Though many of them had made light of the bill, all but two legislators fell prey to the same pressures as Pryor. Yancey recalled that legislators would complain that "preachers back home" were giving them the "what for about sodomy."[31] A national backlash had come to Arkansas.

Earlier in the same month that the sodomy bill became law, the Arkansas House of Representatives considered House Bill 32. Introduced by Rep. Albert "Tom" Collier, the legislation applauded singer and Florida orange juice spokeswoman Anita Bryant for her opposition to equal housing and employment legislation for homosexuals in the Sunshine State. It drew the attention even of White House aides who, after receiving dozens of phone calls and letters from gays and lesbians, called Collier, according to his own account, to ask what the resolution had to say. Collier also noted that in response to his legislation, he received "a real nice letter" from Bryant thanking him and the Arkansas House of Representatives for the resolution. House Bill 32 easily cleared the Arkansas House of Representatives.[32]

The actions taken by Pryor and Collier earned the pair commendations from the Independence Baptist Association of Arkansas. In a letter to Pryor, the association, seeking to preserve "moral and spiritual purity" in the state, noted that it had passed a similar resolution commending Bryant for her adamant stand "against the immoral practices of homosexuality and similar activities." The letter encouraged both Pryor and Bryant to "uphold always the Biblical teachings concerning these immoral practices."[33]

At the same time the Arkansas legislature debated the sodomy law, Bryant had been making national headlines campaigning against gay rights. Bryant had long been a popular performer in the American South, making a name by singing at conventions and state fairs and wooing audiences with patriotic numbers such as the "Battle Hymn of the Republic" and "God Bless America." However, by 1977, the native of Barnsdall, Oklahoma, had become most recognizable as the spokeswoman for the Florida Citrus Commission. Most memorably, she appeared in television commercials singing: "Come to Florida sunshine tree! Florida sunshine naturally!"[34] At the prompting of the citrus commission, she had made Miami, Florida, her home. Once there, she became alarmed upon learning from her local pastor that the Dade County Metro Commission, the legislative body for the city of Miami, was planning to add "affectional or sexual preference" to the city's civil rights ordinance. Adding this phrase would essentially protect homosexuals from discrimination in housing, public accommodations, and employment. Enraged, Bryant determined to defeat the measure. However, time was short and Bryant and her allies were only able to sway a few votes on the commission before the proposal was passed on a vote of five to three. In response, Bryant created the "Save Our Children" campaign aimed at toppling the legislation. In the campaign's literature, Bryant stated: "I don't hate homosexuals! But as a mother, I must protect my children from their evil influence. . . . *They want to recruit your children and teach them the virtues of becoming a homosexual.*"[35] This rhetoric proved highly effective. Bryant convinced many voters in the Miami area that the law would allow homosexuals employed in the county's public schools to freely advertise their sexuality. Bryant and her "Save Our Children" campaign pressed for a referendum to decide if the ordinance forbidding discrimination against lesbians and gays should be allowed to stand. She got it, and 70 percent of voters supported the ordinance's repeal in a special referendum on June 9, 1977. Bryant pledged to continue her crusade. "We will now carry our fight against similar laws throughout the nation that attempt to legitimize a lifestyle that is both perverse and dangerous to the sanctity of the family, dangerous to our children, dangerous to our freedom of religion and freedom of choice, dangerous to our survival as a nation."[36]

Though Arkansas, at the time, hardly boasted a gay community as sizable and conspicuous as that of Miami, certain changes in the traditional family were clearly taking place. In September 1977, the cover of the *Arkansas Times,* a popular alternative magazine, featured an article by Jim Ranchino entitled "The Arkansas of the '70s: The Good Ole Boy Ain't Whut He Used to Be." Ranchino, a native of Arkadelphia, noted that "pre-marital sex, the use of marijuana and unfaithfulness to marriage vows are becoming more the rule than the exception."[37] The departure from traditional institutions of marriage and family that the article broadcast was not altogether lost on Arkansans. In fact, many had been observing it with growing anxiety for some time, as evidenced by the host of bills dealing with sexual conduct and the pressure put on legislators by "preachers back home."[38]

The backlash in Arkansas was swift, and it seems that it only took that isolated incident in the Little Rock city jail to incite action from the legislature. Apparently few were willing to have a vote against an antisodomy ordinance on their legislative record. An episode in southeast Arkansas suggested that legislators may well have had to pay a price had they possessed the courage to take a stand against the homophobic tide swelled by Bryant. On January 5, 1978, the *Lincoln Ledger,* the principal newspaper for Lincoln County and Star City, Arkansas, published an editorial by Ross Dennis. It urged Bryant to "sit down and shut up," insisting that she had no right to save the world from what she considered to be sin. The editorial set off a small firestorm. The small paper and its editors were bombarded with phone calls and visits from local pastors, who threatened a boycott if the editorial was not retracted. In the next issue, the *Ledger's* general manager and owner, Thomas Roark, apologized, stating that he was "very wrong in letting this material be published." In the same issue, Dennis published "An Open Letter to the Readers," in which he apologized for having caused offense by his editorial. He explained that he chose Bryant simply "because she is such a controversial figure and I needed someone to point a finger at" and admitted that he "chose the wrong person for this part of the country." Despite his apology, Dennis was fired from the *Lincoln Ledger* one month later.[39]

Ironically, for all of her crusade's seeming efficacy, Bryant paid a high price for her outspokenness. Under pressure from a gay-organized boycott, she lost her lucrative orange juice contract. Bryant suddenly found it hard to find venues for her concerts. In its July 1977 issue, the *Ladies Home Journal* published the results of a survey that asked high school students to identify the man and woman who have "done the most damage to the world." The man ranking first was Adolf Hitler. The woman was Anita Bryant.[40]

By late the following year, Bryant could not even draw a crowd in Little Rock. Wearing a red and white dress with a long, flowing cape and carrying a red velvet-covered Bible, Bryant arrived in the state capital on Saturday, October 21, 1978. After the state's recriminalization of sodomy and the House of Representatives' passage of a resolution applauding her, Bryant probably assumed Arkansas would welcome her. Bryant may have been surprised then to find only three hundred in attendance for her performance at the three thousand seat Robinson Center Auditorium. Despite the rather poor turnout, Bryant continued with the show, entertaining the faithful few with such songs as "How Great Thou Art," "God Bless America," and "This Is My Country."[41]

It might have seemed that Bryant's influence in Arkansas and across the nation was fading fast. Yet the die had been cast, and Arkansas's sodomy law and similar antigay laws remained in force. Perhaps lawmakers, unwilling to take a stand on the issue, thought they could simply wait for a court to declare the laws unconstitutional, sparing them legislative hardship and political complications. A court challenge did occur, but its outcome would be far different than many expected. The case would become one of the more notorious ever heard before the Supreme Court of the United States.

In the summer of 1982, twenty-nine-year-old Michael Hardwick was arrested in Atlanta, Georgia, by a policeman sent to his home after he failed to show up for a court appearance related to a charge of public drunkenness. After entering the home, the policeman observed Hardwick and another man engaged in oral sex. The officer arrested Hardwick for violating the state's 1816 statute that made oral and anal sex, on the part of either homosexuals or heterosexuals, punishable by a prison term of one to twenty years. An arrest in a private home for consensual fellatio among adults was an extraordinary event, and Hardwick's case would find its way to the U.S. Supreme Court. Those looking to challenge the constitutionality of such sodomy statutes could hardly have imagined a better case. There were no other issues, such as the participation of minors, prostitution, or public indecency, that could obscure the fact that the state of Georgia presumed to regulate sexual behavior in the bedroom. Georgia attorney general Michael Bowers argued before the Supreme Court that "the most profound legislative finding that can be made is that homosexual sodomy is anathema to the basic units of our society: marriage and the family." Bowers concluded that the possible decriminalization of sodomy would demote "those sacred institutions to merely alternative lifestyles."[42]

The Supreme Court handed down the *Bowers v. Hardwick* decision on June 30, 1986. The next day the *Arkansas Democrat* ran a bold three-column headline: "High Court Upholds Georgia Sodomy Law." The *Democrat* reported that the ruling dealt only with homosexual sodomy, noting that by a five-to-four decision the court upheld the principle that "consenting adults have no constitutional rights to private homosexual conduct."[43] Associate Justice Byron R. White, writing for the majority, argued that the "issue presented is whether the Federal Constitution confers the fundamental right upon homosexuals to engage in sodomy and hence invalidates the laws of the many states that still make such conduct illegal and have done so for a very long time." After asserting that Hardwick was asking the Supreme Court to establish "a fundamental right to engage in homosexual sodomy," White declared, "This we are quite unwilling to do."[44]

Although White's opinion promoted the state's role as guardian of traditional morality, his argument dealt mainly with the question of privacy and the individual and was written in coldly objective prose. It was Chief Justice Warren Burger, writing a separate concurring opinion, who went further in condemning the crime of sodomy, and indeed homosexuality, on the grounds of religious ideology. Burger called sodomy an "infamous crime against nature," an offense of "deeper malignity" than rape, and a heinous act "the very mention of which is a disgrace to human nature." For Burger, sodomy was truly a "crime not fit to be named." Invalidating the Georgia statute would "cast aside millennia of moral teaching."[45]

Commentary soon followed the front-page article in the *Democrat*. The newspaper published an essay by the syndicated columnist William Raspberry that remarked that "you don't have to be gay or kinky to believe that the state has no business sticking its nose into private bedrooms."[46] The *Democrat* itself, however, was not as quick to disagree with the court. Eighteen days after the Supreme Court handed down the *Bowers v. Hardwick* decision, the newspaper offered a final opinion on the case. The editorial stated, "the court has made good public policy by flinching away from any declaration that a sick, socially valueless, widely outlawed minority practice merits constitutional protection as a social good." The *Democrat* went on to say that Arkansas should look to the Supreme Court's decision as a forerunner to overturning *Roe v. Wade*, the 1973 U.S. Supreme Court decision that invalidated state laws prohibiting abortions.[47]

Clearly, the pendulum had swung to the right, given a push, perhaps, by the state of Arkansas. In the wake of the Stonewall riots in New York City in June 1969, a gay rights movement had formed and succeeded in promoting tolerance of homosexuality among millions of Americans.[48] Between 1971 and 1980, twenty-two states repealed their sodomy laws. Large cities such as Seattle and Detroit adopted legislation forbidding discrimination on the grounds of sexual orientation. But these gains would be short-lived in the midst of the backlash conjured up by Bryant in Miami. Arkansas would be the only state to first repeal its sodomy law and then reinstate it targeting only homosexual acts, but it was part of a larger pattern.[49] Many states, as well as a host of large urban areas across the nation, would soon use legal methods to crack down on nascent queer visibility. Cities such as St. Paul and Wichita saw civil rights ordinances that included protection for gays and lesbians struck down only months after they had been passed.[50] As the conservative 1980s replaced the tumultuous 1970s, and the religious right began to gain further strength, the American legal establishment now considered it a legal duty to regulate homosexual behavior.

Curiously, though, in the twenty-five years after its passage, defenders of the Arkansas sodomy law often emphasized not its putative benefits but the fact that it was rarely enforced and thus presumably did gay people no harm. No one had been convicted under the law for private, consensual acts. Yet the rare instances in which sodomy arrests were made seem to have been peculiarly well-timed. During the legislative session of 1991, state senator Vic Snyder proposed legislation to remove the sodomy law from Arkansas's criminal code. Shortly after Snyder's bill was accorded a "do not pass" recommendation by the judiciary committee, Pulaski County sheriff's deputies arrested four men for sodomy at an Interstate 40 rest area near Morgan, only a few miles north of Little Rock. Another eleven men were charged with loitering for the purpose of committing a sexual act.[51] It might appear that authorities wanted to illustrate to the public that there was still a need for a state sodomy law.

Regardless of whether that was the case, sodomy laws—however irregularly they were enforced—remained the bedrock for discrimination against anyone in the homosexual minority.[52] First, and perhaps most clearly, there would always be the threat of criminal prosecutions looming over gays and lesbians as long as they were sexual beings. Second, such laws served to support a number of explicit legal disabilities. In addition to branding lesbians and gay men as criminals, sodomy laws have been used to deny employment, access to housing, child custody and visitation rights, and a host of other privileges and public benefits to gay applicants. At the University of Arkansas, Fayetteville, for example, in 1983 the student senate denied funding to a gay and lesbian student group seeking money for a series of films and lectures promoting tolerance of homosexuality. Although the gay and lesbian student group met all of the criteria for funding, the student senate insisted that they could not fund a program which promoted an illegal act.[53] The laws also served as a rationale against enacting local civil rights laws that would bar discrimination based on sexual orientation, and they supplied warrant for countless private discriminations, which lacked any explicit sanction in the law. As homosexuals had been defined as criminal and abnormal by the law, they might be treated as such by private individuals.

These were among the arguments made by seven gay and lesbian Arkansans who gathered in the rotunda of the state capitol building on Wednesday, January 28, 1998, to announce a lawsuit seeking to have the state's sodomy law declared to be in violation of the Arkansas Constitution. Though the plaintiffs acknowledged that there had not been a single instance of anyone being arrested for violating Arkansas's sodomy law in a private place, one of them, Vernon Stokay, argued that the law "is always an overriding threat. . . . You never know what kind of regime will come around. . . . It's always hanging over your head." The seven—Stokay, Elena

Picado, Robin White, George Townsand, Charlotte Downey, Bryan Manire, and Randy McCain, all residing in different locations throughout the state—were backed by Little Rock attorney David Ivers and the Lambda Legal Defense and Education Fund, a national gay rights organization. They believed that any future efforts to topple the law through the state legislature would fail, as had two subsequent attempts by Vic Snyder, in 1993 and 1995 (the bills died in committee). The challenge would have to come through the courts.[54]

There followed four years of legal jousting, which saw the plaintiffs win a ruling from Pulaski County circuit court judge David Bogard that the law was unconstitutional. On July 5, 2002, the Arkansas Supreme Court, in a five to two decision, affirmed Bogard's ruling. A sodomy law that had been on the books for twenty-five years was declared unconstitutional. The majority opinion, written by Associate Justice Annabelle Clinton Imber, stated that Arkansas could not use its police powers to "enforce a majority morality on persons whose conduct does not harm others." Citing Article II of the state constitution—particularly its guarantees of life, liberty, the pursuit of happiness, and the right of Arkansans to be secure in their persons and homes against unreasonable searches and seizures—as well as numerous laws passed by the state legislature indicating the value it placed on personal privacy, Imber wrote, "it is clear to the court that Arkansas has a rich and compelling tradition of protecting individual privacy and that a fundamental right to privacy is implicit in the Arkansas Constitution." This right extended to "all private, consensual, noncommercial acts of sexual intimacy between adults." The court also ruled that the 1977 sodomy law violated the state constitution's guarantees of equal protection in that it criminalized sexual acts between homosexuals that would be perfectly legal if engaged in by heterosexuals.[55]

The Arkansas Supreme Court had thus found more expansive guarantees of liberty, privacy, and equality in the state's constitution than the U.S. Supreme Court had been willing to find in the federal constitution. Shortly after the decision, one of the seven who had challenged the law, Randy McCain, declared, "I'm proud of the Supreme Court. I've always been proud to be an Arkansan, but I'm even more proud today."[56]

At the same time, Attorney General Mark Pryor, the son of the governor who had signed the sodomy bill into law, issued a statement from his office that he would not seek a review of the case by the United States Supreme Court. His spokesman noted simply: "The issue is settled."[57]

The Big Three of Late-Twentieth-Century Arkansas Politics

Dale Bumpers, Bill Clinton, and David Pryor

DIANE D. BLAIR

In this essay, Professor Blair profiles the political careers of three of the most prominent Arkansans of the last century: David Pryor, Dale Bumpers, and Bill Clinton—the "Big Three." She does so because she has a desire to share her thoughts, generated over decades of work as a social scientist and political activist, about each of them with her readers, and because the argument she makes later in the essay about the impact of The Big Three on Arkansas politics in the late twentieth century requires this individual, and somewhat personal, treatment.

Blair notes that Arkansas is unique in the extent to which it has resisted the "rising tide of southern Republicanism" that swept across the region over the last generation or so and that has come to define contemporary politics in the South and, to a lesser extent, the nation. As a result, Arkansas remains quite possibly the most one-party-dominated state in the nation. The central argument of the essay is that this particular brand of Arkansas exceptionalism stems in large part from the collective impact of the Big Three on Arkansas politics during roughly this same time period. As she puts it, "in sustaining their own appeal to the Arkansas electorate the Big Three helped prolong the appeal of the Democratic label."

Diane D. Blair, "The Big Three of Late-Twentieth-Century Arkansas Politics: Dale Bumpers, Bill Clinton, and David Pryor," *Arkansas Historical Quarterly* 54 (Spring 1995): 53–79. Reprinted with permission.

The most publicized outcome of the 1994 national elections was the Republican Party's capture of both houses of the U.S. Congress for the first time in forty years. A subsidiary, but no less consequential, story was evidence that the long-predicted realignment of the South, from its once solidly Democratic status to a partiality toward Republicans, had finally materialized. The southern preference for Republican presidential candidates, well established by the 1980s, penetrated in 1994 to congressional choices as well, with Republicans capturing a majority of all southern seats in both the House and the Senate. Republicans also held a majority of southern governorships in the aftermath of 1994 contests, and for the first time since Reconstruction, control of some southern state legislative chambers. As columnist David Broder observed, the Republicans "may have put the finishing touches on the 30-year-old effort to make the South their new foundation."[1]

Arkansas was not entirely immune to the rising tides of southern Republicanism. For the second time in a row its four seats in the U.S. House of Representatives were split evenly between Republicans (Jay Dickey in the Fourth District, Tim Hutchinson in the Third) and Democrats (Blanche Lambert Lincoln in the First District, Ray Thornton in the Second). Republican Mike Huckabee, first elected lieutenant governor in a special 1993 election, was resoundingly reelected with a comfortable 59 percent majority. Republicans picked up two seats in the State Senate, two in the state House, and seventeen in assorted county contests. However, compared with what was happening elsewhere in the South, these were marginal rather than momentous gains. Arkansas remained firmly in Democratic hands.

Democratic Governor Jim Guy Tucker, despite a vigorous campaign attempting to discredit his fitness for office, carried all but two counties and was reelected with 60 percent of the vote. Since neither U.S. Senate seat was at stake in 1994, those remained Democratic as well. Indeed, Arkansas is the only state never to have elected a Republican to the U.S. Senate. Of the five other statewide elected positions (attorney general, secretary of state, auditor, treasurer, and land commissioner), all five were filled by Democrats, the latter two uncontested and the others being won by margins, respectively, of 80 percent, 53 percent, and 64 percent. Democrats also remained in firm control of both houses of the General Assembly, with eighty-eight of one hundred House seats and twenty-eight of the thirty-five seats in the Senate. In other words, while Democratic majorities were being dramatically reduced or reversed elsewhere in the South, the traditional—some would say tyrannical—grip of the Democratic Party in Arkansas continued to diminish at incremental rather than torrential speed.

The reasons for Arkansas's ongoing resistance to Republicanism have been explored at length elsewhere, with particular emphasis on the state's long Democratic history combined with contemporary demographic characteristics.[2] These and other factors, such as the state's continuing failure to fund party primaries, undoubtedly have important explanatory value. Still, they do not quite suffice. Other southern states have at least some of the same components in their historical traditions, demographic profiles, and political structures, but they have moved much further down the path to realignment than has Arkansas.

What will be suggested here is that an additional factor may help to explain Arkansas's atypical ongoing attachment to Democrats, and that is the extraordinarily long run of three individuals who became the "Big Three" of late–twentieth century Arkansas politics: Dale Bumpers, David Pryor, and Bill Clinton. All three served as governor of Arkansas: Bumpers from 1971 to 1975, Pryor from 1975 to 1979, Clinton from 1979 to 1981 and again from 1983 through 1992. All three were elevated by the Arkansas electorate from the governorship to national office: Bumpers was elected to the Senate in 1974, Pryor to the Senate in 1978, and Clinton to the presidency of the United States in 1992.

None of the Big Three had a political career of absolutely unbroken success. Bumpers, in fact, lost his very first bid for office, a try for the Democratic nomination for state representative in 1962. Pryor's unsuccessful 1972 attempt to capture the Democratic nomination for the Senate away from venerable incumbent John L. McClellan failed so narrowly (Pryor got 48 percent in a runoff) that his political viability was sustained rather than terminated. Similarly, Bill Clinton's 48 percent loss to incumbent Third District Congressman John Paul Hammerschmidt was perceived as an amazing accomplishment for a twenty-seven-year-old law professor with no office-holding experience, and actually advanced rather than arrested Clinton's future political career. Governor Bill Clinton's 1980 loss to challenger Frank White, however, was a crushing defeat and one of the biggest upsets in Arkansas political history.

The Big Three, then, had their stumbles, but their setbacks were far outnumbered by their successes. A brief summary of their political careers and major accomplishments provides important context to the larger thesis here: in providing attractive models of progressive public service and thereby perpetuating their own tenure in public office, the Big Three did much to sustain and prolong the popularity and dominance of the Democratic Party in Arkansas.

First on the political scene was David Pryor. Born and raised in Camden, Pryor's initial venture into politics began when he was elected to the state legislature in 1960 while he was still in law school. He was reelected in 1962 and 1964. When longtime congressman Oren Harris resigned in 1966 to become a federal judge, thirty-two-year-old Pryor defeated four Democrats and one Republican to win the Fourth Congressional District seat, to which he was reelected without opposition in 1968 and 1970. With a seat on the powerful Appropriations Committee and reams of favorable publicity from his exposés of abuses of the elderly in nursing homes, Pryor could easily have extended his stay in the House. He chose instead to challenge Senator John L. McClellan in the 1972 Democratic primary. He lost by a narrow margin. In 1974, however, he successfully sought the governorship, first defeating six-time governor Orval Faubus in the Democratic Primary, (with 51 percent of the vote, thus avoiding a runoff), then Republican Ken Coon (with 66 percent) in the general election.

Pryor served four undramatic but accomplished years as governor. In his first term he continued his longstanding unsuccessful battle for thoroughgoing reform of Arkansas's 1874 Constitution and saw to the establishment of the Department of Local Services, the Department of Natural and Cultural Heritage, a statewide energy conservation plan, and an overseas office (in Belgium) of the Arkansas Industrial Development Commission. Presenting a tightly budgeted but forward-looking record to the electorate, Pryor carried all seventy-five counties and 59 percent of the electorate in his reelection bid in 1976. In Pryor's second term, the legislature did not enact his proposed Arkansas Plan, designed to shift taxing powers and responsibilities from the state to the local level, and lawmakers repealed his antilitter tax shortly after its adoption. However, Pryor's gubernatorial appointments were widely applauded, especially his breakthrough appointments of blacks and women.[3] It was a fiscally prudent, scandal-free gubernatorial record that Pryor presented to the electorate in 1978 when he faced and defeated two attractive opponents (U.S. Reps. Jim Guy Tucker and Ray Thornton) for the Democratic nomination for the Senate.

There he joined Dale Bumpers, who in 1974 had parlayed an extraordinarily successful two terms as governor into a decisive primary victory over thirty-year incumbent J. W. Fulbright for the Democratic nomination to the Senate. Fulbright's towering national and international reputation and years of attentive service to Arkansas might have made him invincible to ordinary challengers. Bumpers, however, had swiftly moved from obscurity to legendary status as a giant-killer.

After nearly twenty successful years practicing law and doing good (teaching Sunday school, serving as city attorney and as school board and chamber of commerce president) in Charleston, Bumpers in 1970 announced what at first seemed a quixotic quest for the Democratic gubernatorial nomination. Three prominent Democrats (former governor Orval Faubus, Attorney General Joe Purcell, and Arkansas House Speaker Hayes McClerkin) were joined by five unknowns (with whom Bumpers was classified) in a very crowded contest. Surprising the Democratic establishment with a second-place finish in the Democratic preferential primary, Bumpers next dispatched the once-invincible Faubus with a healthy 59 percent victory, and then, against one of the most expensive campaigns in Arkansas's history, defeated incumbent governor Winthrop Rockefeller with 62 percent of the vote. Bumpers's attractive personality, masterful use of television, and untainted record struck all the right chords with the Arkansas electorate, grown weary of Rockefeller's gridlock with the legislature yet wary of a return to the Faubus era.

Bumpers' two terms as governor were equally marked by success. In four years he extensively reorganized the executive branch of state government, modernized the budgetary process, and effectively depoliticized the state's personnel system. He persuaded the necessary three-fourths of the state legislature to make the state's income tax both more progressive and more productive, then used the increased revenues for a variety of essential state services such as state-supported kindergartens for preschoolers, free textbooks for high school students, improved social services for elderly, handicapped, and mentally retarded citizens, and an expanded state park system for all. Despite extensive changes and hefty tax increases, neither usually associated with political popularity in Arkansas, Bumpers's gubernatorial performance earned him easy reelection in 1972 (with 67 percent of the vote in the Democratic primary, and 75 percent in the general election) and an astonishing 90 percent approval rating at the end of his second term.[4]

Once in the Senate, both Bumpers and Pryor continued to serve in distinctive and distinguished ways. Bumpers promoted health programs for the poor, aid for rural development, arms control, deficit reduction, and reform of oil and gas drilling rights on federal lands. He opposed deregulation of oil and natural gas prices, attempted to block expensive defense and science projects such as the Star Wars initiative and the Supercollider, and repeatedly attempted reform of the 1872 Mining Act so as to require payment of royalties for mining on federal lands. Pryor continued his attention to the elderly by chairing the Special Committee on Aging and crusading against excessive prices on pharmaceuticals. He won passage of a Taxpayer Bill of Rights, guarded the interests of Arkansas agriculture, attacked government waste, exposed and limited excessive payments to private defense "consultants," and instituted reforms of inefficient Senate scheduling and procedures.[5]

Both senators also earned considerable national attention and acclaim. Bumpers was deemed one of the ten best senators by the national press and was seriously mentioned as a likely presidential candidate for both the 1980 and 1984 contests, with columnist Mary McGrory describing him as the "Senate's premier orator" and Senator Paul Simon expressing the opinion that he "would have more support in the U.S. Senate than any other candidate."[6] Pryor was elevated by his colleagues in 1989 to the third-highest position in the majority leadership ranks, secretary of the Democratic Conference.

Despite repeated attempts by election opponents to characterize Arkansas's senators as too liberal and too leftist for their constituents' tastes, their records were apparently highly acceptable to the electorate: Bumpers was reelected with 59 percent of the vote in 1980, 62 percent in 1986 and 69 percent in 1992; Pryor was reelected by 57 percent of the electorate in 1984 and in 1990 became the first U.S. senator since 1976 to escape opposition in both the primary and the general election. In 1993 the senators were joined in Washington, D.C., by another Arkansas political phenomenon, President Bill Clinton.

Born in Hope, raised in Hot Springs, educated at Georgetown University, Oxford University, and the Yale University School of Law, Clinton returned to Arkansas in 1973 with a faculty position at the University of Arkansas Law School in Fayetteville. His 1974 attempt to unseat Third District Congressman John Paul Hammerschmidt failed. However, in 1976 Clinton defeated (with 56 percent of the vote in the Democratic primary) a former secretary of state and a deputy attorney general to become an active and visible attorney general. In 1978 he overwhelmed opponents in both the Democratic primary and the general election to become, at age thirty-two, the second-youngest governor in Arkansas history.

Clinton's first regular session was action-packed and highly successful as he proposed and persuaded the lawmakers to enact an ambitious and wide-ranging legislative package initiating new programs in economic development, education, conservation, health, and roads. National news magazines hailed him as a "rising star," and his fellow Democratic governors elected him to chair the Democratic Governors Association. However, the major mechanism for financing the road-building program (hefty increases in vehicle registration and license fees) proved highly unpopular, especially in rural areas, and Clinton's popularity further declined when Arkansas was selected by President Carter as a resettlement site for thousands of Freedom Flotilla Cuban refugees. These and other circumstances led in 1980 to Clinton's narrow but stunning defeat by Frank White, a businessman and former Arkansas Industrial Development Commission director. Clinton became only the second twentieth century Arkansas governor to be denied his bid for a second, sometimes called courtesy, two-year term, and the youngest ex-governor in Arkansas (and American) history.[7]

In 1982, however, having apologized to the Arkansas electorate for past "errors" (especially the car tag increases and some controversial commutations) and perceived insensitivity, Clinton fought a vigorous, closely contested, ultimately successful (and in Arkansas unprecedented) campaign to recapture the governorship. Against both primary and general election competition he was reelected governor in 1984, again in 1986 (to Arkansas's first twentieth century four-year term), and again in 1990, becoming only the second governor in Arkansas history (the first was Faubus) to win more than three terms.

Clinton not only reestablished his credentials with the Arkansas electorate, but was increasingly turned to by his fellow governors to be their spokesman and leader. He was elected chair of the National Governors' Association in 1986, chair of the Education Commission of the States in 1987, and chair of the Democratic Governors' Association in 1988. He led the governors' attempts to restructure national welfare laws in 1988 (securing approval of the Family Support Act of 1988), and, as cochair of the President's Education Summit in 1989, played a critical role in drafting the National Education Goals. In 1987 a survey of practitioners and observers of state politics conducted by *U.S. News and World Report* found Clinton to be one of the nation's six best governors, citing particularly his "striking accomplishments" in education in a state lacking prosperity and his reputation as "probably the best-liked chief executive among his peers."[8] In 1991 a poll of all the nation's governors by *Newsweek* ranked Clinton "the most effective" governor in the country.[9]

In October 1991 Clinton declared his candidacy for the Democratic nomination for president. Clinton's record as governor came under exhaustive scrutiny during both the Democratic nomination battle and the three-way general election contest between incumbent Republican George Bush, independent billionaire businessman Ross Perot, and Democratic nominee Clinton, with Bush and Perot competing by campaign's end as to who could portray Arkansas in the most unflattering light. Opponents charged that despite 128 tax and fee increases during Clinton's governorship, Arkansas still ranked last or next to last in family median income and average weekly wages, in literacy rates, teacher pay, infant health, and environmental quality. In the third and final presidential debate, Bush said that what worried him most was for Clinton to "do to America what he did to Arkansas . . . We do not want to be the lowest of the low."[10]

The Clinton campaign issued data-filled documents arguing to the contrary: that Arkansas had the second-lowest state and local tax burden in the country, with taxes as a percent of personal income actually lower than when Clinton took office; that by July 1992, due in part to Clinton's numerous economic development initiatives, the state ranked fifth nationally in job creation and ninth in wage and salary growth, with median income growing at twice the rate of the nation's generally; that as a result of Clinton's education reforms, Arkansas had achieved the highest high school graduation rate in the region, was sending 34 percent more students to college than it did ten years previously, that Arkansas teachers received the highest percentage salary increase in the country the preceding year; that Arkansas's infant mortality rate had declined 43 percent from 1978 to 1990 to virtual parity with the national average, while over 60 percent of the state's children were being served in free preschool programs resulting from Clinton initiatives; and that Arkansas, one of only eight states meeting all federal standards under the Clean Air Act, had developed some of the most progressive water quality standards in the nation and was among the top ten states in wetlands protection and energy research.[11]

Perhaps most telling was the behavior of Arkansans themselves. They traveled by the hundreds with and for Clinton around the country, volunteered by the thousands at the campaign's national headquarters in Little Rock, dug deeply and contributed generously (Arkansas ranked first in per capita contributions in the 1992 presidential election campaign cycle), gave Clinton his single biggest majority (53.8 percent in a three-person race) of any of the fifty states, and celebrated wildly with him on election night when he claimed victory and thanked the people of "this wonderful, small state" for their support.[12]

Returning now to the central assertion of this article, that in sustaining their own appeal to the Arkansas electorate the Big Three helped prolong the appeal of the Democratic label, the sheer numbers tell a significant part of the story. Between 1970 and 1994 this trio of Democrats presented themselves to statewide electorates thirty-six times, and won in thirty-four of those instances. The average percentage received in those thirty-six contests (which included several crowded Democratic primaries and two losses) was an impressive 59.5 percent. Looking only at those seventeen instances when Bumpers, Pryor, or Clinton faced a Republican opponent, the average percentage of the vote received was an astonishing 64.1 percent. If Clinton's 1976 attorney general win and Pryor's 1990 return to the Senate, both without Republican opposition, are calculated in, the average percentage of the vote is an even higher 67.8 percent. From 1970 (Bumpers's first election to the governorship) to 1992 (Bumpers' fourth election to the Senate and Clinton's presidential victory) at least one and often two of these three familiar names were on the ballot every two years (except in 1988, when Clinton was in the middle of his first four-year term and neither Bumpers nor Pryor was up for reelection to the Senate).

Until Clinton's favorite-son candidacy brought Arkansas back to the Democratic column, Arkansas, like the rest of the once solidly Democratic South, had begun voting Republican in presidential contests. Unlike the rest of the South, however, as noted above, Arkansas Republicans had made little progress below the presidential level. What is being suggested here is that the cumulative draw of the Big Three at the top of the ticket sustained and strengthened the popularity of the Democratic label in Arkansas, thereby withstanding the general southern trend toward Republican realignment. But what were the particular characteristics of the Big Three that gave them such strong appeal to the Arkansas electorate? In the presence of many possible alternatives, why did Arkansans so repeatedly and decisively demonstrate their preference for Bumpers, Pryor, and Clinton?

What did these men offer to the electorate in apparently greater measure than did their many opponents? Interestingly, while each of these men followed a very singular career path, the three also possess some striking similarities.

The ability of some people rather than others to elicit electoral support remains, perhaps fortunately, more mystery than science. Still, the most obvious and perhaps best explanation for the extraordinarily long run of the Big Three is that their accomplishments in office, briefly reviewed above, convinced the voters that these politicians were as interested as were their constituents in producing a better life for most Arkansans. Their devotion to public service seems self-evident. Why else would talented lawyers who could (and did) make much more money in the private sector seek an office, such as the governorship, which paid so little? (The Arkansas governorship paid ten thousand dollars annually until 1976. It was increased by constitutional amendment to thirty-five thousand dollars annually until raised by constitutional amendment in 1992, to sixty thousand dollars annually.) As governor, all three proposed ambitious initiatives for economic development, educational and health improvements, environmental protection, and government reform, and secured passage of well over three-fourths of their proposals.[13] Additionally, as they solidified and strengthened the reform style of state government begun in the Rockefeller years, all three ran scandal-free administrations. Good government producing a better Arkansas is a fairly obvious common key to the Big Three's electoral success.

In addition to policy responsiveness, successful politicians must also be able to connect with people, to provide some bonds of empathy and identification between the citizen and the office-holder. Bumpers, Pryor, and Clinton all possess the gift for connecting in abundance. Perhaps this partially reflects a common element in their backgrounds: all were born and raised in small towns where they attended public schools. As many other eminent Arkansans can attest, such beginnings provide a superb training ground for future success. Small-town life exposes one at an early age to the whole spectrum of human accomplishment and failure, the lives of the few who are affluent, the ways of the many who live carefully and modestly, and the needs of those who are still struggling to survive. Pryor, Clinton, and Bumpers were all deeply imprinted with and grounded in the particulars of ordinary, everyday life in Arkansas, and they clearly drew deeply upon this motherlode of observation and understanding to inform their subsequent political decisions.

All three were also raised in households where issues and ideas were discussed and where public service was presented as a desirable undertaking. In numerous public addresses Bumpers told audiences that he had been taught by his father that "public service was the noblest of all professions."[14] Pryor's father, grandfather, and great-grandfather on his mother's side all served as sheriff of Ouachita County, and Pryor often referred proudly to the fact that his mother, Susie, was the first Arkansas woman to seek an elective county office (circuit clerk in 1926). Clinton's mother, a hardworking nurse, still found time to debate ideas with her son and encouraged him to share her interest in public affairs.

Furthermore, all were raised in households that were unashamedly Democratic. This is unsurprising in a state where almost everyone, and certainly everyone who "did" politics, was a Democrat. Pryor recalls accompanying his father to the post office to collect the mail and, upon inquiring about the identity of someone across the room, being told: "You don't want to know him, son. He's a Republican."[15]

However, unlike many Arkansans who were Democrats purely by reflex and tradition, in these three instances there was a philosophical underpinning as well. Bumpers, for example, often recalled how his father had sent him and his brother to get a glimpse of Franklin D. Roosevelt when the president was making a whistle-stop appearance nearby. Bumpers never forgot what the New Deal and later governmental initiatives had meant to his family:

> Born poor, but to devout and loving parents, my father was a small-town merchant whose business was barely surviving when REA came to the rural southland. It enabled him to start selling electrical appliances to a new market. In a small town where we choked on dust in the summer and bogged down in mud in the winter, where sewage ran down the ditches from overflowing outhouses and a few septic tanks, it was a caring Government in the 30s that gave us loans and grants to pave our streets and build a waste treatment facility. And when I returned from three years in the Marine Corps following World War II, it was a thankful and magnanimous Government that allowed my brother and me to attend the best universities in this Nation on the GI Bill—without which I would not be standing here today. And when Betty and I returned to our little hometown to begin my law practice and small business, and raise our beautiful children, we raised them free of the fear of polio and other childhood diseases that had been conquered because of vaccines developed with Government grants.[16]

Clinton also "grew up in the legacy of Roosevelt, where people talked about what government could do for people. My grand-daddy ran a little country store and fed hungry people before the advent of food stamps. He thought he was going to Roosevelt when he died."[17] Pryor was also imbued with the "superior" traits of a Democratic party that incorporated the best of the populist tradition. He ascribed the strength of that tradition in large part to Huey Long's whirlwind campaign through Arkansas in 1932, in which he successfully engineered Hattie Caraway's reelection to the Senate.[18] The governing philosophy all three men eventually brought to office might be called progressive populism—a willingness to use the power of government to counterweight the power and privileges of the economic elite, or in other words, a partiality toward those striving to climb the economic ladder rather than those who had already arrived at the top. This identification with the underdog, with its suspicion of concentrated wealth and the use of government to right the balance, is a powerful part of the Arkansas political tradition and one of the most recurrent themes in the rhetoric and careers of the Big Three.[19]

Clinton's first gubernatorial inaugural address in 1979 articulated themes that continued to characterize his political career, and those of Pryor and Bumpers as well:

> For as long as I can remember, I have believed passionately in the cause of equal opportunity, and I will do all I can to advance it.
>
> For as long as I can remember, I have wished to ease the burdens of life for those who, through no fault of their own, are old or weak or needy, and I will try to help them.
>
> For as long as I can remember, I have been saddened by the sight of so many of our independent, industrious people working too hard for too little because of inadequate economic opportunities, and I will do what I can to enhance them.[20]

Clinton, Bumpers, and Pryor share not only a common political philosophy but uncommon political skills. By the late twentieth century, success in achieving and maintaining major political office in Arkansas depended partially on the same sophisticated, professional paraphernalia that had become the hallmark of politics everywhere: skilled pollsters, paid media consultants, computer-generated mailings, and phone banks. Bumpers, as noted above, was the first Arkansas gubernatorial candidate to demonstrate how one could use television to reach voters directly, over the heads of unfriendly local bosses and a hostile political establishment.

By the time Clinton left the governorship he had demonstrated the effectiveness of the new high-tech politics in governance as well as campaigns: building public support for gubernatorial initiatives, advertising what had been accomplished at the end of a legislative session, and testing a variety of messages for making a program more acceptable and popular.

However, while all of the Big Three demonstrated their mastery of the new mass media politics, they also demonstrated their grasp of and incomparable proficiency at the personal, almost intimate aspect of Arkansas politics, which remains equally important to success. Pryor's remarks announcing his bid for reelection in 1990 simply but eloquently capture this familial flavor:

> It was . . . thirty years ago this month that I first asked the people of Ouachita County for one of the most precious possessions they owned . . . their vote. I wanted to be their State Representative.
>
> As spring came and summer engulfed, the election to that job became our life. Barbara and I divided up the neighborhoods, then the county, and together we literally went door to door and person to person. Even then, this type of "electioneering" was branded as "old-fashioned" and "out of step." But for us it became the rhythm and poetry of what America is all about. From the oil fields in the south to the Red Hills of Chidister and Reader and White Oak, we asked for every vote. On Friday and Saturday nights there were pie suppers and political speakings. On Sunday afternoon there was gospel singings and cake raffles.
>
> Dee, our oldest son, was just a baby. We carried him everywhere we went in a wicker basket. And we still have that wicker basket. . . . America is not about Presidents or Congress or Senators. It's not about statistics, policies, or programs, or even politicians like me. It's about neighbors, whether across the street or across the ocean. People who want to educate their children . . . people who need health care . . . farmers who want a chance . . . elderly who crave dignity . . . taxpayers who deserve fairness . . . and people who want to be free. I want to help.[21]

All of the Big Three became personally acquainted with tens of thousands of their constituents and made them feel like part of an extended family—calling them by name, inquiring about their jobs and health and parents and children, offering hugs as well as handshakes. All graced the stage at hundreds of high school commencements (even the smallest of which, according to Bumpers, takes the same length of time as the largest, as the achievements of each and every graduate are recounted).[22] All made the constant round of civic club speeches, community festival appearances, groundbreaking ceremonies,and political rallies. And they managed to do so with a good humor, grace, and gusto suggesting that there was nothing else they would rather be doing.[23]

Furthermore, they frequently used these personal appearances to advance their programs and defend their records in language that Arkansans easily understood and appreciated and with a style that invited listeners' attention and admiration. As the author has observed elsewhere:

> Continuing longstanding southern and Arkansas traditions, the present "Big Three" of Arkansas politics . . . are all superb story-tellers, who rarely use a prepared address, who quote easily and effectively from Scripture, and who can bring down the house with wry, self-deprecating humor. They have very different oratorical styles: Clinton lists debating points against invisible opponents; Pryor chats and charms; Bumpers educates and preaches. All however, quickly establish a strong rapport with the tens of thousands of Arkansans they encounter each year, thereby building powerful insulation against challengers' suggestions that they are "too intellectual" or "too liberal" or of dubious patriotism.[24]

It was, of course, more than well-liked programs and engaging styles that established and sustained the political lives of the Big Three. In building the large circles of friends, supporters, and contributors essential to sustained political success, they were able early in their careers to make excellent use of the gubernatorial appointment power.

Each Arkansas governor, it is estimated, makes approximately one thousand appointments a year to various boards and commissions. While some positions may seem obscure and unimportant, most are highly prized, as they afford opportunities to have some impact in a particular sphere of interest and carry a connotation of inside status.[25] Counting the combined gubernatorial years of the Big Three translates into a conservative estimate of ten thousand people who, by virtue of their appointments, felt some tie to their benefactors, some obligation to work for and contribute to their continued political success, and perhaps, some partisan loyalty.

All governors in all states have always used their appointive power to political advantage. However, one very distinctive aspect of the appointments made by the Big Three was their deliberate use to advance and empower two groups that had been traditionally excluded from Arkansas's political power structure—blacks and women. Gov. Winthrop Rockefeller had made some significant breakthrough appointments of blacks to such boards as correction, pardons and paroles, and public welfare. Bumpers, Pryor, and Clinton, however, took this practice to new levels and literally changed the face of Arkansas government.

Bumpers appointed a Governor's Commission on the Status of Women in 1971, which reported to him that only 10 percent of those serving on state boards and commissions were women, and most of those dealt with such traditionally women's areas as nursing, cosmetology, and the arts. By the time Bumpers left office, women filled many more appointive slots and did so on boards ranging from correction to the Board of Higher Education. Pryor appointed additional scores of women, including appointments to such previous all-male bastions as the Highway Commission, the Industrial Development Commission, and the Arkansas Supreme Court. As for Clinton, women managed most of his campaigns; his longest-tenured chief of staff (Betsey Wright) was a woman; and women served prominently in his cabinets including the directors of the departments of Education, Health, Pollution Control and Ecology, Parks and Tourism, and Natural Heritage. Furthermore, all of the Big Three supported the proposed Equal Rights Amendment to the U.S. Constitution.

Black voters have become an indispensable component of contemporary Democratic victories in Arkansas, but in the late 1960s, while Democrats (like Lyndon Johnson and Hubert Humphrey) were overwhelmingly favored for president, it was Republican Winthrop Rockefeller who arduously and successfully courted, nourished, and attracted black voters at the state level. A sizable and overwhelmingly Republican black vote was critical to Rockefeller's gubernatorial victories in 1966 and 1968 and loyally remained with him against Bumpers in 1970.[26]

By 1972, however, Bumpers had demonstrated—by refusing requests from white political leaders to shut down a controversial medical clinic in Lee County—that he was not simply a nonsegregationist, but a sympathetic friend, and black voters returned their undivided strength to Bumpers and the Democrats.[27] Pryor, who as a young state representative had sided with the black delegates from Mississippi in a controversial seating dispute at the 1964 Democratic National Convention, was also perceived as a courageous friend. And Clinton, throughout his tenure, named blacks to his staff, to the most powerful and prestigious cabinet positions (finance and administration, health and human services, and the development finance authority), and by the hundreds to state boards, commissions, and judicial posts. By the time the Big Three moved on to national office, there were few appointive positions left that had not been held by women and blacks. Those two groups had become powerful political forces in their own right.

Additionally, the Big Three attracted numerous young voters into their campaigns and causes, thereby socializing a new generation of activists into the ranks of the Democratic Party. As Blytheville native Greg Simon, who was an active teen Republican and now serves as chief domestic policy adviser to Vice President Al Gore, recently observed, "Rockefeller cleaned up the system so . . . you could elect honest Democrats. When you can elect Democrats like David Pryor and Dale Bumpers and Bill Clinton, why vote Republican?"[28]

Furthermore, both Bumpers and Pryor operated substantial internship programs in their Senate offices, which by 1994 had involved well over seven hundred students.[29] Clinton's gubernatorial operations also used student interns, and his campaigns extensively employed hundreds of young people who thereby sharpened their own political skills and reconfirmed their loyalty to the Democratic Party. The Big Three's combination of personal charisma, political success, and programmatic appeal, especially Clinton's decade-long emphasis on education reform in Arkansas, made the Arkansas Democratic Party an attractive option for a young person wanting to be politically involved or considering a political future of his or her own. Whereas by the mid-1980s in some southern states the baton of youthful energy and future leadership seemed to have been passed to the growing ranks of the Republican Party, the Democratic Party still had the look and feel of a winner in Arkansas.

In states dominated by one political party, the dominant party is less an election machine than it is a holding company, a label, under which each candidate organizes his or her own personal coalition.[30] In Arkansas, where both parties as recently as 1985 were ranked among the organizationally weakest in the nation, serious candidates realize that the parties are supplements to rather than substitutes for the candidate's own campaign apparatus.[31] Nevertheless, all of the Big Three willingly and generously performed their assorted party chores (appealing for contributions to lesser-known candidates, drawing a crowd to county rallies, speaking at Jefferson Day or Jackson Day dinners), most of which were of much greater benefit to down-ticket candidates than to themselves. And whereas many Democratic candidates in other southern states by the mid-1980s were creating as much distance as possible between themselves and the party, the Big Three made no secret of their partisan affiliation. In the last weeks of the 1994 elections, both Pryor and Bumpers appeared and spoke at a Washington County fundraising lunch for Third Congressional District Democratic candidate Berta Seitz. Pryor gave passionate praise to President Clinton's legislative achievements, as did Bumpers, who concluded: "I have never been more proud to be a Democrat."[32] It was a phrase rarely heard elsewhere in Dixie in 1994.

This episode exemplifies another trait of the Big Three that contributed to their prolonged success: an amazing ability, over more than two decades of high-powered politics, to, in most instances, work with and for rather than against each other. In the beginning there were occasional and understandable tensions between the principals and among their respective supporters. When Bill Clinton first burst onto the scene, all wondered who might next become victim to his clearly lofty ambitions. In fact, there were rumors (always unconfirmed) that Clinton's narrow margin of defeat in 1980 could have come from the Pryor camp's wanting to squelch young Clinton early before he decided to turn his attention to the seat held by Pryor in the Senate. Many Democrats worried about a possible Bumpers-Clinton contest in 1986 and were bemused when both were mentioned as presidential contestants in 1988. However, considering the agendas and aides and egos involved, what is truly extraordinary is the extent to which relations among the Big Three were not only harmonious and good-humored, but helpful.

When Bumpers announced that he would not be seeking the 1984 presidential nomination, he paid special tribute to the good counsel and supportiveness of Governor and Mrs. Clinton and especially that of Senator Pryor: "To say that David Pryor is a good friend and good colleague would be a gross understatement. He is both and more, and one of the great honors of my life is to serve in the Senate with him."[33] In Clinton's darkest moments in the early 1992 presidential primaries, Pryor appeared by Clinton's side in the snows of New Hampshire, joining him in the kind of personal contact politics they had perfected in Arkansas. By the time of the general election, Pryor had become one of the most frequent and effective surrogate speakers in the Clinton-Gore campaign arsenal and a vital bridge to congressional Democrats. When a lengthy article denigrating Clinton's record in Arkansas appeared in the July 31,

1994, *New York Times Magazine,* Pryor and Bumpers coauthored a vehement response in praise of Clinton's gubernatorial accomplishments.[34] It was Pryor who became known in 1993 as President Clinton's "Best Friend in Congress," but it was Bumpers who took to the Senate floor on October 8, 1994, and spoke at length to his colleagues about Clinton's "intelligence and straightforwardness," his "knowledge and understanding of the problems of this country," and his many legislative accomplishments.[35] While the Big Three did not always see eye to eye, they tended to downplay rather than publicize their differences. With a common philosophical base and passion for Arkansas, they worked closely enough together to reduce the likelihood of some outside challenger's penetrating the winner's circle.

If, as John Brummett has suggested, Arkansas voters by the mid-1960s favored candidates who "would be good ambassadors for the state and representatives of a more sophisticated, intelligent culture than the one people might know from Dogpatch cartoons or the Little Rock Central High School crisis," then the Big Three clearly fit the model. That they generally cooperated with and complimented each other rather than carving each other up added to their positive aura.[36]

There is an additional asset with which each of the Big Three is favored: a wife who departs from the traditional "smile rapturously and say nothing" model of political wives. For each of these politicians a participating wife proved to be a significant advantage. Betty Flanagan Bumpers, during her husband's tenure as governor, led a statewide effort to immunize "every child by two," a program so successful that it was later used by the Centers for Disease Control as a national model for other states. In 1982, drawing on her success with the immunization effort, she founded Peace Links, a peace education group, which she nurtured to life in all fifty states and in other nations. Barbara Lunsford Pryor campaigned door to door, sometimes alone, sometimes by her husband's side, in all his early races. During the congressional and gubernatorial years, she was primarily occupied, between nearly constant campaigns, with raising their three young sons. As a Senate wife, however, she has been a major supporter of Arkansas artists and artisans, using both the Washington and Little Rock offices of Senator Pryor to display and promote their works.[37]

Now most famous is first lady Hillary Rodham Clinton, who will be best remembered in Arkansas for the critical leadership she provided for the centerpiece of her husband's gubernatorial accomplishments—a significant revision and strengthening of Arkansas's public schools. She also, however, founded Arkansas Advocates for Children and Families, helped upgrade and expand Arkansas Children's Hospital, and initiated and chaired other community initiatives to improve the lives of children and women. That she also maintained a private law practice while simultaneously performing the traditional hostessing functions of a governor's spouse, raising a young child, and teaching a Sunday school class left an array of possible options from which future Arkansas first ladies will be more free to choose.[38]

In January 1988 a light airplane in which both Bumpers and Clinton were flying to the annual Gillett Coon Supper came close to disaster, a disaster that would have dramatically altered the last decade of Arkansas's twentieth century politics.[39] Even without such a cataclysm, however, by the last decade of the twentieth century it was clear that further changes were in process or on the horizon and that sooner rather than later a genuinely competitive Arkansas Republican Party would emerge. Northwest Arkansas had become not only one of the fastest growing areas in the state and nation, but as a result of the combined impact of successful entrepreneurs, affluent retirees from northern states, and religious fundamentalists, a bastion of straight-ticket Republicanism. As those with the deepest devotion to the Democratic Party continued to be replaced by new generations not raised on tales of either the Civil War or the New Deal, Republican candidates all over the state became increasingly electable.

Term limits, strongly advocated by Republicans and adopted by Arkansas voters in 1992, not only guaranteed record numbers of open seats in the state legislature by 1996 (always a boon to the out party wishing to get in) but also ensured that future elected executives, limited to two four-year terms, could never amass the political strength that Faubus and Clinton had. The October 1991 death of the *Arkansas Gazette,* which had editorially favored Democrats, and its replacement by the *Arkansas Democrat-Gazette,* meant, according to one longtime observer, "that the real winners of the vaunted newspaper war were the Republicans."[40] The first years of Clinton's presidential administration were both highly productive and highly problematic, bringing pain as well as pride to Arkansas, and whether either Bumpers or Pryor would seek additional Senate terms was uncertain. For nearly twenty-five years, however, Arkansas politics was dominated by three exceptional leaders, who had made many citizens proud to be Arkansans and also proud to be Democrats.

Outsiders and the Amateur Legislature

A Case Study of Legislative Politics

ARTHUR ENGLISH AND JOHN J. CARROLL

The authors of this case study are interested in accounting for the variation across state legislatures in the power and influence of interest groups over the policy-making process in state government. The essence of their argument is that part-time ("amateur") state legislatures tend to be more open to influence by "outsiders," or individuals or groups who have no prior experience in the political arena and few traditional political resources, than are full-time ("professional") state legislatures. They argue that "outsiders" can be more effective in "amateur" legislatures than in "professional" legislatures because, in short, the policy-making process is relatively unstructured—and thus the legislative process is less routine and power is less stratified—in these legislatures.

The focus of this research is the largely successful fight by an "outsider" group to legalize midwifery in Arkansas (Act 838). The study offers a look at the workings of one of the most "amateur" legislatures in the country—and at the politics involved when an "outsider" group challenges established ("insider") groups for influence over that legislature.

Introduction

Political scientists have concentrated their analyses on the United States Congress and legislatures in the larger states, while developing a literature rich in insight on legislative institutions.[1] But this literature has often

Arthur English and John J. Carroll, "Outsiders and the Amateur Legislature: A Case Study of the Legislative Process," *Arkansas Political Science Journal* 6 (Winter 1985): 22–34. Reprinted with permission.

overlooked that most typical, albeit declining, legislative phenomena, the amateur or citizens' legislatures that are found in the smaller and more rural states. The defining difference between these two types of legislative institutions, that is, between the "professionalized" Congress, the California legislature, and the amateur Rhode Island or Arkansas general assemblies, is that in the one legislators "legislate" for a living while in the other members serve part-time and draw their principal paychecks elsewhere.

The difference between the two types of legislative institutions is more than just the "job" orientation of the legislator, however. The difference is structural as well. In general, legislators in amateur chambers work together during the afternoons only a few weeks or months a year, turnover is comparatively high[2], and support staff and institutional resources are few. Professional legislatures in comparison tend to be in session from nine to twelve months every year, they have elaborate and well-paid staffs, and full-time legislators have individual offices, sometimes in their district as well as in the capitol.[3] The result is that citizen legislatures are more loosely structured institutions than professional legislatures[4]—they are not "well integrated" social systems in the sense that the Congress is thought to be[5]—and as a consequence their decision making may be less predictable.

A well-accepted concomitant proposition in the literature describing "professional" or "well institutionalized" legislatures is that the legislative process is long and complex and that it is a specialized arena for highly skilled, experienced and powerful players.[6] The assumption of this literature is that to be successful in the legislative process, external participants need substantial organizational, informational, and monetary resources from which to orchestrate pressure and lobbying campaigns[7] and they are unlikely to be successful without well-developed and previously tested channels of access to legislators, particularly to legislators in positions of formal power, such as committee chairpersons and other legislative leaders. In consequence, persons who lack such resources and who have not developed access to influence are considered to be "outsiders" to the process and are unlikely to affect legislative outcomes.

While this analysis satisfactorily explains the parameters of influence and decision-making in professional legislatures, it does not adequately define these boundaries in amateur institutions. We argue in this case study that "outsiders" in a legislative process can often be effective in amateur legislative settings. We so argue because in amateur legislatures processes tend to be less routinized, power less formally stratified,[8] relationships between members less institutionalized,[9] interest groups fewer, their representation less professional, and their participation more episodic.[10]

Furthermore, in amateur legislatures the unpredictability of voting behavior is often reinforced by undisciplined, fragmented party systems in which voting blocks are factionalized and unstable over time and cohere within relatively narrow issue sets.[11] Of course, this does not imply that amateur legislatures are without their power players and well-organized groups. In amateur legislative systems, including the Arkansas General Assembly, there are usually a coterie of senior members who dominate leadership positions[12] as well as hired lobbyists from a handful of well-financed interest groups.[13]

The concept of outsider is not used here to define those players in the legislative process who hold latent power, choosing to exercise it only at particularly propitious times. Nor do we describe the outsider in terms of deviant, albeit successful, alternative legislative-role orientation.[14] Rather, we conceptualize outsiders in the legislative system as individuals or groups who exhibit the following characteristics: (1) they have had no previous pattern of interaction with the legislature; (2) they are without financial or organizational resources to give them leverage with legislators; (3) the issue they espouse is complex or controversial, so that legislators are apprehensive about supporting it; (4) the issue advanced is staunchly opposed by an interest group that has well-established contacts with legislators.

Our case study of outsider influence in an amateur legislative setting focuses on the Seventy-fourth (1983) session of the Arkansas General Assembly. That session witnessed a confrontation between an initially unorganized group of midwives with few resources who were attempting to legalize the practice of lay midwifery[15] and the Arkansas Medical Society and Department of Health, groups with well established ties to the General Assembly.

Midwifery in Arkansas

While the practice of lay midwifery has deep roots in nineteenth and twentieth century Arkansas, its character was regionally shaped in the state. In the isolated mountain regions of the Ozarks, the Northwest and north central portions of the state, midwifery was exclusively the province of white women who were prominent in their local communities because of their curative powers. Sometimes referred to as "white witches" because of their powers and the good they accomplished in the community, the practice of midwifery in the Ozarks had a mystical and magical quality to it.[16]

The practice of midwifery had a much different character in the Delta counties of south central and Southeastern Arkansas. Flanked by the Mississippi river, the region's economy is almost exclusively agricultural. Many of the counties there are 40 to 50 percent black,[17] although blacks constitute only 16.3 percent of the state's total population.[18] The Delta region is poor; pockets of wealth do exist but these are the larger more prosperous farms operated by whites. Thus, while the per capita income of the region hovers around $7,000,[19] a full $1,000 below the $8,042 for the state and several thousand below Pulaski County ($10,368), where Little Rock is located, it does not fully indicate the high level of black poverty present in the Delta.

In the Ozarks midwifery existed because of tradition and the remoteness of the area from health care facilities. In the Delta, midwifery more than existed—it flourished—not only because of the grim impoverishment of the black population and the lack of health care facilities (1.7 hospital beds per 1,000 population for the state compared to the recommended average of 4.5 per 1,000 population)[20] but because health facilities for blacks were segregated even when they were available, and white hospitals were exceedingly reluctant to accept expectant mothers who were both poor and black. In 1945, only 10 percent of black women in Arkansas gave birth in a hospital, compared to 60 percent of whites[21]. Thus, two of Arkansas's most enduring twentieth century traditions, segregation and poverty, contributed to the growth and legitimacy of midwifery in the state.

During the 1930s and 1940s the state Health Department became exceedingly concerned about the techniques utilized by the black "granny" midwife who was often illiterate and practiced according to superstition. In viewing midwifery as a necessary evil, the department sought to upgrade the practice by more effective training and regulation. The expansion of public health facilities as an outgrowth of cooperative federalism provided the required opening. Midwives were required by the state to attend training sessions conducted by the public health nurses and physicians. Enforcement of these policies would have been impossible had it not been for some astute tactics utilized by the department in dealing with the midwives. First an energetic and able black public health nurse was hired to design and coordinate the instructional program. Second, the instruction itself was designed to instill a sense of duty in the midwives to adhere to the lessons taught by appealing to their state patriotism and their belief in God. Finally, a system was set up in which the patient had to have a blue card stamped by a physician certifying them for delivery by the midwife. The new training and regulations apparently had an impact, because the infant mortality rate in the state soon began to drop and some midwives began writing after their signature, "A Midwife of the State and from God."[22]

In 1952 more explicit regulations were promulgated by the Arkansas State Board of Health pursuant to its broad statutory powers to regulate health in the state. Among the myriad of regulations put forth, midwives had to be of "good moral character (and) have the respect of the majority of the people in the community"; "be not less than 21 years or not over 50 years of age when taking up the practice of midwifery"; "be able to read with understanding and to fill out birth certificates properly"; "attend midwife classes as prescribed by the Maternal and Child Health Division of the Arkansas State Board of Health"; and "wear a clean washed dress when caring for a patient." Violation of any of the regulations constituted a misdemeanor and could result in the revocation of the permit and a fine, imprisonment, or both.[23]

The 1952 regulations defined the structure of midwifery in Arkansas for better than a quarter of a century until January 1979, when the Department of Health, still concerned that its procedures left midwifery essentially unregulated in respect to new "counterculture" midwives entering the state, abolished the program.[24] The remaining grannies, whose numbers had been greatly thinned by attrition, received a form letter telling them that their services were no longer needed and that it was now illegal for them to practice. This edict effectively ended the practice of midwifery by the grannies. Other midwives who were practicing continued to do so without any legitimized status. Thus, by 1979 midwifery in Arkansas had become an illegal and underground occupation, practiced largely by young, counterculture whites.

Midwifery and Politics

At about the time of the 1979 decision to end midwifery in the state, a young woman by the name of Carolyn Vogler moved back to Arkansas from El Paso, Texas, where she had trained in midwifery at the Bethlehem Childbirth Center. Vogler had lived in Arkansas previously and her familiarity with the Delta's poverty and the need for accessible childbirth facilities led her to Dermott, Arkansas. Vogler's charm and intelligence, significant attributes in her fight to legalize midwifery, won her immediate acceptance among elites in the community, and in July 1982, she opened the Delta Maternity Center.[25]

The opening of the center brought a quick response by the Health Department, which believed that Vogler's practice was medically unsafe and thus a threat to maternal and infant care in the region. In particular, the director of the state Department of Health charged that Vogler was in direct violation of the state's Medical Practices Act because she was practicing medicine without a license.[26] A suit instigated by the Arkansas Medical Board was subsequently filed in Chicot County Chancery Court by physicians outside of Dermott to enjoin Vogler from practicing. This tough response to the opening of the Delta Maternity Center in retrospect was not surprising. Vogler represented a direct challenge to the fears of health professionals by overtly practicing midwifery in an institutionalized setting.

Vogler's position was that of the classic outsider. She was new to the state and lacked alliances with Arkansas political leaders or other established groups. She was, in effect, an individual, acting alone on behalf of a cause in which she believed. At the outset, Vogler's financial and organizational resources were minimal, and she was without the funds to launch statewide advertising or lobbying campaigns on her own behalf. Furthermore, her issue was controversial, challenging as it did the historical direction of public policy toward midwifery and the image of her calling as an outdated vestige of a former era. Finally, the Arkansas Medical Association and State Health Department had vested interests in the status quo, both were well connected within Arkansas government, and they would prove themselves formidable foes.

At this point it appeared Vogler would have to yield because she lacked the resources to engage in a lengthy—or even short—legal battle, but despite the difficulty of her situation and her outsider status in the political system, she was able to make considerable headway. First of all, in the campaign to legalize lay midwifery Vogler was her own best advocate. While midwifery certainly has a long tradition in Arkansas, many had come to associate it with the delivery of children under substandard conditions by poorly trained birth assistants. This association hit a sensitive chord among Arkansans wary of the state's reputation as an unsanitary backwater. But Vogler did not fit the stereotype that many lay midwives had previously conveyed as backward, incompetent people. She impressed people as intelligent and extremely knowledgeable. Senator Jack Gibson, who was later to champion her cause in the legislature, found Vogler to be "full of spunk and charm."[27]

Vogler also made convincing arguments. While Arkansas is a poor state, it has good medical facilities, although they are concentrated in the urban areas—Little Rock, Hot Springs, and Fort Smith. Physicians and health care professionals are much sparser in the rural areas of the state, such as the Delta, where there is less money and fewer educational, social, and cultural activities. For example, while there are 2,700 physicians in the state or 118 per 100,000, urban Pulaski County has 322.4 per 100,000, while many of the rural countries have fewer than 70 physicians per 100,000. In two countries, Lee and St. Francis, there are only 38.6 and 29.2 physicians per 100,000, respectively.[28] Similarly, while there are 5,776 nurses in the state, 38.9 per 1,000 population, only 192 nurses served a population of 124,236 in the state's six poorest counties.

Despite these data it would be an exaggeration to say that health care is inaccessible in places like Chicot County, but it is less accessible per person than in the state as a whole, and considering the poverty of the region, the cost for many is prohibitive. Maternity care in Arkansas, including doctor's fee and hospital stay, costs between $1,500 and $2,000; Vogler was offering both pre and post natal care, including delivery, for $300.[29]

Besides her own personal assets and the attractiveness of her issue, Vogler formed an alliance with two of Dermott's most important citizens, Charles S. Gibson, an attorney practicing in Dermott, and his wife Sherri Gibson, one of the town's few community activists. It was the Gibsons who encouraged Vogler to open the Delta Maternity Clinic and let the public judge the merits of her cause. The Gibsons were outraged when Vogler was sued by the medical board and Charles Gibson offered to provide her with free legal help. More importantly, the Gibsons had resources that Vogler did not and were able to provide the legislative connection that Vogler and other midwives needed[30]—a state legislator who would introduce a bill legalizing midwifery and be its advocate in the General Assembly.

Dermott is located in Chicot County, one of the four counties which Senator Jack Gibson either fully or partially represented.[31] Senator

Gibson was Charles Gibson's cousin. These two connections, personal and constituency, became one when Senator Gibson was invited to tour the Delta Maternity Clinic. In a statement which captures the essence of the amateur legislative orientation, Gibson assessed the situation in the following terms: "What she said sounded good to me and I was impressed with her. I did a little research on my own—not too much— and found that we had one of the highest infant mortality rates in the country along with one of the lowest ratios of physicians to population. That convinced me."[32]

With legislative help now available, Vogler and the Gibsons could concentrate on developing a strategy to legalize midwifery in Arkansas. A legal solution through the courts was rejected as being too risky, time consuming, and costly. Winning might help Vogler and the Delta Maternity Clinic, but it might not advance the status of other midwives. It was decided to pursue a campaign to convince the General Assembly to legitimize by law the practice of lay midwifery. An internal-external strategy was devised. Senator Gibson would quietly mobilize support in the Assembly, particularly among Delta legislators, while introducing a bill exempting midwives from the state's Medical Practices Act. Vogler would act as the chief spokesperson for the campaign and deal exclusively with the media; the Gibsons would provide legal and moral support, and attempt to broaden the base of the midwifery coalition.

For groups outside the legislative system, creating a favorable climate of opinion for their issue is essential to the ultimate success of the campaign. Favorable media coverage is crucial because it can legitimize an issue for politically cautious legislators who often look for some indication of mass approval before they get behind an issue.

The media campaign was a *tour de force* for the midwives. The Arkansas Medical Society did not seem to realize that the story of powerful doctors picking on a woman who helps poor women had David and Goliath implications. In consequence, the stories in which the doctors were quoted made them seem shrill and unreasonable compared to those written about Vogler, which described her as a cool, reasonable person with a reasonable issue.

The strategy for the media campaign had been worked out before the campaign began in earnest. Vogler was open to the press, but never critical of her tormentors in the medical community. Indeed, she was frequently quoted as saying she would like to work under a doctor's supervision. When the medical board stated that midwifery was unsafe, she pointed to the high infant mortality rate in the state compared to the low rates in countries where midwives were common. When she was assailed as incompetent she cited the number of babies she had delivered and cared for. When the doctors said that they could do better, she noted that there were few physicians in the Delta region and that maternity care was expensive.[33]

Vogler's media strategy was so effective that her opponents found themselves on the defensive. Indeed, Byron Hawkes, associate director of the Maternal Division in the Arkansas Health Department, wrote Vogler a public letter of apology for remarks he had made before the state medical board:

> There comes a time in everyone's life and professional career, when arrogance comes face to face with humility . . . I cannot condone out-of hospital obstetrical delivery of mother and the newborn but I am realistic enough to realize that segments of today's society wish this experience . . . because of the economic roadblock that now truly exists in Arkansas and in all states. Mrs. Vogler wishes to meet this need and has placed herself into a fighting pose. I admire her stance.[34]

Hawkes went on to apologize for "intemperate statements I have made against her" and concluded with an endorsement of her general aims: "I feel absolutely certain that she agrees with me that her position and that of others in this state must be legalized in a formal manner and status be given to the goals this ancient movement deserves."[35] Hawkes's letter of apology marked a turning point in the campaign. The midwives thought then they had turned the tide but they still had to deal with the legislature and the legislative process.

Midwifery and the Assembly

Given its basic structure and ideological orientation, the Arkansas General Assembly might be considered a forbidding institution by any group seeking to write its preferences into law, and especially by a group with a mixed popular image that has attacked the interest of one of the state's established political forces. The Arkansas legislature is a part-time institution that meets for sixty legislative days every two years. Like other southern legislatures, its membership is senior, heavily Democratic, overwhelmingly male and largely conservative.[36] In recent sessions, for example, it refused to ratify the Equal Rights Amendment and was one of only two states to pass a bill mandating the balanced treatment of creation science.[37]

If the Assembly's reputation was not enough to dissuade Vogler and her allies from seeking a legislative solution, there are pitfalls inherent in the legislative process itself. In the Arkansas General Assembly, a bill may meet a quiet death in several ways. Some bills, for example, are killed by farming them out to an interim committee for "further study." Or a bill may make it to the floor, as most do, only to await action on the calendar indefinitely. This technique allows the sponsor to say a bill got to the floor, even though there was no action on it. And if a bill fails passage a "clincher" motion may be immediately moved, which if adopted means that the previous vote can only be expunged by a two-thirds or better majority.[38] Commonly, a bill will be defeated on the floor or left to languish in committee or on the calendar because its sponsor chooses not to be its advocate.

But the reputation of a legislative body and the pitfalls of the legislative process do not determine the fate of individual bills in an amateur assembly. In an amateur legislative setting, the odds of passing a bill increase sharply because of the deinstitutionalized nature of the body. It would seem, given the short length of the session in amateur legislatures, the relative lack of staff, and the large amount of time that legislators spend home in their districts, that many bills are processed rather than deliberated, and some bills are adopted that would be killed if given less hurried consideration. Alan Rosenthal found, for example, that amateur legislatures, especially those that are southern and rural, had a much higher average bill adoption ratio (from 1963–74) than professional legislatures like Massachusetts, Ohio, Wisconsin, and New York.[39]

Another important consideration that enlarges the opportunities for the successful passage of bills in an amateur legislative setting is the strong constituency orientation of legislators, which can override leadership influences, ideology, and other factors. In Arkansas, legislators spend most of their time in their home districts responding to constituent problems.[40]

Finally, while many legislative bodies—amateur and professional alike—have a conservative bent, some issues like midwifery are not easily reconciled to ideological stereotype. Midwifery is an ideologically complex issue because while it immediately suggests a feminist counterculture orientation, it also taps legislators' pragmatic desires to provide services to constituents.

Thus, when the bill exempting midwifery from the state's Medical Practices Act was introduced by Gibson in the Senate, the midwives found many of the legislators receptive to it. They also found the medical community inattentive and unorganized. The Arkansas Medical Association had concentrated their early efforts on a judicial remedy and had not paid adequate attention to the impending legislative battle.[41] With the medical establishment unprepared, the midwifery forces lobbied the legislators directly by organizing a network of supporters, friends, and clients.

This lobbying coalition consisted of Vogler, the Gibsons, Father Joe Blitz, director of the office of justice and peace in the Catholic Diocese of Little Rock, and Dr. John Wolverton, a supportive physician. This group lobbied the legislators individually in addition to going on the record at a public hearing before the Senate's Public Health, Welfare, and Labor Committee on the need for and merits of midwifery.[42] For his part, Senator Gibson practiced pluralistic politics with his colleagues to a T: "I got me a midwife, a doctor, a Catholic priest and went to work."[43] The bill (SB203) to exempt midwives from the state's Medical Practice Act streaked through the Senate 25–7.[44]

By the time the bill reached the House, however, the legislative climate had drastically changed. The medical profession was now alerted to the possible passage of a bill legalizing midwifery in the state and legislators supportive of midwifery were less numerous and influential in the lower chamber. The bill got an early "do pass" from the House Public Health Committee, but by the time it reached the floor the doctors were prepared for it. Despite an unusual suspension of the rules (again illustrating the unpredictable nature of the legislative process in Arkansas), which allowed Vogler, Father Joe Blitz, and Dr. Wolverton to address the entire House, a grassroots lobbying campaign by the Arkansas Medical Society, which mobilized local doctors to call their legislators, culminated in a thirty-three to forty-three defeat.[45] The resistance of the House to the Senate's bill mandated a compromise strategy by the midwifery forces. Representative Gino Mazzanti, another Delta legislator, forged the compromise in the House. Initially, he proposed an amendment to the bill, based on the national poverty line, which would have legalized midwifery in thirty counties. When this amendment failed to win support, Mazzanti changed the poverty threshold to permit midwifery in those counties in which 30 percent or more of the population had incomes below the poverty line.[46] This would have legalized the practice of midwifery in eleven counties. This version did not pass either. Finally, a 32.5 percent poverty threshold was agreed upon, legalizing midwifery in six counties.[47] The vote on the unamended midwifery bill was then expunged and the bill as amended passed by a vote of 52–20.

The bill was signed into law as Act 838 by Gov. Bill Clinton, who expressed his reservation that midwives provide substandard care. Despite this objection, Governor Clinton, with a reputation as a progressive but pragmatic governor, chose not to oppose the bill because a large number of midwives were practicing in the state and because he had strong electoral support in Southeastern Arkansas, which he did not wish to jeopardize.[48] Thus, the practice of lay midwifery was legalized in just six of Arkansas's seventy-five counties, all located in the south central and Southeastern portion of the state. The midwives had not been able to legalize midwifery throughout the entire state, but they had been able to legitimize its status in six counties despite strong opposition from the medical community.

Discussion

This legislative history demonstrates the remarkable fluidity of politics in an amateur legislative system. Act 838 was placed on the legislative agenda and passed by a midwife who had never been active in politics before, an activist priest, a promidwifery physician, a junior Delta legislator, and two dedicated Dermott activists. These were meager resources by the standards of a professional legislature, yet sufficient to thwart the interests of the medical community as represented by the Arkansas Medical Society and the Department of Health.

This case demonstrates that a victory of this kind, incomplete though it was, can be secured in a legislative setting that lacks the well-institutionalized structures of professionalized bodies. In the Arkansas Assembly, specialization among legislators is a valued trait, as it is in professional legislatures,[49] but amateur legislators have wider discretion. Senator Gibson waged a successful campaign among his colleagues despite only two years' experience in the Senate and a seat on the Committee on Agricultural Economics and Industrial Resources, a specialization presumably not well suited to leadership on a public health measure.[50]

In addition, as in local legislatures such as city councils and school committees, the ideological nature of issues is likely to be obscured by amateur legislators' concerns about constituency needs and practicality. Midwifery, for example, is a "new" issue among feminists who oppose the invasion of their persons by the male-dominated technology of the modern obstetrical ward,[51] and it is sometimes viewed as a liberal issue because its services are primarily for the poor. In the Assembly, many legislators saw midwifery as a constituency measure of direct benefit to persons who could not otherwise afford health care. Carolyn Vogler presented it well in her statement to the press: "Midwifery is a feminist issue, a rich person's issue, a right to life issue, a religious issue, a survivalist issue, and a poor people's issue. It cuts across all classes of people. It's everybody's issue."[52]

This case also illustrates that incrementalism is an intrinsic characteristic of the state legislative process. The midwives did have some resources in the fight to legalize their craft: a highly skilled spokesperson, a legislative champion, and free legal advice; the Arkansas Medical Association had established legislative contacts, substantial resources, and a grassroots lobbying network as their chief weapons. Both sides would have conceded nothing if they didn't have to, but faced with each other's "real" power position, some change was inevitable. Indeed, an axiom of the legislative process is that if you can't get a full loaf, get half, and if you can't get half, get something.

Most significantly, this case study also demonstrates that outsiders in an amateur legislative system can win political battles if they are willing to develop coalitions and to define their issues carefully. Perhaps the single most disturbing aspect of our national political system is its dominance by large groups to the exclusion of individual citizens. But in the amateur state legislative system, interest groups are not as systematically represented as they are in professionalized institutions. Interest groups, including potentially powerful organizations, may be intermittently represented and inadequately informed about matters of concern to them. This was crucial to the outcome in this case. In consequence, this group of legislators, in the absence of strong voting pressures to the contrary,[53] proved receptive to a novel legislative proposal which they believed was convincingly presented.

Thus, the midwifery struggle in Arkansas belies the axiom that many Americans hold about the political system—that little can be done to influence it. This case shows that citizens can influence their public officials if they organize, and that tenacity and constituency contacts will be persuasive in what is often an interest group vacuum. Indeed, legislators continue to believe that elections are decided by how responsive they've been to constituents,[54] and they will listen if pushed.

The idea has also become current that legislators may risk popular support if they become identified with vested interests. This populist sentiment was echoed by a public health department official who at the end lamented: "We got beat by a little girl and a country legislator."[55]

IV

Policy Issues and Political Patterns for the Twenty-first Century in Arkansas Politics and Government

Arkansas

More Signs of Momentum for
Republicanism in Post–"Big Three" Arkansas

JAY BARTH

The 1990s looked promising for the arrival of a competitive, two-party system in Arkansas. The adoption of term limits for state executives and legislators, a long-overdue switch to publicly funded primary elections, and a handful of high-profile Republican victories would, according to most observers, make the state more fertile for Republicans. In this examination of the Arkansas portion of a 2001 survey of party activists in eleven southern states, Barth finds additional support for a strengthened Arkansas GOP in the party's ideological cohesion and strong activism at the grassroots level. He cautions, however, that the strong conservatism of rank-and-file GOP activists may impede the party's growth in a state long partial to ideological moderation, a conclusion receiving support in the 2006 Democratic sweep.

A decade ago, the first Southern Grassroots Party Activists Project gave initial insights into the nature of local party activists—both chairs and members of party county committees—in Arkansas. In her analysis of the data from that survey, Diane Blair a noted a number of hints of momentum for the Republican Party in the state at the grassroots level despite its being the "other party" in a one-party state (below the presidential level).[1] The second wave of the Southern Grassroots Party Activists Project survey, completed in 2001, presents a valuable opportunity to check in on the comparative strength of the two parties at the local level and the political, social,

Jay Barth, "Arkansas: More Signs of Momentum for Republicanism in Post–'Big Three' Arkansas" *The American Review of Politics* 24 (Spring and Summer 2003): 111–26. Reprinted with permission.

and behavioral differences in those positions of formal leadership from the two parties at the beginning of the twenty-first century. Perhaps even more importantly, it allows a reexamination of the Republican organizational momentum shown a decade ago. Indeed, once again the comparative vibrancy of Arkansas Republicanism is shown in the 2001 data, boding well for its eventual achievement of a true two-party system in Arkansas politics. That said, the GOP's ideological coherence—a source of strength for an organization *qua* organization—does threaten to push the Arkansas Republican Party to the right of the political mainstream in a state where the votes of moderate independents are essential for any candidate's success.

Development of Political Parties in Arkansas
Electoral Patterns in Arkansas Since 1991

Much has transpired in Arkansas politics since the time of the 1991 survey.[2] Most historic, of course, was the election of an Arkansan to the presidency the following year. While the native son campaigns of 1992 and 1996 did return Arkansas to the Democratic fold in presidential elections following GOP victories in 1980, 1984, and 1988, the last decade has marked a series of modern high points for the Arkansas Republican Party. Table 1 presents some key historical electoral data for the state since the time of the first wave of the Southern Grassroots Party Activists Survey.

Despite the unprecedented national prominence gained by Democrat Clinton, a good deal of the Republican success during this period is, somewhat ironically, connected to Clinton's election. Clinton's move to Washington removed the best-developed Democratic electoral organization from the state. Moreover, any number of prospective candidates for political office in the state traveled to Washington with him, leaving behind (at least for eight years) their own electoral ambitions in Arkansas. Mike Huckabee, who would become the state's newest political star, used an opening created by Clinton's departure to take a close special election victory for lieutenant governor in 1993. Finally, the Whitewater investigation led, in 1996, to the elevation of Huckabee to the governorship after Gov. Jim Guy Tucker's conviction by a federal jury. Huckabee took full advantage of this opportunity, ably handling the crisis surrounding Tucker's fickleness about actually departing the office and, in 1998, gaining the most impressive electoral victory by a GOP governor in the modern era. At

TABLE I

Republican Strength in Arkansas, 1960–2000

YEAR	PERCENT OF PRESIDENTIAL VOTE	PERCENT OF GUBER-NATORIAL VOTE	PERCENT OF U.S. SENATE VOTE	PERCENT OF U.S. HOUSE DELE-GATION	PERCENT OF STATE HOUSE DELE-GATION	PERCENT OF STATE SENATE DELE-GATION
1960	43.1	31.8	n/a	0.0	0.0	0.0
1962		26.7	31.3	0.0	1.0	0.0
1964	43.4	43.0		0.0	1.0	0.0
1966		54.4	n/a	25.0	2.0	0.0
1968	31.0	52.4	40.9	25.0	4.0	2.9
1970		32.4		25.0	2.0	2.9
1972	68.8	24.6	39.1	25.0	1.0	2.9
1974		34.4	15.1	25.0	2.0	2.9
1976	34.9	16.7		25.0	5.0	2.9
1978		36.6	16.6	50.0	6.0	0.0
1980	48.2	51.9	37.5	50.0	7.0	2.9
1982		45.3		50.0	7.0	8.6
1984	60.5	37.4	42.7	25.0	9.0	11.4
1986		36.1	37.7	25.0	9.0	11.4
1988	54.0			25.0*	11.0	11.4
1990		42.5	n/a	25.0	9.0	11.4
1992	35.5		39.8	50.0	10.0	14.3
1994		40.2		50.0	12.0	20.0
1996	36.8		52.7	50.0	14.0	20.0
1998		59.8	41.8	50.0	25.0	17.1
2000	51.3			25.0	30.0	22.9

n/a—No Republican candidate fielded.
* U.S. Rep. Tommy Robinson changed parties from Democrat to Republican on July 28, 1989.

present, Huckabee moves toward probable reelection in 2002 with the Democratic Party desperately seeking a legitimate standard bearer to challenge the overwhelmingly popular incumbent.

The retirements of two of Arkansas's most consistent vote getters—Democratic U.S. Senators David Pryor (in 1996) and Dale Bumpers (in 1998)—provided additional chances for Republican success. And, in 1996, the GOP filled the vacuum left by Pryor's departure by gaining its first U.S. Senate seat at the ballot box with the elevation of U.S. House member Tim Hutchinson. The GOP was unable to take advantage of the similar opening created by Bumpers's retirement in 1998, as former U.S. Rep. Blanche Lincoln gained the seat. Still, the period between these two surveys marks an era in which all three of the masterful Democratic politicians whom Blair termed the "Big Three" of Arkansas politics left Arkansas's political battlefields, leaving a vacuum into which the Republican party (led by Huckabee) has partially been able to move.[3] Huckabee is a politician who shares much of the ability of the "Big Three" to relate to rank-and-file Arkansans, particularly in an era where the mass media is increasingly relevant in the state's politics.

Even after Republicans had broken the Democrats' lock on victories in statewide elections, election cycle after election cycle passed in Arkansas with little change in the partisan composition of the state legislature. A happening somewhat lost in the intensity of the Clinton victory of 1992 was the passage, via an initiated amendment to the state constitution, of term limits for Arkansas's elected officials. This reform—which fully impacted the state House of Representatives in the 1998 election cycle—assisted Arkansas Republicans in finally making clear inroads into the state House and Senate. As shown in table 1, three times as many Republicans now hold state House seats than a decade ago. The expansion of term limits to the state Senate will likely have similar ramifications over the next four years, particularly in those sections of the state—northwest Arkansas and the suburbs of Little Rock—that are fast-growing and most open to Republicanism. These demographic patterns (as well as the increasing openness of younger Arkansas voters to Republican candidates) bode well for the future of the party in the state, although the GOP's continued difficulty in recruiting quality candidates at all levels of state politics serves as a barrier that will be debilitating in the future.

Party Organization in Arkansas

The long tradition of weak party organizations in Arkansas, exceptional even by the standards of the one-party South, joins the candidate-centered nature of modern Arkansas politics in limiting the development of Arkansas's political parties as organizations. All successful candidates in Arkansas in the modern era—Democrat or Republican—have developed ongoing campaign organizations almost totally independent of their state parties.[4] And, in both parties, because successful candidates' organizations are independent they are occasionally the seeds of dissention within the party even when those candidates are not in direct competition.

Still, at least at the state level, with some assistance from their national party (particularly in the case of the GOP), both state parties have developed over the past generation the basic infrastructure and staffing to legitimize themselves. For a brief period in the late 1960s and early 1970s, Gov. Winthrop Rockefeller poured money into the state Republican Party and his moderate "Rockefeller Republican" followers populated its activists. But, Rockefeller's 1973 death and the Democrats' return to dominance (with a more progressive outlook) left the party, according to one informed analysis a few years later, "perhaps the weakest in the South."[5] After the 1980 election, the moderate wing of the GOP was effectively "purged" from leadership roles in the party and, as the Reagan era continued, the state GOP began to rebuild as an ideologically cohesive (and unambiguously conservative) party.[6] Despite regular financial crises and constant turnover in leadership, the state GOP began to assemble into an organization that could at least be of assistance to the candidates running under the party label. And, of even more importance, the party began playing a hands-on role in recruiting potential candidates in a purposeful manner through a targeting system that had first shown success in Texas.[7] After Clinton's election to the White House, the national Republican Party began pushing resources into the Arkansas state party for projects that could potentially lead to home-state "black eyes" for the president, and state party fundraising was facilitated by Clinton's visibility as a national figure.

The strong personal organizations of Democratic governors throughout the 1970s and 1980s left little independent role for the state Democratic Party, though it too began to develop an infrastructure akin to parties elsewhere in the country. While weak compared to its brethren state parties in most of the nation, the Arkansas Democratic party fought through a devastating debt in the mid-1990s and has—like the state GOP—become an organization that can supplement still-dominant candidate organizations by offering increasingly sophisticated electoral assistance (direct mail, phone banks, donor lists, opponent and issue research) to its nominees particularly through "coordinated campaigns" that employ a significant number of paid employees in election years. It was, however, much slower to engage in candidate recruitment of the sort carried out, with some success, by the state GOP.

More directly relevant to this project, there is considerable inconsistency for both parties in terms of local party organizational presence. Midway through the last decade, the Democratic Speaker of the House of Representatives said, "You would be surprised how many House members tell me that their county committees do nothing."[8] Because of a 1995 federal court ruling deeming the Arkansas primary election system, which required the parties to conduct and fund their own primaries, unconstitutional, one of the traditional reasons for the local Democratic county committees' activity has disappeared. The state now pays for primary elections and both parties' primary ballots are available at all precincts in the state, a shift that presents an opportunity (unfulfilled to this point) to enhance the relevance of the GOP primary in Arkansas. So, while electoral and demographic forces would suggest that the Republican Party has continued to mature at the local level in the state in the last decade, other trends in the way campaigns and elections operate in the state would make it unsurprising if neither parties' local organizations have developed significantly since 1991. This second wave of the Southern Grassroots Party Activists—that, at many points, explicitly replicates the 1991 study—promises some insights into these competing possibilities.

Grassroots Party Activists, 1991 and 2001

With only minor exceptions, today's Democratic and Republican party activists look remarkably similar to their 1991 counterparts in terms of characteristics near the surface. However, in terms of less-visible political traits, Arkansas's party activists have changed in marked ways over the last decade. These shifts—particularly among GOP activists—promise to have significant implications for the future of party politics in the state.

Who are Arkansas's Party Activists?

Democratic Party activists have become more diverse in terms of race and gender since 1991, while almost no changes are evident in demographic characteristics for Republicans. In 1991, despite their vital role in a biracial coalition that had protected Arkansas's Democrats from Republican incursions, only 4.6 percent of Democratic Party activists were African American. Now, as 9.5 percent of the Democratic activists are African Americans, the party's grassroots leadership more closely resembles the demographics of the state as a whole (according to the 2000 Census, African Americans composed 12.3 percent of the Arkansas population) although blacks remain slightly underrepresented. Almost no change has occurred on the Republican side, with 96 percent of Republicans identifying themselves as white. Despite the attention given to the increase in the Hispanic American population in certain Arkansas communities, essentially no Latino/Latina presence is yet shown in the ranks of either party's most active members.

In 1991, a larger percentage of Republican than Democratic Party activists were female. Now, the reverse is true. The percentage of Republican Party activists who are male has increased slightly, from 57.5 to 58.7 percent. But the percentage of male Democratic activists has decreased sharply, from 65 to 52.5 percent, making that party closely reflective of the general population.

As shown in table 2, neither party has been particularly successful at bringing younger citizens into their cadre of local leaders, as the population of both parties' activists has aged in the past decade. While the aging of its grassroots leadership continues to be a larger problem for the state's Democrats (Democratic activists over 80 years of age now actually outnumber its activists under 40), the relatively youthful Republican Party of a decade ago is also grayer. A slight majority (51.7 percent) of GOP activists are now over the age of 60.

While Arkansas's Democratic local leaders have begun to look more like the state in terms of race and gender, they diverge from their fellow Arkansans more than they did a decade ago on two other key characteristics: family income and education. These results are also shown in table 2. While the latest Census estimates the average household income in the state to be just over $37,000, a majority of Arkansas's Democratic activists have family incomes over $50,000. Similarly, while 13.3 percent of Arkansas's general population has completed a college degree, three times

TABLE 2

Demographic Characteristics of Arkansas Party Activists,
1991 and 2001

DEMOGRAPHIC CHARACTERISTIC	DEMOCRATS		REPUBLICANS	
	1991	2001	1991	2001
Age				
Under 40	10.5	7.1	17.8	9.5
40–49	16.4	13.1	14.5	17.7
50–59	20.1	27.3	19.1	21.1
60–69	27.4	28.1	28.9	29.9
70–79	20.9	19.7	16.2	17.0
Over 80	4.7	7.4	3.5	4.8
(N)	(762)	(366)	(456)	(147)
Education				
High school or less	43.2	26.1	19.6	10.1
Some college	28.8	31.2	32.9	22.2
College graduate	13.6	18.3	25.9	29.5
Graduate degree	14.4	24.5	21.6	26.2
(N)	(784)	(372)	(459)	(149)
Family income				
<$25,000		11.9		4.3
$25,000–49,999		31.2		22.2
$50,000–74,999		23.7		32.9
$75,000–99,999		15.2		20.7
$100,000–149,999		8.8		7.9
>$150,000		4.4		9.3
(N)		(362)		(140)
Religion				
Mainstream Protestant		36.1		41.4
Evangelical Protestant		44.9		50.3
Black Protestant		9.6		—
Roman Catholic		6.4		5.5
Other		2.9		2.8
(N)		(374)		(140)

Note: Entries are percentages.

as many Democratic Party activists have completed college, with nearly a quarter now holding a graduate or professional degree. Thus, by these measures, the "party of the people" does not reflect the people of Arkansas.

Democratic activists do remain poorer and less educated than their Republican counterparts, however. A majority of GOP activists are now at least college graduates. And upper income political activists are considerably more likely to be Republican than Democrat, with only 4.3 percent of Republican activists falling in the lowest income cohort.

A decade ago, nearly half of Republican Party activists spent their formative years outside of Arkansas. Now, the Arkansas Republican Party is increasingly a home-grown organization. While 38.7 percent of Republican activists in the most recent survey lived the first eighteen years of their life outside of the state (as compared to 16.9 percent of Democrats), there is a decreasing reliance on in-migration for that party. The roots of these non-native Republicans are still most likely to be in the Midwest, as was the case a decade ago. Those few Democrats not native to Arkansas are more evenly distributed in their birthplaces, with 2.1 percent from a country other than the United States.

Like other Arkansans, party activists worship almost entirely as Protestants. As shown in table 2, basic denomination identification is an area of significant overlap for the two parties' local leaders. The one exception in this religious mirroring is the fact that nearly 10 percent of Democratic activists are active within the African American Protestant tradition, a form of religiosity absent from the nearly all-white Republican Party. While the questions tapping the religious lives of party activists are slightly different than in the 1991 survey, there is little evidence of shifts in that aspect of activists' nonpolitical identifications.

So, nearest the surface—with only a few exceptions—2001 activists look much like their party's activists in 1991. The differences between Democrats and Republicans in these demographics tend to replicate the patterns of a decade ago. Scratching below the surface, as this extensive survey attempts to do, shows distinct shifts in the political attitudes of Arkansas's party activists. The picture presented by this data shows a consistent, increasing polarization of the grassroots workers of the two parties.

Ideology and Issues

This increased polarization is evidenced first by the activists' self-placement on the ideological spectrum. A decade ago, just under 85 percent of Republican activists described themselves as "conservative," with slightly less than half of that group choosing the term "very conservative." On the other hand, Democratic activists in 1991 were clumped in three fairly even groups: 35.6 percent were "conservative"; 33.1 percent, "moderate"; and slightly less than one-third, "liberal." The ideological gap of a decade ago has grown into a chasm, according to this survey. As shown in table 3, Arkansas's Democratic activists have liberalized over the past decade, with 44.7 percent now calling themselves "liberals." Conservative Democrats, a decade ago the plurality of grassroots party activists, now make up a meager one-fourth of Democratic activists.

TABLE 3

Ideological Self-identification of Arkansas Party Activists,
1991 **and** 2001

POLITICAL BELIEFS	DEMOCRATS		REPUBLICANS	
	1991	2001	1991	2001
Very conservative	7.5	5.5	39.5	67.3
Conservative	28.1	24.9	45.2	29.3
Moderate	33.1	30.4	12.4	3.4
Liberal	24.0	32.6	2.6	—
Very liberal	7.4	12.1	0.2	—
(N)	(759)	(365)	(458)	(147)

Note: Entries are percentages.

In contrast, over two-thirds of Arkansas Republicans now choose the term "very conservative" to describe themselves. The most "liberal" of Republican activists are now the tiny 5.5 percent who describe themselves as "moderates." Any vestige of the Rockefeller Republicanism that had been an important foundation of the Arkansas GOP in the 1960s is now history. While both parties' activists have polarized, a key question now comes into focus: is the Arkansas Republican party in danger of becoming too extreme for a mass electorate that has shown a fondness for political candidates—both Democratic and Republican—who have emphasized their moderation and independence?

This increasing polarization is brought home to an even greater degree as we move below the more conceptual self-identification of ideology and examine a series of vital political issues. Table 4 shows the percentage of

Democratic and Republican activists, respectively, who indicate either agreement or strong agreement with the policy stances presented. In those situations where the questions replicated those on the 1991 survey, that data is included to give insight into the shifts that have occurred within these grassroots activists. And, as can be seen, important shifts have occurred during this period.

On most of the questions that are replicated, Democratic activists have shifted in a more liberal direction. However, these Democratic shifts typically are smaller—and in some cases *much* smaller—than are the shifts by Republicans in the opposite direction. For example, Republican activists of 2001 are 22 percentage points more "pro-life" than were GOP activists in 1991; Democratic activists have shifted 9 points in the "pro-choice" direction. On two other issues—the importance of improving the status of women in society and sanctioning prayer in America's public schools—

TABLE 4

Position on Issues (Agree) for Arkansas Party Activists,
1991 **and** 2001

ISSUE AGREEMENT	DEMOCRATS		REPUBLICANS	
	1991	2001	1991	2001
Improve position of women	84.8	81.7	52.8	28.9
Abortion personal choice	64.9	73.0	39.8	17.7
Fewer services/reduce spending	29.9	17.0	74.8	78.4
Permit public school prayer	77.8	77.3	84.1	98.6
Private school vouchers	n/a	13.4	n/a	77.0
Improve position of blacks/minorities	58.7	71.9	37.2	28.4
Ensure job/good living standard	44.4	32.7	15.3	5.4
Women equal role with men	85.4	94.0	77.0	86.4
Homosexual job protection	n/a	54.6	n/a	10.1
Flat tax	n/a	43.7	n/a	76.9
Regulate HMOs	n/a	68.0	n/a	10.7
Blacks preference hiring/promotion	10.6	12.3	4.6	0.7
Stricter gun control	n/a	61.7	n/a	5.3
Death penalty for murder	n/a	66.4	n/a	85.7
Average N	(723)	(363)	(443)	(148)

Note: Entries are percentages of those agreeing with the stated issue positions.

Democratic activists are essentially unchanged in their level of support, but these issues are ones on which Republicans have two of their sharpest changes. Among GOP activists, there is now absolutely no dispute on school prayer and there has been a precipitous drop in their support for government activism to promote the economic and social status of women. Thus, party activist polarization in Arkansas results disproportionately from Republican shifts during the decade.

Some of the sharpest divergence between the Democratic and Republican activists shows itself on topics that were not surveyed in 1991. Gaps of more than 50 percentage points in the levels of support show themselves on gun control (with three-quarters of Democratic activists supporting gun limitations), private school vouchers (with the vast majority of Republican activists supporting this form of school choice), and expanded government regulation of HMOs (with the overwhelming majority of Democratic activists favoring this government activism). Finally, while a majority of Arkansas Democrats favor legislation protecting gay men and lesbians from job discrimination, only a small percentage of Republican activists (10.1 percent) share this view.

The case of gun control serves as an example of the potential dangers that accompany the ideological unity seen among contemporary Republican grassroots activists. Recent surveys of the mass electorate in the state show that nearly half of Arkansans support stricter gun control.[9] Thus, both parties' local elites are out of step with Arkansans as a whole, but Republicans diverge from rank-and-file Arkansas voters to a considerably larger degree. Indeed, 37 percent of Republican Party identifiers support stricter gun control measures. At least on this salient issue, the GOP organization is in danger of disconnecting from the base of voters on which it depends for electoral victories, and to an even greater degree from the independents who are crucial to win in a state now lacking a majority political party.

The apparent stability of the demographic characteristics of Arkansas party activists masks sharp divergence and dramatic shifts in the political worldviews of the activists from the two parties. Arkansas's Republican Party is now a profoundly conservative political party at the grassroots level, while Democratic activists are increasingly in sync with their counterparts in other parts of the country on a variety of issues.

Activists and Their Political Parties

By a variety of additional measures, the 2001 survey results show that the ideologically united Arkansas Republican Party shows itself to be healthier at the local level than the Democratic Party and healthier than the local GOP was in Arkansas in 1991. In her analysis of the 1991 data, Blair noted the variety of ways in which Republican activists perceived their state and local organizations as moving in the right direction in terms of the key roles that those organizations are expected to play. Such optimism remains firmly in place on the part of activists in Arkansas's upstart party, boding well for the future of Republicanism in the state. In contrast, just as was the case a decade ago, Democratic activists see many flaws in the recent effectiveness of their party. More important, this relative optimism by Republicans is matched by higher levels of activism and commitment on the part of GOP grassroots workers and lower rates of factionalism within the Republican Party at both the state and local levels.

First, majorities of Republican activists perceive that their party is stronger as an organization, as a recruiter of candidates, as a fund-raising entity, as a campaign operation, and as a media presence than a decade earlier. Democrats are much more pessimistic about their party's recent work. For example, only 25.2 percent of Democratic activists see their party as having become stronger as a recruiter of candidates for public office; over two-thirds of Republicans have this perception of their party. Combined with the results from the 1991 survey, Arkansas's Republicans now have at least two decades of consistent momentum in organizational development.

Just as Republican Party activists are more united ideologically, they are also more allegiant to their party as they self-report their partisan identification. While traces of dual partisanship are shown by Democratic activists' marginally stronger identification with their party at the state level (contrasting with notable rates of dual partisanship exhibited by both parties' activists a decade ago), examining identification with the *national* party offers a fair representation of activists' party identification. Arkansas Republican activists are amazingly united in their level of commitment to their political party, with over 96 percent describing themselves as "strong Republicans." While Democrats indicate loyalty to their party (78.9 percent are strong Democrats), the Republican allegiance is unmatchable. Indeed, almost as large a percentage of Democrats identify themselves as

Republicans or leaners to the GOP (2.6 percent of total) as Republican activists who describe themselves as anything other than "strong" Republicans (3.4 percent total). Similarly, while 99.3 percent of GOP activists reported voting for George W. Bush in the 2000 presidential election, over 10 percent of Democratic activists bolted their party to support Bush.

Another measure of attitudes toward the parties—activists' description of their feelings of "closeness to" or "distance from" the parties— reinforces these findings. For instance, almost 85 percent of Republican activists put themselves at one of the two points (on a seven-point scale) closest to the Arkansas state Republican Party and a slightly larger percentage of those activists place themselves at the two most distant points from the state Democratic Party. By contrast, only 62.6 percent of Democrat activists place themselves at one of the two closest points to their state party, although over three-quarters do similarly distance themselves from the state GOP. This suggests two things: Republicans are more fervent in their party allegiance, and Democrats are driven as much by their animosity toward the political opposition as by their positive feelings about their own party.

This conclusion is reinforced by the survey's results related to the forces that inspire party activists to become and stay involved in their parties. To a much greater degree than their Democratic counterparts, Republican activists claim to have been driven by their interest in and desire to reshape public policies in explaining their involvement in politics. For example, 69.6 percent of GOP activists "see working in the political party generally as a way to influence politics and government" as being "very important"; this is the case for only 43.5 percent of Democrats. These trends are much like the results from the 1991 survey on similar questions.

Republican activists are also much more likely to "walk the walk" on behalf of their party than are Democrats. The survey asked activists whether they had engaged in thirteen different campaign activities in recent campaigns. As shown in table 5, on every one of the thirteen, a larger percentage of Republicans than Democrats had engaged in the particular work. Somewhat surprisingly, however, both Republican and Democratic activists report being more active than those who held these positions a decade ago were. Then, a majority of Democrats reported engaging in a lone activity (distributing literature). Now, majorities of Democrats report distributing literature (64.3 percent), distributing lawn signs (60.1 percent), and contributing financially to campaigns (65.1 percent). At least half of Republican activists engage in those three activities, plus sending mailings to voters (50 percent), organizing campaign events (56.7 percent), and arranging fund-raising activities (64.6 percent). Particularly relevant in an era where fundraising is perhaps the best measure of the health of a party organization, the gap between the levels of activity between activists from the two parties was greatest on this last activity, with less than one-fourth of Democrats engaging in an activity that is relatively commonplace for Republicans in Arkansas.[10]

It is also interesting to examine the levels of politics where activists place their energies. A decade ago, a majority of Democratic activists described themselves as "very active" at the local level, outpacing Republican respondents. However, Democratic activists were less likely to be active than were Republicans at the state level and, in particular, in

TABLE 5

Campaign Activities of Arkansas Party Activists, 2001

	DEMOCRATS	REPUBLICANS
Contributed money to campaign	65.1	88.0
Distributed posters or lawn signs	60.1	82.7
Distributed campaign literature	64.3	82.0
Arranged fund-raising activities	24.4	64.6
Organized campaign events	33.6	56.7
Sent mailings to voters	35.4	50.0
Organized door-to-door canvassing	24.1	38.0
Dealt with campaign media	18.9	36.0
Organized telephone campaigns	24.1	34.0
Conducted voter registration drives	19.7	23.3
Utilized public opinion surveys	7.6	10.0
Purchased billboard space	3.4	9.7
Helped construct or maintain a campaign website	2.6	3.3
N	(381)	(150)

Note: Entries are the percent who said that they engaged in the campaign activity in recent elections.

national politics. Republicans were consistent in their activism (ranging between 43 and 46 percent) at the three levels.

At present, Republicans remain generally consistent in the level of politics in which they are most engaged, with a slight bias toward state politics. However, the percentage of Republicans who describe themselves as "very active" has jumped considerably, with nearly seven in ten of them claiming that level of activity in state politics. Republicans also outpace Democrats in activism at the local level. Showing some additional evidence that the increased Republican activity is being matched by that of the party's competition, some increase in the percentage of Democrats describing themselves as being "very active" has shown itself at all three levels since 1991, but it has been no match for the Republican shifts.

The more diverse Democratic Party is more likely to be viewed as factionalized by its activities than is the Republican Party. A slight majority of Democrats see the state party as having "very" or "moderately" high levels of factionalism as compared with 41.7 percent of Republicans. Considering the fact that rifts between the Huckabee and Hutchinson factions within the GOP have occasionally become public in the last several years, it is not surprising that Republicans identify divisions between supporters of different party leaders as one of the greatest sources of factionalism in the party. Over 60 percent of Republican activists said that a "great deal" or "fair amount" of disagreement within the party resulted from those divisions. Meanwhile, at the county level, Republicans see minimal factionalism (less than a quarter of activists see signification of factionalism); Democrats are much more likely to identify factionalism within the local party (43.6 percent).

Finally, the Republican Party in Arkansas shows itself to be a more vibrant party organizationally than are the Democrats through considerably greater levels of communication within the party both at the county level and among party actors at the state and federal level. While over 80 percent of Republicans report communicating with the party chair and other county committee members "very often" or "often," this is true among fewer than two-thirds of Democrats. And, while a majority of Republican activists communicate regularly with state government officials, only 41.6 percent of Democrats interact with the more numerous Democratic state government officials.

Conclusion

By almost all measures, this analysis of activists on the front lines of party politics in Arkansas indicates that the Republican Party is a healthier party than it was a decade ago and shows more vibrancy than does the Democratic Party at the local level in Arkansas. It is a more united party and a more active party at the grassroots level. There are some hints of Democratic Party enhancement as well when comparing the 2001 data to the 1991 survey results, however, indicating that—at least to a small degree—sharper partisan competition may be promoting increased party development by the traditionally dominant party.

These results, however, suggest there is a potential danger for the Republican Party in its cohesiveness. The Arkansas GOP is now a remarkably conservative party across the board. From salient social issues to taxation and spending policies, Republicans are deeply ideological in a conservative direction. The key barrier to Republican success in Arkansas over the past generation has been its difficulty in recruiting candidates with sufficient experience and personal charisma to offer voters increasingly open to voting Republican. While still a challenge to the party, the GOP is more consistently fielding legitimate candidates for political office in Arkansas. One wonders, however, whether the doctrinaire conservativism of the candidates who will be able to gain GOP activists' support may develop into just as significant a barrier to those candidates' ultimate success in the years to come.

Arkansas: Still Swingin' in 2004

JAY BARTH AND JANINE PARRY

Arkansas has been a fickle friend to both Democratic and Republican presidential candidates for decades. Between 1960 and 2000, Arkansans' electoral college votes were awarded to Republicans five times, Democrats five times, and to independent candidate George Wallace in 1968. Though most of the Republican victories occurred in recent elections, the state's overwhelmingly Democratic composition at every other level of politics and a narrow victory for George W. Bush in 2000 led many observers to believe 2004 would see Arkansas anointed as a "battleground" state once again. Instead, President Bush doubled his 2000 margin of victory over the Democratic challenger.

In this analysis, the authors draw upon preelection surveys, news accounts, exit poll data, and county-level election results to chronicle and explain a 9-point margin for the GOP in an otherwise Democratic state. They conclude that a population explosion in the state's most affluent, Republican regions, together with the polarizing appeal of an anti-gay-marriage ballot measure among white voters in the state's "rural swing" counties, led to the state's stronger-than-expected right turn that year.

Introduction

Arkansas—a state that George W. Bush won by just fifty thousand votes in 2000—flirted in 2004 with joining Florida as a southern state with "battleground" potential.[1] This status as a prospective swing state was driven

Jay Barth and Janine Parry, "'Still Swingin': Arkansas and the 2004 Presidential Race," *American Review of Politics* 26 (Spring and Summer 2005): 133–54. Reprinted with permission.

not just by the close 2000 presidential outcome, but also by the continued strength of Democratic candidates in Arkansas in recent election cycles. Mark Pryor, for example, was the sole Democrat to defeat an incumbent U.S. senator in 2002, prevailing over Tim Hutchinson by eight percentage points. Moreover, Arkansas Republicanism continues to be geographically shackled to the fast growing communities of Northwest Arkansas (from which the party gets its sole Arkansas U.S. congressman) and the suburbs encircling Little Rock; the GOP only occasionally fields candidates, much less wins posts, elsewhere in the state. At a time then when Republicanism elsewhere in the South shows new strength with each election cycle, nearly three in four Arkansas state legislators continue to wear the Democratic label, and even larger percentages of local officeholders remain in the Democratic fold.[2]

In the spring and summer of 2004, both the John Kerry and Bush campaigns sent staffers into the state, and the campaigns and their allied 527 groups spent funds on television advertising in the Little Rock and Northwest Arkansas markets. By Labor Day, however, advertising had come to a stop, the Bush team had departed for Colorado, and the Kerry staff remained tiny. Still, state Democrats hoped that a grassroots campaign focused on turnout and showcasing ex-president Bill Clinton could pull out a photo finish win among an electorate in which a cultural disconnect with John Kerry competed with doubts about the economic and foreign policy record of George Bush. Instead, voters were moved in a different direction, particularly in the crucially important "swing" counties of the state, awarding the incumbent a win margin that doubled that of four years earlier. While this outcome signals a further cementing of presidential Republicanism in Arkansas, our analysis suggests that a different Democratic candidate and the absence of a galvanizing ballot initiative could have led to a different result in what remains the region's most reliably Democratic state.

The Campaign
The Primary Season: The National Press
Returns (Briefly) to Little Rock

As has become the norm, the state's late May primary meant that Arkansas's rank-and-file voters were irrelevant in determining the Democratic nominee. Still, Arkansas Democrats basked in nostalgia as an Arkansan with a campaign based in a historic downtown Little Rock building played a central role in the party's nomination battle. An Internet-fueled, months-long wooing (equal parts spontaneous and stage-managed) of retired supreme allied commander and CNN analyst Wesley K. Clark, who had casually flirted with a race for Arkansas's governorship in 2002, culminated in his joining the large field of Democratic candidates on September 17.[3] While Clark's announcement at the Little Rock Boys Club occurred almost at exactly the same time in the election cycle as had Clinton's twelve years previous, the increasing frontloading of the nomination process meant that it was decidedly "later." Consequently, despite considerable attention from the national press and millions of dollars in immediate fundraising, the lateness of the entry quickly showed itself as Clark made missteps on issues in the glare of attention and as his campaign was forced to make choices among the crucial first contests, including taking a pass on Iowa's caucuses.

Still, for six months, dozens of Arkansans became full-time volunteers at Clark's headquarters.[4] Elected Democrats in the state—including the entire Democratic congressional delegation—endorsed the Arkansan and campaigned for him as dozens of Arkansans "maxed out" their campaign contributions to the cause.[5] "Arkansans for Clark" yard signs soon populated Little Rock lawns, and state and national opinion polls tracking the candidate's standing appeared daily in the state's largest newspaper. While Bill and Hillary Clinton's support was never explicitly expressed (and, some contended, was not present at all), Clinton's key African American operatives—the so-called "Buffalo Soldiers"—traveled to South Carolina and a version of the "Arkansas Travelers" hit the road for New Hampshire and states closer to home to stump for "the General."[6]

By January's close, however, the nomination momentum had swung to John Kerry. The Massachusetts senator's Iowa victory zapped the energy out of the Clark campaign and led to a third-place showing in New Hampshire. While he eked out a single, narrow victory in Arkansas's neighboring state of Oklahoma, it was not enough to justify remaining in the race, and Clark returned to Little Rock to announce his departure from the race on February 11. Unlike the Clinton "war room" that had became the stuff of Democratic lore and presidential library exhibits, the Clark campaign's infrastructure was unceremoniously auctioned off. With the Arkansan out of the race, Kerry trounced his sole remaining primary opponent, Congressman Dennis Kucinich, on May 18.

A Real Campaign or Not?

Around the time of the primary vote, all signs pointed to full-fledged battleground status for Arkansas. A combination of candidate and high-profile surrogate visits, television advertising, and preparations for large ground operations intimated that Arkansas would see its most intense presidential campaign ever.

President Bush had visited Little Rock for the third time in 2003 for a five hundred thousand dollar fundraiser in November and returned to the city in January 2004 for a health care event, but these looked to be just the beginning.[7] In early April, the president visited El Dorado, in the most reliably Republican county in south Arkansas, for a community-college-based event on economic revitalization.[8] Then, Bush and Vice President Dick Cheney both visited Northwest Arkansas in early May. Cheney gave a sharply partisan talk in a visit to the Wal-Mart headquarters in Bentonville, and the president touted his No Child Left Behind policy in a visit to a high school in Van Buren.[9] The visits to spots in the state that are consistently Republican in their presidential voting suggested that the Bush campaign felt compelled to shore up the GOP base as the campaign began.

Kerry made his second visit of the campaign, the first in nearly a year, to Little Rock in early May. The two-day schedule included an airport rally, a major fundraiser, and a health care event.[10] While Arkansas Democrats were thrilled to have the attention of the Democratic nominee and the signals that he planned to work hard for the state's electoral votes, considerable second-guessing about Kerry's personal style followed the visit.[11] While there was no doubt that Kerry needed to connect culturally with Arkansans (Senator Mark Pryor would later invite his colleague to the state to go hunting), there was a real sense that the Massachusetts senator had forced the issue, appearing overly scripted in his numerous mentions of the Arkansas Razorbacks and his visit to the legendary political hangout Doe's Eat Place.

Arkansas voters also saw a flurry of television advertisements during the spring as the Bush campaign spent just over one million dollars in the Little Rock and Northwest Arkansas markets and the Kerry campaign spent over seven hundred thousand dollars.[12] The principal Bush advertisement targeted Kerry's votes against weapons programs while in the U.S. Senate, taking particular aim at those weapons systems, such as Patriot missiles and Black Hawk helicopters, with components built in the state. Kerry parried with 60 second biographical advertisements emphasizing his military record.[13]

It was that Vietnam heroism that provided the one potential cultural connection with the avidly patriotic white rural voters of Arkansas. It is for this reason that the questions raised by the controversial advertisements of Swift Boat Veterans for Truth (and the subsequent national media coverage of them) were so effective in a state like Arkansas. Arkansan Fred Short, the Vietnam boatmate with whom Kerry had reconnected during a May 2003 visit to Little Rock, served as a key respondent to the Swift Board charges for Kerry in the state, but his appearances—and firsthand account—were no match for the intense media attention given the ads.[14]

Still, the fact that Democrats were serious about contesting for Arkansas's electoral votes was made clear with consideration of an Arkansan for the number two spot on the national ticket. While Wesley Clark's performance as a presidential candidate had been shaky, his military credentials and his southern home kept him on the list of potential vice presidential nominees and garnered him an interview (perfunctory or not) with Kerry. Much longer lists of prospective candidates also included the name of Arkansas Senator Blanche Lincoln.[15]

But, Clark's hopes of a place on the 2004 ticket ended with John Edwards's selection as Kerry's veep candidate. Soon after gaining the spot on the ticket, Edwards made two visits to the state to campaign. An Arkansas Riverbank rally in Little Rock and a Fort Smith appearance a few days later showed a greater comfort by Kerry's new number two in campaigning in the Arkansas context than his ticketmate had shown in May.[16] The Edwards visits were matched by visits by Dick Cheney to Hot Springs and Fort Smith during the same period.[17] These would be the final visits to the state in 2004 of any of the presidential and vice presidential nominees.

Although the Kerry national campaign committed again and again to adding Arkansas to the list of states that would receive television advertising dollars, as the weeks went by it became obvious that the official ticket would never make that investment.[18] Feeling that their opponents needed an air assault to shift the state in Kerry's direction, the Bush/Cheney campaign responded to the Democrats' media inaction by sending the bulk of their staffers in the Little Rock campaign office to more-competitive states; six went to Colorado and two to Florida.[19]

Arkansas's Kerry campaign consisted of a handful of Kerry staffers and a relatively large (by Arkansas standards) field operation of the state Democratic Party. The Democrats' coordinated campaign opened a dozen field offices staffed with about 40 full-time staffers around the state. Along with allied groups, they focused on new voter registration (over 120,000 voters were added to the rolls between 2000 and 2004 in the state, primarily in Democratic counties) and developing a volunteer base that made nearly one million phone calls during the fall.[20] Lawyers also played visible roles in the grassroots strategies of the parties as election day neared, in an unprecedented effort to monitor precincts for voter intimidation or ballot shenanigans.[21] The left-leaning Election Protection Coalition placed Arkansas near the top of its list of targeted states, bringing in numerous out-of-state volunteers to assist in the monitoring and voter education efforts. The state parties focused on using home-state attorneys to assist with their efforts. The Democrats recruited nearly three hundred attorneys, and the Republicans recruited a smaller number of lawyers to serve as precinct monitors, particularly in heavily African American precincts in the traditionally Democratic counties in the state.[22]

A handful of public polls showing a tightened race around the time of the first fall presidential debate (see table 1) encouraged state Democrats, led by former U.S. senators Dale Bumpers and David Pryor, to make their own advertising investment to win the state. The fundraising effort—dubbed the "Doe's Eat Place Pact" because of where it was hatched—quickly raised about $130,000 for the state Democratic Party.[23] Radio advertisements featuring Arkansas political celebrities Bill Clinton, failed presidential candidate Clark, and former transportation secretary Rodney Slater in support of the national ticket followed. A handful of other, relatively small investments were made by the Democratic National Committee and allied 527 groups in the last several days of the race.

The state Democratic Party also invested resources in removing Ralph Nader from the state ballot via court action in September. Their case, claiming fraud and irregularities in the gathering of the signatures that got his name on the ballot as the nominee of the defunct Arkansas Populist Party, enjoyed a brief victory when a Little Rock district court judge agreed with the Democratic lawyers and ordered Nader and his running mate removed from the ballot.[24] A month before the election, however, the state Supreme Court reinstated the ticket by a four to three vote.[25] Much more consequential was a separate ballot decision around

TABLE 1

Selected Polls in Arkansas, Presidential Race 2004

POLL AND POLLING DATES	BUSH	KERRY	SPREAD
Survey USA, April 14–15	47	45	**Bush +2**
Zogby/*Wall Street Journal*, May 18–23	49	45	**Bush +4**
Zogby/*Wall Street Journal*, June 1–6	51	44	Bush +7
Zogby/*Wall Street Journal*, June 15–20	45	47	Kerry +2
Rasmussen, July 1–31	46	46	tie
Zogby/*Wall Street Journal*, July 6–10	47	45	**Bush +2**
Zogby/*Wall Street Journal*, July 26–30	48	46	**Bush +2**
Zogby/*Wall Street Journal*, August 16–21	46	48	**Kerry +2**
Rasmussen, August 1–26	49	43	Bush +6
Zogby/*Wall Street Journal*, August 16–21	46	48	**Kerry +2**
Zogby/*Wall Street Journal*, August 30 September 3	48	46	**Bush +2**
Rasmussen, September 12–25	51	44	Bush +7
Survey USA, September 27–29	53	44	Bush +9
Arkansas News Bureau/Opinion Research, October 4–6	52	43	Bush +9
Zogby, October 10–11	46	45	**Bush +1**
Arkansas Poll (Blair Center, University of Arkansas), October 5–20	53	44	Bush +9
Arkansas News Bureau/Opinion Research, October 18–20	48	48	**tie**
Survey USA, October 23–25	51	45	Bush +6
Mason-Dixon, October 27–29	51	43	Bush +8
Survey USA, October 31-November 1	51	46	Bush +5

Note: Bolded results are within the reported margin of error.
Source: Polling results compiled by RealClearPolitics.com throughout the election cycle; accessed at www.realclearpolitics.com/Presidential_04/ar_polls.html on December 2, 2004.

the same time. Another divided court rejected the ACLU of Arkansas's claims that the proposed state constitutional amendment (Amendment 3) defining marriage as between one woman and one man and barring state recognition of same-sex marriages or other similar legal partnerships was improperly on the ballot because voters could not understand the scope of the measure; the amendment proceeded to a vote.[26]

Aside from the presidential race in the state, the Arkansas ballot item that received the greatest attention during the year was Amendment 3. The proposition flexed its muscles through a church-based petition campaign, which gathered two hundred thousand signatures, a number more than twice that needed for placement on the ballot. The campaign for passage of the amendment did not invest in major media buys, relying instead on a grassroots campaign that evidenced itself mainly in the form of supportive bumper stickers that popped up around the state. The issue also received an exceptional amount of coverage in the statewide media, elevating its place in the campaign in the state.[27] While recognizing that President Bush might well benefit from the amendment's presence on the ballot, Amendment 3's primary backers said they only cared about running up a large margin on the amendment vote. But Bush's surrogates in the state, such as his Arkansas campaign chair Gov. Mike Huckabee and his wife Janet Huckabee, centered on attitudes towards same-sex marriage as a "clear difference" between Kerry and Bush, thereby unmistakably linking the amendment vote to the presidential campaign.[28] Moreover, Arkansas was one of two states where the Republican National Committee distributed mailers focused on the partisan division on the issue of same-sex marriage (and merging that issue with other moral issues).[29] The most striking visuals on a flyer portraying the evils of the "liberal agenda" showed a Bible emblazoned with the word "BANNED" next to a kneeling man slipping a ring onto another man's finger under the word "ALLOWED."

When Bill Clinton, still recovering from heart surgery, was able to return to his home state for a large Halloween evening rally just blocks from his nearly completed presidential library, he showed deep awareness that the issue of same-sex marriage had gained traction in Arkansas as a symbol of John Kerry's cultural disconnect from Arkansans. In his speech, Clinton emphasized that "[t]his election is not about guns and gay marriage," which he called "bull issues."[30] He also tried to turn the emphasis away from emotion-laden cultural issues to bread-and-butter economics.

In referring to the large-scale construction project he had brought to Little Rock, Clinton said sharply: "In the last four years as a private citizen I created more jobs in Arkansas that the Bush administration ever did."[31] While Clinton may have helped further energize the Democratic base, it was a newer Arkansas political star, GOP Gov. Mike Huckabee, who proved more accurate in summing up the tough chore that the "great campaigner" ultimately had: "[S]elling John Kerry in . . . Arkansas is tougher than selling Red Sox fans souvenirs in Manhattan."[32]

The Outcome

All but a handful of public opinion polls gave Bush a relatively robust lead during the final months of the campaign (see table 1). Expenditures and activities by candidates, parties, and interlopers during the final stretch of 2004 consequently paled in comparison to the attention lavished on the state in 2000. It is curious then that turnout bounced back to native son Bill Clinton–era levels. Sixty-four percent of registered Arkansans cast a ballot in the Bush-Kerry contest as compared with 59 percent in the Bush-Gore race four years earlier (see table 2). We suspect the boost was mainly a product of the highly polarized nature of Election 2004 nationwide; whether their own state was in play was far less important to Arkansans than the charged partisan environment nationally. We should add that while we argue later in this section that the antigay-marriage amendment influenced candidate preference among many Arkansas voters, there is limited evidence that the issue had a substantial mobilizing effect on the electorate. When vote likelihood was regressed on the standard battery of turnout predictors plus the respondent's position on Amendment 3 using preelection survey data, the anti-gay position had a significant, but negligible, effect.[33]

TABLE 2
General Election Voter Turnout in Arkansas, Registered Voters, 1972–2004

YEAR	PERCENT TURNOUT
1972	69 (g)
1976	71 (g)
1980	77 (g)
1984	76 (g)
1988	69 (p)
1992	72 (p)
1996	65 (p)
2000	59 (p)
2004	64 (p)

Key: Voter turnout figures are based on gubernatorial voting (g) or presidential voting (p) depending on the highest turnout race of the year.
Source: Data compiled from the official website of the Arkansas Secretary of State at www.arelections.org, accessed January 24, 2005, and from various volumes of *America Votes* (Washington, D.C.: Congressional Quarterly).

"W" Stands for Wide Margin

The outcome in the presidential contest was clearer even than most expected. Fifty-four percent of Arkansas voters cast their ballots for the Republican incumbent; his Democratic challenger garnered the support of 45 percent (see table 3). The resulting 9-point gap nearly doubled Bush's margin of victory in 2000; while Gore fell short by about fifty thousand votes, Kerry lost by more than twice that number. There was greater stability in the performance of minor party candidates. Ralph Nader, running on the state's rejuvenated Populist Party ticket (only after the bare-knuckled court challenge by Democrats), took in barely six thousand votes, or 0.06 percent of those cast. The Libertarian, Constitutional, and Green Party candidates collectively scooped up the remaining 0.05 percent.

TABLE 3

Results of the 2004 Arkansas Presidential and Congressional Elections

CANDIDATE (PARTY)	VOTE PERCENTAGE	VOTE TOTAL
President		
George W. Bush/Dick Cheney (R)	54.3	572,898
John F. Kerry/John Edwards (D)	44.6	469,953
Ralph Nader/Peter Miguel Camejo (P)	0.6	6,171
Michael Badnarik and Richard V. Campagna (L)	0.2	2,352
Michael Anthony Peroutka and Chuck Baldwin (C)	0.2	2,083
David Cobb and Patricia LaMarche (G)	0.1	1,488
U.S. Senate		
Blanche Lincoln (D)*	55.9	580,973
Jim Holt (R)	44.1	458,036
Glen A. Schwarz (W)	0.0	212
Gene Mason (W)	0.0	128
U.S. House of Representatives		
First District		
Marion Berry (D)*	66.6	162,388
Vernon Humphrey (R)	33.4	81,556
Second District		
Vic Snyder (D)*	58.2	160,834
Marvin Parks (R)	41.8	115,655
Third District		
John Boozman (R)*	59.3	160,629
Jan Judy (D)	38.1	103,158
Dale Morfey (I)	2.6	7,016
Fourth District		
Mike Ross (D)	Unopposed	

Key: * denotes incumbent; R = Republican; D = Democrat; P = Populist;
L = Libertarian; C = Constitutional; G = Green; I = independent; W = write-in
Source: Data compiled from the official website of the Arkansas Secretary of State at
www.arelections.org, accessed January 24, 2005.

Within-state variation played an important role in 2004, though in ways more nuanced than in elections past. Arkansas politics long have had a regional quality, reflected, roughly, in the state's four congressional districts.[34] The First and Fourth, in the eastern and southern portions of the state, respectively, are poor, rural regions that remain—for the most part—Democratic strongholds despite residents' social conservatism. Portions of the Second and most of the Third districts of central and Northwest Arkansas are high-growth areas of relative prosperity that are, or are becoming, dependably Republican.[35] But the regional differences in presidential party preference many have come to expect did not materialize in 2004. Though Gore won majority support in the First and Fourth districts in 2000 only to lose statewide, President Bush swept all four regions in his reelection bid, stretching his lead over Kerry to 25 points in the Third (see table 4).[36]

TABLE 4

Presidential Contest by Congressional District, 2004

CONGRESSIONAL DISTRICT	BUSH		KERRY	
	%	VOTES	%	VOTES
First (eastern and north central)	51.7	127,179	47.1	115,994
Second (central)	51.5	145,392	47.6	134,478
Third (Northwest)	62.3	171,853	36.5	100,656
Fourth (south and Southeast)	51.4	128,474	47.5	118,825

Note: Candidate percentages were calculated as a portion of all votes cast minus over- and under-votes.
Source: Data compiled by the authors from the official website of the Arkansas Secretary of State at www.arelections.org, accessed January 25, 2005.

To begin to understand the causes and consequences of this shift, consider the data in table 5. The ten most populous Arkansas counties together contain about 1.2 million people, nearly half the state's total population. The fastest growing of these counties—those topping a 30 percent population increase between 1990 and 2000—are in the Second (Faulkner and Saline) and Third (Washington and Benton) congressional districts. All four counties produced clear victories for the incumbent Republican, with the home of global retail giant Wal-Mart (Benton County) giving Bush nearly 70 percent of the vote. Kerry, in contrast, managed to win only two of Arkansas's biggest prizes, one of which (Jefferson) is actually losing pop-

Table 5

Registered Voter Turnout and Presidential Vote in the Ten Most Populous Arkansas Counties, 2004

COUNTY AND POPULATION	PERCENT POP. CHANGE 1990–2000	TURNOUT (%)	TOTAL VOTES (PERCENT)	
		VOTERS (#)	TOTAL VOTES (RAW NUMBER) BUSH (R)	KERRY (D)
Pulaski (361,474)	3.4	59.6	44.2	55.0
		257,589	67,903	84,532
Washington (157,715)	39.1	72.5	55.7	43.1
		88,380	35,726	27,597
Benton (153,406)	57.3	70.5	68.4	30.5
		96,612	46,571	20,756
Sebastian (115,071)	15.5	69.0	61.7	37.3
		64,111	27,303	16,479
Garland (88,068)	20.0	57.0	54.1	44.9
		70,393	21,734	18,040
Craighead (82,148)	19.1	58.2	53.1	45.9
		51,202	15,818	13,665
Faulkner (86,014)	43.3	62.3	58.6	39.6
		58,882	21,514	14,538
Jefferson (84,278)	-1.4	53.1	33.5	64.5
		57,407	10,218	19,675
Saline (83,529)	30.1	66.1	63.2	35.9
		59,585	24,864	14,153
Pope (54,469)	18.7	60.5	65.1	34.0
		34,557	13,614	7,100

Source: Data compiled from the U.S. Bureau of the Census and the official website of the Arkansas Secretary of State at www.arelections.org, accessed January 24, 2005.

ulation. The importance of the state's political map is compounded further by the equally regional nature of turnout rates. Voters in the high-growth, Republican counties featured in the table substantially outperform their peers, a pattern also evident in 2000.[37] While nearly 73 percent of Washington County residents cast ballots in 2004 (56 percent of them for the Republican incumbent), for example, just 53 percent of those in Jefferson County did.

Arkansas's Swingers

The significance of the state's shifting regionalism for 2004's headliner contest is illustrated further in table 6. In 1988, Blair identified twenty-six "rural swing" counties that have remained stalwartly Democratic even when attractive Republican candidates at the top of the ticket persuaded many of their peers to take a walk on the wild side. The few aberrations in this pattern are telling. Predominantly white, sparsely populated, and "dry" (meaning liquor sales are illegal), this collection of counties swung hard for the "states' rights" campaign of George Wallace in 1968, against George McGovern in 1972, and back again for Jimmy Carter in 1976. Though they remained in the Democratic fold in 1980, they swung wildly again for Ronald Reagan's reelection in 1984 and George Bush's in 1988, then back again to Arkansan's own Bill Clinton in 1992 and 1996. Their role in close state-level contests has been even more decisive, often delivering wins to Democratic and Republican candidates in the same year.[38] Most important for the purposes of this analysis, while George Bush fell short of mustering a majority of their votes in 2000, his support in these counties grew to nearly 54 percent in 2004, nearly even with his statewide average.

TABLE 6

Bush Vote in Arkansas, 2000 and 2004, by County

COUNTY	BUSHVOTE %		R SENATE VOTE %		BUSH GAIN, 2000–2004 (#)	REPUB. GAIN, '98–04 (#)	PERCENT, AMEND. 3
	2000	2004	1998	2004			
Arkansas	52.6	54.6	30.8	35.2	203	809	76.5
Ashley	46.9	53.7	33.8	42.8	1063	1390	81.6
Baxter	57.1	60.1	53.2	52.8	977	2129	75.4
Benton	64.9	68.4	66.5	58.3	8254	13589	74.6
Boone	62.8	66.3	53.5	55.6	1077	2429	80.4
Bradley	45.1	47.3	33.0	63.4	134	1661	79.2
Calhoun	51.6	58.2	37.2	45.0	288	456	79.9
Carroll	57.9	59.0	52.7	51.7	62	1461	71.9
Chicot	35.1	36.3	24.5	28.1	-12	350	72.6
Clark	43.8	44.9	32.0	35.5	27	1216	73.3
Clay	38.2	45.3	23.7	33.1	768	769	81.2
Cleburne	56.1	59.2	46.5	50.2	689	2395	78.6
Cleveland	52.8	57.5	35.3	47.7	295	748	81.4
Columbia	53.9	57.8	42.8	44.2	606	1340	80.1
Conway	49.0	49.6	35.8	39.1	-15	1026	73.4
Craighead	48.3	53.1	36.9	42.1	2371	5213	78.1
Crawford	61.3	65.6	53.0	56.9	2111	4956	80.1
Crittenden	44.3	45.3	28.7	34.2	20	2640	80.3
Cross	48.8	54.6	30.0	43.6	792	1470	79.4
Dallas	47.2	50.2	32.4	37.6	171	477	78.3
Desha	35.7	37.2	26.4	26.0	51	282	65.6
Drew	46.5	52.2	33.1	39.5	614	926	77.5
Faulkner	55.0	58.6	46.4	48.5	2871	7848	74.0
Franklin	53.4	57.4	45.2	48.2	570	1122	77.0
Fulton	49.6	50.9	35.4	38.2	92	778	81.3
Garland	53.1	54.1	46.0	44.3	436	5250	72.6
Grant	54.6	62.1	38.7	49.9	931	1746	82.6
Greene	46.7	51.9	31.7	42.0	1259	3016	83.0
Hempstead	44.7	48.0	33.8	36.1	443	891	77.2
Hot Spring	45.9	49.4	35.6	42.1	544	2102	76.9
Howard	52.2	55.4	36.7	42.0	307	931	83.2

COUNTY	BUSHVOTE %		R SENATE VOTE %		BUSH GAIN, 2000–2004 (#)	REPUB. GAIN, '98–04 (#)	PERCENT, AMEND. 3
	2000	2004	1998	2004			
Independence	**53.0**	**57.1**	**39.1**	**42.8**	**988**	**1992**	**81.6**
Izard	**45.7**	**51.8**	**34.2**	**41.0**	**533**	**520**	**77.7**
Jackson	**37.5**	**42.3**	**26.1**	**32.1**	**380**	**680**	**76.8**
Jefferson	32.2	33.5	28.4	26.7	-506	1763	71.5
Johnson	**51.1**	**53.6**	**41.5**	**46.0**	**302**	**1314**	**77.7**
Lafayette	**45.5**	**50.3**	**30.7**	**37.2**	**305**	**322**	**80.3**
Lawrence	**43.5**	**44.6**	**27.3**	**36.5**	**36**	**1004**	**82.0**
Lee	32.8	36.6	20.3	20.8	820	116	74.6
Lincoln	43.0	46.8	26.4	32.0	203	507	81.5
Little River	43.4	48.6	31.7	37.2	498	788	80.3
Logan	55.4	59.4	42.3	49.6	511	1287	81.5
Lonoke	59.1	65.4	44.2	51.4	3189	5327	80.0
Madison	60.2	60.7	52.5	52.8	120	406	79.1
Marion	56.6	60.1	49.9	53.1	356	1187	77.7
Miller	52.9	57.6	41.4	44.3	311	2307	80.7
Mississippi	41.3	43.3	27.2	34.0	436	1882	75.7
Monroe	40.4	43.3	27.5	29.7	118	252	79.4
Montgomery	**56.9**	**59.8**	**42.4**	**51.2**	**153**	**765**	**78.5**
Nevada	48.0	50.4	31.5	35.0	129	388	72.7
Newton	64.4	63.5	45.2	57.1	-101	1020	78.6
Ouachita	**45.6**	**50.2**	**32.3**	**36.3**	**882**	**842**	**74.9**
Perry	**52.8**	**55.0**	**40.1**	**46.7**	**48**	**883**	**72.6**
Phillips	33.9	35.6	18.3	23.9	383	672	72.8
Pike	**57.3**	**59.8**	**37.6**	**52.6**	**32**	**544**	**81.8**
Poinsett	**41.3**	**46.0**	**28.2**	**36.2**	**600**	**1112**	**80.6**
Polk	64.0	66.6	50.4	57.2	434	1554	81.1
Pope	61.0	65.1	46.6	51.9	1939	4394	79.7
Prairie	**53.1**	**56.0**	**31.7**	**40.7**	**169**	**497**	**80.0**
Pulaski	43.9	44.6	39.1	34.2	-2684	14894	63.8
Randolph	**45.5**	**47.4**	**32.9**	**37.9**	**92**	**1139**	**84.3**
Saline	57.5	63.2	47.9	51.3	4792	8588	76.3
Scott	**60.3**	**62.3**	**41.9**	**50.2**	**86**	**547**	**80.7**
Searcy	64.3	64.3	51.7	51.9	-186	283	82.0

COUNTY	BUSHVOTE %		R SENATE VOTE %		BUSH GAIN, 2000–2004 (#)	REPUB. GAIN, '98–04 (#)	PERCENT, AMEND. 3
	2000	2004	1998	2004			
Sebastian	58.5	61.8	54.1	52.7	2896	6958	76.7
Sevier	49.2	54.7	34.0	42.7	465	786	82.2
Sharp	51.9	54.9	43.3	45.3	370	966	82.1
St. Francis	40.2	39.8	25.1	37.8	-297	2124	74.9
Stone	**54.0**	**57.5**	**36.4**	**48.6**	**353**	**1283**	**77.4**
Union	55.4	58.9	48.7	45.7	-939	2783	79.0
Van Buren	49.9	54.1	41.2	45.9	395	1164	74.9
Washington	54.9	55.7	54.7	47.6	1323	9258	66.2
White	**59.5**	**64.3**	**53.0**	**55.9**	**3044**	**5586**	**80.5**
Woodruff	33.9	33.7	20.9	24.8	-150	260	73.9
Yell	**49.7**	**55.2**	**34.6**	**40.3**	**604**	**804**	**76.6**
Avg. (all counties)	50.1	53.3	37.9	43.0	na	na	77.7
Avg. (RSC)	49.6	53.6	35.3	42.7	na	na	79.4
Statewide Vote	51.3	54.3	42.2	44.1	99958	162166	75.0

Key: Bolded counties denote Blair's "rural swing counties." *Source:* Data compiled by the authors from the official website of the Arkansas Secretary of State at www.arelections.org, accessed January 27, 2005, and from Richard M. Scammon, Alice V. McGillivray, and Rhodes Cook. *America Votes 23* (Washington, D.C.: Congressional Quarterly Press, 1999), 34–35.

It is worth noting that Arkansas's rural swingers played a key role in the 2004 election in two additional—and, we believe—related ways. The first lies in the performance of Jim Holt, a state legislator and the Republican nominee for the U. S. Senate against the incumbent Democrat, Blanche Lincoln. We use 1998 as a baseline for Holt's expected support because his background was remarkably similar to the Republican candidate that year, Fay Boozman. Boozman, like Holt, was in just his first term as a state senator when he made a bid for the U.S. Senate seat being vacated by Democratic giant Dale Bumpers; he garnered 42 percent of the vote statewide. It was a respectable showing in an off-year election against a conservative Democrat, Blanche Lincoln, who already had served three terms in the U.S. House of Representatives and outspent him nearly three to one. The seat was open that year, however, and Lincoln's approval rating climbed steadily throughout her first term.[39] Consequently, few observers of the 2004 cycle expected Holt to break 40 percent (see table 7), and even that projection may have been generous in light of the fact that he raised only $154,000 compared to Lincoln's $5.5 million. In the end, however, 44 percent of the vote went to Holt, an outcome that seemed to earn more press coverage in the state than Bush's reelection. Tellingly, rural swing voters contributed disproportionately to his surprise showing. As the bottom of table 6 reveals, Holt bested Boozman's 1998 performance by 5.1 percentage points across the state. In rural swing counties, however, the margin increased to 7.4 percentage points.

TABLE 7

Selected Polls in Arkansas, U.S. Senate Race 2004

POLL AND POLLING DATES	HOLT (R)	LINCOLN (D)	SPREAD
Survey USA, August 20–22	34	58	Lincoln +24
Survey USA, September 27–29	40	54	Lincoln +14
Arkansas News Bureau/Opinion Research, October 4–6	32	60	Lincoln +28
Zogby, October 10–11	32	60	Lincoln +28
Arkansas News Bureau/Opinion Research, October 18–20	32	60	Lincoln +28
Survey USA, October 23–25	38	57	Lincoln +19
Survey USA October 29–31	42	55	Lincoln +13
Survey USA, October 31-November 1	43	53	Lincoln +10

Source: Polling results compiled by RealClear Politics.com throughout the election cycle; accessed at www.realclearpolitics.com/ Presidential_04/ar_polls.html on December 2, 2004.

Because elections are not conducted in laboratories, it is of course impossible to pin down the reason for Holt's unexpected performance. The pains he took to hitch his wagon to the state's antigay-marriage vote, however, are instructive. A conservative evangelical who employed the "Christian fish" symbol on his campaign materials, Holt said in September that voter support for the proposed state constitutional amendment to prohibit gay marriages and civil unions would boost his popularity against an incumbent who, while favoring an existing state statute that defined marriage as a male-female union, said she opposed amending the federal constitution.[40] Holt hammered away at this distinction, pairing seven hundred bright red "Protect Marriage" placards with his larger campaign signs just a few weeks before the election and initiating a last-minute nontargeted "robocall" campaign declaring his commitment to prohibiting gay and lesbian marriages.[41] It seems likely these efforts were especially influential in Arkansas's rural swing counties. As table 6 demonstrates, more than 79 percent of voters in these areas supported Amendment 3, exceeding by four percentage points the measure's statewide support.

Table 8 (last column) presents additional information about Amendment 3's support among various segments of the Arkansas electorate. Though the measure garnered the approval of three in four voters, it clearly held special appeal for Republicans, conservatives, white evangelicals, frequent churchgoers, high wage-earners, suburbanites, "moral values" voters, those not enamored of Senator Lincoln's job performance, and Bush supporters. In light of these findings, it is no wonder many observers concluded that the measure sprouted coattails in Arkansas, boosting the performance of both a long-shot challenger in the state's U.S. Senate race and an incumbent president who pressed publicly for a national "marriage protection" amendment throughout the campaign. These coattails appear to have been especially significant in the "rural swing counties." A January 2005 analysis by *USA Today* identified 153 counties that switched to Bush after voting Democratic the previous two presidential elections (only a handful switched for Kerry). Of the eleven such counties identified in Arkansas, six of them belong to the "swingin'" category, and all but one surpassed the state average for Amendment 3 support.[42] It is important to emphasize here that vote choice, not voter mobilization, is the dynamic for which we find evidence in these counties. Turnout was up four points in the state's rural swing regions from 2000, virtually the same as the statewide increase.

"Survey Says"—Arkansas's Exit Polls

Other factors—including partisanship, ideology, sex, income, ethnicity, and age—certainly joined population shifts and the gay marriage debate in influencing the 2004 presidential vote in Arkansas. The polling data presented in table 8 not only reflect the key sources of support for both major party candidates but also afford an opportunity to compare Bush's 2004 base with that in 2000. Though most Democrats and liberals (82 and

TABLE 8

Vote Choice by Various Characteristics,
Presidential/Amendment 3 Vote (percent)

CHARACTERISTIC	ALL	BUSH	BUSH '00	KERRY	AMEND. 3
Party identification					
Democrat	41	18	+3	82	65
Republican	31	97	+3	3	89
Independent	29	60	-2	38	72
Ideology					
Liberal	13	19	+1	79	47
Moderate	45	40	-2	58	68
Conservative	42	82	+4	18	89
White conservative Protestant?					
Yes	31	88	n/a	12	92
No	69	39	n/a	60	67
White evangelical/born again?					
Yes	53	71	n/a	29	87
No	47	35	n/a	63	62
Church attendance					
Weekly-plus	n/a	n/a	n/a	n/a	93
Weekly	n/a	n/a	n/a	n/a	87
Monthly	n/a	n/a	n/a	n/a	62
Once a year	n/a	n/a	n/a	n/a	60
Never	n/a	n/a	n/a	n/a	54
Sex					
Male	44	59	+6	40	76
Female	56	50	+1	49	73
White Males	38	67	+9	32	79
White Females	46	60	+6	40	75
Racial/ethnic identity					
White	83	63	+7	36	77
Black	15	6	-6	94	66
Latino	1	*	*	*	*
Asian	0	*	*	*	*
Other	1	*	*	*	*
Age					
18–29	16	47	-6	51	69
30–44	29	60	+5	39	79
45–59	29	57	+10	42	75
60 or older	26	48	-1	52	74
65 or older	16	46	-1	54	73
Income					
Under $15,000	10	23	-11	74	63
$15–30,000	22	44	-1	55	71
$30–50,000	27	59	+5	41	76
$50–75,000	22	63	+12	37	77

CHARACTERISTIC	ALL	BUSH	BUSH '00	KERRY	AMEND. 3
$75–100,000	10	64	+4	36	82
$100–150,000	5	79	n/a	18	83
$150–200,000	2	*	n/a	*	*
$200,000 or more	2	*	n/a	*	*
Married					
Yes	53	71	n/a	38	78
No	47	35	n/a	63	66
Size of community					
Urban	20	47	n/a	52	63
Suburban	7	61	n/a	38	82
Rural	73	55	n/a	44	77
Antigay-marriage vote					
Yes (to ban gay marriage)	75	88	n/a	58	n/a
No (to ban gay marriage)	25	12	n/a	42	n/a
Most Important Issue					
Taxes	5	35	n/a	65	71
Education	4	30	n/a	67	58
Iraq	13	26	n/a	74	65
Terrorism	12	83	n/a	17	74
Economy/jobs	20	13	n/a	86	66
Moral values	33	92	n/a	8	90
Health care	5	17		81	56
Decision to go to war in Iraq					
Strongly approve	30	95	n/a	5	89
Somewhat approve	25	82	n/a	18	86
Somewhat disapprove	14	21	n/a	77	68
Strongly disapprove	29	6	n/a	93	56
Vote for U.S. Senate					
Lincoln (D)	56	22	n/a	77	n/a
Holt (R)	44	94	n/a	5	n/a
Approve of Senator Lincoln					
Yes	n/a	n/a	n/a	n/a	72
No	n/a	n/a	n/a	n/a	91

Key: * denotes a statistically insignificant number of respondents; "n/a" = not available or, in some cases, not applicable.

Source: Most data are based on 1,459 respondents and are compiled from 2004 National Election Pool data reported at CNN.com (Arkansas), accessed at www.cnn.com/ELECTION/2004/pages/results/states/AR/P/00/epolls.0.html on November 4, 2004. Some comparative data was taken from the Voter News Service Exit Poll (Arkansas), November 7, 2000. Some data in the final column are taken from the 2004 Arkansas Poll conducted between October 5 and October 20 and accessible at: http://plsc.uark.edu/arkpoll.

79 percent, respectively) dutifully cast their ballots for the Democratic nominee as they had in the previous election, they proved far less cohesive than Republicans, who gave fully 97 percent of their support to the party's choice. And while Kerry gained a sound victory among self-identified moderates in the state, independents (who constitute as much as 40 percent of the Arkansas electorate) threw their support behind the Republican nominee just as they had in 2000.

With respect to demographic characteristics, Arkansas saw its gender gap double between the two elections, with men—particularly white men—significantly more likely than women to support President Bush. Both groups, however, preferred the Republican (if barely among women), with white male support for the incumbent ballooning by nine points from four years previous.[43]

An income gap also is evident with Arkansans in the lowest and highest income categories voting overwhelmingly for Kerry and Bush, respectively. The latter's twelve-point increase over his 2000 performance among voters with household incomes of $50,000 to $75,000 is particularly noteworthy. Arkansas's relatively small black population (16 percent) registered its disapproval of the administration by halving the support Bush received in 2000; only six percent of the state's African American voters backed the Republican. White voters more than made up the difference, however, by throwing nearly two-thirds of their support to the president; they delivered a paltry 36 percent of their votes to John Kerry. Finally, while many of the state's current demographic patterns favor Republicans, exit polls reveal that Kerry won the support of the youngest Arkansans, reversing their preference from the last two presidential election cycles.[44]

Issues, too, left their mark on election 2004 in Arkansas, much as they did nationwide. Nearly a third of exit poll respondents selected "moral values" as the most important issue, an enigmatic category, to be sure, but one indisputably caught up in the "marriage protection" juggernaut. A quarter cited either "Iraq" or "terrorism," terms that as neatly sorted Kerry from Bush supporters in Arkansas as elsewhere. One in five voters, overwhelmingly Kerry voters, reported being most concerned with the economy. Taxes, education, and healthcare failed to light many fires within the state's electorate, despite a fair amount of attention to each during the campaign.

Conclusion

Early on, there was every indication that Arkansas's dance card would be even more full in 2004 than it had been in 2000. It was, after all, a battleground state in the Bush-Gore contest, and many believed the latter could have engineered a victory had he more vigorously and publicly aligned his campaign with native son Bill Clinton. Gen. Wesley Clark's declaration of his candidacy sparked the kind of excitement among Arkansans that many projected would return the state to the Democratic column in the race for the presidency. Mark Pryor's upset of the Republican incumbent in the U.S. Senate race just two years earlier, as well as the continued dominance of the Democratic party among state and local officeholders, likewise signaled that Arkansas would be in play in 2004. By Labor Day, however, the momentum was with the Bush campaign. Visits by candidates and surrogates slowed, and ad buys were canceled. The radio spots purchased by the states' leading Democrats in response to the suggestion of a tightened race in late October and a grassroots effort from the left came to naught. Instead, the Bush campaign, propelled by massive growth in the state's Republican strongholds, plus the one-two punch of a cultural disconnect with the Democratic nominee and a "protect marriage" crusade among the state's rural, white "swingers," carried Arkansas by a wide margin.

The party balance in Arkansas is likely to deliver future surprises in terms of both election outcomes and, as in 2004, win magnitudes. The relatively easy reelection of George W. Bush, the unexpected popularity of Holt's social conservatism, and the combination of rapid population growth and high voter turnout in the state's few Republican strongholds, bode well for the future of the GOP. Yet, Lincoln's victory leaves Arkansas as the only state in the South with two Democratic U.S. senators. The continued service of the three Democratic House members—after a surprisingly decisive victory by the Second District's Vic Snyder—means that five of the state's six representatives in Washington, D.C., are Democrats. Moreover, the Democratic Party made marginal gains in the state legislature, a first since the implementation of the state's stringent term limits law in the mid-1990s. So, despite an outcome at the presidential level that moves Arkansas closer to its southern peers, the state remains unpredictable as it moves into 2006, an election cycle in which a battle royale already is brewing in the race for governor, an office held by Arkansas's traditional "out" party since 1996.

Education Reform in Arkansas

Hitting a Moving Target

GARY W. RITTER

Because public schools long have been the chief priority of state governments in the United States, education nearly always tops the policy priority lists of both citizens and lawmakers. Here, Professor Ritter, a former schoolteacher who is now a professor of education policy, recounts Arkansas's recent efforts to improve the state's educational situation. The author sees forward motion, much of it at the prompting of repeated court decisions declaring the state's system of public education both "inequitable" and "inadequate." Though the state's Lake View litigation, spanning more than a decade, receives the bulk of the attention, Ritter also provides a useful examination of recent changes to Arkansas's school standards and curricula, assessment and accountability efforts, structural matters (including consolidation), and teacher training and compensation.

Despite decades of effort, and some gains, Arkansans remain "undereducated" compared to their peers around the nation. The most recent census data revealed that only 18 percent of the state's adults (age twenty-five and older) had bachelor's degrees. Only West Virginia could claim a lower percentage. While policymakers earnestly discuss the need to prepare all of our students for college-level work, four out of five Arkansas voters and taxpayers do not themselves possess college degrees. Many may not share the same sense of urgency about the priority that education should

An early version of this article appeared as Gary W. Ritter, "Education Reform in Arkansas: Past and Present," in *Reforming Education in Arkansas: Recommendations from the Koret Task Force,* eds. John Brown and Gary Ritter, (Stanford, Calif.: Hoover Institution Press, 2005), 27–42. This revision is used with permission.

TABLE 1

How Does Arkansas Compare?

	ARKANSAS	U.S.	AR RANK (HIGH = 1)
Adult attainment measures			
% of population (age 25+) with high school diploma, 2005	84.9%	86.8%	42 of 51
% of population (age 25+) with Bachelor's degree, 2007	18.2%	27.0%	50 of 51
NAEP exams, percent at or above proficient			
Reading grade 4, 2007	29%	33%	36 of 52
Reading grade 8, 2007	25%	31%	42 of 52
Math grade 4, 2007	37%	39%	34 of 52
Math grade 8, 2007	24%	32%	42 of 52
Science grade 4, 2005	24%	29%	34 of 45
Science grade 8, 2005	23%	29%	32 of 45
High school outcome measures			
Graduation rate, 2006	76%	68%	25 of 50
ACT composite score, 2007	20.6	21.1	40 of 50
ACT math score, 2007	19.9	20.8	41 of 50

Sources: Census Data for the State of Arkansas, http://www.census.gov/, retrieved June 12, 2008; National Assessment of Educational Progress, *The Nation's Report Card.* Past reports available online at http://nces.ed.gov/nationsreportcard, retrieved June 12, 2008; ACT Average Composite Scores by State, Index to Annual Data Reports, available online at http://www.act.org/, retrieved June 12, 2008.

command. This creates one of the greatest challenges facing state leaders and policymakers.

Our students have shown improvement in recent years, but Arkansas, like many rural southern states, continues to rank near the bottom on many of America's main indices of educational attainment: National Assessment scores, college entrance exam scores, and high-school graduation and college matriculation rates. The results of the spring 2007 administration of the ACT college entrance exam, for example, placed Arkansas fortieth among fifty states. Similarly, the most recent administrations of

National Assessment exams found Arkansas in the middle tier for elementary students and in the bottom tier for middle school students, ranking anywhere from thirty-second to forty-second.

FIGURE 1

National Assessment of Educational Progress, Average Scaled Scores, Arkansas and the United States

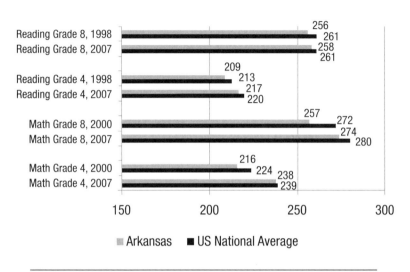

Source: National Assessment of Educational Progress, *The Nation's Report Card.*

Despite some recent successes on in-state assessments and Advanced Placement exams, results from the national benchmark National Assessment of Educational Progress exam make clear how far we still have to go. While the 2007 NAEP results reveal the good news that our state's fourth graders have nearly "caught up" to the national average in reading and math, the results also highlight persistent problems in serving middle school students and minority youngsters. In eighth-grade math, for example, the state continues to rank in the bottom quintile, as only 24 percent of our students scored at or above NAEP's "proficient" level; worse yet, fewer than 10 percent of Arkansas's black students met this standard. Cries for reform should come as no surprise in light of such challenges, and the state's *Lake View* litigation seems—finally—to be serving as a catalyst for change.

Lake View: Catalyst for Reform

In Arkansas, as in more than forty other states, the school finance system has been challenged in court by disgruntled districts. Here as elsewhere, the plaintiffs argue that the state is remiss in its constitutional duty to provide an equitable and adequate system of public schooling to all students. In approximately half of these cases, including in Arkansas, the courts have found in favor of the litigants and demanded changes in funding systems. Thus Arkansas policymakers now live under a "constitutional mandate" to reform the state's system of public schools.

The series of lawsuits, appeals, and court orders known as Lake View began in 1992 when plaintiff districts sued over disparities in state funding. In 1994, a lower-court judge found the school funding system unconstitutionally inequitable.[1] After further turnings of the wheel, a definitive ruling came in 2001, when Chancery Court Judge Collins Kilgore declared that Arkansas had failed to fulfill its constitutional obligation to provide a "general, suitable and efficient system of free public schools."[2] A November 2002 state Supreme Court ruling substantially upheld the Kilgore ruling, made clear that the legislature bore fiduciary responsibility for public education, and gave lawmakers until January 1, 2004, to improve the system. The high court's indictment of the state's school funding system cited multiple shortcomings, including district-to-district disparities in teacher salaries, dramatic differences in the breadth and quality of curricula and the condition of school facilities, and starkly uneven per-pupil expenditures.[3]

Importantly, Arkansas judges borrowed the definition of "efficiency" used by Kentucky's courts, namely "substantial uniformity, substantial equality of financial resources and substantial equal educational opportunity for all students." Known as the "Rose" standards (after the 1989 Kentucky school-funding lawsuit), the seven capacities that an efficient system of education is expected to provide were defined thus:

(i) sufficient oral and written communication skills to enable students to function in a complex and rapidly changing civilization

(ii) sufficient knowledge of economic, social, and political systems to enable the student to make informed choices

(iii) sufficient understanding of governmental processes to enable the student to understand the issues that affect his or her community, state, and nation

(iv) sufficient self knowledge and knowledge of his or her mental and physical wellness

(v) sufficient grounding in the arts to enable each student to appreciate his or her cultural and historical heritage

(vi) sufficient training or preparation for advanced training in either academic or vocational fields so as to enable each child to choose and pursue life work intelligently

(vii) sufficient levels of academic or vocational skills to enable public school students to compete favorably with their counterparts in surrounding states, in academics, or in the job market[4]

The Arkansas court not only found the existing K-12 system wanting on multiple levels, but in invoking the Rose standards described the outcomes an "adequate, efficient, suitable" school system would produce in and for the state's children. Plainly, this demanded that policymakers contemplate far-reaching, systemwide changes in addition to greater and more equitably distributed resources.

Gov. Mike Huckabee summoned lawmakers to action in his opening address before the 2003 legislative session. To his credit, the governor did not try to evade the judicial mandate or rail against the courts for usurping the prerogatives of the executive and legislative branches, as a few suggested he should. Whatever he may have thought or preferred, the handwriting was now clearly on the statehouse wall and the governor chose to commit himself to action.

In his "State of the State" address, Huckabee noted that many of his predecessors had made great pronouncements on education reform that had led to little. He quoted seven gubernatorial inaugural addresses since 1923, including Bill Clinton's 1983 exhortations, then drew this sharp conclusion:

> Every legislative session, every decade, every governor, every General Assembly gathers just as we have, and they talk about their constitutional responsibility to provide the kind of education that our Constitution says we must provide. And minor changes are made. And people go home having congratulated themselves for minor adjustments to a system that for 100 years at least every single governor and legislator has said is broken.[5]

The governor then called upon the legislature to "join me in not being another footnote in the pages of Arkansas history. . . . [W]e'll continue to lose until we finally . . . fulfill the constitutional mandate for an adequate, efficient, suitable, equitable education for every single boy and girl in this state."[6]

The Legislative Response

The Arkansas legislature—which meets every other year—had its first opportunity to respond to the Supreme Court's mandate when it convened for the 2003 session. Governor Huckabee opened with a proposal for far-reaching school consolidation, arguing that this would yield the efficiency necessary to comply with the court's ruling. However, the contentious debate over consolidation so divided the state's policymakers that, by the end of the 2003 regular session, the legislature had failed not only to resolve that issue but also to address the school funding challenges.

With the court deadline looming, Governor Huckabee convened a special session of the legislature on December 8, 2003, and laid four issues before it:

- restructure or consolidate smaller districts
- increase school accountability for student performance
- revise the existing school funding formula
- raise the revenue to pay for these reforms

The central tenet of the *Lake View* ruling, he reminded the General Assembly, was equitable and adequate funding. All Arkansas districts, regardless of size, demographics, or location, were obligated to provide equivalent and adequate educational opportunities, teacher salaries, and school facilities.

In response, lawmakers passed Act 59, which established that school funding would be determined by attendance during the previous year and provided both base funding for essential needs and supplemental resources for specialized needs. For 2004–5, base funding was set at $5,400 per student, with districts to receive additional resources for various categories of disadvantaged students, including low-income students, English-language learners, and those in alternative secondary school programs. Moreover, funding for teacher professional development was set at $50 per student and districts were required to pay higher minimum base salaries ($27,500 for a new bachelor's degree holder, $31,625 for a new teacher holding a master's degree).

Overall, the implementation of Act 59 was projected to require $438 million more (though an outside study had concluded in 2003 that a fully adequate system would cost the state nearly twice that much). Overcoming its reluctance to raise taxes, the legislature devised a three-part package intended to raise at least $417 million more. The state sales tax rate of 5.125 percent was increased to 6 percent, some services were subjected to taxation for the first time, and the corporate franchise tax was increased.

The total state appropriation for elementary and secondary education in 2003–4 had been $1.84 billion; thanks to the new tax dollars and other appropriations, the 2004–5 budget was $2.29 billion. That represented an increased state commitment of more than 24 percent in a single year. After the conclusion of the special session in June 2004, the Supreme Court signaled its satisfaction by removing itself from a direct supervisory role, declaring the Lake View case closed, and turning matters over to the legislature.

The saga did not end there however. In the 2005 session, lawmakers devoted much attention (and some resources) to school facilities and teacher health insurance, but left the per-pupil foundation amount at $5,400 for the 2005–6 school year. This so angered some educators that forty-nine districts appealed to the Supreme Court to reopen the lawsuit. By a four to three vote, the judges agreed in early June 2005 to do so (the court was so fractured, however, that every justice wrote his or her own opinion) and reappointed two "special masters"—who a year earlier had advised the court to give the legislative changes time to bear fruit—to look into the matter once again and advise the court by October 2005.

Their eighty-three-page report reads as if written by the plaintiffs, and concludes that state lawmakers had fallen asleep at the wheel. The main point of contention was, in fact, the unchanged foundation amount. The masters maintained that the legislature had set the $5,400 level for only one year and subsequent years would require additional funding to counter inflation and handle increased teacher salaries. With a one hundred million dollar surplus remaining in state coffers at the end of fiscal 2005, the unchanged school-funding level generated even more anger among the plaintiffs.[7]

On December 15, 2005, the court sided with the plaintiffs in a five to two decision, ruling that the legislature failed to make education spending its top priority in that year's regular session and underfunded school building repairs and construction. The court did not direct the legislature to appropriate a specific funding increase, but instead gave the state a December 1, 2006, deadline to "correct the constitutional deficiencies." The key points of the court's ruling were the following:

- The General Assembly could not have provided adequate funding for the 2005–6 and 2006–7 school years, because it made no effort to comply with Act 57 and to determine what adequate funding should be. Furthermore, the General Assembly failed to consult the state Department of Education for any information before or during the 2005 regular session, and the court "has no doubt that the decision to freeze the previous year's figure of $5,400 for purposes of 2005–2006 is a direct result of this lack of information."

- Education needs were not funded first, as required by Act 108 of the Second Extraordinary Session of 2003. Rather, both foundation funding aid and categorical funding "were established based upon what funds were available—not by what was needed."

- Appropriations for the repair and construction of safe, dry, and healthy facilities were grossly underfunded and, thus, inadequate. The court observed that Immediate Repair Program funding equaled only one half (twenty million dollars) of the forty million dollars needed and only a hundred and twenty million dollars was appropriated for priority one facilities, despite an estimated need of over $205 million.[8]

To address the December 2005 ruling, Arkansas lawmakers would need to meet in special session prior to the December 2006 deadline. At the same time, the consulting team of Lawrence Picus and Allan Odden had been commissioned in 2005 to investigate—among other things—school resource use across the state to examine how the schools had been using the new funding. There was disagreement among some regarding whether the lawmakers should address the question of additional funding while awaiting the results of a second adequacy study. Some lawmakers argued that the state should wait for the results of this study, due in the fall of 2006, before meeting in special session. However, Governor Huckabee and many other state lawmakers preferred to quickly address the concerns of the court and worked for a special session in the spring.

The governor called the legislature into session in April 2006 after much behind-the-scenes legislative work to develop proposals with a good chance of satisfying the lawmakers. The special session moved quickly, beginning on April 3 and concluding April 7. The legislature passed education-related legislation that appropriated an additional two hundred million dollars to public schools for the 2005–6 school year and the 2006–7 school years. The per-student foundation funding level was increased from $5,400 to $5,486 in 2005–6 and to $5,620 in 2006–7. The legislation also increased the minimum teacher salary for each year and appropriated an additional fifty million dollars for school facilities.

In December 2006 the Arkansas Supreme Court—in a five to two decision—declined to put an end to the *Lake View* case, arguing that the legislature had not provided enough information as to whether it had complied with the court's mandate. The court gave legislators thirty days to comply with its latest order. In addition, to oversee the General Assembly's reform efforts in the 2007 legislative session, the court renominated its special masters, a ruling that, predictably, stirred public outcry from policymakers. Governor Huckabee described the court as "out of control," and claimed that it was "usurping the constitutionally stated limitations and separations of powers."[9]

Despite this, the governor and the legislature expressed confidence that their actions effectively addressed the concerns of the court, confidence that—after an additional investment of one hundred million dollars by the Arkansas legislature in the spring of 2007—appears to have been merited. On May 31, 2007, a unanimous decision of the state Supreme Court officially closed the long-running *Lake View* case. Many are hopeful the state will now be able to refocus its attention from arguing over dollars to considering how best to deploy these resources to ensure that all students in Arkansas actually learn more in the years to come. Meanwhile, the work of school reform marches on in numerous areas, four of which are considered next.

FIGURE 2

Arkansas School Finance Litigation Timeline

DATE	ACTION
1979	The Alma School District and ten other school districts file a lawsuit over the school-funding formula.
1983	The Arkansas Supreme Court strikes down the state's public school–funding formula, leading to a special legislative session later in the year.

1984	State raises sales tax by one cent to help fund public education.
1992	The Lake View School District in Phillips County sues the state over gross disparities in public school funding, including teacher salaries, school facilities, and curriculum.
1994	Pulaski County Chancellor Annabelle Clinton Imber finds in favor of Lake View, ruling Arkansas's education system violates equity provisions of the state constitution.
1995	Gov. Jim Guy Tucker signs a bill to create a school-funding system that sends money to districts equally on a per-student basis.
1996	Voters approve Amendment 74 to the state constitution, mandating at least twenty-five mills of property tax in each school district for maintenance and operation.
1998	After amended complaints by Lake View, the state Supreme Court orders a new trial to determine if the state's reforms have met the requirements of the 1994 order.
September–October 2000	Pulaski County Chancellor Collins Kilgore conducts the *Lake View* trial. Thirty-six witnesses testify, and the court record totals 20,878 pages.
2001	Kilgore declares the school-funding system to be not only unconstitutionally inequitable but also inadequate and orders the state to fund a preschool program.
2002	The state Supreme Court unanimously upholds most of Kilgore's ruling, noting that the state has the ultimate authority over schools. But it overrules Kilgore on preschool, saying there is no such constitutional mandate. The court gives the state until January 1, 2004, to come up with a solution.
September 2003	Consultants issue a school finance adequacy report, which calls for nearly $850 million in new spending.
December 2003	The legislature convenes in a special session called by Gov. Mike Huckabee to take up education reform after making little progress toward meeting the court's mandate during the 2003 regular session.
January 2004	The Lake View School District files a motion with the state Supreme Court to hold the state in contempt for failing to comply with the Lake View ruling. The court decides to consider Lake View's motion, finds the state in "noncompliance," and retakes jurisdiction of the case. It decides to

appoint two special court "masters" to evaluate actions of the legislature and Huckabee, later naming former justices Bradley Jesson and David Newbern as masters.

February 2004   The legislature wraps up the special session. It passes about $380 million a year in new taxes, a new funding formula that sends more money to districts with a higher percentage of low-income students, and consolidation of districts with fewer than three hundred and fifty students. Huckabee calls legislative accomplishments "maximum taxes for minimum reform."

April 2004   Jesson and Newbern release their report calling many of the legislative acts "laudable" but adding that the state will likely continue to have inequities as long as districts are permitted to raise additional money locally.

May 2004   Huckabee's lawyer, Leon Holmes, urges the court to keep control over the case and order more school district consolidation. Attorney General Mike Beebe's office asks for the court to pull out of the case.

June 2004   The court removes itself from the case in a four to three decision, citing concerns over separation of powers. It compliments the state's education-reform measures.

November 2004   After assessing nearly six thousand school buildings in Arkansas, consultants find $2.3 billion in immediate needs. Legislators later debate this figure as unrealistic.

April 2005   The 2005 regular legislative session ends. Huckabee and lawmakers focus on increasing state aid to colleges and universities but delay increasing base funding for public schools. However, $104 million is set aside as state aid to improve public school facilities and $35 million to subsidize teacher health insurance. On April 14, the day after the session ends, the Rogers School District files a request for the Supreme Court to reopen the *Lake View* case, accusing the legislature of not adequately increasing school funding. Forty-six school districts join the Rogers district in asking the court to reopen the case. The number of districts eventually grows to forty-nine.

May 2005   The Supreme Court hears oral arguments on whether to reopen the case.

June 2005   In a four to three decision, the Supreme Court agrees to reopen the case, reappointing Jesson and Newbern to take

	testimony on legislative actions. The court sets a deadline of September 1, 2005, for the masters to complete a report.
August 2005	Court hears testimony. The deadline for the special masters' report is postponed to October 1, 2005.
September 2005	Legislature rehires consulting firm to conduct adequacy study.
October 2005	Special masters release report finding that the Eighty-fifth General Assembly did not adequately fund public schools or facilities improvements.
December 2005	In a five to two decision, the Supreme Court sides with the plaintiffs and retains jurisdiction of the case. The court concludes that the legislature failed to make education its top priority during the 2005 regular session and did not provide adequate funding for 2005–6 or 2006–7 because it made no effort to define an adequate level of funding. The court sets a deadline of December 1, 2006 for the state to "correct constitutional deficiencies."
April 2006	The legislature meets in special session from April 3 through April 7 and passes education-related legislation that appropriates approximately two hundred million dollars to public schools for the 2005–6 school year and the 2006–7 school year. The legislation increases the per-student foundation funding level from $5,400 to $5,486 in 2005–6 and to $5,620 in 2006–7. The legislature also increases the minimum teacher salary for each year and appropriates an additional fifty million dollars for school facilities.
December 2006	The Arkansas Supreme Court declines to end the case, arguing that it needs more information before it can say whether reforms approved by the legislature during the April 2006 special session had sufficiently addressed problems.

In a five to two decision, the Court gives the state thirty days to demonstrate that it has complied with their order. The court also reappoints special masters to review the legislature's work. |
| January 2007 | The special masters issue their report to the Arkansas Supreme Court. |
| February 2007 | The Arkansas General Assembly lays out its plan to uphold the mandates set by the special masters, issuing two adequacy reports outlining its progress. |

May 2007   In the 2007 session, the General Assembly made the follow-
            ing funding reforms:

- Per-pupil foundation funding increased from the
  current level of $5,662 to $5,789 in 2009.

- Additional per-pupil funding for students in
  "alternative learning environments" (such as special
  education programs) increased from $3,750 to $4,063.

- Funding for students in poverty increased depending
  on the concentration of impoverished students in a
  particular school district.

The court also argued that teacher salaries had risen to an
appropriate level when compared to neighboring states.
The average Arkansas teacher earned $42,931 in 2006—
which puts the state second among neighboring states, and
ninth among all southern states.

May 2007   The Arkansas Supreme Court, acting on the recommenda-
            tion of the reappointed special masters, unanimously
            declares that "our system of public school financing is now
            in constitutional compliance."

Recent Reforms
Standards and Curricula

In the 1980s, as Americans focused on the message of *A Nation at Risk,*
Arkansas awakened to the idea that it needed to strengthen its education
system and boost its students' performance[10]. The reform era opened
with sundry initiatives by then-governor Bill Clinton (and first lady
Hillary Rodham Clinton), including initial efforts to set standards, test
teachers, and focus on school leadership.

In hindsight, however, just about all of those high-profile moves were
cosmetic, superficial endeavors that didn't begin to tackle the underlying problems and were quickly weakened or undone. For example, the
state's first set of statewide curricular standards—called course content
guides—were developed in the 1980s but readily proved to be inadequate.

In the early 1990s, the state moved from course content guides to
today's system of curricular frameworks, which were gradually phased in
by the State Board of Education based on the advice of a curriculum task
force. These frameworks are now in their second and third incarnation

for the various discipline areas and, in some subjects, are still in need of
work. For example, recent revisions of math and English language arts
frameworks provide grade-specific standards, but the science and social
studies frameworks are still organized by grade clusters, which are far less
helpful to teachers in the classroom. (This is to be changed in the third
incarnation of these frameworks, occurring over the next two years.)

In 1999, the standards issue again was tackled by lawmakers with the
passage of the Arkansas Comprehensive Testing, Assessment, and
Accountability Program (ACTAAP). That measure required that all public school students demonstrate proficiency in core academic subjects on
standardized assessments aligned with state standards. Today, the state has
published frameworks in seven areas (consolidated from ten). But in recent
years these have earned low marks from external reviewers such as
Education Week and the Thomas B. Fordham Foundation. In the *Education
Week* ratings, which employ a composite grade to rate each state on its
overall system of standards and accountability, the Arkansas grade has
ranged from a D to a B -, placing it in the lower half of all states.[11]

While such external reviews understandably concern policymakers,
there are also some bright signs to be noted. Recent iterations of English
(2003) and math (2004) standards appear to be improved. Moreover, the
state takes some justifiable pride in its "Smart Core" curriculum, a set of
college-prep course requirements that becomes the "default" curriculum
for the graduating class of 2010. A recent report by Achieve, Inc., praised
Arkansas as one of only three states that automatically enroll students in
a rigorous curriculum of college- and work-preparatory courses in both
math and science.[12]

Assessment and Accountability

The 1999 ACTAAP legislation signaled Arkansas's entry into the national
school accountability movement. Upon its passage, the state embarked
upon the development of criteria-referenced "benchmark" assessments
in math and English language arts in grades four, six, and eight. As of
the 2004–5 school year, these exams also were administered to all students in grades three, five, and seven in compliance with the federal No
Child Left Behind (NCLB) act. Recent legislation driven by state business leaders also mandates a national norm-referenced exam (currently
the Iowa Test of Basic Skills) for all students in grades three through nine

so the progress of Arkansas students can be compared with their peers around the country.

Alongside these assessments is a growing accountability structure. During the 2003 legislative session, despite their focus on the school consolidation dispute, lawmakers passed an important measure known as "the Omnibus Act" that created the framework for the state education department to develop accreditation standards in conformity with NCLB and gave that agency the teeth to intervene in schools and districts not meeting standards. Additional legislation that year required all schools be rated in three areas: current student test scores, growth in student test scores, and financial management.

Overall, though the testing system remains cumbersome and contentious, Arkansas has made an effort to be conscientious in defining "proficiency," in setting its NCLB "cut-scores" for gauging adequate yearly progress, and in evenly spacing the requisite gains to meet NCLB's fourteen-year period goal rather than back-loading them until late in that timeframe. The state also has refrained from seeking a host of waivers or exceptions from Washington. As it continues to reconstruct its testing systems—reconciling the competing demands of NCLB, norm-based testing, criteria-referenced testing, end-of-course exams, and other assessments—Arkansas will have the opportunity to think afresh about powerful options such as value-added analysis.

Structure and Governance

Here the main engine of change has been Governor Huckabee's drive to consolidate tiny rural districts in the name of "efficiency." Two months after the Supreme Court handed down its November 2002 indictment of the state's schools, the governor opened the 2003 session with a proposal for far-reaching school consolidation. His original plan called for consolidation of school districts with fewer than 1,500 students and would have reduced the number of districts from 310 to 116. This proposal caused much consternation, and no consolidation legislation was passed during the 2003 regular session.

The debate centered on the question of how large a district needed to be to maintain a baseline of educational adequacy and fiscal efficiency. During the special legislative session of 2003–4, a compromise bar was set at a minimum enrollment of 350 students districtwide. While Huckabee

maintained this was too low, he allowed the measure to become law without his signature. Since that time, the number of school districts in
Arkansas had decreased from 308 to 252 as of August 2005. This subject,
like so many others, is likely to be revisited. however.

Legislators also tinkered with the Arkansas charter school law in
2005. While the state still has a weak charter law, the recent amendments
double the existing cap on open-enrollment charters to twenty-four
statewide and raise the maximum term for charter authorization from
three to five years. Additionally, the success of the KIPP (Knowledge is
Power Program) Delta College Preparatory School in Helena led policymakers to exempt KIPP schools from the charter cap. The state can now
charter as many KIPP schools as it wants. Beyond charters, however,
there are few "choice" opportunities in the state, which poses a problem
for students hoping to transfer out of schools that fail to make adequate
yearly progress in the years to come.

Teachers

Teachers and teacher recruitment in Arkansas made national headlines in
the 1980s. In an attempt to ensure the quality of teachers in Arkansas classrooms, then-governor Bill Clinton pushed through an education reform
plan in 1983 and famously appointed his wife, Hillary Rodham Clinton,
to lead the effort. It included raises for teachers, new taxes to pay for them,
and mandatory competency tests for both new and working teachers.
When the teachers were finally required to sit for the National Teachers
Examination two years later, reports emerged that more than one-third of
the teachers in parts of the state failed to earn a passing score. Because of
the potential political fallout, as many tell the story, the cutoff score was
quietly lowered so that fewer than ten percent actually failed—and many
of those teachers retained their jobs after retaking the exam.[13] In the end,
the plan generated a great deal of controversy but not much change in the
state's teaching corps.

Today, Arkansas trains, recruits, and pays its teachers in much the
same way as most other states. Most teachers in the state emerge from the
seventeen National Council for Accreditation of Teacher Education-–
accredited institutions of teacher training. Due to the NCLB mandate,
new teachers must show subject-area competency by passing a rigorous
test or earning an academic major in the core academic area taught.

However, the requirements for subject-area competency for experienced teachers are less well-defined. In Arkansas, they can be deemed "highly qualified" in various ways, including having more than five years of experience or obtaining ninety hours of professional development credit. These requirements may be too lax. For example, the December 2003 Education Trust report—*Telling the Whole Truth (or Not) About Highly Qualified Teachers*—suggests that many states are over-reporting the numbers of highly qualified teachers. Arkansas was highlighted as a suspect state because it reported having highly qualified teachers staffing 97 percent of its schools and 97 percent of its high-poverty classrooms.[14]

While many have voiced concern over a teacher shortage in Arkansas, the problem is perhaps better described as a distribution problem. In other words, teachers are concentrated in some areas and subjects, while there remains a dearth of teachers in low-income, high-minority schools and in certain fields, such as math and science. A recent survey of Arkansas superintendents suggests that administrators face little difficulty finding qualified elementary school teachers but find it very difficult to track down qualified math or science teachers.

Faced with such distribution challenges, the Arkansas Department of Education has had to allow more teachers to teach out-of-field. In the 2004–5 school year, the department received out-of-field waiver requests from 249 teachers in sixty-nine districts. More than half of these requests were for teachers of core subjects (for example, math, science, language, social studies) who were not trained in those areas.

Other than simply waiving requirements, how else have Arkansas policymakers dealt with these challenges? As mentioned earlier, the court-mandated strategy has been to simply increase minimum teacher salaries so that compensation in Arkansas remains competitive with surrounding states to stave off the possibility of Arkansas teachers defecting across the borders for better pay.

Of course, there are many innovative strategies for attracting and retaining good teachers that are policy options, such as alternative certification or merit pay for teachers in areas of great need. The state does offer an alternative licensure program: the NTLP, or Non-Traditional Licensure Program, through which bachelor's degree holders can work toward a teaching license while employed as classroom teachers. The program extends over a two-year period and involves assessment, teaching, and portfolio development, as well as summer and weekend instructional modules.

There are approximately thirty thousand teachers in Arkansas schools; currently, there are five hundred participants in the first year of the two-year NTLP program. We must wait, then, to assess this approach.

There have been no statewide ventures in merit pay at the individual teacher level, although there have been interesting local attempts. Most recently, an elementary school in Little Rock incorporated a pay-for-performance plan in which teachers received bonuses—funded by an outside donor—for student gains on standardized assessments during the 2004–5 school year. In 2005–6, an additional Little Rock school adopted a similar program, and the program is expected to expand to five schools in 2006–7, with a mix of funding from private and public sources. It is not clear whether the bonuses lead to improved student performance for the school, but as the program grows more data will become available and researchers will be able to appraise its effectiveness.

Conclusion

Observers of school reform in Arkansas encounter few dull days. Despite the many ups and downs, there is good reason for optimism. In reaction to the Supreme Court's mandate to mend an unconstitutional funding system, Arkansas policymakers took a proactive stance. While those in other states have dug in their heels and resisted court-mandated reform, Arkansas leaders seized the opportunity to enact broad changes.

During the 2003 legislative session, lawmakers were willing to compromise on district consolidation, educators compromised on testing and accountability, and business leaders agreed to support increased spending in accordance with these reforms. After long, argumentative sessions in 2003 and 2004, legislators emerged justifiably proud of the reforms that were passed into law with respect to school funding, school organization and governance, and assessment and accountability.

When the 2004–5 school year began, students were attending much more generously funded schools. The state boosted K-12 education spending by almost 30 percent and, on average, schools had an additional one thousand dollars per pupil in state dollars. Early analyses of school district funding figures reveal that these increases have been successfully targeted to students in disadvantaged districts. That is, while additional school resources have been distributed to all districts around the state, districts benefiting from the greatest increases are those that serve poor students, minority students, and students struggling on state exams.

After further increases before the 2005–6 school year, the additional annual education funding from the state had reached nearly $650 million. With another $200 million in increases passed into law during the 2006 special legislative session and another $100 million in the 2007 regular session (including $40 million for preschool programs), the funding increases that followed the last round of the Lake View litigation exceeded $900 million.

Arkansas has made a good faith effort to revitalize its elementary and secondary education system by providing needed resources and encouraging efficiencies and reforms in several areas. All that remains—for the educators around the state—is the formidable task of figuring out how best to use the resources so all schools can succeed and all children can learn.

NOTES

Political Culture, Political Attitudes, and Aggregated Demographic Effects

1. A draft of this paper was delivered at the annual meeting of the Arkansas Political Association, Little Rock, Arkansas, February 18–19, 2000; it was awarded the association's Best Paper Award at the 2001 meeting. The authors would like to thank the conference participants and the anonymous reviewers for their insightful comments. We also wish to acknowledge Collis Geren, Will Miller, Todd Shields, Susan Thomas, and Molly Longstreth for their assistance with this research.

2. For the latest voter turnout statistics in Arkansas by county, see the secretary of state's website at http://sos.state.ar.us/vc98.

3. See, for example, Richard Yates, "Arkansas: Independent and Unpredictable," in *The Changing Politics of the South,* ed. William C. Havard (Baton Rouge: Louisiana State University Press, 1972); Robert L. Savage and Richard J. Gallagher, "Politicocultural Regions in a Southern State: An Empirical Analysis," *Publius* 7 (Winter 1977): 91–105; Robert L. Savage and Diane D. Blair, "Regionalism and Political Opinion in Arkansas: An Exploratory Survey," *Arkansas Political Science Journal* 5 (Winter 1984): 59–85; Diane D. Blair, William D. Mangold, and Robert L. Savage, "Further Explorations of Regionalism and Political Opinion in Arkansas," *Midsouth Political Science Journal* 9 (Winter 1988): 92–109; and Diane D. Blair, *Arkansas Politics and Government: Do the People Rule?* (Lincoln: University of Nebraska Press, 1988).

4. Daniel J. Elazar, *American Federalism: A View From the States* (New York: Thomas Y. Crowell, 1966), 84.

5. See for example Ira Sharkansky, "The Utility of Elazar's Political Culture: A Research Note," *Polity* 1 (Autumn 1969): 66–83; Joel Lieske, "Regional Subcultures in the United States," *Journal of Politics* 55 (November 1993): 888–913; Robert Erikson, John P. McIver, and Gerald C. Wright, "State Political Culture and Public Opinion," *American Political Science Review* 81 (September 1987): 797–813; Thomas J. Volgy, John E. Schwarz, and Hildy Gottlieb, "Female Representation and the Quest for Resources: Feminist Activism and Electoral Success," *Social Science Quarterly* 67 (1986): 156–68; David Young Miller, "The Impact of Political Culture on Patterns of State and Local Government Expenditures," *Publius* (1991): 83–100; Keith Boeckelman, "Political Culture and State Development Policy," *Publius* (1991): 49–62; and Joel Paddock, "Research Note: Political Culture and the Partisan Style of State Party Activists," *Publius: The Journal of Federalism* (1997): 127–32.

6. Between September 15th and October 2nd of 1999, the Survey Research Center at the University of Arkansas, Fayetteville dialed 3,738 randomly selected Arkansas telephone numbers. These attempts yielded 885 completed surveys. A completed survey consisted of sixty-eight questions and the margin of error was plus or minus 3 percentage points. The text of the survey protocol is available online at http://new-www3.uark.edu/arkpoll.

7. Savage and Gallagher, "Politicocultural Regions in a Southern State."

8. Savage and Blair, "Regionalism and Political Opinion in Arkansas"; Blair, Mangold, and Savage, "Further Explorations of Regionalism."

9. Five counties in the Ozarks also received component scores above the median: Fulton, Newton, Searcy, Stone, and Van Buren.

10. The Pearson's correlation coefficient between the conservatism index and our simple three-option ideology question on the poll was .209 (p<.01).

11. Blair, *Arkansas Politics and Government*.

12. V. O. Key Jr., *Southern Politics in State and Nation* (New York: Knopf, 1949), 185.

13. For a spirited discussion of the use of Elazar's ideas in public opinion research see, Robert L. Savage, "Looking for Political Subcultures: A Critique of the Rummage-Sale Approach," *The Western Political Quarterly*, 34 (June 1981): 331–36.

The Proposed Arkansas Constitution of 1970

1. For the best analysis of the 1874 Constitution, see Walter H. Nunn, "Revision of the Arkansas Constitution" (master's thesis, Department of Political Science, University of Kansas, 1966) housed at University of Central Arkansas, Torreyson Library Archive, Nunn Papers, File Box 2. Conway, Arkansas.

2. Abe Collins, "Reminiscences of the Constitutional Convention of 1917–18." *Arkansas Historical Quarterly* 1, no. 2 (1942): 117–23.

3. Ralph C. Barnhart, "A New Constitution for Arkansas?" Arkansas Law Review 17, no. 1, (Winter, 1962): 1–15.

4. The late Dr. Alexander was the author of the only recent book on Arkansas government: *Government in Arkansas: Organization and Function at State, County, and Municipal Levels*. (Fayetteville: University of Arkansas, Bureau of Research, 1957).

5. *Act 121*, Regular Session of the Arkansas General Assembly (1967).

6. There were two studies on the work of the commission: Judy Jones Jordan, "The Arkansas Constitutional Revision Study Commission: A Case Study" (senior honor thesis, Department of History and Political Science, Hendrix College, 1969); and Walter H. Nunn, "The Commission Route to Constitutional Reform: The Arkansas Experience" *Arkansas Law Review* 22, no. 1 (Spring 1968): 317–39.

7. Arkansas Constitutional Revision Study Commission, "Revising the Arkansas Constitution," 1968.

8. *Act 3*, First Extraordinary Session of the Arkansas General Assembly (1968).

9. *Act 42*, First Extraordinary Session of the Arkansas General Assembly (1968).

10. Pages for the convention were supplied through the offices of the Arkansas Association of Student Councils on a volunteer basis. Not only did this save the convention money, but the high school students made excellent pages.

11. The rules of the Arkansas Convention and of eighteen other state constitutional conventions held since 1943 may be found in a collection reproduced by the National Municipal League, "Constitutional Convention Rules" (1970).

12. Seventh Arkansas Constitutional Convention, "Proposed Arkansas Constitution of 1970 with Comments: A Report to the People of the State of Arkansas" (1970).

13. Two delegates had ten thousand tabloids distributed by the local newspapers in their three-county district.

14. National Municipal League, *Model State Constitution,* 6th ed. (New York: National Municipal League, 1963), 36–38.

15. An amendment adopted in 1958 sets legislators' salaries at twelve hundred dollars per year, plus twenty dollars per day for regular sessions, six dollars per day for special sessions, and five cents per mile round trip once each session. The General Assembly gets around the parsimonious sum by voting "expense allowances" and "public relations" sums.

16. An amendment adopted in 1946 set the governor's salary at sixteen thousand dollars per year, the lowest in the nation. The lieutenant governor receives twenty-five hundred dollars, the attorney general six thousand dollars, and others five thousand dollars per year.

17. There are now some 180 boards, commissions, bureaus, and departments in the state executive branch.

18. Recently, Governor Bumpers expressed his regret that these two agencies could not be included in his reorganization plan. Noting their independence from the governor, the General Assembly, and the people, Bumpers commented that, evidently, the two commissions "look only to God."

19. Arkansas is one of four states with separate courts of law and equity. See George C. Smith and Walter W. Nixon, "La Dolce Vita—Law and Equity Merged at Last!," *Arkansas Law Review* 24, no. 2 (Summer 1970): 162–81. The entire Summer 1970 edition of the *Arkansas Law Review* was devoted to the proposed constitution.

20. A provision in the executive branch article also prohibited the attorney general from the private practice of law.

21. Arkansas Judiciary Commission, "Report to the 1965 General Assembly," (1965), 163–88.

22. At present, the Arkansas justices of the peace form the quorum court, which is limited to levying county taxes already approved by the voters and making appropriations over which it has very little discretion. Any Arkansas county judge who cannot control his Quorum Court is in a bad way. The Pulaski County Quorum Court has over 350 members.

23. Herbert Sydney Duncombe, *County Government in America.* (Washington, D.C.: National Association of Counties Research Foundation, 1966).

24. John P. Wheeler Jr. and Melissa Kinsey, "Magnificent Failure: The Maryland Constitutional Convention of 1967–68," *National Municipal League* (now the National Civic League), (Winter 1970): 211–12.

25. The 1874 Constitution limits Arkansas municipalities to a five-mill property tax for general operations. Property is supposed to be assessed at 20 percent of its market value.

26. The Arkansas Council of the American Federation of State, County, and Municipal Employees would probably have supported the revised charter, but was prohibited from taking any political stand separate from the state AFL-CIO's Committee on Political Education.

27. In 1970, Arkansas began using a "black patch" to cover the numbers and provide a more-secret ballot.

28. At the insistence of Governor Bumpers, the fair trade liquor law was repealed by the 1971 General Assembly.

29. Walter H. Nunn and Kay Collett of the University of Arkansas are currently writing a book-length study of the constitutional revision movement in Arkansas for

the National Municipal League. *Editor's note: See Walter Nunn and Kay G. Collett, Political Paradox: Constitution Revision in Arkansas, (New York: National Municipal League, 1973).*

30. The Farm Bureau was the one major state organization that fought the calling of a convention, because it feared the proposed document would be too "liberal" and "urban-oriented." Pleasantly surprised with the convention's product, the Farm Bureau supported it strongly, believing that if it failed another convention ten years later would advance a much less acceptable charter.

Intelligible, Honest, and Impartial Democracy

1. A recent spate of books interpreting and reinterpreting the history of American law highlights the tensions between these strains in American legal thought. Larry Kramer has written an exciting book emphasizing the populism of American law from root to branch, while May Sarah Bilder and John Philip Reid have written careful and historically unimpeachable books that emphasize the structural nature of early American law, making it a limit on elite and popular will. Compare Larry D. Kramer, *The People Themselves* (Oxford: Oxford University Press, 2004) and John P. Reid, *The Rule of Law: The Jurisprudence of Liberty in the Seventeenth and Eighteenth Centuries* (DeKalb, Illinois: Northern Illinois Press, 2004).

2. Robert G. Reaves, "Amending the Arkansas Constitution by the Initiative Process" (master's thesis, University of Arkansas, 1949); Timothy J. Kennedy, *Initiated Constitutional Amendments in Arkansas: Strolling Through the Mine Field,* 9 U. Ark. Little Rock L.J. 1 (1986–87); Stephen B. Niswanger, *A Practitioner's Guide to Challenging and Defending Legislatively Proposed Constitutional Amendments in Arkansas,* 17 U. Ark. Little Rock L.J. 17 (1995).

3. Amendment 7 was not always Amendment 7 but was occasionally number five, nine, ten, or thirteen. First proposed in 1909 and based on an earlier Oregon law, the amendment went through several incarnations before being finally designated in 1927 by the Arkansas Supreme Court as Amendment 7 because it was the seventh amendment that the various amendments had modified. See *Schichtel v. Uda,* 292 S.W. 981 (Ark. 1927). Though the amendment was approved in 1920, it appears to have been first used in 1925. See *Brickhouse v. Hill,* 268 S.W. (Ark. 1925); *Wright v. Ward,* 280 S.W. 369 (Ark. 1926). A brief history of the provision is in J. Kennedy, *Initiated Constitutional Amendments in Arkansas.* For useful thoughts on its future see Thomas B. Cotton, *The Arkansas Ballot Initiative: An Overview and Some Thoughts on Reform,* 53 Ark. L. Rev. 759 (2000). Of course, amendments to the constitution had been passed by ballot long before Amendment 7 subsumed both procedures.

4. Reaves, "Amending the Arkansas Constitution by the Initiative Process"; Kennedy, *Initiated Constitutional Amendments in Arkansas*; Stephen B. Niswanger, *A Practitioner's Guide to Challenging and Defending Legislatively Proposed Constitutional Amendments in Arkansas,* 17 U. Ark. Little Rock L.J. 17 (1995).

5. "The veto power of the Governor or mayor shall not extend to measures initiated by or referred to the people." Ark. Const., Art. 5 § 1.

6. Nathan Cree, *Direct Legislation by the People* (Chicago: A. C. McClurg and Co., 1892); Ellis Oberholtzer, *The Referendum in America: Together with Some Chapters on the History of the Initiative and Other Phases of Popular Government in the United States* (New York: Charles Scribner's Sons, 1900); Charles Beard and Bril Shultz,

Documents on the State-Wide Initiative, Referendum and Recall (New York: MacMillan Co., 1912).

7. James Boyle, *The Initiative and Referendum: Its Folly, Fallacies, and Failure* (Columbus, Ohio: A. H. Smythe, 1912). In Arkansas, for example, various measures to limit civil rights were passed at midcentury by referendum, not least being the 1956 petition, which succeeded 61 percent to 39 percent, to "prohibit the Federal Government from exercising power of public schools."

8. See the table, "Laws Brought to the Ballot Box" at the end of this chapter.

9. See http://www.sosweb.state.ar.us/elections _inititatives.html, which is summarized in the table, "Laws brought to the Ballot Box."

10. Ark. Const. Art. 5 § 1 (2005) (incorporating Amendment 7).

11. Article 5 further provides: "The first power reserved by the people is the initiative. Eight per cent of the legal voters may propose any law and ten per cent may propose a constitutional amendment by initiative petition and every such petition shall include the full text of the measure so proposed. Initiative petitions for state-wide measures shall be filed with the Secretary of State not less than four months before the election at which they are to be voted upon; provided, that at least thirty days before the aforementioned filing, the proposed measure shall have been published once, at the expense of the petitioners, in some paper of general circulation. . . . Upon all initiative or referendum petitions provided for in any of the sections of this article, it shall be necessary to file from at least fifteen of the counties of the state, petitions bearing the signature of not less than one-half of the designated percentage of the electors of such county." Ark. Const. Art. 5 § 1.

12. "The second power reserved by the people is the referendum, and any number not less than six per cent of the legal voters may, by petition, order the referendum against any general Act, or any item of an appropriation bill, or measure passed by the General Assembly, but the filing of a referendum petition against one or more items, sections or parts of any such act or measure shall not delay the remainder from becoming operative. . . ." Ark. Const. Art. 5 § 1. Note the legislature is barred from presenting statutes for adoption through referendum, although it is required to enact amendments to the constitution by referendum.

13. Ark. Const. Art. 5 § 1. See also Ark. Code Ann. § 7–9-107 (2005).

14. Ark. Code Ann. § 7–9-107 (2005). To require redrafting, the attorney general must find that "the ballot title, or the nature of the issue, is presented in such manner that the ballot title would be misleading" or liable for the voter to cast a ballot contrary to the "viewpoint that the voter believes himself casting a vote for."

15. Ark. Code Ann. § 7–9-114 (2005) (abstract).

16. "Any legal action against such certification shall be filed with the Supreme Court within forty-five (45) days of the Secretary of State's publication." Ark. Code Ann § 7–9-107(B) (2005). See also Ark. Code Ann. § 7–9-1112 (2005) (mandamus).

17. See table, "Selected Actions Challenging Ballots in Arkansas, 1912–2004" at the end of this chapter.

18. See, for example, *Hodges v. Dawdy,* 149 S.W.656 (Ark. 1912).

19. *Hodges,* 149 S.W.656 at 658.

20. *Westbrook v. McDonald,* 43 S.W.2d 356 (Ark. 1931).

21. *Westbrook,* 43 S.W.2d at 360.

22. *Walton v. McDonald,* 97 S.W.2d 81 (Ark. 1936).

23. *Walton,* 97 S.W.2d at 83.

24. *Bradley v. Hall,* 251 S.W.2d 470, 472 (Ark. 1952).

25. *May v. Daniels,* 194 S.W.3d 771 (Ark. 2004).

26. *May,* 194 S.W.3d at 775. The text of Amendment 3 is:

> "SECTION 1: Marriage
> "Marriage consists only of the union of one man and one woman.
>
> "SECTION 2: Marital Status
> "Legal status for unmarried persons which is identical or substantially similar to marital status shall not be valid or recognized in Arkansas, except that the Legislature may recognize a common law marriage from another state between a man and a woman.
>
> "SECTION 3: Capacity, rights, obligations, privileges, and immunities.
> "The Legislature has the power to determine the capacity of persons to marry, subject to this amendment, and the legal rights, obligations, privileges, and immunities of marriage." *May,* 194 S.W.3d at 774.

27. Kathy Kiely, "Gay Issues on Ballots Add twist to Election." *USA Today,* August 11, 2004. The Massachusetts decision is *Goodridge v. Department of Public Health,* 440 Mass. 309, handed down March 4, 2003.

28. *May,* 194 S.W.3d at 775.

29. The amendment proved popular with voters, garnering nearly 75 percent of the vote. See http://www.sosweb.state.ar.us/elections_initiatives.html.

30. *Arkansas Women's Political Caucus v. Rivieve,* 677 S.W.2d 846 (1984), striking down the popular name, "The Unborn Child Amendment".

31. *May,* 194 S.W.3d at 776.

32. "Even Section 2 concerns marriage in that it prohibits recognition of marital status for unmarried persons, except that the legislature may recognize certain common law marriages." *May,* 194 S.W.3d at 777.

33. *May,* 194 S.W.3d at 778–79.

34. *May,* 194 S.W.3d at 780.

35. *May,* 194 S.W.3d at 781–83.

36. *May,* 194 S.W.3d at 786.

37. *May,* 194 S.W.3d at 786.

38. *May,* 194 S.W.3d at 787.

39. *May,* 194 S.W.3d at 787.

40. *May,* 194 S.W.3d at 790.

41. Moreover, both Justice Hannah and Justice Thornton believed the amendment's ballot problems were rooted only in section two, rather than the amendment as a whole. See *May,* 194 S.W.3d at 788. This is, at least as I read the precedents, very generous indeed.

42. *Walton v. McDonald,* 97 S.W.2d 81 (Ark. 1936).

43. *Johnson v. Hall,* 316 S.W.2d 197 (Ark. 1958).

44. See Appendix, Note 6.

45. *Bradley,* 251 S.W.2d at 470.

46. See also *Moore v. Hall,* 316 S.W.2d 207 (Ark. 1958).

The Antievolution Law

1. *Epperson v. Arkansas,* 393 U.S. 97, 89 Sup. Ct. 266 (1968).

2. Pine Bluff *Commercial,* September 2, 1965, 8.

3. *Arkansas Gazette,* February 13, 1959, 1B.

4. *Arkansas Gazette,* February 17, 1959, 1A.

5. *Arkansas Gazette,* February 17, 1959, 1A.

6. *Arkansas Gazette* June 28,1966, 1A.

7. Arkansas Constitution (1874), Amendment 7 (1920).

8. *Arkansas Gazette,* September 22, 1965, 18B. The Scopes quoted is the Scopes of the famous Dayton, Tennessee, "monkey trial."

9. Gail Kennedy, ed., *Evolution and Religion: The Conflict Between Science and Theology in Modern America,* Problems in American Civilization Series (Boston: Heath, 1957), viii.

10. Richard Hofstadter, *Anti-Intellectualism in American Life (*New York: Knopf, 1964), 126.

11. George Brown Tindall, *The Emergence of the New South, 1913–1945 (*Baton Rouge, La.: Louisiana State University Press, 1967), 200.

12. Kennedy, *Evolution and Religion,* ix.

13. Hofstadter, *Anti-Intellectualism in American Life,* 125.

14. Kennedy, *Evolution and Religion,* viii.

15. W. J. Cash, *The Mind of the South (*New York: Knopf ,1941), 337–38.

16. Francis Butler Simkins, *A History of the South (*New York: Knopf, 1956), 417.

17. Simkins, *A History of the South.*

18. Maynard Shipley, "The Forward March of the Anti-Evolutionists," *Current History* 29 (January 1929): 579–580.

19. Tindall, *Emergence of the New South,* 206.

20. R. Halliburton Jr., "The Adoption of the Arkansas Anti-Evolution Law," *Arkansas Historical Quarterly,* 23 (Autumn 1964): 272–73.

21. Kennedy, *Evolution and Religion,* ix.

22. Simkins, *History of the South,* 418.

23. William Foy Lisenby, "Brough, Baptists, and Bombast: The Election of 1928," *Arkansas Historical Quarterly* 32 (Summer 1973): 127.

24. *Arkansas Gazette,* April 24, 1966, 1E.

25. Halliburton, "The Adoption of the Arkansas Anti-Evolution Law," 273.

26. *Arkansas Gazette,* November 11, 1927, 18.

27. *Arkansas Gazette,* December 19, 1926, 28.

28. *Arkansas Gazette,* January 9, 1927, 24.

29. *Arkansas Gazette,* January 9, 1927, 19. Hay Watson Smith outraged some fundamentalist Presbyterians by his outspoken opposition to any attempt to outlaw the teaching of evolution, and they brought formal charges of heresy against him. He was finally cleared of these charges in 1934 after a series of hearings before various Presbyterian courts. See Leo Thomas Sweeney, "The Anti-Evolution Movement in Arkansas" (master's thesis, University of Arkansas, 1966), 119–21.

30. *Arkansas Gazette,* January 10, 1927, 7.

31. *Arkansas House Journal,* 1927, 60.

32. *Arkansas House Journal,* 1927 68–69.

33. The Tennessee antievolution statute that resulted in the Scopes trial was worded similarly.

34. *Arkansas Democrat,* January 29, 1927, 3.

35. *Arkansas House Journal,* 1927, 82.

36. *Arkansas Democrat,* January 27, 1927, 1.

37. *Arkansas Gazette,* January 29, 1927, 1. For a more detailed account of the hearing, see Sweeney, "The Anti-Evolution Movement in Arkansas," 51–54.

38. *Arkansas Gazette,* February 3, 1927, 1.

39. *Arkansas Gazette,* February 3, 1927, 1.

40. *Arkansas Gazette,* February 3, 1927, 3

41. *Arkansas Gazette,* February 3, 1927, 14

42. *Arkansas Gazette,* February 3, 1927, 14.

43. *Arkansas House Journal,* 1927, 263.

44. *Arkansas Gazette,* February 4, 1927, 3.

45. *Arkansas House Journal,* 1927, 272.

46. *Arkansas House Journal,* 1927, 292.

47. *Arkansas House Journal,* 1927, 293.

48. *Arkansas Gazette,* February 10, 1927, 5.

49. *Arkansas Gazette,* February 10, 1927, 5.

50. *Arkansas House Journal,* 1927, 324.

51. *Arkansas Democrat,* February 10, 1927, 1.

52. *Arkansas Gazette,* February 11, 1927, 1.

53. *Arkansas Senate Journal,* 1927, 351.

54. *Arkansas Democrat,* February 11, 1927, 14.

55. Maynard Shipley, "A Fear of the Monkey War," *Independent* 119 (October 1927): 327.

56. Shipley, "A Fear of the Monkey War."

57. Arkansas Constitution (1874) Amendment 7 (1920).

58. Arkansas Secretary of State, *Historical Report.* 1958, 194.

59. *Arkansas Democrat,* May 6,1928, 11.

60. *Arkansas Acts,* 1929, Initiated Act No. 1, Section 1. Sections 1 and 2 of the act are as follows: "Section 1. That it shall be unlawful for any teacher or other instructor in any University, College, Normal, Public School, or other institution of the State, which is supported in whole or in part from public funds derived by State and local taxation to teach the theory or doctrine that mankind ascended or descended from a lower order of animals and also it shall be unlawful for any teacher, textbook commission, or other authority exercising the power to select textbooks for above mentioned educational institutions to adopt or use in any such institution a textbook that teaches the doctrine or theory that mankind descended or ascended from a lower order of animals.

"Section 2. Be it further enacted that any teacher or other instructor or textbook commissioner who is found guilty of violation of this Act by teaching the theory or doctrine mentioned in Section 1 hereof, or by using or adopting any such textbooks in any such educational institution shall be guilty of a misdemeanor and upon conviction shall be fined not exceeding five hundred dollars ($500.00); and upon conviction shall vacate the position thus held in any educational institutions of the character above mentioned or any commission of which he may be a member."

61. *Arkansas Gazette,* April 24, 1966, 1E.

62. *Arkansas Gazette,* November 11, 1927, 18.

63. *New York Times,* May 6, 1928, section 3, 2.

64. *Arkansas Gazette,* April 24, 1966, 1E.

65. *Arkansas Democrat,* October 14, 1928, 8.

66. *Arkansas Gazette,* October 17, 1928, 1.

67. *Arkansas Gazette,* November 3,1928, p. 6.

68. Ralph W. Widener Jr., "Charles Hillman Brough," *Arkansas Historical Quarterly* 34 (Summer 1975): 113.

69. Widener, "Charles Hillman Brough," 114.

70. *Arkansas Gazette,* October 31, 1928, 19.

71. *Arkansas Gazette,* November 4, 1928, 4.

72. *Arkansas Gazette,* November 4, 1928, 4.

73. *Arkansas Acts,* 1929, p. 1,519.

74. Election Return Abstracts, Arkansas Secretary of State's Office.

75. *Arkansas Gazette, November* 9, 1929, 1.

76. Maynard Shipley, "The Forward March of the Anti-Evolutionists," *Current History* 29 (January 1929): 578.

77. Quoted in the *Literary Digest,* December 1, 1928, 28.

78. *Arkansas Gazette,* November 9, 1928, 1.

79. *Arkansas Democrat,* November 11, 1928, 1.

80. *Arkansas Gazette,* November 9, 1928, 1.

81. *Arkansas Gazette,* November 21, 1928, 8.

82. *Arkansas Democrat,* March 31, 1966, 10.

83. *Arkansas House Journal,* 1937, 859.

84. See introduction to this article. For a more extensive treatment of the 1937 and 1959 legislative attempts, see Sweeney, "The Anti-Evolution Movement in Arkansas," 123–24.

85. *Arkansas Daily Legislative Digest* (1965), 88.

86. *Arkansas Gazette,* February 2, 1965, 1B.

87. *Arkansas Gazette,* February 3, 1965, p. 6A.

88. Forrest Rozzell, executive secretary of the Arkansas Education Association until 1976, interview with author, Little Rock, Arkansas, June 15, 1978. There were also two other interviews, one on June 21 and the other on June 22.

89. Hubert Blanchard, associate executive secretary of the Arkansas Education Association during the *Epperson* case, interview with author Little Rock, Arkansas, June 20, 1978.

90. Rozzell, interview.

91. Rozzell, interview.

92. *Arkansas Democrat,* September 4, 1965, 3

93. *Arkansas Gazette,* September 8, 1965, 1A.

94. *Arkansas Gazette,* September 7, 1965, 6A.

95. *Arkansas Democrat,* September 11, 1965, 3.

96. *Arkansas Gazette,* December 7, 1965, 1A.

97. Eugene Warren, attorney for the Arkansas Education Association, interview with author, Little Rock, Arkansas, June 16, 1978.

98. Rozzell, interview.

99. Rozzell, interview.

100. Warren, interview.

101. *Arkansas Democrat,* December 7, 1965, 2.

102. *Arkansas Democrat,* December 7, 1965, 2.

103. Blanchard, interview.

104. *Arkansas Gazette,* March 18, 1966, 2A.

105. *Arkansas Gazette,* March 19, 1966, 5A.

106. *Arkansas Gazette,* March 19, 1966, 5A.

107. See *Arkansas Gazette,* March 25, 1966, 29A; *Arkansas Gazette,* March 30, 1966, 8A, and *Arkansas Gazette,* March 31, 1966, 8A; and *Arkansas Democrat,* March 24, 1966, 2.

108. *Arkansas Gazette,* March 29, *1966,* 1B.

109. *Arkansas Democrat,* March 27, 1966, 13A.

110. *Arkansas Democrat,* March 31, 1966, 10.

111. Warren, interview.

112. *Arkansas Gazette,* April 2, 1966, 1A, 2A.

113. *Arkansas Democrat,* May 28, 1966, p. 2.

114. Rozzell, interview; *Arkansas Democrat,* April 2, 1966, 2; *Arkansas Gazette,* April 3, 1966, 2E.

115. *Epperson v. McDonald,* No. 131575 Pulaski Chancery Court, First Div. (May 27, 1966), 7.

116. *Epperson,* No. 131575 at 5.

117. *Scopes v. State of Tennessee,* 154 Tenn. 105, 298 S.W. 363 (1927). In this case, the Tennessee Evolution Law was held to be constitutional, but the fine levied upon Scopes was held not to be within the power of the court, and his conviction was reversed on this ground.

118. *Epperson,* No. 131575 at, 6.

119. *Scopes,* 154 Tenn.

120. *State v. Epperson,* 242 Ark. 922, 416 S.W. 2nd 322 (1967). Appellant's brief in this case (No. 4127), 3.

121. *Epperson,* 242 Ark. 922, 416 S.W. 2nd at 81

122. *Epperson,* 242 Ark. 922, 416 S.W. 2nd.

123. *Epperson,* 242 Ark. 922, 416 S.W. 2nd

124. Rozzell, interview; Warren, interview.

125. *Arkansas Gazette,* March 5, 1968, 1B.

126. *Arkansas Gazette,* October 17, 1968, 1A.

127. *New York Times,* October 17, 1968, 49.

128. *New York Times,* October 17, 1968, 49.

129. Warren, interview.

130. Warren, interview.

131. *New York Times,* October 17, 1968, 49.

132. *Arkansas Democrat,* October 17, 1968, 3A.

133. *Epperson v. Arkansas,* 393 U.S. 97 (1968).

134. *Epperson,* 393 U.S. at 104.

135. *Epperson,* 393 U.S. at 107.

136. *Epperson,* 393 U.S. at 107.

137. *Epperson,* 393 U.S. at 109.

138. *Epperson,* 393 U.S. at 109.

139. *Epperson,* 393 U.S. at 114.

140. *Epperson,* 393 U.S. at 112.

141. *Epperson,* 393 U.S. at 114.

142. *Epperson,* 393 U.S. at 115.

143. *Epperson,* 393 U.S. at 116.

144. *Arkansas Gazette,* November 13, 1968, 1A.

146. *Arkansas Gazette,* November 13, 1968, 1A.

146. Rozzell, interview.

147. *Arkansas Gazette,* November 14, 1968, 6A.

148. *Arkansas Gazette*, November 13, 1968, 1A.

Low Villains and Wickedness in High Places

1. For the proplanter perspective, see J. W. Butts and Dorothy James, "The Underlying Causes of the Elaine Riot of 1919," *Arkansas Historical Quarterly* 20 (Spring 1961): 95–104. For a black perspective, see Walter White, "'Massacring Whites' in Arkansas," the *Nation,* December 6, 1919, 715–16. Other important accounts include Arthur I. Waskow, *From Race Riot to Sit-In, 1919 and the 1960s: A Study in the Connections between Conflict and Violence* (Garden City, N.Y.: Doubleday & Company, 1966); O. A. Rogers Jr., "The Elaine Race Riots of 1919," *Arkansas Historical Quarterly* 19 (Summer 1960): 142–50; B. Boren McCool, *Union, Reaction, and Riot: A Biography of a Race Riot* (Memphis: Bureau of Social Research, Division of Urban and Regional Studies, Memphis State University, 1970), 23–52; Richard C. Cortner, *A Mob Intent on Death: The NAACP and the Arkansas Riot Cases* (Middletown, Conn.: Wesleyan University Press, 1988); Nan Elizabeth Woodruff, "African American Struggles for Citizenship in the Arkansas and Mississippi Deltas in the Age of Jim Crow," *Radical History Review* 55 (1993): 33–51; and Carl H. Moneyhon, *Arkansas and the New South: 1874–1929* (Fayetteville: University of Arkansas Press, 1997), 107–8.

2. Francis I. Gwaltney, *The Quicksand Years* (London: Seker & Warburg, 1965).

3. Waskow, *From Race Riot to Sit-In,* 143–44; Cortner, *Mob Intent on Death,* 25–26.

4. White, "'Massacring Whites in Arkansas,'" 715–16.

5. McCool, *Union, Reaction, and Riot,* 23–52. There is considerable controversy over the number of blacks killed, with some contemporaries and historians concluding that hundreds may have died. In an eccentric book L. S. Dunaway argued 856 blacks were killed. Dunaway, *What a Preacher Saw Through a Key-Hole in Arkansas* (Little Rock: Parke-Harper Publishing Company, 1925), 102.

6. Butts and James, "The Underlying Causes," 95–104. The mysterious black detectives from Chicago allegedly reported that certain planters were slated to be killed. Sebastian Straub, a prominent merchant in Helena who had many plantation accounts, was said to have hired at least one of these detectives. His son, Charles W. Straub, was interviewed by Butts and James in October 1960, and claimed to have been with his father when he met with the black detective prior to the riot and claimed to have seen the detective's report. These reports, however, were never entered as evidence and their existence cannot be confirmed. If they did exist, the reports would raise interesting questions about the activities and motivations of these black detectives and their willingness to play to the fears of white leaders in Phillips County. Butts and James, 97–98. See also Cortner, *Mob Intent on Death, 7.*

7. Rogers, "The Elaine Race Riots," 142–47.

8. McCool seems also to have based his narrative of the riot on trial testimony later shown to be unreliable.

9. Levon Helm with Stephen Davis, *This Wheel's on Fire: Levon Helm and the Story of the Band* (New York: William Morrow and Company, 1993), 15. The Helms were farm renters. Helm indicates that his maternal grandfather, Wheeler Wilson, who alternated between the life of a logger and a farmer, was opposed to Ku Klux

Klan activity, and Helm credits him (and his mother) with "saving me from having to wear that whole damn load of racism that a lot of people had to carry." Helm and Davis, 17.

10. John Elvis Miller, interview by Walter Brown, Bruce Parnham, and Samuel A. Sizer, Fort Smith, Ark., March 18, 1976, transcript pp. 16, 21, MC 279, Special Collections Division, University of Arkansas Libraries, Fayetteville.

11. For Thomas's efforts to investigate the causes of the riot, see A. C. Miller (a prominent Methodist preacher and editor and manager of the *Arkansas Methodist*) to D. Y. Thomas, December 23, 1919; a letter dated January 1, 1920, from D. Y. Thomas with a marginal note saying "copy of a letter sent to two people at Helena," which asks for information; E. M. Allen [a prominent Helena businessman, on "Business Men's League" stationery] to Thomas, January 4, 1920; Greenfield Quarles (a Helena attorney) to Thomas, January 5, 1920; U. S. Bratton to Thomas, March 1, 1920; Bratton to Thomas, September 15, 1921; Letter to Editor of the *New York Times,* "About Race Troubles in Arkansas," February 9, 1920. All in David Y. Thomas Papers, Series 1, Box 1, Folder 2, Special Collections Division, University of Arkansas Libraries, Fayetteville. For his book, see D. Y. Thomas, *Arkansas and Its People: A History, 1541–1930* (New York: The American Historical Society, Inc., 1930), 1–294.

12. Butts and James, "The Underlying Causes," 97. On the unreliability of the evidence presented against the Elaine defendants, see Cortner, *Mob Intent on Death,* 123–25.

13. The Smitty and Jones affidavits are themselves problematic, however. As Cortner reveals, the NAACP knew these witnesses were vulnerable, partly because both men took money from the NAACP and from Scipio Jones, the black attorney from Arkansas who assisted in the appeals, and partly because they were both afraid to return to the state if a new trial was ordered. Although the funds extended to them were not in return for their testimony, but rather in recognition of the fact that they could not find work and support their families because they had recanted, the "appearance" of collusion could have materially damaged the case. Despite threats of violence and loss of income, the two men persisted in their revised stories, and, as Waskow suggests, there is more reason to believe them than to suspect them. Waskow, *From Race Riot to Sit-In,* 125–26, 134; Cortner, *Mob Intent on Death,* 167–72.

14. Waskow, *From Race Riot to Sit-In,* 125–26.

15. Cited in *Moore v. Dempsey,* 261 U.S. 86 (1923), Brief for the Appellants, 12.

16. *Moore,* 261 U.S. 86

17. Miller, interview, 15.

18. McCool read the letter to suggest that whites had long "feared a Negro rebellion," and entirely neglected the more direct evidence it contained of a white impulse to attack the black community; McCool, *Union, Reaction, and Riot,* 20; Harry Anderson to C. H. Brough, October 7, 1919, Charles Brough Collection, Series 1, Box 4, Folder 55, Item 87, Special Collections Division, University of Arkansas Libraries, Fayetteville. Sheriff Kitchens was incapacitated by illness at the time of the shootings at the Hoop Spur Church, and Sebastian Straub was acting as sheriff in his place. Kitchens became involved in the events as they unfolded, however, and became a member of the Committee of Seven, made up of prominent white Helena men who investigated the causes of the riot. For the Committee of Seven, see Greenfield Quarles to D. Y. Thomas, January 5, 1920, Thomas Papers; McCool, *Union, Reaction, and Riot,* 22; Cortner, *Mob Intent on Death,* 13.

19. Waskow, *From Race Riot to Sit In,* 128–129.

20. Waskow, *From Race Riot to Sit In,* 125. Butts and James found planters were alarmed about the union long before the riot. Butts and James, "The Elaine Riot," 97–98. See also McCool, "Union, Reaction, and Riot," 20, 22.

21. Gwaltney's portrait of a divided white community, however, did not move much beyond familiar literary representations of Snopes-like crackers and Compsonesque patricians. Gwaltney, *The Quicksand Years.*

22. For a study that recognizes divisions within the black community, see Cortner, *Mob Intent on Death.* To suggest an unusual unity within the white community is by no means to suggest unanimity. There were a number of examples of Phillips County whites warning or otherwise protecting blacks during the riots.

23. For figures on 1880 cotton production, see *Report of the Productions of Agriculture, Tenth Census* (Washington, D.C.: Government Printing Office, 1883), vol. 13, 214. For figures on 1920 cotton production, see *Fourteenth Census of the United States, 1920, Agriculture,* vol. 6, Part 2, table 4, 580 (Washington, D.C.: Government Printing Office, 1922); For figures on percentage of farm owners in 1880, see *Miscellaneous Documents of the House of Representatives* (Washington D.C.: Government Printing Office, 1896), table 94, 248. For figures on percentage of farm owners in 1920, see *Fourteenth Census, Agriculture,* vol. 4, table 1, 565.

24. Bessie Ferguson, "The Elaine Race Riot" (master's thesis, George Peabody College for Teachers, 1927), 22.

25. *Helena World,* February 23, 1898.

26. For a lengthier discussion of the Cross and Poinsett county cases, see Jeannie Whayne, *A New Plantation South: Land, Labor, and Federal Favor in Twentieth-Century Arkansas* (Charlottesville: University Press of Virginia, 1996), 47–54. For whitecapping elsewhere, see, for example, William F. Holmes, "Moonshiners and Whitecaps in Alabama, 1893," *Alabama Review* 34 (January 1981): 31–49; Holmes, "Moonshining and Collective Violence: Georgia, 1889–1895," *Journal of American History* 67 (December 1980): 588–611; Holmes, "Whitecapping: Agrarian Violence in Mississippi, 1902–1906," *Journal of Southern History* 35 (1969): 165–85; Holmes, "Whitecapping in Georgia: Carroll and Houston Counties, 1893," *Georgia Historical Quarterly* 64 (1980): 388–404; and Holmes, "Whitecapping in Mississippi: Agrarian Violence in the Populist Era," *Mid-America* 55 (1973): 134–48.

27. In 1900 these were Mooney and Searcy townships. Between 1910 and 1920, Tappan township was carved out of both. Elaine was within Tappan township. "Manuscript Census of Population," Phillips County, Ark., 1900 and 1920. For a note on the creation of Tappan township, see *Fourteenth Census of the United States Taken in the Year 1920,* vol. I (Washington, D.C.: Goverment Printing Office, 1921), 849.

28. Race relations, it should be noted, remained extraordinarily complicated in these turbulent Delta communities. Whites and blacks, particularly single males, might interact with one another in honkytonks at the same time as nightriders were attacking black sharecroppers. See Whayne, *A New Plantation South,* 27–28.

29. This version of events is reported in McCool, *Union, Reaction, and Riot,* 31. McCool is quoting a private interview J. W. Butts had with J. M. Countiss in October 1960.

30. Ferguson, "The Elaine Race Riot," 55. Although Ferguson reported that Dr. Johnston's reputation was not spotless—he was said to have been charged with breaking the prohibition statutes and with "other minor offenses"—she concluded that "if only one made the attempt [to escape] it was surely cowardice to kill three other persons who were bound and possessed no means of defense." On Johnston's police

record, Ferguson cites "the records of the police court," in the text, but she does not footnote that citation. In fact, druggists in those years often sold liquor, so there may be some truth to her assertion. As to Ferguson's overall study of the Elaine Race Riot, it is a curious document that reveals some understanding of the economic exploitation visited upon black people, but betrays the author's prejudices in declaring that Robert Hill "simply played upon the ignorance and superstition of a childlike race." McCool, *Union, Reaction, and Riot,* 38.

31. Ferguson, "Elaine Race Riot," 54; Ida B. Wells-Barnett, *The Arkansas Race Riot,* (Chicago: Hume Job Print, 1920), 25. Black oral tradition in Phillips County supports the notion that the Johnstons had innocently been out hunting. See C. Calvin Smith, "Serving the Poorest of the Poor: Black Medical Practitioners in the Arkansas Delta, 1880–1960," *Arkansas Historical Quarterly* 57 (Autumn 1998): 302.

32. *Arkansas Gazette,* October 4, 1919, as quoted in Cortner, *Mob Intent on Death,* 9.

33. Nor was any cache of guns offered in evidence against the twelve black men convicted of murder, though they were similarly reported in the newspapers to have had a stockpile of arms. Miller, interview, 22.

34. For a view critical of the black middle class and its failure to address the problems of poor blacks, see Fon Gordon, *Caste and Class: The Black Experience in Arkansas, 1880–1920* (Athens: University of Georgia Press, 1995). For more sympathetic views, see John William Graves, *Town and Country: Race Relations in an Urban-Rural Context, Arkansas, 1865–1905* (Fayetteville: University of Arkansas Press, 1990); Tom Dillard, "Scipio A. Jones," *Arkansas Historical Quarterly* 31 (Autumn 1972): 201–19; Dillard, "Golden Prospects and Fraternal Amenities: Mifflin W. Gibbs's Arkansas Years," *Arkansas Historical Quarterly* 35 (Winter 1976): 307–33; and Dillard, "To the Back of the Elephant: Racial Conflict in the Arkansas Republican Party," *Arkansas Historical Quarterly* 33 (Spring 1974): 3–15.

35. E. M. Allen to D. Y. Thomas, January 4, 1920, Thomas Papers.

36. E. M. Allen to D. Y. Thomas, January 21, 1920; and E. M. Allen to D. Y. Thomas, January 4, 1920, Thomas Papers, Series 1, Box 1, Folder 2. In the January 21, 1920, letter, Allen indicated that Morris had been involved in organizing a cooks' union of Negro women "to demand that their mistresses use the title of Miss or Mrs. in addressing them." This seems a highly unlikely venture for the distinguished Dr. Morris. A. C. Miller, a white preacher, claimed that Morris had "somewhat discredited himself by clamoring for repeal of separate coach law." A. C. Miller to D. Y. Thomas, December 23, 1919, Thomas Papers. For biographical information on Morris, see Jack Salzman, David Lionel Smith, and Cornel West, *Encyclopedia of African-American Culture and History* (New York: MacMillian, 1996), 1885–86. See also *The Booker T. Washington Papers,* Volume 7, (Urbana: University of Illinois Press, 1972), 387.

37. See Morris quoted in Waskow, *From Race Riot to Sit-In,* 146. On black assurances to the white community, see Cortner, *Mob Intent on Death,* 45–46.

38. Solidarity within the black community might also have been enhanced in these years by the progress of the "lily white" faction in the state Republican Party. The "lily whites" shunned cross-racial alliances even with elite blacks, further diminishing the latter's opportunities to make common cause with those outside the African American community. See Dillard, "Back of the Elephant"; Dillard, "Scipio Jones."

39. Brough's actions and official position on the riot, which was that it was an insurrection and that whites acted reasonably in the face of the threat, have been the subject of some controversy. As his biographer, Foy Lisenby, suggests, this posture was

in keeping with his white supremacist ideology but "one might have expected a more empirical attitude from a former professor who had chaired the University Commission on Race Questions." Brough had been on the faculty at the University of Arkansas prior to his election as governor. Foy Lisenby, *Charles Hillman Brough: A Biography* (Fayetteville: University of Arkansas Press, 1996), 48, 115.

40. McCool, *Union, Reaction, and Riot,* 27–28.

41. Waskow, *From Race Riot to Sit-In,* 129.

42. Waskow, *From Race Riot to Sit-In,* 130–131. O. S. Bratton, son of U. S. Bratton, the lawyer retained by the Progressive Farmers Union to sue unscrupulous planters, was arrested while on his way to interview union members interested in the litigation.

43. Anderson to Brough, October 7, 1919, Brough Papers.

44. "Manuscript Census of Population," Mooney, Searcy and Tappan townships, Phillips County, 1920.

45. As Nan Woodruff suggests, this indebted those blacks to the planters who had paid their bond and thus tied them ever more firmly to the plantation system. Woodruff, "African American Struggles," 42.

46. Bessie Ferguson has it that Jones was a deputy sheriff. It may be that he was both a deputy sheriff and a special agent for the railroad. Ferguson, "The Elaine Race Riot," 46.

47. *Moore,* 261 U.S. 86 at 546. McReynolds used this language in his dissent from the court's ruling overturning the convictions of six of the black defendants. Interestingly, Butts and James quote McReynolds without indicating that his was the one dissenting opinion on the court.

48. Bratton, referring to the case at hand, hoped to see the party "landed in the penitentiary, where he belongs." The accused lived in Wilmot, Arkansas and was later convicted in Texas. U. S. Bratton to Henry Terrell, U.S. Attorney, San Antonio, Texas, July 5, 1905, Justice Department Papers, Record Group 60, National Archives and Records Administration, Washington, D.C.

49. Bratton to Thomas, September 15, 1921, Thomas Papers.

50. Miller interview, 11. See *Arkansas Code of 1987,* annotated, for a description of laws establishing the landlord's lien on the crop (1868); and the superiority of the landlord's lien (1876, 1878, and 1881), 216–24.

51. Glen T. Barton and J. G. McNealy, "Recent Changes in Farm Labor Organization in Three Arkansas Plantation Counties," Preliminary Report, University of Arkansas College of Agriculture, Agricultural Experiment Station, Fayetteville, Arkansas, September 1939, 32, Special Collections Division, University of Arkansas Libraries, Fayetteville.

52. Miller, interview, 11, 21.

53. U.S. Department of Agriculture, "Farm Tenancy in Arkansas," Bureau of Agricultural Economics, in cooperation with the Arkansas Agricultural Experiment Station, (Washington, D.C., 1941), 11. Economic historians Roger Ransom and Richard Sutch concluded that credit arrangements were such that the interest rates charged by merchants "ranged from 40 to 70 percent" for the south as whole. Planters who did not themselves have commissaries made agreements with merchants to supply their share-croppers. Roger L. Ransom and Richard Sutch, *One Kind of Freedom: The Economic Consequences of Emancipation* (New York: Cambridge University Press, 1977), 130.

54. Ferguson, "The Elaine Race Riot," 17.

55. George P. Rawick, *The American Slave: A Composite Autobiography* (Westport, Conn.: Greenwood Publishing, 1972), Vol. 9, part 4, 248.

56. U. S. Industrial Commission, *Industrial Commission Report on Agriculture and Agricultural Labor* (Washington, D.C.: Government Printing Office, 1901), xviii.

57. Bratton to D. Y. Thomas, September 15, 1921, Thomas Papers.

58. Bratton to Thomas. See, more generally, Pete Daniel, *Shadow of Slavery: Peonage in the South, 1901–1969* (Urbana: University of Illinois Press, 1972).

59. *Helena World,* July 21, 1916, cited in Susan E. C. Huntsman, "Race Relations in Phillips County, 1895–1920" (honor's thesis, University of Arkansas, Fayetteville, 1996), 16.

60. Rogers. "The Elaine Race Riots." 144.

61. The black literacy rate had been 64.6% in 1900. The white rate was far higher—91.9percent in 1900 and 94.7 percent in 1920. "Manuscript Census of Population," Searcy and Mooney townships, Philips County, 1900; Searcy, Mooney, and Tappan townships, Phillips County, 1920.

62. *Helena World,* October 12, 1898, cited in Huntsman, "Race Relations in Phillips County," 11 -12.

63. Huntsman, "Race Relations in Phillips County,"13–14. For disputes between tenants and planters elsewhere in the Arkansas Delta, see Whayne, *A New Plantation South,* 55–59.

64. "Memorandum on Tenancy in the Southwestern States (Extracts from the Final Report of the United States Industrial Relations, 1916)" NAACP manuscripts, cited in Waskow, *From Race Riot to Sit-In,* 122.

65. Butts and James, "The Underlying Causes," 104.

66. U. S. Bratton, who was a native Arkansan, was forced to leave the state with his family after a series of threats. He joined another son, Guy Bratton, who was practicing law in Detroit, Michigan. U. S. worked for a time as attorney for a labor union, the United Brotherhood of Maintenance-of-Way Employes (sic) and Railway Shop Laborers. During the crisis, while O. S. Bratton was still jailed in Helena, friends advised the senior Bratton to refrain from traveling to Phillips County because he would be "shot down without any ceremony" if he did. His son Guy traveled to Helena to confer with local officials concerning his brother's release, and apparently barely escaped a plot against his life. U. S. Bratton to D. Y. Thomas, September 15, 1921, Thomas Papers. U. S. Bratton later became a member of the team of lawyers appealing the convictions of the men sentenced to death.

67. Gwaltney to Alan D. Williams, January 10, 1963, Francis Gwaltney Papers, Special Collections Division, University of Arkansas Libraries, Fayetteville.

68. See Alan D. Williams (Little, Brown & Company) to John Schaffner (Gwaltney's literary agent at the time), January 4, 1963, Box 17, File 20; and Margaret Cousins (Doubleday & Company, Inc.) to John Schaffner, August 15, 1963, Box 17, File 20, Gwaltney Papers. Cousins's blistering critique of the novel greatly angered Gwaltney, and his friend, Norman Mailer, wrote to caution him against trying to write while angry and to express an interest in seeing the rejected manuscript. Norman Mailer to Francis Irby Gwaltney, December 20, 1963, Gwaltney-Mailer Correspondence, Special Collections Division, University of Arkansas Libraries, Fayetteville. McGraw-Hill also rejected the manuscript; Harold Scharlatt to John Schaffner, December 16, 1963, Box 17, File 20, Gwaltney Papers.

69. He began negotiating with Seger & Warburg in London in 1964. See Schaffner to Gwaltney, March 12, 1964, Box 17, File 20, Gwaltney Papers. According to Gwaltney in a letter to Mailer, by December 1965, the book "has received two bad

reviews and a batch of glowing ones. *Punch* and the *Times* were especially nice." Gwaltney to Mailer, November 2, 1965, Gwaltney-Mailer Correspondence.

70. Stu Robinson to Francis Gwaltney, October 8, 1965, Box 17, File 21, Gwaltney Papers.

A Place at the Table

1. *Arkansas Gazette*, June 14, 1946.

2. For treatments of the GI Revolt, see, for example, Dee Brown, *The American Spa: Hot Springs* (Little Rock: Rose Publishing, 1982), 88; T. Harri Baker and Jane Browning, *An Arkansas History for Young People* (Fayetteville: University of Arkansas Press, 1991), 336; Michael B. Dougan, *Arkansas Odyssey: The Saga of Arkansas from Prehistoric Times to Present* (Little Rock: Rose Publishing, 1994), 480; and Diane D. Blair, *Arkansas Politics and Government: Do the People Rule?* (Lincoln: University of Nebraska Press, 1988), 17, 50.

3. Jim Lester, *A Man for Arkansas: Sid McMath and the Southern Reform Tradition* (Little Rock: Rose Publishing, 1976), 19–33; V. O. Key, *Southern Politics in State and Nation* (New York: Knopf, 1949), 201–4.

4. Shirley Abbott, *The Bookmaker's Daughter: A Memory Unbound* (New York: Ticknor and Fields, 1991), 206–15.

5. Brown, *American Spa,* 50–60.

6. Inez E. Cline and Fred Mark Palmer, "Belvedere," *The Record: Garland County Historical Society* 33 (1992): 2–5.

7. Lester, *McMath,* 22.

8. Abbott, *Bookmaker's Daughter,* 206–15.

9. Brown, *American Spa,* 87–88.

10. Lester, *McMath,* 22; *Arkansas Gazette,* October 11, 1947.

11. Lester, *McMath,* 22.

12. Key, *Southern Politics in State and Nation,* 593–94.

13. Lester, *McMath,* 22–23.

14. Sid McMath, interview with author, Little Rock, Arkansas, October 16, 1996.

15. McMath, interview.

16. Richard W. Hobbs, "GI Regime," *The Record: Garland County Historical Society* 36 (1995): 129–30.

17. Richard Hobbs, telephone interview with author, June 25, 1997.

18. Lester, *McMath,* 23–24.

19. Hot Springs *Sentinel Record,* April 28, 1946.

20. Q. Byrum Hurst, interview with author, Hot Springs, Arkansas, October 17, 1996.

21. *Sentinel Record,* April 28, 1946.

22. *Arkansas Gazette,* April 28, 1946.

23. *Sentinel Record,* June 30, 1946.

24. A contemporary of the GIs, preeminent political scientist V. O. Key, emphasized in 1949 that the broader GI effort in the state was not an attempt to introduce new issues into Arkansas politics but was instead simply an effort to gain honest elections. Key found nothing in the veterans' political doctrines or philosophies that substantiated the charges of radicalism leveled against them by their opponents.

Admittedly, free and honest elections in some Arkansas counties would have been a radical change, Key wrote, noting that election fraud in Arkansas was surpassed only by that in Tennessee. Key, *Southern Politics in State and Nation,* 184–203, 443.

25. Hurst, interview; McMath, interview.

26. Hurst, interview; Dallas Herndon, *Annals of Arkansas* (Hopkinsville, Ky.: Historical Record Association, 1947), 1,422–24.

27. McMath, interview.

28. Hurst, interview.

29. McMath, interview.

30. Mark Palmer, interview with author, Hot Springs, Ark., January 29, 1997.

31. Hurst, interview.

32. Lester, *McMath,* 26.

33. *Arkansas Gazette,* July 5, 1946.

34. Lester, *McMath,* 28.

35. Abbott, *Bookmaker's Daughter,* 209.

36. *Arkansas Democrat,* July 8, 1946.

37. *Arkansas Democrat,* July 7, 1946.

38. Hobbs, "GI Regime"; Hobbs, interview. Hobbs remembers that campaign workers Birdie Fulton and Walter McLavey were the men robbed by Spears, but the *Arkansas Democrat* identified Livingston and Fulton as the victims.

39. *Arkansas Gazette,* July 10, 1946.

40. *Arkansas Gazette,* July 10, 1946; *Arkansas Gazette,* July 11, 1946; *Arkansas Democrat,* July 9, 1946.

41. Lester, *McMath,* 27–28.

42. *Arkansas Democrat,* July 8, 1946; Lester, *McMath,* 28.

43. *Arkansas Democrat,* July 12, 1946.

44. *Arkansas Democrat,* July 15, 1946.

45. *Arkansas Gazette,* August 1, 1948.

46. *Arkansas Democrat,* July 30, 1946.

47. *Arkansas Gazette,* August 1, 1946.

48. James Holt, interview with author, Hot Springs, Arkansas, June 12, 1997.

49. Lester, *McMath,* 29.

50. *Arkansas Democrat,* July 31, 1946.

51. *Arkansas Gazette,* August 1, 1946.

52. *Arkansas Gazette,* August 1, 1946.

53. *Arkansas Gazette,* August 1, 1946; *Arkansas Gazette,* November 6, 1946.

54. *Arkansas Gazette,* November 7, 1946.

55. *Arkansas Gazette,* November 6, 1946.

56. *Arkansas Gazette,* November 7, 1946.

57. *Arkansas Gazette,* November 7, 1946.

58. *Arkansas Gazette,* November 6, 1946.

59. *Arkansas Gazette,* April 2, 1947.

60. *Arkansas Gazette,* March 18, 1947

61. *Arkansas Gazette,* March 18, 1947; Abbott, *Bookmaker's Daughter,* 229.

62. *Sentinel Record,* October 11, 1947; *Arkansas Gazette,* November 12, 1947.

63. *Arkansas Gazette,* November 12, 1947.

64. *Sentinel Record,* November 21, 1948; *Arkansas Gazette,* November 20, 1947.

65. Abbott, *Bookmaker's Daughter,* 216.

66. *Arkansas Gazette,* October 1, 1947.

67. Lester, *McMath,* 37–42.

68. Kelly Bryant, *Historical Report of the Secretary of State: Arkansas* (Little Rock: State of Arkansas, 1968), 484.

69. Hobbs, interview; Holt, interview.

70. Hobbs, interview; Hurst, interview. Stories of stuffed ballot boxes and fraudulent poll tax receipts were common in Garland County, as they were in other Arkansas counties, right up to 1965, when the poll tax was removed. Despite rumors, however, there is no proof that any GIs other than Ray Owen were directly involved.

71. Holt, interview; Hurst, interview; McMath, interview.

72. *Arkansas Gazette,* December 8, 1948.

73. *Sentinel Record,* July 29, 1948.

74. Hurst, interview; Hobbs, interview.

75. Holt, interview; interview by author with retired casino owner who wished to remain unidentified, November 3, 1996. Information provided by this source was corroborated by other sources.

76. *Arkansas Gazette,* January 30, 1948.

77. Hot Springs city jail docket, 1946–1947, Garland County Historical Society. There were no gambling arrests entered after the date of July 5, 1947, in this ledger. No ledgers for later years are available.

78. *Arkansas Gazette,* January 16, 1948.

79. Holt, interview; Hurst, interview; anonymous casino owner, interview.

80. Roy Reed, *Faubus: The Life and Times of an American Prodigal* (Fayetteville: University of Arkansas Press, 1997), 318–19.

81. Hurst, interview.

82. Hurst, interview.

"The Great Negro State of the Country"?

1. Lawrence Bobo and Gilliam Franklin Jr., "Race, Socio-Political Participation and Black Empowerment," *American Political Science Review* 84 (1990): 377–93; Michael W. Combs, John R. Hibbing, and Susan Welch, "Black Constituents and Congressional Roll Call Votes," *Western Political Quarterly* 37 (1984): 427–34; Arthur B. Levy and Susan Stoudinger, "Sources of Voting Cues for the Congressional Black Caucus," *Journal of Black Studies* 7 (1976): 29–45; Neil Pinney and George Serra, "The Congressional Black Caucus and Vote Cohesion: Placing the Caucus within House Voting Patterns," *Political Research Quarterly* 52 (1999): 583–608; Robert Singh, *The Congressional Black Caucus: Racial Politics in the U.S. Congress* (Thousand Oaks, Calif.: Sage, 1998); Carol M. Swain, *Black Faces, Black Interests: The Representation of African-Americans in Congress* (Cambridge: Harvard University Press, 1993); Katherine Tate, "Black Political Participation in the 1984 and 1988 Presidential Elections, *The American Political Science Review* 85 (1991): 1,158–76; and Kenny J. Whitby, *The Color of Representation: Congressional Behavior and Black Interests* (Ann Arbor: University of Michigan Press, 1997).

2. Kathleen A. Bratton, "The Effect of Legislative Diversity Agenda Setting: Evidence from Six State Legislatures," *American Politics Research* 30 (2002): 115–42; Kathleen A. Bratton and Kerryl L. Haynie, "Agenda Setting and Legislative Success in State Legislatures: The Effects of Gender and Race," *The Journal of Politics* 61 (1999): 658–79; Charles E. Menifield, "Black Political Life in the Missouri General Assembly,"

Journal of Black Studies 31 (2000): 20–38; Bryron D'Andra Orey, "Black Legislative Politics in Mississippi," *Journal of Black Studies* 30 (2000): 791–814.

3. Diane Blair, *Arkansas Politics and Government: Do the people rule?* (Lincoln: University of Nebraska Press, 1988), 4.

4. V. O. Key, *Southern Politics in State and Nation.* (New York, Vintage Books, 1949). Blair, *Arkansas Politics and Government,* 4.

5. We also included one special session—called in the fall of 1983 to address Gov. Bill Clinton's education reform plan—because of its lasting significance in the state's politics and policy.

6. News articles were inconsistent in the identification of bill (and act) numbers for both chambers. Thus, before examining roll call votes, we first double-checked and/or supplemented the identification of all measures in the *Arkansas Legislative Digest* for each legislative session. Then, we turned to the House and Senate journals of the Arkansas General Assembly to record the votes of individual members.

7. A 1973 study by the Voter Education Project, however, reported that Arkansas trailed only Alabama in the number of African Americans elected to public office at all levels (P. Strickland, "State Second in Electing Black Officials," *Arkansas Gazette,* April 3, 1987). It retained its position, bested only by Mississippi, in the project's 1974 report and the Arkansas Black Political Caucus hosted the second National Black Political Convention that year ("Arkansas Ranks 2d in South in Elected Black officials," *Arkansas Gazette,* March 4, 1974, 5A; *Chicago Tribune,* "Blacks Hope LR Sessions Hardworking," *Arkansas Gazette,* March 11, 1974, 7A).

8. "Jewell Defeats Sparks to Win Senate Race," *Arkansas Gazette,* November 8, 1972, 10A.

9. Townsend was nominated in 1969 by governor Winthrop Rockefeller to serve on the State Board of Education; the state senate refused to confirm the appointment, however ("Two Blacks, Johnston Win in District 3," *Arkansas Gazette,* November 8, 1972, 11A).

10. "Jewell Defeats Sparks."

11. Jim Ranchino, "The Arkansan of the '70s: The Good Ole Boy Ain't Whut He Used to be," *Arkansas Times,* September 1977, 40–43.

12. *Jeffers v. Clinton* 730 F. Supp. 196 (E.D. Ark. 1989).

13. Tony Moser, "Arkansas Case Lies at Heart of Fight over Redistricting," *Arkansas Democrat-Gazette,* February 20, 1995, 1A.

14. Mark Oswald, "Blacks Must Stand Up for Rights to Achieve Success, Lawyer Says," *Arkansas Gazette,* September 22, 1990, 4A.

15. Elizabeth Caldwell and Rachel O'Neal, "Say Farewells' at Legislature," *Arkansas Democrat-Gazette,* August 25, 1994, 8A; Noel Oman, "Voter Outrage at Jewell Helped Push Walker Over Top," *Arkansas Democrat Gazette,* May 29, 1994. Retrieved December 22, 2002, from http://web.lexis-nexis.com/universe.

16. Seth Blomeley, "Race Emerges as Issue for Democrats Vying in Redrawn LR Senate District," *Arkansas Democrat-Gazette,* May 14, 2002, 1B.

17. Rachel O'Neal, "Seven Freshman Senators Take Oath," *Arkansas Democrat-Gazette,* January 10, 1995, 5B.

18. Arkansas Legislative Black Caucus, "History," from the now-defunct caucus website, retrieved June 3, 2002. Can be viewed at http://web.archive.org/web/20020604174851/http://www.arklegblackcaucus.org/.

19. Arkansas Legislative Black Caucus, "History."

20. Doug Thompson, "Tax Cuts Not High on List for Legislators This Year," *Arkansas Democrat-Gazette,* January 9, 2001, 1A.

21. Tracy Steele, telephone interview with Parry, June 3, 2002.

22. Democratic Party of Arkansas, "About DPA," retrieved June 7, 2002, http://www.arkdems.org. The article appears to no longer be on the website, but can be viewed at http://web.archive.org/web/20020812090026/www.arkdems.org/about/about_auxiliaries.html.

23. The caucus also sponsors an internship opportunity for undergraduate students during the legislative session and a scholarship program honoring Dr. William Townsend. A five hundred dollar scholarship is awarded to one student from each district represented by a member of the Arkansas Legislative Black Caucus (Arkansas Legislative Black Caucus, "History"). Kerry L. Haynie, *African American Legislators: The American States* (New York: Columbia University Press, 2001).

24. Seth Blomeley, "Candidate Criticizes Lawmakers," *Arkansas Democrat-Gazette,* April 5, 2002, 1B.

25. John V. Pennington, "Legislative Black Caucus Meeting Draws Competitors in Senate Race," Hot Springs *Sentinel-Record,* August 3, 2002, 1B.

26. Kern Alexander and James Hale, "Educational Equity, Improving School Finance in Arkansas" (Report to the Advisory Committee of the Special School Formula Project of the Joint Interim Committee on Education, Little Rock, General Assembly, 1978).

27. *Dupree v. Alma School District,* 279 Ark. 340, 651 S.W.2d 90 (1983).

28. David Osborne, *Laboratories of Democracy: A New Breed of Governor Creates Models for National Growth* (Boston: Harvard Business School Press, 1990).

29. Long-time observer of Arkansas politics Diane Blair commented that "Teachers felt like they were being bit by their own dog" when the Clintons backed teacher testing in exchange for the rest of the education reform package (see Osborne, *Laboratories of Democracy,* 94).

30. Bob Wells, "Black Caucus Listens to Clinton: Pay Plan, Tax, Tests Opposed," *Arkansas Gazette,* October 2, 1983, 4A.

31. Wells, "Black Caucus Listens to Clinton."

32. Wells, "Black Caucus Listens to Clinton."

33. Wells, "Black Caucus Listens to Clinton."

34. Irma Hunter Brown, telephone interview with Parry, June 5, 2002.

35. Michael Arbanas, "Senate Approves 50% Increase in Retirement Pay; Bill Passes 26–8 with No Debate," *Arkansas Gazette,* February 15, 1991. Retrieved May 20, 2002 from http://web.lexis-nexis.com/universe/.

36. Brown, interview; John Reed, "School Choice Passes Senate after Tie Vote," *Arkansas Gazette,* March 10, 1989, 11A.

37. Lori McElroy, "Education Bills Fly by Panel in Senate," *Arkansas Gazette,* January 31, 1991. Retrieved May 20, 2002 from http://web.lexis-nexis.com/universe.

38. Ben McGee, telephone interview with Parry, May 25, 2002.

39. David Kern and Noel Oman, "With Day Left, Chambers Split on Condom Ban," *Arkansas Democrat,* March 27, 1991, 13A.

40. Democrat Capitol Bureau, "Compromise on Clinics Sends Assembly Home," *Arkansas Democrat,* March 28, 1991, 1A; David F. Kern, "Brownlee Opposes Condom Ban," *Arkansas Democrat,* March 27, 1991, 1E.

41. Democratic Capitol Bureau, "Compromise on Clinics"; Scott Morris, "Session

Comes to an End," *Arkansas Gazette,* March 28, 1991, 1A; "Resolution Supports Call for Session," *Arkansas Gazette,* March 15, 1980, 6A.

42. Jocelyn Elders, telephone interview with Parry, May 24, 2002.

43. McGee, interview.

44. Lisa Ferrell, telephone interview with Parry, May 29, 2002.

45. Ferrell, interview; Elizabeth Caldwell and Rachel O'Neal, "Bill Cuts Parental Strings on Police Questioning, Would be OK Without Notice," *Arkansas Democrat-Gazette,* August 18, 1994, 1A.

46. Brown, interview.

47. A. L. May, "Senate Has Long, Full Day of Work," *Arkansas Democrat,* March 18, 1977, 12B.

48. Joan Duffy, "House Rejects School Settlement," *Arkansas Democrat,* March 17, 1989a, 1A; Joan Duffy, "68-Day Legislative Session Ends," *Arkansas Democrat,* March 18, 1989, 1A

49. Knight News Service, "School Case Cost May Hit $59 Million," *Arkansas Gazette,* February 9, 1989, 1A.

50. Joan Duffy, "Struggle Looms as Arkansas House Passes Separate Civil Rights Bills," Memphis *Commercial Appeal,* February 27, 1993, A7.

51. Joan Duffy, "Lack of Action on Civil Rights Bill: Leaves Lewellen Measure in Limbo," *Commercial Appeal,* March 10, 1993, A8.

52. Joan Duffy, "Competing Bills, Lawmakers May Doom Law on Civil Rights," *Commercial Appeal,* March 25, 1993, A14.

53. Joan Duffy, "Minority Lawmakers Blast Arkansas Rights Bill," *Commercial Appeal,* March 28, 1993, B1.

54. At the April 8 signing ceremony, Walker praised Lewellen for his role in the "tremendous scuffle to get something substantive done." Lewellen stood on the edge of the crowd, opting not to speak though invited, saying only "It was Bill Walker's day," to a reporter covering the event (Joan Duffy, "Civil Right Law Signed to cap Ark. Legislature," *Commercial Appeal,* 1993, A1).

55. Ernest Dumas, "Enterprise Zones Aid Firms, Not Workers," *Arkansas Gazette,* December 9, 1983.

56. Dumas, "Enterprise Zones."

57. Brown, interview.

58. Brown, interview.

59. Pam Strickland, "Panel's Approval Moves Sales Tax Closer to Final Test in Full House," *Democrat,* April 3, 1987, 1A.

60. "Comments Indicate Job Tough, Not Impossible," *Arkansas Gazette,* March 31, 1987, 9A

61. Grant Tennille, "Necessary Taxes or Highway Robbery? Better Roadways Carry Divisive Price," *Arkansas Democrat-Gazette,* March 20, 1995, 1A.

62. Joe Stumpe, "House Passes Senate Redistricting Plan," *Arkansas Democrat,* March 27, 1991, 1A.

63. Michael Arbanas, "5 Redistricting Plans Discussed in Committee," *Arkansas Gazette,* March 12, 1991, 3G.

64. McGee, interview.

65. Mark Oswald, "New District Plan Issued," *Arkansas Gazette,* March 2, 1991, 2B; less overtly, Democrats and many journalists also alleged that representative McGee's motivations were transparently self-interested: A concentration of black voters into one congressional district would be conducive to his national-level political

aspirations (Max Brantley, "GOP District Plan Has Two Faces," *Arkansas Gazette,* March 14, 1991, 11; Scott Morris, "House Decides to OK 2 Redistricting Plans," *Arkansas Gazette,* March 22, 1991, 21; Mark Oswald, "Black House Members, GOP Join Forces," *Arkansas Gazette,* March 13, 1991, 31A.)

66. Mark Oswald and Scott Morris, "House Accepts Plan for Districts," *Arkansas Gazette,* March 27, 1991, 3H.

67. Scott Morris, "12 Blacks Ask to Intervene in Redistricting Suit," *Arkansas Gazette,* June 19, 1991, 6B.

68. Linda Satter, "Lawsuit Says Bias Corrupted Primaries," *Arkansas Democrat-Gazette,* May 24, 2002, 15A.

69. Satter, "Lawsuit says bias corrupted primaries."

70. C. S. Murphy, "Steele's Style Found Favor with Voters, Pundits Say," *Arkansas Democrat-Gazette,* May 23, 2002. Retrieved May 24, 2002, from http://web.lexis-nexis.com/universe.

71. Blair, *Arkansas Politics and Government,* especially chapter 9.

72. The redistricting responsibility was handed off to an interim committee for resolution by 2003.

73. Elders, interview.

74. McGee, interview, May 25, 2002.

75. McGee, interview.

76. For more on the significance of seniority, see Robert Johnston and Mary Storey, "The Arkansas Senate: An Overview," *Arkansas Political Science Review* 4 (1983): 69–81.

77. Steele, interview.

78. A similar plan was later that year crafted into a statewide initiative, touted by Gov. Mike Huckabee and adopted by voters at the polls. The appropriations bills necessary for its implementation, however, went right back to the state legislature, at which point the black Caucus negotiated several key concessions. These included the funding of an Addiction Studies Program at the University of Arkansas, Pine Bluff, a 15percent set-aside for minority-targeted prevention and cessation initiatives, and more money to a Minority Health Commission. Steele, interview.

79. Brown, interview.

80. Ferrell, interview.

81. Steele, interview.

82. Such alliances can, and do, take colorful twists as whites battle for black support in southern states. In Louisiana, for example, conservative lawmakers recently attempted to secure African American support for their cause by arguing that Darwin was a racist, and therefore evolution should be excluded from the state's textbooks (Melinda Deslatte, "Louisiana Lawmakers Say Darwin's Ideology Racist," *Oak Ridger,* May 2, 2001. Accessed online, June 1, 2002, http://oakridger.com/stories/050201/stt_0502010060.html).

83. In an interview, former representative Brown cautioned that the advent of term limits makes black members newly dependent on the favor of their white colleagues—instead of the seniority many were finally developing by the close of the 1990s—for their election, or selection, to leadership posts. Whether term limits, and the subsequent loss of seniority as the prevailing criterion for legislative power, serves to the advantage or disadvantage the black caucus members in the long run remains to be seen.

Term Limits in Arkansas

1. Art English and Linda Goss, "Follow the Leader: Leadership Structure in the Arkansas Senate" (Little Rock: Annual meeting of the Arkansas Political Science Association, 1986).

2. Interviews with members and staff of the Arkansas General Assembly were conducted by Brian Weberg of the National Conference of State Legislatures and Art English of the University of Arkansas at Little Rock, between November 2001 and May 2002. The data collected are part of the National Conference of State Legislatures' Joint Term Limits Project.

3. Bill introductions and adoptions from data compiled by the Bureau of Legislative Research of the Arkansas General Assembly.

4. Data collected from Southwestern Bell Legislative Directories and Legislative Digests from the Secretary of the Senate.

5. Art English and Matthew Warriner, "The Transformation of Political Marginals: Quorum Court Evolution in Arkansas," (San Antonio, Texas: Annual Meeting of the Southwestern Political Science Association, 1999).

6. Bill Paschall and Associates, "The Arkansas Legislature: A 2001 Retrospective," (Little Rock, nd).

7. Data collected from Southwestern Bell Legislative Directories.

Arkansas Governors in the Twentieth Century

1. Arthur M. Schlesinger, "Our Presidents: A Rating by 75 Historians." *New York Times Magazine,* July 9, 1962, 41.

2. See Ark. Const. Art. 6 (1874).

3. Louis Koenig, *The Chief Executive,* 3rd ed. (New York: Harcourt, Brace, Jovanovich. 1975), 34.

4. Ralph C. Barnhart, "A New Constitution for Arkansas," *Arkansas Law Review* 17 (Winter 1962–63): 3.

5. Ark. Const. Art. 8 (1868).

6. Ark. Const. (1874), Amend. 35 (1944) and 42 (1952).

7. Arkansas Constitutional Revision Study Commission, *Revising the Arkansas Constitution* (Little Rock, 1968), 56.

8. The persons who were asked to participate, their occupations, and affiliations are given below. (For occupations, H = Historian, J = journalist, P = political scientist, L = lawyer, C = citizen.)

Kenneth Walker	H	Arkansas Tech University
Michael Dougan	H	Arkansas State University
J. E. Griner	H	Arkansas State University
Robert Hargraves	PS	Garland County Community College (part-time)
Ray Muncy	H	Harding University
Boyce Drummond	H	Henderson State University
George Thompson	H	Hendrix College
Robert Meriwether	PS	Hendrix College
Richard Yates	PS	Hendrix College

Daniel Grant	PS	Ouachita Baptist University
Bob Riley	PS	Ouachita Baptist University
Robert Johnston	PS	University of Arkansas at Little Rock
William C. Nolan	PS	Southern Arkansas University
Robert Waltz	H	Southern Arkansas University
Walter Brown	H	University of Arkansas, Fayetteville
Diane Kincaid Blair	PS	University of Arkansas, Fayetteville
Don Holley	H	University of Arkansas at Monticello
Henry Wilkins	PS	University of Arkansas at Pine Bluff
Waddy Moore	H	University of Central Arkansas
Foy Lisenby	H	University of Central Arkansas
Simms McClintock	PS	University of Central Arkansas
John Ferguson	H	Arkansas History Commission
Marcus Holbrook	C	Director of Arkansas Legislative Council
Henry Woods	L	U.S. District Judge
Walter Nunn	PS	Arkansas Institute of Politics & Government
Kay Goss	PS	Constitutional Convention Research Director
Willard Gatewood	H	University of Arkansas, Fayetteville
Tom Dillard	H	State Parks & Tourism
Norman Hodges	PS	Southwest Missouri State University
Robert Leflar	L	University of Arkansas, Fayetteville, Law School
Leland Duvall	J	*Arkansas Gazette*
Margaret Ross	J	*Arkansas Gazette*
Robert McCord	J	*Arkansas Democrat*
Harry Ashmore	J	Center for Democratic Studies, California
Jim Lester	H	University of Arkansas at Little Rock (part time)
John Ward	J	*Log Cabin Democrat*—Conway
Mary Hudgins	C	Hot Springs
Bob Lancaster	J	*Arkansas Democrat*
Ernest Dumas	J	*Arkansas Gazette*
Brooks Hays	C	Chevy Chase, Maryland
Boyd Johnson	H	Retired from Henderson State
Dan Durning	PS	University of Arkansas at Little Rock (part-time)
Dale Enoch	C	Little Rock
Sam Harris	J	*Arkansas Gazette*
Bill Smith	C	Little Rock
Pauline Hoeltzel	C	Little Rock
Hal Douglas	J	*Northwest Arkansas Times*—Fayetteville
Page Muhollan	H	Arizona State, Tempe
Harri Baker	H	University of Arkansas at Little Rock
George Douthit	J	*Arkansas Democrat*
Elsie Jane Roy	L	U.S. District Judge
Cal Ledbetter Jr.	PS	University of Arkansas at Little Rock
C. Fred Williams	H	University of Arkansas at Little Rock

9. Respondents were given these suggested guidelines for use in evaluating Arkansas governors: (1) Did he have a sense of history? (2) What did he achieve as governor? (3) What kind of people did he appoint to office? (4) What kind of leadership did he provide? (5) Was any significant corruption associated with his administration(s)? (6) Did he abuse the power of his office? (7) How did his program fare with the legislature? (8) What was his impact on the state and the office of governor? (9) Did he use the power of his office to advance the public welfare? (10) What kind of national image did he project for the state? (11) What kind of administrative ability did he have? (12) How sensitive was he to human needs? (13) Other—please specify.

10. A copy of the instructions and questionnaire will be furnished upon request to either author at this address: University of Arkansas at Little Rock, 33rd and University, Little Rock, Arkansas 72204.

11. The following works on Arkansas history served as principal sources for the Background and Analysis section of this paper: Dallas T. Herndon, *Centennial History of Arkansas* (Little Rock: S. J. Clarke Publishing Co., 1922); John I. Ferguson and James H. Atkinson, *Historic Arkansas* (Little Rock: Arkansas History Commission, 1966); O. E. McKnight and Boyd Johnson, *The Arkansas Story* (Oklahoma City: Harlow Publishing Corp., 1956); Walter S. McNutt, *A History of Arkansas* (Little Rock: Democrat Printing and Lithography Co., 1933); David Yancy Thomas, *Arkansas and Its People: A History,* 1541–1930 (New York: American Historical Society, 1930); Janice Wegener ed., *Historical Report of the Secretary of State,* (Little Rock: Office of the Secretary of State, 1978).

A Practitioner's Guide to Arkansas's New Judicial Article

1. Larry Brady and J. D. Gingerich, "A Practitioner's Guide to Arkansas's New Judicial Article," *University of Arkansas at Little Rock Law Review* 24 (2002): 715–26.

2. "In re Implementation of Amendment 80: Admin. Plans Pursuant to Admin. Order No. 14," 345 Ark. Adv. app. (June 28, 2001) (per curiam) [hereinafter "In re Implementation of Amendment 80"].

3. Amendment 80 to the Arkansas Constitution appeared on the 2000 general election ballot as "Referred Amendment 3." It was approved by a vote of 431,137 (57 percent) for and 323,547 (43 percent) against. "Publisher's Notes: Ark. Const. amend. 80."

4. An elected constitutional convention proposed a new constitution for the state, including a judicial article with provisions very similar to those found in Amendment 80. See State of Arkansas, "Proposed Arkansas Constitution of 1970 with Comments: A Report to the People of the State of Arkansas by the Seventh Arkansas Constitutional Convention" (1970); and Ronald L. Boyer, "A New Judicial System for Arkansas," *University of Arkansas Law Review* 24 (1970): 221. The proposal was defeated at the 1970 general election.

5. A similar proposal was drafted by a constitutional convention in 1980, submitted to the voters, and defeated. See State of Arkansas, "Proposed Arkansas Constitution of 1980 with Comments: A Report to the People of the State of Arkansas by the Seventh Arkansas Constitutional Convention" (1980). The Arkansas General Assembly also attempted to place a constitutional amendment on the 1980 general election ballot that would have revised the limitations on jurisdiction and venue of state courts. Prior to the election, the Arkansas Supreme Court struck this proposal from the ballot. See *Wells v. Riviere,* 269 Ark. 156, 599 S.W.2d 375 (1980).

6. In 1991, the Arkansas Bar Association developed, as a part of its legislative package, a proposed judicial article to the Arkansas Constitution and sought to have the issue referred to a public vote by the General Assembly. Senate Joint Resolution 10 of 1991 was one of three amendments referred by the Joint State Agencies and Governmental Affairs Committee for full consideration by the Arkansas House and Senate. The proposal was approved by the senate, but was defeated in the House by one vote.

7. Former governor Jim Guy Tucker initiated a process in 1995 to draft and submit for voter approval a revised constitution, including a judicial article. A draft was produced and the question was submitted to the voters on whether to call a constitutional convention. Act of Oct. 19, 1995, No. 1, 1995 Ark. Acts 1. The vote failed in a special election in December of 1995.

8. Five items appeared on the 2000 general election ballot. They included constitutional amendments to allow city and county governments to issue short-term redevelopment bonds, to adjust real property assessments and provide a property tax credit, to revise the judicial article, and to establish a state lottery and casino gambling. An initiated act on tobacco settlement proceeds also appeared. Only the gambling amendment failed to secure approval by the voter. Arkansas Secretary of State, "History of Initiatives and Referenda 1938–2000," at http://sosweb.state.ar.us/bi38–00.xls (retrieved March 7, 2002).

9. What was obviously a typographical error in the final and official legislation that referred Amendment 80 to the voters resulted in the lack of a specific effective date for the amendment. Section 21 of Amendment 80 provides that the amendment shall become effective on "July, 2001." In actions by the Supreme Court and General Assembly to implement the amendment, this omission of a particular date has not been noted and the presumed effective date had been July 1, 2001.

10. See "In re Appointment of Special Supreme Court Committee to Be Known as 'Amendment 80 Committee,'" 343 Ark. app. 877 (2000) (per curiam).

11. See "In re Appointment." The members are Ronald D. Harrison, Jim L. Julian, Judge Robert J. Gladwin, Judge David B. Bogard, Judge John F. Stroud Jr., Judge Andree L. Roaf, Justice Annabelle Clinton Imber, Justice Robert L. Brown, and Chief Justice Dub Arnold, Chair.

12. Act 914 of March 19, 2001, [codified at Ark. Code Ann. § 16–10–136 (LEXIS Supp. 2001)].

13. Act 915 of March 19, 2001, (repealing Ark. Code Ann. § § 16–16–201 to -1115).

14. Act 951 of March 20, 2001.

15. Act 1582 of April 13, 2001, [codified at Ark. Code Ann. § § 9–27–213, -318, -352, -507 to -508, 510 (LEXIS Supp. 2001)].

16. Act 1789 of April 19, 2001, [codified at Ark. Code Ann. § § 7–10–101 to -103, 7–5–205, -704, 7–7103, -401, 14–42–206, 7–5–405, -407 (LEXIS Supp. 2001)].

17. "In re Adoption of Admin. Order No. 14," 344 Ark. app. 747 (2001) (per curiam).

18. See "In re Implementation of Amendment 80: Amendments to Admin. Orders," 345 Ark. Adv. app. (May 24, 2001) (per curiam).

19. See "In re Implementation of Amendment 80: Amendments to Rules of Civil Procedure & Inferior Court Rules," 345 Ark. Adv. app. (May 24, 2001) (per curiam) [hereinafter "In re Amendments"].

20. "In re Ark. Rules of Criminal Procedure 1.5 & 8.2," 345 Ark. Adv. app. (May 17, 2001) (per curiam).

21. "In re Implementation of Amendment 80: Amendments to Rules of Appellate Procedure—Civil & Rules of the Supreme Court & Court of Appeals," 345 Ark. Adv. app. (June 7, 2001) (per curiam).

22. "In re Arkansas Rules of Civil Procedures & Rules of the Supreme Court & Court of Appeals," 347 Ark. Adv. app. (Jan. 24, 2002) (per curiam).

23. "Administrative Order No. 14," para. 4(b), 344 Ark. app. 747, 750 (2001) (per curiam).

24. For an excellent review of the creation and history of Arkansas's chancery courts, see Morton Gitelman, "The Separation of Law and Equity and the Arkansas Chancery Courts: Historical Anomalies and Political Realities," *University of Arkansas at Little Rock Law Journal* 17 (1995): 215.

25. "Administrative Order No. 14."

26. "In re Implementation of Amendment 80."

27. States that continue to separate law and equity jurisdiction and maintain chancery courts are Delaware, Mississippi, and Tennessee. David Rottman et al., *State Court Organization* (Washington, D.C.: U.S. Department of Justice, 1998), 342, 361.

28. Ark. Const. amend. 80, § 19(B)(1).

29. "Administrative Order No. 14," para. 1, 344 Ark. app. at 748. Section 6 of Amendment 80 provides as follows: "Subject to the superintending control of the Supreme Court, the Judges of a Circuit Court may divide that Circuit Court into subject matter divisions, and any Circuit Judge within the Circuit may sit in any division." Ark. Const. amend. 80, § 6.

30. "Administrative Order No. 14," para. 1, 344 Ark. app. at 747–48.

31. Letter from Bob Tobin, National Center for State Courts, to J. D. Gingerich, Director, Administrative Office of the Courts, December 15, 2000, on file with author.

32. See "Administrative Order No. 14," paras. 2, 4(b), 344 Ark. app. at 748–50. After submission of the initial plans in June, 2001, subsequent plans are to be submitted by March 1 of each year following the year in which the judicial election of circuit judges is held. See para. 3, 344 Ark. app. at 749.

33. As a result, the Supreme Court failed to adopt the National Center for State Court's recommendation of a system of local administrative judges as suggested in Tobin to Gingerich. Arkansas joins New York and Wyoming as the only states with no system of administrative judges for the courts of general jurisdiction. See Rottman, *State Court Organization,* 34. In other states, administrative judges are provided a wide range of authority and responsibility. This range includes the assignment of judges, the assignment of cases, the supervision of employees, and the management of the court budget.

34. "Administrative Order No. 14," para. 2, 344 Ark. app. at 748–49.

35. Single-judge circuits include the Ninth-East, Eleventh-East, Eighteenth-West and Nineteenth-East circuits.

36. The judges in the Sixth, Tenth, and Eleventh-West circuits could not reach an agreement at the local level. In each case, more than one proposal was submitted to the Supreme Court, none of which had the support of all of the judges in the circuit.

37. See "In re Implementation of Amendment 80."

38. The Arkansas Supreme Court requested further information from judges in the Twenty-first and Twenty-third circuits.

39. Circuits whose plans were initially rejected by the Supreme Court were the First, Thirteenth, Fifteenth, Nineteenth-West and Twenty-second circuits.

40. Arkansas Judiciary, "Circuit Court Administrative Plans," at http://courts.state.ar.us/ courts/circuitplans.html (accessed August 8, 2001).

41. Note, however, that cases filed prior to January 1, 2002, that receive a case number under the former version of Administrative Order No. 2 shall maintain their original case numbers. For example, a chancery case that was filed in 2001 and received case number "E-20011" will continue to use that case number in proceedings that take place after January 1, 2002, even though the case is now being heard in the civil or domestic relations division of circuit court.

42. "Administrative Order No. 8," para. 2(c), 345 Ark. Adv. app. (May 24, 2001) (per curiam).

43. "Administrative Order No. 8."

44. "Administrative Order No. 8."

45. "Administrative Order No. 8."

46. See Ark. Const. art. 7, § 19.

47. See Ark. Const. amend. 80.

48. Act 997 of March 21, 2001, [codified at Ark. Code Ann. § 14–14–502(a)(2)(B) (LEXIS Supp. 2001)].

49. "In re Amendments."

50. "In re Amendments."

51. See "In re Amendments to Admin. Orders Numbers 8 & 14," 346 Ark. Adv. app. (Nov. 1, 2001) (per curiam).

52. Ark. Const. amend. 80, § § 7, 19.

53. Ark. Const. amend. 80, § 8.

54. "In re Implementation of Amendment 80."

55. "In re Implementation of Amendment 80."

56. "In re Implementation of Amendment 80."

57. "In re Implementation of Amendment 80."

58. "In re Implementation of Amendment 80."

History, Political Culture, and Constitutional Reform in Arkansas

1. David Easton, *A Systems Analysis of Political Life* (New York: John Wiley, 1965).

2. Vincent Ostrom, *The Political Theory of a Compound Republic* (Lincoln, Neb.: University of Nebraska Press, 1987), 70.

3. Ricahrd E. Neustadt, *Presidential Power: The Politics of* Leadership (New York: Wiley, 1960). Merle Black, David M. Kovenock, and William C. Reynolds, *Political Attitudes in the Nation and the States* (Chapel Hill, N.C.: Institute for Research in Social Science, 1974); M. Kent Jennings and Richard G. Niemi, *The Political Character of Adolescence* (Princeton, N.J.: Princeton University Press, 1974). Jennings and Niemi report that their 1965 sample of seventeen-year-olds in several American cities found that 74.5 percent had the most confidence in the national government, 13 percent had the most confidence in their states, and 11 percent had the most confidence in their local governments. Youth, however, are typically more idealistic in this regard than adults (see Robert J. Blendon, John M. Benson, Richard Morin, Drew E. Altman, Mollyann Brodie, Mario Brossard, and Matt James, "Changing Attitudes in

America," in *Why Americans Don't Trust Government*, eds. Joseph S. Nye Jr., Philip D. Zelikow, and David C. King (Cambridge Mass.: Harvard University Press, 1997), 208-9. Data from the 1968 Comparative State Elections Project, reported in Black, Kovenock and Reynolds, indicate that 44 percent of the respondents had the most confidence in the national government, 18 percent in the states, and 17 percent in local governments. This rank-order of confidence in the three levels continued to hold firm, although the percentages had changed, in the 1972 NES study, as well; see Phillip W. Roeder, *Public Opinion and Policy Leadership in the American States* (Tuscaloosa: University of Alabama Press, 1994), 41.

4. When Jennings and Niemi replicated their study of seventeen year-olds in 1973 (the year of televised Watergate hearings, vice president Spiro Agnew's plea bargain, and American withdrawal from Vietnam), the percentage of youths indicating most confidence in the national government had fallen to 27 percent, while the percentage indicating greatest confidence in state or local government had risen to 32 and 41 percent, respectively. The 1976 NES study found that local government, at 39 percent, ranked first in confidence, followed by national government at 33 percent, and state government at 28 percent; see Roeder, 41. On the erosion of public evaluation, see also Benjamin Ginsberg, *The Consequences of Consent: Elections, Citizen Control, and Popular Consent* (Reading Mass.: Addison-Wesley, 1982), 236-37 and Nye, Zelikow, and King, *Why Americans Don't Trust Government*.

5. Larry J. Sabato, *Goodbye to Good-Time Charlie: The American Governor Transformed*, 2nd ed. (Washington D.C.: Congressional Quarterly Press, 1983); Alan Rosenthal, *Legislative Performance in the States* (New York: The Free Press, 1974); ACIR, *Measuring State Fiscal Capacity* (Washington D.C.: Advisory Commission on Intergovernmental Relations, September 1986); see also Benjamin Ginsberg and Martin Shefter, *Politics by Other Means: The Declining Importance of Elections in America* (New York: Basic Books, 1990).

6. Blendon et al., "Changing Attitudes in America," 208.

7. Blendon et al., "Changing Attitudes in America;" see also Gary Orren, "Fall from Grace: The Public's Loss of Faith in Government," in Nye, Zelikow, and King, *Why Americans Don't Trust Government*, 81.

8. Diane D. Blair, *Arkansas Politics and Government: Do the People Rule?* (Lincoln Neb.: University of Nebraska Press, 1988), 122.

9. Blair, *Arkansas Politics and Government*.

10. Donald E. Whistler, "Arkansas General Assembly" (unpublished manuscript).

11. Timothy B. Donovan, Willard B. Gatewood Jr., and Jeannie M. Whayne, eds., *The Governors or Arkansas*, 2nd ed. (Fayetteville: University of Arkansas Press, 1995).

12. Roy Reed, "Orval Faubus: Out of Socialism into Realism," in *Arkansas Politics*, eds. Richard P. Wang and Michael B. Dougan (Fayetteville: M and M Press, 1997), 352-69.

13. The Arkansas Household Research Panel of the University of Arkansas at Fayetteville is a randomly selected sample of households across the state that have agreed to respond to at least four omnibus mail surveys per year. Obviously, the panel requirements and use of self-administered mail surveys result in over-representation of white, educated, older, and wealthy Arkansans.

14. Further note that when Arkansas respondents' level of confidence in various nongovernmental as well as governmental institutions is investigated, local government (46.6) continues to be preferred to institutions such as the state Legislature (40.1) and the governor's office (38.9), but fares less well than churches (80.8), medi-

cine (72.6), banks (70.8), higher education (69.0), television news (50.9), and newspapers (49.1). The only nongovernmental institutions trailing local government, the legislature, and the governor in public confidence were utilities (29.8), organized labor (28.2), and oil companies (23.1). Pairing this set of findings with those preceding, Savage and Blair conclude that "more altruistic, less remote, and more decentralized institutions receive stronger votes of confidence" from Arkansans. Robert L. Savage and Diane D. Blair, "Regionalism and Political Opinion in Arkansas: An Exploratory Survey," *Arkansas Political Science Journal* 5 no. 1 (1984): 65.

15. Savage and Blair, "Regionalism and Political Opinion in Arkansas".

16. Donald E. Whistler and Gary D. Wekkin, "The Political Socialization of Central Arkansas High School Seniors: Jennings and Niemi Revisited" (paper delivered at the annual meeting of the Arkansas Political Science Association, Russellville, Ark., February 14, 1998).

17. Roeder, *Public Opinion and Policy Leadership*, 56.

18. Tom J. Terral, *Biennial Report of the Secretary of State, Arkansas* (Little Rock: H. G. Pugh and Co., 1921), 104; Calvin R. Ledbetter Jr., George E. Dyer, Robert E. Johnston, Wayne R. Swanson, and Walter H. Nunn, *Politics in Arkansas: The Constitutional Experience* (Little Rock: Academic Press of Arkansas, 1972), 221; Blair, *Arkansas Politics and Government,* 128; Rachel O'Neal, "Voters Say No to Constitution," *Arkansas Democrat Gazette,* December 13, 1995, 1A.

19. Blair, *Arkansas Politics and Government,* 130.

20. Ledbetter, et al., *Politics in Arkansas*184.

21. Blair, *Arkansas Politics and Government,* 130; see also Robert W. Meriwether, "The Proposed Arkansas Constitution of 1970," *Nebraska Law Review* 50 (1971): 600-621.

22. Blair, *Arkansas Politics and Government,* 130.

23. Murphy Commission (Arkansas Citizens' Commission to Streamline State Government), *The Current Structure of State Government in Arkansas: Trends in Growth, Organization, and Spending* (Little Rock: Murphy Commission, 1997), 1-8.

24. Gary D. Wekkin, "'Hogtied': The Powers of the Arkansas Governor's Office" (paper presented at the annual meeting of the Arkansas Political Science Association, Pine Bluff, Ark., February 13, 1999).

25. Not to mention another elected statewide office—the state commissioner of lands—that was labeled "obsolete" almost a century ago by then-governor George Donaghey, who however failed in his declared intention to eliminate the post. See Calvin R. Ledbetter Jr., *Carpenter from Conway: George Washington Donaghey as Governor of Arkansas, 1909-1913* (Fayetteville: University of Arkansas Press, 1993), 106.

26. Such scandals can have a powerful impact upon short-run public opinion, as illustrated for example by the fall of Governor Tucker from a 63 percent favorable (compared to 16 percent unfavorable) opinion share in April 1994 to a 28 percent favorable (compared to 48 percent unfavorable) opinion share as his trial approached in March 1996; see Arthur J. Finkelstein and Associates, *Survey of Arkansas Voters* (professional consultant report prepared for the Republican Party of Arkansas), (University of Central Arkansas Archives, Conway, April 24, 1994); and Kieran Mahoney Associates, *Survey of Arkansas Voters* (professional consultant report prepared for the Republican Party of Arkansas), (University of Central Arkansas Archives, Conway, 1996). The latter sample also found that 41 percent of the respondents believed "The charges against Jim Guy Tucker are true," compared to 18 percent who disagreed, and 41 percent who either didn't know or didn't respond.

27. Kieran Mahoney Associates, *Survey of Arkansas Voters* (professional consultant report prepared for the Republican Party of Arkansas), (University of Central Arkansas Archives, Conway, May 30, 1996).

28. Kieran Mahoney Associates, *Survey of Arkansas Voters* (professional consultant report prepared for the Republican Party of Arkansas), (University of Central Arkansas Archives, Conway, August 28, 1996)

29. Center for the Study of Representation, "Arkansas Poll" (University of Arkansas, http://plsc.uark.edu/arkpoll, 1999).

30. Wekkin, "'Hogtied'."

31. The rest of the agencies have directors whose appointment is determined by statute (four agencies), appointed by boards without any confirmation (seven agencies), or appointed by boards, subject to gubernatorial confirmation (ten agencies).

32. The election of a State Commissioner of Lands, on the other hand, was endorsed by only 45 percent of the sample, inasmuch as fully 17 percent of the sample responded that the position should be eliminated (in accordance with governor George W. Donaghey's opinion).

33. See, for example, Murphy Commission (Arkansas Citizens' Commission to Streamline State Government), *The Current Structure of State Government*; Murphy Commission, *Making Arkansas' State Government Performance Driven and Accountable* (Little Rock: Murphy Commission, 1998); Keith S. Berry, *Taxes and Savings in Arkansas: A Report to the Murphy Commission* (Little Rock: Murphy Commission, 1998); John Ronald Hy and Gary D. Wekkin, *Mandate for Public Education Reform: Arkansas' Attitudes Toward Public Education, Parental Choice, Charter Schools, and Academic Performance Issues: A Report to the (Murphy) Arkansas Citizens' Commission for Streamlining State Government* (Little Rock: Arkansas Policy Foundation, May 1997); John Ronald Hy and R. Lawson Veasey, *Improving Productivity by Reducing Taxes: A Report to the Murphy Commission* (Little Rock: Murphy Commission, 1998); Charles Mazander, *The Arkansas Highway Transportation Department: Improving Performance, Restructuring, and Saving Taxpayer Dollars* (Little Rock: Murphy Commission, 1998); and Charles Morgan, *The Role of Function of State Government in Arkansas* (Little Rock: Murphy Commission, 1996).

34. Indeed, such distrust of political elites may very well help explain the other great mystery of Arkansas electoral behavior, which is the state electorate's notorious political independence, as illustrated in the confounding three-way ticket-splitting that went on during the 1968 general election (in which the state reelected the Democrat, Fulbright, to the U.S. Senate, the Republican, Rockefeller, to the governorship, and gave its electoral college votes to the third-party candidate, Wallace) and in the electoral musings of Savage and Blair, "Regionalism and Public Opinion." The two major American political parties are, after all, quasi-public utilities since they not only organize government but are protected as well as regulated in state constitutions and election laws, and their organizational members are regarded as "elites" not only by the public but also by the professional literature. See Leon Epstein, *Political Parties in the American Mold* (Madison, Wis:: University of Wisconsin Press, 1986); Herbert McCloskey, Paul J. Hoffman, and Rosemary O'Hara, "Issue Conflict and Consensus among Party Leaders and Followers," *American Political Science Review* 54 (1960): 406-427; John S. Jackson III, Barbara L Brown, and David Bositis, "Herbert McCloskey and Friends Revisited: 1980 Republican and Democratic Elites Compared to the Mass Public," *American Politics Quarterly* 10 (1982): 158-80; and Michael A. Maggiotto and Gary D. Wekkin, *Partisan Linkage in Southern Politics: Elites, Voters and Identifiers*

(Knoxville, Tenn.: University of Tennessee Press, 2000). The relationship between popular distrust of government and political partisanship/independence in Arkansas is a question worth future exploration by Arkansas political scientists.

Orval E. Faubus

1. V. O. Key Jr., *Southern Politics In State and Nation,* (Knoxville: University of Tennessee Press, 1984), 8. Populism was not restricted to the hill country, but, as Key points out, radical politics had a more marked influence in the thin-soiled uplands than in the planter-controlled Delta.

2. Bonnie Pace, interview with author, November 9, 1990, Combs, Ark.

3. Pace, interview; Orval E. Faubus, interview with author, June 14, 1988, Conway, Ark.

4. *Madison County Record* (Ark.), March 9, 1933, from the Combs news column by "Jimmie Higgins," Sam Faubus's nom de plume, March 16, 1933, article by Arch Cornett.

5. Orval E. Faubus to author, May 28, 1993.

6. Faubus speech to University of Arkansas Young Democrats, April 30, 1993, Fayetteville.

7. Faubus to author, February 11, 1993.

8. Walt W. Rostow, *The Stages of Economic Growth* (Cambridge: Cambridge University Press, 1963), 18.

9. *Arkansas Recorder,* January, 18, 1957, p. 8.

10. *Arkansas Recorder,* October 19, 1956, p. 2.

11. Key, *Southern Politics,* 666.

12. Key, *Southern Politics,* 669. For a discussion of the negative influence of race in shaping the black belt's domination of southern politics, see chapters 1 and 31.

13. Key, *Southern Politics,* 672.

14. U.S. Bureau of the Census, *Seventeenth Census of the United States, 1950, Vol. 2: Characteristics of the Population* (Washington, D.C.: Government Printing Office, 1952), pt. 4, 65.

15. Faubus, interview with author, November 29, 1993, Arkansas Educational Television Network, Conway, Ark., videocassette.

16. Faubus to John Connally, March 27, 1980, Orval Eugene Faubus Papers, Special Collections, Mullins Library, University of Arkansas (hereafter cited as OEF Papers); Faubus to author, May 27, 1994.

17. Faubus to Harry Dent, January, 10, 1973, OEF Papers.

18. Faubus memorandum to staff, October, 11, 1965, OEF Papers.

19. For various perspectives on Southern populism and some of its adherents, see the following: W. Scott Morgan, *History of the Wheel and Alliance and the Impending Revolution* (Fort Scott, Kan.: J. H. Rice & Sons, 1889); Theodore Saloutos, *Farmer Movements in the South 1865-1933* (Berkeley and Los Angeles: University of California Press, 1960); Francis Butler Simkins, *The Tillman Movement in South Carolina* (Durham, N.C.: Duke University Press, 1926); C. Vann Woodward, *Tom Watson: Agrarian Rebel* (Oxford, England: Oxford University Press, 1938); James Turner, "Understanding the Populists," *The Journal of American History* 67 (September 1980): 354-73; Robert C. McMath Jr., *Populist Vanguard: A History of the Southern Farmers Alliance* (Chapel Hill: University of North Carolina Press, 1975); John D. Hicks, *The*

Populist Revolt (Minneapolis: University of Minnesota Press, 1931); Paul Rogin, "Populism," in *The Intellectuals and McCarthyism* (Cambridge: MIT Press, 1967); Bruce Palmer, *Man Over Money: The Southern Populist Critique of American Capitalism* (Chapel Hill: University of North Carolina Press, 1980); Lawrence Goodwyn, *Democratic Promise: The Populist Moment in America* (New York: Oxford University Press, 1976); and Norman Pollack, *The Populist Mind* (Indianapolis: Bobbs-Merrill, 1967).

20. *Madison County Record,* March 9, 1933.

21. *Madison County Record,* March 16, 1933.

22. For various perspectives on the relative radicalism of southwestern Socialists, see Garin Burbank, *When Farmers Voted Red: The Gospel of Socialism in the Oklahoma Countryside, 1910-1924* (Westport, Conn.: Greenwood Press, 1976); David A. Shannon, *The Socialist Party of America,* (New York: MacMillan, 1955); James R. Green, *Grass-Roots Socialism: Radical Movements in the Southwest 1894–1943* (Baton Rouge: Louisiana State University Press, 1978); and George Gregory Kiser, "The Socialist Party in Arkansas, 1900–1912," (master's thesis, University of Arkansas, 1980).

23. Shannon, *Socialist Party in America,* 3, 35.

24. Kiser, "Socialist Party in Arkansas," 87–88, 110–11.

25. Shannon, *Socialist Party of America,* 266.

Noblesse Oblige and Practical Politics

1. *Arkansas Democrat,* April 8, 1968.

2. Taylor Branch, *Parting the Waters: America in the King Years, 1954–63* (New York: Simon and Schuster, 1988), 27–29; Peter Collier and David Horowitz, *The Rockefellers: An American Dynasty* (New York: Holt Rinehart and Winston, 1976), 101.

3. Winthrop Rockefeller to Rodman Rockefeller, May 16, 1969, Winthrop Rockefeller Collection, University of Arkansas at Little Rock Archives and Special Collections, University of Arkansas at Little Rock Library (hereafter cited as WR Papers), Record Group III, Box 571, File 3; *New York Times,* September 26, 1946; *New York Times,* April 18, 1947.

4. Winthrop Rockefeller to Robert W. Dowling, president, National Urban League, December 24, 1952, Rockefeller Family Archives, Rockefeller Archive Center, North Tarrytown, New York (hereafter cited as Rockefeller Family Archives), Record Group II, Office of the Messrs. Rockefeller (hereafter cited as OMR), National Urban League, Box 40, Folder 111.4; memo, David F. Freeman to Dana S. Creel, 27 April 1960, Rockefeller Family Archives, Record Group II, OMR, National Urban League, Box 41, Folder 111.43; Rt. Rev. Msgr. James E. O'Connell, President, Urban League of Greater Little Rock to Winthrop Rockefeller, August 14, 1967, WR Papers, Record Group III, Box 84, File 9; *New York Times,* February 16, 1956; *New York Times,* June 19, 1956.

5. Winthrop Rockefeller to John D. Rockefeller Jr., September 4, 1936, and John D. Rockefeller Jr. to Raymond B. Fosdick, president, Rockefeller Foundation, September 17, 1936, Rockefeller Family Archives, Record Group II, OMR, Rockefeller Boards, Box 26, Folder 261; Winthrop Rockefeller, "A Letter to My Son," 74–78, unpublished manuscript, WR Papers.

6. Oral history interview conducted by the Rockefeller Archive Center with James Hudson, May 1, 1973, at 30 Rockefeller Plaza, New York, New York, Rockefeller

Archive Center, Rockefeller family tape; Alvin Moscow, *The Rockefeller Inheritance* (Garden City, New York: Doubleday, 1977), 204; *New York Times,* December 6, 1946.

7. *New York Times,* September 5, 1952; *New York Times,* January 2, 1949; *New York Times,* December 22, 1948; *New York Times,* September 26, 1946; (New York) *Amsterdam News,* January 1, 1949.

8. *Arkansas Gazette,* April 13, 1956; *Arkansas Gazette*, April 23, 1956.

9. *New York Times,* October 6, 1957; *Arkansas Gazette,* October 5, 1957; Robert Sherrill, *Gothic Politics in the Deep South: Stars of the New Confederacy* (New York: Grossman, 1968), 75.

10. Closing the city's high schools shocked the more moderate citizens of Little Rock into action, and when the schools reopened in 1959, all the high schools were integrated on a limited basis. *Arkansas Gazette,* October 3, 1957; *Arkansas Gazette,* October 5, 1957; Orval Eugene Faubus, *Down from the Hills Two* (Little Rock: Democrat Printing and Lithographing, 1986), 5; Tony Freyer, *The Little Rock Crisis: A Constitutional Interpretation* (Westport, Conn.: Greenwood Press, 1984), 148; Harry S. Ashmore, *Arkansas: A History* (New York: W. W. Norton, 1978; reprint, 1984), 152, 155.

11. Belden Associates, "A Study of Voter Opinion in Arkansas October 3– October 10, 1964," WR Papers, Record Group IV, Box 73.

12. "Arkansas Republican Party Platform, 1964," WR Papers, Record Group III, Box 1, File 2; "Meet the Press" transcript, May 3, 1964, WR Papers, Record Group IV, Box 47, File 4.

13. "Meet the Press" transcript; "WR Statement Regarding Federal Guidelines," August 30, 1966, WR Papers, Record Group III, Box 30, File 3; *New York Times,* May 4, 1964.

14. Arkansas Governor's Race, 1966, breakdown of vote by counties, WR Papers, Record Group III, Box 174, File 6; *New York Times,* October 26, 1966; *New York Times,* November 10, 1966; *Arkansas Gazette,* December 13, 1966; *Arkansas Democrat,* December 18, 1966.

15. *Arkansas Gazette,* March 11, 1967.

16. Rockefeller to O'Connell, September 14, 1967, WR Papers, Record Group III, Box 116, File 2.

17. John Ward, *The Arkansas Rockefeller* (Baton Rouge: Louisiana State University Press, 1978), 165.

18. Memo, William T. Kelly, chairman, Governor's Council on Human Resources, to Rockefeller, April 29, 1968, WR Papers, Box 52, File 2c; memo, Ozell Sutton to officials, civic leaders, and concerned persons, September 13, 1968; memo, Sutton to mayors, city managers, and chiefs of police, September 13, 1968; newsletter, Governor's Council on Human Resources, December 1968, WR Papers, Record Group III, Box 116, File 2.

19. Memo, Sutton to Rockefeller, January 6, 1969; memo, Sutton to mayors, September 13, 1968; memo, Sutton to officials, September 13, 1968; newsletter, Governor's Council on Human Resources, December 1968; memo, Sutton to Rockefeller, November 19, 1968; memo, Sutton to W. Rockefeller, January 16, 1969; James A. Madison, U.S. Department of Justice, to Sutton, March 5, 1969; press release, Governor's Office, July 10, 1969, WR Papers, Record Group III, Box 88, File 11; *Arkansas Democrat,* June 16, 1968; *Arkansas Gazette,* September 18, 1968.

20. Remarks by Odell Pollard, Republican state chairman, to the Urban League of Greater Little Rock, May 12, 1967; "A Public Progress Report on Advancement of the

Negro in State Government," Arkansas Republican State Committee, September 1967, WR Papers, Record Group III, Box 43, File 3; *New York Times,* December 5, 1965; *Arkansas Democrat,* December 18, 1966; *Arkansas Democrat,* May 21, 1967.

21. W. A. Hawkins to Rockefeller, January 15, 1968, WR Papers, Record Group III, Box 97, File 1; Rockefeller to Lt. Gen. Lewis B. Hershey, Selective Service System, June 19, 1968, WR Papers, Record Group III, Box 492, File 3; Hawkins to Hon. Edward M. Kennedy, November 4, 1969, WR Papers, Record Group III, Box 489, File 3.

22. Hawkins to Truman Altenbaumer, December 6, 1968, WR Papers, Record Group III, Box 233, File 2.

23. *Arkansas Gazette,* December 31, 1970; *Arkansas Democrat,* November 11, 1969; *Arkansas Democrat,* January 30, 1970.

24. *Memphis Commercial Appeal,* April 12, 1968; *Arkansas Gazette,* November 12, 1967; *Arkansas Gazette,* August 30, 1969.

25. United Press International wire copy, WR Papers, Record Group III, Box 326, File 2.

26. Hawkins to Rockefeller, January 15, 1968, WR Papers, Record Group III, Box 97, File 1.

27. Alfredo Garcia, civil rights coordinator, to Walter Richter, regional director, Office of Economic Opportunity, Austin, Texas, November 11, 1967; Garcia to Richter, April 29, 1968, WR Papers, Record Group III, Box 323, File 3; *Arkansas Democrat,* February 5, 1967.

28. *Arkansas Gazette,* April 10, 1968; *Arkansas Gazette,* April 12, 1968; *Arkansas Gazette,* April 16, 1968; *Arkansas Democrat,* April 10, 1968; *Arkansas Democrat,* April 11, 1968; Rev. C. B. Knox, Rev. Cecil Cone, and Rev. John H. Corbitt to W. Rockefeller, April 12, 1968, WR Papers, Record Group III, Box 86, File 13.

29. *New York Times,* July 25, 1968.

30. *Arkansas Gazette,* August 30, 1969.

31. George T. Smith to Rockefeller, April 8, 1968, Arkansas Republican Party Archives, University of Arkansas at Little Rock Archives and Special Collections, University of Arkansas at Little Rock Library, Series II, Box 1 File 11; Ralph D. Scott, Director, Arkansas State Police, to Rockefeller, April 8, 1968, WR Papers, Record Group III, Box 86, File 13; telegram, Rockefeller to David Lawrence, *U.S. News and World Report,* April 18, 1968, WR Papers, Record Group III, Box 98, File 2a; Cathy Kunzinger Urwin, *Agenda for Reform: Winthrop Rockefeller as Governor of Arkansas, 1967–71* (Fayetteville: University of Arkansas Press, 1991), 106.

32. State of Arkansas, Executive Proclamation, August 10, 1968, WR Papers, Record Group III, Box 337, File 4; Ralph D. Scott to Rockefeller, August 12, 1968, WR Papers, Record Group III, Box 579, File 5; *Arkansas Democrat,* August 10, 1968; *Arkansas Democrat,* August 15, 1968; *Arkansas Gazette,* August 10, 1968; *Arkansas Gazette,* August 12, 1968; *Arkansas Gazette,* 14, 1968.

33. Patricia Washington McGraw, Grif Stockley, and Nudie E. Williams, "We Speak for Ourselves, 1954 and After," in Tom Baskett Jr., ed., *Persistence of the Spirit: The Black Experience in Arkansas* (Little Rock: Arkansas Endowment for the Humanities, 1986), 40–43; *Arkansas Gazette,* March 21, 1969; *Arkansas Gazette,* March 22, 1969; *Arkansas Gazette,* April 8, 1969.

34. *Arkansas Gazette,* April 8, 1969.

35. *Arkansas Gazette,* June 6, 1969.

36. *Arkansas Gazette,* August 11, 1969.

37. "A Special Meeting in the Governor's Conference Room in Regard to the

Racial Situation in Forrest City," transcript, August 6, 1969, WR Papers, Record Group III, Box 328, File 1; telegram, Rockefeller to Rev. E. A. Williams, August 5, 1969, WR Papers, Record Group III, Box 98, File 2a.

38. *Arkansas Gazette,* August 20, 1969. The march was cancelled by Brooks and Cooley in September. *Pine Bluff Commercial,* September 16, 1969.

39. Statement by Rockefeller, August 18, 1969, WR Papers, Record Group III, Box 116, File 2; telegram, Rockefeller to Cato Brooks Jr., August 9, 1969, WR Papers, Record Group III, Box 424; *New York Times,* August 17, 1969; *New York Times,* August 20, 1969; *Arkansas Gazette,* August 14, 1969; *Arkansas Gazette,* August 17, 1969; *Arkansas Gazette,* August 20, 1969.

40. Memo, Bob Fisher to Rockefeller, September 24, 1969; memo, Fisher to Rockefeller, September 9, 1969, WR Papers, Record Group III, Box 86, File 13; memo, Charles Allbright to John Ward, August 19, 1969, WR Papers, Record Group III, Box 116, File 2; Ralph D. Scott to Rockefeller, August 18, 1969; memo, Sgt. Jim Wooten to Scott, August 18, 1969, WR Papers, Record Group III, Box 86, File 13; *Arkansas Gazette,* August 14, 1969.

41. Memo, Scott to Lt. Col. Bill Miller, August 19, 1969; Scott to Rockefeller, August 19, 1969, WR Papers, Record Group III, Box 86, File 13; *New York Times,* August 22, 1969.

42. State of Emergency Declaration, August 22, 1969, WR Papers, Record Group III, Box 205, File 10; *Arkansas Gazette,* August 20, 1969; *Arkansas Gazette,* August 22, 1969; *Arkansas Gazette,* August 25, 1969; *Arkansas Democrat,* August 20, 1969; *Arkansas Democrat,* August 21, 1969; *Arkansas Democrat,* August 25, 1969; *Washington Post,* August 23, 1969.

43. *New York Times,* August 29, 1969; *New York Times,* August 30, 1969; State of Arkansas, Executive Department Proclamation, August 27, 1969, WR Papers, Record Group III, Box 207. File 5; *Arkansas Gazette,* August 27, 1969; *Arkansas Gazette,* August 28, 1969.

44. *Arkansas Gazette,* September 3, 1969; *Arkansas Gazette,* September 17, 1969; *Arkansas Gazette,* September 19, 1969; *Arkansas Gazette,* September 20, 1969; *Arkansas Gazette,* October 28, 1969; *Arkansas Democrat,* September 15, 1969; *Arkansas Democrat,* September 20, 1969; Memphis *Commercial Appeal,* September 18, 1969; *Commercial Appeal,* October 3, 1969.

45. *Arkansas Gazette,* November 30, 1969.

46. *Commercial Appeal,* September 18, 1969.

47. "Meet the Press" transcript.

48. "WR Statement Regarding Federal Guidelines: Given KTHV," August 30, 1966; memo, Ward to Rockefeller, August 27, 1966, WR Papers, Record Group III, Box 30, File 3; memo, Tom Eisele to Rockefeller, August 23, 1966, WR Papers, Record Group III, Box 460, File 3.

49. *Arkansas Gazette,* May 29, 1968; *Arkansas Gazette,* May 22, 1968.

50. Telegram, John W. Walker to Rockefeller, May 23, 1968, WR Papers, Record Group III, Box 608; telegram, T. E. Patterson to Rockefeller, May 27, 1968, WR Papers, Record Group III, Box 557; *Arkansas Gazette,* June 2, 1968.

51. Telegram, Rockefeller to Richard M. Nixon, June 26, 1969, WR Papers, Record Group III, Box 550, File 2; William "Sonny" Walker and Dr. Elijah E. Palnick to Rockefeller, July 2, 1969, WR Papers, Record Group III, Box 608; *New York Times,* June 28, 1969; *Arkansas Gazette,* June 28, 1969.

52. *New York Times,* July 4, 1969.

53. Jerris Leonard, assistant attorney general, to Arkansas State Board of Education, April 14, 1970; Leonard to Rockefeller, April 14, 1970; Rockefeller to Leonard, April 3, 1970, WR Papers, Record Group III, Box 521, File 1.

54. State Board of Education to T. E. Patterson, September 9, 1968, WR Papers, Record Group III, Box 323, File 1.

55. *Arkansas Gazette,* April 4, 1970; *Arkansas Gazette,* May 14, 1970; *Arkansas Gazette,* June 6, 1970; *Arkansas Gazette,* June 18, 1970; *Arkansas Gazette,* July 28, 1970; *Arkansas Gazette,* August 1, 1970; *Arkansas Gazette,* August 30, 1970; *Arkansas Gazette,* October 15, 1970.

56. *New York Times,* October 30, 1969; *New York Times,* December 14, 1969.

57. *New York Times,* September 18, 1969; Ward, *The Arkansas Rockefeller,* 176.

58. *Arkansas Gazette,* January 24, 1970.

59. Petition to Rockefeller, February 5, 1970, WR Papers, Record Group III, Box 83, File 2b; *Arkansas Gazette,* February 5, 1970; *Commercial Appeal,* February 19, 1970.

60. Memo, Dona Williams to Bob Faulkner and John L. Ward, February 20, 1970, WR Papers, Record Group III, Box 324, File 1.

61. Statement by Rockefeller, February 21, 1970, WR Papers, Record Group IV, Box 165, Folder 4.

62. Robert Faulkner, interview with author, February 9, 1988, Little Rock.

63. Memo, Greg Simon to Fisher and Charles Allbright, August 5, 1970, WR Papers, Record Group III, Box 640, File 3; Mid-South Opinion Surveys, April 20, 1970, and September 13, 1970, WR Papers, Record Group IV, Box 82; *New York Times,* July 28, 1970; *New York Times,* August 11, 1970; *New York Times,* August 26, 1970; *New York Times,* September 6, 1970; *New York Times,* September 10, 1970; *Arkansas Gazette,* February 24, 1970; *Arkansas Gazette,* September 2, 1970; *Arkansas Gazette,* September 3, 1970; *Arkansas Gazette,* September 4, 1970; *Arkansas Gazette,* September 9, 1970; *Pine Bluff Commercial,* February 24, 1970.

64. Jim Ranchino, *Faubus to Bumpers: Arkansas Votes, 1960–1970* (Arkadelphia, Ark.: Action Research, 1972), 71.

65. Numan V. Bartley and Hugh D. Graham, *Southern Politics and the Second Reconstruction* (Baltimore: Johns Hopkins University Press, 1975), 122, 149. Numan and Bartley base this figure on the voting returns of predominantly black precincts in Little Rock. Racially mixed precincts were eliminated from their analysis. In *Faubus to Bumpers,* Jim Ranchino asserts that Rockefeller held onto 88 percent of the black vote statewide. But Ranchino does not explain how he arrived at this figure. Rockefeller almost certainly received a higher percentage of the black vote in the Delta than he did in Little Rock. The only two counties he carried in 1970 were in the Delta. Statewide, the percentage of the black vote carried by Rockefeller probably lies somewhere between the 49 and 88 percent figures. But the statistical analysis necessary to verify this is not available. Numan V. Bartley and Hugh D. Graham, *Southern Elections County and Precinct Data, 1950–1972* (Baton Rouge: Louisiana State University Press, 1978), x, 353; Ranchino, *Faubus to Bumpers,* 72, 74.

66. *Arkansas Gazette,* March 5, 1973; *New York Times,* March 5, 1973.

67. Cal Ledbetter Jr., interview with author, September 15, 1987, Little Rock.

68. *Arkansas Democrat,* September 9, 1969.

69. *Arkansas Democrat,* September 12, 1969; *Arkansas Democrat,* September 17, 1969.

70. *Arkansas Democrat,* April 11, 1968; *Arkansas Gazette,* April 12, 1968; *Arkansas Gazette,* April 16, 1968.

71. J. H. Bond, regional director, to Rockefeller, December 12, 1968, WR Papers, Record Group III, Box 420, File 1.

72. Report, U.S. Commission on Civil Rights, August 1965, WR Papers, Record Group III, Box 84, File 3.

73. *Arkansas Gazette,* May 25, 1968; *Arkansas Gazette,* September 24, 1967; J. B. Garrett, Superintendent, Arkansas Training School for Girls, to Bob Scott, governor's office, July 29, 1968, WR Papers, Record Group III, Box 334, File 4.

74. *Arkansas Gazette,* September 27, 1967.

The Arkansas Electorate

1. The descriptive information in this section is based on two surveys taken in 1968 and 1970, and U.S. Census material. Both surveys were taken in selected precincts according to current demographic and political information. Random samples were then taken in each precinct of registered voters. All surveying was conducted through personal interviews. The 1968 survey was taken in November, immediately after the general election, and contained over 3,200 samples; the 1970 survey was taken the month before the November general election and 2,500 persons were interviewed.

2. It is highly unusual for more votes to be cast in the race for governor than in the presidential contest. Only 609,593 votes were counted in the Humphrey/Nixon/Wallace election. The reason for the discrepancy was an error in reporting Jefferson County results by the Jefferson County Election Commission. Some ten thousand votes were somewhere omitted in the presidential race.

"What Women Wanted"

1. Cynthia Harrison, *On Account of Sex: The Politics of Women's Issues* (Berkeley: University of California Press, 1988); Vicky Randall, *Women and Politics* (New York: St. Martin's Press, 1982); Patricia Zelman, *Women, Work, and National Policy: The Kennedy-Johnson Years* (Ann Arbor, Mich.: UMI Research Press, 1982); Barbara Ryan, *Feminism and the Women's Movement: Dynamics of Change in Social Movement Ideology and Activism* (New York: Routledge, 1992); Esther Peterson, "The Kennedy Commission," in Irene Tinker, ed. *Women in Washington: Advocates for Public Policy* (Beverly Hills: Sage Publications, 1983). For a discussion of women's commissions, or women's policy units, in comparative perspective, see also Dorothy McBride Stetson and Amy G. Mazur, eds., *Comparative State Feminism* (Thousand Oaks, Calif.: Sage, 1995).

2. Margaret Mead and Frances Balgley Kaplan, eds., *American Women: The Report of the President's Commission on the Status of Women and Other Publications of the Commission* (New York: Scribner, 1965).

3. For an account of the Women's Bureau (a unit within the U.S. Department of Labor) as the central national-level women's policy agency in the United States, see Dorothy McBride Stetson, "The Oldest Women's Policy Agency: The Women's Bureau in the United States," in Stetson and Mazur, *Comparative State Feminism,* 254–71.

4. Mim Kelber, ed., *Women and Government: New Ways to Political Power* (Westport, Conn.: Praeger, 1994); Catherine East, "Newer Commissions," in Tinker, *Women in Washington;* Martin Gruberg, "Official Commissions on the Status of

Women: A Worldwide Movement," unpublished paper, Annual Meeting of the American Political Science Association, New Orleans, September 1973; U.S. Women's Bureau, *National Conference of Governors' Commissions on the Status of Women, Progress and Prospects: The Report of the Second National Conference of Governors' Commissions on the Status of Women* (Washington, D.C.: U.S. Women's Bureau, 1966); Kathryn Clarenbach and Marian L. Thompson, *Handbook for Commissions on the Status of Women* (Madison: University of Wisconsin-Extension, in cooperation with the Women's Bureau, Employment Standards Division, U.S. Department of Labor, 1974); Harrison, *On Account of Sex.*

5. *Arkansas Gazette,* January 18, 1964, 2A.

6. *Arkansas Gazette,* November 13, 1965, 2A.

7. *Arkansas Gazette,* November 16, 1967, 1B.

8. *Arkansas Gazette,* February 9, 1968, 1B.

9. See also Sara Murphy, "Distaff Note: The Ladies of the Legislature," *Arkansas Gazette,* January 29, 1967, 5E.

10. Jeane Lambie, telephone interview with author, June 25, 2000. See also Cathy Kunzinger Urwin, *Agenda for Reform: Winthrop Rockefeller as Governor of Arkansas, 1967–1971* (Fayetteville: University of Arkansas Press, 1991), especially chapter 5.

11. Dorothy Stuck, telephone interview with author, June 26, 2000.

12. A state women's commission was revived by the Arkansas legislature in 1997. By 1999, its members had voted that it not be renewed, however, due to conflicts over abortion, gay foster parenting, and contraceptive access for teens—conflicts not unlike those of the 1970s. See Leslie Newell Peacock, "Divided They Sit," *Arkansas Times,* December 4, 1998, 8; Jan Cottingham, "Women's Commission Votes to Dissolve," *Arkansas Times,* February 2, 1999, 10; *Arkansas Democrat-Gazette,* February 28, 1999, 1B, 3B.

13. Diane D. Blair, personal interview with author, Fayetteville, Arkansas, May 10, 1998.

14. Blair, interview.

15. Blair, interview; Governor's Commission on the Status of Women (GCSW), *The Status of Women in Arkansas* (Little Rock: GCSW, 1973). Other staffers listed in the 1973 report of the GCSW were Eleanor Crawford and Carolyn Auge.

16. GCSW, *The Status of Women,* i.

17. *Arkansas Gazette,* May 31, 1971, 19A; *Arkansas Gazette,* December 12, 1971, 1B; *Arkansas Democrat,* June 2, 1971, 8A.

18. *Arkansas Gazette,* September 22, 1971, 1B.

19. *Arkansas Gazette,* September 22, 1971, 1B.

20. Lambie, interview.

21. *Arkansas Gazette,* October 1, 1971, 9A.

22. *Arkansas Gazette,* December 12, 1971, 7A.

23. *Arkansas Gazette,* December 12, 1971, 7A

24. Blair, interview.

25. *Arkansas Gazette,* December 12, 1971, 17A.

26. The Arkansas legislature granted women the right to vote in primary elections only. But in a one-party state this meant that white women, at least, might influence elections in a meaningful way. All of the important decisions were made among Democrats in the party primaries (which throughout the South were limited to white participation until 1944). The general election in the south was long a mere formality. See V. O. Key Jr., *Southern Politics in State and Nation* (New York: Knopf, 1949).

27. See, for example, Zelman, *Women, Work, and National Policy;* Harrison, *On Account of Sex;* Vivien Hart, *Bound by Our Constitution: Women, Workers, and the Minimum Wage* (Princeton, N.J.: Princeton University Press, 1994); and Judith Sealander, *As Minority Becomes Majority: A Federal Reaction to the Phenomenon of Women in the Work Force, 1920–1963* (Westport, Conn.: Greenwood Press, 1983).

28. See *Arkansas Gazette,* November 28, 1970, 8A; *Arkansas Gazette,* March 19, 1971, 8A; *Arkansas Gazette,* December 12, 1971, 17A; see also, Murphy, "Distaff Note."

29. Henry M. Alexander, *Government in Arkansas: Organization and Function at State, County, and Municipal Levels* (Little Rock: Pioneer Press, 1963), chapter 9; IWY Research Project, *Arkansas Women Together: A Study of the Status of Women in Arkansas* (Little Rock: IWY Research Project, 1977). Late enfranchisement (relative to men) and restricted access to the professions, however, did not mean that Arkansas women were ever "apolitical" on the scale often presumed. For an excellent example of female political activism in twentieth-century Arkansas, see Sara Alderman Murphy (former GCSW vice chair), *Breaking the Silence: Little Rock's Women's Emergency Committee to Open Our Schools, 1958–1963* (Fayetteville: University of Arkansas Press, 1997).

30. *Arkansas Gazette,* December 12, 1971, 17A

31. Diane Kincaid and Gordon Herrington, *Women: Rights, Roles, Reasons: Final Report* (Little Rock: GCSW, 1973).

32. Kincaid and Herrington, *Final Report,* 2.

33. Kincaid and Herrington, *Final Report,* 2; *Banner-News* (Magnolia), January 24, 1972, 1, 5.

34. Kincaid and Herrington, *Final Report,* 12.

35. Kincaid and Herrington, *Final Report,* 12.

36. Nan Snow, interview with author, Little Rock, May 13, 1998.

37. Kincaid and Herrington, *Final Report;* GCSW, *The Status of Women.*

38. See, for example, *Arkansas Gazette,* January 16, 1972, 10A; *Arkansas Gazette* February 23, 1972, 16A; *Arkansas Gazette* April 11, 1972, 7A; *Arkansas Gazette* July 2, 1972, 16A; *Arkansas Gazette* September 12, 1972 1B; *Arkansas Gazette* April 22, 1973, 1D, 12D,; *Arkansas Gazette* June 1, 1973, 33A; and *Arkansas Gazette* July 13, 1973, 1B.

39. *Arkansas Gazette* June 19, 1971, 12A.

40. Blair, interview.

41. *Arkansas Gazette,* February 7, 1973, 14A. See also Mead and Kaplan, *American Women;* Harrison, *On Account of Sex;* and Peterson, "The Kennedy Commission."

42. *Arkansas Gazette,* May 31, 1971, 19A.

43. News reports reveal, for example, that most, if not all, of the women speakers at the conferences were married. See "Commitment to Human Responsibility," *Arkansas Alumnus,* April 1972, 8–9; *Banner News,* January 24, 1972, 1, 5.

44. Blair, interview.

45. *Arkansas Gazette,* December 12, 1975, 20B.

46. Snow, interview, 1998; Tracy McKay, "The Equal Rights Amendment in Arkansas: Activism, Fundamentalism, and Traditionalism" (honors thesis, Hendrix College, 1997); Brenda Blagg, "Diane Kincaid Blair," in Arkansas Press Women Association, Inc., *Horizons: 100 Arkansas Women of Achievement* (Little Rock: Rose Publishing, 1980); see also Carol Felsenthal, *The Sweetheart of the Silent Majority: The Biography of Phyllis Schlafly* (Garden City, N.Y.: Doubleday and Company, 1981).

47. Jane Mansbridge, *Why We Lost the ERA* (Chicago: University of Chicago Press, 1986), especially chapter 2.

48. McKay, "The Equal Rights Amendment in Arkansas"; *Arkansas Gazette,*

January 11, 1973, 4A; *Arkansas Gazette,* January 13, 1973, 12A; *Arkansas Gazette,* January 16, 1973, 1A, 8A (quotes). See also David W. Brady and Kent L. Tedin, "Ladies in Pink: Religion and Political Ideology in the Anti-ERA Movement," *Social Science Quarterly* 56 (March 1976): 564–75.

49. Though *Gazette* accounts do not note it, a *Democrat* reporter interviewed three female opponents to the ERA who were present at its January 12, 1973, debut on the floor of the House. They were Una Piver and Cynthia Scott Dorsey of Jacksonville and Hope Andrews of Sylvan Hills. See *Arkansas Democrat,* January 11, 1973, 10A (photograph with caption), January 12, 1973, 1A-2A.

50. See *Arkansas Gazette,* January 17, 1973, 1B; *Arkansas Gazette,* January 18, 1973, 6A.

51. *Arkansas Gazette,* January 16, 1973, 8A.

52. *Arkansas Gazette,* January 16, 1973, 8A.Jones also introduced a resolution proposing a two-year study of the amendment before consideration of ratification. *Arkansas Gazette,* January 17, 1973, 4A. The full text of the amendment was: "Section 1. Equality of rights under the law shall not be denied or abridged by the United States or by any state on account of sex. Section 2. The Congress shall have the power to enforce, by appropriate legislation, the provisions of this article."

53. See *Arkansas Gazette,* January 18, 1973, 6A; *Arkansas Gazette,* February 1, 1975, 6A,; *Arkansas Gazette,* February 10, 1975, 4A; *Arkansas Gazette,* February 18, 1975, 6A (editorial); and *Arkansas Gazette,* February 24, 1975, 4A (editorial). Other newspapers whose editorial staff came out in favor of ratification included the *Baxter Bulletin* at Mountain Home, the Searcy *Daily Citizen,* the Dumas *Clarion,* and the Benton *Courier.*

54. *Arkansas Democrat,* February 14, 1975, 1A, 12A,; *Arkansas Democrat,* February 15, 1975, 1A, 3A.

55. *Arkansas Democrat,* February 18. 1975, 6A (editorial).

56. *Arkansas Gazette,* February 15, 1975, 3A.

57. *Arkansas Gazette,* February 12, 1975, 6A.

58. *Arkansas Gazette,* January 24, 1973, 8A.

59. *Arkansas Gazette,* February 2, 1973, 1A.

60. *Arkansas Gazette,* January 26, 1973, 1A.

61. *Arkansas Gazette,* January 21, 1973, 4A; *Arkansas Gazette,* January 24, 8A.

62. U.S. Congress, Senate, Judiciary Committee, Equal *Rights for Men and Women,* 92d Congress, 2d sess., 1972, 13.

63. *Arkansas Gazette,* January 24, 1973, 8A

64. *Arkansas Gazette,* January 23, 1973, 4A.

65. *Arkansas Gazette,* January 11, 1973, 4A.

66. *Arkansas Gazette,* January 18, 1973, 5A.

67. *Arkansas Gazette,* March 2, 1972, 3A.

68. *Arkansas Gazette,* January 29, 1975, 4A.

69. Bob Lancaster, "The Fight for Inequality," *Arkansas Gazette,* January 17, 1973, 1B.

70. Rachael Roland McKinney, telephone interview with author, June 25, 2000.

71. Nan Snow, telephone interview with author, June 26, 2000.

72. Lancaster, "The Fight," 1B.

73. *Arkansas Gazette,* March 14, 1975, 24A.

74. *Arkansas Gazette,* January 25, 1973, 8A; *Arkansas Gazette,* January 26, 1973, 1A,

2A; *Arkansas Gazette,* February 2, 1973, 1A, 2A; *Arkansas Gazette,* February 7, 1973, 3A; *Arkansas Gazette,* February 22, 1973, 3A.

75. *Arkansas Gazette,* November 15, 1973, 9A.

76. *Arkansas Gazette,* December 22, 1973, 17A.

77. Shirley McFarlin, telephone interview with author, June 26, 2000.

78. *Arkansas Gazette,* August 25, 1974, 1A, 2A.

79. *Arkansas Gazette,* August 28, 1974, 13A.

80. *Arkansas Gazette,* September 10, 1974, 8A.

81. *Arkansas Gazette,* December 11, 1974, 10A.

82. *Arkansas Gazette,* January 12, 1975, 8A. It is difficult to determine whether it was the women involved or the legislators they were lobbying who had treated the issue flippantly in Christie's estimation. Christie did later chide the *Gazette* for its "cheap shots at both opponents and proponents" in an editorial glibly ridiculing the "antic debate" over the ERA. See *Arkansas Gazette,* February 10, 1975, 10A; *Arkansas Gazette,* February 18, 1975, 6A. Also listed as being members of the "Men for the ERA" group's steering committee were James B. Blair, whom Diane Kincaid later married, and Bill Clinton, "a lawyer and law professor at the University of Arkansas Law School and unsuccessful candidate for Congress."

83. *Arkansas Gazette,* January 21, 1975, 3A.

84. *Arkansas Gazette,* January 12, 1977, 16A.

85. *Arkansas Gazette,* February 1, 1975, 3A.

86. *Arkansas Gazette,* February 12, 1975, 10A; *Arkansas Gazette,* February 15, 1975, 1A, 3A; *Arkansas Democrat,* February 14, 1975, 1A.

87. *Arkansas Gazette,* March 4, 1975, 4A. Hoffman never revealed whether he was for or against the amendment. He repeatedly said only that he had introduced the measure "for the people in my district who asked me to do it." See *Arkansas Gazette,* January 16, 1975, 4A.

88. Blagg, "Diane Kincaid Blair," 14.

89. The specific phrase with which Van Dalsem was "credited" was "We don't have any of these university women in Perry County, but I'll tell you what we do up there when one of our women starts poking around in something she doesn't know anything about. We get her an extra milk cow. If that doesn't work, we give her a little more garden to tend. And then if that is not enough, we get her pregnant and keep her barefoot." Passage quoted in Diane D. Blair *Arkansas Politics and Government: Do the People Rule?* (Lincoln: University of Nebraska Press, 1988), 6. For a more detailed treatment of Van Dalsem, see Robert Thompson, "Barefoot and Pregnant: The Education of Paul Van Dalsem," *Arkansas Historical Quarterly* 57 (Winter 1998): 377–407.

90. *Arkansas Democrat,* January 12, 1973, 1A. Pro-ERA activist McFarlin vaguely recalled the conflict, asserting "Oh, we were going to win until . . . members got in a fight," (McFarlin, interview).

91. This is not to say that the GCSW's other activities went unnoticed by the women's policy community at the time. Rhobia Taylor, the regional director of the U.S. Women's Bureau in Dallas, was quoted in June of 1973 as calling Arkansas a "five-star state" of the region. She said Blair's GCSW had accomplished more than any other in her five state area. See *Arkansas Gazette,* June 1, 1973, 33A.

92. *Arkansas Gazette,* December 12, 1975, 20B.

93. At least one, the Washington State Women's Council, was terminated by citi-

zen action. See Janine A. Parry, "Putting Feminism to a Vote: The Washington State Women's Council (1963–1978)," *Pacific Northwest Quarterly* 91 (Fall 2000): 171–82.

94. Gruberg, "Official Commissions."

95. U.S. Women's Bureau, Commissions *on the Status of Women: A Progress Report* (Washington, D.C.: U.S. Women's Bureau, Department of Labor, 1975); Lyndon B. Johnson School of Public Affairs, *Regional Workshops for Texas Women: Commissions on the Status of Women* (Austin: The Status of Women Policy Research Project, LBJ School of Public Affairs, University of Texas at Austin, 1976). These sources incorrectly include Arkansas as among those states losing women's commissions in 1976.

96. *Arkansas Gazette,* January 4, 1976, 2D.

97. *Arkansas Gazette,* January 18, 1976, 8C.

98. *Arkansas Gazette,* January 18, 1976, 8C.

99. *Arkansas Gazette,* January 18, 1976, 8C; *Arkansas Gazette,* December 5, 1976, 6A.

100. *Arkansas Gazette,* January 11, 1977, 1A, 2A.

101. *Arkansas Gazette,* January 12, 1977, 2A; *Arkansas Gazette,* January 18, 1977, 3A.

102. *Arkansas Gazette,* January 27, 1977, 1A, 2A; *Arkansas Gazette,* January 28, 1977, 5A; *Arkansas Gazette,* January 29, 1977, 14A.

103. *Arkansas Gazette,* February 3, 1977, 22A.

104. *Arkansas Gazette,* February 17, 1977, 1B.

105. *Arkansas Gazette,* March 1, 1977, 1A, 2A.

106. *Arkansas Gazette,* March 1, 1977, 1A, 2A.

107. *Arkansas Gazette,* March 4, 1977, 1B.

108. *Arkansas Gazette,* March 2, 1977, 6A; see also *Arkansas Democrat,* March 1, 1977, 1A, 14A.

109. *Arkansas Gazette,* March 2, 1977, 16A.

110. *Arkansas Gazette,* March 19, 1977, 12A.

111. *Arkansas Gazette,* April 10, 1977, 28A.

112. *Arkansas Gazette,* December 12, 1976, 6A; *Arkansas Gazette,* June 12, 1977, 22A.

113. Though no longer formally associated with the GCSW, Blair was a member and a temporary convener of the Arkansas Committee for International Women's Year and a delegate to the National Women's Conference in Houston; see Blagg, "Diane Kincaid Blair."

114. *Arkansas Gazette,* June 11, 1977, 1A, 2A.

115. *Arkansas Gazette,* June 12, 1977, 21A.

116. *Arkansas Gazette,* June 13, 1977, 1A, 2A. The heated situation was not particular to Arkansas. Such meetings all over the country were criticized by antifeminists as being pro-ERA, prochoice, and progay rights, charges usually confirmed by the feminist women elected to attend the national meeting in Houston. For more detail about the nationwide struggle surrounding the IWY meetings, see Ellen Goodman, "New Radicals in Feminism," *Seattle Times,* November 9, 1977, A12. Though expressly profeminist, it is revealing.

117. *Arkansas Gazette,* June 13, 1977, 1A, 2A.

118. See Mansbridge, *Why We Lost,* chap. 2; *Arkansas Gazette,* October 7, 1978, 1A, 2A. For examples of continued Arkansas activism on the ERA issue, see *Arkansas Gazette,* January 20, 1979, 4A; *Arkansas Gazette,* March 15, 1979, 14A; *Arkansas Gazette,* July 1, 1981, 9A; *Arkansas Gazette,* December 2, 1981, 17A; *Arkansas Gazette,* June 30, 1982, 1B, 4B; and *Arkansas Gazette,* August 8, 1982, 1A, 12A.

119. *Arkansas Gazette,* October 7, 1979, 1A, 2A; *Arkansas Gazette,* August 8, 1982, 1A, 2A.

120. IWY Research Project, *Arkansas Women Together.*

121. McKay, "The Equal Rights Amendment in Arkansas"; Governor's Commission on the Status of Women (GCSW) Legal Task Force, *The Legal Status of Women in Arkansas: Questions and Answers (on) Women and the Law* (Little Rock, GCSW, 1972); Governor's Commission on the Status of Women (CSW), *Handbook on Legal Rights for Arkansas Women* (Little Rock: GCSW, 1977); Arkansas Department of Labor, Office on Women and Work, *Handbook on Legal Rights for Arkansas Women* (Little Rock: Arkansas Department of Labor, 1980, 1987).

122. IWY Research Project, *Arkansas Women Together.*

123. IWY Research Project, *Arkansas Women Together;* Blair, interview.

124. Blair, interview. According to Blair, "we were advancing an egalitarian agenda for women. These other women wanted to put women back into a subordinate status . . . [at least] what we saw as a subordinate status."

125. Betsey Wright, personal communication with author, May 24, 2000.

126. Lambie, interview; McFarlin, interview; Snow, interview, 2000.

127. Blair, interview; Wright, personal communication; Snow, interview, 1998.

128. Snow, interview, 1998; Snow, interview, 2000.

129. Blair, interview.

130. Snow, interview, 1998; Snow interview, 2000.

131. McFarlin, interview.

132. *Arkansas Gazette,* December 22, 1973, 17A.

133. *Arkansas Gazette,* February 14, 1978, 4A.

134. *Arkansas Gazette,* July 10, 1978, 3A.

135. See East, "Newer Commissions."

136. Marilyn Simmons, telephone interview with author, June 27, 2000.

137. *Arkansas Gazette,* February 15, 1972, 8A; *Arkansas Gazette,* March 2, 1973, 3A.

138. *Arkansas Gazette,* January 21, 1973, 4A.

139. Snow, interview, 2000.

140. *Arkansas Democrat,* January 12, 1977, 16A.

141. *Arkansas Gazette,* January 24, 1973, 2A.

A Crime Unfit to be Named

1. In this sense, "queer" is a technical term used in queer theory and studies. The word, which obviously has several definitions, is here meant as a descriptor, encompassing both those who would claim to be gay and lesbian, as well as those who engage in homosexual sex but would not necessarily label themselves as gay or lesbian. For a useful treatment of the term as employed in gay and lesbian studies, see John Howard, *Men Like That: A Southern Queer History* (Chicago: University of Chicago Press, 1997), xviii–xix.

2. *Cabaret* won several Academy Awards and was hailed by many critics as a cinematic masterpiece. Actor Michael York's depiction of a British man dealing with his homosexuality is considered the first gay character in mainstream cinema not to be a "sexual pervert" or the stereotypical "sissy."

3. David Bianco, *Gay Essentials* (Los Angeles: Alyson, 1999), 228–30.

4. "Cohabitation Tax, Other Bills Aimed at 'Deviate Acts,'" *Arkansas Gazette,* January 23, 1977, A6.

5. "Cohabitation Tax." Speaking of cohabitating couples, Tyer declared: "They may have a desire for each other, physically and maybe even spiritually, but they don't want to conform. This country was built on conformity."

6. "Cohabitation Tax"; George Bentley, "New Justice Code Turns the Tables for Novel Ruling," *Arkansas Gazette,* March 26, 1976, A16.

7. Bentley, "New Justice Code.".

8. Bentley, "New Justice Code."

9. Bentley, "New Justice Code."

10. Bentley, "New Justice Code."

11. Ibid.

12. "Jail not Public Place, Charges Dismissed," *Arkansas Gazette,* June 25, 1976, A5.

13. *Carter & Burkhead v. State,* 255 Ark. 255, 500 S.W.2d (1973).

14. Arkansas's first sodomy law mandated a life sentence for whites found guilty. Blacks, whether free or slave, faced a much harsher punishment: death. After the Civil War, the death penalty provision disappeared under mysterious circumstances, having never been debated or acted on by the legislature. George Painter, "The Sensibility of Our Forefathers: The History of Sodomy Laws in the United States" http://www. sodomylaws.org/sensibilities/html. Also see *Revised Statutes of the State of Arkansas* (Boston: Weeks, Jordan and Co., 1838), 182.

15. Rafael Guzman, "1976 Criminal Code: General Principles," *Arkansas Law Review* 30 (1976): 111–13. Guzman, a law professor at the University of Arkansas, Fayetteville, served as a member of the Arkansas Criminal Code Revision Commission.

16. David Frum, *How We Got Here: The 70's, the Decade That Brought You Modern Life (For Better or Worse)* (New York: Basic, 2000), 205–6.

17. Guzman, "1976 Criminal Code," 111–13. The most notable and recognizable revision came in legal classification. Each felony was placed in one of four classifications: A, B, C, or D. Each misdemeanor was placed in one of three classifications: A, B, or C. For a complete list of revisions as adopted by the legislature, consult the *Arkansas Statutes Annotated,* 41–901–1101 (Criminal Code of 1976).

18. "Cohabitation Tax."

19. "Cohabitation Tax."

20. "Sodomy Bill Amended to Define Restrictions; House Passage Urged," *Arkansas Gazette,* January 26, 1977, A3.

21. "Sodomy Bill Amended."

22. "Sodomy Bill Amended."

23. "Sodomy Bill Amended."

24. "Bill Fails, Would Punish Tenants for No Notice," *Arkansas Gazette,* January 27, 1977, B1.

25. "House Supports Abortion Foes With Voice Vote," *Arkansas Gazette,* February 11, 1977, A1. The only representatives to vote against the bill were Jodie Mahony of El Dorado and Henry Wilkins of Pine Bluff; Ted Holder, interview with author, Little Rock, AR, September 23, 2001.

26. "Senate Passes Measures in Drive to Adjourn," *Arkansas Gazette,* March 17, 1977, A21.

27. *The Advocate,* vol. 210, April 1977, 7.

28. "Deadline Nears on Sex Bill Veto; Inquiries Made," *Arkansas Gazette,* March 28, 1977, B6.

29. Ark. Code Ann. § 5–14–122.

30. Lawrence Yancey, telephone interview with author, January 31, 2002. In an interview, Pryor claimed he had no recollection of signing the sodomy bill into law; he declined to comment beyond that. David Pryor, telephone interview with author, January 31, 2002.

31. Yancey, interview.

32. "Resolution Draws Call from Aide," *Arkansas Gazette*, March 30, 1977, B1.

33. The letter, dated April 10, 1977, was sent directly to Governor Pryor and was signed by the clerk of the executive board, S. D. Hacker. The letter is included in David Pryor's gubernatorial papers, series 2, Gubernatorial Correspondence, subseries 2, box 63, Special Collections Division, University of Arkansas Libraries, Fayetteville.

34. Dudley Clendinen and Adam Nagourney, *Out for Good: The Struggle to Build a Gay Rights Movement in America* (New York: Simon and Schuster, 1999), 291–338.

35. Tina Fetner, "Working Anita Bryant: The Impact of Christian Anti-Gay Activism on Lesbian and Gay Movement's Claims," *Social Problems* 48 (2001): 411. The quotation was taken from a direct mail fundraising letter from Bryant's Save Our Children organization, which existed from 1977 until 1979. The emphasis is in the original.

36. Clendinen and Nagourney, *Out for Good,* 299.

37. Jim Ranchino, "The Arkansas of the '70s: The Good Ole Boy Ain't Whut He Used to Be," *Arkansas Times,* September 1977, 40.

38. Yancey, interview.

39. Ross Dennis, "We Hold These Truths to be Self Evident . . ." *Lincoln Ledger* (Star City, Ark.), January 5, 1978, A2; Thomas Roark, "I Want to Clear Things Up" *Lincoln Ledger,* January 12, 1978, A 2; Ross Dennis, "An Open Letter to the Readers" *Lincoln Ledger,* January 12, 1978, A 1; Doug Smith, "Orange-juice Horseshoe Is Dropped Rapidly" *Arkansas Gazette,* January 19, 1978, B 1.

40. Clendinen and Nagourney, *Out for Good,* 329.

41. "She's 'Prolife,' Not 'Antigay,' Singer Asserts" *Arkansas Gazette,* October 22, 1978, A 16.

42. *Bowers v. Hardwick,* 478 United States 186 (1986), 6–7.

43. "High Court Upholds Georgia Sodomy Law," *Arkansas Democrat* (Little Rock), July 1, 1986, A 1.

44. *Bowers v. Hardwick,* 15–16. Chief Justice Warren Burger, and justices Lewis F. Powell, William H. Rehnquist, and Sandra Day O'Connor concurred. Justice Harry Blackmun wrote the dissenting opinion and was joined by justices William J. Brennan, Thurgood Marshall, and John Paul Stevens.

45. *Bowers v. Hardwick,* 17–18.

46. William Raspberry, "Enforcement of Sodomy Law Difficult," *Arkansas Democrat,* July 8, 1986, A 6.

47. "The Sodomy Ruling," *Arkansas Democrat,* July 17, 1986, A10.

48. The riots following a police raid at the Stonewall Inn on June 28, 1969, are considered to be the beginning of the modern gay rights movement. For a detailed account of the riots and their social ramifications, see Martin Duberman, *Stonewall* (New York: Dutton, 1993).

49. By July 2002, Arkansas was one of only six states with sodomy laws applying solely to same-sex behavior. The others were Missouri, Michigan, Kansas, Texas, and Oklahoma. Missouri, when adopting its new criminal code, simply let the sodomy law cross over. The Missouri Supreme Court decided in 1977 that the phrase "crime against nature" was understood by the majority of the population of the state and that

the law, which still treated sodomy as felony carrying a life sentence, did not need to be rewritten. *Griffith v. State of Missouri,* 504 S.W. 2nd 324 (1977).

50. The laws were struck down as follows: St. Paul on April 25, 1978; Wichita on May 9, 1978; and Eugene, Oregon, on May 23, 1978; Clendinen and Nagourney, *Out for Good,* 316–19, 327–29.

51. Mark Oswald, "Committee Rejects Sodomy Law Repeal," *Arkansas Gazette,* January 31, 1991, A1, A3; John Hoogester, "Deputies Acting to Remove Gays from Rest Area," *Arkansas Gazette,* February 2, 1991B1.

52. For a discussion of sodomy laws and their social impact, see John D'Emilio, *Sexual Politics, Sexual Communities: The Making of a Homosexual Minority in the United States, 1940–1970* (Chicago: University of Chicago Press, 1983), 42–44.

53. *Northwest Arkansas Times* (Fayetteville), March 31, 1983.

54. Seth Blomeley, "Seven Sue to Void State Sodomy Law," *Arkansas Democrat-Gazette,* January 29, 1998, B2.

55. *Jegley v. Picado et. al.,* 2002 Ark. LEXIS 401.

56. Traci Shurley, "Justices Strike Down Sodomy Law," *Arkansas Democrat-Gazette,* July 5, 2002, A1.

57. Shurley, "Justices Strike Down Sodomy Law."

The Big Three of Late-Twentieth-Century Arkansas Politics

1. David Broder, "The GOP Earthquake," *Washington Post National Weekly Edition,* November 14–20, 1994, 6.

2. See, for example, Diane D. Blair, *Arkansas Politics and Government: Do the People Rule?* (Lincoln: University of Nebraska Press, 1988), 69–87, 264–80.

3. For additional details on Pryor's record as governor see Diane Blair, "David Hampton Pryor," in *The Governors of Arkansas,* eds. Timothy P. Donovan and Willard B. Gatewood Jr. (Fayetteville: University of Arkansas Press, 1981), 242–47.

4. For additional details on Bumpers's gubernatorial record see Dan Durning, "Dale Leon Bumpers," in *The Governors of Arkansas,* 235–41.

5. For additional details on Senate accomplishments, chairmanships, and voting records see Michael Barone and Grant Ujifusa, *The Almanac of American Politics, 1994* (Washington, D.C.: National Journal, 1993), 59–61; and *Politics in America, 1994,* ed. Phil Duncan (Washington, D.C.: Congressional Quarterly, 1993), 81–87.

6. Mary McGrory, "Is Bumpers the Answer for the Democratic National Committee," *Washington Post,* December 10, 1988; Simon quoted in *Arkansas Gazette,* January 27, 1987, 6A. See also William Greider, "Of Virtue, Quality, and the White House," *Rolling Stone,* March 31, 1983, 9–10; and "Senator Bumpers for President in 1984," *Arkansas Gazette,* December 9, 1982.

7. The most thorough treatment of Clinton's first gubernatorial term is in Phyllis F. Johnston, *Bill Clinton's Public Policy for Arkansas: 1979–80* (Little Rock: August House, 1982). A summary of Clinton's subsequent gubernatorial record and extensive bibliographic guide to additional materials can be found in Diane D. Blair, "William Jefferson Clinton," in *The Governors of Arkansas,* ed. Timothy P. Donovan, Willard B. Gatewood Jr., and Jeannie M. Whayne (Fayetteville: University of Arkansas Press, 1995).

8. *U.S. News and World Report,* December 21, 1987, 52–53.

9. *Newsweek,* July 1, 1991, 27.

10. For this and many similar anti-Arkansas charges by Clinton's opponents in the 1992 contest, see Diane D. Blair, "Arkansas: Ground Zero in the Presidential Race," in *The 1992 Presidential Election in the South,* eds. Robert P. Steed, Laurence W. Moreland, and Tod A. Baker (Westport, Conn.: Praeger, 1994), 103–118.

11. Analyses of the validity of such charges and countercharges include Jerry Dean, "Bush Hits Clinton at Home, But is He on Target?" *Arkansas Democrat-Gazette,* September 17, 1992; David Lauter and James Gerstenzang, "Accuracy of Bush, Clinton Accusations," *Los Angeles Times,* October 11, 1992, A36, A38.

12. On campaign contributions see *Arkansas Democrat-Gazette,* December 29, 1992, B1; Clinton's election night comments in *Arkansas Democrat-Gazette,* November 4, 1992, A15.

13. For Bumpers's and Pryor's legislative success rates see Robert Johnston and Dan Durning, "The Arkansas Governor's Role in the Policy Process, 1955–79," *Arkansas Political Science Journal* 2 (1981): 16–39. Clinton's legislative success rates of 83 percent, 90 percent, and 100 percent documented in *Arkansas Gazette,* May 15, 1983; *Arkansas Gazette,* April 7, 1985; and *Arkansas Gazette,* April 1, 1991.

14. A recent example is in Senator Bumpers' commencement address at Arkansas State University, August 5, 1994.

15. David Pryor, telephone interview with author, January 2, 1995. Notes in author's possession. When Pryor's brother took the daughter of Ouachita County's only known Republican, Skidmore Willis, to the movies, Pryor's father brought him home with a reprimand.

16. Excerpts from speech by Senator Dale Bumpers to U.S. Chamber of Commerce, Washington, D.C., April 3, 1984, in author's possession.

17. Speech by Gov. Bill Clinton to Conference on Early Childhood Issues, Frankfort, Kentucky, May 11, 1987, in author's possession.

18. Speech by Senator David Pryor delivered to the Old State House Museum Associates, Little Rock, November 18, 1988, in author's possession.

19. The depth and strength of the progressive, populist Arkansas tradition is described and explained in Roy Reed, "Clinton Country," *New York Times Magazine,* September 6, 1992, 32. See also Blair, *Arkansas Politics and Government,* 93–95, 270–72.

20. "Gov. Bill Clinton's Inaugural Address," January 9, 1979, in author's possession.

21. "Remarks Made by Senator David Pryor on Saturday, February 17, 1990, Announcing His Bid for Re-election to the United States Senate," in author's possession.

22. Related by Bumpers to William R. Kincaid on stage at Fayetteville High School commencement, May, 1984, notes in author's possession.

23. See Rex Nelson, "On the road with David Pryor," *Arkansas Magazine, Arkansas Democrat,* April 26, 1987; "Folksy, Caring Image Major Forces Behind Pryor's Success," *Arkansas Democrat,* February 18, 1990.

24. Blair, *Arkansas Politics and Government,* 269–70.

25. For details on the Arkansas governor's appointive powers see "Arkansas Boards and Commissions, A Fact Sheet," (Little Rock: Arkansas League of Women Voters, 1987); Diane D. Blair, "Gubernatorial Appointment Power: Too Much of a Good Thing?" *State Government* 55 (Summer 1982), 88–91.

26. For additional details see Blair, *Arkansas Politics and Government,* 80–81.

27. On the importance of the Marianna clinic, see "Lee County Clinic Defied Times," *Arkansas Gazette,* September 19, 1991, 1A.

28. "Ex-Republican's Tennessee Link Led to White House," *Arkansas Democrat-Gazette,* November 22, 1994.

29. Number estimated by Henry Woods, special projects and intern coordinator for Senator Bumpers and Senator Pryor.

30. On the organizational weakness of parties in one-party states, see V. O. Key Jr., *Southern Politics in State and Nation* (New York: Random House, 1949), 15–18; on the particular "paralysis and disorganization" in Arkansas, see 183–204.

31. In terms of local organizational strength, Arkansas Democrats were ranked forty-fourth in the nation, Republicans fortieth, by James L. Gibson, Cornelius P. Potter, John F. Bibby, and Robert J. Huckshorn, "Whither the Local Parties?" *American Journal of Political Science* 29 (1985), 152, 154–55.

32. From notes taken by author at event, Kelly's Barn, Fayetteville, Arkansas, October 23, 1993, notes in author's possession.

33. Statement by Senator Dale Bumpers, Little Rock, Arkansas, April 5, 1983, typescript in author's possession.

34. See "Mr. Clinton Moved the State Forward," *New York Times,* September 5, 1994.

35. *U.S. Congressional Record,* October 8, 1994, S15002–S15005.

36. John Brummett, *High Wire: From the Back Roads to the Beltway, the Education of Bill Clinton,* (New York: Hyperion, 1994), 235.

37. For additional details see Anne McMath, *The First Ladies of Arkansas* (Little Rock: August House, 1989), 219–37.

38. McMath, *The First Ladies of Arkansas,* 248–56. See also Rex Nelson, *The Hillary Factor: The Story of America's First Lady* (New York: Gallen Publishing Group, 1993).

39. See "Clinton, Bumpers Had a Scare in Light Plane," *Arkansas Gazette,* January 10, 1988; John Brummett, "Plane Scare Simply Part of the Job," *Arkansas Gazette,* January 12, 1988.

40. John Brummett, "Republican Newspaper," *Arkansas Times,* November 5, 1992.

Outsiders and the Amateur Legislature

1. Students of political science are familiar with the emphasis in the literature on congressional studies. Recent impressions, however, bolstered by the greater number of political scientists working with state data, suggest that there are an increasing number of studies on state legislative politics being published. While this may be true, we found in a survey of the articles published from 1980 through the first two issues of 1985 in the *American Political Science Review* and the *Journal of Politics* but eleven articles that dealt with state legislative politics, compared to forty-five on the Congress. For these two prestigious journals, the emphasis on congressional studies continues.

2. Douglas C. Chaffey and Malcolm E. Jewell, "Selection and Tenure of State Legislative Party Leaders: A Comparative Analysis," *The Journal of Politics* 34, no. 4 (November, 1972).

3. Council of State Governments, *The Book of the States* 1984–85 Vol. 25 (Lexington, Ky: The Council of State Governments, 1984).

4. Comparing some of the structural characteristics of the Arkansas and Rhode Island general assemblies with the California legislature is revealing. The biennial salary for California legislators is $56,220 while it is $15,000 and $600 for Arkansas

and Rhode Island legislators respectively. In terms of staff, California legislators have available central staff in the legislature as well as individual staff in the legislature and in their home districts. Arkansas and Rhode Island legislators have access to central staff but must either share support staff with other legislators year round (Rhode Island) or, in the Arkansas legislator's case, may employ individual part-time staff through his or her regular session or interim maintenance allowance ($308 weekly in session; $420 monthly interim). Length of session provides perhaps the starkest structural contrast among these legislatures. The Arkansas General Assembly meets biennially for sixty days, although regular sessions are almost always a bit longer. The Rhode Island General Assembly is constitutionally mandated for sixty days and members are not paid for additional days in session. The California legislature, on the other hand, is in session on a year-round basis.

5. *The Book of the States,* 1984–85 specifically notes the following legislatures as professional bodies according to their criteria of time in session, compensation, and occupational self-definition of members: California, Illinois, Massachusetts, Michigan, New Jersey, New York, Ohio, Pennsylvania, and Wisconsin.

6. Nelson W. Polsby. "The Institutionalization of the U.S. House of Representatives," *American Political Science Review* 62, no. 1 (March 1968); Malcolm E. Jewell and Samuel L. Patterson, *The Legislative Process in the United States* (New York: Random House, 1977); T R. Reid, *Congressional Odyssey: The Saga of a Senate Bill* (San Francisco: W. H. Freeman, 1980); Eric Redman, *The Dance of Legislation* (New York: Simon and Schuster, 1973); Erwin L. Levine and Elizabeth M. Wexler, *PL 94–142, An Act of Congress* (New York: McMillan Publishing Co., Inc., 1981).

7. Ronald J. Hrebenar and Ruth K. Scott, *Interest Groups Politics in America* (Englewood Cliffs, New Jersey: Prentice-Hall, 1982).

8. John J. Carroll and Arthur English, "Governing the House: Leadership of the State Legislative Party" paper delivered at the 1981 Annual Meeting of the Midwest Political Science Association, Cincinnati, Ohio, April 16–18, 1981.

9. John J. Carroll and Arthur English, "Rules of the Game in Ephemeral Institutions: U.S. State Constitutional Conventions," *Legislative Studies Quarterly* 6, no. 2 (May 1981).

10. Arthur English and John J. Carroll, *Citizens Manual to the Arkansas General Assembly* (Little Rock, Arkansas: Institute of Politics and Government, 1983); Robert E. Johnston and Mary Story, "The Arkansas Senate, An Overview," *Arkansas Political Science Journal* 4, no. 1 (Winter 1983), 69–80.

11. John Comner, ed. *Nonpartisanship in the Legislative Process: Essays on the Nebraska Legislature* (Washington: University Press of America, 1978).

12. Loren P. Beth and William C. Harvard, "Committee Stacking and Political Power in Florida," *Journal of Politics* 23, no. 2 (1961); Linda Goss, "Leadership Influence in a One-Party Legislature: The Arkansas Senate" (unpublished independent study paper, Department of Political Science, University of Arkansas at Little Rock, 1985).

13. English and Carroll, *Citizens Manual to the Arkansas General Assembly.*

14. Ralph K. Huitt, "The Outsider in the Senate: An Alternative Role," *American Political Science Review* 55, no. 2 (1961); Samuel C. Patterson, "The Role of the Deviant in the State Legislative System," *Western Political Quarterly* 14, no. 2 (1961).

15. The practice of midwifery in Arkansas has been defined in several ways by law and administrative regulation. In 1952 the State Board of Health acting under the authority of Acts 1913, No. 96 (Arkansas Statutes of 1974) promulgated rules and

regulations which said "The term midwife shall be held to mean any female other than a physician who shall attend or agree to attend any woman during childbirth and who shall accept any pay or other remuneration for services." According to Act 838, adopted in 1983, "The practice of lay midwifery means and includes any act or practice of attending women at or during childbirth." And according to the regulations promulgated on August 3, 1984, by the Arkansas Department of Health, a lay midwife is "any person, other than a physician or licensed nurse midwife who shall manage care during the ante-partum, intrapartum or postpartum periods; or who shall advertise as a midwife by signs, printed cards or otherwise. This definition shall not be construed to include unplanned services provided under emergency, unplanned circumstances."

16. Zoe Oakleaf, "A Study of White Witches" (unpublished paper for the Comprehensive Examination in the Field of Social History, Dept. of History, University of Iowa, 1976).

17. According to the U.S. Bureau of Census, *County and City Data Book,* 1983, the percentage of black population in each of the six counties in which midwifery was legalized is Chicot, 52.9; Monroe, 40.8; Phillips, 52.9; Lee 54.8; St. Francis, 46; and Woodruff, 31.

18. U.S. Bureau of the Census, *County and City Data Book* (Washington, D.C.: Government Printing Office, 1983).

19. We averaged the per capita incomes of the six counties in which midwifery was legalized to derive a per capita for these counties of $6,908.

20. Sarah Hudson, "Thoroughly Modern Midwives: Black 'Granny' Midwives and Public Health in Arkansas 1920 to the Present" (unpublished History Departmental Essay: Yale University, 1984).

21. Hudson, "Thoroughly Modern Midwives."

22. Hudson, "Thoroughly Modern Midwives."

23. The regulations specifically indicated, in accordance with Act No. 96 of 1913, Section 28, that a fine of not less than ten dollars nor more than one hundred dollars be assessed or imprisonment not exceeding one month, or both.

24. Dr. Byron Hawkes, former Director of the Maternal Division in the Arkansas Health Department, telephone interview with English, June 5, 1985.

25. Sherry Gibson, a Dermott community activist, telephone interview with English, September 2, 1983.

26. Chapter 72–604 of the Arkansas Statutes notes a number of occupations that are exempt from the Medical Practices Act, although they may be subject to other pertinent state laws, for example, physician therapist, osteopath, cosmetologist. Midwifery was not included in the statute.

27. Senator Jack Gibson, telephone interview with English, September 4, 1983.

28. *County and City Data Book,* 1983.

29. Testimony by Carolyn Vogler before the Senate's Public Health, Welfare and Labor Committee, February 2, 1983.

30. Arthur English attended a workshop of the Arkansas Association of Midwives in October, 1982, at the Delta Maternity Center. Attending that meeting were about eight midwives, not including two grannies who briefly stopped in.

31. Senator Gibson represents District 35 in the Arkansas Senate, which consists of Desha, Drew, and parts of Ashley and Chicot counties.

32. Gibson, interview.

33. For an example of this strategy, see Vogler's letter to the editor, "Hospitals and Doctors, Yes, but Not Actual Care," *Arkansas Gazette,* September 16, 1982.

34. See "An Apology to Vogler," *Arkansas Gazette* (September 25, 1982).

35. "An Apology to Vogler."

36. English and Carroll, *Citizens Manual to the Arkansas General Assembly.*

37. The other state to have passed a creation-science law was Louisiana. The Arkansas law was found unconstitutional in the case of *McLean, et al. vs. the Arkansas Board of Education, et al.,* U.S. District Court, Eastern District Arkansas, January 5, 1982.

38. *Rules of the House of Representatives of the State of Arkansas* (1977). Committee on Rules, G. W. "Buddy" Turner Jr., chairman.

39. Alan Rosenthal, *Legislative Life* (New York: Harper and Row, 1981). Rosenthal's data from 1963 to 1974 show that amateur legislatures pass a substantially higher percentage of bills introduced than professional legislatures, although certain legislatures do not fit the generalization. Georgia and Arkansas, for example, had .60 and .58 rate of adopted bills; Nebraska, .63; South Dakota, .51; and Idaho, .55. On the other hand, Rhode Island during this period only had a .20 rate, Wyoming, .38, and Mississippi, .36. On the professional legislature side, all of those noted by the 1984–85 *The Book of the States* had rates of .26 and below, with the exception of California and Illinois, which had rates of .42 and .43 respectively. More recent data drawn from *The Book of the States* show that Arkansas, for the 1981 session, had a .63 adoption rate, California, for the 1980–82 session, had a .48 rate; and Rhode Island, for its 1981 annual session including resolutions had a .43 rate and a .52 rate for the 1982 session.

40. English and Carroll, *Citizens Manual to the Arkansas General Assembly.*

41. Ken LeMatis, lobbyist for the Arkansas Medical Association, telephone interview with English, September 11, 1983.

42. See statements of Carolyn Vogler, Father Joe Blitz, and Dr. John Wolverton in favor of SB203 before the Public Health, Welfare, and Labor Committee of the Arkansas General Assembly, February 2, 1983.

43. Gibson, interview.

44. See "Senate Approves Bill to Legalize Midwifery," *Arkansas Gazette,* February 25, 1983.

45. See "Physician Opposition Kills Bill to Legalize Midwifery," *Arkansas Gazette,* March 9, 1983.

46. "Physician Opposition Kills Bill."

47. "Physician Opposition Kills Bill."

48. See "Clinton Signs Midwife Bill, Cites Concern," *Arkansas Gazette,* March 29, 1983. It is interesting to note that Clinton also signed into law that same day a bill which permitted nurse-midwives to practice in the state under the regulation of the state nursing board. That bill had been introduced by the medical community to short-circuit the lay midwifery bill. It also is interesting to note that Clinton had unexpectedly been upset by Frank White in the 1980 gubernatorial election because of what many thought was inattention to voter interests. Clinton regained the governorship in 1982 after apologizing for his mistakes. His attention to the midwifery issue therefore suggests that he did not wish to repeat his earlier mistake and risk alienating the large number of citizens living in Southeastern Arkansas who were most directly affected by the bill.

49. English and Carroll, *Citizens Manual to the Arkansas General Assembly;*

Donald E. Whistler and Charles DeWitt Dunn, "Institutional Representation and Institutional Accountability in the Arkansas General Assembly," *Arkansas Political Science Journal* 4, no. 1 (Winter 1983).

50. John C. Wahlke et al., *The Legislative System: Explorations in Legislative Behavior* (New York: John Wiley and Sons, 1962); John J. Carroll and Arthur English, "Rules of the Game in Ephemeral Institutions: U.S. State Constitutional Conventions," *Legislative Studies Quarterly* 6, no. 2 (May 1981).

51. Robin Warshaw, "The American Way of Birth: High-Tech Hospitals, Birthing Center or No Options at All," *Ms* 13, no. 3 (September 1984).

52. Carolyn Vogler, telephone interview with English, September 11, 1983.

53. On the effect of party on voting see Susan Welch and Eric H. Carlson, "The Impact of Party on Voting Behavior in a Non-partisan Legislature," *American Political Science Review* 67 no. 3, (September, 1993): 854–67; and John J. Carroll and Arthur English, "Constitution-Making Roles and Delegates Behavior," *Polity* 17, no. 3, (Spring 1985): 586–94.

54. Whistler and Charles Dunn, "Institutional Representation and Institutional Accountability," 47; Richard F. Fenno Jr., *Home Style: House Members in Their Districts* (Boston: Little Brown and Company, 1978).

55. Vogler, interview, September 11, 1983, and February 20, 1984. This quote was repeated to Vogler by John B. Currie, the consumer representative on the State Medical Board who heard Joe K. Verser, Secretary of the Medical Board, say it in a meeting after the midwifery bill passed.

Arkansas: More Signs of Momentum for Republicanism

1. Diane D. Blair, "Arkansas: Emerging Party Organizations," in *Southern Party Organizations and Activists,* eds. Charles D. Hadley and L. Bowman (Westport, Conn.: Praeger, 1995).

2. For fuller analyses of the key political happenings in Arkansas during this era, see Jay Barth, Diane D. Blair, and Ernie Dumas, "Arkansas: Characters, Crises, and Partisan Change," in *Southern Politics in the 1990s,* ed. Alexander P. Lamis (Baton Rouge: Louisiana State University Press, 1999); Jay Barth, "Arkansas: The Last Hurrah for a Native Son," in *The 1996 Presidential Election in the South: Southern Party Systems in the 1990s,* eds. Laurence W. Moreland and Robert P. Steed (Westport, Conn.: Praeger, 1997); and Jay Barth, Todd Shields, and Janine Parry, "Arkansas: Nonstop Action in Post-Clinton Arkansas," in *The 2000 Presidential Election in the South,* eds. Robert P. Steed and Laurence W. Moreland (Westport, Conn.: Praeger, 2002).

3. Diane D. Blair, "The Big Three of Late–Twentieth Century Politics: Dale Bumpers, Bill Clinton, and David Pryor" *Arkansas Historical Quarterly* 54 (Spring 1995): 53–79.

4. For a full discussion of the nature of Arkansas's state and local party organizations at the midpoint of the decade under consideration, see Diane D. Blair and W. Jay Barth, "Arkansas," in *State Party Profile: A 50-State Guide to Development, Organization, and Resources,* eds. Daniel S. Ward and Andrew Appleton (Washington, D.C.: Congressional Quarterly Press, 1996).

5. Jack Bass and Walter DeVries, *The Transformation of Southern Politics* (New York: New American Library, 1977), 40.

6. On the purge of "Rockefeller Republicans" after the 1980 election cycle, see

Alexander P. Lamis, *The Two-Party South,* exp. ed. (New York: Oxford University Press, 1988), 120–30.

7. Andrew M. Appleton, and Daniel S. Ward, "Understanding Organizational Innovation and Party-Building," in *The Changing Role of Contemporary American Parties,* eds. Daniel Shea and John Green (Lanham, N.C.: Rowman and Littlefield, 1994).

8. Blair and Barth, "Arkansas," 29.

9. See the Arkansas Poll, University of Arkansas, fall 1999, at http://plsc.uark.edu/arkpoll/fall99/policy/GUN3.HTM.

10. It is important to note that while the same population of activists was used in 2001 as in 1991 for the Democrats—all county party chairs and committee members—and a list that was more expansive in terms of counties covered for the Republicans than in 1991 was employed for that party, the number of individuals on those mailing lists was significantly smaller. This suggests that both parties may have culled their lists to only the most loyal—and therefore, most active—party activists. This does raise questions related to the exactness of the 2001 replication on these questions.

Arkansas: Still Swingin' in 2004

1. The authors wish to thank a host of readers, but especially Hal Bass and Ann Clemmer, for their helpful suggestions. All errors in fact or interpretation rest with the authors.

2. For overviews and analysis of contemporary Arkansas political patterns, see Jay Barth, Diane D. Blair, and Ernie Dumas, "Arkansas: Characters, Crises, and Change," in *Southern Politics in the 1990s,* ed. Alexander P. Lamis (Baton Rouge: Louisiana State University Press, 1999); Gary D. Wekkin, "Arkansas: Electoral Competition and Reapportionment in the 'Land of Opportunity,'" in *The New Politics of the Old South: An Introduction to Southern Politics* 2nd ed., eds. Charles S. Bullock III and Mark J. Rozell (New York: Rowman & Littlefield, 2005); and Diane D. Blair and Jay Barth, *Arkansas Politics and Government: Do the People Rule?* 2nd ed. (Lincoln, Neb.: University of Nebraska Press, 2005).

3. *Arkansas Times,* July 11, 2003; *Commercial Appeal,* September 15, 2003; Arkansas News Bureau, July 14, 2003; *Arkansas Democrat-Gazette,* September 18, 2003; Arkansas News Bureau, September 18, 2003.

4. *Washington Post,* October 13, 2003.

5. Arkansas News Bureau, September 18, 2003.

6. The *State,* January 7, 2004; Arkansas News Bureau, September 28, 2003.

7. *Arkansas Democrat-Gazette,* September 18, 2003.

8. *Arkansas Democrat-Gazette,* April 7, 2004.

9. Arkansas News Bureau, May 4, 2004; Arkansas News Bureau, August 4, 2004.

10. *Arkansas Democrat-Gazette,* May 13, 2004.

11. *Arkansas Times,* September 9, 2004; *Arkansas Times,* March 21, 2004.

12. *Arkansas Business,* November 1, 2004.

13. *Arkansas Democrat-Gazette,* April 28, 2004; Arkansas News Bureau, May 4, 2004.

14. Arkansas News Bureau, August 29, 2004.

15. *Arkansas Democrat-Gazette,* March 15, 2004.

16. Arkansas News Bureau, August 5, 2004.

17. Arkansas News Bureau, August 4, 2004; *Washington Post,* August 5, 2004.

18. Arkansas News Bureau, September 10, 2004.

19. Arkansas News Bureau, September 22, 2004.

20. Democratic Party of Arkansas, *2004 Post Election Report* (Little Rock: Democratic Party of Arkansas, 2005).

21. Arkansas News Bureau, October 30, 2004; *Arkansas Democrat-Gazette,* October 6, 2004.

22. Democratic Party of Arkansas, *Post Election Report.*

23. Democratic Party of Arkansas, *Post Election Report,* 21

24. Arkansas News Bureau, September 11, 2004; *Arkansas Democrat-Gazette,* September 21, 2004.

25. *Arkansas Democrat-Gazette,* October 2, 2004.

26. *Arkansas Democrat-Gazette,* October 8, 2004.

27. Tim Davis, "Same-Sex Marriage: The Social Wedge Issue of the New Century?" (unpublished manuscript, Harvard University, 2005).

28. Arkansas News Bureau, March 5, 2004.

29. *Arkansas Democrat-Gazette,* September 25, 2004.

30. *New York Times,* November 1, 2004.

31. Arkansas News Bureau, November 1, 2004.

32. *Washington Post,* November 1, 2004.

33. Janine A. Parry and William D. Schreckhise, *The Arkansas Poll 2004: Summary Report* (Fayetteville, Ark.: Diane D. Blair Center of Southern Politics and Society, 2004).

34. Janine A. Parry and William D. Schreckhise, "Political Culture, Political Attitudes, and Aggregated Demographic Effects: Regionalism and Political Ideology in Arkansas," *Midsouth Political Science Review* 5 (2001): 61–75.

35. Byron E. Shafer and Richard G. C. Johnston. "The Transformation of Southern Politics Revisited: The House of Representatives as a Window," *British Journal of Political Science* 31 (Oct. 2001): 601–25.

36. For a comprehensive look at the 2000 election in Arkansas, see Jay Barth, Janine A. Parry, and Todd G. Shields, "Arkansas: Nonstop Action in Post-Clinton Arkansas," in ed. Robert P. Steed and Laurence W. Moreland, *The 2000 Presidential Election in the South* (Westport, Conn.: Praeger, 2002).

37. Barth, Parry, and Shields, "Arkansas: Nonstop Action."

38. Blair and Barth, *Arkansas Politics and Government.*

39. Parry and Schreckhise, *The Arkansas Poll 2004.* The prospect of presidential coattails did not look promising either, with Bush's statewide—and rural swing county—approval rating hovering stubbornly at 50 percent.

40. Associated Press State and Local Wire, September 20, 2004; Associated Press State and Local Wire, November 20, 2004.

41. *Arkansas Democrat-Gazette,* October 6, 2004.

42. Unless otherwise indicated, data on various demographic and other voter groups are drawn from the exit poll data from the 2004 National Election Pool, conducted by Edison Media Research and Mitofsky International.

43. *USA Today,* January 31, 2005.

44. The overwhelming African American support for Kerry is particularly striking considering some evidence of diminished enthusiasm for his candidacy among this crucial voting group during the year; see *Salon.com,* October 27, 2004.

Education Reform in Arkansas

1. *Lake View School District No. 25 v. Tucker,* 92–5318 (Pulaski County Chancery Court Ark. 1994).

2. *Lake View School District No. 25 v. Huckabee,* 2001 92–5318 (Pulaski County Chancery Court Ark. 2001).

3. *Lake View School District No. 25 v. Huckabee,* 91 S.W.3d 472 (Ark. 2002).

4. *Rose v. Council for Better Education, Inc.*, 790 S.W.2d 186 (Ky. 1989).

5. Governor Mike Huckabee, "State of the State Address," January 14, 2003. Available online at http://www.arkansas.gov/governor/media/releases/press/011403–1.html. Retrieved January 9, 2007.

6. Huckabee, "State of the State Address."

7. Special Masters' Report to the Supreme Court of Arkansas, *Lake View School District No. 25 v. Huckabee,* S.W.3d (Ark. 2005).

8. *Lake View School District No. 25 v. Huckabee,* S.W.3d (Ark. 2005).

9. Rob Morrow, "Court Leaves Lake View Case Open, Masters Reappointed," *Arkansas News Bureau,* December 1, 2006. Available online at http://arkansasnews.com/archive/2006/12/01/News/338670.html. Retrieved January 8, 2007.

10. National Commission on Excellence in Education. *A Nation at Risk: A Report to the Nation.* (Washington, D.C.: U.S. Government Printing Office, 1983).

11. *Quality Counts 1999: Rewarding Results, Punishing Failure.* Available online at http://counts.edweek.org/sreports/qc99. Retrieved January 9, 2007. A summary of subsequent *Education Week* rankings can be accessed online at http://www.uark.edu/ua/oep/briefs/quality_counts_2006.pdf.

12. Achieve, Inc., *Closing the Expectations Gap, 2006,* report released February, 2006. Available online at http://www.achieve.org/files/50-statepub-06.pdf. Retrieved January 8, 2007.

13. Keith B. Richburg, "Arkansan Defends Tests for Teachers; Need to Oust 'Incompetents' Cited," *Washington Post,* July 13, 1985, A3; see also Robert L. Kennedy, "Arkansas Teacher Testing: A Penny for Your Scores," paper presented at the Annual Meeting of the American Evaluation Association (Boston, Mass., October 14–17, 1987); George J. Church, "Is Bill Clinton For Real?" *Time,* January 27, 1992. Available online at http://www.time.com/time/magazine/article/0,9171,1101920127–158882,00.html. Retrieved January 8, 2007.

14. The Education Trust, *Telling the Whole Truth (or Not) About High School Graduation: New State Data,* report released December 22, 2003. Available online at http://www2.edtrust.org/NR/rdonlyres/4DE8F2E0–4D08–4640-B3B0–013F6 DC3865D/0/tellingthetruthgradrates.pdf. Retrieved January 8, 2007.

CONTRIBUTORS

JAY BARTH is the M. E. and Ima Graves Peace Distinguished Professor of Politics and director of civic engagement projects at Hendrix College. He is the coauthor (with the late Diane D. Blair) of the second edition of *Arkansas Politics and Government: Do the People Rule?* (University of Nebraska Press, 2005). His articles have appeared in such journals as *American Politics Research, Political Research Quarterly, Political Psychology, Political Behavior, Women and Politics,* and *State Politics and Policy Quarterly.*

DIANE D. BLAIR studied and taught political science at the University of Arkansas for more than thirty years. She wrote *Arkansas Politics and Government: Do the People Rule* (now in a second edition with Jay Barth) and edited *Silent Hattie Speaks: The Personal Journal of Senator Hattie Caraway,* in addition to authoring and coauthoring dozens of scholarly journal articles and book chapters, mainly on the subjects of Arkansas politics and women in politics. Her public service also was considerable, including substantial contributions to the Arkansas Governor's Commission on the Status of Women, the Arkansas Political Science Association, and the National Corporation for Public Broadcasting.

LARRY BRADY is the research and court services director for the Arkansas Administrative Office of the Courts. He earned a bachelor's degree at the University of Arkansas in 1977 and his law degree from Washington University in 1980. Prior to his service at the AOC he was in private practice in Little Rock.

JOHN J. CARROLL is emeritus professor of political science at the University of Massachusetts Dartmouth. He has also taught at the University of Detroit and Providence College. His research interests include state government and constitutional processes, with a special emphasis on civil liberties. His work has appeared in a number of journals, among them *Polity* and *Legislative Studies Quarterly.*

ART ENGLISH is a professor of political science at the University of Arkansas at Little Rock. His research has appeared in *Polity, Legislative Studies Quarterly, American Review of Politics, MidSouth Journal of Political Science, Arkansas Political Science Journal, State Legislatures, National Civic Review,* and *Spectrum.* He has earned several university and community awards for public service.

J. D. GINGERICH has served as the director of the Arkansas Administrative Office of the Courts since 1988. He received his undergraduate degree from the University of Central Arkansas, his law degree from the University of Arkansas, and a postgraduate degree in international law from the University of Bristol in England. Prior to going to the AOC he served as chief legal counsel and professor of political science at UCA.

CAL LEDBETTER is a professor emeritus in political science at the University of Arkansas at Little Rock. He served five terms in the Arkansas House of Representatives and was a delegate and a vice president of the Arkansas Constitutional Convention of 1979–80. His research has focused on Arkansas governors and Arkansas constitutions, and he is the author of eighteen articles published in the *Arkansas Historical Quarterly*. Other articles have appeared in the *Arkansas Law Review, Social Science Journal, Arkansas Political Science Journal*, and *National Civic Review*. He has written a biography of Arkansas Governor George Donaghey entitled *The Carpenter from Conway*.

ROBERT W. MERIWETHER is an emeritus professor of education, history, and political science at Hendrix College, where he taught from 1959 to 1993. In addition to authoring many scholarly publications, Meriwether served as an elected delegate to an Arkansas Constitutional Convention, a member of the state Ethics Commission and the state Board of Election Commissioners, and as a Justice of the Peace in Faulkner County, among other positions. He also directed the Arkansas Governor's School from 1981 to 1982.

WILLIAM H. MILLER is an associate professor of public administration, chair of the public administration program and director of the DPA program at the University of Illinois at Springfield. His research focuses on political and economic minorities and public policy analysis. His work has been published in *Public Administration Review, American Review of Public Administration, State and Local Government Review*, and elsewhere.

JANINE A. PARRY is associate professor of political science and director of the Arkansas Poll at the University of Arkansas. Her research on state politics, elections and participation, and gender and politics has appeared in *Political Behavior, State Politics and Policy Quarterly, Social Science Quarterly*, the *Arkansas Historical Quarterly*, and many other outlets.

PATSY HAWTHORN RAMSEY has a sociology degree from Ouachita Baptist University, a master's in history from the University of Arkansas, and currently is working on an Ed. D. in higher education curriculum at the University of Arkansas at Little Rock. She is an instructor in the University of Central

Arkansas's Department of History, where she serves as the social studies education program coordinator and the state coordinator of National History Day in Arkansas.

JIM RANCHINO studied and taught political science at Ouachita Baptist University. In addition to his teaching, scholarship, and service duties at OBU, he operated a polling and political research firm and served as a regular commentator on Arkansas politics for local, state, and national media.

ROY REED is a professor emeritus of journalism at the University of Arkansas. He was a reporter at the *Arkansas Gazette* during the Faubus years. He spent most of his newspaper career as a national and foreign correspondent for the *New York Times*. He is the author of *Faubus: The Life and Times of an American Prodigal.*

GARY W. RITTER holds the 21st Century Chair in Education Policy in the Department of Education Reform at the University of Arkansas, where he serves as the director of the Office for Education Policy. His articles on issues such as teacher pay, school accountability, school finance, and racial integration in schools have appeared in such journals as *Education Finance and Policy, Review of Educational Research, Education Next, Educational Evaluation and Policy Analysis, Journal of Education Finance, Georgetown Public Policy Review, Educational Leadership, Black Issues in Higher Education, Journal of Research in Education, International Journal of Testing,* and *Education Week.*

WILLIAM D. SCHRECKHISE is an associate professor of political science at the University of Arkansas. He has published articles on public policy, public law, and public opinion in journals such as *Social Science Quarterly, Public Administration Quarterly, Public Integrity, American Review of Politics, Justice Journal,* and *State and Local Government Review.*

STEVE SHEPPARD is William Enfield Professor of Law and member of the graduate faculty in political science in the University of Arkansas. He recently wrote *I Do Solemnly Swear: The Moral Obligations of Legal Officials* (Cambridge University Press, 2009) and revised Karl Llewellyn's *The Bramble Bush: The Classic Lectures on the Law and Law School* (Oxford University Press, 2008).

BROCK THOMPSON, a native of Conway, Arkansas, holds degrees from Hendrix College and the University of Arkansas. He recently completed his doctorate in American Studies at Kings College, University of London. His studies focus on Southern gay and lesbian history, identity politics, and queer theory.

CATHY KUNZINGER URWIN is the author of *Agenda for Reform: Winthrop Rockefeller as Governor of Arkansas 1967–1971*. She holds a Ph.D. from the University of Notre Dame and is a former member of the Board of Trustees of the Arkansas Historical Association. She has written most recently for *America in World War II* magazine.

GARY D. WEKKIN is a professor of political science at the University of Central Arkansas, where he specialized in partisanship and voting behavior in Arkansas and the South before narrowing his focus to the American presidency. His research has borne fruit in the forms of three titled volumes and articles in *American Politics Quarterly, American Review of Politics, British Journal of Political Science, Western Political Quarterly,* and other venues.

JEANNIE M. WHAYNE is a professor of history at the University of Arkansas. She has published more than a dozen essays and has authored, coauthored, or edited nine books, including *A New Plantation South: Land, Labor, and Federal Favor in Twentieth Century Arkansas* (winner of the Arkansiana Award for best book published in 1996); *Shadows over Sunnyside: An Arkansas Plantation in Transition, 1830–1945*; and *Arkansas Delta: A Land of Paradox,* (winner of the Virginia Ledbetter Prize in Arkansas History).

DONALD E. WHISTLER is a professor of political science at the University of Central Arkansas. He is the author of a forthcoming book *Citizen Legislature: The Arkansas General Assembly* and a coeditor of *Building Democracy in One-Party Systems* (Praeger, 1993). His articles have appeared in journals such as *Politics & Policy, Political Research Quarterly,* and *Women & Politics.* He is a past editor of the *Midsouth Political Science Journal.*

C. FRED WILLIAMS is a professor of history at the University of Arkansas at Little Rock. He received an undergraduate degree in history from East Central State College, Ada, Oklahoma, a master's in history from Wichita State University, and a PhD in history from the University of Oklahoma. He began his professional career as an assistant professor of history at the University of Arkansas at Little Rock in 1969, where he has taught the History of the American West and the History of Arkansas. He has published numerous monographs and articles including *Historic Little Rock: An Illustrated History* (San Antonio, Texas: Historical Publishing Network, 2008), and *Arkansas: Independent and Proud* (Sun Valley, California: American Historical Press, 2002).

INDEX

JANINE A. PARRY is associate professor of political science at the University of Arkansas and director of the Arkansas Poll. She has published articles in *Social Science Quarterly, Policy Studies Journal, Arkansas Historical Quarterly, Political Behavior,* and *State Politics and Policy Quarterly.*

RICHARD P. WANG is associate professor and chair of the Department of Political Science at Arkansas State University and coeditor of *Arkansas Politics: A Reader.* He has published articles in the *International Journal of Public Administration* and *Current Regional Issues.*

DAVID PRYOR is a former governor and U.S. senator for Arkansas and the author of *A Pryor Commitment.*